THE FIRST AMENDMENT

A READER

Second Edition

By

John H. Garvey
Professor of Law
Notre Dame Law School

Frederick Schauer
Frank Stanton Professor of the First Amendment
John F. Kennedy School of Government
Harvard University

AMERICAN CASEBOOK SERIES®

WEST GROUP

Bancroft-Whitney • Clark Boardman Callaghan
Lawyers Cooperative Publishing • WESTLAW® • West Publishing

For Customer Assistance Call 1-800-328-4880

 *TEXT IS PRINTED ON 10% POST CONSUMER RECYCLED PAPER*

3rd Reprint — 2004

Preface

Back when Constitutional Law was a one semester course, and when that one semester included all of criminal procedure and most of state and local taxation, study of the First Amendment rarely took more than two weeks. Now, however, it frequently occupies a course of its own, or comprises quite a large chunk of other courses. Those who lament the demise of required courses in Bills and Notes, Equity, and Agency will resent Constitutional Law's increasing hegemony over the law school curriculum. Yet the First Amendment provides a good example of the fact that this phenomenon is not (only) a function of the shifting interests of the professoriate. Issues of free speech, free press, and freedom of religion increasingly pervade the business of courts at all levels, increasingly occupy a prominent place in political debate and nonjudicial policymaking, and increasingly intrude themselves into such seemingly alien subjects as Securities Regulation and Taxation.

Perhaps because of the intrinsic importance of the subject, and perhaps because so much of it relates directly to the kinds of things that academics *do*, First Amendment law has both disproportionately attracted and been disproportionately influenced by academic writing. Much of this scholarship is, however, quite simply too lengthy to make it convenient for classroom use. When law review articles routinely contain tables of contents, and when many law reviews relegate anything shorter than thirty pages to the status of "Essay" or "Commentary," it is increasingly difficult to integrate this scholarship into the First Amendment part of the curriculum.

Part of our goal, therefore, was to provide a vehicle for the integration of serious scholarship into the classroom treatment of the First Amendment. Yet as producers of legal scholarship ourselves, we are uncomfortable with the notion that most of what is important in an article can be reduced to a paragraph, a sentence, a phrase, or a label. We think that arguments matter, and we think that reasons matter, and thus we think that there is more of importance in a good piece of scholarship than simply its conclusions.

Faced therefore with the often competing demands of conciseness and depth, we have attempted in editing the included selections from the academic literature to give enough of the argument that the argument itself can be appreciated and evaluated. And we have also tried to wield a heavy enough editing knife so that repetition from the case law and among selections is minimized, and so that a reasonably large number of articles could be made available

Our principles of selection were numerous. Some number of articles have attained the status of "classics," and these were included regardless of our own views about whether that status is deserved or not. Others presented the issues with such clarity that their pedagogical value seemed obvious, even if they did not offer strikingiy new or important perspectives. Still others staked out distinct positions that can and should be debated in the classroom. And although we have tried to recognize that articles written by us or by our friends will appear more likely to us to satisfy these criteria than they do to others, we cannot claim to have been totally successful in avoiding the distortions of this phenomenon.

Selection inevitably entails exclusion, and we are uncomfortable about some of our exclusions. Some articles simply do not edit down to five or six pages without losing all that is of importance, and we have inevitably but unfortunately preferred those articles that can be so encapsulated to those that can not, without in any way wishing to claim that the former are in any way "better" than the latter. Considerations of topic balance and space allocation have also mandated use of merely one or two articles in some areas, even though more might plausibly have been included in a larger volume. In making all of our selections, therefore, we have tried to avoid claiming to be arbiters of "good" legal scholarship, preferring instead to claim only that these are the articles that when edited down to five or six pages might seem to many teachers to be particulariy suitable for classroom use. We hope that the introductions and bibliographies will provide suitable signposts for those who wish to go further into any of the areas we deal with here.

In producing this volume, we are admitted parasites. Without the work of the scholars whose efforts we cut, paste, describe, and appropriate, this book could not exist. All have been generous in allowing their work to be used, and even more so in acceding to our editing, and in allowing the reproduction now of words they might wish they had not used, or ideas they now do not hold. To all of the authors used here we are most grateful. And we are grateful as well to the Notre Dame Law School and to the Joan Shorenstein Center on the Press, Politics and Public Policy of the John F. Kennedy School of Government, Harvard University, for numerous forms of tangible and intangible support.

JOHN H. GARVEY
FREDERICK SCHAUER

August, 1995

Acknowledgments

We would like to thank the authors and copyright holders of the following works, who permitted their inclusion in this book:

Larry A. Alexander, Trouble on Track Two: Incidental Regulations of Speech and Free Speech Theory. Copyright © 1993 by University of California, Hastings College of the Law. Reprinted from Hastings Law Journal Vol. 44, No. 4, pp. 921–25, 931–36, by permission.

Akhil Reed Amar, The Case of the Missing Amendments: R.A.V. v. City of St. Paul. Copyright © by the Harvard Law Review Association.

David A. Anderson, The Origins of the Press Clause. Originally published in 30 UCLA Law Review 455 (1983), The Regents of the University of California. All Rights Reserved.

C. Edwin Baker, Scope of the First Amendment Freedom of Speech. Originally published in 25 UCLA Law Review 964 (1978), The Regents of the University of California. All Rights Reserved.

Robert N. Bellah, Civil Religion in America. Reprinted by permission of Daedalus, Journal of the American Academy of Arts and Sciences, from the issue entitled, "Religion in America," Winter 1967, Volume 96 Number 1.

Walter Berns, The First Amendment and the Future of American Democracy. Copyright © 1977 by Basic Books, Inc. Reprinted by permission of Basic Books, a division of HarperCollins Publishers Inc.

Lillian R. BeVier, Rehabilitating Public Forum Doctrine: In Defense of Categories. 1992 Supreme Court Review 79. Copyright © by The University of Chicago. All Rights Reserved.

Vincent Blasi, The Checking Value in First Amendment Theory. Copyright © 1977 by the American Bar Foundation. Reprinted with permission of the University of Chicago Press.

Vincent Blasi, The Pathological Perspective and the First Amendment. Copyright © 1985 by the Directors of the Columbia Law Review Association, Inc. All Rights Reserved. This article originally appeared at 85 Columbia Law Review 449 (1985). Reprinted by permission.

Vincent Blasi, Toward a Theory of Prior Restraint: The Central Linkage. Copyright © 1981 by the Minnesota Law Review.

Lee C. Bollinger, The Tolerant Society: Freedom of Speech and Extremist Speech in America.

Copyright © 1986 by Oxford University Press, Inc. Reprinted by permission.

Robert H. Bork, Neutral Principles and Some First Amendment Problems, 47 Indiana Law Journal 1 (1971). Copyright © 1971 by the Trustees of Indiana University. Reprinted by Permission.

Gerard V. Bradley, Church–State Relationships in America. Reprinted by permission of Greenwood Publishing Group, Inc., Westport, CT. Copyright © 1987 by Gerard v. Bradley and published in 1987 by Greenwood Press.

Kingsley R. Browne, Title VII as Censorship: Hostile-Environment Harassment and the First Amendment. Reprinted with permission of the author and the Ohio State Law Journal.

Edmond Cahn, The "Establishment of Religion" Puzzle. Reprinted with permission of the New York University Law Review.

Stephen L. Carter, Evolutionism, Creationism, and Treating Religion as a Hobby. Copyright © 1987, Duke University School of Law.

Robert C. Casad, The Establishment Clause and the Ecumenical Movement. Reprinted with permission of the Michigan Law Review.

Ronald A. Cass, The Perils of Positive Thinking: Constitutional Interpretation and Negative First Amendment Theory. Originally published in 34 UCLA Law Review 1405 (1987). The Regents of the University of California. All Rights Reserved.

Jesse Choper, The Religion Clauses of the First Amendment: Reconciling the Conflict. Reprinted with permission of the author and the University of Pittsburgh Law Review.

R.H. Coase, The Market for Goods and the Market for Ideas. Copyright © 1974 by the American Economic Association.

Richard Delgado, Campus Antiracism Rules: Constitutional Narratives in Collision. Reprinted by special permission of Northwestern University School of Law, Northwestern University Law Review, Volume 85, Issue 2, (1991)—343, 345–348.

Walter Dellinger, The Sound of Silence: An Epistle on Prayer and the Constitution. Reprinted by permission of The Yale Law Journal Company and Fred B. Rothman & Company from The Yale Law Journal, Vol. 95, pp. 1631, 1634–1637.

John Hart Ely, Flag Desecration: A Case Study in the Roles of Categorization and Balancing in First Amendment Analysis. Copyright © 1975 by the Harvard Law Review Association.

Thomas I. Emerson, Toward a General Theory of the First Amendment. Reprinted by permission of The Yale Law Journal and Fred B. Rothman & Company from The Yale Law Journal, Vol. 72, pp. 877, 878–887.

Cynthia L. Estlund, Speech on Matters of Public Concern: The Perils of an Emerging First Amendment Category. Reprinted with the permission of the George Washington Law Review 1990.

Daniel A. Farber, Commercial Speech and First Amendment Theory. Reprinted with permission of Daniel A. Farber.

Daniel A. Farber, Free Speech Without Romance: Public Choice and the First Amendment. Copyright © by the Harvard Law Review Association.

Daniel A. Farber & Philip P. Frickey, Practical Reason and the First Amendment. Originally published in 34 UCLA Law Review 1615 (1987), The Regents of the University of California. All Rights Reserved.

Owen Fiss, Why the State? Copyright © 1987 by the Harvard Law Review Association.

Mayer G. Freed & Daniel D. Polsby, Race, Religion, and Public Policy: Bob Jones University v. United States, 1983 Supreme Court Review 1. Copyright © 1984 by The University of Chicago. All Rights Reserved.

Paul A. Freund, Public Aid to Parochial Schools. Copyright © 1969 by the Harvard Law Review Association.

John H. Garvey, Another Way of Looking at School Aid, 1985 Supreme Court Review 61. Copyright © 1985 by The University of Chicago. All Rights Reserved.

John H. Garvey, Freedom and Choice in Constitutional Law. Copyright © 1981 by the Harvard Law Review Association.

John H. Garvey, Free Exercise and the Values of Religious Liberty. Reprinted with permission of the Connecticut Law Review.

John H. Garvey, The Pope's Submarine. Copyright © 1993 San Diego Law Review Association. Reprinted with the permission of the San Diego Law Review.

Frederick Mark Gedicks, Public Life and Hostility to Religion. Reprinted with permission of the author and the Virginia Law Review.

Steven G. Gey, The Apologetics of Suppression: The Regulation of Pornography as Act and Idea. Reprinted with permission of the Michigan Law Review.

Donald A. Giannella, Religious Liberty, Nonestablishment, and Doctrinal Development Part II. The Nonestablishment Principle. Copyright © 1968 by the Harvard Law Review Association.

Steven Goldberg, The Constitutional Status of American Science. Copyright © 1979 by the Board of Trustees of the University of Illinois.

Kent Greenawalt, O'er the Land of the Free: Flag Burning as Speech. Originally published in 37 UCLA Law Review 925 (1990), The Regents of the University of California. All Rights Reserved.

Kent Greenawalt, Religion as a Concept in Constitutional Law. Copyright © 1984 by California Law Review Inc. Reprinted from California Law Review Vol. 72 No. 5, (Sept. 1984), pp. 753–816, by permission.

Kent Greenawalt, Religious Convictions and Lawmaking. Reprinted with permission of the author and the Michigan Law Review.

Kent Greenawalt, Speech and Crime. Copyright © 1980 by the American Bar Foundation. Reprinted with permission of the University of Chicago Press.

Abner S. Greene, The Political Balance of the Religion Clauses. Reprinted by permission of The Yale Law Journal Company and Fred B. Rothman & Company from The Yale Law Journal, Vol. 102, pp. 1611–1644.

Gerald Gunther, Learned Hand and the Origins of Modern First Amendment Doctrine: Some Fragments of History. Copyright © 1975 by the Board of Trustees of the Leland Stanford Junior University.

Mark DeWolfe Howe, The Garden and the Wilderness. Reprinted with permission of the Hebrew Union College—Jewish Institute of Religion.

Stanley Ingber, Rethinking Intangible Injuries: A Focus on Remedy. Copyright © 1973 by California Law Review Inc. Reprinted from California Law Review Vol. 73 No. 3, (May 1985), pp. 772–856, by permission.

Thomas H. Jackson and John Calvin Jeffries, Commercial Speech: Economic Due Process and the First Amendment. Reprinted with permission of the Virginia Law Review Association and Fred B. Rothman & Co.

Phillip E. Johnson, Concepts and Compromise in First Amendment Religious Doctrine. Copyright © 1984 by California Law Review Inc. Reprinted from California Law Review Vol. 72 No. 5, (Sept. 1984), pp. 817–846, by permission.

Harry Kalven, Jr., The Metaphysics of the Law of Obscenity, 1960 Supreme Court Review 1. Copyright © 1960 by The University of Chicago. All Rights Reserved.

Harry Kalven, Jr., The New York Times Case: A Note on "The Central Meaning of the First Amendment", 1964 Supreme Court Review 191. Copyright © 1964 by The University of Chicago. All Rights Reserved.

Kenneth L. Karst, Equality as a Central Principle in the First Amendment. Reprinted with permission of the University of Chicago Law Review.

Charles R. Lawrence, III, If He Hollers Let Him Go: Regulating Racist Speech on Campus. Copyright © 1990 by Charles R. Lawrence, III.

Douglas Laycock, Formal, Substantive, and Disaggregated Neutrality Toward Religion. Copyright © 1990 by Douglas Laycock. Reprinted with permission of the DePaul Law Review.

Douglas Laycock, The Remnants of Free Exercise, 1990 Supreme Court Review 1. Copyright © 1991 by The University of Chicago. All Rights Reserved.

Paul A. LeBel, Reforming the Tort of Defamation: An Accommodation of the Competing Interests Within the Current Constitutional Framework. Reprinted with permission of the Nebraska Law Review.

Pierre N. Leval, The No-Money, No-Fault Libel Suit: Keeping Sullivan in Its Proper Place. Copyright © 1988 by the Harvard Law Review Association.

Leonard W. Levy, Emergence of a Free Press. Copyright © 1985 by Leonard W. Levy. Reprinted by permission of Oxford University Press, Inc.

Hans A. Linde, "Clear and Present Danger" Reexamined: Dissonance in the Brandenburg Concerto. Copyright © 1970 by the Board of Trustees of the Leland Stanford Junior University.

Ira C. Lupu, The Lingering Death of Separationism. Reprinted with the permission of The George Washington Law Review © 1994.

Catharine A. MacKinnon, Feminism Unmodified: Discourses on Life and Law. Reprinted by permission of the publishers, Cambridge, Mass.: Harvard University Press, Copyright © 1987 by the President and Fellows of Harvard College.

Catharine A. MacKinnon, Only Words. Reprinted by permission of the publishers from Only Words by Catharine A. MacKinnon, Cambridge, Mass.: Harvard University Press, Copyright © by Catharine A. MacKinnon.

Catharine A. MacKinnon, Pornography, Civil Rights and Speech. Permission granted by the Harvard Civil Rights Civil Liberties Law Review. Copyright © 1985 by the President and Fellows of Harvard College.

Mari J. Matsuda, Public Response to Racist Speech: Considering the Victim's Story. Reprinted with permission of the Michigan Law Review.

Michael W. McConnell, Accommodation of Religion, 1985 Supreme Court Review 1. Copyright © 1985 by The University of Chicago. All Rights Reserved.

Michael W. McConnell, The Origins and Historical Understanding of Free Exercise of Religion. Copyright © 1990 by the Harvard Law Review Association.

Alexander Meiklejohn, Political Freedom. Copyright © 1948, 1960 by Harper & Brothers. Reprinted by permission of HarperCollins Publishers.

Frank I. Michelman, Conceptions of Democracy in American Constitutional Argument: The Case of Pornography Regulation. The full text of this article appears at 56 Tenn.L.Rev. 291 (1989) and is reprinted here by permission of the Tennessee Law Review Association, Inc.

Henry P. Monaghan, Constitutional Fact Review. Copyright © 1985 by the Directors of the Columbia Law Review Association, Inc. All Rights Reserved. This article originally appeared at 85 Colum.L.Rev. 229 (1985). Reprinted by permission.

Henry P. Monaghan, First Amendment "Due Process". Copyright © 1970 by the Harvard Law Review Association.

Henry P. Monaghan, Overbreadth, 1981 Supreme Court Review 1. Copyright © 1981 by The University of Chicago. All Rights Reserved.

Melville B. Nimmer, The Right to Speak from Times to Time: First Amendment Theory Applied to Libel and Misapplied to Privacy. Copyright © 1968 by California Law Review Inc. Reprinted from California Law Review, Vol. 56 No. 4, (Aug. 1968), pp. 935–967, by permission.

Note, Civil Religion and the Establishment Clause. Reprinted by permission of The Yale Law Journal Company and Fred B. Rothman & Company from The Yale Law Journal, Vol. 95, pp. 1237–1257.

Note, Toward a Constitutional Definition of Religion. Copyright © 1978 by the Harvard Law Review Association.

Dallin H. Oaks, Separation, Accommodation and the Future of Church and State. Copyright © 1985 by Dallin H. Oaks. Reprinted with permission of the DePaul Law Review.

Michael Stokes Paulsen, Lemon Is Dead. Reprinted with permission of the author and the Case Western Reserve Law Review.

James R. Pielemeier, Constitutional Limitations on Choice of Law: The Special Case of Multistate Defamation. Copyright © 1985, James R. Pielemeier. Reprinted with permission of the University of Pennsylvania Law Review.

Robert C. Post, Racist Speech, Democracy, and the First Amendment. Reprinted with permission of the William & Mary Law Review.

Robert C. Post, The Constitutional Concept of Public Discourse: Outrageous Opinion, Democratic Deliberation and Hustler Magazine v. Falwell. Copyright © 1990 by the Harvard Law Review Association.

Robert C. Post, The Social Foundations of Defamation Law: Reputation and the Constitution. Copyright © 1986 by California Law Review Inc. Reprinted from California Law Review, Vol. 74 No. 3, (May 1986), pp. 691–742, by permission.

David M. Rabban, The First Amendment in Its Forgotten Years. Reprinted by permission of The Yale Law Journal Company and Fred B. Rothman & Company from The Yale Law Journal, Vol. 90, pp. 514–595.

Martin H. Redish, The First Amendment in the Marketplace: Commercial Speech and the Values of Free Expression. Reprinted with the permission of The George Washington Law Review. Copyright © 1971.

Martin H. Redish, The Proper Role of the Prior Restraint Doctrine in First Amendment Theory. Reprinted with permission of the Virginia Law Review Association and Fred B. Rothman & Co.

Martin H. Redish, The Value of Free Speech. Copyright © 1982 by the University of Pennsylvania Law Review.

Martin H. Redish, The Role of Pathology in First Amendment Theory: A Skeptical Examination. Reprinted with permission of the Case Western Reserve Law Review.

David A.J. Richards, Free Speech and Obscenity Law: Toward a Moral Theory of the First Amendment. Copyright © 1974 by the University of Pennsylvania Law Review.

Thomas Scanlon, A Theory of Freedom of Expression. Copyright © 1972 by Princeton University Press. Reprinted by permission of Princeton University Press.

Frederick Schauer, Categories and the First Amendment: A Play in Three Acts. Reprinted with permission of the Vanderbilt Law Review.

Frederick Schauer, Causation Theory and the Causes of Sexual Violence. Copyright © 1987 by the American Bar Foundation. Reprinted with permission of the University of Chicago Press.

Frederick Schauer, Codifying the First Amendment: New York v. Ferber, 1982 Supreme Court Review 285. Copyright © 1983 by The University of Chicago. All Rights Reserved.

Frederick Shauer, Free Speech: A Philosophical Enquiry. Copyright © Cambridge University Press 1982. Reprinted with permission of the Cambridge University Press.

Frederick Schauer, Must Speech Be Special? Reprinted by special permission of Northwestern University School of Law, Northwestern University Law Review, Volume 78, Issue 5, (1983)—1284–1306.

Frederick Schauer, Slippery Slopes. Copyright © 1985 by the Harvard Law Review Association.

Frederick Schauer, Speech and "Speech"—Obscenity and "Obscenity": An Exercise in the Interpretation of Constitutional Language. Reprinted with the permission of the publisher. Copyright © 1979 The Georgetown Law Journal Association and Georgetown University.

Frederick Schauer, Uncoupling Free Speech. This article originally appeared at 92 Columbia Law Review (1992). Reprinted by permission.

Alan Schwarz, No Imposition of Religion: The Establishment Clause Value. Reprinted by permission of The Yale Law Journal Company and Fred B. Rothman & Company from The Yale Law Journal, Vol. 77, pp. 692–737.

Suzanna Sherry, Lee v. Weisman: Paradox Redux, 1993 Supreme Court Review 123. Copyright © 1993 by The University of Chicago. All rights reserved.

Steven Shiffrin, The First Amendment and Economic Regulation: Away from a General Theory of the First Amendment. Reprinted with permission of the Northwestern University School of Law.

Steven H. Shiffrin, The First Amendment, Democracy, and Romance. Reprinted by permission of the publishers, Cambridge, Mass.: Harvard University Press, Copyright © 1990 by Steven H. Shiffrin.

Gary J. Simson, The Establishment Clause in the Supreme Court: Rethinking The Court's Approach. Copyright © 1987 by Cornell University. All Rights Reserved. Reprinted with permission of the Cornell Law Review and Fred B. Rothman & Co.

Rodney K. Smith, Now is the Time for Reflection: Wallace v. Jaffree and Its Legislative Aftermath. Copyright © 1986 by Rodney K. Smith. Reprinted with permission of the Alabama Law Review.

Steven D. Smith, Symbols, Perceptions, and Doctrinal Illusions: Establishment Neutrality and the "No Endorsement" Test. Reprinted with permission of the author and the Michigan Law Review.

Steven D. Smith, The Restoration of Tolerance. Copyright © 1990 by California Law Review Inc. Reprinted from California Law Review Vol. 78 No. 2, (October 1990), pp. 305–356, by permission.

Rodney Smolla, Let the Author Beware: The Rejuvenation of the American Law of Libel. Copyright © 1983 by the University of Pennsylvania Law Review.

Geoffrey R. Stone, Content Regulation and the First Amendment. Reprinted by special permission of Northwestern University School of Law, Northwestern University Law Review, Volume 81, Issue 1, (1986) —168–172.

Geoffrey R. Stone, The Equal Access Controversy: The Religion Clauses and the Meaning of "Neutrality". Reprinted with permission of the William & Mary Law Review.

David A. Strauss, Why Be Tolerant? Reprinted with permission of the University of Chicago Law Review.

Kathleen M. Sullivan, Religion and Liberal Democracy. Reprinted with permission of the University of Chicago Law Review.

Cass R. Sunstein, Free Speech Now. Reprinted with permission of the University of Chicago Law Review.

Cass R. Sunstein, Pornography and the First Amendment. Copyright © 1986 Duke University School of Law.

*

Summary of Contents

Table of Contents

THE FIRST AMENDMENT

A READER

Second Edition

Congress shall make no law respecting an establishment of religion, or prohibiting the free exercise thereof; or abridging the freedom of speech, or of the press; or the right of the people peaceably to assemble, and to petition the Government for a redress of grievances.

*

Chapter I

HISTORICAL ORIGINS OF THE SPEECH AND PRESS CLAUSES

Much of contemporary First Amendment theory, doctrine, and commentary treats the speech and press clauses as being distinct from the religion clauses. But it was not always so. The modern treatment of speech and religion as substantially separate constitutional domains is a departure from early historical understandings of free speech as being concerned primarily with religious (or anti-religious) speech. Thus Milton's *Areopagitica* in 1644, perhaps the earliest sustained defense of freedom of speech and press, was focused almost exclusively on the importance of freeing from licensing those writings that might diverge from accepted religious teachings.[1] For much of the next two centuries, both up to and beyond the adoption of the First Amendment, discussions of freedom of speech and its limits in England, in North America, and elsewhere were arguments centered on heresy and blasphemy, and on the desirability or undesirability of an officially imposed religious orthodoxy.

Although much that has now been assimilated into a secular free speech tradition thus had its roots in debates about religious dissent, there developed early in the eighteenth century a distinct tradition about political dissent—one that informed much of the colonial understanding about freedom of the press. In *A Theologico–Political Treatise* (1670), Spinoza's argument "That in a Free State Every Man May Think What He Likes, and Say What He Thinks" was concerned mostly with politics and not with religion. But it was not until the work of the pseudonymous Cato, the similar arguments of John Wilkes, and the trial of John Peter Zenger and the accompanying commentary in 1732, that there developed the modern tradition of freedom of the press as a form of political dissent. Vincent Blasi traces and analyzes this history in the

---

1. By modern standards, the range of religious opinion that Milton wished to protect was spectacularly narrow. Like Locke in An Essay concerning Toleration (1667) and Letter concerning Toleration (1689), Milton would not have extended the liberty of speech and belief to Roman Catholics and others he thought equally beyond the pale.

selection included here. He extracts from it the view that a primary purpose of the freedoms of speech and press, then and now, has been to check government as a way of preventing abuse.

Although Blasi seems accurately to capture a widely held understanding of *why* the freedoms of speech and press were thought important, dispute remains about the historical understanding of the strength of the principle. Some of this dispute is captured in the accompanying contributions by Leonard Levy and David Anderson. Levy argues that the original understanding of the First Amendment was far narrower than is now commonly supposed: much evidence supports the proposition that the framers (following Milton and Blackstone) intended to restrict prior restraints but not to prevent subsequent punishment, including prosecution for seditious libel. Anderson attributes to the framers a more generous understanding of the strength of the protection. And there is little doubt that, although early cases expressed some appreciation for the narrower view,[2] developments since 1919 have made it clear that even if Levy is right as a matter of history, contemporary interpretations would not (and Levy would not say they should) adhere to this narrow an understanding.

The relevant history of the Speech and Press Clauses does not end in 1791, however, and (as with any area of law that is developed in largely common-law fashion) subsequent social and political developments have been as important as subsequent doctrinal developments in shaping the modern understanding. David Rabban tracks the importance of political events, lower court rulings, and scholarly commentary in forming the American understanding of free speech that was in place when the Supreme Court first actively entered the First Amendment arena in 1919. Gerald Gunther's important recovery and analysis of the correspondence between Learned Hand and Oliver Wendell Holmes demonstrates Hand's effect on the development of Holmes's thought, and on the doctrine relating to speech thought likely to lead to illegal activity.

VINCENT BLASI, THE CHECKING VALUE IN FIRST AMENDMENT THEORY

1977 A.B.F.Res.J. 521, 528–538.

In this article, I examine the sources and premises of the idea that free expression is valuable in part because of the function it performs in checking the abuse of official power, an idea I shall hereafter refer to as "the checking value." * * *

* * *

The tendency of officials to abuse their public trust is a theme that has permeated political thought from classical times to the present. John Locke devoted much of his *Second Treatise on Civil Government*,

---

2. See especially Patterson v. Colorado, 205 U.S. 454 (1907) (Holmes, J.).

first published in 1690, to this specific problem. But although Locke set forth an influential theory that the general citizenry has a right to overthrow rulers who abuse the public trust, he did not emphasize the role of the press in the process of checking governmental authority. In the decades immediately after Locke wrote, however, two institutions—the newspaper and the opposition party—developed into major forces in the politics of the times; partly as a result, the idea that free expression serves as a check on the behavior of incumbents assumed a prominent place in the political discourse of eighteenth-century England.

Among the English essayists of this period who were read by the colonists, four deserve special mention. The most important was "Cato," the pen name of coauthors John Trenchard and Thomas Gordon, who in the 1720s published a series of essays attacking the overbearing and manipulative administration of Sir Robert Walpole. The essays were widely read and discussed in both England and the colonies. * * *

Cato's discussion of the values underlying free expression is contained primarily in his Letter Number 15, entitled "Of Freedom of Speech." * * *. Cato's emphasis is on the need for popular recourse against evil officials:

> Whoever would overthrow the Liberty of a Nation must begin by subduing the Freeness of Speech; a Thing terrible to publick Traytors.

> . . . .

> That Men ought to speak well of their Governours, is true, while their Governours deserve to be well spoken of, but to do publick Mischief without Hearing of it is only the Prerogative and Felicity of Tyranny . . . .

The essay next proceeds to a didactic review of ancient Roman and English history to make the point that while free expression poses no threat to enlightened rulers, it helps to check abuses of official power by "Traytors and Oppressors." The concluding portion of the essay mentions in passing the value of free expression in nurturing "excellent Writers" and "Men of Genius" but rests its argument ultimately on the checking value: "Freedom of Speech is the great Bulwark of Liberty; they prosper and Die together . . . . Freedom of Speech therefore being of such infinite importance to the Preservation of Liberty; every one who loves Liberty ought to encourage Freedom of Speech."

While Cato probably was the English political writer most influential among the American colonists, the English political figure who most excited their admiration was the flamboyant John Wilkes. In 1763 Wilkes published the forty-fifth issue of his journal, the *North Briton,* which included a stinging attack on a speech given by George III. This prompted the king's ministers to file an information for seditious libel and to issue general warrants for the arrest and search of some 200 persons involved in the publication and dissemination of Number 45.

Wilkes's private study was ransacked, his papers were seized, and Number 45 was ordered burned. A member of Parliament at the time, Wilkes was expelled from the House of Commons and prosecuted for seditious libel. He fled to France from whence he sent back to London numerous tracts and letters defending his cause and setting himself up as a martyr. A shrewd propagandist, he built a large following in England and the colonies.

Wilkes was a politician and a polemicist, not an original political theorist. His only discussion of freedom of the press, contained in the first issue of the *North Briton,* follows Cato in emphasizing the checking value of free expression:

> The liberty of the press is the birth-right of a Briton, and is justly esteemed the firmest bulwark of the liberties of this country. It has been the terror of all bad ministers; for their dark and dangerous designs, or their weakness, inability, and duplicity, have thus been detected and shewn to the public, generally in too strong and just colours for them long to bear up against the odium of mankind....
> A wicked and corrupt administration must naturally dread this appeal to the world; and will be for keeping all the means of information equally from the prince, parliament and people.

The controversy over the prosecution and expulsion of Wilkes produced a lively debate among pamphleteers. Probably the two most important defenders of Wilkes's freedom of expression were "Father of Candor" and "Junius," anonymous writers whose identities have yet to be conclusively established. Father of Candor, whose essay *An Enquiry into the Doctrine Lately Propagated Concerning Libels, Warrants, and the Seizure of Papers* went through seven editions between 1764 and 1771, presented a detailed criticism of the doctrine of seditious libel. He conceded that "libels on particular persons in their private capacities" should be punishable, but contended that "the case is totally different with respect to an administration; for the country in general is always the better or worse for its conduct, and therefore every man has a right to know, to consider and to reflect upon it." He based his argument directly on the checking value: "The liberty of exposing and opposing a bad administration by the pen is among the necessary privileges of a free people, and is perhaps the greatest benefit that can be derived from the liberty of the press."

The *Letters of Junius* are renowned not only for their contribution to political thought but also for the litigation that ensued over crown efforts to suppress them. To the chagrin of Lord Mansfield, the prosecutions of various publishers of the *Letters* were aborted by rebellious verdicts, which are now celebrated as leading examples of the practice of jury nullification. * * *

Like Wilkes's *North Briton,* the *Letters of Junius* were more concerned with immediate political issues than with abstract theories of government and liberty. But Junius did present one general discussion of liberty of press and in it he emphasized the checking value:

A considerable latitude must be allowed in the discussion of public affairs, or the liberty of the press will be of no benefit to society. As the indulgence of private malice and personal slander should be checked and resisted by every legal means, so a constant examination into the characters and conduct of ministers and magistrates should be equally promoted and encouraged. They, who conceive that our newspapers are no restraint upon bad men, or impediment to the execution of bad measures, know nothing of this country. In that state of abandoned servility and prostitution, to which the undue influence of the crown has reduced the other branches of the legislature, our ministers and magistrates have in reality little punishment to fear, and few difficulties to contend with, beyond the censure of the press, and the spirit of resistance which it excites among the people.

Cato and Wilkes and Father of Candor and Junius probably did not represent the thinking of most Englishmen. They were opposition figures. But according to Bernard Bailyn's luminous book *The Ideological Origins of the American Revolution:*

To say simply that this tradition of opposition thought was quickly transmitted to America and widely appreciated there is to understate the fact. Opposition thought, in the form it acquired at the turn of the seventeenth century and in the early eighteenth century, was devoured by the colonists. From the earliest years of the century it nourished their political thought and sensibilities. There seems never to have been a time after the Hanoverian succession when these writings were not central to American political expression or absent from polemical politics.[43]

From his study of the pamphlets of the American revolution, Bailyn concludes that the colonists were preoccupied with the fragility of constitutional government. Thus, they frequently drew lessons from ancient history but "their detailed knowledge and engaged interest" was confined to the relatively narrow period when the Roman republic "was being fundamentally challenged or when its greatest days were already past and its moral and political virtues decayed." Similarly, the colonists were fascinated by modern Venice, Sweden, and Denmark, "despotic states that had within living memory been free and whose enslavement, being recent, had been directly observed...." The escape from Stuart tyranny represented by the Glorious Revolution of 1689 was viewed by the colonial pamphleteers as a close call, and anything but secure. Most important, Americans were appalled by the corruption of the Walpole ministry in England, particularly the way Walpole was able to manipulate Parliament. In short, the allocation of political power was a central concern to the colonists, and "[m]ost commonly the discussion of power centered on its essential characteristic of aggressiveness: its

---

43. [Bernard Bailyn, The Ideological Origins of the American Revolution 43 (Cambridge, Mass.: Harvard University Press, 1967).]

endlessly propulsive tendency to expand itself beyond legitimate boundaries.''

Thus, the colonial pamphleteers, like the opposition leaders in England whom they so admired, organized much of their political thought around the need they perceived to check the abuse of governmental power. The First Amendment was an outgrowth of this body of thought, as can be discerned from a brief examination of the most important eighteenth-century American writings on freedom of speech and freedom of the press.

The dispute over liberty of the press which most captured the imagination of the colonists was unquestionably the seditious libel prosecution in 1735 of the New York printer John Peter Zenger. A poorly educated tradesman, Zenger was printer for the *New York Weekly Journal,* a newspaper that served as the mouthpiece for the chief opposition faction in New York state politics. The paper's managing editor and chief contributor was James Alexander, a highly skillful lawyer * * *. Alexander frequently printed essays on freedom of the press in the pages of the *Journal,* including Cato's Letter Number 15. * * *

When the *Journal* published a particularly stinging series of anonymous articles satirizing the incumbent administration, an indictment was returned charging Zenger with seditious libel. Alexander secured the services of the renowned Philadelphia lawyer Andrew Hamilton as counsel for the defense. In his brilliant closing argument to the jury, Hamilton defended the right of all freemen "publicly to remonstrate the abuses of power in the strongest terms, to put their neighbors upon their guard against the craft or open violence of men in authority ...." The jurors, instructed to rule only on the indisputable question whether Zenger had published the offending issues, returned a verdict of not guilty. The jury's defiance was greeted by loud cheers in the courtroom and has ever since been celebrated as one of the great events in the history of freedom of the press.

* * *

The draftsman of the First Amendment was James Madison. His most fully developed discussion of freedom of the press is contained in the Virginia Report of 1799–1800, a document he prepared for the Virginia House of Delegates in criticism of the federal Alien and Sedition Acts. Elaborating on a theory he had sketched out ten years earlier in presenting his proposed draft of the Bill of Rights to the United States House of Representatives, Madison argued that the British legal doctrine of freedom of the press, which consisted mainly in the prohibition of prior restraints and permitted criminal punishment for seditious libel, represented a narrow conception of liberty inapplicable to the American system of government. For in England, he observed, "[t]he representatives of the people in the legislature are not only exempt themselves from distrust, but are considered as sufficient guardians of the rights of their constituents against the danger from the executive." In contrast, "[i]n the United States, the executive magistrates are not held to be infallible, nor the legislatures to be omnipotent; and both being elective, are both responsible." "Is it not natural and necessary," asked Madison, "under such different circumstances, that a different degree of freedom in the use of the press should be contemplated?"

Madison proceeded to explain why the federal Sedition Act claimed "a power which, more than any other, ought to produce universal alarm." His principal argument was that the freedom to criticize government officials is essential to the process by which the electorate turns out of office those who fail to discharge their trusts. When public officials fail in this respect, said Madison, "it is natural and proper, that, according to the cause and degree of their faults, they should be brought into contempt or disrepute, and incur the hatred of the people." Whether and to what extent the public trust has been breached "can only be determined by a free examination thereof, and a free communication among the people thereon." Madison placed more emphasis than earlier theorists on the role of the electorate in the checking process, and also on the need to check errors of judgment as well as illegal or despotic actions by government officials. Nonetheless, the Virginia Report constitutes a detailed argument by the author of the First Amendment that one of the principal purposes of freedom of the press is to permit intensive scrutiny of the behavior of public officials.

Thomas Jefferson also tended to view liberty of the press in terms of the checking value. In a 1790 letter to Noah Webster, Jefferson distinguished between rights that individuals retain because their enjoyment is not inconsistent with the purposes of government, and other rights that constitute "certain fences which experience has proved peculiarly efficacious against wrong." He then gave examples: "Of the first kind, for instance, is freedom of religion; of the second, trial by jury, habeas corpus laws, free presses." Thirty-three years later, in a letter to Adamantios Coray, Jefferson once again stressed the checking value in explaining his commitment to freedom of the press: "This formidable censor of the public functionaries, by arraigning them at the tribunal of public opinion, produces reform peaceably, which must otherwise be done by revolution." He added, almost as an afterthought, "It is also the best instrument for enlightening the mind of man and improving him as a rational, moral, and social being ...."

* * * These authorities * * * do not establish that the generation of Americans which enacted the First Amendment built its whole philosophy of freedom of the press around the checking value. Then, as now, the commitment to free expression embodied a complex of values. There can be no doubt, however, that one of the most important values attributed to a free press by eighteenth-century political thinkers was that of checking the inherent tendency of government officials to abuse the power entrusted to them. Insofar as the views prevalent at the time of adoption have relevance to contemporary interpretation, the checking value rests on a most impressive foundation.

LEONARD W. LEVY, EMERGENCE
OF A FREE PRESS

173, 183–186, 198–202, 204–205, 220, 262, 266–267 (1985).

[The common law crime of seditious libel forbade malicious criticism of the government. It embraced defamation or ridicule of public officials, laws, or policies—anything that tended to lower the government in the public esteem. Truth was no defense to the charge of libel. Indeed, truth made the libel worse, because it exacerbated the scandal.

[At the trial of a seditious libel the jury decided only the fact of publication—i.e., whether the defendant published the remarks charged, and whether they carried the innuendo alleged. The judge decided as a matter of law whether the remarks were seditious—i.e., whether they were maliciously intended and had a bad tendency.

[Blackstone's *Commentaries* maintained that seditious libel was entirely consistent with freedom of the press. As he put it: [a]

Where blasphemous, immoral, treasonable, schismatical, seditious, or scandalous libels are punished by the English law ... the liberty of the press, properly understood, is by no means infringed or violated. The *liberty of the press* is indeed essential to the nature of a free state; but this consists in laying no *previous* restraints upon publications, and not in freedom from censure for criminal matter when published. Every freeman has an undoubted right to lay what sentiments he pleases before the public: to forbid this is to destroy the freedom of the press: but if he publishes what is improper, mischievous, or illegal, he must take the consequences of his own temerity.

[Zechariah Chafee, the author of an early influential work on freedom of speech, argued that the First Amendment was intended to obliterate the common law of sedition.[b] Leonard Levy disputes this view of First Amendment history. He argues that the common law understanding was taken over by the states after they separated from England, and that it was not changed by the tepid free press clauses some of them adopted. He also maintains that the Framers of the First Amendment gave no indication that they intended to change the received learning on the subject.]

From the Revolution to the First Amendment

* * *

In the period between the Declaration of Independence and the ratification of the First Amendment (1776–1791), America had its first opportunity to develop a legal system and a society in which all men

---

a. Sir William Blackstone, Commentaries on the Laws of England (London, 1765–69), book 4, chap. II, 151–152.

b. Free Speech in the United States (Cambridge, Mass., 1948), 21.

were free to express their opinions, however unpopular, on any subject, short of direct and immediate incitement to crime. No doubt America during this period, as earlier, was as free as, and probably freer than, any other place in the world. Yet the American states did not take the opportunity of abandoning or seriously limiting the oppressive common law of seditious libel.

On the contrary, twelve of the thirteen original states, all but Connecticut, expressly adopted the common-law system after separating from England. Virginia did it by statute in 1776: "The common law of England shall be the rule of decision, and shall be considered in full force until the same shall be altered by the legislative power of the colony." New Jersey did it by a provision in its Constitution of 1776: "The common law of England, as well as so much of the statute law, as have been heretofore practiced in this colony, shall remain in force, until they shall be altered by a future law." The independent republic of Vermont at first adopted the common law as it was "understood in the New England states," but three years later, in 1782, followed the prevailing model of adopting "so much of the common law of England, as is not repugnant to the constitution, or to any act of the legislature of this State." No state abolished or altered the common law of criminal defamation in general or seditious libel in particular, and no state court ruled that the free press clause of its state constitution rendered void the prosecution of a libel.

The Revolution generated the most creative constitutional achievements in history, including the world's first written constitutions and bills of rights that limited all branches of government. Virginia included in its Declaration of Rights, which preceded that of any other state, a provision "That the freedom of the Press is one of the greatest bulwarks of liberty, and can never be restrained but by despotic Governments." Presumably the second clause meant that a free state should not restrain the freedom of the press. Virginia established a pattern for all American free press clauses: it gave no hint of what it meant by freedom of the press or by the word "restrained." Its free press clause * * * did not apply to Tory opinions, nor did its other constitutional protections, nor did those of other states. Virginia's free press clause served as a model for that of North Carolina, although North Carolina substituted a namby-pamby "ought" for the word "can." "Ought," which was hardly enforceable, reflected an ideal, not a prescription or a command. The word "ought" instead of "shall" appeared in the revolutionary constitutions of seven of the nine states that had a free press clause, including Vermont, thereby expressing a hope rather than a constitutional injunction. None used "shall."

* * *

Some of our best constitutional authorities have argued that one object of the Revolution was "to get rid of the English common law on liberty of speech and of the press." [50] * * * [This thesis] is not without supporting evidence. That evidence consists chiefly of, first, a declaration that the states constitutionally protected freedom of speech and press; second, an assumption that such protection superseded the common law; and, third, the hard fact that most states tolerated a press whose caustic conduct belied the existence of the common law. The explanation of the third point is that even in England, where the existence and repressiveness of the law of seditious libel were not in doubt, prosecutions were "occasional," as Madison later wrote, and "the freedom exercised by the press, and protected by public opinion, far exceeds the limits prescribed by the ordinary rules of law." [51] * * * No state explicitly adopted the common law on the press or the doctrine of criminal libels, although no state explicitly rejected either. Only two states prosecuted seditious libel after adopting a constitution with a free press clause, but prosecutions for criminal libel fit the law of every state. Drawing a conclusion from the mere fact that a state's constitution had a free press clause is difficult. In major states—Virginia, Pennsylvania, Massachusetts, and New York—prosecutions suggested a compatibility between free government and punishing libel as a crime.

* * *

[Consider the interpretation given to the free press guarantee in Massachusetts.] In 1789 William Cushing, who had been an influential member of the convention that framed the Massachusetts constitution, was serving his twelfth year as chief justice of his state. He addressed a long, thoughtful letter to John Adams, giving his interpretation of their state constitution's free-press clause which had been originally drafted by Adams. The clause affirmed, "The liberty of the press is essential to the security of freedom in a state; it ought not, therefore, to be restrained in this commonwealth." Cushing worried about the question whether a publication aspersing the conduct of officeholders could be punished under the free-press clause, "when such charges are supportable by the truth of fact." Cushing called this clause "very general and unlimited," and asked, "What guard or limitation can be put upon it?" He was certain it did not * * * render immune from prosecution "*injuring* the public or individuals by propagating falsehoods." But he wanted Adams's opinion on his belief that the clause did guarantee a freedom to discuss all subjects and characters "within the bounds of truth." Blackstone, he admitted, had defined the liberty of the press as a freedom from previous restraints and not as a freedom from punishment for the publication of criminal matter.

But the words of our article understood according to plain English, make no such distinction, and must exclude *subsequent* restraints, as much as *previous restraints*. * * *

50. Henry Schofield, Essays on Constitutional Law and Equity (Boston, 1921), 2:251–522; Zechariah Chafee, Jr., Free Speech in the United States (Cambridge, Mass., 1948), 20.

51. The Virginia Report of 1799–1800 (Richmond, Va., 1850), 221.

Adams replied as follows:

> The difficult and important question is whether the truth of words can be admitted by the court to be given in evidence to the jury, upon a plea of not guilty? * * * I * * * am very clear that under the Articles of our Constitution which you have quoted, it would be safest to admit evidence to the jury of the Truth of accusations, and if the jury found them true and that they were published for the Public good, they would readily acquit.

* * * [I]t is clear that even though Cushing partially repudiated Blackstone when arguing that a guarantee of freedom of the press meant an exclusion of subsequent as well as previous restraints, the chief justice was only going as far as * * * a new generation of English writers who were active in the 1780s. Each had a harp with two strings to it: truth should be a defense against a charge of criminal utterance; the jury should decide whether the defendant's words were criminal. As noted earlier, truth as a defense meant a modification of the common law in substance as well as procedure. Unquestionably it would have liberalized the common law by expanding the scope of permissible expression to include even derogatory and scandalous publications if they were true and presumably written for the public good, or at least, without malice.

But truth is a mischievous, often an illusory, standard that defies knowledge and understanding. It cannot always be proved. * * * Jurors can judge whether the evidence proves the truth of a charge that some official has taken a bribe, but their fallibility is too great to entrust to them a judgment on the truth of an accusation that the government, or one of its policies, or a member of its administration is unjust, tyrannical, or repugnant to the public interest. Accusations of the latter order, not charges of bribes, constituted almost without exception the subject of prosecutions, the very fact that made the doctrine of seditious libel such an oppressive fetter on freedom of expression. The best and most relevant illustration is the entire corpus of prosecutions for seditious libel under the Sedition Act of 1798.

That statute, which nearly abolished freedom of speech and press, embodied the reform proposed by Cushing and Adams. As Zechariah Chafee pointed out, the Sedition Act

> entrusted criminality to the jury and admitted truth as a defense.
> * * * [93]

President Adams willingly signed the Sedition Act and eagerly urged its enforcement, and Cushing, then an associate justice of the Supreme Court of the United States, presided over some of the trials and charged juries on the constitutionality of the statute. Both men acted in full consistency with the opinions expressed in their correspondence of 1789, because they accepted then, as in 1798–1799, the concept of seditious

---

93. Chafee, Free Speech, 23.

libel. They believed then, as Cushing said, that falsehoods and scandals against the government should be punished "with becoming rigour."

* * *

[The views of Adams and Cushing were, if anything, more libertarian than the views held by] James Wilson of Pennsylvania. Excepting James Madison, Wilson was probably the most influential Framer of the United States Constitution and as great a legal expert as anyone in the new nation. At the Pennsylvania ratifying convention of 1787 Wilson had occasion, like his fellow Framers in other state ratifying conventions, to deny an Anti–Federalist accusation that the failure to guarantee freedom of the press meant that oppression of opinion was constitutionally possible. [But, he went on to say,]

> I presume it was not in the view of the honorable gentleman to say that there is no such thing as libel, or that the writers of such ought not to be punished. The idea of the liberty of the press is not carried so far as this in any country—*what is meant by liberty of the press is that there should be no antecedent restraint upon it;* but that every author is responsible when he attacks the security or welfare of the *government,* or the safety, character and property of the individual. * * *

Here, in the most explicit language, is James Wilson, a major figure, restating the English or Blackstonian definition of freedom of the press. His statement leaves no doubt that he believed the law of seditious libel to be in force, because he spoke of the legal responsibility of writers who attacked the security or welfare of the government, and he added that for such attacks the remedy was prosecution. * * * No one at the Pennsylvania convention essayed to deny Wilson's exposition of the law. Thus, in the only state among the original thirteen to guarantee both freedom of speech and press in a constitution drawn before the Federal Bill of Rights, those guarantees did not imply an abandonment of the common law's injunction against criminal libels.

* * *

FROM THE FIRST AMENDMENT TO THE SEDITION ACT

* * *

Did the Framers of the First Amendment intend "to wipe out the common law of sedition, and make further prosecutions for criticism of the government, without any incitement to law-breaking, forever impossible in the United States of America"?[1] The immediate history of the drafting and adoption of the First Amendment's freedom of speech and press clause does not suggest an intent to institute broad reform.

* * *

1. [*Id.* at] 21.

* * * Congress debated the clauses on religion, but on the remainder of the First Amendment considered only whether the right of peaceable assembly vested the people with the power to instruct their representatives how to vote. In the course of that discussion, Madison made the only recorded statement on the subject of speech or press. If by peaceable assembly, he said, "we mean nothing more than this, that the people have a right to express and communicate their sentiments and wishes, we have provided for it already. The right of freedom of speech is secured; the liberty of the press is expressly declared to be beyond the reach of this Government. ...." Any interpretation of the meaning and compass of freedom of speech-and-press drawn from this vague statement would strain credulity. Apathy, ambiguity, and brevity characterize the comments of the few Congressmen who spoke on the First Amendment. The House did not likely understand the debate, care deeply about its outcome, or share a common understanding of the finished amendment.

The Senate, which kept no record of its debates, had deliberated on seventeen amendments submitted by the House. One the Senate killed, the proposal Madison thought "the most valuable": protection against state infringement of speech, press, religion, or trial by jury. The motion to adopt failed to receive the necessary two-thirds vote, although by what margin is unknown. The Senate included many members jealous of state prerogatives and who believed that the Constitution already imposed too many limitations on the states. As a result of the Senate's rejection of the ban on the states, the Constitution offered against state violation no protection whatever to speech, press, and religion. The Senate also weakened the House's ban on establishments of religion. Someone made a proposal that would have critically weakened the free press clause. The Senate voted down a motion to alter the amendment so that freedom of the press should be protected "in as ample a manner as hath at any time been secured by the common law." There is no way of knowing whether the motion was defeated on the ground that it was too narrow or simply unnecessary. Its phraseology reflects a belief in the mind of its proposer that the common law adequately protected freedom of the press; its defeat suggests the Senate's unwillingness to make the amendment embody merely an explicit Blackstonianism. Otherwise the Senate accepted the House proposals, although the Senate combined several, reducing the total number from seventeen to twelve. * * * c

The state legislatures that ratified the First Amendment offer no enlightenment either. Without the records of their legislative debates, we do not know what the state legislatures understood the First Amendment freedoms to mean. Private correspondence, newspapers, and tracts do not help. Most people undoubtedly cared about protecting freedom of speech-and-press, but no one seems to have cared enough to clarify what he meant by the subject upon which he lavished praise. If

c. Relocated paragraph.

definition were unnecessary because of the existence of a tacit and widespread understanding of "liberty of the press," only the received or traditional understanding could have been possible. To assume the existence of a general, latitudinarian understanding that veered substantially from the common-law definition is incredible, given the total absence of argumentative analysis of the meaning of the clause on speech and press. Any novel definition expanding the scope of free expression or repudiating, even altering, the concept of seditious libel would have been the subject of public debate or comment. Not even the Anti-Federalists offered the argument that the clause on speech and press was unsatisfactory because it was insufficiently protective against prosecutions for criminal defamation of the government.

DAVID A. ANDERSON, THE ORIGINS OF THE PRESS CLAUSE

30 UCLA L.Rev. 455, 493–496, 499, 509–513 (1983).

The legislative history of the press clause * * * supports Professor Blasi's assertion that "one of the most important values attributed to a free press by eighteenth-century political thinkers was that of checking the inherent tendency of government officials to abuse the power entrusted to them." [229]   * * *

* * * [Blasi's] view of the press clause seems so thoroughly supported by the legislative history that one may wonder why it has not been universally accepted. The answer lies, I think, in the puzzle of seditious libel and in the hegemony of Leonard Levy's interpretation of first amendment history. If the Framers expected the press to operate as an effective check on government, how could they have tolerated the law of seditious libel, which made criticism of government a crime? And if they really understood the value of a free press, how could they have behaved so repressively toward it when they held power?

* * *

Until 1960, the common assumption was that freedom of the press was one of the key reforms for which the American Revolution had been fought. Professor Chafee in 1941 expressed the generally accepted view: "The First Amendment was written by men ... who intended to wipe out the common law of sedition, and make further prosecutions for criticism of government, without any incitement to law-breaking, forever impossible in the United States of America." [238]

This view was shattered in 1960 with the publication of Levy's book, *Legacy of Suppression*. Levy concluded that the Framers had no intention of instituting any broad reform regarding freedom of expression and, in fact, intended to leave intact the law of seditious libel. The book was widely reviewed and, together with Levy's later writings on the

---

229. Blasi, [*The Checking Value in First Amendment Theory*, 1977 Am.B.Found.Research J. 521,] 538. * * *

238. Z. Chafee, Free Speech in the United States 21 (1941).

subject, has dominated discussion of first amendment history for the past twenty years.[a]

Levy interprets the phrase "freedom of the press" as a mere prohibition against restraints in advance of publication. His conclusion is based on the assertions that in 1789 this was the common law meaning of the phrase, that the few contemporaries who attempted to explain what they meant mentioned nothing more than freedom from prior restraint, and that none of the Framers articulated a more expansive meaning. The prevalent restriction on the press at the time was post-publication punishment for seditious libel, and none of the Framers condemned that as inconsistent with freedom of the press; therefore a general guarantee of press freedom * * * would have prohibited only prior restraints.

* * *

The Press Clause and the Common Law

The legislative history of the press clause casts doubt on * * * Levy's thesis. His [basic] proposition—that the press clause merely constitutionalized the common law—was not expressed in any of the drafts of the first amendment or in any of its antecedents. The only time such an expression was attempted—in the Senate motion to protect press freedom "in as ample a manner as hath at any time been secured by the common law"—it was rejected.

That does not prove Levy wrong, of course. The Senate may have rejected the reference to common law because it understood the press clause precisely as he suggests, and therefore considered the reference unnecessary. It is also possible, however, that the Senate rejected the limitation on the substantive ground that freedom of the press should not be limited to its common law meaning. Given two plausible explanations, with no extrinsic proof of either, there is no apparent reason to presume that the legislature's action was nonsubstantive. And, as we can see from the seventh amendment, when Congress intended the rules of the common law to control, it was capable of saying so. Indeed, the Senate approved the reference to "rules of the common law" in the seventh amendment on the same day that it defeated the attempt to limit freedom of the press to its common law meaning.

* * *

The legislative history does not support Levy's interpretation of the press clause, but he never claimed that it did. His theory rests instead on the proposition that freedom of the press could only have meant freedom from prior restraint, because in 1789 the concept of seditious libel—criminal punishment for criticism of government—was almost universally accepted and because no more expansive theory of press freedom was current. Once again, Levy's scholarship is the dominant

a. Levy issued a second, revised version of his book, entitled Emergence of a Free Press, in 1985. We have drawn the excerpt in this chapter from that version. (Eds.)

source of information. We therefore may profitably begin by examining his historical evidence.

Seditious Libel in America, Pre-1798

Levy asserts that the validity of seditious libel had never been challenged in America prior to 1781, but his own evidence shows that seditious libel, in fact, became ineffectual during the eighteenth century primarily because of popular opposition. This suggests that the Blackstonian view was not universal, and that there was opposition to the notion that it was criminal to criticize government.

Levy correctly points out that seditious libel was part of the received law in colonial America and that no state had repudiated it by 1791. But although the law of seditious libel remained in effect, in practice the doctrine was impotent by the time of the revolution. Criminal prosecutions for seditious libel were virtually unknown in the lifetimes of the Framers.[305] Professor Nelson suggests that "[c]ourt trials for seditious libel ended as a serious threat to printers in the American colonies with the decision in the Zenger case in 1735." Nelson was able to find only one successful prosecution before *Zenger* and none after. Indeed, few prosecutions were even attempted. Nelson found only nine attempts in the entire colonial period.

* * *

Criminal prosecution in the courts was not the only method of punishing seditious libel in colonial America, however. As Levy points out, the judges were "angels of self-restraint" compared to the legislatures, which claimed power to punish as "breaches of parliamentary privilege" statements reflecting adversely on the legislature, its members, or on the government generally.

Parliamentary privilege was an extension of the freedom of speech guaranteed to Parliament by the English Bill of Rights of 1689. In addition to freedom from arrest and freedom of speech for themselves, members of the colonial legislatures, like their English models, claimed the right to punish nonmembers who displayed contempt for the reputation or authority of the assembly. Suspected contemnors were summoned before the assembly and summarily tried.

Although parliamentary privilege was used in colonial America more frequently and more successfully than criminal prosecution, it too was eventually rendered ineffective by popular opposition. For example, the Massachusetts House in 1754 attempted to punish printer Daniel Fowle for satirizing a House debate. Fowle fought back by publishing a tract condemning the proceedings against him as unjust and describing as tyrannical the House's role as accuser, judge, and jury. His case became

---

305. Nelson, *Seditious Libel in Colonial America,* 3 Am.J.Legal Hist. 160, 170 (1959).

a local cause celebre, and the House was forced by public pressure to drop the charges. * * *

* * *

In any event, use of seditious libel to suppress criticism in the colonies proves little about the meaning of the press clause. The prosecutions occurred before there were any state constitutional provisions protecting freedom of the press, so they do not necessarily suggest that seditious libel was believed to be consistent with freedom of the press. They do indicate that someone approved of seditious libel, but they do not necessarily reflect the view of the public. The fact that legislatures and judges employed seditious libel hardly proves that the Framers intended to permit them to continue to do so; the very purpose of constitutional limitations is to restrain legislators and judges from acts they would otherwise consider proper. The popular resistance mentioned above makes it obvious that the views of the judges, and sometimes even the legislators, were at variance with those of many Americans. The offense of seditious libel "was one that seems to have been condemned on the statute books but not by the moral consciousness of the community. When the better men in the community openly break the law, it is a law which is destined to be replaced, for it is already dying." [325]

DAVID M. RABBAN, THE FIRST AMENDMENT IN ITS FORGOTTEN YEARS

90 Yale L.J. 514, 516–20, 522–24, 558–62, 579 (1981).

Contemporary scholars of the free speech clause of the First Amendment generally trace its modern development from the Espionage Act passed shortly after the United States entered World War One. They regard the resulting cases as the first important judicial decisions, and the articles and book published by Zechariah Chafee, Jr., from 1918 through 1920 as the seminal legal scholarship. Chafee's writings were prompted by and concentrated on the highly controversial Espionage Act prosecutions and decisions. Although he devoted some attention to the origins and early history of the First Amendment, Chafee essentially ignored the years between the Sedition Act of 1798 and the Espionage Act of 1917.

For decades, scholars and judges accepted Chafee's interpretation of First Amendment history. In 1960, however, Leonard Levy wrote *Legacy of Suppression,* which effectively challenged Chafee's libertarian understanding of the original meaning of the First Amendment. Scholars have also refuted the libertarian connotation Chafee ascribed to the phrase "clear and present danger" in the opinion Justice Holmes wrote in *Schenck v. United States,* one of the first Espionage Act cases decided by the Supreme Court. More recently, Gerald Gunther has stressed the

325. Anastaplo, [Book Review, 39 N.Y.U.L.Rev. 735, 738 (1964).]

importance of Judge Learned Hand's earlier opinion in *Masses Publishing Co. v. Patten,* decided the month after Congress passed the Espionage Act.　But the period between 1798 and 1917 has remained inadequately explored.

* * *

The impression left by Chafee and reinforced by subsequent scholars thus persists, and analysis of the modern development of free speech doctrine still generally begins with the Espionage Act litigation.

There was, in fact, a marked increase in legal analysis of the First Amendment in the years following World War One.　There were more prosecutions, more judicial decisions, and more scholarly articles and books.　Perhaps of greatest importance, World War One and its aftermath made a greater number of influential people sensitive to First Amendment concerns.

This postwar activity, however, did not spring from a void.　During the generation that preceded World War One, the consequences of industrialization led to substantial social unrest and radical activity. The industrial violence associated with the Homestead and Pullman strikes in the 1890s, the fear of anarchists generated by the Haymarket riot of 1886 and revived by the assassination of President McKinley in 1901, the nativist response to mass immigration, and the notoriety of the IWW and Emma Goldman in the early 1900s are among the best known examples.　It is not surprising that this turbulent period tested the legal meaning of free speech.　The subsequent neglect of the prewar years has left a distorted view of the social and intellectual history of the First Amendment.

Scholarship and judicial decisions before the war often foreshadowed and influenced subsequent developments in ways that the post-war civil libertarians never fully understood and occasionally misrepresented.　In the decades prior to *Schenck,* a rather wide range of free speech cases, including several arising out of radical activity, did reach the Supreme Court.　Some referred directly to the First Amendment.　Others raised questions that courts today would recognize as free speech issues, although the Supreme Court, and sometimes even the litigants, often did not identify them as such.　A few scattered hints of doctrine emerged from this litigation, particularly judicial reliance on the possible "bad tendency" of speech as a justification for penalizing it.　The Supreme Court, with one minor exception, uniformly found against the free speech claimants.　Decisions by other courts were generally as restrictive, although some did support free speech.

Legal scholarship before the war also explored the meaning of freedom of expression, often in remarkably sophisticated terms and often with considerable concern for the importance of free speech to the individual and to society.　Important scholars such as Thomas Cooley, Ernst Freund, Roscoe Pound, and Henry Schofield analyzed these issues before Zechariah Chafee, Jr., entered the field.　Theodore Schroeder, the principal figure in the Free Speech League, an important precursor of the American Civil Liberties Union, wrote extensively on freedom of expression during this period.[19] These scholars strongly criticized the prevalent judicial insensitivity to free speech.

* * *

I. Free Speech Before the Courts

Scholars generally assume that courts were not asked to resolve free speech issues until Congress passed the Espionage Act in 1917. No major casebook on constitutional law highlights a First Amendment decision before 1917, and few casebooks even refer to any prior free speech developments. * * *

Scores of decisions reported from all levels of the judicial system in the generation before World War One demonstrate that this assumption is incorrect. These cases arose in a striking variety of factual contexts. Many grew out of the social unrest of the period: workers, anarchists, socialists, and religious minorities produced much of the free speech litigation before the war. But cases involving editors and publishers, businessmen, movie distributors, candidates for political office, and government employees also brought First Amendment issues to judicial attention. These decisions provide fascinating proof that litigation about freedom of expression is not just a relatively recent phenomenon.

The overwhelming majority of prewar decisions in all jurisdictions rejected free speech claims, often by ignoring their existence. No court was more unsympathetic to freedom of expression than the Supreme Court, which rarely produced even a dissenting opinion in a First Amendment case. Most decisions by lower federal courts and state courts were also restrictive, although there were some notable exceptions. Radicals fared particularly poorly, but the widespread judicial hostility to the value of free speech transcended any individual issue or litigant.

This pervasive hostility did not emerge from a coherent theoretical framework. The cases were as doctrinally sparse as they were factually

---

19. The Free Speech League, founded in 1902 and incorporated in 1911, was the leading defender of free speech prior to World War One. The League was an informal organization consisting of a few intellectuals and professionals who lived in New York City. Its members dedicated themselves to protecting freedom of expression for all groups and in all contexts at a time when almost all Americans, including the future leaders of the American Civil Liberties Union and other postwar civil libertarians, were generally unconcerned about this issue. Most of the information available on the League is contained in the private papers of Theodore Schroeder, its most important member. Schroeder's papers are locat-

ed in the Library of Southern Illinois University at Carbondale. Other active members of the League included the well-known journalists Hutchins Hapgood and Lincoln Steffens, and Gilbert E. Roe, a former law partner of Senator Robert M. LaFollette and a practicing attorney who handled many free speech cases, including Fox v. Washington, 236 U.S. 273 (1915), State v. Boyd, 86 N.J.L. 75, 91 A. 586 (Sup.Ct.1914), *rev'd on other grounds,* 87 N.J.L. 560, 94 A. 807 (Ct.Err. & App.1915), People v. Sinclair, 86 Misc. 426, 149 N.Y.S. 54 (Ct.Gen. Sess.1914), Masses Publishing Co. v. Patten, 244 F. 535 (S.D.N.Y.), *rev'd,* 246 F. 24 (2d Cir.1917), and Debs v. United States, 249 U.S. 211 (1919) * * *.

diverse. Like many decisions in all areas of the law before World War
One, these First Amendment cases typically invoked formal pieties at the
expense of rigorous analysis, thus precluding the interchange and criticism necessary to the evolution of doctrine. At the same time that they
issued platitudes about the importance of First Amendment values,
judges failed to recognize free speech claims. Even when the courts
addressed the free speech issues presented, they generally resolved them
on an ad hoc basis. Courts rarely went beyond the facts of a particular
case to articulate fundamental principles of interpretation. As Chafee
pointed out, "[n]early every free speech decision ... appears to have
been decided largely by intuition," and the intuitions of conservative
judges rarely supported freedom of expression.

The absence of systematic judicial thought makes it difficult to
divide the prewar cases into analytical categories, but some generalizations are possible. Opinions constantly reiterated that the First Amendment and analogous provisions of state constitutions do not protect
"license" or the "abuse" of speech. Using this rationale without defining the boundary between "free" speech and "license" or "abuse,"
courts routinely restricted speech in public places and developed the
labor injunction. Courts also punished libel, obscenity, and "indecent"
publications, pointing out that the First Amendment did not abolish
preexisting liability at common law. Many decisions, including an
important Supreme Court opinion by Justice Holmes, followed Blackstone's conclusion that free speech precludes prior restraints, but permits the punishment of publications, regardless of truth, for their
tendency to harm the public welfare.[27] In striking contrast to their
increased oversight of economic and social legislation, judges gave great
deference to the "police power" of legislators and administrators to
determine the tendency of speech. Judges also readily found that
speech, even if not directly prohibited, had a tendency to produce an
action proscribed by statute and therefore could be penalized as a
violation of the more general law.

The judicial landscape, however, was not unrelievedly bleak. A few
Supreme Court opinions contained some fragments of theory and hints
of a more tolerant attitude toward freedom of expression. In addition, a
minority of state and lower federal courts provided substantial protection for free speech, and several evaluated the meaning of the First
Amendment with extraordinary care and sophistication, even by more
recent standards.

* * *

* * * For the most part, however, the few relatively libertarian
opinions were not analytically more rigorous than the norm for this
period. Even when supporting free speech claims, they generally did not
explain in any meaningful detail the basis for the result. They did not
attempt to develop guidelines for determining what constitutes speech or

---

27. Patterson v. Colorado, 205 U.S. 454,
462 (1907).

when speech may be unlawful, perhaps because they devoted so little attention to considering the interests the First Amendment was designed to safeguard.

The analytical sterility of most opinions, regardless of outcome, was self-perpetuating. Judges did not challenge each other to think deeply about the First Amendment and were therefore less likely to revise their views. But there were a sufficient number of libertarian decisions to suggest that judges were not simply unable to conceive of more generous approaches to the First Amendment. It seems likely that many judges who reached restrictive decisions knew some of the protective precedents and consciously, if seldom explicitly, rejected them. In any event, the fact that some prewar judges could be sympathetic to free speech claims suggests that the tradition of insensitivity was not so dominant that only an intellectual breakthrough in First Amendment interpretation could have created the possibility of different results. The existence of protective decisions, even more than their relative paucity, emphasizes the general judicial hostility toward free speech before World War One.

The prewar cases also demonstrate that the decisions in Selective Draft Law and Espionage Act prosecutions during and immediately after World War One were neither a temporary aberration from a libertarian tradition nor the consequence of an initial encounter with the First Amendment. The wartime and postwar decisions were depressingly similar to their prewar antecedents. They continued an existing tradition of hostility to free speech claims by reaching restrictive results through simplistic justifications that rarely considered the meaning of the First Amendment. To give the most obvious examples, Justice Holmes' decisions in the first Espionage Act cases are not appreciably different in analysis or result from his prewar decisions in *Patterson v. Colorado* and *Fox v. Washington*. On the other hand, this established tradition of hostility makes even more dramatic the rapid reorientation of First Amendment theory by the postwar civil libertarians, whose ranks Justices Holmes and Brandeis soon joined.

II. LEGAL SCHOLARSHIP

Scholars as well as judges considered the meaning of freedom of expression in the generation before Congress passed the Espionage Act. Just as case law preceded *Schenck*, treatises and articles anticipated Chafee. This legal scholarship stands in striking contrast to the tradition of judicial hostility to First Amendment values. Unlike the prewar decisions, which were generally restrictive and poorly reasoned, much of the legal writing of this period used sophisticated analyses to reach protective standards. Relatively libertarian theory, moreover, was not the province of eccentric iconoclasts. The authors included some of the most eminent scholars in the country. They offered convincing doctrinal support for free speech claims, but their ideas did not gain significant judicial acceptance until after the United States entered World War One.

Within this scholarship, five authors were particularly important.[235] Two respected and widely cited treatises, Thomas Cooley's *Constitutional Limitations* and Ernst Freund's *The Police Power,* included sections on freedom of speech. At the annual meeting of the American Sociological Society in 1914, Henry Schofield, a professor at Northwestern University Law School, presented a comprehensive paper on "Freedom of the Press in the United States." Roscoe Pound, perhaps the most influential legal scholar of his generation, wrote two articles in the *Harvard Law Review* that, while limited in scope, offered highly original and provocative interpretations of the First Amendment.[239] The prodigious theoretical writings of Theodore Schroeder, the guiding force behind the Free Speech League, were the most extensive and libertarian treatments of freedom of speech in the prewar period.[241] Despite their often convoluted style and hysterical tone, Schroeder's writings were an early and comprehensive statement of what modern scholars would describe as an "absolutist" approach to the First Amendment. Unfortunately, they have failed to receive the serious scholarly attention they deserve.

These scholars rarely described or criticized each other's arguments. They sometimes cited cases as raw material for the presentation of free speech issues, but rarely as guides to analysis, an understandable approach given the poor quality of judicial precedents. Nor did they rely on prior scholarly treatment of the First Amendment perhaps because none of significance existed. Nevertheless, all five discussed a number of similar themes and, despite differences in emphasis, their published work reveals broad areas of agreement.

Like their modern counterparts, these scholars were most united in their criticisms of judicial decisions. They castigated American courts for adopting as a constitutional standard Blackstone's position that free speech means nothing more than the prohibition of prior restraints. Pound and Schofield accused judges of failing to make useful distinctions

---

235. * * *

Given the current assumption that there was little or no First Amendment activity before World War One, it is interesting to read in a law review note published in 1916 that, except for the Fourteenth Amendment, the First Amendment is "the most popular as well as the most versatile of the constitutional guaranties." Note, *Constitutional Law—Freedom of Speech and of the Press—Recent Decisions,* 65 U.Pa.L.Rev. 170, 170 (1916). This note identified the growing "struggle between capital and labor" and "the increase of reform legislation of doubtful constitutionality" as the two major sources of First Amendment litigation. *Id.* at 174.

Case and Comment devoted its November 1915 issue to a "Free Speech Number." The articles are essentially descriptive, but several characterized from different per-

spectives the state of the law on free speech. Two authors approved of existing case law, Ackerly, *Constitutional Freedom of Speech and of the Press,* 22 Case & Com. 457 (1915); Chamberlain, *Freedom of Speech in Public Streets, Parks and Commons,* 22 Case & Com. 461 (1915), while two others criticized the prevailing judicial tradition as overly restrictive, Morton, *Free Speech and Its Enemies,* 22 Case & Com. 471 (1915); Shepard, *Freedom of Speech in Industrial Controversies,* 22 Case & Com. 466 (1915).

239. Pound, *Equitable Relief Against Defamation and Injuries to Personality,* 29 Harv.L.Rev. 640 (1916); Pound, *Interests of Personality,* 28 Harv.L.Rev. 343, 445 (1915).

241. *See, e.g.,* T. Schroeder, *Free Speech for Radicals* (enl. ed. 1916); T. Schroeder, *"Obscene" Literature and Constitutional Law* (1911).

between protected and unprotected speech. Pound pointed out the courts' occasional "over-insistence" upon the state's interest in security, and Schofield called the practice of holding newspaper editors in contempt for criticizing judicial conduct "intolerable" and a reestablishment of the Star Chamber. "When judges in solemn and deliberate opinions," Schofield further complained, "bracket striking and boycotting workmen with anarchists, then the *tu quoque* hot retort of the workmen that the judges are tools of the corporations is essentially human." Cooley, observing that the courts traditionally adapted "the plastic rules of the common law" to accommodate change, criticized judges for not developing the law of libel to provide greater protection for newspapers, "one of the chief means for the education of the people."

Schroeder was the most vitriolic in his criticism of judicial decisions. "[J]udicial history," he concluded, "abundantly shows that courts have destroyed and evaded the constitutional guarantee of freedom of speech and of the press" by "dogmatically" creating "new exceptions and limitations, which are not represented by a single word in the constitution itself." Judges, in Schroeder's opinion, had suffered from "an epidemic of respectable hysteria" that "incapacitate[d] them for critical thinking," as demonstrated by their reliance on "stupid" and "meaningless epithets" such as "licentiousness." When judges complained that free speech could not be defined, they undertook "authoritatively to make their own intellectual bankruptcy the limit of the intellectual evolution of the race."

These scholars did not simply criticize the courts. They attempted to construct theoretical support for their free speech values by investigating the meaning and limitations of the First Amendment. And though they evidently thought and wrote independently, a substantial degree of consensus emerged from their articles and books. They emphasized social interests in freedom of expression, including the positive influence of the exchange of ideas on the development of civilization and, particularly, the importance of political discussion to democratic government. Most of them distinguished "public" from "private" concerns and argued that the First Amendment provides greater safeguards for the discussion of public affairs, especially by political and religious minorities. Several believed that broad protection for freedom of speech would reduce the threat of disorder and that its repression would be more likely to lead to actual violence. Consistent with these views, they generally rejected, as incompatible with the First Amendment, the English common-law crime of seditious libel, other tests based on the alleged bad tendency of speech, and Blackstone's opinion that free speech prohibits only prior restraints. With various degrees of explicitness, several recognized incitement to unlawful action as the point at which speech may constitutionally be punished. Most of these scholars also agreed that the First Amendment did not abolish common-law crimes such as libel and obscenity. However, they generally maintained that the First Amendment provides basic safeguards that could be expanded, but not limited, as society develops.

* * *

The work of these five authors illustrates the chasm that existed before World War One between the world of legal scholarship and the judiciary. The restrictive results and the analytic poverty of the prewar decisions reflected the pervasive judicial hostility to the value of free speech. Those cases bear little resemblance to recent First Amendment adjudication. Much of the legal scholarship of that period, on the other hand, hardly seems the product of an earlier age. Scholars identified and addressed many of the issues that continue to generate judicial and scholarly commentary. From historical and functional analyses of the purposes of the First Amendment, they derived practical tests for determining its scope.

These prewar writings, generally ignored in contemporary judicial decisions, are today largely forgotten. Chafee is now considered the seminal scholar of the First Amendment. Chafee himself, however, relied on his scholarly predecessors, and Holmes and Brandeis in turn relied on Chafee in developing a libertarian tradition in their dissenting opinions in the 1920s. As a result, these prewar scholars exerted belated yet significant influence on the development of First Amendment theory in a more receptive era.

GERALD GUNTHER, LEARNED HAND AND THE ORIGINS OF MODERN FIRST AMENDMENT DOCTRINE: SOME FRAGMENTS OF HISTORY

27 Stan.L.Rev. 719–22, 755–61 (1975).

This Essay grows out of my research for a biography of Judge Learned Hand.[a] My main purpose is to put into print significant portions of the largely unpublished correspondence between Judge Hand and two other major contributors to the evolution of first amendment doctrine, Justice Oliver Wendell Holmes and Professor Zechariah Chafee, Jr. Sixteen of their letters—the first group between Hand and Holmes, the second between Hand and Chafee—constitute the Appendix to this Essay. Here I want not only to sketch the background and describe the substance of the exchanges, but also to offer my tentative interpretation of their meaning and impact.

I believe these are letters of historical fascination and continuing importance. They are fascinating for their behind-the-scenes glimpses of personal interactions and intellectual struggles in the formative era of free speech law, little more than a half century ago. They are important because the writers then debated at a level of analytical sophistication

---

a. Now published as Learned Hand: Knopf, 1994).
The Man and the Judge (New York: Alfred

and philosophical insight not surpassed in judicial opinions or academic commentary to this day. And they are especially important because they illuminate the quite different speech-protective formulas advanced by Hand and Holmes—formulas that have recently coalesced in unanticipated ways to form the core of today's first amendment doctrine.

This correspondence centering on Learned Hand throws light on two major themes, one beginning to be explored in the literature, the other more novel. The first pertains to the perceptions and contributions of Justice Holmes at the time of the Supreme Court's first significant encounter with first amendment problems, in cases involving agitation against United States participation in World War I. In the spring of 1919, Justice Holmes announced the clear and present danger test in the Court's opinion in *Schenck v. United States.* The correspondence between Hand and Holmes confirms what revisionist commentators have recently suggested: that Holmes was at that time quite insensitive to any claim for special judicial protection of free speech; that the *Schenck* standard was not truly speech-protective; and that it was not until the fall of 1919, with his famous dissent in *Abrams v. United States,* that Holmes put some teeth into the clear and present danger formula, at least partly as a result of probing criticism by acquaintances such as Learned Hand.

The second theme pertains to the meaning and persistence of Learned Hand's *Masses* alternative for the solution of seditious speech problems. In 1917, District Judge Hand decided *Masses Publishing Co. v. Patten,*[6] holding that the radical magazine *The Masses* could not be banned from the mails under the World War I Espionage Act. It was a rare judicial effort to stem the mounting tide of suppression of dissent, in an articulation of first amendment values and an elaboration of free speech doctrine announced 2 years before the Supreme Court's first opportunity to grapple with the same issues.

These letters make clear what has long been doubted or ignored: that the *Masses* approach was indeed a distinctive, carefully considered alternative to the prevalent analyses of free speech issues. According to the usual arguments, the punishability of speech turned on an evaluation of its likelihood to cause forbidden consequences. Varying formulations—"natural and probable" consequences and "bad tendency" were the favorites—authorized suppression upon different showings of the closeness of speech to illegal action. But all of those approaches shared the common characteristic of requiring factfinders—typically, juries—to assess circumstances and to guess about the risks created by the challenged speech.

Learned Hand thought this characteristic of the prevalent formulas too slippery, too dangerous to free expression, too much at the mercy of factfinders reflecting majoritarian sentiments hostile to dissent. Instead, he urged, in *Masses* and for several years thereafter, the adoption of a strict, "hard," "objective" test focusing on the speaker's words: if

---

6. 244 F. 535 (S.D.N.Y.), *rev'd,* 246 F. 24 (2d Cir.1917).

the language used was solely that of direct incitement to illegal action, speech could be proscribed; otherwise, it was protected.

In the received wisdom about our first amendment tradition, *Masses* has been overshadowed by the clear and present danger criterion that emerged 2 years later, in the Holmes opinions in *Schenck* and *Abrams*. The tendency has been to view the *Masses* approach as a precursor of clear and present danger, essentially similar to Holmes' test. It has seemed to me for some time that sharp differences are perceptible on the face of the Hand and Holmes opinions. But not until these letters became available was there convincing evidence that the differences were from the beginning deeply felt and clearly perceived. When I prepared an edition of my constitutional law casebook a few years ago, before I began my research in the Hand Papers, I included *Masses* as the only principal case that was not a Supreme Court decision, and I called attention to the differences between the *Masses* incitement test and clear and present danger. At that time, I feared—and others admonished me—that I might be exaggerating the differences, that I might be reading too much into the words of the opinions.

The correspondence removes those doubts. Hand was fully aware of the distinctiveness of his approach. He adopted it with considerable concern and thought, and he persisted in urging it despite the coolest reception from the profession. Perhaps most intriguingly, the correspondence demonstrates that Hand was among the very few who did not wholly join the chorus of libertarian acclaim for Holmes' dissent in *Abrams*. Instead, in his letters to Chafee, he lucidly and persuasively articulated flaws in the clear and present danger test and continued for some years to advocate the *Masses* alternative.

In the early 1920's, Hand gave up. He was resigned to seeing his analysis condemned to oblivion. Yet he proved a better prophet than he knew. Clear and present danger did indeed become the dominant libertarian doctrine for the three decades after *Schenck*: it was increasingly invoked in Supreme Court opinions and widely hailed in off-the-Court commentaries, led by those of Zechariah Chafee, Jr. But in the late 1950's, the popularity of clear and present danger waned. The Supreme Court set off in new directions; and the perceptions and doctrines of its new outlook proved to be strikingly similar to those Learned Hand had urged from 1917 to 1921. Indeed, today's operative first amendment doctrine, as first enunciated in *Brandenburg v. Ohio* in 1969, can be viewed as a coalescing of the best features of the two contending approaches: Hand's incitement analysis has become a central theme; elements of Holmes' clear and present danger test provide additional safeguards for free expression.

* * *

Document No. 1.   *Learned Hand to Oliver Wendell Holmes, June 22, 1918*

Windsor, Vermont

June 22, 1918.

Dear Mr. Justice

I gave up rather more easily than I now feel disposed about Tolerance on Wednesday. Here I take my stand. Opinions are at best provisional hypotheses, incompletely tested. The more they are tested, after the tests are well scrutinized, the more assurance we may assume, but they are never absolutes. So we must be tolerant of opposite opinions or varying opinions by the very fact of our incredulity of our own. (This may be left for deductive demonstration in accord with the inexorable rules of formal logic by E.D.W., C.J. U.S. Sup. Ct.).[199]

You say that I strike at the sacred right to kill the other fellow when he disagrees. The horrible possibility silenced me when you said it. Now, I say, "Not at all, kill him for the love of Christ and in the name of God, but always realize that he may be the saint and you the devil. Go your way with a strong right arm and a swift shining sword, in full consciousness that what you kill for, and what you may die for, some smart chap like Laski may write a book and prove is all nonsense." I agree that in practical application there may arise some difficulty, but I am a philosopher and if Man is so poor a creature as not to endure the truth, it is no concern of mine. I didn't make him; let the Galled Jade wince, speaking reverently of course.

I sat under the Bo Tree and these truths were revealed unto me. Tolerance is the twin of Incredulity, but there is no inconsistency in cutting off the heads of as many as you please; that is a natural right. Only, and here we may differ, I do say that you may not cut off heads, (except for limited periods and then only when you want to very much indeed), because the victims insist upon saying things which look against Provisional Hypothesis Number Twenty–Six, the verification of which to date may be found in its proper place in the card catalogue. Generally, I insist, you must allow the possibility that if the heads are spared, other cards may be added under that sub-title which will have, perhaps, an important modification.

All this seems to me so perfectly self-evident, self-explanatory and rigidly applicable to the most complicated situations that I hesitate to linger upon it, lest I should seem tolerant of any different of opinion concerning it.

I greatly enjoyed my good fortune in meeting you on the train.

Faithfully yours,
Learned Hand.

---

199. Chief Justice Edward Douglass White. White's opinions typically had a surface appearance of formal logic but were widely thought to be unsatisfactory.

Document No. 2. *Oliver Wendell Holmes to Learned Hand, June 24, 1918*

Beverly Farms, Mass.

June 24, 1918

Dear Hand

Rarely does a letter hit me so exactly where I live as yours, and unless you are spoiling for a fight I agree with it throughout. My only qualification, if any, would be that free speech stands no differently than freedom from vaccination. The occasions would be rarer when you cared enough to stop it but if for any reason you did care enough you wouldn't care a damn for the suggestion that you were acting on a provisional hypothesis and might be wrong. That is the condition of every act. You tempt me to repeat an apologue that I got off to my wife in front of the statue of Garrison on Commonwealth Avenue, Boston, many years ago. I said—If I were an official person I should say nothing shall induce me to do honor to a man who broke the fundamental condition of social life by bidding the very structure of society perish rather than he not have his way—Expressed in terms of morals, to be sure, but still, his way. If I were a son of Garrison I should reply—Fool, not to see that every great reform has seemed to threaten the structure of society,—but that society has not perished, because man is a social animal, and with every turn falls into a new pattern like the Kaleidoscope. If I were a philosopher I should say—Fools both, not to see that you are the two blades (conservative and radical) of the shears that cut out the future. But if I were the ironical man in the back of the philosopher's head I should conclude— Greatest fool of all, Thou—not to see that man's destiny is to fight. Therefore take thy place on the one side or the other, if with the added grace of knowing that the Enemy is as good a man as thou, so much the better, but kill him if thou Canst. All of which seems in accord with you. If I may repeat another chestnut of ancient date and printed in later years—When I say a thing is true I mean that I can't help believing it—and nothing more. But as I observe that the Cosmos is not always limited by my Cant Helps I don't bother about absolute truth or even inquire whether there is such a thing, but define the Truth as the system of my limitations. I may add that as other men are subject to a certain number, not all, of my Cant Helps, intercourse is possible. When I was young I used to define the truth as the majority vote of that nation that can lick all others. So we may define the present war as an inquiry concerning truth. Of course you won't suspect me of thinking with levity on that subject because of my levitical speech. I enjoyed our meeting as much as you possibly could have and should have tried to prolong it to Boston but that I feared my wife would worry.

Sincerely Yours

O.W. Holmes

Document No. 3. *Oliver Wendell Holmes to Learned Hand, Feb. 25, 1919*

Supreme Court of the United States,
Washington, D.C.

Feb. 25, 1919

Dear Judge Hand

Instead of the letter I intended to write to you some new work makes it necessary that I should confine myself to a word. I read your Masses decision—I haven't the details in my mind and will assume for present purposes that I should come to a different result—but I did want to tell you after reading it that I thought that few judges indeed could have put their view with such force or in such admirable form.

Sincerely yours
O.W. Holmes

Hon. Learned Hand

Document No. 4. *Learned Hand to Oliver Wendell Holmes, (late Mar.) 1919*

JUDGE LEARNED HAND'S CHAMBERS

Dear Mr. Justice

I have read Debs v. U.S. and the other case [203] and this is positively my last appearance in the role of liberator. I haven't a doubt that Debs was guilty under any rule conceivably applicable. As to the rule actually laid down my dying words are these, now already fast receding in the seas of forgotten errors, and a crazy Saragossa that would be, wouldn't it? All the mad freaks of past contrivance.

The thing against which the statute aims is positive impediments to raising an army. Speech may create such by its influence on others' conduct. In nature the causal sequence is perfect, but responsibility does not go pari passu. I do not understand that the rule of responsibility for speech has ever been that the result is known as likely to follow. It is not,—I agree it might have been,—a question of responsibility dependent upon reasonable forecast, with an excuse when the words, had another possible effect. The responsibility only began when the words were directly an incitement. If I am wrong about that, it is mere matter of history. I confess I have no present access to the history.

Assuming that I am not wrong, then it was a question of extending the responsibility, and that was fairly a matter of better and worse. All I say is, that since the cases actually occur when men are excited and since juries are especially clannish groups,—are they societates perfectae?,—it is very questionable whether the test of motive is not a dangerous test. Juries wont much regard the difference between the probable result of the words and the purposes of the utterer. In any case, unless one is rather set in conformity, it will serve to intimidate,—

203. Frohwerk v. United States, 249 U.S. 204 (1919).

throw a scare into,—many a man who might moderate the storms of popular feeling. I know it did in 1918.

The rule coupled w. Burleson's [204] legal irresponsibility certainly terrorized some of the press whose voices were much needed.

There, that is all! Absolutely and irrevocably all in saecula saeculorum! I bid a long farewell to my little toy ship which set out quite bravely in the shortest voyage ever made.

I was amused at the Harrison law decision,[205] which showed the vast importance of the sacred doctrine of "Imputation." That means the "Mystery" or "Sacrament" of being able to impute to Congress purposes you know they didn't have.

Sincerely yours
L. Hand

Document No. 5. *Oliver Wendell Holmes to Learned Hand, Apr. 3, 1919*

Supreme Court of the United States,
Washington, D.C.

April 3, 1919

Dear Judge Hand

Since your letter came I have been so busy propagating new sophistries &c. that I haven't had time to defend the old ones. And now I am afraid that I don't quite get your point. As to intent under the Espionage Act I believe I have said nothing except to note that under the instructions the jury must be taken to have found that Debs's speech was intended to obstruct and tended to obstruct—and except further that evidence was held admissible as bearing on intent. Even if absence of intent might not be a defence I suppose that the presence of it might be material. Leaving that on one side, you say "the responsibility only began when the words were directly an incitement"—I am afraid I do not know exactly what history you have in mind—but I don't see how you differ from the test as stated by me Schenck v. U S (March 3, 1919). "The question in every case is whether the words used are used in such circumstances and are of such a nature as to create a clear and present danger that they will bring about the substantive evils that Congress has a right to prevent. It is a question of proximity and degree."—I haven't time even now to recur to your decision but I take it that you agree that words may constitute an obstruction within the statute, even without proof that the obstruction was successful to the point of preventing recruiting. That I at least think plain. So I don't know what the

204. Albert Sidney Burleson—Postmaster General of the United States, 1913–1921—was responsible for mail bans such as that challenged in the *Masses* case.

205. *See* United States v. Doremus, 249 U.S. 86 (1919).

matter is, or how we differ so far as your letter goes. With which I send you my blessing and don't hold you bound by your adieu to this stage.

As to the Harrison Drug Act, (*between ourselves*) I am tickled at every case of that sort as they seem to me to confirm the ground of my dissent in the Child Labor case last term. Hammer v. Dagenhart, 247 U.S. 257, 277. Also I think the drug act cases rightly decided. In my opinion Congress may have what ulterior motives they please if the act passed in the immediate aspect is within their powers—though personally, were I a legislator I might think it dishonest to use powers in that way.

Yours sincerely
O.W. Holmes

Document No. 6. *Learned Hand to Oliver Wendell Holmes, Nov. 25, 1919*

JUDGE LEARNED HAND'S CHAMBERS

Dear Mr. Justice

I was greatly pleased with your dissent in the Abrams case, especially with the close which, if I may say so, was in your very highest vein. I am quite confident that whether it is avowed or not, in the end your views must prevail, after people get over the existing hysteria. It will not be the first time that you have formed the law by a minority opinion. I also agree with enthusiasm with your analysis of motive & intent about which there has been much too meagre discussion in the books. It was with a strong emotion that I read your words, stronger because I had found so little professional support for my own beliefs which would always have been expressed so, had I had the power to express them. I cannot help feeling like thanking you, even though I recall the annoyance it gives me when anyone undertakes to thank me for what I may say in an opinion. I always want to answer, "You fool, *I* didn't do it, it just came that way, quite simply and inevitably. If you thank me, you only show that you haven't the remotest idea of what I am doing." So I shall refrain—expressly anyway.

Meanwhile the merry sport of Red-baiting goes on, and the pack gives tongue more and more shrilly. I really can't get up much sympathy for the victims, but I own to a sense of dismay at the increase in all the symptoms of apparent panic. How far people are getting afraid to speak, who have anything really worth while to say, I don't know, but I am sure that the public generally is becoming rapidly demoralized in all its sense of proportion and toleration. For men who are not cock-sure about everything and especially for those who are not damned cock-sure about anything, the skies have a rather sinister appearance.

Nov. 25, 1919   Faithfully yours
Mr. Justice Holmes   Learned Hand

_____

Document No. 7. *Oliver Wendell Holmes to Learned Hand, Nov. 26,
1919*

Supreme Court of the United States,
Washington, D.C.

Nov. 26, 1919

My dear Judge

Your letter gives me the greatest pleasure and I am very much
obliged to you for writing to me. Sympathy and agreement always are
pleasant but they are much more than that when they come from one
that I have learned to think of as I do of you. Accept my thanks.

Ever sincerely yours
Hon. Learned Hand   O.W. Holmes

BIBLIOGRAPHY

The English Heritage

William Blackstone, COMMENTARIES ON THE LAWS OF ENGLAND
(vol. IV, pp. 151–52).

John Bagnell Bury, A HISTORY OF FREEDOM OF THOUGHT (1913).

William M. Clyde, THE STRUGGLE FOR THE FREEDOM OF THE
PRESS FROM CAXTON TO CROMWELL (1934).

Alec Craig, THE BANNED BOOKS OF ENGLAND AND OTHER
COUNTRIES (1962).

Thomas A. Green, VERDICT ACCORDING TO CONSCIENCE, PER-
SPECTIVES ON THE ENGLISH CRIMINAL TRIAL JURY, 1200–
1800 (1985).

James Paterson, THE LIBERTY OF THE PRESS, SPEECH AND PUB-
LIC WORSHIP (1880).

Fredrick Siebert, FREEDOM OF THE PRESS IN ENGLAND 1476–1776
(1952).

Van Vechten Veeder, *The History of the Law of Defamation,* in 3
SELECT ESSAYS IN ANGLO–AMERICAN LEGAL HISTORY 447
(1907).

William H. Wickwar, THE STRUGGLE FOR THE FREEDOM OF THE
PRESS, 1819–1832 (1928).

American Origins of Free Speech and Free Press

James Alexander, A BRIEF NARRATIVE OF THE CASE AND TRIAL
OF JOHN PETER ZENGER (S. Katz 2d ed. 1972).

David Anderson, *Levy v. Levy*, 84 Mich.L.Rev. 777 (1986).

David Anderson, *The Origins of the Press Clause*, 30 UCLA L.Rev. 455 (1983).

Walter Berns, *Freedom of the Press and the Alien and Sedition Laws*, 1970 Sup.Ct.Rev. 109.

Richard Buel, Jr., *Freedom of the Press in Revolutionary America: The Evolution of Libertarianism 1760–1820*, in THE PRESS AND THE AMERICAN REVOLUTION 59 (B. Bailyn & J. Hench eds. 1980).

Thomas F. Carroll, *Freedom of Speech and of the Press in the Federalist Period: The Sedition Act*, 18 Mich.L.Rev. 615 (1920).

Zechariah Chafee, FREE SPEECH IN THE UNITED STATES (1942).

Clyde A. Duniway, THE DEVELOPMENT OF FREEDOM OF THE PRESS IN MASSACHUSETTS (1906).

Murray Dry, *Free Speech and Republican Government*, 6 Const. Comm. 355 (1989).

Philip Hamburger, *The Development of the Law of Seditious Libel and the Control of the Press*, 37 Stan.L.Rev. 661 (1985).

E. Hudon, FREEDOM OF SPEECH AND PRESS IN AMERICA (1963).

Leonard Levy, EMERGENCE OF A FREE PRESS (1985).

Leonard Levy, LEGACY OF SUPPRESSION: FREEDOM OF SPEECH AND PRESS IN EARLY AMERICAN HISTORY (1960).

Leonard Levy, *The Legacy Reexamined*, 37 Stan.L.Rev. 661 (1985).

Leonard Levy, ed., FREEDOM OF THE PRESS FROM ZENGER TO JEFFERSON (1966).

Leonard Levy, JEFFERSON AND CIVIL LIBERTIES: THE DARKER SIDE (1963).

Rutherford Livingston, JOHN PETER ZENGER, HIS PRESS, HIS TRIAL, AND A BIBLIOGRAPHY OF ZENGER IMPRINTS (1904).

William Mayton, *Seditious Libel and the Lost Guarantee of a Freedom of Expression*, 84 Colum.L.Rev. 91 (1984).

David Rabban, *The Ahistorical Historian: Leonard Levy on Freedom of Expression in Early American History*, 37 Stan.L.Rev. 795 (1985).

William Van Alstyne, *Congressional Power and Free Speech: Levy's Legacy Revisited*, 99 Harv.L.Rev. 1089 (1986).

The Roots of Modern Doctrine

Vincent Blasi, *The First Amendment and the Ideal of Civic Courage: The Brandeis Opinion in Whitney v. California*, 29 Wm. & Mary L.Rev. 653 (1988).

Vincent Blasi, *Learned Hand and the Self–Government Theory of the First Amendment:* Masses Publishing Co. v. Patten, 61 U.Colo. L.Rev. 1 (1990).

David Bogen, *The Free Speech Metamorphosis of Mr. Justice Holmes,* 11 Hofstra L.Rev. 97 (1982).

Robert Cover, *The Left, the Right and the First Amendment: 1918–1928,* 40 Md.L.Rev. 349 (1981).

Richard H. Eliel, *Freedom of Speech During and Since the Civil War,* 18 Am.Pol.Sci.Rev. 712 (1924).

Daniel Hildebrand, *Free Speech and Constitutional Transformation,* 10 Const.Commentary 133 (1993).

Harry Kalven, *Professor Ernst Freund and Debs v. United States,* 40 U.Chi.L.Rev. 235 (1973).

William B. Lockhart & Robert C. McClure, *Literature, the Law of Obscenity, and the Constitution,* 38 Minn.L.Rev. 295 (1954).

James C. Paul and Murray L. Schwartz, FEDERAL CENSORSHIP: OBSCENITY IN THE MAIL (1961).

David Rabban, *The Emergence of Modern First Amendment Doctrine,* 50 U.Chi.L.Rev. 1205 (1983).

David M. Rabban, *The Free Speech League, the ACLU, and Changing Conceptions of Free Speech in American History,* 45 Stan.L.Rev. 47 (1992).

David M. Rabban, *The IWW Free Speech Fights and Popular Conceptions of Free Expression Before World War I,* 80 Va.L.Rev. 1055 (1994).

Yosal Rogat & James O'Fallon, *Mr. Justice Holmes: A Dissenting Opinion—The Speech Cases,* 36 Stan.L.Rev. 1349 (1984).

Marc Rohr, *Communists and the First Amendment: The Shaping of Freedom of Advocacy in the Cold War Era,* 28 San Diego L.Rev. 1 (1991).

Henry Schofield, *Freedom of the Press in the United States,* 9 Pub.Am. Sociological Soc. 67 (1914).

Edward F. Waite, *The Debt of Constitutional Law to Jehovah's Witnesses,* 28 Minn.L.Rev. 209 (1944).

David Yassky, *Eras of the First Amendment,* 91 Colum.L.Rev. 1699 (1991).

Chapter II

PHILOSOPHICAL FOUNDATIONS OF FREEDOM OF SPEECH

A. INTRODUCTION

We have reviewed the history of the First Amendment at some length in Chapter I because it has an obvious bearing on the meaning we give to the speech and press clauses. Exactly how much it should constrain our interpretation is a hard question, one which we do not propose to address in this volume. Still, it would be simply a mistake to assume that what the legal system considers the *purpose* of a constitutional provision is coincident with the intentions of its creators. It is impossible to engage in coherent constitutional decisionmaking without some view of the goals that different clauses are deemed to serve. And even those committed to the view that original intent can answer *some* questions do not maintain that it solves all issues likely to wind up in the courts. It is too often ambiguous, or just silent.

It should come as no surprise, therefore, that inquiring into the purposes served by the freedoms of speech and press has been a major preoccupation of scholars and judges. We review some of that work in this chapter. Though there is little scholarly or judicial agreement about the theory of the First Amendment, it is necessary to understand the debates in this area before dealing with the doctrinal issues discussed in Chapters III and IV.

B. THE THEORY OF FREE SPEECH

The First Amendment's speech and press clauses have generated a particularly large literature exploring the underlying rationales for those clauses. The reasons for this are complex. First, free speech theorists have inherited a literature that is among the most important in liberal political theory, including not only John Milton's *Areopagitica* and John Stuart Mill's *On Liberty*, the latter excerpted in this chapter, but also works by Benedict de Spinoza,[1] John Locke,[2] David Hume,[3] and, more

1. A Theologico–Political Treatise (1670).

2. Letter Concerning Toleration (1689); Essay Concerning Toleration (1667).

3. *Of the Liberty of the Press,* in Essays, Moral, Political and Literary (1963).

recently, Bertrand Russell,[4] Karl Popper,[5] and Alexander Meiklejohn.[6]

But however strong the tradition that contemporary free speech theorists inherit, the pressure to theorize comes from the Constitution itself. The relevant text ("Congress shall make no law * * * abridging the freedom of speech, or of the press") is extraordinarily open-ended. We need a theory to apply it to concrete cases, much more than we do for those constitutional provisions, such as the qualifications for holding office and the limitations on the number of terms a President may serve, that in most instances can be applied just as they are written. Moreover, even those who are inclined to see the language of the First Amendment as comparatively determinate have to acknowledge that that determinacy is far too inclusive to provide any realistic assistance. Vast areas of law—including much of criminal law, contracts, evidence, commercial law, antitrust, securities, trade regulation, and many more— involve laws, regulations, or official action in some way restricting the use of language. Faced with the prospect that a First Amendment taken literally in scope would constitutionalize far more of American law than most are comfortable with, First Amendment theory has developed in part as a way of reducing the literal scope of the speech and press clauses to more manageable and more plausible proportions. Thus the initial question of free speech theory is just what task any theory must serve. Kent Greenawalt argues that it must distinguish free speech cases from numerous others involving penalties on the use of language. Frederick Schauer maintains that it must, in order to avoid triviality, explain why harm-producing communication is to be protected despite the harm it may cause. Thomas Emerson notes that there is no reason why a satisfactory theory of the First Amendment needs to be unitary; it may be that the First Amendment has different purposes, no one of which is necessarily more important than the others.

KENT GREENAWALT, SPEECH AND CRIME

1980 Am.B.Found.Res.J. 645, 647–55, 657, 662, 742–43, 750, 784.*

This article concerns communications that may cause antisocial behavior. The main focus is on criminal counseling and vaguer advocacy of crime, that is, expressions encouraging criminal actions; but the discussion also covers provocative comments that trigger hostile violent responses, and disclosures of facts that provide incentives to commit crimes or aid in their commission. Whether such communications can be punished is a troublesome question for a liberal society, given the

---

4. The Practice and Theory of Bolshevism (1949).

5. The Open Society and Its Enemies (5th ed. 1966).

6. Free Speech and Its Relation to Self-Government, in Political Freedom: The Constitutional Powers of the People (1965).

* For a fuller development of the themes in this article, see Greenawalt's more recent Speech, Crime, and the Uses of Language (Oxford, 1989). [Eds.]

central place of freedom of expression and the necessity for any government to enforce the criminal law with a modicum of success. In the
United States, this clash of values is largely resolved through interpretation of the First Amendment, and my analysis is directed to that
constitutional problem, though much I say also has relevance for legislative decisions.

* * *

If on a dark path a person holding the only flashlight tells another
to "step to the right," knowing that the abyss lies in that direction, the
speaker has committed murder when the follower plummets to death
even though all the actor has done is to speak. Unlike murder, crimes
such as perjury and criminal fraud are actually defined in terms of
communication. The behavior they reach is deemed harmful, not because the listener is likely to do something wrongful, but because the
forbidden deception may injure the listener or lead him to engage in
innocent acts that injure others, as when a jury trustingly relies on
perjured testimony to convict.

Though these examples show the obvious untenability of any assertion that communication is always constitutionally protected, serious
questions arise whether feared injuries warrant suppression of particular
kinds of speech. Can racial epithets be punished because they cause
psychological pain, or libels because they damage reputation? Since
such utterances inflict direct harm *and* may provoke criminal responses,
a full analysis of whether they may be punished has to include both
matters.

One way in which communication may cause antisocial action is that
linguistic and photographic representations of various events may engender responsive criminal behavior among recipients.

* * *

Brandenburg v. Ohio,[3] decided in 1969, contains the Supreme
Court's most recent general standard concerning constitutional protection for speech that encourages criminal action. For over 60 years, the
Court has indicated that the Constitution imposes some limits on the
occasions when such speech may be punished. Without clear explanation of its shifts, the Court has wavered over the content of those limits.
In *Brandenburg,* the Court overturned a local Ku Klux Klan leader's
state conviction for advocacy in violation of a criminal syndicalism
statute. Per curiam, and to no one's surprise, the Court held that the
statute impermissibly intruded upon the freedom of expression. From
previous cases, the majority drew this lesson: "These . . . decisions have
fashioned the principle that the constitutional guarantees of free speech
and free press do not permit a State to forbid or proscribe advocacy of
the use of force or of law violation except where such advocacy is
directed to inciting or producing imminent lawless action and is likely to

3. 395 U.S. 444.

incite or produce such action." As we shall see later, this principle was not easy to draw from the earlier cases, but what we want to scrutinize here are its apparent implications. The test in *Brandenburg* was so unnecessary to decision and was presented so summarily that we cannot be sure whether it was intended as the comprehensive standard it appears to be. One who takes the formulation literally and suggests very grave difficulties with it may be accused of being inattentive to what the Court was actually deciding in that case. But if, instead, one writes off some implications as not intended, he may be charged with wishing away what the opinion deliberately states.

The Court tells us that advocacy of law violation is punishable only upon two conditions: the advocacy must be (1) "directed to inciting or producing imminent lawless action" and (2) "likely to incite or produce such action." Since no narrower definition was suggested, "advocacy" as used by the Court apparently includes all urgings of the appropriateness of illegal action, of which remarks directed to inciting or to producing imminent lawless action are a subcategory. One who unambiguously urges specific criminal action is still protected so long as he does not urge *imminent* lawless action. In *Hess v. Indiana* [6] a majority of the Burger Court gave content to the notion of imminency in applying the *Brandenburg* test. During an antiwar demonstration, Hess had remarked to demonstrators blocking the street, "We'll take the fucking street later." At least for purposes of argument, the Supreme Court accepted the state court's view that the statement might be taken to urge the illegal action of taking the street to be performed at some subsequent time. But the Court said that "at worst" the statement "amounted to nothing more than advocacy of illegal action at some indefinite future time," and that there was no evidence it was intended to produce "imminent disorder." Now, if Hess really did mean to urge illegal action, common sense tells us that "later" must have meant later during the day of the demonstration; so the opinion seems to mean that in that setting at least, illegal action some hours hence is not imminent. Even if "imminent" contains some degree of flexibility, the term connotes and is used by the Court to suggest a very short time span between an incitement and the hoped-for action. Suppose then a local racist starts urging in early June and continues to urge publicly through the evening of July 3 that each white in the community identify a particular black and make plans for killing that black on July 4 to celebrate the country's Independence Day, and further suppose that the leader is so effective that some whites faithfully attempt to carry out his proposal. If *Brandenburg* and *Hess* really purport to make such speech constitutionally protected, their principle is subject to grave doubts. If imminence in that hypothetical context would constitute a longer period than in *Hess*, the Court has failed to explicate the factors in the street demonstration setting—e.g., the short attention span of the audience, distractions, the presence of the police—that led to the conclusion that activity proposed to be done later in the day would not be imminent.

6. 414 U.S. 105 (1973).

Under the Court's test, advocacy is protected unless it is actually likely to produce illegal action. Suppose a radical speaker in a university setting is inveighing against authority and says to his emotionally aroused audience, "I want you to show me right now how you spit on the lackeys of imperialism by beating that university guard, the one standing right there, to death." Even if the speaker fully intends that his words be carried out to the letter, his comments are protected if it is "not likely" that the audience will act upon his counsel. Although such a result may be defensible, the Court has failed to explain why a clear purpose to have a serious crime committed immediately should not be a sufficient basis for punishment.

A third troublesome aspect of the Court's standard is that the words must be *directed* toward inciting or producing illegal action. To say that someone's words are directed toward producing a result implies that the purpose of the speaker is to produce that result and, perhaps more, that this purpose is evident in the words that he uses. So long as the speaker does not actually intend to produce imminent lawless action, the Court's standard bars punishment even though the speaker is fully aware that his words may provoke illegal action and that such action is virtually certain to follow. And perhaps it protects the speaker who cleverly avoids conveying to the audience his approval of illegal action, but speaks for the very purpose of producing it. Each of these limitations lies in some tension with the Court's apparent assumption in other cases that a person may be punished for using "fighting words" likely to provoke a violent response.[8] Sometimes the person who hurls an offensive remark at another actually wants a fight, but usually he does not. If A may be punished for saying things to B that are likely to provoke B to strike A, even though A is only reckless about that possibility, why should A be immune from punishment for saying things to B that make it likely that B will commit a crime against someone else? Perhaps the answer is that fighting words make no contribution to social discourse, but one cannot give that answer comfortably in light of what else the Court has said in recent years.

The fourth and by far most pervasive difficulty about the *Brandenburg* test is its failure to qualify its reference to advocacy of law violation. The simple point is that criminal acts are urged upon various people in all sorts of settings that have never been assumed to raise First Amendment problems at all. In a private letter, A urges B to kill their rich uncle upon the uncle's return from Europe so that both can share in the proceeds of the uncle's will. Can the Court possibly have meant that this sort of communication is protected speech if the uncle's return is not imminent or if B is unlikely to act upon A's suggestion? It may be responded, probably accurately, that the Court was not thinking of ordinary private solicitations to commit crimes. Conceivably the Court's use of the term "advocacy" was meant to imply some principled, ideological basis for illegal action in contrast to the usual grounds of private

---

8. See, e.g., Gooding v. Wilson, 405 U.S. 518 (1972).

gain or revenge. But the point here is that any viable approach to the subject of encouragements to crime that gives such encouragements extensive First Amendment protection must somehow distinguish encouragements that raise substantial First Amendment issues from those that do not. That is no easy task, yet in neither *Brandenburg* nor *Hess* does the Court even acknowledge the need to address it. * * *

Communications from other human beings are among the most important causes of human behavior, but the criminal law cannot concern itself with every communication that may fortuitously lead to the commission of a crime. If any communications are to be punished, they must bear some reasonably close connection to the commission of crime. Sometimes, as noted in the introduction, the utterance of words with a proscribed intent may be the sole means by which an ordinary "nonspeech" crime is committed [11] or may constitute a crime, like perjury, that is defined in terms of communication. On other occasions, one person's participation in a criminal activity may be to assign responsibilities and instruct others what physical acts to perform. So long as the underlying crime is acceptably defined, these actors who may do no more than communicate are punishable under present law and would be subjects of punishment under any rational penal theory.

Present law also makes punishable those who have jointly agreed to commit a crime. Even in jurisdictions that require an overt act as well as an agreement, persons who have conspired to commit a crime typically will be punishable well before the point at which the acts of either or both of them would constitute an attempt. Lying behind this distinction is the premise that agreement marks a clear intent to commit a crime, a firmness of purpose, and a social danger that may be lacking when only individual preparatory acts are involved. By agreeing with someone else to do something, a person commits himself to that course of action and he finds it much more difficult to withdraw from an original plan than if he is acting on his own. A substantial portion of people who have once agreed to commit specific crimes will do so unless interventions occur; and it is rational to treat someone's agreement to commit a crime as an indication of his social dangerousness. Objection might, nevertheless, be made to the present extent of liability on the grounds that the law need not reach so far back from the ultimate commission of substantive crimes, that genuine agreement is often difficult to ascertain, and that agreement in many contexts does not connote fixity of purpose. Some of these doubts, much like ones that may be raised about the crime of solicitation, are discussed below in that context. Some may be recast in a manner related to freedom of expression and are so considered in subsequent sections of the article. In any event, solid reasons plainly exist for imposing criminal liability on the basis of communications that convey agreement to commit criminal acts.

---

11. E.g., the murder committed by a direction to step to the right, a step that carries the unaware victim over a cliff.

Encouragements to commit specific crimes may not be as closely connected to ultimate criminal acts as the categories of communication so far discussed, but they also are rather obvious candidates for punishment. When such encouragements have been acted upon, the law has made the speaker liable for the actions of his listeners; and most jurisdictions have also made the speaker criminally liable for unsuccessful encouragements of serious crimes. * * *

The essential argument for making solicitation criminal is straightforward. Without doubt people sometimes act in response to the encouragements of other people; if all urgings to commit criminal acts were stopped, fewer criminal acts would be committed. The person who urges another to commit a criminal act has a criminal intent and has manifested a certain degree of dangerousness. If his solicitation is a "but for" cause of the commission of a crime, he bears some moral responsibility for it, but even if the urging is unsuccessful his intentionally dangerous behavior makes criminal punishment appropriate. * * *

A speaker may communicate factual information for the purpose of increasing the chances that his listener will commit a crime. What is the speaker's liability if he manages to convey the information without signifying his approval of the crime? If the information, say the location of jewelry, assists in the commission of the crime, then the speaker is liable as an accessory or accomplice. If the information is not acted upon, the speaker may still be liable for attempting to aid, a ground of liability recognized by some jurisdictions, including those following the model code. Since even those who are skeptical about the harm done by encouragements would acknowledge that on occasion the success of a criminal actor depends on an important piece of information derived from someone else, ordinary penal policy would suggest that the person who conveys information for the purpose of aiding commission of a crime should be punishable. * * *

When the speaker offers money to the listener if the listener will commit a crime, the proposed financial reward so plainly alters any existing situation, so plainly goes beyond the communication of facts and evaluative opinion, that no one would consider such an offer to be expression that should be protected against government interference. From the perspective of penal policy, persons who offer financial inducements to others to commit crimes pose an obvious social threat; and the appropriateness of their punishment is not subject to any of the constitutional doubts that might be raised about simple encouragements and requests. The same considerations apply to other tangible inducements and to threats of specific harms communicated for the purpose of getting the listener to commit a crime. Of course, even simple requests or encouragements often carry the implicit message that a failure by the listener to act as proposed will be followed by disapproval; and the listener may fear that disapproval will then produce undefined harms. But in such circumstances, the situation-altering aspect is much less pronounced, the evaluative aspect much more prominent.[369]   Thus, the denial of constitutional protection to explicit inducements and threats does not necessarily mean that other encouragements must be treated similarly.

Orders by those in positions of authority are, however, much more like explicit threats than like simple encouragements.   Orders are meant to be carried out, and penalties typically attach to subordinates who fail to obey orders.   Orders also work an important change in the normative situation that faces the listener with respect to the act in question.   He has been trained to believe that subordinates should obey superiors; the superior's order, without more, is a strong reason that did not previously exist in favor of performing the act.   When superiors issue orders to subordinates to perform illegal behavior that bears some relation to the superior's general area of authority, such orders are also properly viewed as action beyond the scope of the First Amendment.

When two or more persons agree to do something they ordinarily effect a significant change in their normative relations, binding each of the participants to do his part in return for the other's carrying out his. Words of agreement that alter a situation in this way should not be considered expression protected by the First Amendment.   As the Iowa Supreme Court said, when defendants convicted of conspiring to fix prices urged that their conviction was improper under *Brandenburg,* "entering into an *agreement* to fix prices may hardly be said to be speech, symbolic speech, or expression under the ambit of Amendment 1." [371]

* * *

These principles for dealing with private nonideological solicitations may seem barred by the literal import of the *Brandenburg* test, under which "advocacy of the use of force or of law violation" cannot be made punishable "except where such advocacy is directed to inciting or producing imminent lawless action and is likely to incite or produce such action."

But it would be astonishing to suppose that the per curiam majority really considered and meant to protect secretive nonideological counseling to crime, and perhaps its talk of advocacy of law violation was meant to suggest ideological advocacy, not every reason that might be given in favor of an act.

* * *

369.   In social contexts in which it is mutually understood that an explicit benefit or harm will follow the listener's performance or nonperformance, a request could be treated like an inducement.   Suppose A, an important criminal, has five times asked B to commit crimes without offering an explicit inducement.   Each time upon B's successful completion A gives B $1,000. When A asks B the sixth time to commit a crime, his request is like an explicit inducement.

371.   State v. Blyth, 226 N.W.2d 250, 263 (1975).

Language serves a variety of functions, only some of which are covered by the special reasons for freedom of speech. Drawing constitutional lines of inclusion and exclusion is vastly complicated by the multiple purposes and effects particular communications can have, but we can identify utterances that have much less claim to protection than the claims of fact and value that the amendment obviously embraces. Words are sometimes used to alter normative relations, the utterances themselves establishing new duties and rights. I have suggested that although such situation-altering utterances as orders and agreements may involve implicit assertions of fact and value, their dominant purpose to change reality puts them outside the First Amendment. This is a point not much addressed in the cases and literature on freedom of speech, but the conclusion coincides with the long-standing assumption that punishment of agreements to commit ordinary crimes does not raise any constitutional difficulties.

FREDERICK SCHAUER, MUST SPEECH BE SPECIAL?

78 Nw.U.L.Rev. 1284, 1285–89, 1303–06 (1983).

From 1919 until about twenty years ago, discussion about freedom of speech in the context of the first amendment took place largely in the "How much?" mode. The courts and first amendment theorists commonly acknowledged, as Holmes put it, that the first amendment was not "intended to give immunity for every possible use of language."[1] Thus, the various exceptions to the coverage[2] of the first amendment— commercial advertising, defamation, obscenity, and fighting words—were rarely called into serious question. Moreover, even with respect to political and other speech that the first amendment plainly covered, the battle lines were narrowly drawn. No one doubted that free speech was a good thing, at least in the abstract, and consequently there was little concern for *why* free speech was valued. Instead the problems centered around the weight to be given freedom of speech when it conflicted with other universally acknowledged values, most commonly national security and public order. Although in retrospect it seems that this debate could have been illuminated by closer attention to the philosophical foundations of the principles of free speech, that was not the course taken. Rather, the tired metaphors of the marketplace of ideas and the search for truth served as stage props for a debate over how much the values of free speech would have to yield in the face of exigent public concerns.

1. Frohwerk v. United States, 249 U.S. 204, 206 (1919).

2. I use the word "coverage" to refer to those activities the regulation of which is to be measured against the standards of the first amendment. It is quite possible that certain conduct, even when measured against the standards of the first amendment, will remain unprotected. Yet the distinction between coverage and protection is designed to point out that there is a big difference between those activities (some of which are verbal) that have nothing to do with the first amendment, and those that at least require that governmental action be tested against relatively stringent first amendment standards.

* * * Although the accepted assumptions, traditional metaphors, and standard platitudes about the value of free speech might have been largely sufficient to deal with the issues of the past, they are clearly inadequate to confront the questions we must ask when trying to determine the extent to which, if at all, the courts should broaden the coverage of the first amendment to encompass a wide range of activities seemingly so far from the comprehension of the classical free speech theorists that the relevance of classical theory has become attenuated. In the place of the classical theories have come new attempts to ask about the "Why?" of the first amendment, in the hope of developing a theory that will explain the values that the concept of free speech is designed to serve. With such a theory in place, of course, it becomes much easier to confront the questions raised by the broadening of the first amendment. For if we know *why* we have the principles of free speech, then we can determine in the new case whether that class of activities is the type that the first amendment is designed to promote.

* * * I want to deal with the question of whether, and if so to what extent, an adequate theory of free speech must explain the way in which the activities encompassed by the first amendment are importantly distinct from activities that do not receive such uniquely cherished protection. In other words, must speech be special?

In asking whether speech is or must be special, we must start by clarifying the nature of the question. That is, no one could plausibly claim that the activities covered by the first amendment share no characteristics whatsoever with activities not covered by the first amendment. Rather, the claim I want to consider is more modest. Do the activities covered by the first amendment possess at least one and maybe more theoretically relevant differences from those activities not so covered? If they do, then we can say that the activities covered by the first amendment are in some sense special. But if they do not—if they are an analytically indistinguishable subset of a larger category, not all of which is protected by the first amendment—then we can say that speech is not special.

The question of whether speech is special has a descriptive side and a normative side. On the descriptive side, the question is whether one can identify relevant differences between speech and activities not covered by the first amendment. But on the normative side, the question is whether such a difference is necessary for a satisfactory underlying theory of the first amendment. For it is by no means inconceivable, and indeed may very well be the case, that what is analytically necessary for a satisfactory theory of the first amendment is unattainable given the existing state of the world. Yet that is getting ahead of things. For the moment, it is sufficient to note that the question "Must speech be special?" is analytically distinct from the question "Is speech special?".

[Schauer questions whether a principle of self-expression, self-fulfillment, or self-development distinguishes self-expressing, self-fulfilling, or self-developing speech from a much larger range of not-necessarily-communicative self-expressing, self-fulfilling, or self-developing conduct.] Thus, it is freedom of speech and press, and not freedom of liberty in general, that is specifically set forth in the text for special protection. Even if the justification would, to be fully consistent, have to be applied to a far wider range of cases, only part of this range is picked out by the constitutional text for special attention. The reason we do not apply the self-development arguments to their full reach is that we lack the constitutional mandate for so doing. Because we have that mandate in the case of speech, we can proceed to apply that justification in speech cases. The relevant distinction under this argument—what makes speech special—is the very fact that the constitutional text says it is.

One might call this the argument from coincidence. Even if there is no good reason for treating speech specially, the text says we must, and that is sufficient to justify the special protection for speech. And to the extent that the text is clear, we cannot legitimately avoid it. Thus, there may be no completely justifiable reason for limiting the presidency to those thirty-five years old or older, or for giving equal representation in the Senate to Delaware and California, but these are the mandates from the text, so we follow them. And so too, picking out speech for special treatment is the mandate from the text, and that's that. Speech is special by stipulation, even though now the stipulation may seem a bit odd.

But this loses sight of why we are looking at justifications at all. The very reason we are concerned about the underlying theoretical justification for the principle of freedom of speech, in a way that we are not with respect to the age of the presidency and equal representation in the Senate, is that the text is not clear, and we are therefore required to work out a theory of free speech so that we can intelligently apply the vague words of the document. The argument from coincidence is therefore circular. It calls upon us to note the presence of speech and not action in general in the text, but it is the very unclarity of the text that is the impetus for the entire enterprise. If we assume we cannot have a literal interpretation of the first amendment, then we must interpret it in light of some underlying purpose or theory. But if that underlying theory says nothing in particular about speech, if it does not set speech apart from a vast range of other conduct, then there is no principled stopping point after we leave the domain of what is very specifically and unequivocally mentioned in the text. To put it bluntly, the argument from coincidence might support applying the first amendment to all self-expressive or self-fulfilling instances of *speech* (taken literally) or press (taken literally), but the argument is of no assistance if we are trying to figure out why or how to apply the first amendment to oil paintings and handwritten manuscripts but not to nude bathing or riding a motorcycle without a safety helmet.

* * *

Thus, we cannot distinguish free speech, or speech itself, from all other activities. That is undoubtedly impossible. It nevertheless remains crucial that we treat freedom of speech as being independent from general liberty, because of two interrelated problems. First, we want to protect speech *more* than we protect many other activities that are part of some conception of general liberty. For example, we want to protect speech more than we protect economic activity, although under some theories economic activity is an important and perhaps even central part of liberty in general. We also want to protect free speech more than we want to protect a wide range of non-communicative lifestyle choices, although once again these choices are to some an important component of liberty in general. The second point, inseparable from the first, is that we are unwilling to disable ourselves from dealing with harmful, offensive, obnoxious, dangerous behavior in general in the way that we are with reference to speech.

Thus there exists in current free speech doctrine a difference in both the type and probability of harms that will justify government intervention. Harms that are sufficient outside the coverage of the first amendment are non-cognizable within the coverage of the first amendment; and even with respect to harms that are entitled to consideration both inside and outside the first amendment, the first amendment requires a likelihood of harm much higher than we otherwise require. It is this difference that is in need of theoretical justification, at least as we continue to contemplate broadening the first amendment, and thus it is important to see why speech might be special with respect to general liberty. Fortunately, this is an easier task than trying to see if speech is special *simpliciter,* but that does not mean that we have already achieved success.

* * *

In searching for an underlying theoretical justification for the principle of freedom of speech, it is possible that we will find a number of different justifications. Although some theories are indeed unitary, and although there need not be anything inherently wrong with a unitary theory, so, too, there need not be anything wrong with a multi-valued theory.

When I refer to a multi-valued theory of the first amendment, I am actually including two different types of multi-valued theories. One type views the language of the free speech and free press clauses of the first amendment as the umbrella under which are located a number of more or less distinct separate principles, each with its own justification, and each directed towards a separate group of problems. Under such a view, for which I acknowledge considerable sympathy, we might in fact have several first amendments. We might have one first amendment directed primarily to the problem of government suppression of its critics. The justifications for this first amendment might be largely of the democratic theory and abuse of governmental power varieties. * * * Another first amendment might be directed primarily towards the problem of open inquiry in the sciences and at academic institutions, being based primarily on the heritage of Galileo and the search for truth/marketplace of ideas justifications for the principle of free speech. * * * A third first amendment might be a reaction to an excess of historical censorship of the arts. * * * This list of possible first amendments is of course representative rather than exhaustive, but I think I have made the point.

Alternatively, the other variety of multi-valued theory might say that speech represents a unique mix of various different characteristics, not duplicated in other human endeavors. This unique mix of self-expression, self-realization, capacity for influencing political change, and so on, is then said to justify special protection for speech. This is by no means an implausible view, but it seems somewhat sticky in application, at least at the margin. That is, what do we do when we are unsure of first amendment coverage in a close case? I suspect that here it would be futile to inquire into whether this instance presents the same kind of unique mix of characteristics that justifies the special protection of speech. Rather, we would look at the particular components of that mix that were present in the case at hand, and when that happens this second type of multi-valued theory collapses into the first.

* * *

There is an intellectual ache in all of this, and it may be shared by many people now engaged in the process of trying to explore the theoretical foundations of the principle of freedom of speech. As we reject many of the classical platitudes about freedom of speech and engage in somewhat more rigorous analysis, trying to discover why speech—potentially harmful and dangerous, often offensive, and the instrument of evil as often as of good—should be treated as it is, our intuitions about the value of free speech, solid as they may be, are difficult to reconcile with this analysis. The ache, it seems to me, is caused by the fact that although the answer to "Must speech be special?" is probably "Yes," the answer to "*Is* speech special?" is probably "No." Reconciling this inconsistency is the agenda we cannot avoid.

THOMAS I. EMERSON, TOWARD A GENERAL THEORY OF THE FIRST AMENDMENT
72 Yale L.J. 877, 878–87 (1963).

The right of the individual to freedom of expression has deep roots in our history. But the concept as we know it now is essentially a product of the development of the liberal constitutional state. It is an integral part of the great intellectual and social movement beginning with the Renaissance which transformed the Western world from a feudal and authoritarian society to one whose faith rested upon the dignity, the reason and the freedom of the individual. The theory in its modern form has thus evolved over a period of more than three centuries, being applied under different circumstances and seeking to deal with different problems. It is sufficient for our purposes to restate it in its final, composite form, as it comes to us today.

The values sought by society in protecting the right to freedom of expression may be grouped into four broad categories. Maintenance of a system of free expression is necessary (1) as assuring individual self-fulfillment, (2) as a means of attaining the truth, (3) as a method of securing participation by the members of the society in social, including political, decision-making, and (4) as maintaining the balance between stability and change in the society. We consider these in their affirmative aspects, without regard at this time to the problems of limitation or reconciliation with other values.

A. Individual Self-Fulfillment

The right to freedom of expression is justified first of all as the right of an individual purely in his capacity as an individual. It derives from the widely accepted premise of Western thought that the proper end of man is the realization of his character and potentialities as a human being. Man is distinguished from other animals principally by the qualities of his mind. He has powers to reason and to feel in ways that are unique in degree if not in kind. He has the capacity to think in abstract terms, to use language, to communicate his thoughts and emotions, to build a culture. He has powers of imagination, insight and feeling. It is through development of these powers that man finds his meaning and his place in the world.

The achievement of self-realization commences with development of the mind. But the process of conscious thought by its very nature can have no limits. An individual cannot tell where it may lead nor anticipate its end. Moreover, it is an *individual* process. Every man is influenced by his fellows, dead and living, but his mind is his own and its functioning is necessarily an individual affair.

From this it follows that every man—in the development of his own personality—has the right to form his own beliefs and opinions. And, it also follows, that he has the right to express these beliefs and opinions. Otherwise they are of little account. For expression is an integral part of the development of ideas, of mental exploration and of the affirmation of self. The power to realize his potentiality as a human being begins at this point and must extend at least this far if the whole nature of man is not to be thwarted.

Hence suppression of belief, opinion and expression is an affront to the dignity of man, a negation of man's essential nature. What Milton said of licensing of the press is equally true of any form of restraint over expression: it is "the greatest displeasure and indignity to a free and knowing spirit that can be put upon him."

The right to freedom of expression derives, secondly, from basic Western notions of the role of the individual in his capacity as a member of society. Man is a social animal, necessarily and probably willingly so. He lives in company with his fellow men; he joins with them in creating a common culture; he is subject to the necessary controls of society and particularly of the state. His right to express his beliefs and opinions, in this role as a member of his community, follows from two fundamental principles. One is that the purpose of society, and of its more formal aspect the state, is to promote the welfare of the individual. Society and the state are not ends in themselves; they exist to serve the individual. The second is the principle of equality, formulated as the proposition that every individual is entitled to equal opportunity to share in common decisions which affect him.

From these concepts there follows the right of the individual to access to knowledge; to shape his own views; to communicate his needs, preferences and judgments; in short, to participate in formulating the aims and achievements of his society and his state. To cut off his search for truth, or his expression of it, is thus to elevate society and the state to a despotic command and to reduce the individual to the arbitrary control of others. The individual, in short, owes an obligation to cooperate with his fellow men, but that responsibility carries with it the right to freedom in expressing himself.

Two basic implications of the theory need to be emphasized. The first is that it is not a general measure of the individual's right to freedom of expression that any particular exercise of the right may be thought to promote or retard other goals of the society. The theory asserts that freedom of expression, while not the sole or sufficient end of society, is a good in itself, or at least an essential element in a good society. The society may seek to achieve other or more inclusive ends— such as virtue, justice, equality, or the maximum realization of the potentialities of its members. These problems are not necessarily solved by accepting the rules for freedom of expression. But, as a general proposition, the society may not seek to solve them by suppressing the beliefs or opinions of individual members. To achieve these other goals it must rely upon other methods: the use of counter-expression and the regulation or control of conduct which is not expression. Hence the right to control individual expression, on the ground that it is judged to promote good or evil, justice or injustice, equality or inequality, is not, speaking generally, within the competence of the good society.

The second implication, in a sense a corollary of the first, is that the theory rests upon a fundamental distinction between belief, opinion and communication of ideas on the one hand, and different forms of conduct on the other. For shorthand purposes we refer to this distinction hereafter as one between "expression" and "action." As just observed, in order to achieve its desired goals, a society or the state is entitled to exercise control over action—whether by prohibiting or compelling it— on an entirely different and vastly more extensive basis. But expression occupies a specially protected position. In this sector of human conduct, the social right of suppression or compulsion is at its lowest point, in most respects non-existent.

This marking off of the special area of expression is a crucial ingredient of the basic theory for several reasons. In the first place thought and communication are the fountainhead of all expression of the individual personality. To cut off the flow at the source is to dry up the whole stream. Freedom at this point is essential to all other freedoms. Hence society must withhold its right of suppression until the stage of action is reached. Secondly, expression is normally conceived as doing less injury to other social goals than action. It generally has less immediate consequences, is less irremediable in its impact. Thirdly, the power of society and the state over the individual is so pervasive, and construction of doctrines, institutions and administrative practices to limit this power so difficult, that only by drawing such a protective line between expression and action is it possible to strike a safe balance between authority and freedom.

B.   ATTAINMENT OF TRUTH

In the traditional theory, freedom of expression is not only an individual but a social good. It is, to begin with, the best process for advancing knowledge and discovering truth.

Considered in this aspect, the theory starts with the premise that the soundest and most rational judgment is arrived at by considering all facts and arguments which can be put forth in behalf of or against any proposition. Human judgment is a frail thing. It may err in being subject to emotion, prejudice or personal interest. It suffers from lack of information, insight, or inadequate thinking. It can seldom rest at the point any single person carries it, but must always remain incomplete and subject to further extension, refinement, rejection or modification. Hence an individual who seeks knowledge and truth must hear all sides of the question, especially as presented by those who feel strongly and argue militantly for a different view. He must consider all alternatives, test his judgment by exposing it to opposition, make full use of different minds to sift the true from the false. Conversely, suppression of information, discussion, or the clash of opinion prevents one from reaching the most rational judgment, blocks the generation of new ideas, and tends to perpetuate error. This is the method of the Socratic dialogue, employed on a universal scale.

The process is a continuous one. As further knowledge becomes available, as conditions change, as new insights are revealed, the judgment is open to reappraisal, improvement or abandonment.

The theory demands that discussion must be kept open no matter how certainly true an accepted opinion may seem to be. Many of the most widely acknowledged truths have turned out to be erroneous. Many of the most significant advances in human knowledge—from Copernicus to Einstein—have resulted from challenging hitherto unquestioned assumptions. No opinion can be immune from challenge.

The process also applies regardless of how false or pernicious the new opinion appears to be. For the unaccepted opinion may be true or partially true. And there is no way of suppressing the false without suppressing the true. Furthermore, even if the new opinion is wholly false, its presentation and open discussion serves a vital social purpose. It compels a rethinking and retesting of the accepted opinion. It results in a deeper understanding of the reasons for holding the opinion and a fuller appreciation of its meaning.

The only justification for suppressing an opinion is that those who seek to suppress it are infallible in their judgment of the truth. But no individual or group can be infallible, particularly in a constantly changing world.

It is essential to note that the theory contemplates more than a process for arriving at an individual judgment. It asserts that the process is also the best method for reaching a general or social judgment. This is true in part because a social judgment is made up of individual judgments. It will therefore be vitally conditioned by the quality of the individual judgments which compose it. More importantly, the same reasons which make open discussion essential for an intelligent individual judgment make it imperative for rational social judgments. Through the acquisition of new knowledge, the toleration of new ideas, the testing of opinion in open competition, the discipline of rethinking its assumptions, a society will be better able to reach common decisions that will meet the needs and aspirations of its members.

C. Participation in Decision-Making

The third main function of a system of freedom of expression is to provide for participation in decision-making through a process of open discussion which is available to all members of the community. Conceivably the technique of reaching the best common judgment could be limited to an elite, or could be extended to most members of the society excluding only those who were felt to be clearly unworthy. In its earlier forms the theory was often so restricted. But as the nineteenth century progressed it came to be accepted that all men were entitled to participate in the process of formulating the common decisions.

This development was partly due to acceptance of the concept that freedom of expression was a right of the individual, as discussed previously. But it was also inherent in the logic of free expression as a social good. In order for the process to operate at its best, every relevant fact must be brought out, every opinion and every insight must be available for consideration. Since facts are discovered and opinions formed only by the individual, the system demands that all persons participate. As John Stuart Mill expressed it, "If all mankind minus one, were of one opinion, and only one person were of the contrary opinion, mankind would be no more justified in silencing that one person, than he, if he had the power, would be justified in silencing mankind."

But in addition to these reasons, the right of all members of society to form their own beliefs and communicate them freely to others must be regarded as an essential principle of a democratically-organized society. The growing pressures for democracy and equality reinforced the logical implications of the theory and demanded opportunity for all persons to share in making social decisions. This is, of course, especially true of political decisions. But the basic theory carried beyond the political realm. It embraced the right to participate in the building of the whole culture, and included freedom of expression in religion, literature, art, science and all areas of human learning and knowledge.

In the field of political action, as just mentioned, the theory of freedom of expression has particular significance. It is through the political process that most of the immediate decisions on the survival, welfare and progress of a society are made. It is here that the state has a special incentive to repress opposition and often wields a more effective power of suppression. Freedom of expression in the political realm is usually a necessary condition for securing freedom elsewhere. It is in the political sector, therefore, that the crucial battles over free expression are most often fought.

As the general theory makes clear, freedom of discussion in public affairs serves an important function regardless of whether the political structure of a nation is democratic or not. Every government must have some process for feeding back to it information concerning the attitudes, needs and wishes of its citizens. It must, therefore, afford some degree of freedom at least to some of its citizens, to make known their wants and desires. Indeed in a more formal aspect—as a petition for redress of grievances—this right of communicating to the government in power was one of the earliest forms of political expression. The Magna Carta and the Bill of Rights of 1689, for instance, were promulgated in response to such petitions. In general, the greater the degree of political discussion allowed, the more responsive is the government, the closer is it brought to the will of its people, and the harder must it strive to be worthy of their support.

The crucial point, however, is not that freedom of expression is politically useful, but that it is indispensable to the operation of a democratic form of government. Once one accepts the premise of the Declaration of Independence—that governments derive "their just powers from the consent of the governed"—it follows that the governed must, in order to exercise their right of consent, have full freedom of expression both in forming individual judgments and in forming the common judgment. Together with the argument for freedom of religious belief, this proposition was the one most frequently and most insistently urged in support of freedom of expression.

The proponents of freedom of political expression often addressed themselves to the question whether the people were competent to perform the functions entrusted to them, whether they could acquire sufficient information or possessed sufficient capacity for judgment. The men of the eighteenth century, with their implicit faith in the power of reason and the perfectibility of man, entertained few doubts on this score. Political theorists of the nineteenth and twentieth centuries have been more cautious. And there was some disagreement as to whether the right of political expression could safely be extended to societies which had not reached a certain point in the development of education and culture. But these problems were actually questions concerning the viability of democracy itself. And once a society was committed to democratic procedures, or rather in the process of committing itself, it necessarily embraced the principle of open political discussion.

D. BALANCE BETWEEN STABILITY AND CHANGE

The traditional doctrine of freedom of expression, finally, embodies a theory of social control. The principle of open discussion is a method of achieving a more adaptable and at the same time more stable community, of maintaining the precarious balance between healthy cleavage and necessary consensus. This may not always have been true, and may not be true of many existing societies. But where men have learned how to function within the law, an open society will be the stronger and more cohesive one.

The reasons supporting this proposition can only be stated here in summary form. In the first place, suppression of discussion makes a rational judgment impossible. In effect it substitutes force for logic. Moreover, coercion of expression is likely to be ineffective. While it may prevent social change, at least for a time, it cannot eradicate thought or belief; nor can it promote loyalty or unity. As Bagehot observed, "Persecution in intellectual countries produces a superficial conformity, but also underneath an intense, incessant, implacable doubt."

Furthermore, suppression promotes inflexibility and stultification, preventing the society from adjusting to changing circumstances or developing new ideas. Any society, and any institution in society, naturally tends toward rigidity. Attitudes and ideas become stereotyped; institutions lose their vitality. The result is mechanical or arbitrary application of outworn principles, mounting grievances unacknowledged, inability to conceive new approaches, and general stagnation. Opposition serves a vital social function in offsetting or ameliorating this normal process of bureaucratic decay.

Again, suppression of expression conceals the real problems confronting a society and diverts public attention from the critical issues. It is likely to result in neglect of the grievances which are the actual basis of the unrest, and thus prevent their correction. For it both hides the extent of opposition and hardens the position of all sides, thus making a rational compromise difficult or impossible. Further, suppression drives opposition underground, leaving those suppressed either apathetic or desperate. It thus saps the vitality of the society or makes resort to force more likely. And finally it weakens and debilitates the majority whose support for the common decision is necessary. For it hinders an intelligent understanding of the reasons for adopting the decision and, as Mill observed, "beliefs not grounded on conviction are likely to give way before the slightest semblance of an argument." In short, suppression of opposition may well mean that when change is finally forced on the community it will come in more violent and radical form.

The argument that the process of open discussion, far from causing society to fly apart, stimulates forces that lead to greater cohesion, also rests upon the concept of political legitimation. Stated in narrower and perhaps cruder terms, the position is that allowing dissidents to expound their views enables them "to let off steam." The classic example is the Hyde Park meeting where any person is permitted to say anything he wishes to whatever audience he can assemble. This results in a release of energy, a lessening of frustration, and a channeling of resistance into courses consistent with law and order. It operates, in short, as a catharsis throughout the body politic.

The principle of political legitimation, however, is more broadly fundamental. It asserts that persons who have had full freedom to state their position and to persuade others to adopt it will, when the decision goes against them, be more ready to accept the common judgment. They will recognize that they have been treated fairly, in accordance with rational rules for social living. They will feel that they have done all within their power, and will understand that the only remaining alternative is to abandon the ground rules altogether through resort to force, a course of action upon which most individuals in a healthy society are unwilling to embark. In many circumstances, they will retain the opportunity to try again and will hope in the end to persuade a majority to their position. Just as in a judicial proceeding where due process has been observed, they will feel that the resulting decision, even though not to their liking, is the legitimate one.

In dealing with the problem of social control, supporters of free expression likewise emphasize that the issue must be considered in the total context of forces operating to promote or diminish cohesion in a society. By and large, they theorize, a society is more likely to be subject to general inertia than to volatile change. Hence resistance to the political order is unlikely to reach the stage of disorder unless a substantial section of the population is living under seriously adverse or discriminatory conditions. Only a government which consistently fails to relieve valid grievances need fear the outbreak of violent opposition. Thus, given the inertia which so often characterizes a society, freedom of expression, far from causing upheaval, is more properly viewed as a leavening process, facilitating necessary social and political change and keeping a society from stultification and decay.

Moreover, the state retains adequate powers to promote political unity and suppress resort to force. For one thing it shares the right to freedom of expression with its citizens. While there may be some limits on this power, the state is normally in a much better position to obtain information and in a much more authoritative position from which to communicate its official views than the ordinary citizen or group of citizens. More importantly, the state possesses the authority to restrict or compel action. The right with which we are concerned, as already noted, extends only to expression; when the stage of action is reached the great power of the state becomes available for regulation or prohibition. And finally the state has not only the power but the obligation to control the conditions under which freedom of expression can function for the general welfare. This includes not only responsibility for eliminating grievances which may give rise to disorder but also a responsibility for maintaining economic and social conditions under which the ground rules of democracy can operate.

Proponents of the theory acknowledge that the process of full discussion, open to all, involves some risks to the society that practices it. At times there may be substantial delay in the working out of critical problems. There can be no ironclad guarantee that in the end a decision beneficial to society will be reached. The process, by encouraging diversity and dissent, does at times tend to loosen the common bonds that hold society together and may threaten to bring about its dissolution. The answer given is that the stakes are high and that the risks must be run. No society can expect to achieve absolute security. Change is inevitable; the only question is the rate and the method. The theory of freedom of expression offers greater possibilities for rational, orderly adjustment than a system of suppression. Moreover, they urge, as the lesson of experience, that the dangers are usually imaginary; that suppression is invoked more often to the prejudice of the general welfare than for its advancement. To this they add that the risks are the lesser evil, that the alternatives are worse, that the only security worth having is that based on freedom.

Thus, the theory of freedom of expression involves more than a technique for arriving at better social judgments through democratic procedures. It comprehends a vision of society, a faith and a whole way of life. The theory grew out of an age that was awakened and invigorated by the idea of a new society in which man's mind was free, his fate determined by his own powers of reason, and his prospects of creating a rational and enlightened civilization virtually unlimited. It is put forward as a prescription for attaining a creative, progressive, exciting and intellectually robust community. It contemplates a mode of life that through encouraging toleration, skepticism, reason and initiative, will allow man to realize his full potentialities. It spurns the alternative of a society that is tyrannical, conformist, irrational and stagnant. It is this concept of society that was embodied in the first amendment.

It is not within the scope of this article to demonstrate the soundness of the traditional theory underlying freedom of expression, or its viability under modern conditions. The writer believes that such a demonstration can be made. But the significant point here is that we as a nation are presently committed to the theory, that alternative principles have no substantial support, and that our system of freedom of expression must be based upon and designed for the realization of the fundamental propositions embodied in the traditional theory.

In constructing and maintaining a system of freedom of expression, the principal problems and major controversies have arisen when the attempt is made to fit the affirmative theory—that is, the affirmative functions served by the system—into a more comprehensive scheme of social values and social goals. The crucial issues have revolved around the question of what limitations, if any, ought to be imposed upon freedom of expression in order to reconcile that interest with other individual and social interests sought by the good society. Most of our efforts in the past to formulate rules for limiting freedom of expression have been seriously defective through failure to take into consideration the realistic context in which such limitations are administered. The crux of the problem is that the limitations, whatever they may be, must be applied by one group of human beings to other human beings. In order to take adequate account of this factor it is necessary to have some understanding of the forces in conflict, the practical difficulties in formulating limitations, the state apparatus necessary to enforce them, the possibility of distorting them to attain ulterior purposes, and the impact of the whole process upon achieving an effective system of free expression.

The starting point is a recognition of the powerful forces that impel men toward the elimination of unorthodox expression. Most men have a strong inclination to suppress opposition even where differences in viewpoint are comparatively slight. But a system of free expression must be framed to withstand far greater stress. The test of any such system is not whether it tolerates minor deviations but whether it permits criticism of the fundamental beliefs and practices of the society. And in this area the drives to repress, both irrational and rational, tend to become overwhelming.

The human propensity to curb unwanted criticism has long been noted by the theorists of freedom of expression. Thus John Stuart Mill, early in his essay *On Liberty,* remarked:

> The disposition of mankind, whether as rulers or as fellow-citizens, to impose their own opinions and inclinations as a rule of conduct on others, is so energetically supported by some of the best and by some of the worst feelings incident to human nature, that it is hardly ever kept under restraint by anything but want of power.

The strong innate drive to suppress deviant opinion has also been stressed in modern studies of the authoritarian personality. An attack upon cherished premises tends to create anxiety, especially in those who have a strong inner need for certainty. The deviant opinion is felt as a threat to personal security. And the response tends to be fear, hatred or a similar emotion, from which springs a compulsion to eliminate the source of the danger. In such circumstances it is natural to turn to the state for protection against the supposed evil. Such factors play a prominent part in the formulation of restrictions upon expression and, equally important, in their administration.

BIBLIOGRAPHY

Lawrence Alexander & Paul Horton, *The Impossibility of a Free Speech Principle,* 78 Nw.U.L.Rev. 1319 (1983).

J.M. Balkin, *Some Realism About Pluralism: Legal Realist Approaches to the First Amendment,* 1990 Duke L.J. 375.

Ronald K.L. Collins & David M. Skower, *The First Amendment in an Age of Paratroopers,* 68 Tex.L.Rev. 1087 (1990).

Thomas I. Emerson, THE SYSTEM OF FREEDOM OF EXPRESSION (1970).

Alvin I. Goldman, *Epistemic Paternalism: Communication Control in Law and Society*, 88 J. Phil. 113 (1991).

R. Kent Greenawalt, SPEECH, CRIME, AND THE USES OF LANGUAGE (1989).

R. Kent Greenawalt, *Free Speech Justifications*, 89 Colum.L.Rev. 119 (1989).

Pnina Lahav, *Holmes and Brandeis: Libertarian and Republican Justifications for Free Speech*, 4 J.L. & Politics 451 (1988).

Sanford Levinson, *First Amendment, Freedom of Speech, Freedom of Expression: Does It Matter What We Call It?*, 80 Nw.U.L.Rev. 767 (1985).

Catharine MacKinnon, FEMINISM UNMODIFIED: DISCOURSES ON LIFE AND LAW, Chs. 11–16 (1987).

Catharine A. MacKinnon, ONLY WORDS (1993).

Richard Posner, *Free Speech in an Economic Perspective*, 20 Suffolk U.L.Rev. 1 (1986).

Joseph Raz, *Free Expression and Personal Identification*, 11 Oxford J. Legal Stud. 303 (1991).

Frederick Schauer, FREE SPEECH: A PHILOSOPHICAL ENQUIRY, Ch. 1 (1982).

Frederick Schauer, *Mrs. Palsgraf and the First Amendment*, 47 Wash. & Lee L.Rev. 161 (1990).

Frederick Schauer, *The Phenomenology of Speech and Harm*, 103 Ethics 635 (1993).

David A. Strauss, *Persuasion, Autonomy, and Freedom of Expression*, 91 Colum.L.Rev. 334 (1991).

Laurence Tribe, *Toward a Metatheory of Free Speech*, 10 Sw.U.L.Rev. 237 (1978).

Harry Wellington, *On Freedom of Expression*, 88 Yale L.J. 1105 (1979).

C. THE SEARCH FOR TRUTH IN THE MARKETPLACE OF IDEAS

A considerable amount of traditional free speech theory has seen free speech as the instrument of the search for truth, and the standard "marketplace of ideas" characterization,[1] embodied most famously in Holmes's dissent in *Abrams v. United States*,[2] identifies the relationship

1. See Abrams v. United States, 250 U.S. 616 (1919).

2. 250 U.S. 616, 630 (1919) (Holmes, J., dissenting) ("the best test of truth is the power of the thought to get itself accepted in the competition of the market").

between governmental non-intervention and the identification of truth. Indeed, this is perhaps the earliest basis for a defense of freedom of speech and freedom of the press, as Milton's *Areopagitica* makes clear ("let [Truth] and Falsehood grapple; who ever knew Truth put to the worse, in a free and open encounter? "), and it is likely also the most enduring, with Mill's variant in *On Liberty* continuing to occupy a dominant position in free speech thought. More recently, works such as Karl Popper's *The Open Society and Its Enemies* [3] and much of popular discourse about speech and press freedom has perpetuated the view that truth will most easily be located and falsehood or error most easily rejected if only the non-intervention of the state ensures that human rationality will not be constrained by governmental self-interest.

However prevalent the metaphor and the theory, however, the principle of the marketplace of ideas is not without its detractors. If the principle is one that *defines* truth in terms of success in the market, then, Schauer argues, it seems at odds with our ordinary epistemological assumptions. But if instead the principle is taken to support the empirical proposition that the marketplace of ideas is the mechanism most likely to locate an independently defined truth, then empirical inquiry rather than simple assumption seems required. Here the inquiry is likely to note the non-metaphorical qualities of the marketplace of ideas, with the marketplace of ideas being a market in a more literal sense. Ronald Coase sees this as justification for extending outside the free speech arena the same marketplace assumptions that free speech doctrine applies within, but first Catharine MacKinnon and then Owen Fiss reach the opposite conclusion from the same initial insight. They ask why the skepticism applied by liberals to the economic market ought not to be applied as well to the market in ideas. If the same market distortions based on wealth, class, power, race, and gender are applicable to the marketplace of ideas as to the marketplace of goods and services, then free speech theory is in need of a major overhaul.

JOHN STUART MILL, ON LIBERTY
Chapter 2 ("Of the Liberty of Thought and Discussion") (1859).

If all mankind minus one were of one opinion, and only one person were of the contrary opinion, mankind would be no more justified in silencing that one person, than he, if he had the power, would be justified in silencing mankind. Were an opinion a personal possession of no value except to the owner; if to be obstructed in the enjoyment of it were simply a private injury, it would make some difference whether the injury was inflicted only on a few persons or on many. But the peculiar evil of silencing the expression of an opinion is, that it is robbing the human race; posterity as well as the existing generation; those who dissent from the opinion, still more than those who hold it. If the opinion is right, they are deprived of the opportunity of exchanging error

3. (5th ed. 1966).

for truth: if wrong, they lose, what is almost as great a benefit, the clearer perception and livelier impression of truth, produced by its collision with error.

It is necessary to consider separately these two hypotheses, each of which has a distinct branch of the argument corresponding to it. We can never be sure that the opinion we are endeavouring to stifle is a false opinion; and if we were sure, stifling it would be an evil still.

First: the opinion which it is attempted to suppress by authority may possibly be true. Those who desire to suppress it, of course deny its truth; but they are not infallible. They have no authority to decide the question for all mankind, and exclude every other person from the means of judging. To refuse a hearing to an opinion, because they are sure that it is false, is to assume that *their* certainty is the same thing as *absolute* certainty. All silencing of discussion is an assumption of infallibility. Its condemnation may be allowed to rest on this common argument, not the worse for being common.

Unfortunately for the good sense of mankind, the fact of their fallibility is far from carrying the weight in their practical judgment which is always allowed to it in theory; for while every one well knows himself to be fallible, few think it necessary to take any precautions against their own fallibility, or admit the supposition that any opinion, of which they feel very certain, may be one of the examples of the error to which they acknowledge themselves to be liable. Absolute princes, or others who are accustomed to unlimited deference, usually feel this complete confidence in their own opinions on nearly all subjects. People more happily situated, who sometimes hear their opinions disputed, and are not wholly unused to be set right when they are wrong, place the same unbounded reliance only on such of their opinions as are shared by all who surround them, or to whom they habitually defer; for in proportion to a man's want of confidence in his own solitary judgment, does he usually repose, with implicit trust, on the infallibility of "the world" in general. And the world, to each individual, means the part of it with which he comes in contact; his party, his sect, his church, his class of society; the man may be called, by comparison, almost liberal and large-minded to whom it means anything so comprehensive as his own country or his own age. Nor is his faith in this collective authority at all shaken by his being aware that other ages, countries, sects, churches, classes, and parties have thought, and even now think, the exact reverse. He devolves upon his own world the responsibility of being in the right against the dissentient worlds of other people; and it never troubles him that mere accident has decided which of these numerous worlds is the object of his reliance, and that the same causes which make him a Churchman in London, would have made him a Buddhist or a Confucian in Pekin. Yet it is as evident in itself, as any amount of argument can make it, that ages are no more infallible than individuals; every age having held many opinions which subsequent ages have deemed not only false but absurd; and it is as certain that many opinions now general will be rejected by future ages, as it is that many, once general, are rejected by the present.

The objection likely to be made to this argument would probably take some such form as the following. There is no greater assumption of infallibility in forbidding the propagation of error, than in any other thing which is done by public authority on its own judgment and responsibility. Judgment is given to men that they may use it. Because it may be used erroneously, are men to be told that they ought not to use it at all? To prohibit what they think pernicious, is not claiming exemption from error, but fulfilling the duty incumbent on them, although fallible, of acting on their conscientious conviction. If we were never to act on our opinions, because those opinions may be wrong, we should leave all our interests uncared for, and all our duties unperformed. An objection which applies to all conduct can be no valid objection to any conduct in particular. It is the duty of governments, and of individuals, to form the truest opinions they can; to form carefully, and never impose them upon others unless they are quite sure of being right. But when they are sure (such reasoners may say), it is not conscientiousness but cowardice to shrink from acting on their opinions, and allow doctrines which they honestly think dangerous to the welfare of mankind, either in this life or in another, to be scattered abroad without restraint, because other people, in less enlightened times, have persecuted opinions now believed to be true. Let us take care, it may be said, not to make the same mistake: but governments and nations have made mistakes in other things, which are not denied to be fit subjects for the exercise of authority: they have laid on bad taxes, made unjust wars. Ought we therefore to lay on no taxes, and, under whatever provocation, make no wars? Men and governments, must act to the best of their ability. There is no such thing as absolute certainty, but there is assurance sufficient for the purposes of human life. We may, and must, assume our opinion to be true for the guidance of our own conduct: and it is assuming no more when we forbid bad men to pervert society by the propagation of opinions which we regard as false and pernicious.

I answer, that it is assuming very much more. There is the greatest difference between presuming an opinion to be true, because, with every opportunity for contesting it, it has not been refuted, and assuming its truth for the purpose of not permitting its refutation. Complete liberty of contradicting and disproving our opinion is the very condition which justifies us in assuming its truth for purposes of action; and on no other terms can a being with human faculties have any rational assurance of being right.

When we consider either the history of opinion, or the ordinary conduct of human life, to what is it to be ascribed that the one and the other are no worse than they are? Not certainly to the inherent force of the human understanding; for, on any matter not self-evident, there are ninety-nine persons totally incapable of judging of it for one who is capable; and the capacity of the hundredth person is only comparative;

for the majority of the eminent men of every past generation held many opinions now known to be erroneous, and did or approved numerous things which no one will now justify. Why is it, then, that there is on the whole a preponderance among mankind of rational opinions and rational conduct? If there really is this preponderance—which there must be unless human affairs are, and have always been, in an almost desperate state—it is owing to a quality of the human mind, the source of everything respectable in man either as an intellectual or as a moral being, namely, that his errors are corrigible. He is capable of rectifying his mistakes, by discussion and experience. Not by experience alone. There must be discussion, to show how experience is to be interpreted. Wrong opinions and practices gradually yield to fact and argument; but facts and arguments, to produce any effect on the mind, must be brought before it. Very few facts are able to tell their own story, without comments to bring out their meaning. The whole strength and value, then, of human judgment, depending on the one property, that it can be set right when it is wrong, reliance can be placed on it only when the means of setting it right are kept constantly at hand. In the case of any person whose judgment is really deserving of confidence, how has it become so? Because he has kept his mind open to criticism on his opinions and conduct. Because it has been his practice to listen to all that could be said against him; to profit by as much of it as was just, and expound to himself, and upon occasion to others, the fallacy of what was fallacious. Because he has felt, that the only way in which a human being can make some approach to knowing the whole of a subject, is by hearing what can be said about it by persons of every variety of opinion, and studying all modes in which it can be looked at by every character of mind. No wise man ever acquired his wisdom in any mode but this; nor is it in the nature of human intellect to become wise in any other manner. The steady habit of correcting and completing his own opinion by collating it with those of others, so far from causing doubt and hesitation in carrying it into practice, is the only stable foundation for a just reliance on it: for, being cognisant of all that can, at least obviously, be said against him, and having taken up his position against all gainsayers—knowing that he has sought for objections and difficulties, instead of avoiding them, and has shut out no light which can be thrown upon the subject from any quarter—he has a right to think his judgment better than that of any person, or any multitude, who have not gone through a similar process.

It is not too much to require that what the wisest of mankind, those who are best entitled to trust their own judgment, find necessary to warrant their relying on it, should be submitted to by that miscellaneous collection of a few wise and many foolish individuals, called the public. The most intolerant of churches, the Roman Catholic Church, even at the canonisation of a saint, admits, and listens patiently to, a "devil's advocate." The holiest of men, it appears, cannot be admitted to posthumous honours, until all that the devil could say against him is known and weighed. If even the Newtonian philosophy were not permitted to be questioned, mankind could not feel as complete assurance of its truth as they now do. The beliefs which we have most warrant for have no safeguard to rest on, but a standing invitation to the whole world to prove them unfounded. If the challenge is not accepted, or is accepted and the attempt fails, we are far enough from certainty still; but we have done the best that the existing state of human reason admits of; we have neglected nothing that could give the truth a chance of reaching us: if the lists are kept open, we may hope that if there be a better truth, it will be found when the human mind is capable of receiving it; and in the meantime we may rely on having attained such approach to truth as is possible in our own day. This is the amount of certainty attainable by a fallible being, and this the sole way of attaining it.

* * *

Let us now pass to the second division of the argument, and dismissing the supposition that any of the received opinions may be false, let us assume them to be true, and examine into the worth of the manner in which they are likely to be held, when their truth is not freely and openly canvassed. However unwillingly a person who has a strong opinion may admit the possibility that his opinion may be false, he ought to be moved by the consideration that, however true it may be, if it is not fully, frequently, and fearlessly discussed, it will be held as a dead dogma, not a living truth.

There is a class of persons (happily not quite so numerous as formerly) who think it enough if a person assents undoubtingly to what they think true, though he has no knowledge whatever of the grounds of the opinion, and could not make a tenable defence of it against the most superficial objections. Such persons, if they can once get their creed taught from authority, naturally think that no good, and some harm, comes of its being allowed to be questioned. Where their influence prevails, they make it nearly impossible for the received opinion to be rejected wisely and considerately, though it may still be rejected rashly and ignorantly; for to shut out discussion entirely is seldom possible, and when it once gets in, beliefs not grounded on conviction are apt to give way before the slightest semblance of an argument. Waiving, however, this possibility—assuming that the true opinion abides in the mind, but abides as a prejudice, a belief independent of, and proof against, argument—this is not the way in which truth ought to be held by a rational being. This is not knowing the truth. Truth, thus held, is but one superstition the more, accidentally clinging to the words which enunciate a truth.

If the intellect and judgment of mankind ought to be cultivated, a thing which Protestants at least do not deny, on what can these faculties be more appropriately exercised by any one, than on the things which concern him so much that it is considered necessary for him to hold opinions on them? If the cultivation of the understanding consists in one thing more than in another, it is surely in learning the grounds of one's own opinions. Whatever people believe, on subjects on which it is of the first importance to believe rightly, they ought to be able to defend against at least the common objections. But, some one may say, "Let them be *taught* the grounds of their opinions. It does not follow that opinions must be merely parroted because they are never heard controverted. Persons who learn geometry do not simply commit the theorems to memory, but understand and learn likewise the demonstrations; and it would be absurd to say that they remain ignorant of the grounds of geometrical truths, because they never hear any one deny, and attempt to disprove them." Undoubtedly: and such teaching suffices on a subject like mathematics, where there is nothing at all to be said on the wrong side of the question. The peculiarity of the evidence of mathematical truths is that all the argument is on one side. There are no objections, and no answers to objections. But on every subject on which difference of opinion is possible, the truth depends on a balance to be struck between two sets of conflicting reasons. Even in natural philosophy, there is always some other explanation possible of the same facts; some geocentric theory instead of heliocentric, some phlogiston instead of oxygen; and it has to be shown why that other theory cannot be the true one: and until this is shown, and until we know how it is shown, we do not understand the grounds of our opinion. But when we turn to subjects infinitely more complicated, to morals, religion, politics, social relations, and the business of life, three-fourths of the arguments for every disputed opinion consist in dispelling the appearances which favour some opinion different from it. The greatest orator, save one, of antiquity, has left it on record that he always studied his adversary's case with as great, if not still greater, intensity than even his own. What Cicero practised as the means of forensic success requires to be imitated by all who study any subject in order to arrive at the truth. He who knows only his own side of the case, knows little of that. His reasons may be good, and no one may have been able to refute them. But if he is equally unable to refute the reasons on the opposite side; if he does not so much as know what they are, he has no ground for preferring either opinion. The rational position for him would be suspension of judgment, and unless he contents himself with that, he is either led by authority, or adopts, like the generality of the world, the side to which he feels most inclination. Nor is it enough that he should hear the arguments of adversaries from his own teachers, presented as they state them, and accompanied by what they offer as refutations. That is not the way to do justice to the arguments, or bring them into real contact with his own mind. He must be able to hear them from persons who actually believe them; who defend them in earnest, and do their very utmost for them. He must know them in their most plausible and persuasive form; he must feel the whole force of the difficulty which the true view of the subject has to encounter and dispose of; else he will never really possess himself of the portion of truth which meets and removes that difficulty. Ninety-nine in a hundred of what are called educated men are in this condition; even of those who can argue fluently for their opinions. Their conclusion may be true, but it might be false for anything they know: they have never thrown themselves into the mental position of those who think differently from them, and considered what such persons may have to say; and consequently they do not, in any proper sense of the word, know the doctrine which they themselves profess. They do not know those parts of it which explain and justify the remainder; the considerations which show that a fact which seemingly conflicts with another is reconcilable with it, or that, of two apparently strong reasons, one and not the other ought to be preferred. All that part of the truth which turns the scale, and decides the judgment of a completely informed mind, they are strangers to; nor is it ever really known, but to those who have attended equally and impartially to both sides, and endeavoured to see the reasons of both in the strongest light. So essential is this discipline to a real understanding of moral and human subjects, that if opponents of all important truths do not exist, it is indispensable to imagine them, and supply them with the strongest arguments which the most skilful devil's advocate can conjure up.

* * *

It still remains to speak of one of the principal causes which make diversity of opinion advantageous, and will continue to do so until mankind shall have entered a stage of intellectual advancement which at present seems at an incalculable distance. We have hitherto considered only two possibilities: that the received opinion may be false, and some other opinion, consequently, true; or that, the received opinion being true, a conflict with the opposite error is essential to a clear apprehension and deep feeling of its truth. But there is a commoner case than either of these; when the conflicting doctrines, instead of being one true and the other false, share the truth between them; and the nonconforming opinion is needed to supply the remainder of the truth, of which the received doctrine embodies only a part. Popular opinions, on subjects not palpable to sense, are often true, but seldom or never the whole truth. They are a part of the truth; sometimes a greater, sometimes a smaller part, but exaggerated, distorted, and disjointed from the truths by which they ought to be accompanied and limited. Heretical opinions, on the other hand, are generally some of these suppressed and neglected truths, bursting the bonds which kept them down, and either seeking reconciliation with the truth contained in the common opinion, or fronting it as enemies, and setting themselves up, with similar exclusiveness, as the whole truth. The latter case is hitherto the most frequent, as, in the human mind, one-sidedness has always been the rule, and many-sidedness the exception. Hence, even in revolutions of opinion, one part of the truth usually sets while another rises. Even progress, which ought to superadd, for the most part only substitutes, one partial and incomplete truth for another; improvement consisting chiefly in this, that the new fragment of truth is more wanted, more adapted to the needs of the time, than that which it displaces. Such being the partial character of prevailing opinions, even when resting on a true foundation, every opinion which embodies somewhat of the portion of truth which the common opinion omits, ought to be considered precious, with whatever amount of error and confusion that truth may be blended. No sober judge of human affairs will feel bound to be indignant because those who force on our notice truths which we should otherwise have overlooked, overlook some of those which we see. Rather, he will think that so long as popular truth is one-sided, it is more desirable than otherwise that unpopular truth should have one-sided assertors too; such being usually the most energetic, and the most likely to compel reluctant attention to the fragment of wisdom which they proclaim as if it were the whole.

* * *

We have now recognised the necessity to the mental well-being of mankind (on which all their other well-being depends) of freedom of opinion, and freedom of the expression of opinion, on four distinct grounds; which we will now briefly recapitulate.

First, if any opinion is compelled to silence, that opinion may, for aught we can certainly know, be true. To deny this is to assume our own infallibility.

Secondly, though the silenced opinion be an error, it may, and very commonly does, contain a portion of truth; and since the general or prevailing opinion on any subject is rarely or never the whole truth, it is only by the collision of adverse opinions that the remainder of the truth has any chance of being supplied.

Thirdly, even if the received opinion be not only true, but the whole truth; unless it is suffered to be, and actually is, vigorously and earnestly contested, it will, by most of those who receive it, be held in the manner of a prejudice, with little comprehension or feeling of its rational grounds. And not only this, but, fourthly, the meaning of the doctrine itself will be in danger of being lost, or enfeebled, and deprived of its vital effect on the character and conduct; the dogma becoming a mere formal profession, inefficacious for good, but cumbering the ground, and preventing the growth of any real and heartfelt conviction, from reason or personal experience.

FREDERICK SCHAUER, FREE SPEECH: A PHILOSOPHICAL ENQUIRY

Chapter 2 ("The Argument From Truth"), 19–29 (1982).

Stipulating that increased knowledge is a valuable end does not help to answer the central question—does granting a special liberty of discussion and communication aid us in reaching that end? Is the marketplace of ideas more likely to lead to knowledge than to error, ignorance, folly, or nonsense?

To many people this question answers itself. They assert that free and open discussion of ideas is the only rational way of achieving knowledge, and they assume that the mere assertion of this proposition is proof of its truth. This is of course unsatisfactory. Without a causal link between free speech and increased knowledge the argument from truth must fail. Examining this link is the primary purpose of this chapter.

One way of avoiding the difficult task of establishing this connexion between discussion and knowledge is by *defining* truth in terms of the process of discussion; that is, define truth as that which survives the process of open discussion. Whatever is rejected after full, open enquiry is, by definition, false, wrong, or unwise. Whatever is agreed or accepted is, conversely, true, good, or sound. One might call this a consensus theory of truth. Under this theory there is no test of truth other than the *process* by which opinions are accepted or rejected.

When truth is defined in this way, the 'marketplace of ideas' metaphor is most apt, because the economic analogy is strongest. Under the purest theory of a free market economy the worth of goods is determined solely by the value placed on them by operation of the market. The value of an object is what it will fetch in a free market at leisurely sale. Similarly, the consensus or 'survival' theory of truth holds that truth is determined solely by the value that ideas or opinions are given in the intellectual marketplace. Under this view the results are defined by the process through which those results are produced. The goal is then not so much the search for knowledge as it is the search for rational thinking. Given this definition of truth, knowledge flows from rational thinking as a matter of logical necessity. The argument substitutes a tautology for the problematic causal link between discussion and knowledge. Since the result is defined by the process, it is the process and not the result that matters.

* * *

The survival theory of truth is alluringly uncomplicated; but as the basis for the principle of free speech it suffers from crippling weaknesses. Foremost among these weaknesses is that the argument begs the question. If truth is defined by reference to and in terms of a process, then why is the process of open discussion preferable to any other process, such as random selection or authoritarian fiat? Why is open discussion taken to be the only rational method of enquiry?

The survival theory, in refusing to acknowledge independent criteria for truth, provides no guidance for preferring one method of decision to any other. The survival theory does not purport to demonstrate *why* open discussion leads to knowledge, because it rejects any objective test of truth. Moreover, the survival theory does not tell us why open discussion leads to more desirable results of any kind. Thus the theory prompts us to ask why we should prefer rational thinking to any other form of thinking. But then the theory *defines* rationality as willingness to participate in open discussion and receptiveness to a variety of ideas. The survival theory thereby skirts the entire question by assuming open enquiry as valuable *a priori*. But we are still left with no criteria for evaluating whether this method of enquiry is better than any other. By taking open enquiry as sufficient *ex hypothesi,* the survival or consensus theory provides no assistance in answering the question of why free discussion should be preferred.

In his essay *On Liberty,* Mill suggests a version of the survival theory of truth in referring to the complete liberty to contradict a proposition as "the very condition which justifies us in assuming its truth for purposes of action". Perhaps rational assurance flows more easily from hearing opposing views. Perhaps freedom of contradiction is an important consideration in assuming the truth of any proposition. But that does not transform freedom to contradict into a sufficient condition, or even a necessary condition, for truth. We presuppose, at the very least, independent criteria of verifiability and falsifiability. Geoffrey Marshall has noted in response to Mill's argument that we should still have rational assurance "that the Earth is roundish" even "if the Flat Earth Society were an illegal organization". In those circumstances we would certainly want to look closely at why the contrary view was banned, so as more carefully to scrutinize the received view. But the very fact of allowing the expression of the opposing opinion is not what provides us with our assurance about the shape of the Earth.

The consensus theory seems slightly less bizarre in the context of ethical rather than factual or scientific propositions. But even with respect to ethics, a consensus theory incorporates a strange and unacceptably extreme subjectivism. If we define moral truth as what in fact survives, then we are committed to saying that Nazism was "right" in Germany in the 1930s, and that slavery was equally "correct" or "wise" in parts of the United States prior to the Civil War. Nor is it satisfactory to respond by saying that these were not fully open systems, and that only propositions arising out of open systems can properly be recognized as sound. If that were the case, then any prevailing American view on anything in the last thirty years would have been correct, because there has been virtually unlimited freedom of discussion in the United States during that time.

A form of subjectivism that defines truth solely in terms of the strength of an opinion in the marketplace of ideas is so totally at odds with the idea of truth embodied in our language of evaluation as to be virtually useless. A theory of majority rule for truth distorts out of all recognition our use of words like 'true', 'good', 'sound', or 'wise'. Subjectivism may argue for greater freedom of speech, but not in a way related to the argument from truth. I will return to this theme in later chapters, but we can confidently pass over the consensus theory here. Defining truth (and, in turn, knowledge) solely in terms of a process answers none of the important questions about free speech. If free speech is justified because it defines the process that produces knowledge, and if that knowledge is in turn defined by the very same process, we are saying nothing at all. It is entirely possible that the process of open discussion is the best way of arriving at knowledge. But this is the causal link that the survival theory of truth fails even to address.

The focus on this causal link between freedom of speech and increased knowledge is arguably the greatest contribution of Mill's *On Liberty*. Earlier writers simply assumed that truth would reveal itself in the interplay of competing belief. Truth was considered self-evident, needing only to be expressed to be recognized. By contrast, Mill saw the importance of explaining the way in which error would be replaced by knowledge. A paraphrase of Mill's argument may aid in precise analysis:

> The relationship between discussion and truth is a product of the uncertain status of our beliefs and the fallibility of the human mind. Because we can not be absolutely certain of any of our beliefs, it is possible that any given belief might be erroneous, no matter how firmly we may be convinced of its truth. To hold otherwise is to assume infallibility. Because any belief might be erroneous, the suppression of the contrary belief entails the risk of upholding the erroneous belief and suppressing the true belief. The risk is magnified in practice because most beliefs are neither wholly true nor wholly false, containing instead elements of both truth and falsity. Only by allowing expression of the opinion we think false do we allow for the possibility that that opinion may be true. Allowing contrary opinions to be expressed is the only way to give ourselves the opportunity to reject the received opinion when the received opinion is false. A policy of suppressing false beliefs will in fact suppress some true ones, and therefore a policy of suppression impedes the search for truth.

* * *

On Liberty can be read as assuming that there is some objective truth, even if we are never sure we have found it. As a result, Mill has been criticized by those who reject the notion of objective truth. If we are always uncertain, they say, then we never know if we have identified truth. These critics accuse Mill of inconsistency in saying that we can never be certain, but that we can search for truth. Apart from the fact that these arguments confuse truth with certainty, confuse a state of the world with a state of mind, the arguments are largely irrelevant to the issue at hand. The question is not certainty, but epistemic advance.

This point is brought out in much of the work of Karl Popper. By stressing falsifiability rather than verifiability, and by characterizing the advance of knowledge as the continual process of exposing error, Popper frees the argument from truth from the problem of certainty. The identification of error may not bring us closer to truth, but the identification of an error is still desirable, and the rejection of an erroneous belief is still an epistemic advance. Popper's argument from the identification of error thus parallels Mill's argument from truth. Both share the same core principle—allowing the expression of contrary views is the only rational way of recognizing human fallibility, and making possible the rejection or modification of those of our beliefs that are erroneous.

* * *

Mill, Popper, and their followers have refined the argument from truth by explaining how knowledge is more likely to be gained in a society in which all views can be freely expressed. But they have still neglected the critical question—does truth, when articulated, make itself known? Does truth prevail when placed side-by-side with falsity? Does knowledge triumph over ignorance? Are unsound policies rejected when sound policies are presented? The question is whether the theory accurately portrays reality. It does not follow as a matter of logical entailment that truth will be accepted and falsehood rejected when both are heard. There must be some justification for assuming this to be an accurate description of the process, and such a justification is noticeably absent from all versions of the argument from truth.

The argument from truth may well be the statement of an ideal. Listening to other positions, suspending judgment (if possible) until opposing views are expressed, and considering the possibility that we might be wrong virtually defines, in many contexts, the process of rational thinking. At least it is a substantial component of the definition. Rationality in this sense may not always lead to increased knowledge, and there may at times be better methods of searching for truth. But all academic disciplines presuppose that this type of rationality has value, and it would be difficult to prove this presupposition unwarranted. When such rational thinking can be assumed, maximum freedom of discussion is a desirable goal. In systems of scientific and academic discourse, the argument from truth has substantial validity. Those who occupy positions in these fields may not always think rationally, but we are at least willing to say they should, and are inclined to try to replace those who do not think rationally with those who will.

* * *

It is hardly surprising that the search for truth was so central in the writings of Milton, Locke, Voltaire, and Jefferson. They placed their faith in the ability of reason to solve problems and distinguish truth from falsehood. They had confidence in the reasoning power of *all* people, if only that power were allowed to flourish. The argument from truth is very much a child of the Enlightenment, and of the optimistic view of the rationality and perfectibility of humanity it embodied. But the naïveté of the Enlightenment has since been largely discredited by history and by contemporary insights of psychology. * * *

I do not mean to be taken as saying that falsity, ignorance, or evil have inherent power over truth, knowledge, or goodness. Rather, I mean only to deny the reverse—that truth has inherent ability to gain general acceptance. The argument from truth must demonstrate either that true statements have some intrinsic property that allows their truth to be universally apparent, or that empirical evidence supports the belief that truth will prevail when matched against falsehood. The absence of such a demonstration, in the face of numerous counter-examples, is the most prominent weakness of the argument from truth. History provides too many examples of falsity triumphant over truth to justify the assertion that truth will inevitably prevail. Mill noted that "the dictum that truth always triumphs over persecution is one of those pleasant falsehoods which men repeat after one another till they pass into commonplaces, but which all experience refutes". My point is that, *contra* Mill, the point would be the same if we removed the persecution and instead let truth battle with falsehood rather than the forces of oppression. Mill's assumption that the removal of persecution will allow truth to triumph in all cases is every bit as much a "pleasant falsehood".

Of course we know that falsity at times prevailed over truth only by having finally discovered truth with respect to a particular issue. Thus discussions along this line usually distinguish between the long run and the short run. Those who reject the assumptions of the Enlightenment point to instances in which truth and reason have not prevailed. In response, those who place their faith in the power of reason observe that when erroneous views have at times been accepted they have also been discredited in the long run. But the validity of this response depends on just how long the long run is. If there is no limit to its duration, the assertion that knowledge advances in the long run is both irrefutable and meaningless. Yet if the relevant time period is discrete and observable, history furnishes far too many counter-examples for us to have much confidence in the power of truth consistently to prevail.

In discussing fallibilist theory, we often forget that it is only *possible* that the received opinion is erroneous, and therefore only *possible* that the rejected opinion is true. When we say that all views should be permitted expression so that knowledge may advance, this necessitates being willing to achieve *some* increase in knowledge at the expense of tolerating a great deal of falsity. In order to locate all the sound ideas, we must listen to many unsound ideas. When we allow the expression of an opinion that is only possibly true, we allow the expression of an opinion that is also possibly, perhaps *probably,* false. If the expression of the opinion in question involves no unpleasant consequences even if it is false, unsound, or useless, then there is a potential benefit at no cost. But it is simply a mistake to say that the expression of false or unsound opinions can never have unpleasant consequences.

The predominant risk is that false views may, despite their falsity, be accepted by the public, who will then act in accordance with those false views. The risk is magnified in those circumstances in which people have seemed particularly disposed towards the acceptance of unsound ideas. One good example is race relations. History has shown us that people unfortunately are much more inclined to be persuaded of the rectitude of oppressing certain races or certain religions than they are likely to accept other unsound and no less palpably wrong views.

Moreover, unpleasant side effects may accompany the expression of erroneous views even when there is no risk of widespread acceptance. By side effects I mean those consequences that are not directly attributable to the *falsity* of the views expressed. People may be offended, violence or disorder may ensue, or reputations may be damaged. It is foolish to suppose that the expression of opinions never causes harm. Generally, but not always, the expression of unsound opinions causes greater harm than the expression of sound opinions. When we allow the expression of an opinion because it is possibly true, we often accept an appreciably higher probability of harm than the probability of the truth of a seemingly false opinion. As a result, the strength of protection of the right to dissent afforded by the argument from fallibilism is directly proportionate to the value placed on the goal of searching for knowledge. There is absolute protection only if the search for knowledge is the transcendent value in society. If the search for knowledge does not have a lexical priority over all other values, the possibility that the rejected view may be correct will often be insufficient to justify allowing it to be expressed—depending, of course, on the evaluation of the harm expected to flow from its dissemination.

To cut off access to possible knowledge is undoubtedly a harm. But the question to be asked is whether we should take a large risk in exchange for what may be a minute possibility of benefit. Unfortunately, we cannot be sure we have properly weighed the harms and benefits unless we know what benefits the suppressed opinion might bring. And this is impossible to assess so long as that opinion is suppressed. Therefore we are merely guessing when we suppress; but we are also guessing when we decide not to suppress. If the expression of an opinion possibly causes harm, allowing that expression involves some probability of harm. If the suppression of that opinion entails the possible suppression of truth, then suppression also entails some probability of harm. Suppression is necessarily wrong only if the former harm is ignored. Therefore a rule absolutely prohibiting suppression is justified only if speech can never cause harm, or if the search for truth is elevated to a position of priority over all other values.

Mill assumed that in all cases we could act in furtherance of the policy embodied in the received opinion, while at the same time permitting the expression of the contrary opinion. But in some cases the very act of allowing the expression of the contrary opinion is inconsistent with acting on the received opinion. For example, we prohibit slavery in part because of a received opinion that racial equality and respect for the dignity of *all* people is the morally correct position. If we allow people to argue that slavery is morally correct, many others will be offended, their dignity will be insulted, and there is likely to be increased racial disorder. The expression is thus detrimental to acting on the received opinion, to furthering racial equality and respect for the dignity of all. A strong version of the argument from truth would hold that the possibility, however infinitesimal, that slavery is good makes tolerating the harm that will flow from the expression of that opinion worthwhile. But the size of that possibility and the extent of the potential harm are irrelevant only if the search for knowledge must always prevail over other values.

CATHARINE A. MACKINNON, FEMINISM UNMODIFIED: DISCOURSES ON LIFE AND LAW

140, 155–58, 195 (1987).

The First Amendment absolutist position is very different from this position. Absolutism supposes that we all have an equal interest in the marketplace of ideas it supposedly guarantees. This is not the case for women. First of all, the marketplace of ideas is literal: those with the most money can buy the most speech, and women are poor. Second, protecting pornographers, as the First Amendment now does, does not promote the freedom of speech of women. It *has* not done so. Pornography terrorizes women into silence. Pornography is therefore not in the interest of our speech. We do not, as women, have the stake in the existing system we have been said to have. The First Amendment has also been interpreted to support the speech of Nazis, as if that would promote the rights of Jews. I doubt that, too, although the issues are specific to each case. Jews are not lying down for anti-Semitism any more than women are lying down for misogyny. But that isn't a victory for the First Amendment; it's a victory for Jews and women against odds that the First Amendment has been used to stack. What I think is that people who are absolutely interested in the First Amendment should turn their efforts to getting speech for people, like women, who have been denied that speech almost entirely, who have not been able to speak or to get themselves heard. Understanding free speech as an abstract system is a liberal position. Understanding how speech also exists within a substantive system of power relations is a feminist position.

* * *

The theory of the First Amendment under which most pornography is protected from governmental restriction proceeds from liberal assumptions that do not apply to the situation of women. First Amendment theory, like virtually all liberal legal theory, presumes the validity of the distinction between public and private: the "role of law [is] to mark and guard the line between the sphere of social power, organized in the form of the state, and the area of private right." On this basis, courts distinguish between obscenity in public (which can be regulated, even if some attempts founder, seemingly in part *because* the presentations are public) and the private possession of obscenity in the home. The problem is that not only the public but also the private *is* a "sphere of social power" of sexism. On paper and in life pornography is thrust upon unwilling women in their homes. The distinction between public and private does not cut the same for women as for men. It is men's right to inflict pornography upon women in private that is protected.

The liberal theory underlying First Amendment law further believes that free speech, including pornography, helps discover truth. Censorship restricts society to partial truths. So why are we now—with more pornography available than ever before—buried in all these lies? Laissez faire might be an adequate theory of the social preconditions for knowledge in a nonhierarchical society. But in a society of gender inequality, the speech of the powerful impresses its view upon the world, concealing the truth of powerlessness under that despairing acquiescence that provides the appearance of consent and makes protest inaudible as well as rare. Pornography can invent women because it has the power to make its vision into reality, which then passes, objectively, for truth. So while the First Amendment supports pornography, believing that consensus and progress are facilitated by allowing all views, however divergent and unorthodox, it fails to notice that pornography (like the racism, in which I include anti-Semitism, of the Nazis and the Klan) is not at all divergent or unorthodox. It is the ruling ideology. Feminism, the dissenting view, is suppressed by pornography. Thus, while defenders of pornography argue that allowing all speech, including pornography, frees the mind to fulfill itself, pornography freely enslaves women's minds and bodies inseparably, normalizing the terror that enforces silence from women's point of view.

To liberals, speech must never be sacrificed for other social goals. But liberalism has never understood that the free speech of men silences the free speech of women. It is the same social goal, just other *people*. This is what a real inequality, a real conflict, a real disparity in social power looks like. The law of the First Amendment comprehends that freedom of expression, in the abstract, is a system, but it fails to comprehend that sexism (and racism), *in the concrete,* are also systems. That pornography chills women's expression is difficult to demonstrate empirically because silence is not eloquent. Yet on no more of the same kind of evidence, the argument that suppressing pornography might chill legitimate speech has supported its protection.

* * *

The most basic assumption underlying First Amendment adjudication is that, socially, speech is free. The First Amendment says, "Congress shall not abridge *the freedom of speech.*" Free speech exists. The problem for government is to avoid constraining that which, if unconstrained by government, *is* free. This tends to presuppose that whole segments of the population are not systematically silenced *socially,* prior to government action. The place of pornography in the inequality of the sexes makes such a presupposition untenable and makes any approach to *our* freedom of expression so based worse than useless. For women, the urgent issue of freedom of speech is not primarily the avoidance of state intervention as such, but finding an affirmative means to get access to speech for those to whom it has been denied.

* * *

Those who wrote the First Amendment *had* speech—they wrote the Constitution. *Their* problem was to keep it free from the only power that realistically threatened it: the federal government. They designed the First Amendment to prevent government from constraining that which, if unconstrained by government, was free, meaning *accessible to them.* * * * If everyone's power were equal to theirs, if this were a nonhierarchical society, that might make sense.

R.H. COASE, THE MARKET FOR GOODS AND THE MARKET FOR IDEAS

64 Am.Ec.Rev. 384–86, 389–90 (1974).

The normal treatment of governmental regulation of markets makes a sharp distinction between the ordinary market for goods and services and the activities covered by the First Amendment—speech, writing, and the exercise of religious beliefs—which I call, for brevity, "the market for ideas." The phrase, "the market for ideas," does not describe the boundaries of the area to which the First Amendment has been applied very exactly. Indeed, these boundaries do not seem to have been very clearly drawn. But there can be little doubt that the market for ideas, the expression of opinion in speech and writing and similar activities, is at the center of the activities protected by the First Amendment, and it is with these activities that discussion of the First Amendment has been largely concerned.

* * *

What is the general view that I will be examining? It is that, in the market for goods, government regulation is desirable whereas, in the market for ideas, government regulation is undesirable and should be strictly limited. In the market for goods, the government is commonly regarded as competent to regulate and properly motivated. Consumers lack the ability to make the appropriate choices. Producers often exercise monopolistic power and, in any case, without some form of government intervention, would not act in a way which promotes the public interest. In the market for ideas, the position is very different. The government, if it attempted to regulate, would be inefficient and its motives would, in general, be bad, so that, even if it were successful in achieving what it wanted to accomplish, the results would be undesirable. Consumers, on the other hand, if left free, exercise a fine discrimination in choosing between the alternative views placed before them, while producers, whether economically powerful or weak, who are found to be so unscrupulous in their behavior in other markets, can be trusted to act in the public interest, whether they publish or work for the *New York Times,* the *Chicago Tribune* or the Columbia Broadcasting System. Politicians, whose actions sometimes pain us, are in their utterances beyond reproach. It is an odd feature of this attitude that commercial advertising, which is often merely an expression of opinion and might, therefore, be thought to be protected by the First Amendment, is considered to be part of the market for goods. The result is that government action is regarded as desirable to regulate (or even suppress) the expression of an opinion in an advertisement which, if expressed in a book or article, would be completely beyond the reach of government regulation.

This ambivalence toward the role of government in the market for goods and the market for ideas has not usually been attacked except by those on the extreme right or left, that is, by fascists or communists. The Western world, by and large, accepts the distinction and the policy recommendations that go with it. The peculiarity of the situation has not, however, gone unnoticed, and I would like to draw your attention to a powerful article by Aaron Director.[a]

* * *

Director remarks of the attachment to free speech that it is "the only area where *laissez-faire* is still respectable."

Why should this be so? In part, this may be due to the fact that belief in a free market in ideas does not have the same roots as belief in the value of free trade in goods.

* * *

Because of the view that a free market in ideas is necessary to the maintenance of democratic institutions and, I believe, for other reasons also, intellectuals have shown a tendency to exalt the market for ideas and to depreciate the market for goods. * * *

But leave aside the question of the relative importance of the two markets; the difference in view about the role of government in these two markets is really quite extraordinary and demands an explanation. It is not enough merely to say that the government should be excluded from a sphere of activity because it is vital to the functioning of our society. Even in markets which are mainly of concern to the lower orders, it would not seem desirable to reduce the efficiency with which they work. The paradox is that government intervention which is so harmful in the one sphere becomes beneficial in the other. The paradox is made even more striking when we note that at the present time it is usually those who press most strongly for an extension of government regulation in other markets who are most anxious for a vigorous enforcement of the First Amendment prohibitions on government regulation in the market for ideas.

What is the explanation for the paradox? Director's gentle nature does not allow him to do more than hint at it: "A superficial explanation for the preference for free speech among intellectuals runs in terms of vertical interests. Everyone tends to magnify the importance of his own occupation and to minimize that of his neighbor. Intellectuals are engaged in the pursuit of truth, while others are merely engaged in earning a livelihood. One follows a profession, usually a learned one,

a. Aaron Director, *The Parity of the*   (1964).
Economic Market Place, 7 J.L. & Econ. 1

while the other follows a trade or a business." I would put the point more bluntly. The market for ideas is the market in which the intellectual conducts his trade. The explanation of the paradox is self-interest and self-esteem. Self-esteem leads the intellectuals to magnify the importance of their own market. That others should be regulated seems natural, particularly as many of the intellectuals see themselves as doing the regulating. But self-interest combines with self-esteem to ensure that, while others are regulated, regulation should not apply to them. And so it is possible to live with these contradictory views about the role of government in these two markets. It is the conclusion that matters. It may not be a nice explanation, but I can think of no other for this strange situation.

* * *

I do not believe that this distinction between the market for goods and the market for ideas is valid. There is no fundamental difference between these two markets and, in deciding on public policy with regard to them, we need to take into account the same considerations. In all markets, producers have some reasons for being honest and some for being dishonest; consumers have some information but are not fully informed or even able to digest the information they have; regulators commonly wish to do a good job, and though often incompetent and subject to the influence of special interests, they act like this because, like all of us, they are human beings whose strongest motives are not the highest.

When I say that the same considerations should be taken into account, I do not mean that public policy should be the same in all markets. The special characteristics of each market lead to the same factors having different weights, and the appropriate social arrangements will vary accordingly. It may not be sensible to have the same legal arrangements governing the supply of soap, housing, automobiles, oil, and books. My argument is that we should use the same *approach* for all markets when deciding on public policy. In fact, if we do this and use for the market for ideas the same approach which has commended itself to economists for the market for goods, it is apparent that the case for government intervention in the market for ideas is much stronger than it is, in general, in the market for goods. For example, economists usually call for government intervention, which may include direct government regulation, when the market does not operate properly— when, that is, there exist what are commonly referred to as neighborhood or spillover effects, or, to use that unfortunate word, "externalities." If we try to imagine the property rights system that would be required and the transactions that would have to be carried out to assure that anyone who propagated an idea or a proposal for reform received the value of the good it produced or had to pay compensation for the harm that resulted, it is easy to see that in practice there is likely to be a good deal of "market failure." Situations of this kind usually lead economists to call for extensive government intervention.

Or consider the question of consumer ignorance which is commonly thought to be a justification for government intervention. It is hard to believe that the general public is in a better position to evaluate competing views on economic and social policy than to choose between different kinds of food. Yet there is support for regulation in the one case but not in the other. Or consider the question of preventing fraud, for which government intervention is commonly advocated. It would be difficult to deny that newspaper articles and the speeches of politicians contain a large number of false and misleading statements—indeed, sometimes they seem to consist of little else. Government action to control false and misleading advertising is considered highly desirable. Yet a proposal to set up a Federal Press Commission or a Federal Political Commission modeled on the Federal Trade Commission would be dismissed out of hand.

* * *

Whatever one may think of the motives which have led to the general acceptance of the present position, there remains the question of which policies would be, in fact, the most appropriate. This requires us to come to some conclusion about how the government will perform whatever functions are assigned to it. I do not believe that we will be able to form a judgment in which we can have any confidence unless we abandon the present ambivalence about the performance of government in the two markets and adopt a more consistent view. We have to decide whether the government is as incompetent as is generally assumed in the market for ideas, in which case we would want to decrease government intervention in the market for goods, or whether it is as efficient as it is generally assumed to be in the market for goods, in which case we would want to increase government regulation in the market for ideas. Of course, one could adopt an intermediate position—a government neither as incompetent and base as assumed in the one market nor as efficient and virtuous as assumed in the other. In this case, we ought to reduce the amount of government regulation in the market for goods and might want to increase government intervention in the market for ideas.

OWEN FISS, WHY THE STATE?
100 Harv.L.Rev. 781, 783, 787–89, 791 (1987).

As part of the contemporary assault on state activism that so dominates our politics, Ronald Coase and Aaron Director have confronted New Deal liberals with the free speech tradition in order to remind them of the virtues of laissez faire and to build a case against state intervention in economic matters. My inclination is, of course, just the reverse. It occurred to me that if Coase and Director can celebrate the libertarian element in the free speech tradition as a way of arguing against state intervention in the economic sphere, we should be able to start at the other end—to begin with the fact of state intervention in economic matters, and then use that historical experience to understand why the state might have a role to play in furthering free speech values. Such an approach might not only clarify and enrich our understanding of the first amendment, but might also yield a more general and perhaps more important insight. It might undermine the larger assault on the state. Because speech has been used as a lever for laissez faire, on the theory that it identifies an area where the demand for limited government is strongest and most appealing, a conclusion that state regulation of speech is consistent with, and may even be required by, the first amendment might well throw the entire critique of the activist state into question.

* * *

Today, public debate is dominated by the television networks and a number of large newspapers and magazines. The competition among these institutions is far from perfect, and some might argue for state intervention on a theory of market failure. There is a great deal of force to those arguments, but they obscure a deeper truth—a market, even one that is working perfectly, is itself a structure of constraint. A fully competitive market might produce a diversity of programs, formats, and reportage, but, to borrow an image of Renata Adler's, it will be the diversity of "a pack going essentially in one direction."

The market constrains the presentation of matters of public interest and importance in two ways. First, the market privileges select groups, by making programs, journals, and newspapers especially responsive to their needs and desires. One such group consists of those who have the capital to acquire or own a television station, newspaper, or journal; another consists of those who control the advertising budgets of various businesses; and still another consists of those who are most able and most likely to respond enthusiastically to advertising. The number in the last group is no doubt quite large (it probably includes every nine-year-old who can bully his or her parents into purchasing one thing or another), but it is not coextensive with the electorate. To be a consumer, even a sovereign one, is not to be a citizen.

Second, the market brings to bear on editorial and programming decisions factors that might have a great deal to do with profitability or allocative efficiency (to look at matters from a societal point of view) but little to do with the democratic needs of the electorate. For a businessman, the costs of production and the revenue likely to be generated are highly pertinent factors in determining what shows to run and when, or what to feature in a newspaper; a perfectly competitive market will produce shows or publications whose marginal cost equals marginal revenue. Reruns of *I Love Lucy* are profitable and an efficient use of resources. So is MTV. But there is no necessary, or even probabilistic, relationship between making a profit (or allocating resources efficiently) and supplying the electorate with the information they need to make free and intelligent choices about government policy, the structure of government, or the nature of society. This point was well understood when we freed our educational systems and our universities from the grasp of the market, and it applies with equal force to the media.

None of this is meant to denigrate the market. It is only to recognize its limitations. The issue is not market failure but market reach. The market might be splendid for some purposes but not for others. It might be an effective institution for producing cheap and varied consumer goods and for providing essential services (including entertainment) but not for producing the kind of debate that constantly renews the capacity of a people for self-determination. The state is to act as the much-needed countervailing power, to counteract the skew of public debate attributable to the market and thus preserve the essential conditions of democracy. The purpose of the state is not to supplant the market (as it would under a socialist theory), nor to perfect the market (as it would under a theory of market failure), but rather to supplement it. The state is to act as the corrective *for* the market. The state must put on the agenda issues that are systematically ignored and slighted and allow us to hear voices and viewpoints that would otherwise be silenced or muffled.

To turn to the state for these reasons does not presuppose that the people who staff a government agency are different in moral quality or in personality from those who control or manage the so-called private media. The state has no corner on virtue. What the theory of countervailing power does presuppose, however, is that simply by virtue of their position government employees are subject to a different set of constraints than those who run the media. They are public officials. We know that sometimes the word "public" becomes hollow and empty, a mere cover for the advancement of private interests, and that systems of public accountability are not perfect. But that is not to deny the force of these systems of accountability altogether. They may be imperfect but nonetheless of some effect. There is also an important difference of aspiration. It is one thing to empower someone called a public official and to worry whether the power entrusted is being used for public ends; it is another thing simply to leave that power in the hands of those who openly and unabashedly serve institutions that rest on private capital and are subject to market pressures.

* * *

We began, you will recall, with the claim that left to itself public debate will not be "uninhibited, robust, and wide open," but instead will be skewed by the forces that dominate society. The state should be allowed to intervene, and sometimes even required to do so, I argued, to correct for the market. In saying this, I assumed that the state would act as a countervailing power, but there is a danger, so the leftist critic insists, that it will not act in this way but will instead become the victim of the same forces that dominate public debate. There is a risk that the state will reinforce rather than counteract the skew of the market, because it is as much an object of social forces as it is an agent of change. The state might do some good, but the prospect of it doing so is so slim, and the danger of it doing just the opposite is so great, that it would be best, the leftist critic concludes, to bar state intervention altogether or at least to create a strong presumption against it—not to secure autonomy, but to insure the richness of public debate.

In the late 1970s, Charles Lindblom published an important book, *Politics and Markets,* which described with great force and clarity the so-called danger of "circularity." The state was supposed to govern business, but there was good reason to believe that the system of control largely worked the other way around. The picture that Lindblom painted was a sobering one—the danger of circularity is indeed real—but my own view of the facts and, more particularly, of our historical experience with the activist state in the sixties leads me to believe that the elements of independence possessed by the state are real and substantial. This independence is not complete, but it is nonetheless sufficient to make the theory of countervailing power viable. I also believe that we might cope with the danger of circularity in ways other than creating the strong presumption against state action urged by the leftist critic. To begin with, we might recognize that some state agencies are more independent of market forces than others and accordingly allocate more power to them.

BIBLIOGRAPHY

Carl Auerbach, *The Communist Control Act of 1954: A Proposed Legal–Political Theory of Free Speech,* 23 U.Chi.L.Rev. 173 (1956).

C. Edwin Baker, *Scope of the First Amendment Freedom of Speech,* 25 UCLA L.Rev. 964 (1978).

C. Edwin Baker, *Advertising and a Democratic Press,* 140 U.Pa.L.Rev. 2097 (1992).

C. Edwin Baker, *Of Course, More Than Words,* 61 U.Chi.L.Rev. 1181 (1994).

J.M. Balkin, *Some Realism About Pluralism: Legal Realist Approaches to the First Amendment,* 1990 Duke L.J. 375.

Mary Becker, *Conservative Free Speech and the Uneasy Case for Judicial Review,* 64 U.Colo.L.Rev. 975 (1993).

David O. Brink, *Mill's Deliberative Utilitarianism,* 21 Phil. & Pub. Aff. 67 (1992).

R.D. Coase, *Advertising and Free Speech,* 6 J.Leg.Stud. 1 (1977).

Aaron Director, *The Parity of the Economic Market Place,* 7 J. Law & Econ. 1 (1964).

Benjamin DuVal, *Free Communication of Ideas and the Quest for Truth: Toward a Teleological Approach to First Amendment Adjudication,* 41 Geo.Wash.L.Rev. 161 (1972).

Stanley Fish, THERE'S NO SUCH THING AS FREE SPEECH: AND IT'S A GOOD THING TOO (1994).

Owen Fiss, *Free Speech and Social Structure,* 71 Iowa L.Rev. 1405 (1986).

Stanley Ingber, *The Marketplace of Ideas: A Legitimizing Myth,* 1984 Duke L.J. 1.

H.J. McCloskey, *Liberty of Expression: Its Grounds and Limits,* 13 Inquiry 219 (1970).

Catharine MacKinnon, *Pornography, Civil Rights and Speech,* 20 Harv. C.R.–C.L.L.Rev. 1 (1985).

Frances Olsen, *Feminist Theory in Grand Style,* 89 Colum.L.Rev. 1147 (1989).

Lucas A. Powe, Jr., *Scholarship and Markets,* 56 Geo.Wash.L.Rev. 172 (1987).

Norman L. Rosenberg, *Another History of Free Speech: The 1920s and the 1940s,* 7 L. & Inequality 333 (1989).

Frederick Schauer, *Language, Truth, and the First Amendment: An Essay in Memory of Harry Canter,* 64 Va.L.Rev. 263 (1978).

James Fitzjames Stephen, LIBERTY, EQUALITY, FRATERNITY (R.J. White ed. 1967).

Richard Wright, *A Rationale from J.S. Mill for the Free Speech Clause,* 1985 Sup.Ct.Rev. 149.

D. SELF-EXPRESSION AND PERSONAL LIBERTY

Edwin Baker, who joins some of the authors noted in the previous section in questioning the assumptions of the marketplace-of-ideas model, rests the principle of free speech not on the search for truth, but instead on individual liberty and the value of personal self-expression. In slightly different versions the same focus on the individual rather than on social utility dominates the perspectives of Martin Redish and David Richards, both of whom share with Baker the sense that what is important about free speech is the way in which it liberates the individual to pursue her faculties to the greatest possible degree. These various self-realization or individual liberty perspectives have also been the subject of criticism. The most common criticism, exemplified by Robert Bork, is not that liberty and self-realization are not valuable, but rather that these values are not served uniquely or specially by speech, as compared to non-speech forms of activity. The result, say Bork and others, is that the idea of personal liberty is insufficient to generate a distinct principle of freedom of speech.

C. EDWIN BAKER, SCOPE OF THE FIRST AMENDMENT FREEDOM OF SPEECH

25 UCLA L.Rev. 964–66, 990–98, 1009, 1039–40 (1978).

This paper develops three theories of the scope of speech protected by the first amendment: two different marketplace of ideas theories, which I will call the *classic model* and the *market failure model,* and a third, the *liberty model.* The classic model depends on implausible assumptions for its coherence. The market failure model is unworkable, dangerous, and inconsistent with a reasonable interpretation of the purpose of the first amendment. Although the Court consistently has used and proclaimed the classic theory and though most modern reformist proposals recommend a market failure model, the liberty model provides the most coherent theory of the first amendment. Adoption of this theory, which delineates a realm of individual liberty roughly corresponding to noncoercive, nonviolent action, would have major, salutary implications for judicial elaboration of the first amendment.

* * *

The liberty model holds that the free speech clause protects not a marketplace but rather an arena of individual liberty from certain types of governmental restrictions. Speech is protected not as a means to a collective good but because of the value of speech conduct to the individual. The liberty theory justifies protection because of the way the protected conduct fosters individual self-realization and self-determination without improperly interfering with the legitimate claims of others. Of course, the liberty theory must specify what conduct is protected. After investigating the nature of speech—its uses and the manner in which it typically affects the world—and after reviewing generally accepted notions of the values of first amendment protected activities, I argue that the constitutional protection of free speech bars certain governmental restrictions on noncoercive, nonviolent, substantively valued conduct, including nonverbal conduct. In this liberty interpretation, first amendment protections of speech, assembly, and religion are merely different markers illustrating or bounding a single realm of liberty of self-expression and self-determination. Although any one of these three concepts illuminates this realm, the concept of protected speech most clearly delineates its scope. Finally, the broadened scope of protection required by the liberty theory cures the major inadequacies of the marketplace of ideas as a model for finding or creating societal "truth," thereby providing protection for a progressive process of change.

* * *

* * * Professor Emerson, probably the most thoughtful and influential first amendment scholar, finds first amendment freedom essential for four values: 1) individual self-fulfillment, 2) advancement of knowledge and discovery of truth, 3) participation in decision making by all members of the society (which "embraces the right to participate in the building of the whole culture"), and 4) achievement of a "more adaptable and hence stable community."

Emerson's list is acceptable. However, it is informative to see that the first value, self-fulfillment, and the third, participation in change, are key values and to understand why conduct promoting these two values ought to receive constitutional protection.

The values of self-fulfillment and participation in change impose somewhat different requirements on a satisfactory theory. The emphasis on "self" in self-fulfillment requires the theory to delineate a realm of liberty for self-determined processes of self-realization. The participation in change value requires the theory to specify and protect activities essential to a democratic, participatory process of change. Emerson's other two values are derivative. Given that truth is chosen or created, not discovered, advancement of knowledge and discovery of truth are merely aspects of participation in change. Also, one apparently achieves a "more flexible and thereby more stable community" by providing for individual self-fulfillment and participation in change. Thus, henceforth, I will refer to individual self-fulfillment and participation in change as the key first amendment values.

* * *

An exploration of the uses of speech will clarify both *how* and *when* speech contributes to the key values of the first amendment. * * *

To engage voluntarily in a speech act is to engage in self-definition or expression. A Vietnam war protestor may explain that when she chants "Stop This War Now" at a demonstration, she does so without any expectation that her speech will affect the continuance of war or even that it will communicate anything to people in power; rather, she participates and chants in order to *define* herself publicly in opposition to the war. This war protestor provides a dramatic illustration of the importance of this self-expressive use of speech, independent of any effective communication to others, for self-fulfillment or self-realization. Generally, any individually chosen, meaningful conduct, whether public or private, expresses and further defines the actor's nature and contributes to the actor's self-realization.

Speech is not merely communicative but also creative. * * * For example, the creative use of language is particularly prominent in: 1) making up new rules for a game or practice, as well as the language embodying the new rules; 2) coining a word, forming a new verbal image; 3) writing a poem or a play; 4) verbally formulating an analysis in order to "discover" new relationships or possibilities, or a dialogue through which *both* participants gain insights which *neither* possessed before; 5) "creating" or planning a new strategy; 6) persuading another of something; 7) teaching or developing new capabilities in another. The creative aspect, the new aspect of the world which results, varies in these examples. But in each case either the speaker or the listener or both possess something new—new images, new capacities, new opportunities, new amusements—which did not exist before and which were created by people's speech activity. Often the new creation will influence behavior. And in each case the creation has changed the social world, the world of meanings, opportunities, and restraints, in which people live.

Self-expressive and creative uses of speech *more fully and uniformly* promote the two key first amendment values, self-fulfillment and participation in both societal decision making and culture building, than does speech which communicates propositions and attitudes. First, *solitary uses* of speech contribute to self-fulfillment. Also, people's private analysis of their own character or of how to accomplish some goal, or people's practice of singing or of creating or viewing obscenity for private entertainment or relaxation, are all private speech activities which, by changing or defining people, change or modify the culture. Second, *communications* not intended to communicate propositions or attitudes of the speaker—such as story telling intended merely to entertain the listener, or singing intended merely to show the accomplishments of the singer, or group singing or a verbal ritual possibly intended to develop group solidarity—may both contribute to self-fulfillment and affect the culture.

* * *

The first amendment could not possibly protect all the manifold activities, some of which involve violence or coercion, that further self-fulfillment or contribute to change. The logic of constitutionally protecting speech relates to the common sense perceptions both of the importance of speech for realizing certain values and of the method by which speech advances those values. In fact, * * * the first amendment protects non-verbal, creative and self-expressive activities when they advance first amendment values in a manner relevantly similar to speech. Here, the central problem is to determine what *methods* or *manner* of using speech deserve constitutional protection.

Speech, unlike other behavior, is seldom thought of as physically violent or destructive [104]—the shrill voice breaking a glass is an aberrant example not typical of our normal notions of speech use. Similarly, using high decibel levels of sound to physically interfere with another's activities belies, rather than exemplifies, our characteristic image of speech; few urge constitutional protection for sheer noise used to disrupt a meeting. Speech may harm others; but normally, speech differs from most other harm-producing conduct in the way it causes the harm. Both the amiable interchange which leads to replacing old with new friendships (consider the tort of alienation of affection) and the destructive interchange well illustrated in Edward Albee's *Who's Afraid of Virginia Woolf* create an effect by influencing the mind—the percep-

104. Compare "sticks and stones may   me."
break my bones but names will never hurt

tions, feelings, beliefs or understandings—of the listener (or the speaker).

Law is typically used to prohibit certain harmful actions. But if the Constitution limits the government's power to restrict people's liberty, then either some harms or some methods of causing harms must not suffice to justify legal restrictions on behavior. This conclusion cannot be controversial. Under existing doctrine, harms caused by speech normally do not justify a restriction on speech, while harms that result from invading another's area of decision authority (*e.g.*, destruction of another's property or coercing another's behavior) normally justify outlawing the invading conduct. The theoretical justification for this doctrine, as well as the explication of its scope, depends upon showing that the principle of respecting the equality and autonomy of individuals, which justifies limiting the collective's decision-making authority, requires that people have the right to cause harms by certain means (speech caused harms) but not by others. This can be done. The key aspect distinguishing harms caused by protected speech acts from most other methods of causing harms is that speech harms occur only to the extent people "mentally" adopt perceptions or attitudes. Two factors deserve emphasis. First, the speech act does not interfere with another's legitimate decision authority, assuming that the other has no right to decide what the speaker should say or believe. This assumption is a necessary consequence of our respecting people's autonomy. Second, outlawing acts of the speaker in order to protect people from harms that result because the listener adopts certain perceptions or attitudes disrespects the responsibility and freedom of the listener. Both of these observations follow from our typical concept of the person which identifies a person, at least in part, with the person's perceptions and feelings; we hold a person responsible for actions that are based on the opinions or perceptions the person accepts. In fact, respecting the listener's integrity as an individual normally requires holding the listener responsible for her conduct unless she has been coerced or forced into the activity.

This explanation for protecting speech suggests the uses which do not merit protection. (Of course, one must be very careful not to find exceptions too easily—one must guard against the easy conclusion of those in authority that a particular "harmful" use of speech must fit into an exception.) The reasons why speech is protected do not apply if the speaker *coerces* the other or *physically interferes* with the other's rights.

* * *

If one concludes that the first amendment does not protect all speech, the literalist argument that all speech and *only* speech is protected loses force. Nevertheless, no accepted criteria exist to evaluate claims of first amendment protection for nonverbal conduct. I think, however, that a persuasive argument for protection of a particular type of conduct could be made by showing that: 1) the experience conduct furthers key first amendment values; 2) protection of this type of conduct is essential for an adequate realization of these values; 3) this conduct and protected verbal conduct promote first amendment values in a relevantly similar manner, and 4) principled lines can identify which conduct should be protected in what ways.

* * *

Concluding that freedom of speech requires protecting self-chosen, nonverbal conduct from certain forms of government abridgement involves a considerable revision of first amendment theory. However, this conclusion appears to be the only principled interpretation of the first amendment once one demonstrates the inadequacy of both the classic marketplace of ideas theory and the market failure theory.

The argument for this liberty theory of freedom of speech involved, first, a review of the basic functions or values of the first amendment. The two key values were individual self-fulfillment and individual participation in public decision making. These values did not provide a coherent distinction between "expression," which Professor Emerson argued is protected, and "action," which he argued is not. Instead, the category of protected speech was better described as "noncoercive" expressive conduct. Neither the key first amendment values nor the noncoercive method by which clearly protected verbal conduct advances these values suggested any constitutionally relevant difference between verbal conduct and noncoercive, nonviolent, and expressive nonverbal conduct. This implies that both should be protected.

MARTIN H. REDISH, THE VALUE OF FREE SPEECH

130 U.Pa.L.Rev. 591, 593–94, 601–04, 627–29 (1982).

The position taken in this Article is that the constitutional guarantee of free speech ultimately serves only one true value, which I have labeled "individual self-realization." This term has been chosen largely because of its ambiguity: it can be interpreted to refer either to development of the individual's powers and abilities—an individual "realizes" his or her full potential—or to the individual's control of his or her own destiny through making life-affecting decisions—an individual "realizes" the goals in life that he or she has set. In using the term, I intend to include both interpretations. I have, therefore, chosen it instead of such other options as "liberty" or "autonomy," on the one hand, and "individual self-fulfillment" or "human development," on the other. The former pair of alternatives arguably may be limited to the decisionmaking value, whereas the latter could be interpreted reasonably as confined to the individual development concept.

That the first amendment serves only one ultimate value, however, does not mean that the majority of values thought by others to be fostered by free speech—the "political process," "checking," and "marketplace-of-ideas" values—are invalid. I have not chosen from a list of mutually exclusive possibilities, nor do I argue that the value that I have selected supersedes these alternatives. My contention is that these other values, though perfectly legitimate, are in reality subvalues of self-realization. To the extent that they are legitimate, each can be explained by—and only by—reference to the primary value: individual self-realization. It thus is inaccurate to suggest that "the commitment to free expression embodie[s] a complex of values."

This Article attempts to establish that this first principle—individual self-realization—can be proven, not merely by reference to some unsupportable, conclusory assertions of moral value, but by reasoning from what we in this nation take as given: our democratic system of government. It demonstrates that the moral norms inherent in the choice of our specific form of democracy logically imply the broader value, self-realization. It then concludes that all forms of expression that further the self-realization value, which justifies the democratic system as well as free speech's role in it, are deserving of full constitutional protection.

* * *

It is not hard to understand why constitutional protection of speech would be greater than that of conduct. If we were to draw a rough distinction—the kind that must necessarily have been drawn by the framers—we could reasonably decide that speech is less likely to cause direct or immediate harm to the interests of others [48] and more likely to develop the individual's mental faculties, and that speech thus deserves a greater degree of constitutional protection than does conduct. [Robert] Bork's assumption [a] that any principled first amendment theory must rely solely on values that are *uniquely* protected by speech drastically undercuts this status by effectively removing all categories of speech from the amendment's protection.

* * *

The primary flaw in the analysis of Bork and [Alexander] Meiklejohn [b] is that they never attempt to ascertain what basic value or values

---

48. Dean Wellington has correctly noted that "speech often hurts. It can offend, injure reputation, fan prejudice or passion, and ignite the world. Moreover, a great deal of other conduct that the state regulates has less harmful potential." Wellington, *On Freedom of Expression*, 88 Yale L.J. 1105, 1106–07 (1979) (footnote omitted). He cites, as one example of the latter, laws prohibiting certain forms of sexual relations between consenting adults. *Id.* 1107. But (as noted in the text), in establishing a constitutional rule that is to provide a guide for future generations, it is impossible to enumerate the specific instances that deserve a greater degree of protection and those that deserve a lesser degree. It is almost certainly true in the overwhelming majority of cases that speech is less immediately dangerous than conduct. In any event, I would argue, with respect to the example of laws regulating consensual sexual practices cited by Dean Wellington, that such conduct should (at least as a matter of logic and morals) be deemed fully protected by the self-realization principle. To the extent that it is not protected, it is probably because there is no constitutional provision giving it the high level of protection given speech by the first amendment.

a. Bork, *Neutral Principles and Some First Amendment Problems*, 47 Ind.L.J. 1 (1971).

b. Political Freedom (1960).

the democratic process was designed to serve. Examination of the "process" values inherent in our nation's adoption of a democratic system reveals an implicit belief in the worth of the individual that has first amendment implications extending well beyond the borders of the political world. Indeed, political democracy is merely a means to—or, in another sense, a logical outgrowth of—the much broader value of individual self-realization. The mistake of Bork and Meiklejohn, then, is that they have confused one means of obtaining the ultimate value with the value itself.

The logic employed by Meiklejohn and Bork to reach their conclusion that the protection of speech was designed to aid the political process would have absolutely no relevance except in a democratic system. For a monarchy or dictatorship to function politically, it of course is not necessary that the general public be able to speak freely or receive information about pressing political questions, because private individuals will have no say in decisions. Even a benevolent dictator would be more likely to allow free expression in traditionally nonpolitical areas such as art, literature, and music than in the political realm. The free speech value emphasized by Meiklejohn and Bork, then, is inherently linked to a democratic form of government.

Democracy is by no means the only system that could have been chosen when our nation was founded. Indeed, it is probably safe to say that the overwhelming majority of organized societies throughout history have not chosen it, even in its most diluted form. It would seem, then, that there must be some values that the founding fathers believed to be uniquely fostered by a democracy, values that succeeding generations of political leaders presumably have shared, since there has been little or no effort to alter substantially our system of government by constitutional processes.

One conceivable value is "consequentialist" in nature: efficiency. One could believe that the results of a democratic system are somehow better than any other system's. Such an argument, however, would be very difficult to prove, for several reasons. Initially, it would probably be difficult to obtain agreement on the criteria for measuring results. How are we to decide what is "better"? Higher gross national product? More international influence? And better for whom? Elites? A majority? Oppressed minorities? Secondly, it is doubtful that we could establish empirically that throughout history democracies have fared better than other forms of government. After all, we do know that the trains ran on time in Mussolini's Italy; can the Chicago Transit Authority make the same claim? Moreover, it may well be counter-intuitive to believe, especially in a modern, highly technological society, that decisions made by the masses or their elected representatives—who are rarely chosen because of any degree of real expertise—would be either the wisest or the most efficient. Finally, it is doubtful that many of us would be anxious to discard democracy even if it were established definitely that an alternative political system was more efficient. It is likely, then, that the values inherent in a democratic system are "process-oriented," rather than related to some objective standard of governmental efficiency.

These "process" values seem to translate into two forms: an "intrinsic" value and an "instrumental" value. The "intrinsic" value is one that is achieved by the very existence of a democratic system. It is the value of having individuals control their own destinies. For if one does not accept the morality of such a proposition, why bother to select a democratic system in the first place? As Meiklejohn said, "[i]f men are to be governed, we say, then that governing must be done, not by others, but by themselves. So far, therefore, as our own affairs are concerned, we refuse to submit to alien control." The point is so obvious that it requires no further elaboration, except to say that the core concept of "self-rule" appears to have formed the cornerstone of every theory of democracy to date. It would seem to be so as a matter of definition.

The second value of a democratic system is labeled "instrumental," because it is a goal to which a democratic system is designed to lead, rather than one that is attained definitionally by the adoption of a democratic system. It is a goal that is associated primarily with "classical" (fully participatory) democracy: development of the individual's human faculties.

* * *

My thesis is that: (1) although the democratic process is a means of achieving both the intrinsic and instrumental values, it is only one means of doing so; (2) both values (which, as noted previously, may be grouped under the broader heading of "self-realization") may be achieved by and for individuals in countless nonpolitical, and often wholly private, activities; and (3) the concept of free speech facilitates the development of these values by directly fostering the instrumental value and indirectly fostering the intrinsic value. Free speech fosters the former goal *directly* in that the very exercise of one's freedom to speak, write, create, appreciate, or learn represents a use, and therefore a development, of an individual's uniquely human faculties. It fosters the latter value *indirectly* because the very exercise of one's right of free speech does not in itself constitute an exercise of one's ability to make life-affecting decisions as much as it *facilitates* the making of such decisions.

This conceptual framework indicates that the appropriate scope of the first amendment protection is much broader than Bork or Meiklejohn would have it. Free speech aids all life-affecting decisionmaking, no matter how personally limited, in much the same manner in which it aids the political process. Just as individuals need an open flow of information and opinion to aid them in making their electoral and governmental decisions, they similarly need a free flow of information and opinion to guide them in making other life-affecting decisions. There thus is no logical basis for distinguishing the role speech plays in the political process. Although we definitely need protection of speech to aid us in making political judgments, we need it no less whenever free speech will aid development of the broader values than the democratic system is designed to foster.

* * *

There is more to self-realization, however, than private self-government. For it is highly doubtful that fine art, ballet, or literature can be thought to aid one in making concrete life-affecting decisions, yet all three seem deserving of full first amendment protection. This is because of the other branch of self-realization: the development of one's human faculties, recognized as an end in itself. Once this form of self-realization is acknowledged, it becomes significantly more difficult to exclude many of the categories of expression deemed irrelevant to the private self-government branch.

Of course, we might conclude that, whereas art, literature, and ballet are proper means of developing one's mental faculties, a mere stream of obscenities or advocacy of crime is not. But, although it may well be appropriate to distinguish among different forms of expression on the ground that some of them present greater danger of harming society, it is considerably more doubtful that an arm of the state should have the authority to decide for the individual that certain means of mental development are better than others. If two consenting individuals wish to engage in a conversation consisting of little more than a stream of obscenities, assuming no harm to others, it is dangerous to provide the state with the power to prohibit such activity on the ground that such discourse is not "valuable." For, if the state can make that decision, what is logically to prevent it from deciding that the works of Henry Miller are not "valuable" because of their constant use of obscenities? Or why could not the state similarly set up an administrative board to decide that certain works of literature, art, dance, or music are not as "valuable" as others, and can therefore be suppressed? Most of us would no doubt find such a process intuitively repugnant, presumably even if we agreed with the censor about the lack of quality of a particular book, movie, or performance. We would explain this feeling of repugnance, I suppose, by reasoning that it is simply not the state's business to decide for each individual what books, movies, or shows are "valuable"; that is a decision for the individual to make for himself or herself. But once we have gone that far, how could we rationally distinguish the stream of obscenities between consenting adults? There, too, we would have to reason that perhaps that particular form of discourse is not our cup of tea, but that this gives the state no more inherent right to suppress it than it would have to suppress a particular book or movie we found distasteful. A stream of obscenities may not develop one's *intellectual* abilities (though it could conceivably increase one's vocabulary), but neither does music, art, or dance. An individual's "mental" processes cannot be limited to the receipt and digestion of cold, hard theories and facts, for there is also an emotional element that is uniquely human and that can be "developed" by such "non-rational" forms of communication.

DAVID A.J. RICHARDS, FREE SPEECH AND OBSCENITY LAW: TOWARD A MORAL THEORY OF THE FIRST AMENDMENT

123 U.Pa.L.Rev. 45, 59–63, 68–69 (1974).

Whatever the historical obscurities which surround the proposal and adoption of the first amendment, there is little question that the amendment was part of and gives expression to a developing moral theory regarding the equal liberties of men which had been given expression by Milton and Locke and which was being given or was to be given expression by Rousseau and Kant. The technical legal history of free speech in England and America prior to the adoption of the first amendment obviously renders doubtful any consensus on the specific application of the amendment; a consensus, to the extent it existed, was one on the generalities of a political compromise that concealed future divergences of interpretation. In such circumstances, the explanation of underlying moral theory is a fortiori useful. But even if the legal history appeared to be definitive, it would, in fact, be seriously incomplete if it were not understood in the light of a history of evolving moral ideas to which the first amendment, like all laws, gives expression.

* * *

An adequate moral theory would express the intuitive features of the common sense notion of morality, organizing these features in a constructive and determinate way. The central intuitive features of morality are mutual respect—treating others as you would like to be treated in comparable circumstances; universalization—judging the morality of principles by the consequences of their universal application; and minimization of fortuitous human differences, like clan, caste, ethnicity, and color, as a basis for differential treatment.

This Article employs a contractarian analysis, following the model of John Rawls,[89] that incorporates the intuitive features of morality in this way: Moral principles are those that perfectly rational men, irrespective of historical or personal age, in a hypothetical position of equal liberty and having all knowledge and reasonable belief except that of their specific personal situation, would agree to as the ultimate standards of conduct that are applicable at large. Mutual respect is inherent in the idea of moral principles as standards to which all men would consent, defining the ways in which they, as well as others, should be treated in comparable circumstances. Universalization is expressed by the idea that the morality of any principle is to be judged on the assumption that it is generally accepted and acted on. The minimization of fortuity is guaranteed by the ignorance of specific identity.

* * *

89. [A Theory of Justice (1971).]

The original position presents a problem of rational choice under uncertainty: rational men in the original position have no way of predicting the probabilities that they may end up in any given situation of life. If a person agrees to principles of justice that permit deprivations of liberty and property rights and later discovers that he occupies a disadvantaged position, he will have no just claim against deprivations which may render his entire life prospects meager and bitterly servile. To forestall such consequences, the rational strategy in choosing the basic principles of justice would be the conservative "maximin" strategy: make certain that the worst position in the system adopted is the best of all conceivable worst positions, that is, maximize the minimum condition. Thus, if a person is born into the worst possible situation of life allowed by the adopted moral principles, he or she will still be better off than in the worst situation allowed by any other possible principles.

The application of the maximin strategy requires us to consider the interpretation and relative weight assigned the general goods by those in the original position. These dimensions will crucially determine the principles governing the distribution of general goods.

Consider, for example, the liberties of thought and expression, in speech, the press, religion or association. The idea here is that people are not to be constrained to communicate or not to communicate, to believe or not to believe, to associate or not to associate. The value placed on this cluster of ideas derives from the notion of self-respect that comes from a mature person's full and untrammelled exercise of capacities central to human rationality. Thus, the significance of free expression rests on the central human capacity to create and express symbolic systems, such as speech, writing, pictures, and music, intended to communicate in determinate, complex and subtle ways. Freedom of expression permits and encourages the exercise of these capacities: it supports a mature individual's sovereign autonomy in deciding how to communicate with others; it disfavors restrictions on communication imposed for the sake of the distorting rigidities of the orthodox and the established. In so doing, it nurtures and sustains the self-respect of the mature person.

Further, freedom of expression protects the interest of the mature individual, with developed capacities of rational choice, in deciding whether to be an audience to a communication and in weighing the communication according to his own rational vision of life. This idea was expressed by Kant by the moving thought that each rational being is a sovereign legislator in the realm of ends. It is a contempt of human rationality for any other putative sovereign, democratic or otherwise, to decide to what communications mature people can be exposed.

The value of free expression, in this view, rests on its deep relation to self-respect arising from autonomous self-determination without which the life of the spirit is meager and slavish. Other arguments for the moral value of free expression, for example, its relation to the discovery of truth, seem, by contrast, less powerful and often unhappily overused when they will not bear the fundamental weight they are expected to support. Such arguments, to the extent they are valid, at best provide additional reasons to value freedom of communication. The value of free expression is, however, as strong as its best moral argument, which is more potent than many another political banality now used in its defense.

One can clarify the nature and weight of other liberties in similar ways. Voting rights importantly confirm a person's sense of autonomous self-direction, without which the spirit shrivels into apathy. Access to the criminal and civil law affords basic security of the person. The liberty of physical, social, and economic movement frees a person from the fortuitous place and class of his birth, thereby granting effort and aspiration open horizons. In short, all these liberties, like the liberties of expression, nurture a basic sense of self-respect, a belief in the competent independence and integrity of one's person.

* * *

Attempts by the state to prohibit certain contents of communication *per se* are fundamentally incompatible with the moral and constitutional principle of equal liberty. Notwithstanding the detestation of and outrage felt by the majority toward certain contents of communication, the equal liberty principle absolutely forbids the prohibition of such communications on the ground of such detestation and outrage alone. Otherwise, the liberty of expression, instead of the vigorous and potent defense of individual autonomy that it is, would be a pitifully meager permission allowing people to communicate only in ways to which no one has any serious objection. The interest of the few in free expression is not to be sacrificed on such grounds to the interest of the many, notwithstanding utilitarian calculations to the contrary. Conventional attitudes are not to be the procrustean measure of the exercise of human expressive and judgmental competence.

On this view, the constitutionally protected liberty of free expression is the legal embodiment of a moral principle which ensures to each person the maximum equal liberty of communication compatible with a like liberty for all. Importantly, if the first amendment freedoms rest on a fundamental moral principle, they have no necessary justificatory relation to the liberty of equal voting rights. No doubt, the existence of equal voting rights advances values of self-direction and autonomy that are also advanced by the liberties of expression and thought. But a maximum equal liberty of self-expression is neither a necessary nor a sufficient logical or factual condition of democratic voting rights or of the competent exercise of those rights. Voting rights may exist and be competently exercised in a regime where expression is not in general free, but is limited to a small class of talented technicians who circulate relevant data on policy issues to the electorate. Similarly, free expression may exist in a political aristocracy or in a democracy where voting rights are not competently exercised because of illiteracy or political apathy.

The independent status of the value of free expression from the value of voting rights shows not that free expression is not valuable, but that its value is not intrinsically political. It rests, rather, on deeper moral premises regarding the general exercise of autonomous expressive and judgmental capacity and the good that this affords in human life. It follows that the attempt to limit the constitutional protection of free expression to the political must be rejected on moral and constitutional grounds.

ROBERT H. BORK, NEUTRAL PRINCIPLES AND SOME FIRST AMENDMENT PROBLEMS
47 Ind.L.J. 1, 20–28 (1971).

The law has settled upon no tenable, internally consistent theory of the scope of the constitutional guarantee of free speech. Nor have many such theories been urged upon the courts by lawyers or academicians. Professor Harry Kalven, Jr., one whose work is informed by a search for theory, has expressed wonder that we should feel the need for theory in the area of free speech when we tolerate inconsistencies in other areas of the law.[45] He answers himself:

> If my puzzle as to the First Amendment is not a true puzzle, it can only be for the congenial reason that free speech is so close to the heart of democratic organization that if we do not have an appropriate theory for our law here, we feel we really do not understand the society in which we live.

Kalven is certainly correct in assigning the first amendment a central place in our society, and he is also right in attributing that centrality to the importance of speech to democratic organization. Since I share this common ground with Professor Kalven, I find it interesting that my conclusions differ so widely from his.

I am led by the logic of the requirement that judges be principled to the following suggestions. Constitutional protection should be accorded only to speech that is explicitly political. There is no basis for judicial intervention to protect any other form of expression, be it scientific, literary or that variety of expression we call obscene or pornographic. Moreover, within that category of speech we ordinarily call political, there should be no constitutional obstruction to laws making criminal any speech that advocates forcible overthrow of the government or the violation of any law.

I am, of course, aware that this theory departs drastically from existing Court-made law, from the views of most academic specialists in the field and that it may strike a chill into the hearts of some civil libertarians. But I would insist at the outset that constitutional law, viewed as the set of rules a judge may properly derive from the document and its history, is not an expression of our political sympathies or of our judgments about what expediency and prudence require.

45. H. Kalven, The Negro and the First Amendment 4–5 (1966).

When decision making is principled it has nothing to say about the speech we like or the speech we hate; it has a great deal to say about how far democratic discretion can govern without endangering the basis of democratic government. Nothing in my argument goes to the question of what laws should be enacted. I like the freedoms of the individual as well as most, and I would be appalled by many statutes that I am compelled to think would be constitutional if enacted. But I am also persuaded that my generally libertarian commitments have nothing to do with the behavior proper to the Supreme Court.

In framing a theory of free speech the first obstacle is the insistence of many very intelligent people that the "first amendment is an absolute." Devotees of this position insist, with a literal respect they do not accord other parts of the Constitution, that the Framers commanded complete freedom of expression without governmental regulation of any kind. The first amendment states: "Congress shall make no law ... abridging the freedom of speech ...." Those who take that as an absolute must be reading "speech" to mean any form of verbal communication and "freedom" to mean total absence of governmental restraint.

Any such reading is, of course, impossible. Since it purports to be an absolute position we are entitled to test it with extreme hypotheticals. Is Congress forbidden to prohibit incitement to mutiny aboard a naval vessel engaged in action against an enemy, to prohibit shouted harangues from the visitors' gallery during its own deliberations or to provide any rules for decorum in federal courtrooms? Are the states forbidden, by the incorporation of the first amendment in the fourteenth, to punish the shouting of obscenities in the streets?

No one, not the most obsessed absolutist, takes any such position, but if one does not, the absolute position is abandoned, revealed as a play on words. Government cannot function if anyone can say anything anywhere at any time. And so we quickly come to the conclusion that lines must be drawn, differentiations made. Nor does that in any way involve us in a conflict with the wording of the first amendment. Laymen may perhaps be forgiven for thinking that the literal words of the amendment command complete absence of governmental inhibition upon verbal activity, but what can one say of lawyers who believe any such thing? Anyone skilled in reading language should know that the words are not necessarily absolute. "Freedom of speech" may very well be a term referring to a defined or assumed scope of liberty, and it may be this area of liberty that is not to be "abridged."

* * *

We are, then, forced to construct our own theory of the constitutional protection of speech. We cannot solve our problems simply by reference to the text or to its history. But we are not without materials for building. The first amendment indicates that there is something special about speech. We would know that much even without a first amendment, for the entire structure of the Constitution creates a representative democracy, a form of government that would be meaningless without freedom to discuss government and its policies. Freedom for political speech could and should be inferred even if there were no first amendment. Further guidance can be gained from the fact that we are looking for a theory fit for enforcement by judges. The principles we seek must, therefore, be neutral in all three meanings of the word: they must be neutrally derived, defined and applied.

* * *

* * * I wish to begin the general discussion of first amendment theory with consideration of a passage from Justice Brandeis' concurring opinion in * * * *Whitney* [.] * * *

As a starting point Brandeis went to fundamentals and attempted to answer the question why speech is protected at all from governmental regulation. If we overlook his highly romanticized version of history and ignore merely rhetorical flourishes, we shall find Brandeis quite provocative.

> Those who won our independence believed that the final end of the state was to make men free to develop their faculties; and that in its government the deliberative forces should prevail over the arbitrary. They valued liberty both as an end and as a means. They believed liberty to be the secret of happiness and courage to be the secret of liberty. They believed that freedom to think as you will and to speak as you think are means indispensable to the discovery and spread of political truth; that without free speech and assembly discussion would be futile; that with them, discussion affords ordinarily adequate protection against the dissemination of noxious doctrine. ... They recognized the risks to which all human institutions are subject. But they knew ... that it is hazardous to discourage thought, hope and imagination; that fear breeds repression; that repression breeds hate; that hate menaces stable government; that the path of safety lies in the opportunity to discuss freely supposed grievances and proposed remedies; and that the fitting remedy for evil counsels is good ones.

We begin to see why the dissents of Brandeis and Holmes possessed the power to which Professor Kalven referred. They were rhetoricians of extraordinary potency, and their rhetoric retains the power, almost half a century latter, to swamp analysis, to persuade, almost to command assent.

But there is structure beneath the rhetoric, and Brandeis is asserting, though he attributes it all to the Founding Fathers, that there are four benefits to be derived from speech. These are:

1. The development of the faculties of the individual;

2. The happiness to be derived from engaging in the activity;

3. The provision of a safety valve for society; and,

4. The discovery and spread of political truth.

We may accept these claims as true and as satisfactorily inclusive. When we come to analyze these benefits, however, we discover that in terms of constitutional law they are very different things.

The first two benefits—development of individual faculties and the achievement of pleasure—are or may be found, for both speaker and hearer, in all varieties of speech, from political discourse to shop talk to salacious literature. But the important point is that these benefits do not distinguish speech from any other human activity. An individual may develop his faculties or derive pleasure from trading on the stock market, following his profession as a river port pilot, working as a barmaid, engaging in sexual activity, playing tennis, rigging prices or in any of thousands of other endeavors. Speech with only the first two benefits can be preferred to other activities only by ranking forms of personal gratification. These functions or benefits of speech are, therefore, to the principled judge, indistinguishable from the functions or benefits of all other human activity. He cannot, on neutral grounds, choose to protect speech that has only these functions more than he protects any other claimed freedom.

The third benefit of speech mentioned by Brandeis—its safety valve function—is different from the first two. It relates not to the gratification of the individual, at least not directly, but to the welfare of society. The safety valve function raises only issues of expediency or prudence, and, therefore, raises issues to be determined solely by the legislature or, in some cases, by the executive. The legislature may decide not to repress speech advocating the forcible overthrow of the government in some classes of cases because it thinks repression would cause more trouble than it would prevent. Prosecuting attorneys, who must in any event pick and choose among cases, given their limited resources, may similarly decide that some such speech is trivial or that ignoring it would be wisest. But these decisions, involving only the issue of the expedient course, are indistinguishable from thousands of other managerial judgments governments must make daily, though in the extreme case the decision may involve the safety of the society just as surely as a decision whether or not to take a foreign policy stand that risks war. It seems plain that decisions involving only judgments of expediency are for the political branches and not for the judiciary.

This leaves the fourth function of speech—the "discovery and spread of political truth." This function of speech, its ability to deal explicitly, specifically and directly with politics and government, is different from any other form of human activity. But the difference exists only with respect to one kind of speech: explicitly and predominantly political speech. This seems to me the only form of speech that a principled judge can prefer to other claimed freedoms. All other forms of speech raise only issues of human gratification and their protection against legislative regulation involves the judge in making decisions of the sort made in *Griswold v. Connecticut.*

* * *

* * * I agree that there is an analogy between criticism of official behavior and the publication of a novel like *Ulysses,* for the latter may form attitudes that ultimately affect politics. But it is an analogy, not an identity. Other human activities and experiences also form personality, teach and create attitudes just as much as does the novel, but no one would on that account, I take it, suggest that the first amendment strikes down regulations of economic activity, control of entry into a trade, laws about sexual behavior, marriage and the like. Yet these activities, in their capacity to create attitudes that ultimately impinge upon the political process, are more like literature and science than literature and science are like political speech. If the dialectical progression is not to become an analogical stampede, the protection of the first amendment must be cut off when it reaches the outer limits of political speech.

Two types of problems may be supposed to arise with respect to this solution. The first is the difficulty of drawing a line between political and non-political speech. The second is that such a line will leave unprotected much speech that is essential to the life of a civilized community. Neither of these problems seems to me to raise crippling difficulties.

The category of protected speech should consist of speech concerned with governmental behavior, policy or personnel, whether the governmental unit involved is executive, legislative, judicial or administrative. Explicitly political speech is speech about how we are governed, and the category therefore includes a wide range of evaluation, criticism, electioneering and propaganda. It does not cover scientific, educational, commercial or literary expressions as such. A novel may have impact upon attitudes that affect politics, but it would not for that reason receive judicial protection. This is not anomalous, I have tried to suggest, since the rationale of the first amendment cannot be the protection of all things or activities that influence political attitudes. Any speech may do that, and we have seen that it is impossible to leave all speech unregulated. Moreover, any conduct may affect political attitudes as much as a novel, and we cannot view the first amendment as a broad denial of the power of government to regulate conduct. The line drawn must, therefore, lie between the explicitly political and all else. Not too much should be made of the undeniable fact that there will be hard cases. Any theory of the first amendment that does not accord absolute protection for all verbal expression, which is to say any theory worth discussing, will require that a spectrum be cut and the location of the cut will always be, arguably, arbitrary. The question is whether the general location of the cut is justified. The existence of close cases is not a reason to refuse to draw a line and so deny majorities the power to govern in areas where their power is legitimate.

The other objection—that the political-nonpolitical distinction will leave much valuable speech without constitutional protection—is no more troublesome. The notion that all valuable types of speech must be protected by the first amendment confuses the constitutionality of laws with their wisdom.   Freedom of non-political speech rests, as does freedom for other valuable forms of behavior, upon the enlightenment of society and its elected representatives.   That is hardly a terrible fate. At least a society like ours ought not to think it so.

BIBLIOGRAPHY

C. Edwin Baker, HUMAN FREEDOM AND LIBERTY OF SPEECH (1989).

C. Edwin Baker, *Commercial Speech: A Problem in the Theory of Freedom,* 62 Iowa L.Rev. 1 (1976).

C. Edwin Baker, *The Process of Change and the Liberty Theory of the First Amendment,* 55 S.Cal.L.Rev. 293 (1981).

C. Edwin Baker, *Realizing Self–Realization: Corporate Political Expenditures and Redish's* The Value of Free Speech, 130 U.Pa.L.Rev. 646 (1982).

Meir Dan–Cohen, *Freedoms of Collective Speech: A Theory of Protected Communications by Organizations, Communities, and the State,* 79 Calif.L.Rev. 1229 (1991).

Richard H. Fallon, Jr., *Two Senses of Autonomy,* 46 Stan.L.Rev. 875 (1994).

Sheldon H. Nahmod, *Artistic Expression and Aesthetic Theory: The Beautiful, The Sublime and The First Amendment,* 1987 Wis.L.Rev. 221.

Martin H. Redish, FREEDOM OF EXPRESSION: A CRITICAL ANALYSIS (1984).

Martin H. Redish, *Self–Realization, Democracy, and Freedom of Expression: A Reply to Professor Baker,* 130 U.Pa.L.Rev. 678 (1982).

David A.J. Richards, TOLERATION AND THE CONSTITUTION (1986).

Frederick Schauer, FREE SPEECH: A PHILOSOPHICAL ENQUIRY, Ch. 4 (1982).

Steven H. Shiffrin, *The First Amendment and Economic Regulation: Away From a General Theory of the First Amendment,* 78 Nw. U.L.Rev. 1212 (1983).

E.   FREE SPEECH AND DEMOCRATIC THEORY

The theories we have so far considered, despite their important differences, are alike in two respects. They both hold that speech has broad-based importance throughout human thought; and they consequently both offer protection to a broad spectrum of speech. The argument from democratic theory differs on both points. It holds that speech has a narrower and even more instrumental significance. And so it offers very strong protection to a quite limited class of speech.

The argument from democratic theory for a free speech principle rests on the assumption of popular sovereignty. If the people are going to exercise their sovereign power intelligently they need to be well informed, and to debate before deciding. Freedom of speech allows this to happen. Notice that this argument does not work for all political systems. Free speech is unnecessary in a monarchy like Saudi Arabia. Notice too that under this argument speech matters more for the audience than for the speaker. We value speech because it is a way of educating the sovereign assembly.

Of course people don't spend all their time talking about politics. It is not clear whether this theory offers any protection to the works of Jane Austen and Red Barber. It all depends on how narrowly we define the domain of politics and the influences that shape our political preferences. If we make the circle too small we are being unrealistic: art, sports, and science are not only proper subjects of legislation, they also influence our ambitions, beliefs, and values. But one of the virtues of the argument from democratic theory is the very strong protection it gives to political speech. If we define that term too broadly we will weaken the First Amendment protection by spreading it too thin.

The name most prominently associated with the argument from democracy is that of Alexander Meiklejohn. The paradigm upon which he would build free speech theory is the New England town meeting. That institution exhibits popular sovereignty in an unmediated way. The people (not their representatives) assemble in a communal parliament, debate matters of public interest, and vote. Here freedom of speech serves the role that the Speech or Debate Clause serves in Article I of the United States Constitution: it allows legislators to examine all sides of an issue without fear of reprisal.

Harry Kalven obviously shares Meiklejohn's view about the political significance of speech. But he stresses a different paradigm—seditious libel. Kalven suggests that the important speech is not the legislator's contribution to pending legislation but the outsider's criticism of government behavior. He invites us to think of the government and the people as different groups existing in conflict.

Cynthia Estlund does not dispute the contributions of democratic theory, but she offers several reasons for not making it the centerpiece of free speech law. It is very hard to separate matters of public and private concern; and attempts to do so usually run the risk of underinclusion.

Although there are differences, there are also important affinities between traditional arguments from democratic theory and more contemporary reliance on public discourse or dialogue as the foundation of freedom of speech. Many who write in the modern republican tradition have seen free speech and press as centrally related to public deliberation. The selections from Robert Post and Cass Sunstein exemplify this trend.

ALEXANDER MEIKLEJOHN, POLITICAL FREEDOM
24–28 (1960).

[We will better understand the principle of freedom of speech if we] examine the procedure of the traditional American town meeting. That institution is commonly, and rightly, regarded as a model by which free political procedures may be measured. It is self-government in its simplest, most obvious form.

In the town meeting the people of a community assemble to discuss and to act upon matters of public interest—roads, schools, poorhouses, health, external defense, and the like. Every man is free to come. They meet as political equals. Each has a right and a duty to think his own thoughts, to express them, and to listen to the arguments of others. The basic principle is that the freedom of speech shall be unabridged. And yet the meeting cannot even be opened unless, by common consent, speech is abridged. A chairman or moderator is, or has been, chosen. He "calls the meeting to order." And the hush which follows that call is a clear indication that restrictions upon speech have been set up. The moderator assumes, or arranges, that in the conduct of the business, certain rules of order will be observed. Except as he is overruled by the meeting as a whole, he will enforce those rules. His business on its negative side is to abridge speech. For example, it is usually agreed that no one shall speak unless "recognized by the chair." Also, debaters must confine their remarks to "the question before the house." If one man "has the floor," no one else may interrupt him except as provided by the rules. The meeting has assembled, not primarily to talk, but primarily by means of talking to get business done. And the talking must be regulated and abridged as the doing of the business under actual conditions may require. If a speaker wanders from the point at issue, if he is abusive or in other ways threatens to defeat the purpose of the meeting, he may be and should be declared "out of order." He must then stop speaking, at least in that way. And if he persists in breaking the rules, he may be "denied the floor" or, in the last resort, "thrown out" of the meeting. The town meeting, as it seeks for freedom of public discussion of public problems, would be wholly ineffectual unless speech were thus abridged. It is not a Hyde Park. It is a parliament or congress. It is a group of free and equal men, cooperating in a common enterprise, and using for that enterprise responsible and regulated discussion. It is not a dialectical free-for-all. It is self-government.

These speech-abridging activities of the town meeting indicate what the First Amendment to the Constitution does not forbid. When self-governing men demand freedom of speech they are not saying that every individual has an unalienable right to speak whenever, wherever, however he chooses. They do not declare that any man may talk as he pleases, when he pleases, about what he pleases, about whom he pleases, to whom he pleases. The common sense of any reasonable society would deny the existence of that unqualified right. No one, for example, may, without consent of nurse or doctor, rise up in a sickroom to argue for his principles or his candidate. In the sickroom, that question is not "before the house." The discussion is, therefore, "out of order." To you who now listen to my words, it is allowable to differ with me, but it is not allowable for you to state that difference in words until I have finished my reading. Anyone who would thus irresponsibly interrupt the activities of a lecture, a hospital, a concert hall, a church, a machine shop, a classroom, a football field, or a home, does not thereby exhibit his freedom. Rather, he shows himself to be a boor, a public nuisance, who must be abated, by force if necessary.

What, then, does the First Amendment forbid? Here again the town meeting suggests an answer. That meeting is called to discuss and, on the basis of such discussion, to decide matters of public policy. For example, shall there be a school? Where shall it be located? Who shall teach? What shall be taught? The community has agreed that such questions as these shall be freely discussed and that, when the discussion is ended, decision upon them will be made by vote of the citizens. Now, in that method of political self-government, the point of ultimate interest is not the words of the speakers, but the minds of the hearers. The final aim of the meeting is the voting of wise decisions. The voters, therefore, must be made as wise as possible. The welfare of the community requires that those who decide issues shall understand them. They must know what they are voting about. And this, in turn, requires that so far as time allows, all facts and interests relevant to the problem shall be fully and fairly presented to the meeting. Both facts and interests must be given in such a way that all the alternative lines of action can be wisely measured in relation to one another. As the self-governing community seeks, by the method of voting, to gain wisdom in action, it can find it only in the minds of its individual citizens. If they fail, it fails. That is why freedom of discussion for those minds may not be abridged.

The First Amendment, then, is not the guardian of unregulated talkativeness. It does not require that, on every occasion, every citizen shall take part in public debate. Nor can it even give assurance that everyone shall have opportunity to do so. If, for example, at a town meeting, twenty like-minded citizens have become a "party," and if one of them has read to the meeting an argument which they have all approved, it would be ludicrously out of order for each of the others to insist on reading it again. No competent moderator would tolerate that wasting of the time available for free discussion. What is essential is not that everyone shall speak, but that everything worth saying shall be said. To this end, for example, it may be arranged that each of the known conflicting points of view shall have, and shall be limited to, an assigned share of the time available. But however it be arranged, the vital point, as stated negatively, is that no suggestion of policy shall be denied a hearing because it is on one side of the issue rather than another. And this means that though citizens may, on other grounds, be barred from speaking, they may not be barred because their views are thought to be false or dangerous. No plan of action shall be outlawed because someone in control thinks it unwise, unfair, un-American. No speaker may be declared "out of order" because we disagree with what he intends to say. And the reason for this equality of status in the field of ideas lies deep in the very foundations of the self-governing process. When men govern themselves, it is they—and no one else—who must pass judgment upon unwisdom and unfairness and danger. And that means that unwise ideas must have a hearing as well as wise ones, unfair as well as fair, dangerous as well as safe, un-American as well as American. Just so far as, at any point, the citizens who are to decide an issue are denied acquaintance with information or opinion or doubt or disbelief or criticism which is relevant to that issue, just so far the result must be ill-considered, ill-balanced planning for the general good. *It is that mutilation of the thinking process of the community against which the First Amendment to the Constitution is directed.* The principle of the freedom of speech springs from the necessities of the program of self-government. It is not a Law of Nature or of Reason in the abstract. It is a deduction from the basic American agreement that public issues shall be decided by universal suffrage.

If, then, on any occasion in the United States it is allowable to say that the Constitution is a good document it is equally allowable, in that situation, to say that the Constitution is a bad document. If a public building may be used in which to say, in time of war, that the war is justified, then the same building may be used in which to say that it is not justified. If it be publicly argued that conscription for armed service is moral and necessary, it may likewise be publicly argued that it is immoral and unnecessary. If it may be said that American political institutions are superior to those of England or Russia or Germany, it may, with equal freedom, be said that those of England or Russia or Germany are superior to ours. These conflicting views may be expressed, must be expressed, not because they are valid, but because they are relevant. If they are responsibly entertained by anyone, we, the voters, need to hear them. When a question of policy is "before the house," free men choose to meet it not with their eyes shut, but with their eyes open. To be afraid of ideas, any idea, is to be unfit for self-government. Any such suppression of ideas about the common good, the First Amendment condemns with its absolute disapproval. The freedom of ideas shall not be abridged.

HARRY KALVEN, JR., THE NEW YORK TIMES CASE: A NOTE ON "THE CENTRAL MEANING OF THE FIRST AMENDMENT"

1964 Sup.Ct.Rev. 191, 204–210.

[*New York Times Co. v. Sullivan*[a] dealt with a libel judgment rendered under Alabama law in favor of the police commissioner of

---

a. 376 U.S. 254 (1964).

Montgomery. The Times had run a political advertisement complaining about police misconduct toward Dr. Martin Luther King and black students in the community. The ad contained misstatements of fact. The Supreme Court held that Alabama's law was akin to a rule of seditious libel, and therefore unconstitutional under the First Amendment.]

The exciting possibilities in the Court's opinion derive from its emphasis on seditious libel and the Sedition Act of 1798 as the key to the meaning of the First Amendment. My thesis is dependent on [several] propositions. First, that the importance of the free-speech provision of the Constitution rests on the rejection of seditious libel as an offense. Second, that constitutional history and the traditional analysis had relegated the concept of seditious libel to a curiously unimportant place, although the nagging question of the constitutionality of the Sedition Act of 1798 had never properly been put to rest. Third, that the special virtue of the *Times* opinion is its restoration of seditious libel to its essential role, thus suddenly and dramatically changing the idiom of free-speech analysis and resolving the question of the constitutionality of the Sedition Act. * * * If I am right, the *Times* case represents a happy revolution of free-speech doctrine. Or, to put the matter differently, analysis of free-speech issues should hereafter begin with the significant issue of seditious libel and defamation of government by its critics rather than with the sterile example of a man falsely yelling fire in a crowded theater.

My first proposition need not detain us long. The concept of seditious libel strikes at the very heart of democracy. Political freedom ends when government can use its powers and its courts to silence its critics. My point is not the tepid one that there should be leeway for criticism of the government. It is rather that defamation of the government is an impossible notion for a democracy. In brief, I suggest, that the presence or absence in the law of the concept of seditious libel defines the society. A society may or may not treat obscenity or contempt by publication as legal offenses without altering its basic nature. If, however, it makes seditious libel an offense, it is not a free society no matter what its other characteristics.

My second proposition, the denigration of the importance of seditious libel in establishing First Amendment principles, is more difficult to establish. Perhaps it is only the accident of the sequence in which the speech cases have come to the Court, combined with the fact that the Court never had the sedition laws before it, that leaves the impression of its disregard of seditious libel and its fascination with the clear-and-present danger formula and balancing. Perhaps it is because we have not used functional categories in working out the theory of free speech. In any event, we do not start with the notion that seditious libel is clearly beyond the power of government and develop our ideas from that proposition.

Certainly, the logic of the clear-and-present danger test does not foreclose the matter. It leaves the status of seditious libel in doubt. It does not suggest that severe criticism of government policy could never be sufficiently dangerous. Indeed, one might cite *Schenck*,[57] *Debs*,[58] and *Abrams*[59] as three cases in which the Court itself reached the opposite conclusion.

Moreover, until its disposition by the *Times* case, the status of the Sedition Act of 1798 remained an open question. It has been a term of infamy in American usage, but sober judgments about its constitutionality have been few indeed. * * * My point, for the moment, is not to choose the better view of the history of the First Amendment and the Sedition Act, but rather to call attention to the fact that for over 150 years it was not thought necessary to establish the status of the Act as a first step in getting to the meaning of the First Amendment. It was thus possible for the Espionage Act of 1917, as amended in 1918, to contain sections that oddly echoed the idiom of seditious libel: "language intended to bring the form of government of the United States ... or the Constitution ... or the flag ... or the uniform of the Army or Navy into contempt, scorn, contumely, or disrepute." And it was possible for the Government solemnly to urge that the Sedition Act was constitutional in its argument in the *Abrams* case in 1919.

* * *

I turn, then, to the third proposition concerned with the meaning of the Court's opinion in the *Times* case. I suggest that the critical statement in Mr. Justice Brennan's opinion is: "If neither factual error nor defamatory content suffices to remove the constitutional shield from criticism of official conduct, the combination of the two elements is no less inadequate. This is the lesson to be drawn from the great controversy over the Sedition Act of 1798, 1 Stat. 586, which first crystallized a national awareness of the central meaning of the First Amendment. See Levy, Legacy of Suppression (1960), at *258 et seq.* ...." There follows an extended discussion of the "great controversy," with appropriate quotations from Madison whose views the Court summarizes thus: "The right of free public discussion of the stewardship of public officials was thus, in Madison's view, a fundamental principle of the American form of government."

The Court then, for the first time in its history and some 166 years after the enactment of the Sedition Act, turned squarely to the issue of its constitutionality. The answer was that "the attack upon its validity has carried the day in the court of history." The opinion cited Jefferson, Calhoun, Holmes, Brandeis, Jackson, Douglas, Cooley, and Chafee and concluded: "These views reflect a broad concensus that the Act, because

---

57. Schenck v. United States, 249 U.S. 47 (1919).

58. Debs v. United States, 249 U.S. 211 (1919).

59. Abrams v. United States, 250 U.S. 616 (1919).

of the restraint it imposed upon criticism of government and public officials, was inconsistent with the First Amendment."

The Court did not simply, in the face of an awkward history, definitively put to rest the status of the Sedition Act. More important, it found in the controversy over seditious libel the clue to "the central meaning of the First Amendment." The choice of language was unusually apt. The Amendment has a "central meaning"—a core of protection of speech without which democracy cannot function, without which, in Madison's phrase, "the censorial power" would be in the Government over the people and not "in the people over the Government." This is not the whole meaning of the Amendment. There are other freedoms protected by it. But at the center there is no doubt what speech is being protected and no doubt why it is being protected. The theory of the freedom of speech clause was put right side up for the first time.

Although the total structure of the opinion is not without its difficulties, it seems to me to convey, however imperfectly, the following crucial syllogism: The central meaning of the Amendment is that seditious libel cannot be made the subject of government sanction. The Alabama rule on fair comment is closely akin to making seditious libel an offense. The Alabama rule therefore violated the central meaning of the Amendment.

If the opinion can be read in this way, what emerges as of large importance is the generous sweep of the major premise and not the application of it to the point of defamation law involved in the *Times* case. The touchstone of the First Amendment has become the abolition of seditious libel and what that implies about the function of free speech on public issues in American democracy. The drama of the *Times* case then is that the Court, forced to extricate itself from the political impasse that was presented to it, did so by returning to the essence of the First Amendment to be found in its limitations on seditious libel. It gets to very high ground indeed.

CYNTHIA L. ESTLUND, SPEECH ON MATTERS OF PUBLIC CONCERN: THE PERILS OF AN EMERGING FIRST AMENDMENT CATEGORY

59 Geo.Wash.L.Rev. 1, 40–46 (1990).

[In *Connick v. Myers* [a] the Supreme Court held that a public employee could be discharged for speech that did not relate to "matters of public concern." Two years later in *Dun & Bradstreet v. Greenmoss Builders* [b] the Court held that allegedly libelous speech (a credit report falsely stating that the plaintiff had filed for bankruptcy) enjoyed no special constitutional immunity if it did not deal with a matter of public concern. Estlund argues that these cases subvert the substance and structure of the First Amendment by limiting its protection to matters of public concern.]

a. 461 U.S. 138 (1983). **b.** 472 U.S. 749 (1985).

* * * The notion of a category of speech on matters of public concern does not, at first glance, seem entirely novel. Speech on public issues has often been singled out for special solicitude. Moreover, categorization is a well-established tool of First Amendment analysis. One of the major features of the landscape of modern First Amendment law is the existence of categories of speech deemed "less central" or peripheral to the values of free speech that are left unprotected or less protected. But the superficial similarity of the public concern category to existing tools of First Amendment doctrine is misleading.

The categories of speech that were recognized before *Connick* only defined types of speech that were either excluded from First Amendment protection altogether or disfavored. The burden of demonstrating exclusion fell on the party seeking it and the speaker thus enjoyed a presumption of coverage, or protection. Moreover, the disfavored categories were defined as precisely as possible, and as far removed as possible from the core of speech on public issues, so as to minimize the risk and the consequences of erroneous exclusion. Together these features of the doctrine created a "buffer" between speech at the core of the First Amendment and speech subject to suppression because of its content. The public concern test eliminates that buffer. It transforms the hitherto indistinct boundaries around the core of public issue speech into a rigid threshold barrier that, like the boundaries of the traditional disfavored categories of speech, must be defined and applied in case after case. This doctrinal innovation cuts to the heart of First Amendment doctrine, and, perhaps paradoxically, undermines the protection of speech on public issues.

1. SHIFTING THE BURDEN OF PROOF TO THE SPEAKER

"Mistakes" will inevitably occur in any regime that requires case-by-case application of a threshold test based on the content of speech. It is in part because of the inevitability of error that modern free speech doctrine creates a fundamental presumption that "speech"—verbal or graphic communication of ideas, opinions, and information—is protected by the First Amendment. The exclusion of speech from constitutional scrutiny, or its subjection to a less rigorous regime of protection, is an exception limited to narrow categories of disfavored speech. The burden of persuasion under this scheme falls to the advocate of suppression.

Professor Fred Schauer describes this scheme as a "defining out" approach to setting the boundaries of First Amendment coverage. A "defining in" approach, by contrast, would identify a category of covered speech based upon "the underlying theory of the First Amendment, and would exclude everything else." According to Professor Schauer:

> When we use presumptions and allocate the burden of proof, we attempt to ensure that decisions under uncertainty will be biased away from restriction of those values we hold to be of greatest importance. In the context of the choice between defining in and

and defining out, it seems to follow that we can avoid more errors of underinclusion by defining out rather than defining in.[233]

Modern First Amendment doctrine follows the "defining out" approach: "speech" is presumptively within the realm of the First Amendment unless it is shown to be excluded.

The public concern test abandons this precaution. Unlike the other established categories within First Amendment doctrine, the public concern test creates a category that the speaker has to get *into* rather than stay *out* of. By shifting the burden of proof to the speaker to demonstrate that her message falls within the preferred category, the public concern test shifts the risk of judicial error to the speaker; it creates a heightened risk of underinclusion, or, more to the point, oversuppression of speech that ought to be, but is not, deemed to be of public concern.

2. Imprecision and the Risk of Error

The ability to define categories with a tolerable degree of precision is critical to the soundness of any First Amendment doctrine assigning different levels of protection to different categories of speech. Precision, like the presumption of coverage, is a hedge against errors of oversuppression. Some categories of speech, such as libel, commercial advertising, and fighting words, have generated relatively few disputes over their boundaries. Libel law has deeply divided the Court since *New York Times,* but identifying the category of libel has never posed a difficult problem. Similarly, although the proper level of protection to be accorded commercial advertising has been a source of dispute, the identification of commercial advertising, in the vast majority of cases, has not posed a major difficulty for courts. The fighting words doctrine, to the extent it survives, has also proved to be sufficiently narrow and confined as to generate little litigation.

In marked contrast, "obscenity" has proved intractably difficult to define. Beginning with *Roth v. United States,*[240] the Court's first attempt to define the category of obscenity, one test has followed another, each failing to command the consistent support of a majority. More importantly, each new test has failed utterly to resolve cases in a predictable manner. Justice Stewart's memorable lament—"I know it when I see it"[242]—became the rule of decision as the Court summarily disposed of case after case based upon the Court's private screenings of the speech in question.

* * *

The public concern test poses just this problem. [The] project of defining the appropriate boundaries of public debate is not only without any mooring in the legal and philosophical principles underlying freedom

---

233. [Schauer, *Categories and the First Amendment: A Play in Three Acts,* 34 Vand.L.Rev. 265, 280–81 (1981).]

240. 354 U.S. 476 (1957).

242. Jacobellis v. Ohio, 378 U.S. 184, 197 (1964) (Stewart, J., concurring).

of expression; indeed, it seriously offends those principles. But my point here is a different one. Even if one believes (or accepts for pragmatic reasons) that not all speech can be fairly characterized as speech on matters of public concern, the prospect of reducing that concept to a legal test yielding predictable results is at least as remote as the prospect of successfully defining "obscenity."

* * *

In defining "matters of public concern," the Court faces a spectrum of possibilities. At one end of the spectrum is the extremely narrow definition of political speech once proposed (and later repudiated) by Professor Robert Bork as defining the entire scope of the First Amendment. Professor Bork's proposal would have limited First Amendment protection to "criticisms of public officials and policies, proposals for the adoption or repeal of legislation or constitutional provisions and speech addressed to the conduct of any governmental unit in the country."[251] Such a narrow definition of "matters of public concern" or "public issues" would arguably yield relatively predictable results. It would do so, however, only at the cost of excluding from protection almost all literature, art, science, history, discussion of the economic system and the activities of powerful nongovernment persons and organizations, and much speech on matters of widespread public controversy that had yet to coalesce into specific proposals for government intervention. A definition such as this one, which denies the power of the people, through protest and discussion, to define the government's agenda, would be an intolerable restriction on the freedom of public debate.

But if we expand the definition of matters of public concern to include, for example, speech that shapes political attitudes or that might give rise to demands for government action, it seems to become infinitely elastic; that is, there is no coherent, predictable way of limiting its scope. This dilemma is illustrated by the migration of Professor Alexander Meiklejohn from a narrow and expressly political conception of speech relevant to self-government to a virtually boundless view that would encompass "novels and dramas and paintings and poems."[256] An all-inclusive category of "matters of public concern" would, of course, serve no purpose whatsoever, whether that purpose was conceived as restricting the scope of First Amendment protections in favor of competing interests, or as preserving "speech that matters" from the leveling effect of a uniform test.

251. [Bork, *Neutral Principles and Some First Amendment Problems,* 47 Ind. L.J. 1, 29 (1971).]

256. The view that the First Amendment should protect only speech relevant to self-government is closely identified with the work of Professor Alexander Meiklejohn. *See, e.g.,* A. Meiklejohn, Free Speech and Its Relation to Self–Government 94 (1948). Originally, Professor Meiklejohn would have protected only speech *directly* relevant to self-government. *See id.* at 22–27. But he later adopted a much broader view of the speech that was relevant to self-government, such as "novels and dramas and paintings and poems." Meiklejohn, *The First Amendment is an Absolute,* 1961 Sup.Ct.Rev. 245, 263[.]

Any definition of "matters of public concern" that is to serve the assigned functions of this new category must attempt to chart a middle course between the very narrow, explicitly political definition proffered by Professor Bork, and the almost infinitely expansive definition of speech relevant to self-government eventually adopted by Professor Meiklejohn. Any definition that charts this middle course, however, will be plagued by an irreducible element of vagueness and subjectivity.

ROBERT C. POST, THE CONSTITUTIONAL CONCEPT OF PUBLIC DISCOURSE: OUTRAGEOUS OPINION, DEMOCRATIC DELIBERATION AND *HUSTLER MAGAZINE v. FALWELL*

103 Harv.L.Rev. 601, 626, 634–37, 667–72, 684 (1990).

There has traditionally been a strong affinity between first amendment jurisprudence and the concept of the public. * * *

The concept of the public has a number of different meanings for first amendment doctrine. One important meaning is the designation of speech that will be deemed constitutionally independent of the managerial authority of state institutions.

* * *

A public, in other words, is constituted precisely by the ability of persons to speak to one another across the boundaries of divergent cultures. From this perspective, of course, the social function of first amendment doctrine, as reformulated during the 1930's and 1940's, becomes plain enough: it is to establish a protected space within which this communication can occur. Sociologically viewed, however, the continued existence of this space depends upon at least five preconditions. First, a society must include a plurality of cultures and traditions. A society characterized by the norms of only one community will lack the impetus to liberate its public discourse from the regulation of those norms. * * *

Second, even a culturally heterogeneous society cannot sustain public discourse unless the society values and wishes to preserve that heterogeneity. * * *

Third, those participating in public discourse can communicate with each other only if they have something in common to talk about. Thus persons cannot constitute "a 'public'" unless "they are exposed to similar social stimuli." A primary and continuing source of these stimuli within public discourse is the news. News, as Walter Lippmann noted long ago, "comes from a distance," from beyond the "self-contained community" in which we happen to live. The news functions as a medium of common information that brings together persons of widely disparate traditions and cultures. Thus "news is a public (and a public-generating) social phenomenon." "The emergence of the mass media and of the 'public' are mutually constructive developments." For this reason the first amendment protects not merely the expression of ideas, but also "the free communication of information."

Fourth, persons must have a reason to enter into the realm of public discourse to communicate with those beyond their own communities.
* * *

Fifth, communication requires not merely common information, but also commonly accepted standards of meaning and evaluation, so that the significance of that information can be assessed. The necessity for these standards suggests that the emergence of public discourse rests upon a delicate balance: if persons in public discourse share too much, if they are simply members of the same community, the diversity requisite for the emergence of public discourse will not be present. But if, on the other hand, such persons share too little, if they have absolutely no common standards for the evaluation and assessment of meaning, public discourse cannot be sustained.

The conduct of public discourse, in other words, requires persons to share standards, but not the kind of standards that fuse them into a community. But what can persons in public discourse share in the "absence of interaction in terms of the conventional and traditional definitions" of specific communities? The answer given by sociologists was that persons can share the ability to engage in "intellectual processes," and they thus defined a "public" as "any group . . . that achieves corporate unity through critical interaction." "In the public," it was said, "interaction takes the form of discussion. Individuals act upon one another critically . . . . Opinions clash and thus modify and moderate one another." In the words of a more contemporary theorist, Alvin Gouldner, the very existence of public discourse implies "a cleared and safe space" in which the interpretation of shared stimuli, like news, can occur in a "critical" manner, "meaning that what has been said may be questioned, negated and contradicted."

The identification of public discourse with forms of "critical interaction" rests upon a very abstract logic. If membership in a community is "a constituent of . . . identity," the effort to communicate through public discourse with those who do not share that identity must entail a constant effort to distance oneself from the assumptions and certitudes that define oneself and one's community. By being "critical" and "intellectual," public discourse can strive to generalize its appeal so as to reach persons from disparate cultures and traditions.

The problem, however, is that this conception of public discourse is highly schematic, and its value as an empirical description may be questioned. Even the most casual survey of American public deliberation would lead to the conclusion that it is "intellectual" and "critical" only in fits and starts, and that there are unending attempts by various cultures and traditions to seize control of public discussion and to subject it to particular community values and standards. But the conception does have considerable power as a description of how meaningful public discussion can occur in the face of fundamental and concededly valid cultural divergence. In such circumstances, it may be said, persons ought to strive to engage in a mutual process of critical interaction, because if they do not, no uncoerced common understanding can possibly be attained.

First amendment doctrine attempts to protect an arena for just such a process of critical interaction. Resting upon a deep respect for the "sharp differences" characteristic of American life, it is committed to the maintenance of "the right to differ as to things that touch the heart of the existing order."

* * *

* * * Contemporary doctrine delineates the domain of public discourse primarily through an assessment of the content of speech. The Court has a standard account of this approach: "We have recognized that the First Amendment reflects a 'profound national commitment' to the principle that 'debate on public issues should be uninhibited, robust, and wide-open' and have consistently commented on the central importance of protecting speech on public issues." As a doctrinal matter, therefore, the Court has most comprehensively attempted to define public discourse by distinguishing speech about "matters of public concern" from speech about "matters of purely private concern."

Although the "public concern" test rests on a clean and superficially attractive rationale, the Court has offered virtually no analysis to develop its logic. Indeed, as matters now stand, the test of "public concern" "amounts to little more than a message to judges and attorneys that no standards are necessary because they will, or should, know a public concern when they see it." To begin to comprehend the causes for this failure, one must note the ambiguity in the adjective "public" in the phrase "public concern." Sometimes the adjective signifies that the speech at issue is about matters that ought to be of interest to those who practice the art of democratic self-governance. I shall call this the "normative" conception of public concern. Sometimes, however, the adjective connotes that the speech at issue concerns matters that large numbers of people already know, and thus are "public" in a purely empirical sense. I shall call this the "descriptive" conception of public concern. * * *

(a) The Normative Conception of "Public Concern." The Court is most comfortable with the normative conception of "public concern," and in most instances its use of the phrase signifies that the content of the speech at issue refers to matters that are substantively relevant to the processes of democratic self-governance. But it is not difficult to see why this conception of public concern would lead directly to a doctrinal impasse. Democratic self-governance posits that the people, in their capacity as a public, control the agenda of government. They have the power to determine the content of public issues simply by the direction of their interests. This means that every issue that can potentially agitate the public is also potentially relevant to democratic self-governance, and hence potentially of public concern. The normative concep-

tion of public concern, insofar as it is used to exclude speech from public discourse, is thus incompatible with the very democratic self-governance it seeks to facilitate.

The Court fully recognizes this difficulty. It underlies the Court's firm and correct conviction that "governments must not be allowed to choose 'which issues are worth discussing or debating' .... To allow a government the choice of permissible subjects for public debate would be to allow that government control over the search for political truth." * * *

Certain speech, of course, is clearly and obviously recognizable as substantively relevant to democratic self-government. Most speech about public officials falls into this category. But it does not follow from this fact that speech less easily recognizable can with confidence be ruled out as irrelevant to matters of public concern. Robert Bork, for example, once proposed limiting constitutionally protected speech to that "concerned with governmental behavior, policy or personnel." Bork's proposal was attractive because it seemed to follow so directly from the logic of democratic self-governance, and to offer a clean and precise definition of speech about matters of public concern.

On closer inspection, however, Bork's proposal proved inadequate, because it missed the fundamental point that the first amendment safeguards public discourse not merely because it informs government decisionmaking, but also because it enables a culturally heterogeneous society to forge a common democratic will. The formation of this will depends upon the ability of public discourse to sustain deliberation about our identity as a people, as well as about what specifically we want our government to do. That is why most would unquestionably consider as public discourse the public discussion of such issues as the proper role of motherhood, the disaffection of the young, and the meaning of American citizenship, even if this discussion did not occur within the specific context of any proposed or actual government action.

The public realm, as Hanna Pitkin has eloquently remarked, is where the "people determine what they will collectively do, settle how they will live together, and decide their future, to whatever extent that is within human power." To decide these things, however, is to engage in a process of "collective self-definition," of determining "who we shall be, for what we shall stand." To classify speech as public discourse is, in effect, to deem it relevant to this collective process of self-definition and decisionmaking. There is obviously no theoretically neutral way in which this can be done. Speech can be deemed irrelevant for national self-definition only in the name of a particular, substantive vision of national identity. If this is done with the authority of the law, possible options for democratic development will be foreclosed. * * *

The fundamental theoretical difficulty faced by writers like Warren and Brandeis, who would place limits on what *ought* to be pertinent to the formation of a common democratic will, is that any effort substantively to circumscribe public discourse is necessarily self-defeating, for it displaces the very democratic processes it seeks to facilitate.

(b) The Descriptive Conception of "Public Concern." The descriptive conception of "public concern" promises a way out of this impasse. It appears to offer courts a means of maintaining the boundaries of public discourse in a manner that remains neutral with respect to the competing claims of speech to be relevant to issues of democratic governance. The descriptive conception defines "speech involving matters of public concern" as speech about issues that happen actually to interest the "public," which is to say to "a significant number of persons." The conception thus flows from a purely empirical notion of the public; it classifies as public discourse expression about the common stimuli that in fact establish the existence of a public.

* * *

Public discourse lies at the heart of democratic self-governance, and its protection constitutes an important theme of first amendment jurisprudence. * * * The first amendment preserves the independence of public discourse so that a democratic will within a culturally heterogeneous state can emerge under conditions of neutrality, and so that individuals can use the medium of public discourse to persuade others to experiment in new forms of community life. The ultimate dependence of public discourse upon community life, however, suggests that this neutrality and freedom is always limited, for the very boundaries of public discourse must be located in a manner that is sensitive to ensuring the continued viability of the community norms that inculcate the ideal of rational deliberation.

CASS R. SUNSTEIN, FREE SPEECH NOW

59 U.Chi.L.Rev. 255, 263–65, 267–68, 272–76, 302, 304–09 (1992).[1]

Perhaps we need a New Deal for speech, one that would parallel what the New Deal provided to property rights during the 1930s, and that would be rooted in substantially similar concerns. A brief review follows.

Before the New Deal, the Constitution was often understood as a constraint on government "regulation." In practice, this meant that the Constitution was often invoked to prohibit governmental interference with existing distributions of rights and entitlements. Hence minimum wage and maximum hour laws were seen as unjustifiable exactions— takings—from employers for the benefit of employees and the public at large. The Due Process Clause insulated private arrangements from public control, especially if the government's goals were paternalistic or redistributive. In operating under the police power, government must be neutral in general, and between employers and employees in particu-

---

1. Many of the arguments in this article are expanded in Sunstein's Democracy and the Problem of Free Speech (Free Press, 1993).

lar. A violation of the neutrality requirement, thus understood, would count as a violation of the Constitution.

On the pre-New Deal view, existing distributions marked the boundary not only between neutrality and partisanship, but between inaction and action as well. Government inaction consisted of respect for existing distributions. Government action was understood as interference with them. The rallying cry "laissez-faire" embodied such ideas. The fear of, and more important, the very conception of "government intervention" captured this basic approach.

The New Deal reformers argued that this entire framework was built on fictions. Their response is captured in President Roosevelt's references to "this man-made world of ours" and his insistence that "we must lay hold of the fact that economic laws are not made by nature. They are made by human beings." The pre-New Deal framework treated the existing distribution of resources and opportunities as prepolitical, when in fact it was not. It saw minimum wage and maximum hour laws as introducing government into a private or voluntary sphere. But the New Dealers pointed out that this sphere was actually a creation of law. Rules of property, contract, and tort produced the set of entitlements that ultimately yielded market hours and wages.

To New Deal reformers, the very categories of "regulation" and "government intervention" seemed misleading. The government did not "act" only when it disturbed existing distributions. It was responsible for those distributions in the first instance. What people owned in markets was a function of the entitlements that the law conferred on them. The notion of "laissez-faire" thus stood revealed as a conspicuous fiction.

* * *

These ideas have played little role in the law of free speech. For purposes of speech, contemporary understandings of neutrality and partisanship, or government action and inaction, are identical to those that predate the New Deal.

One response to the recent First Amendment controversies would be to suggest that they confirm the wisdom of the New Deal reformation on this score. On this view, American constitutionalism, with respect to freedom of expression, has failed precisely to the extent that it has not taken that reformation seriously enough. I do not mean to suggest that speech rights should be freely subject to political determination, as are current issues of occupational safety and health, for example. I do not mean to suggest that markets in speech are generally abridgements of speech, or that they usually disserve the First Amendment. I do mean to say that in some circumstances, what seems to be government regulation of speech actually might promote free speech, and should not be treated as an abridgement at all. I mean also to argue, though more hesitantly, that what seems to be free speech in markets might, in some selected circumstances, amount to an abridgement of free speech.

[W]hile the proposals might seem unconventional, they have a clear foundation in no lesser place than *New York Times Co. v. Sullivan,* one of the defining cases of modern free speech law. There the Court held that a public official could not bring an action for libel unless he could show "actual malice," defined as knowledge of or reckless indifference to the falsity of the statements at issue. The *Sullivan* case is usually taken as the symbol of broad press immunity with respect to criticism of public officials. More importantly, observers often understand *Sullivan* to reflect Alexander Meiklejohn's conception of freedom of expression—a conception of self-government connected to the American conception of sovereignty and built on the need to ensure that the government does not inhibit political expression.

It is striking that in *Sullivan,* the lower court held that the common law of tort, and more particularly libel, was not state action at all, and was therefore entirely immune from constitutional constraint. A civil action, on this view, involves a purely private dispute. The Supreme Court quickly disposed of this objection. The use of public tribunals to punish speech is conspicuously state action. What is interesting is not the Supreme Court's rejection of the argument, but the fact that the argument could even be made by a state supreme court as late as the 1960s. How could reasonable judges perceive the rules of tort law as purely private?

The answer lies in the persistence of the pre-New Deal understanding that the common law simply implements existing rights or private desires, and does not amount to "intervention" or "action" at all. The view that the common law of property should be taken as prepolitical and just, and as a refusal to use government power—the view that the New Deal repudiated—was the same as the view of the state supreme court in *Sullivan.* Reputation, after all, is a property interest. Just as in the pre-New Deal era, the state supreme court did not see the protection of that interest as involving government action at all.

The Supreme Court's rejection of that claim seemed inevitable in *Sullivan,* and this aspect of the case is largely forgotten. But courts base much of current law on precisely the forgotten view of that obscure state court. We might even generalize from *Sullivan* the broad idea that courts must always assess the protection of property rights through the common law pragmatically, in terms of its effects on speech.

Consider, for example, the issues raised by a claimed right of access to the media. Suppose that most broadcasters deal little or not at all with issues of public importance, restricting themselves to stories about movie stars or sex scandals. Suppose too that there is no real diversity of view on the airwaves, but instead a bland, watered-down version of conventional morality. If so, a severe problem for the system of free expression is the governmental grant of legal protection—rights of exclusive use—to enormous institutions compromising Madisonian values. Courts usually do not see that grant of power—sometimes made through the common law, sometimes through statute—as a grant of power at all, but instead treat it as purely "private." Thus the exclusion of people and views from the airwaves is immunized from constitutional constraint, on the theory that the act of exclusion is purely private. By contrast, rights of access to the media are thought to involve governmental intervention into the private sphere.

In *Sullivan,* the Supreme Court said, as against a similar claim, that courts should inspect common law rules for their conformity with the principle that government may not restrict freedoms of speech and press. "The test is not the form in which state power has been applied but, whatever the form, whether such power has in fact been exercised."

We can apply this understanding to current problems. If we regard the First Amendment as an effort to ensure that people are not prevented from speaking, especially on issues of public importance, then current free speech law seems ill-adapted to current conditions. Above all, the conception of government "regulation" misstates certain issues and sometimes disserves the goal of free expression itself. Some regulatory efforts, superimposed on the established regulation through common law rules, may promote free speech. Less frequently, the use of statutory or common law rules to foreclose efforts to speak might themselves represent impermissible content-neutral restrictions on speech. We must judge both reform efforts and the status quo by their consequences, not by question-begging characterizations of "threats from government."

* * *

Or consider a case in which a network decides not to sell advertising time to a group that wants to discuss some public issue or to express some dissident view. Under current law, the refusal raises no First Amendment question, in part because a number of the justices—perhaps now a majority—believe that there is no "state action." But government gives broadcasters property rights in their licenses, and their exercise of those rights is a function of law in no subtle sense. It is generally salutary to have a system in which government creates ownership rights or markets in speech, just as in property. The point is not that markets are bad, but that a right of exclusive ownership in a television network is governmentally conferred. The exclusion of the would-be speakers is made possible by the law of civil and criminal trespass, among other things. It is thus a product of a governmental decision.

A market system in which only certain speakers express only certain views is a creation of law. The questions are (1) whether reform efforts eliminating adverse effects of exclusive ownership rights by conditioning the original grant are consistent with the First Amendment, or (2) whether the government grant of exclusive ownership rights itself violates the First Amendment. We cannot answer such questions by saying that ownership rights are governmental; we need to know the purposes and effects of the grant. And we cannot answer that question a priori or in the abstract; we need to know a lot of details.

One might respond that the Constitution creates "negative" rights rather than "positive" ones, or at least that the First Amendment is "negative" in character, granting a right to protection against the government, not to subsidies from the government. The claim certainly captures the conventional wisdom, and an argument for a New Deal for speech must come to terms with it.

There are two responses. First, and most fundamentally, no one is asserting a positive right in these cases. Instead, the claim is that government sometimes cannot adopt a content-neutral rule that imposes a (negative) constraint on who can speak and where they can do so. When someone with view X cannot speak on the networks, it is because the civil and criminal law prohibits him from doing so. This is the same problem that underlies a wide range of familiar claims in content-neutral cases. Consider a ban on door-to-door soliciting. An attack on content-neutral restrictions is not an argument for "positive" government protection. It is merely a claim that courts must review legal rules stopping certain people from speaking in certain places under First Amendment principles. In fact the response that a New Deal for speech would create a "positive right" trades on untenable, *Lochner* era distinctions between positive and negative rights.

The second response is that the distinction between negative and positive rights fails to explain even current First Amendment law. There are two obvious counterexamples. The Supreme Court has come very close to saying that when an audience becomes hostile and threatening, the government is obligated to protect the speaker. Under current law, reasonable crowd control measures are probably constitutionally compelled, even if the result is to require a number of police officers to come to the scene. The right to speak may well include a positive right to governmental protection against a hostile private audience.

The area of libel provides a second example. By imposing constitutional constraints on the common law of libel, the Court in effect has held that those who are defamed must subsidize speakers, by allowing their reputations to be compromised to the end of broad diversity of speech. Even more, the Court has held that government is under what might be seen as an affirmative duty to "take" the reputation of people whom the press defames in order to promote the interest in free speech. The First Amendment requires a compulsory, governmentally produced subsidy of personal reputation (a property interest) for the benefit of speech.

These cases reveal that the First Amendment, even as currently conceived, is no mere negative right. It has positive dimensions. These dimensions consist of a command to government to take steps to ensure that legal rules according exclusive authority to private persons do not violate the system of free expression. In a hostile audience case, the government is obliged to protect the speaker against private silencing. In the libel cases, the government is obliged to do the same thing—to provide extra breathing space for speech even though a consequence is an infringement on the common law interest in reputation. It is incorrect to say that the First Amendment creates merely a right to fend off government censorship as conventionally understood.

* * *

Consider the Court's remarkable opinion in the *Red Lion* case. There the Court upheld the fairness doctrine, which required broadcasters to give attention to public issues and provide a chance for those with opposing views to speak. In *Red Lion,* the Court actually seemed to suggest that the doctrine was constitutionally compelled. According to the Court, the fairness doctrine would "enhance rather than abridge the freedoms of speech and press," for free expression would be disserved by "unlimited private censorship operating in a medium not open to all." The Court suggested that:

> [A]s far as the First Amendment is concerned those who are licensed stand no better than those to whom licenses are refused. A license permits broadcasting, but the licensee has no constitutional right to be the one who holds the license or to monopolize a radio frequency to the exclusion of his fellow citizens. There is nothing in the First Amendment which prevents the Government from requiring a licensee to share his frequency with others and to conduct himself as a proxy or fiduciary with obligations to present those views and voices which are representative of his community and which would otherwise, by necessity, be barred from the airwaves.

* * *

> [T]he people as a whole retain their interest in free speech by radio and their collective right to have the medium function consistently with the ends and purposes of the First Amendment. It is the right of the viewers and listeners, not the right of the broadcasters, which is paramount. It is the purpose of the First Amendment to preserve an uninhibited marketplace of ideas in which truth will ultimately prevail, rather than to countenance monopolization of that market, whether it be by the Government itself or a private licensee. It is the right of the public to receive suitable access to social, political, esthetic, moral, and other ideas and experiences which is crucial here. That right may not constitutionally be abridged either by Congress or by the FCC.[52]

This vision of the First Amendment does not stress the autonomy of broadcasters with current ownership rights. Instead it emphasizes the need to promote democratic self-government by ensuring that people are presented with a broad diversity of views about public issues. A market system may compromise this goal. It is hardly clear that "the freedom

52. Red Lion Broadcasting v. FCC, 395 U.S. 367 (1969).

of speech" is promoted by a regime in which people may speak if and only if other people are willing to pay enough to hear them.

* * *

Instead of or in addition to renovating the free speech tradition in this way, we might offer a more cautious proposal. The most fundamental step would involve an insistence on the original idea that the First Amendment is principally about political deliberation. The fact that words or pictures are involved is not, standing by itself, a sufficient reason for full constitutional protection. Bribery, criminal solicitation, threats, conspiracies, perjury—all these are words, but they are not by virtue of that fact entitled to the highest level of constitutional protection. They may be regulated on the basis of a lesser showing of harm than is required for political speech. They are not entirely without constitutional protection—they count as "speech"—but they do not lie within the core of the free speech guarantee.

[In] order to defend this proposal, we must explore whether there should be a two-tier First Amendment. The view that some forms of speech are less protected than others is frequently met with alarm. Notwithstanding its controversial character, this view derives strong support from existing law. Indeed every Justice has expressed some such view within the last generation.

We must still decide by what standard courts might accomplish the task of distinguishing between low-value and high-value speech. To support an emphasis on politics, we need to define the category of political speech. For present purposes I will treat speech as political *when it is both intended and received as a contribution to public deliberation about some issue.* It seems implausible to think that words warrant the highest form of protection if the speaker does not even intend to communicate a message; the First Amendment does not put gibberish at the core even if it is taken, by some in the audience, to mean something. By requiring intent, I do not mean to require a trial on the question of subjective motivation. Generally this issue can be resolved simply on the basis of the nature of the speech at issue. By requiring that the speech be received as a contribution to public deliberation, I do not mean that all listeners or readers must see the substantive content. It is sufficient if some do. Many people miss the political message in some forms of political speech, especially art or literature. But if no one sees the political content, it is hard to understand why the speech should so qualify.

Finally, the requirements are in the conjunctive, though in almost all cases speech that is intended as a contribution to public deliberation will be seen by some as such. The fact that speech is so seen by some is insufficient if it is not so intended; consider, for example, commercial speech, obscenity, or private libel. If some people understand the speech in question to be a contribution to public deliberation, it cannot follow that the speech qualifies as such for constitutional purposes, without treating almost all speech as political and therefore destroying the whole point of the two-tier model. Of course the definition I have offered leaves many questions unanswered, and there will be hard intermediate cases. I offer it simply as a starting point for analysis.

An approach that affords special protection to political speech, thus defined, is justified on numerous grounds. Such an approach receives firm support from history—not only from the Framers' theory of free expression, but also from the development of that principle through the history of American law. There can be little doubt that suppression by the government of political ideas that it disapproved, or found threatening, was the central motivation for the clause. The worst examples of unacceptable censorship involve efforts by government to insulate itself from criticism. Judicial interpretations over the course of time also support a political conception of the First Amendment.

This approach seems likely as well to accord with our initial or considered judgments about particular free speech problems. Any approach to the First Amendment will have to take substantial account of those judgments, and adjust itself accordingly. It seems clear that such forms of speech as perjury, bribery, threats, misleading or false commercial advertising, criminal solicitation, and libel of private persons—or at least most of these—are not entitled to the highest degree of constitutional protection. No other approach unifies initial or preliminary judgments about these matters as well as a political conception of the First Amendment.

In addition, an insistence that government's burden is greatest when political speech is at issue responds well to the fact that here government is most likely to be biased. The presumption of distrust of government is strongest when politics are at issue. It is far weaker when government is regulating (say) commercial speech, bribery, private libel, or obscenity. In such cases there is less reason to suppose that it is insulating itself from criticism.

Finally, this approach protects speech when regulation is most likely to be harmful. Restrictions on political speech have the distinctive feature of impairing the ordinary channels for political change; such restrictions are especially dangerous. If there are controls on commercial advertising, it always remains possible to argue that such controls should be lifted. If the government bans violent pornography, citizens can continue to argue against the ban. But if the government forecloses political argument, the democratic corrective is unavailable. Controls on nonpolitical speech do not have this uniquely damaging feature.

Taken in concert, these considerations suggest that government should be under a special burden of justification when it seeks to control speech intended and received as a contribution to public deliberation. To be sure, there are some powerful alternative approaches. Perhaps we should conclude that speech is entitled to protection if it involves rational thought. This would extend beyond the political to include not merely literary and artistic work, but commercial and scientific expression as well. But there would be serious problems with any such approach. For example, we should probably not give technological data with potential military applications the same degree of protection as political speech; nor should we give misleading commercial speech the same protection as misleading political speech.

Alternatively, one might think that the free speech principle includes any representation that reflects deliberation or imagination in a way that is relevant to the development of individual capacities. No one has fully elaborated an approach of this sort. It would carry considerable promise. But such an approach would make it hard to distinguish between scientific and political speech. It also might protect such things as child pornography.

Much work must be done to elaborate and evaluate alternatives of this sort. But a conception of free speech that centers on democratic governance appears to be the best way to organize our considered judgments about cases likely to raise hard First Amendment questions.

If the First Amendment offers special protection to political speech, we must of course reject the proposition that all forms of speech stand on the same ground. It would be necessary to draw distinctions between obscenity and political protest, or misleading commercial speech and misleading campaign statements, or proxy statements and party platforms. We must resort far less readily to the view that a restriction on one form of speech necessarily will lead to restriction on another.

Counterarguments.

The difficulties with a political conception of the First Amendment are not unfamiliar; they raise all of the questions that produced the current First Amendment preoccupation with line-drawing. How, for example, are we to treat the work of Robert Mapplethorpe, the music of a rock group, or nude dancing? Both commercial speech and pornography are political in the crucial sense that they reflect and promote a point of view, broadly speaking ideological in character, about how to structure important things in the world. The recent attack on pornography has drawn close attention to its political character, and thus ironically might be thought to invalidate efforts to regulate it.

Is it so clear that speech that has nothing to do with politics is not entitled to First Amendment protection? Must we exclude music or art or science? Surely it is philistine or worse to say that the First Amendment protects only political platforms. Often the deepest political challenges to the existing order can be found in art, literature, music, or sexual expression. Sometimes government attempts to regulate these things for precisely this reason.

These are hard questions without simple solutions. I will venture only some brief remarks in response. The first is that we should not take the existence of hard line-drawing problems to foreclose an attempt to distinguish between political and nonpolitical speech. If the distinction is otherwise plausible, and if systems that fail to make it have severe problems, the difficulty of drawing lines is acceptable.

Even more fundamental, there is no way to operate a system of free expression without drawing lines. Not everything that counts as words or pictures is entitled to full constitutional protection. The question is not whether to draw lines, but how to draw the right ones.

Second, we should understand broadly the category of the political. The definition I have offered would encompass not simply political tracts, but all art and literature that has the characteristics of social commentary—which is to say, much art and literature. Much speech is a contribution to public deliberation despite initial appearances. In addition, it is important to create a large breathing space for political speech by protecting expression even if it does not fall unambiguously within that category. Both *Ulysses* and *Bleak House* are unquestionably political for First Amendment purposes. The same is true of Robert Mapplethorpe's work, which attempts to draw into question current sexual norms and practices, and which bears on such issues as the right of privacy and the antidiscrimination principle.

To say this is emphatically not to say that speech that has political consequences is by virtue of that fact "political" in the constitutional sense. Obscenity is political in that it has political well-springs and effects; the same is true of commercial speech and even bribery—certainly bribery of public officials. An employer's purely verbal sexual or racial harassment of an employee surely has political consequences, including the creation of a disincentive for women and blacks to go to that workplace at all. But these forms of speech are not by virtue of their effects entitled to the highest form of constitutional protection. To say that speech is political for First Amendment purposes because it has political causes and effects is to say that nearly all words or pictures are immunized from legal regulation without the gravest showing of clear and immediate harm. For reasons suggested above, that cannot be right.

For purposes of the Constitution, the question is whether the speech is a contribution to social deliberation, not whether it has political effects or sources. Thus, for example, there is a distinction between a misogynist tract, which is entitled to full protection, and pornographic movies, some of which are in essence masturbatory aids and not entitled to such protection. Personal, face-to-face racial harassment by an employer of an employee is not entitled to full protection, while a racist speech to a crowd is. There is a distinction between a racial epithet and a tract in favor of white supremacy. An essay about the value of unregulated markets in oil production should be treated quite differently from an advertisement for Texaco—even if an oil company writes and publishes both.

BIBLIOGRAPHY

George Anastaplo, THE CONSTITUTIONALIST: NOTES ON THE FIRST AMENDMENT (1971).

C. Edwin Baker, *Advertising and a Democratic Press*, 140 U.Pa.L.Rev. 2097 (1992).

Jerome Barron, *Access to the Press—A New First Amendment Right,* 80 Harv.L.Rev. 1641 (1967).

Walter Berns, THE FIRST AMENDMENT AND THE FUTURE OF AMERICAN DEMOCRACY (1957).

Walter Berns, *Freedom of the Press and the Alien and Sedition Laws: A Reappraisal,* 1970 Sup.Ct.Rev. 109.

Lillian BeVier, *An Informed Public, An Informing Press: The Search for a Constitutional Principle,* 68 Calif.L.Rev. 482 (1980).

Lillian BeVier, *Money and Politics: A Perspective on the First Amendment and Campaign Finance Reform,* 73 Calif.L.Rev. 1045 (1985).

Lillian BeVier, *The First Amendment and Political Speech: An Inquiry Into the Substance and Limits of Principle,* 30 Stan.L.Rev. 299 (1978).

Alexander M. Bickel, THE MORALITY OF CONSENT Ch. 3 (1975).

Vincent Blasi, *The First Amendment and the Ideal of Civic Courage: The Brandeis Opinion in* Whitney v. California, 29 Wm. & Mary L.Rev. 653 (1988).

Edward J. Bloustein, *The Origin, Validity, and Interrelationships of the Political Values Served by Freedom of Expression,* 33 Rutgers L.Rev. 372 (1981).

Lee C. Bollinger, THE TOLERANT SOCIETY Ch. 2 (1986).

Lee C. Bollinger, *Free Speech and Intellectual Values,* 92 Yale L.J. 438 (1983).

Robert H. Bork, *Neutral Principles and Some First Amendment Problems,* 47 Ind.L.J. 1 (1971).

William Brennan, *The Supreme Court and the Meiklejohn Interpretation of the First Amendment,* 79 Harv.L.Rev. 1 (1965).

Zechariah Chafee, *Book Review* (of Meiklejohn), 62 Harv.L.Rev. 891 (1949).

Stephen A. Gardbaum, *Broadcasting, Democracy and the Market,* 82 Geo.L.J. 373 (1993).

Stephen E. Gottlieb, *The Dilemma of Election Campaign Finance Reform,* 18 Hofstra L.Rev. 213 (1989).

Harry Kalven, Jr., A WORTHY TRADITION: FREEDOM OF SPEECH IN AMERICA (J. Kalven ed., 1988).

Paul Kauper, *Book Review* (of Meiklejohn), 58 Mich.L.Rev. 619 (1960).

Judith S. Koffler & Bennett L. Gershman, *The New Seditious Libel,* 69 Corn.L.Rev. 816 (1984).

Pnina Lahav, *Holmes and Brandeis: Libertarian and Republican Justifications for Free Speech,* 4 J.L. & Pol. 451 (1988).

Judith Lichtenberg, ed., DEMOCRACY AND THE MASS MEDIA (1990).

Daniel H. Lowenstein, *Campaign Spending and Ballot Propositions: Recent Experience, Public Choice Theory, and the First Amendment,* 29 UCLA L.Rev. 505 (1982).

William Marshall, *Free Speech and the "Problem" of Democracy,* 89 Nw.U.L.Rev. 191 (1994).

Alexander Meiklejohn, *The First Amendment is an Absolute,* 1961 Sup. Ct.Rev. 245.

Frank Morrow, *Speech, Expression, and the Constitution,* 85 Ethics 235 (1975).

Michael J. Perry, *Freedom of Expression: An Essay on Theory and Doctrine,* 78 Nw.U.L.Rev. 1137 (1983).

Robert C. Post, *Defaming Public Officials: On Doctrine and Legal History,* 1987 Am.B.Found.Res.J. 539.

Robert C. Post, CONSTITUTIONAL DOMAINS: DEMOCRACY, COMMUNITY, MANAGEMENT (1995).

Robert Post, *Managing Deliberation: The Quandary of Democratic Dialogue,* 103 Ethics 654 (1993).

Robert Post, *Meiklejohn's Mistake: Individual Autonomy and the Reform of Public Discourse,* 64 U.Colo.L.Rev. 1109 (1993).

L.A. Powe, Jr., *Mass Speech and the Newer First Amendment,* 1982 Sup.Ct.Rev. 243.

L.A. Powe, Jr., *Tornillo,* 1987 Sup.Ct.Rev. 345.

Martin Redish & Gary Lippman, *Freedom of Expression and the Civic Republican Revival in Constitutional Theory: The Ominous Implications,* 79 Calif.L.Rev. 267 (1991).

Norman L. Rosenberg, PROTECTING THE BEST MEN: AN INTERPRETIVE HISTORY OF THE LAW OF LIBEL (1986).

Frederick Schauer, FREE SPEECH: A PHILOSOPHICAL ENQUIRY Ch. 3 (1982).

Frederick Schauer, *The Role of the People in First Amendment Theory,* 74 Calif.L.Rev. 761 (1986).

Steven Shiffrin, *Government Speech,* 27 UCLA L.Rev. 565 (1980).

Cass R. Sunstein, DEMOCRACY AND THE PROBLEM OF FREE SPEECH (1993).

Cass R. Sunstein, *Government Control of Information,* 74 Calif.L.Rev. 889 (1986).

Jonathan Weinberg, *Broadcasting and Speech,* 81 Calif.L.Rev. 1101 (1993).

J. Skelly Wright, *Politics and the Constitution: Is Money Speech?,* 85 Yale L.J. 1001 (1976).

F. ADDITIONAL PERSPECTIVES

In Sections C, D and E we have reviewed a variety of justifications for protecting freedom of speech. There is much that is persuasive in each account. But in each case we have also seen limitations on the reach of the argument (e.g., democratic theory protects only speech about matters of public concern), and reasons for rejecting it altogether (e.g., it is not clear that truth will prevail in a free market of ideas). It should not be surprising, then, that First Amendment theorists have looked for other ways to explain the common devotion to free speech.

Thomas Scanlon makes an influential argument that combines some of the best elements of the self-expression and the democratic theory models. Like Meiklejohn, Scanlon stresses the importance of sovereign authority for free speech theory; but for Scanlon it is the individual who is sovereign. It is inconsistent with my dignity as an autonomous, rational agent for the government to "protect" me against the influence of what it considers false beliefs.

Steven Shiffrin claims to reject all the justifications we have examined thus far: the marketplace of ideas, the value of self-expression, the argument from democracy, the value of autonomy. He claims that the central function of the First Amendment is to promote individualism, antiauthoritarianism, dissent, and nonconformity. If he is to be believed, the speech we should value most is that which is generally disdained, precisely *because* it is so lowly regarded. The difficult point for a theory of this kind is to explain why we should assign value in this apparently counterintuitive way.

Lee Bollinger suggests an answer to this question. Like Shiffrin, Bollinger focuses on extremist, nonconformist speech. And like Shiffrin he rejects the standard free speech justifications. But Bollinger argues that we should protect extremist speech not (as Shiffrin urges) because it is valuable, but precisely because it is unworthy of protection. He believes that by doing so we can develop a habit of tolerance that will carry over to other activities, and make our communal life less contentious.

Whether this will actually happen is open to question. David Strauss points out that Bollinger has made some assumptions about social psychology that may prove false, in which case his theory falls apart. Bollinger also fails to tell us why speech theory should rest on the virtue of tolerance. He assumes that it is necessary to make democracy work. But Strauss suggests that there may be equally effective substitutes—enlightened self-interest, patriotism, a sense of fair play, even passivity.

Steven Smith takes up this last point where Bollinger leaves off. Smith suggests two reasons why we should value tolerance. One is the prudential case, that it may help us get along on an overcrowded planet. But a second reason is that some good things are valuable only if voluntarily chosen. There is no gain in forcing beliefs upon the unwilling.

Given the increased importance of economic approaches to various areas of law, it is not surprising that economics might inform thinking about both the theory and the doctrine of freedom of speech and freedom of the press. Such a line of inquiry has seemed increasingly fruitful to many theorists, although it is hardly clear where the line of inquiry leads, and hardly clear that considering the economics of communication leads to the libertarian conclusions often associated (often wrongly) with an economic perspective. Consequently, it is not surprising to see Daniel Farber using the economics of information to generate a new and important argument for protecting speech, and Frederick Schauer using economic thinking about cost allocation to question whether the inevitable costs of a free speech system that (properly) protects some harmful speech must necessarily be borne by the victims of the harmful speech.

The concluding piece by Ronald Cass asserts that nearly all the theories reviewed in this chapter begin at the wrong end of the maze. "Affirmative theories," as he calls them, try to deduce First Amendment principles from some (usually one) value that they see as more fundamental. These theories have been remarkably unproductive: they have had little influence on the courts, they rarely make our decisions more certain, and in the cases where they do give clear guidance it is usually unfortunate. Cass proposes that we be guided instead by "negative theory": we should begin with concrete problems, not with fundamental values. We should focus on the concerns that animated the framers and subsequent judicial expositors of the First Amendment.

THOMAS SCANLON, A THEORY OF FREEDOM OF EXPRESSION

1 Phil. & Pub.Aff. 204, 213–219, 222–224 (1972).

I will now state the principle of freedom of expression * * *. The principle, which seems to me to be a natural extension of the thesis Mill defends in Chapter II of *On Liberty,* and which I will therefore call the Millian Principle, is the following:

> There are certain harms which, although they would not occur but for certain acts of expression, nonetheless cannot be taken as part of a justification for legal restrictions on these acts. These harms are: (a) harms to certain individuals which consist in their coming to have false beliefs as a result of those acts of expression; (b) harmful consequences of acts performed as a result of those acts of expression, where the connection between the acts of expression and the subsequent harmful acts consists merely in the fact that the act of expression led the agents to believe (or increased their tendency to believe) these acts to be worth performing.

* * *

I would like to believe that the general observance of the Millian Principle by governments would, in the long run, have more good consequences than bad. But my defense of the principle does not rest on this optimistic outlook. [T]he Millian Principle, as a general principle about how governmental restrictions on the liberty of citizens may be justified, is a consequence of the view, coming down to us from Kant and others, that a legitimate government is one whose authority citizens can recognize while still regarding themselves as equal, autonomous, rational agents. Thus, while it is not a principle about legal responsibility, the Millian Principle has its origins in a certain view of human agency from which many of our ideas about responsibility also derive.

* * *

To regard himself as autonomous in the sense I have in mind a person must see himself as sovereign in deciding what to believe and in weighing competing reasons for action. He must apply to these tasks his own canons of rationality, and must recognize the need to defend his beliefs and decisions in accordance with these canons. * * * An autonomous person cannot accept without independent consideration the judgment of others as to what he should believe or what he should do. He may rely on the judgment of others, but when he does so he must be prepared to advance independent reasons for thinking their judgment likely to be correct, and to weigh the evidential value of their opinion against contrary evidence.

The requirements of autonomy as I have so far described them are extremely weak. They are much weaker than the requirements Kant draws from essentially the same notion,[7] in that being autonomous in my sense (like being free in Hobbes's) is quite consistent with being subject to coercion with respect to one's actions. A coercer merely changes the considerations which militate for or against a certain course of action; weighing these conflicting considerations is still up to you.

An autonomous man may, if he believes the appropriate arguments, believe that the state has a distinctive right to command him. That is, he may believe that (within certain limits, perhaps) the fact that the law requires a certain action provides him with a very strong reason for performing that action, a reason which is quite independent of the consequences, for him or others, of his performing it or refraining. How strong this reason is—what, if anything, could override it—will depend on his view of the arguments for obedience to law. What is essential to the person's remaining autonomous is that in any given case his mere recognition that a certain action is required by law does not settle the question of whether he will do it. That question is settled only by his own decision, which may take into account his current assessment of the

---

7. Kant's notion of autonomy goes beyond the one I employ in that for him there are special requirements regarding the reasons which an autonomous being can act on. (See the second and third sections of Foundations of the Metaphysics of Morals.)

While his notion of autonomy is stronger than mine, Kant does not draw from it the same limitations on the authority of states (see Metaphysical Elements of Justice, sections 46–49).

general case for obedience and the exceptions it admits, consideration of his other duties and obligations, and his estimate of the consequences of obedience and disobedience in this particular case.

Thus, while it is not obviously inconsistent with being autonomous to recognize a special obligation to obey the commands of the state, there are limits on the *kind* of obligation which autonomous citizens could recognize. In particular, they could not regard themselves as being under an "obligation" to believe the decrees of the state to be correct, nor could they concede to the state the right to have its decrees obeyed without deliberation. The Millian Principle can be seen as a refinement of these limitations.

The apparent irrationality of the doctrine of freedom of expression derives from its apparent conflict with the principle that it is the prerogative of a state—indeed, part of its duty to its citizens—to decide when the threat of certain harms is great enough to warrant legal action, and when it is, to make laws adequate to meet this threat. (Thus Holmes's famous reference to "substantive evils that Congress has a right to prevent.") [9] Obviously this principle is not acceptable in the crude form in which I have just stated it; no one thinks that Congress can do *anything* it judges to be required to save us from "substantive evils." The Millian Principle specifies two ways in which this prerogative must be limited if the state is to be acceptable to autonomous subjects. The argument for the first part of the principle is as follows.

The harm of coming to have false beliefs is not one that an autonomous man could allow the state to protect him against through restrictions on expression. For a law to provide such protection it would have to be in effect and deterring potential misleaders while the potentially misled remained susceptible to persuasion by them. In order to be protected by such a law a person would thus have to concede to the state the right to decide that certain views were false and, once it had so decided, to prevent him from hearing them advocated even if he might wish to. The conflict between doing this and remaining autonomous would be direct if a person who authorized the state to protect him in this way necessarily also bound himself to accept the state's judgment about which views were false. * * *

The argument for the second half of the Millian Principle is parallel to this one. What must be argued against is the view that the state, once it has declared certain conduct to be illegal, may when necessary move to prevent that conduct by outlawing its advocacy. The conflict between this thesis and the autonomy of citizens is * * * slightly oblique. Conceding to the state the right to use this means to secure compliance with its laws does not immediately involve conceding to it the right to require citizens to believe that what the law says ought not to be done ought not to be done. Nonetheless, it is a concession that autonomous citizens could not make, since it gives the state the right to deprive

9. In Schenck v. United States.

citizens of the grounds for arriving at an independent judgment as to whether the law should be obeyed.

These arguments both depend on the thesis that to defend a certain belief as reasonable a person must be prepared to defend the grounds of his belief as not obviously skewed or otherwise suspect. There is a clear parallel between this thesis and Mill's famous argument that if we are interested in having truth prevail we should allow all available arguments to be heard.[10] But the present argument does not depend, as Mill's may appear to, on an empirical claim that the truth is in fact more likely to win out if free discussion is allowed. Nor does it depend on the perhaps more plausible claim that, given the nature of people and governments, to concede to governments the power in question would be an outstandingly poor strategy for bringing about a situation in which true opinions prevail.

It is quite conceivable that a person who recognized in himself a fatal weakness for certain kinds of bad arguments might conclude that everyone would be better off if he were to rely entirely on the judgment of his friends in certain crucial matters. Acting on this conclusion, he might enter into an agreement, subject to periodic review by him, empowering them to shield him from any sources of information likely to divert him from their counsel on the matters in question. Such an agreement is not obviously irrational, nor, if it is entered into voluntarily, for a limited time, and on the basis of the person's own knowledge of himself and those he proposes to trust, does it appear to be inconsistent with his autonomy. The same would be true if the proposed trustees were in fact the authorities of the state. But the question we have been considering is quite different: Could an autonomous individual regard the state as having, not as part of a special voluntary agreement with him but as part of its normal powers qua state, the power to put such an arrangement into effect without his consent whenever *it* (i.e., the legislative authority) judged that to be advisable? The answer to this question seems to me to be quite clearly no.

* * *

The Millian Principle is obviously incapable of accounting for all of the cases that strike us as infringements of freedom of expression. On the basis of this principle alone we could raise no objection against a government that banned all parades or demonstrations (they interfere with traffic), outlawed posters and handbills (too messy), banned public meetings of more than ten people (likely to be unruly), and restricted newspaper publication to one page per week (to save trees). Yet such policies surely strike us as intolerable. That they so strike us is a reflection of our belief that free expression is a good which ranks above the maintenance of absolute peace and quiet, clean streets, smoothly flowing traffic, and rock-bottom taxes.

10. In chap. II of On Liberty.

Thus there is a part of our intuitive view of freedom of expression which rests upon a balancing of competing goods. By contrast with the Millian Principle, which provides a single defense for all kinds of expression, here it does not seem to be a matter of the value to be placed on expression (in general) as opposed to other goods. The case seems to be different for, say, artistic expression than for the discussion of scientific matters, and different still for expression of political views.

Within certain limits, it seems clear that the value to be placed on having various kinds of expression flourish is something which should be subject to popular will in the society in question. The limits I have in mind here are, first, those imposed by considerations of distributive justice. Access to means of expression for whatever purposes one may have in mind is a good which can be fairly or unfairly distributed among the members of a society, and many cases which strike us as violations of freedom of expression are in fact instances of distributive injustice. This would be true of a case where, in an economically inegalitarian society, access to the principal means of expression was controlled by the government and auctioned off by it to the highest bidders, as is essentially the case with broadcasting licenses in the United States today. * * *

But [this] tells only part of the story. Access to means of expression is in many cases a necessary condition for participation in the political process of the country, and therefore something to which citizens have an independent right. At the very least the recognition of such rights will require governments to insure that means of expression are readily available through which individuals and small groups can make their views on political issues known, and to insure that the principal means of expression in the society do not fall under the control of any particular segment of the community. But exactly what rights of access to means of expression follow in this way from political rights will depend to some extent on the political institutions in question. Political participation may take different forms under different institutions, even under equally just institutions.

The theory of freedom of expression which I am offering, then, consists of at least four distinguishable elements. It is based upon the Millian Principle, which is absolute but serves only to rule out certain justifications for legal restrictions on acts of expression. Within the limits set by this principle the whole range of governmental policies affecting opportunities for expression, whether by restriction, positive intervention, or failure to intervene, are subject to justification and criticism on a number of diverse grounds. First, on grounds of whether they reflect an appropriate balancing of the value of certain kinds of expression relative to other social goods; second, whether they insure equitable distribution of access to means of expression throughout the society; and third, whether they are compatible with the recognition of certain special rights, particularly political rights.

This mixed theory is somewhat cumbersome, but the various parts seem to me both mutually irreducible and essential if we are to account for the full range of cases which seem intuitively to constitute violations of "free speech."

————

Seven years after he published this article Scanlon revisited the issue, and confessed to a belief that some of his earlier views had been mistaken. Scanlon, *Freedom of Expression and Categories of Expression,* 40 U.Pitt.L.Rev. 519 (1979). One problem with the Millian Principle which he had initially adopted, he said, was its sweeping rejection of paternalism. It would not allow laws against deceptive advertising, for example, or the ban against cigarette advertising on television. Surely rules like these are all right.

A second and more general problem is this. The Millian Principle is designed to protect the important interest in making up one's own mind intelligently. Freedom of expression helps us to do that; so does a good education, access to information (not everyone can afford cable TV), etc. Of course there is a limit to what we are willing to pay for education, public radio, and so on, even if they do enhance our decisionmaking capacity. We usually weigh the costs of better decision-making against the corresponding benefits. But the Millian Principle says that two important kinds of costs should just be ignored. Why? A convincing explanation would have to show that these costs are different from others, and that we would be willing to bear an unlimited amount of them. Scanlon felt he had not given such an explanation.

In a way these two problems are alike, and they point to what Scanlon thought was the basic flaw in his earlier argument. In each case the Millian Principle is too strong. It forces us to accept social costs that are too high—or to put it the other way around, it forbids government intervention when (all things considered) we would prefer to have it. The reason it does all this is that it holds up autonomy as an absolute limit on the exercise of government authority. Autonomy—the ability to exercise independent rational judgment—is indeed a good thing, and we want to promote it. But to make it an absolute constraint is to assign it "greater and more constant weight than we in fact give" it. There are other goods in the world besides autonomy. And there are cases where we might actually promote our interest in autonomy by regulating speech; but the Millian Principle does not allow us to consider this possibility.

————

STEVEN H. SHIFFRIN, THE FIRST AMENDMENT, DEMOCRACY, AND ROMANCE
1–2, 5, 74–75, 77–79, 82–83, 85, 203–204, 210 (1990).

On July 15, 1838, Ralph Waldo Emerson delivered an address to the Harvard Divinity School. The response was outrage. Emerson was not invited to speak again at Harvard for almost thirty years.

The outrage was provoked. In speaking against "historical Christianity," Emerson told the "Unitarian clergy to their faces that they were preaching a dead theology." If Christ was important for religion, Emerson said, it should be because of what he said and not because of who he was. To emphasize the authority of Christ, rather than the power of his message, was to "corrupt" all attempts at communication, to engage in "noxious exaggeration" of the personal, and to adopt "petrified . . . official titles" and a "vulgar tone of preaching" that "degrade[s] the life and dialogues of Christ," and "kills all generous sympathy and liking." Such appeals to authority were denigrated as "appropriated and formal," a "profanation of the soul," an exhibition of the "sleep of indolence" resting amidst the "din of routine."

Emerson's gesture was not merely a revolt against the use of appeals to authority in Christian preaching. The Divinity School Address expressed and exemplified Emerson's general view that you should respect no authority, no custom, no convention, no habit, no institution unless it makes sense to you. If it does not make sense, Emerson counseled, demanded, insisted that you speak out. Emerson believed that everyone faces the question: "Will you fulfil the demands of the soul or will you yield yourself to the conventions of the world?" The Emersonian message was to trust your own intuitions, to speak out in favor of your own ideals, and to oppose the "strait prison-like limits of the Actual," to resist the conventions of the "old, halt, numb, bedrid world."

The Harvard divines thought Emerson went too far; perhaps he did. Dissenters often do. But, as luck would have it, Emerson's message carried beyond the corridors of Cambridge. Indeed, his importance as a cultural figure stems in large part from his emphasis on self-reliance and independence and from his lifelong commitment to the "free expression and dissemination of new ideas."

Although Emerson's perspective has helped to shape our literature and our culture, it has yet to be recognized or realized in American law. Emerson's thought has been presented in thousands of classrooms to millions of students, but no Justice has ever even once referred to the free speech views of Ralph Waldo Emerson in any Supreme Court case.

* * *

If an organizing symbol makes sense in first amendment jurisprudence, it is not the image of a content-neutral government; it is not a town hall meeting or even a robust marketplace of ideas; still less is it liberty, equality, self-realization, respect, dignity, autonomy, or even tolerance. If the first amendment is to have an organizing symbol, let it be an Emersonian symbol, let it be the image of the dissenter. A major purpose of the first amendment, I will claim, is to protect the romantics—those who would break out of classical forms: the dissenters, the unorthodox, the outcasts. The first amendment's purpose and function in the American polity is not merely to protect negative liberty, but also affirmatively to sponsor the individualism, the rebelliousness, the antiau-thoritarianism, the spirit of nonconformity within us all. * * *

* * *

In establishing these claims, I will use the little-noticed case of *Connick v. Myers.*[136] It exhibits the impoverished character of legal discourse about freedom of speech as well as any case I know. Sheila Myers was an Assistant District Attorney in New Orleans for five-and-a-half years. As the Court put it, "She served at the pleasure of . . . Harry Connick, the District Attorney for Orleans Parish." Sometime in 1980 Connick decided to transfer Myers to a different section of the criminal court. Myers objected to the transfer and to a number of other aspects about the managerial policies of the office. She * * * prepared a questionnaire soliciting the views of her co-workers, fifteen district attorneys, "concerning office transfer policy, office morale, the need for a grievance committee, the level of confidence in supervisors, and whether employees felt pressured to work in political campaigns."

* * * Connick fired Myers * * *. Myers argued that her discharge was unconstitutional. She argued that her distribution of the question-naire was a protected exercise of free speech.

* * * [The] Supreme Court agreed with Connick. By a 5–4 vote, it upheld the firing of Myers. * * * After parading a series of quotations about the importance of political speech and self-government, Justice White concentrated on whether Myers's speech addressed a "matter of public concern." The general inquiry was said to be grounded on the issue of whether the subject matter was one upon which " 'free and open debate is vital to informed decisionmaking by the electorate.' " The Court stated that if the speech was not of public concern, there was no first amendment protection against dismissal.

* * *

There is nothing very complex about the values involved [in this case]. I suspect they would be the first resort of anyone who had not been exposed to the reigning judicial precedents. We might imagine how Sheila Myers might have thought about the case before she saw a lawyer. Myers, of course, *is* a lawyer; so that background might have infected her capacity to see the situation clearly. Her vision, too, might have been clouded by the existing community of legal discourse with its paeans to democracy and self-government. If not, I suspect her first reaction would have nothing to do with public issues or private issues. Her assumption might well be that the first amendment guaranteed the right to speak about any subject and that it most especially guaranteed the right to dissent against existing customs, habits, conventions, pro-cesses, and institutions. It is possible that Myers was gathering evi-dence so that she could go to the voters with her information. But she may have had more "modest" goals in mind. She might simply have

136.   461 U.S. 138 (1983).

wanted to speak out against the management of the office. She presumably wanted to stimulate others in the office to begin discussing office policies and management. For all we know, Myers's questionnaire might have spelled the beginning of a union organizing campaign.

* * *

So understood, Myers's claim stands in a great first amendment tradition. It was a tradition well understood by Ralph Waldo Emerson and Walt Whitman. For them, and I would argue for most Americans, the point of Myers's claim has little to do with whether there were voters out there combing the pages of the local *Times–Picayune* to learn about office morale in the District Attorney's office. For them, American democracy meant that Americans could speak out against any of the existing institutions, habits, customs, and traditions. Emerson and Whitman may have celebrated a mythical American, but they celebrated an American who was not wedded to the comforts of the present nor tied by the bonds of the past. They celebrated the courage of the nonconformist, the iconoclast, the dissenter. In urging self-reliance and independence of thought, in praising the heroism of those willing to speak out against the tide, they sided with the romantics—those willing to break out of classical forms. Their conception of democracy had little to do with voting and everything to do with the American spirit. They sided with John Stuart Mill, in recognizing the ease of conformity. And, with Mill, they sponsored nonconformity.

In so doing, they struck a responsive chord. Emerson spoke at a special time in American history. It was a period when there was substantial discussion of the failure of Americans to produce a genuinely independent literature, a period when Tocqueville and others were observing that the abstract American commitment to freedom and civil liberties was not matched by the spirit of its people. Indeed Tocqueville, reacting to his concern about the tyranny of the majority and of public opinion, had insisted that "I know no country in which, speaking generally, there is less independence of mind and true freedom of discussion than in America." [153] For whatever complicated reasons, * * * Emerson's recurrent pleas against the fear of speaking out "came to seem, to a whole generation, [as] an agent of liberation." * * *

It is that tradition to which I appeal. Anyone who takes that tradition seriously must flinch at the Court's mindless observation in *Myers* that, "This is no defeat for the First Amendment." The *Myers* case tells public employees everywhere to shut up or get fired. The loss is not merely that voters will lose information. The loss is the failure to appreciate that the protection of dissent and its nurturance is a major American value.

* * *

153. A. de Tocqueville, Democracy in America, 254–255 (J.P. Mayer ed. 1969).

Cases like *Myers* * * * suffice to show that, judged by the value of dissent, the Court's approach to the first amendment is in disrepair. The dissent value affords a basis for criticizing these decisions, not for explaining them. Nonetheless, the dissent value can assist in explaining some important aspects of first amendment doctrine. The dissent value affords at least a partial explanation for the Court's second-class treatment of commercial advertising. Commercial advertising arguably makes a contribution to the efficient allocation of economic resources, and some regard that contribution as political. But no one would contend that the typical commercial advertisement is an exercise in dissent. When [Myers circulates a petition,] we witness an act of dissent. When General Motors gives us a pitch about the glory of Chevrolet, we run for the refrigerator. To sing "We shall overcome," is to join a protest movement; to sing "Things go better with Coke," is to protest nothing. Moreover, the distinction makes a difference. If protestors are banned from city streets, the first amendment affords protection. If commercial advertising is prohibited on city streets, the first amendment affords no refuge.

The first amendment treatment of literature presents an even better example. One would be hard pressed to say that the value of literature is political. Indeed, Judge Robert Bork once went so far as to argue that the first amendment should be interpreted to protect only explicitly political speech.[177] On this view, he wrote, freedom for literature would depend not on constitutional protection, but "upon the enlightenment of society and its elected representatives. That is hardly a terrible fate. At least a society like ours ought not to think it so."

At one level, Judge Bork might be correct. Even if the first amendment afforded virtually no protection for literature, literary freedom might still be quite expansive in most communities. For most authors, the abolition of the first amendment would have no practical effect on the dissemination of their work. Judge Bork's claim, however, carries plausibility at this point in our history in part because his theory of the first amendment has not ever been accepted in this country.

Suppose a book by D.H. Lawrence, for example, were publicly burned by county officials in some rural area of the United States. There would be a public outcry, of course, and those resisting might well quote from Milton and Holmes in drawing upon a marketplace of ideas rhetoric. Yet, it is at least doubtful that the marketplace of ideas is threatened by the burning. D.H. Lawrence's publications would still be available in the vast majority of American communities. Indeed the actions of zealous prosecutors in provincial towns might, in fact, enhance the demand for his work. The depth of passion against bookburnings, however, runs deeper than fears that truth will ultimately lose out in its battle with falsehood in the proverbial marketplace.

177. Bork, [*Neutral Principles and* L.J. 1, 20 (1971).] *Some First Amendment Problems,* 47 Ind.

Literature is commonly prized for its capacity to broaden our perspective, to challenge our limited ways of looking at the world. Literature challenges and shatters conventions. A provincial community that attacks a book of D.H. Lawrence attacks more than a book. It attacks an American value. People have come to understand that American democracy protects literature even if it is threatening to existing conventions and traditions. The fight to protect a work of D.H. Lawrence is less a fight for truth than it is a struggle to maintain a symbolic understanding of America as a country where people have the right to experiment, to be independent, to dissent from the everyday understandings. If I am right, then Judge Bork is wrong, wrong not only about literature and the first amendment, but also about the principles of American democracy.

As Bork conceives American democracy, the preeminent responsibility of the people acting through their elected representatives is to establish, maintain, and refine the public morality. Accordingly, Judge Bork sees the legislature as the repository of democratic wisdom, and regards it as a part of society's responsibility to decide whether books by D.H. Lawrence appropriately belong within the evolving tradition of civilized discourse. Within this framework the courts pose a threat of interfering with the *democratic* task of defining the public morality and that is why Judge Bork would have them stay their hand when elected representatives seek to purge uncivilized discourse from the public forum.

* * *

* * * [B]oth Emerson and Whitman had a more realistic and more vibrant conception of American democracy than that which has customarily prevailed among American academic lawyers. By the lights of Emerson and Whitman, government could *never* provide an authoritative expression of public morality. Indeed, it is a dangerous idea to suppose that government ever *authoritatively* expresses the popular will on any subject. Government may *purport* to speak *for* the people and in the name of the people, but whether it has successfully done so is always for *us* to decide. * * *

Emerson and Whitman understood that democracy was much more than a set of governmental arrangements. For them, democracy stood against the whole idea of authoritative pronouncements whether they were to emanate from government or were more subtly couched in customs, habits, or traditions. * * * They understood that democracy and orthodoxy are always potentially at war. They knew that democracy and dissent run together.

LEE C. BOLLINGER, THE TOLERANT SOCIETY
8–10, 120–121, 124–126, 133–136 (1986).

Traditionally, the focus of free speech theory has been on identifying the ways in which having the freedom of speech is valuable to us; just as it would be natural to point to the paintings of the great masters to explain why we should permit the activity of painting, so we have been inclined to point to the uses of speech we most value to justify the free speech principle. Attaining truth, exercising our democratic prerogative of self-government, and satisfying our yearnings for self-expression are interests that nearly everyone regards as vital and that can be readily, and reasonably, associated with the activity of speaking. Free speech theory has, in short, been highly successful in uncovering the riches of a policy of treating speech as a zone of liberty.

Yet, a disturbing lacuna appears in our theory as we confront the reality of protecting extremist speech (or what might be referred to as the overprotection of speech). For many of us who regard ourselves as committed to the idea of freedom of speech, the benefits traditionally associated with such a principle—primarily related to the process of discovering "truth"—begin to break down as the speech in question strikes more and more deeply at the personal and social values we cherish and hold fundamental to the society. * * * Despite the inability of conventional theories of free speech to account for this phenomenon of overprotection, there does seem to be a shared intuition that the society adds something important to its identity, that it is significantly strengthened, by these acts of extraordinary tolerance. It is the purpose of this book to try to explore the elements of that intuition; in that inquiry we will be able to reformulate the aims of the modern-day free speech idea.

It may be said of the new perspective offered here that while free speech theory has traditionally focused on the value of the activity protected (speech), it seeks a justification by looking at the disvalue of the response to that activity, by directing our attention to the problematic character of the feelings evoked by, in particular, extremist speech. Such troublesome feelings, however, are not to be understood as the affliction of only a segment of the society but rather as being universal. Nor, on the other hand, can it be said that they always govern our responses to this kind of speech activity. One of the significant points of departure between the perspective taken here and at least some prior theoretical accounts of free speech is the willingness to take as a working premise the idea that a good part of the speech behavior we are talking about is often unworthy of protection in itself and might very well be legally prohibited for entirely proper reasons. To acknowledge that, however, does not mean that a choice to tolerate such speech is irrational or unwise. The rationality and wisdom of choosing the course of tolerance can be derived from a neglected insight—namely, that the problematic feelings evoked by this kind of speech activity are precisely the same kinds of feelings evoked by a myriad of interactions in the society, not the least of which are the reactions we take toward non-speech behavior. Thus, while previous theoretical accounts of free speech have been led to focus on the differences between speech and other behavior (often described as "conduct"), the theory described here locates important social meaning in the similarities between the responses generated by all kinds of behavior. At this stage in our social history, then, free speech involves a special act of carving out one area of social interaction for extraordinary self-restraint, the purpose of which is to develop and demonstrate a social capacity to control feelings evoked by a host of social encounters.

* * *

[A]ny sound theory of free speech must answer three central questions. [Why should we exercise such extraordinary self-restraint in the regulation of speech when we do not with respect to nonspeech behavior? Why, in particular, should we tolerate extremist speech? Why should we vest the interpretative and enforcement functions of the principle in the judicial branch? I will begin with the first of these problems, which is,] to explain why the society has chosen to abide by what amounts to a presumption against regulation of this one area of behavior, that is, the behavior of speech. Apart from a few isolated regions in the area of nonspeech behavior, nowhere else in life do we insist in this way on such a level of self-restraint. [Why should we do this?] From the critical insight into the generality, the universality, of the feelings that generate an excessive response to speech acts, we can see free speech as a limited, or partial, area in which an extraordinary position of self-restraint is adopted by the society as one means of developing a more general capacity with respect to that impulse. Free speech provides a discrete and limited context in which a general problem manifests itself and in which that problem can usefully be singled out for attention. Does it make sense to structure social life in this way?

* * *

In both our private and public lives we often act in certain ways in one area in order to influence our behavior in other areas—in ways that, considered alone and independently from other parts of our lives, would appear strange. We understand, if sometimes only instinctively, that qualities we acquire by stretching ourselves in one area of activity spill over into other areas where those qualities are also needed. We may even separate certain areas of life where we will behave in extraordinary ways in order to develop particular qualities needed elsewhere. The near total restraint in the use of race as a consideration in public decision making, which functions in part as a symbolic counterbalance to the use of race in private decision making, is a good example of this.

* * *

We may now * * * also see why the category of speech behavior seems instinctively such a sensible place in which to undertake this enterprise. That speech generally causes less individual and social injury than does nonspeech behavior, while not in itself a sufficient justification for a free speech principle such as we now have, is nonetheless an important characteristic for explaining why speech is an appropriate setting in which to pursue a greater capacity for tolerance. Speech offers a fairly sharp line for limiting the extraordinary experiment with tolerance and an upper limit of potential for harm that makes unrestrained activity there generally tolerable for these purposes. There is in this sense, then, rational support for the widespread feeling that the reduced harm-producing capacity of speech behavior is somehow relevant to understanding why the culture has developed different rules for the regulation of speech and nonspeech acts. But what of the extremes of speech? Why pursue the principle to this extent, to the very outer perimeter of speech activities, to speech nearly all of us believe immoral and vicious? This is a more complicated question * * *.

* * * The extremes tend to attract attention, and that, as any educator or radical knows, can be pedagogically and symbolically advantageous. They provide, in other words, a useful context in which to impress on people the lesson sought to be communicated, a frame for the message. But there is more to the extreme cases than this.

Given that the very nature of the problem we are dealing with is, as a practical matter, beyond the capacity of law to solve, involving as it does what is essentially a matter of attitude or judgment, it seems reasonable to approach the problem in the limited area selected for symbolic action through a principle of nearly general self-restraint. It is simply too difficult to make a case-by-case examination of legal restraints on speech to ascertain whether the underlying motivations are of an improper variety. The problem of the impulse to excessive intolerance is simply too elusive for that type of scrutiny.

Even apart from the complexity of the inquiry in the free speech area itself, there is the additional point that the problem of the impulse—because it cuts through a variety of social interactions and involves a capacity for toleration in the broadest sense—must really be confronted by creating something of an *ethic* against regulation, which will exert force in the opposite direction, very much like the presumption of innocence does in the context of the criminal jury trial. One way to accomplish this is to hold the society to a position of near complete and total tolerance in a limited area of social intercourse. Therefore, not only does the context of the extreme case provide a desirable educational setting for conveying the general message; it also means that the society has committed itself to a course of action in which the sacrifice demanded will create a psychological environment in which the message will find its most receptive audience. By pursuing the "principle" to its logical end, well beyond what the particulars of individual cases call for under it, the society impresses on itself the importance of the lesson, creating out of it an ethic, or identity, of self-restraint. "To straighten a bent stick you bend it back the other way."

* * *

Finally, it is also the case that we often benefit from the extreme cases by holding up to ourselves, through the act of protecting the speech and permitting it to occur, the very example of the mental process that it is the fundamental purpose of free speech to alter. Extremist speech is very often the product or the reflection of the intolerant mind at its worst and, as such, an illustration to us of what lies within ourselves and of what we are committed, through the institution of free speech, to overcome: Perhaps ironically, but nonetheless powerfully, the principle of "free speech" serves to "protect," and so to hold up before us, that which we aspire to avoid.

* * *

In the end, all this comes down to a simple but nonetheless critical point: extremes are not to be understood as the peripheral cost of an inevitably imperfect world, in which no one can be trusted to draw the proper lines properly, but rather as integral to the central functions of the principle of free speech. The third and last major theoretical issue to be considered is whether it makes sense in a democracy to entrust the interpretation of constitutional norms to the judicial branch. * * * I would like to identify some generally unnoticed advantages of a judicial enforcement system for a principle of free speech such as we have so far outlined * * *. It should be borne in mind that the tolerance principle, as I have thus far described it, is intended and designed to perform a self-reformation function for the general community and not, as is so often assumed as the starting point for discussions about the functions of judicial review, to offer a shield of protection either for the majority against the government or for minorities against unfair treatment at the hands of the majority. In the light of that deeper social function, what can be said about the benefits of having the free speech idea enforced by a judicial branch?

* * *

First, the limited number of voices who pronounce the reasons for tolerance (in written statements) makes a coherent explanation more feasible. Furthermore, it may be regarded as important that judges are members of a professional group whose central intellectual ethic is identical with the aspirations of the free speech principle. To a degree more than with any other group, judges are expected to have mastered the tolerant mind, to have the capacity to set aside their personal beliefs and predilections, and to control the impulses that accompany them * * *.

There are two final attributes of the judicial system that, while difficult to identify or even articulate, are nevertheless of potentially great significance to the actual functioning of free speech. The first involves the fact that the judiciary, having no forces at its disposal for enforcing its judgments, is the one government institution most dependent on its own capacity to secure the "toleration" of others necessary for its acts to become effective. This dependence on others may well induce a greater institutional understanding and appreciation of the process of toleration in general.

The second attribute arises from an ambiguity, an uncertainty, under the free speech principle over the responsibility for the choice for tolerance. * * * [T]he impulse to intolerance * * * arises, at least in part, from the feeling that the choice of tolerance would indicate weakness of belief or will. Such a feeling may be especially strong in the extreme cases, which we now can see are integral to the new free speech principle. The sense, therefore, of having no choice in the decision for tolerance, and thus no part of the responsibility, can help to alleviate the need to act intolerantly. The ambiguity about this ultimate decision maker is very much at the center of the constitutional and judicial system of enforcement of the free speech principle. The "judge," a figure not subject to election or recall, appears to be the final decision maker, and the text interpreted (the Constitution) is itself encased in a set of social attitudes that makes its revision virtually unthinkable. The practical consequence of such a system is that in particular cases, when the needs of intolerance run extremely high, there is in the structure of free speech a means for making tolerance more palatable, which thus helps to preserve the identity of the general principle. Simultaneously, the litigation setting offers a convenient context for those for whom tolerance is troublesome both to articulate their "plea" for intolerance and to dissociate themselves from the result, and thereby from at least part of the "responsibility."

DAVID A. STRAUSS, WHY BE TOLERANT?

53 U.Chi.L.Rev. 1485–1486, 1497–1501, 1505–1506 (1986).

Lee Bollinger argues that the institution of free speech, established by the First Amendment, functions principally as a kind of didactic ritual: by requiring us to be tolerant of the most abhorrent speech, the First Amendment teaches us to be tolerant throughout political life. Bollinger's primary focus is on what he calls "extremist speech." His principal example of extremist speech is the effort a few years ago by a Nazi group to march in Skokie, Illinois, a Chicago suburb with a large Jewish population that includes several thousand survivors of concentration camps. Bollinger rejects, not as worthless but rather as insufficient and obsolete, what he sees as the two principal received justifications for providing legal protection to such extremist speech: the view [the 'classical model'] that all speech, including extremist speech, must be protected so that democratic politics can function successfully; and the theory [the 'fortress model'] that if extremist speech is not tolerated, the government will be able to suppress speech that is unquestionably valuable and worthy of protection. He argues instead that the purpose of free speech is to teach self-control by forcing people to tolerate an activity they would like to suppress. In particular, this enforced toleration teaches us to understand and control the "impulse toward intolerance" that is present in everyone—an impulse that has its legitimate claims, Bollinger says, but that, if unchecked, can have devastating consequences for society.

* * *

[One problem with] Bollinger's theory [is that it] may apply not to First Amendment issues generally but only to extremist speech, and perhaps only to certain cases of extremist speech. If that is true, then the doctrinal implications he draws from his theory, while still important, are substantially less dramatic than they first appear to be.

This difficulty is suggested by Bollinger's quick dismissal of the version of the fortress theory that sees the First Amendment as a bulwark against *government,* as opposed to popular, efforts to suppress speech. Bollinger argues that episodes like Skokie and the McCarthy era involved not independent actions by government officials but attempts at suppression by a genuine democratic majority. Many disputes about freedom of speech, however—and probably most disputes that raise unresolved legal issues—do not involve outpourings of popular intolerance. They often concern relatively low-visibility issues of which most members of the public are probably unaware. They therefore fit the fortress theory's model of government officials limiting speech on their own initiative. This seems to be true, for example, of most "public forum" cases, and in general of many of the Supreme Court's recent First Amendment cases.[18]

In such cases, the fortress model has much to commend it. When free speech conflicts with other interests, government officials may have a tendency systematically to undervalue the interest in protecting speech. One could argue that the role of the courts is to correct this bureaucratic tendency. The tendency to suppress speech comes from numerous sources. Officials may tend to overvalue short-term, concrete interests that conflict with allowing free speech, and to undervalue the more abstract, long-term interests served by speech. Free speech (assuming it does not involve the press) may be less well defended by the kind of organized constituent groups that are effective in influencing government officials. Free speech may tend to create disorder, and officials might place undue emphasis on the need to maintain control. Officials may be less able to sympathize with the relatively powerless outsiders who must resort to somewhat disorderly speech than with the representatives of groups whose interests are in conflict with those of the speakers. Finally, of course, to the extent the speech criticizes the officials themselves, their concern for their own reputations and positions may cause them to be unduly hostile to it.

* * *

Bollinger's own theory might not survive [other] challenges he makes, quite effectively, to the classical and fortress models. One point comes immediately to mind, and Bollinger, characteristically, acknowledges it: the empirical psychological premises underlying his theory are

---

18. See, e.g., Bethel School District No. 403 v. Fraser, 106 S.Ct. 3159 (1986); City of Los Angeles v. Preferred Communications, 106 S.Ct. 2034 (1986); Pacific Gas & Elec. Co. v. Pub. Util. Comm'n of California, 106 S.Ct. 903 (1986); Cornelius v. NAACP Legal Def. and Educ. Fund, 105 S.Ct. 3439 (1985); United States v. Albertini, 105 S.Ct. 2897 (1985); Clark v. Community for Creative Non–Violence, 468 U.S. 288 (1984); Minnesota Bd. for Community Colleges v. Knight, 465 U.S. 271 (1984); Perry Ed. Assn. v. Perry Local Educators' Assn., 460 U.S. 37 (1983); Heffron v. Int. Soc. for Krishna Consc., Inc., 452 U.S. 640 (1981).

not obviously true. It is not at all clear that people who are forced to tolerate speech they abhor will become more tolerant in other contexts; they might easily become *less* tolerant, in which case Bollinger's theory would collapse. Indeed, it would become an argument for suppression.

* * *

Perhaps a more serious difficulty with Bollinger's view is that it is vulnerable to a charge he levels against the fortress theory—indeed, more vulnerable to this objection than the fortress theory itself. Bollinger argues that the fortress model—insofar as it views the First Amendment as a bulwark against popular efforts to squelch dissidence—creates a system that is "manipulative," "alienating," "elitist," and fundamentally at odds with the values of rational discourse that free speech is usually thought to promote. Although Bollinger does not put the point in these terms, he seems to be saying that the fortress model does not satisfy the requirement, emphasized by Kant and Rawls, that the reasons for social institutions must be capable of being made public.[20]

Specifically, Bollinger suggests that the fortress model divides the world between the intolerant masses, who would eradicate all heterodoxy if they had the chance, and an elite that alone understands the value of protecting a wide range of speech. The institutions of free speech are designed by the elite to hold the masses in check. But since the masses obviously cannot be told *that,* the only way to hold them in check is to publicize essentially false stories about free speech—for example, that the language or history of the First Amendment unambiguously prohibits all suppression, or that all speech, even Nazi speech, contributes to progress. Judges and others responsible for maintaining the institution of free speech cannot acknowledge that the original intent of the First Amendment is unclear, or that we do not have a fully satisfactory explanation of why all speech must be protected. Once they admitted that there was some doubt about whether extremist speech must be protected, the waves of mass intolerance would rip through the cracks in the dike and swamp all valuable unorthodox speech.

Bollinger asserts that there is something wrong with an institution that can survive only by propagating a series of noble lies about its absoluteness and necessity. It would be especially ironic, he notes, if the defenders of free speech—whose rhetoric emphasizes the importance of vigorously debating all preconceptions—had to rely on an uncritical acceptance of aspects of the institution of free speech itself.

This is a powerful argument. But a similar argument can be made against Bollinger's theory. Like the fortress model, Bollinger's view begins from the premise that people generally are deficient in their ability to respond rationally to ideas and behavior that they dislike. But where the fortress view prescribes rigid doctrinal barriers to guard against the impulse toward intolerance, Bollinger prescribes a kind of

---

20. See Immanuel Kant, Perpetual Peace, in Hans Reiss, ed., Kant's Political Writings 125–30 (1970); John Rawls, A Theory of Justice 133 & n. 8 (1971).

collective psychotherapy. We are to force ourselves to come face to face with our own impulse toward intolerance so that we can understand and control it better. Both theories can be seen as involving the imposition of a regime—rigid barriers in the one case, therapy in the other—on the ignorant, intolerant masses by an elite that alone understands both the virtues of tolerance and the way to manipulate institutions in order to achieve it.

On the other hand, it is possible to defend both the fortress theory and Bollinger's view against this charge. People can recognize their own deficiencies and voluntarily take actions to deal with them; the institution of free speech might be seen as a collective choice of a way to deal with the impulse toward intolerance. Bollinger's theory would be comparable to a collective decision to submit to the kind of therapy that he believes the tolerance of abhorrent expression supplies. This seems to be the way Bollinger understands it. But by the same token, the fortress model is comparable to the familiar story of Odysseus tying himself to the mast; we recognize that we may be tempted to be intolerant, so we all collectively decide, ahead of time and in a cool hour, to make it more difficult for any of us to give in to that impulse when it occurs.

* * *

Finally, and paradoxically, I am not sure that Bollinger ever explains why tolerance is valuable. For him, of course, tolerance of extremist speech is not intrinsically valuable; it is desirable only because it helps people be more tolerant in other contexts, where tolerance is needed. In particular, Bollinger says that tolerance is crucial to the success of a democracy:

> [A] capacity to contain one's beliefs in the interest of maintaining a continuing community is critical. ... Those who possess the power to see their choices put into effect must decide whether and how far to press ahead in the face of opposition. Those in the minority must decide whether to accede to the will and power of the majority or in what ways to continue the fight. ... In this sense, therefore, the capacity sought through free speech bears a special relevance to the actual functioning of a democratic system of government.

But why is *tolerance* the capacity that democracy requires? Many other capacities seem to be equally effective in causing political winners not to press their advantage to the point of instability, and political losers not to rebel. Enlightened long-term self-interest alone might suffice; both winners and losers may believe that they have more to gain from preserving the system than from disrupting it. Indeed, in most reasonably democratic societies, this seems likely to be true of the losers and is certainly true of the winners. If long-term self-interest is sufficient to maintain the democratic system, we do not need to teach tolerance by tolerating extremist speech; we only need institutions that teach people to be rationally self-interested.

Other qualities also seem sufficient: patriotism; a sense of fair play, comparable to that which causes competitors not to cheat even when they can escape detection; or a belief in democratic institutions. Not all of these qualities will correlate well with tolerance, and there is no reason to believe that tolerating extremist speech—and thus incurring the very real costs that Bollinger emphasizes—is the most efficient way to cultivate these qualities. Bollinger's theory tells us (assuming its empirical premises are correct) *how* to make society more tolerant; but it does not tell us why we would want to do so.

Indeed, it seems that passivity—a quality that Bollinger is careful to distinguish from tolerance—would do at least as well as tolerance in maintaining stability in a democracy. As long as the losers are passive, democracy will survive. And one might ask why Bollinger confines his reasoning to democracies. There are winners and losers in any society, and no society can survive unless the losers submit and the winners do not press their advantage too far. If anything, non-democracies are even more in need of tolerance, because they cannot count on other qualities—such as self-interest among the losers and the sense of fair play—to the same extent as a democracy can. But undemocratic societies do not usually have an institution of free speech to teach tolerance to their citizens.

Bollinger does not address these problems; he does not adequately explain why he sees a close connection between tolerance and democracy.

STEVEN D. SMITH, THE RESTORATION OF TOLERANCE

78 Calif.L.Rev. 304, 334–338 (1990).

Tolerance may seem to be an unstable and perhaps even internally contradictory attitude. Tolerance entails permitting others to hold and disseminate erroneous beliefs, but since they are necessarily wrong, these beliefs represent an evil that individuals and, it would seem, governments should want to combat. If one is convinced that a particular idea is false, practical reason suggests that one should repress that idea. This is the logic of intolerance, which a tolerant regime must overcome.

Various responses to the logic of intolerance have been advanced. The present analysis will not attempt any comprehensive survey but will instead describe two kinds of arguments that historically have carried the greatest influence. These may be described as the prudential and the positive arguments for tolerance.

1. THE PRUDENTIAL CASE FOR TOLERANCE

The prudential argument asserts that because the people living in a community are in fact diverse in their beliefs, values, and ways of life, the adoption of an attitude of mutual tolerance will most effectively promote peaceful coexistence. As E.M. Forster put it, tolerance is "a makeshift, suitable for an overcrowded and overheated planet."[123] This general argument can spawn more specific but similarly pragmatic arguments; for example, that the suppression of dissent is difficult, costly, and not worth the gains, or that repression is politically destabilizing. The pragmatic argument can also be understood in more positive terms: tolerance allows a community to benefit from the skills, resources, and diverse viewpoints of political, religious, or ethnic minorities.

Historically, the prudential argument has substantially influenced the development of toleration. Colonial observers like Crèvecoeur and modern historians like Sidney Mead have attributed the achievement of religious freedom in the United States primarily to the nation's religious diversity and its need to establish some mutually acceptable modus vivendi.[126] The prudential argument is no less relevant today. For example, Lee Bollinger's provocative analysis of tolerance in free speech doctrine accepts the prudential argument and then gives it a novel twist. Bollinger argues that we have only a limited capacity to tolerate,[127] and tolerance is essential in all aspects of social life. He therefore suggests that we strengthen that capacity by singling out a particular human activity—speech—and forcing ourselves to practice tolerance beyond what the intrinsic value of the tolerated speech might warrant. The exercise is largely pedagogical; through our approach to speech we will strengthen the general capacity for tolerance that a diverse community requires.

Despite its historical and continuing importance, the prudential case for tolerance has its limitations. First, its appeal depends upon its context. In some situations, tolerance may indeed be the best way to achieve a harmonious community. But in other situations it might be easier or more effective simply to silence or eliminate an irritating minority. The prudential argument provides no rationale for practicing tolerance in these circumstances.

In addition, the prudential argument cannot respond to zealous citizens who are unwilling to relegate matters involving fundamental beliefs and values to the realm of pragmatic calculation. The true believer does not lay down the sword of God just to avoid unpleasant confrontations; indeed, she may relish such confrontations as an opportunity to test and prove her faith. Thus, the defense of tolerance will be bolstered if the prudential argument can be supplemented by a more positive rationale for tolerance—a rationale founded in principle rather than expediency.

2. THE POSITIVE CASE FOR TOLERANCE

John Locke offered a positive justification for tolerance. * * * Locke contended that Christianity exists to secure the salvation of

---

123. E.M. Forster, [Two Cheers for Democracy 47 (1951)].

126. *See* J. Crèvecoeur, Letters From an American Farmer, 54–57 (Gloucester 1782); S. Mead, The Lively Experiment: The Shaping of Christianity in America, 35–37 (1963).

127. *See* L. Bollinger, [The Tolerant Society (1986).]

souls.[132] But salvation can be attained only by those who voluntarily exercise the requisite faith. Faith cannot be forcibly imposed, and even if it could be, such faith would not secure salvation. Hence, the persecution of heretical religious opinion is futile.

Although Locke focused upon religious belief, the logic of his argument has broader implications. The argument holds that a particular good—for Locke, salvation of the soul—cannot be attained except by voluntary choice or acceptance. But salvation may not be the only good of that kind. For example, while the logic of intolerance sponsors the suppression of false beliefs in order to promote truth, the "truth" thereby contemplated is surely not "truth" in the abstract, whatever that might mean, but rather a distinctively human good—sincere and voluntary belief in true ideas. Yet that particular good cannot be achieved by methods that undermine the sincerity and voluntariness of human opinions.

* * *

The positive argument for tolerance has its limitations. It depends upon an orthodoxy which posits that certain goods are valuable only if voluntarily chosen. Hence, not every orthodoxy will support the positive argument for tolerance, and the proponent of tolerance may therefore not only need to show how an accepted orthodoxy requires tolerance, but may also need to propose or defend another orthodoxy that incorporates this premise.

In addition, the positive case for tolerance does not support absolute toleration. Even when the desired ends can be achieved only voluntarily, there may be reasons for regulating conduct. For example, while Locke's argument suggests that it is senseless to prosecute atheists out of concern for the salvation of their souls, he believed that atheism might nonetheless properly be outlawed because it undermined the sanctity of promises. Likewise, a contemporary community might wish to prevent Nazis from conducting public demonstrations not because it wants to shape the beliefs either of the Nazis or of its own residents, but rather because such demonstrations are likely to cause violence, property damage, or psychic distress.

Still, although the positive case does not support absolute toleration, it does provide a reason for tolerating particular types of conduct. Moreover, the positive rationale examines the very goods or objectives that many brands of intolerance purport to value—salvation, truth, moral virtue—and shows that those values actually endorse, and even require, a policy of tolerance. Where applicable, therefore, the positive case turns the logic of intolerance against itself. As a consequence, the argument for tolerance strengthens proportionally with the strength or fervor with which the orthodoxy itself is held.

132. [J. Locke, *A Letter Concerning Toleration,* in On Politics and Education (H. Penniman ed. 1947).]

DANIEL A. FARBER, FREE SPEECH WITHOUT ROMANCE: PUBLIC CHOICE AND THE FIRST AMENDMENT

105 Harv.L.Rev. 554–55, 558–64, 568–69 (1990).

What is special about speech? Why is it exempt from various types of regulation routinely applied to other activities? For instance, why are there special restrictions on liability for harmful speech and a unique constitutional right to use certain government property for communication, but not for any other purpose?

As Steven Shiffrin emphasizes in his recent book on the First Amendment,[5] one way to answer these questions is to celebrate the Romantic ideals of self-expression and self-realization. Although that is undoubtedly a valuable perspective, this Commentary will explore a different and very *un*romantic understanding of the First Amendment's protection of speech. This understanding derives from public choice theory—that is, the application of economics methodology to political institutions.

The crucial insight of public choice theory is that, because information is a public good, it is likely to be undervalued by both the market and the political system. Individuals have an incentive to "free ride" because they can enjoy the benefits of public goods without helping to produce those goods. Consequently, neither market demand nor political incentives fully capture the social value of public goods such as information. Our polity responds to this undervaluation of information by providing special constitutional protection for information-related activities. This simple insight explains a surprising amount of First Amendment doctrine.

* * *

Over the past twenty years, economists have become increasingly interested in the economics of information. Their most basic finding, subject to some qualifications, is that markets are likely to produce too little information because information, like clean air or national defense, has many of the attributes of a public good. That is, the benefits of information cannot be restricted to direct purchasers but inevitably spread to larger groups. The production of information often produces positive externalities—that is, benefits to third parties. Because the producer does not consider these benefits in his production decision, less information is produced than is socially optimal. There are people who, if they had to, would be willing to pay for the benefits of additional information, but that additional information is not produced because the market is unable to translate those individuals' preferences into an incentive for the producer. Market demand reflects only benefits to

---

5. *See* Steven H. Shiffrin, The First   (1990).
Amendment, Democracy, and Romance

purchasers, not benefits received by free riders. According to this analysis, if the government intervenes in the market at all, it should *subsidize* speech rather than limit it. Legal restrictions on information only further reduce a naturally inadequate supply of information.

Virtually any activity can produce third-party benefits of some kind under the appropriate circumstances. Third-party benefits are least likely to occur in the case of discrete physical goods. Only one person can consume a given meal or drive a certain car at a particular time. Information, however, is perhaps uniquely reproducible. The same idea or the same data can be understood simultaneously by an indefinite number of individuals at relatively little marginal cost. Once information is produced, it can be made available to a broader audience in several ways—through physical reproduction, through paraphrasing, through information-sharing services such as libraries or press reports, and sometimes merely through observing the subsequent behavior of original audience members. These and other phenomena allow many individuals to consume the same item of information without compensating the original producer.

Two more points about this argument deserve mention. First, the argument does not turn on the absolute value of speech compared with other activities but rather on the disparity between the private and social value, which is greater for speech than for typical consumer goods. Thus, it does not matter whether speech (or some category of speech) is more or less important to individuals or to society than some other consumer good, such as food. What is important is that a much greater share of the value of the food flows to the initial purchaser, and less flows to other members of society. Second, some speech may consist of misinformation, and its dissemination throughout society may be a public "bad" rather than a public good. But if individuals are rational, they will usually screen out false information or refuse to rely at all on a communication if they cannot assess its reliability. This screening is by no means a foolproof process, and in some instances government intervention may be warranted to prevent the dissemination of false information. Nevertheless, the presumption should be that the free dissemination of information generally makes individuals more knowledgeable and improves their welfare.

Just as the market will underproduce information, the political system is likely to overregulate information. In general, consumers of information, like all large, diffuse groups of individuals with small personal stakes, face serious organizational problems in lobbying and other political activities. Such collective action problems are due in part to the powerful incentive that individual members of such groups have to free ride. When the product in question is information, this effect is exacerbated because the benefits of improved information are so diffuse. Hence, although consumers of other products are often ineffective as a political force, consumers of information are even more likely to be dismal failures in preventing government from limiting information production.

In the context of nonpublic goods, producers may organize consumer protests or otherwise act as proxies for consumer interests because the producers' sales directly reflect the value of the product to consumers. Consider, for example, a government effort to regulate a new prescription drug. Consumers' willingness to purchase the drug translates directly into a financial stake for the producers (the drug companies) and the distributors (doctors and pharmacists). Because sales reflect most of the social benefits of the consumer good in this case, lobbying by producers can act as a partial proxy for lobbying by consumers. In the context of public goods such as information, however, the total social benefit of the good is not reflected in direct consumer sales. Payments to information producers, such as book publishers, reflect only the benefits received by direct purchasers and do not include the full benefit ultimately enjoyed by the rest of society from receiving the information indirectly. Because sales of information do not fully reflect the ultimate social benefit of information production, the producers' financial stake— and thus the intensity of industry lobbying on behalf of consumers—does not reflect the full social value of the information. Consequently, media lobbying efforts are a less effective proxy for consumer interests than are the efforts of producers in other industries. These barriers to lobbying by producers and consumers of information suggest that, to whatever extent the government may or may not tend to overregulate other behavior, it will be *more* likely to overregulate speech. Like other widely dispersed public benefits, information is likely not only to be underproduced in the private market, but also to be insufficiently protected by the political system. It is precisely this tendency to overregulate speech activities that requires constitutional protection for speech.

On a hasty reading, this argument might seem to suggest that speech produces only benefits and therefore should be virtually immune from regulation. The argument is actually more limited. Like any other activity, speech may impose costs on third parties, and when these externalities exceed the total social value of the speech, regulation may be in order. But regulation of speech should be viewed with special caution because information is already produced at a suboptimal level and legislatures are particularly prone to overregulate speech. Consequently, government regulation of speech should be more restrained than regulation of other activities.

* * *

Everyone seems to agree that political speech lies at the core of the First Amendment's protection. At the periphery are forms of speech such as pornography and commercial advertising. As it turns out, core speech most strongly exhibits the qualities of a public good and therefore most needs protection, while the forms of speech at the periphery are only weak public goods.

Political speech might well be considered a "double" public good. Information contained in political speech is one public good, and political participation, which is often guided by such information, is a second public good. Consider, for example, the supply of information about foreign affairs. To the extent that voters seek such information, they can often obtain it secondhand without paying the original producer. The free rider problem is exacerbated in this context because voters also have an incentive to free ride on the activities of other political participants. Because my vote probably will not change the election results, I have little incentive to seek relevant information. Even if the information were only privately available, I would have little incentive to pay for it. Instead, I might as well sit back and let other people participate in politics. I will obtain whatever benefits exist from a good foreign policy regardless of whether I participate. The result is predictably straightforward: although information in general is likely to be underproduced, political information is even more likely to be underproduced, and underproduced to a greater extent. Furthermore, because information producers will capture only a tiny share of the ultimate benefits of their product in the form of better government, their lobbying activities against censorship similarly will be underfinanced. Therefore, the public good argument for protecting speech applies with particular force to political speech.

This argument for protecting political speech does not assume any special malice or even insensitivity on the part of government officials toward disclosure of adverse political information. Although government officials may have conflicts of interest concerning the regulation of political speech, such conflicts are insufficient by themselves to justify especially stringent protection of political speech. We do not necessarily disallow legislation whenever politicians have a conflict of interest, such as that in cases involving political gerrymandering and public funding for campaign expenses. Thus, at the very least we need further argument to connect the harm (a political conflict of interest) with the remedy (constitutional protection of speech).

Moreover, the conflict of interest is not always as strong as it may appear. Political challengers have strong incentives to oppose restrictions on information. Even for incumbents, suppressing adverse information may not be desirable. Whether suppressing information is a good strategy depends on the expectations people have in the absence of information. For example, if people think most incumbents are crooks, it is to the collective advantage of incumbents to suppress information about corruption only if the situation is even *worse* than people suspect. This is an application of what has been called the "No News Is Bad News" principle in game theory. For this reason, incumbents will often be divided about the desirability of suppressing information.

In addition, politicians' incentive to suppress adverse information can be viewed as a special case of their general incentive to favor politically organized special interests at the expense of the unorganized public. Politicians always have at least a *potential* conflict of interest between their own desire to be reelected and their desire to serve the public, at least to the extent that the politician's honest perception of the public interest does not agree with the latest poll results. Politicians should not be understood as a unique force for suppressing information, but rather as simply another special interest that sometimes wishes to suppress information. Normally, special interests are countered by various other forces, but we have already seen that information producers have an insufficient motive to lobby against restrictions on information and that this motive is especially weak when political speech is concerned because of the "double" public good problem. Additionally, of course, politicians do have advantages that assist them in obtaining legislation favorable to their interests: they have inside political knowledge and an organizational structure designed for taking political action. The likely result of these advantages is that too much political speech will be suppressed.

* * *

Many First Amendment doctrines reflect the fear that certain laws overdeter speech and thus lead to a suboptimal amount of total information disseminated in society. For example, cases such as *New York Times Co. v. Sullivan* [60] provide extraordinary protection for enterprises that harm others through their communications. As the Court in *New York Times* recognized, if newspapers were liable for all inaccuracies, they would strike the wrong balance between the costs of inaccurate information and the benefits of producing additional accurate information.

For example, suppose an editor knows that a story is sixty percent likely to be correct and that publishing the story will increase the paper's profits by $100,000. If the story is true, it will produce a net social benefit of $1 million, but if it is false, the paper will have to pay defamation damages of $500,000. If the decision is based on the total social benefits, the paper should publish the story. Yet if the paper considers only its own economic incentives, it will refuse to publish because it faces an expected loss of $100,000.[64] To prevent overdeterrence, we must provide the paper considerable protection against liability.

FREDERICK SCHAUER, UNCOUPLING FREE SPEECH

92 Colum.L.Rev. 1321, 1326–31, 1334–38, 1356–57 (1992).

Sticks and stones may break your bones, but names will never hurt you. Or so our parents admonished when we were seven years old. By the time we reached nine or ten, however, we realized that our parents were wrong, and that a host of communicative acts could indeed hurt us, the hardly surprising consequence of the essentially social nature of human communication.

---

60. 376 U.S. 254 (1964).

64. The $100,000 loss is arrived at by subtracting the expected costs of defamation damages, 40% of $500,000, or $200,000, from the paper's increased profits of $100,000.

The capacity of speech to cause injury in diverse ways contends with the goal of strong free speech (and free press) protection, and it is a commonplace that robust free speech systems protect speech not because it is harmless, but despite the harm it may cause. Given that existing First Amendment doctrine protects those who negligently and erroneously charge public officials and public figures with criminal behavior,[1] immunizes from tort liability publications causing bodily injury or death,[2] and shields from prosecution those who successfully abet violent criminal acts,[3] it can scarcely be denied that a major consequence of a highly protective approach to freedom of speech and freedom of the press is to shelter from legal reach a set of behaviors that could otherwise be punished and a set of harms that could otherwise be compensated.

Implicit in conventional First Amendment rhetoric is that it could not be otherwise. To put it more precisely, existing understandings of the First Amendment presuppose that legal toleration of speech-related harm is the currency with which we as a society pay for First Amendment protection. Paying a higher price by legally tolerating more harm is thus taken to be necessary in order to get more First Amendment protection. Conversely, it appears equally well accepted that being more concerned about speech-related harm by tolerating less of it requires accepting a commensurately weaker First Amendment. And although people disagree about the amount of free speech protection they wish to have and, consequently, the extent of harm they wish to have their legal system tolerate, they agree about the necessary connection between speeches protected and harms tolerated. Such disagreements as exist are only about the appropriate ratio and not about the structure of the relationship.

I propose to call into question this very relationship, suggesting that the coupling of harm-toleration and speech-protection is by no means inevitable. In questioning the relationship, I do not suggest we can get

---

1. See Ocala Star–Banner Co. v. Damron, 401 U.S. 295, 296 (1971) (plainly erroneous report of indictment for perjury); see also Rood v. Finney, 418 So.2d 1, 2 (La.Ct. App.1982) (plainly erroneous report of drug addiction), cert. denied, 420 So.2d 979 (La. 1982), and cert. denied, 460 U.S. 1013 (1983).

2. See Herceg v. Hustler Magazine, Inc., 565 F.Supp. 802, 803 (S.D.Tex.1983), motion to dismiss denied, 583 F.Supp. 1566 (S.D.Tex.1984), rev'd, 814 F.2d 1017 (5th Cir.1987), cert. denied, 485 U.S. 959 (1988); Olivia N. v. National Broadcasting System Co., 178 Cal.Rptr. 888, 892–93 (Ct.App. 1981), cert. denied sub nom. Niemi v. National Broadcasting Co., 458 U.S. 1108 (1982); Walt Disney Prods., Inc. v. Shannon, 276 S.E.2d 580, 582 (Ga.1981). In all of the foregoing cases (and many others), the relationship between the publication and the injury would have satisfied standard tort requirements of negligence, fore-

seeability, and proximate cause. See generally Frederick Schauer, Mrs. Palsgraf and the First Amendment, 47 Wash. & Lee L.Rev. 161 (1990). In some contrast to the above cases, however, is Berhanu v. Metzger, No. 8911–07007 (Cir.Ct., Multnomah County, Or., Oct. 22, 1990) (appeal pending). There, the victim of an attack by members of the White Aryan Resistance sued the leader of that organization for encouraging the attack, and the jury, finding specific intent, foreseeability, and proximate cause (although not imminence), found for the plaintiff against the leader in the amount of $12,479,000.

3. See Brandenburg v. Ohio, 395 U.S. 444, 448 (1969); American Booksellers Ass'n v. Hudnut, 771 F.2d 323, 333–34 (7th Cir.1985), aff'd, 475 U.S. 1001 (1986). See Kent Greenawalt, Speech, Crime, and the Uses of Language 262–63 (1989); Kent Greenawalt, Speech and Crime, 1980 Am. B.Found Res.J. 645, 650–53.

something for nothing. Still, [existing] understandings of the First Amendment are based on the assumption that, because a price must be paid for free speech, it must be the victims of harmful speech who are to pay it. This assumption, however, seems curious. It ought to be troubling whenever the cost of a general societal benefit must be borne exclusively or disproportionately by a small subset of the beneficiaries. And when in some situations those who bear the cost are those who are least able to afford it, there is even greater cause for concern. If free speech benefits us all, then ideally we all ought to pay for it, not only those who are the victims of harmful speech. Moreover, although much of modern law reform, especially in torts, has reflected attempts to reallocate costs towards those best able to bear them and to adjust incentives in order to achieve optimal patterns of behavior, this trend has as yet failed to influence our understanding of constitutional rights in general and free speech rights in particular.

* * *

In *Ocala Star–Banner Co. v. Damron,*[14] the Supreme Court demonstrated with stunning clarity the costs commonly associated with *New York Times Co. v. Sullivan.*[15] The facts of *Ocala Star–Banner* are straightforward: Leonard Damron was the mayor of the town of Crystal River, Florida, and a candidate for County Tax Assessor of Citrus County. On April 17, 1966, a reporter telephoned the *Star–Banner* with a story that James Damron (who happened to be the brother of Leonard Damron) had been arrested and charged with perjury in the United States District Court in Gainesville, with the trial to take place in the following term of that court. The area editor, who had been working at the paper for just more than a month, wrote up the story for publication, changing the name from James Damron to Leonard Damron, quite possibly on the assumption either that the two were one and the same or that the reporter on the scene had misstated Leonard Damron's name. As it appeared in the next day's paper, under the headline "Damron Case Passed Over to Next U.S. Court Term," the story commenced with: "A case charging local garage owner Leonard Damron with perjury was passed over for the present term of Federal Court after Damron entered a not guilty plea before Federal Judge Harrold Carswell in Gainesville."

Although the *Star–Banner* printed two retractions before the election for County Tax Assessor took place, Leonard Damron lost the election, held two weeks after the article appeared. He sued the *Star–Banner* for libel, and succeeded in establishing falsity, negligence, and a relationship between the falsity and both general damage to his reputation and specific damage to his electoral prospects. Damron ultimately won a jury award of compensatory damages in the amount of $22,000.

The $22,000 award was upheld in the Florida courts, but was then overturned by a unanimous United States Supreme Court. Justice

14. 221 So.2d 459 (Fla.Dist.Ct.App. 1969), cause dismissed, 231 So.2d 822 (Fla. 1970), rev'd, 401 U.S. 295 (1971).

15. 376 U.S. 254 (1964).

Stewart's brief opinion made clear that the case involved little more than a mechanical application of the rule in *New York Times,* since no plausible case for the existence of actual malice could be maintained. Thus, not only is *Ocala Star–Banner* an easy case under the *New York Times* rule, but it also enables us to identify with some precision the cost of the *New York Times* rule—$22,000—since that is what Damron would have received had that rule not been in place. Consequently, in order to prevent the *Ocala Star–Banner* from being excessively chilled in its pursuit of truth, Leonard Damron is compelled to forego an award of $22,000, which is (utility functions and opportunity costs aside) the economic equivalent of compelling him to pay $22,000.

But why Leonard Damron? He is certainly not the primary beneficiary of unchilling the *Star–Banner* and every other American newspaper and magazine. On the contrary, as Justice White's concurrence makes so clear, Leonard Damron is the unfortunate victim of the social benefit coming from the relaxed rule of liability. So at the outset it seems odd that he should have to shoulder the entire cost of a benefit that is society's and not his.

But is there an alternative? [I want] to explore a number of them, continuing to use *Ocala Star–Banner* as my working example. My goal [is] to see whether there are alternatives to Leonard Damron's having to forego $22,000 that do not encourage the self-censorship of the *Ocala Star–Banner*. Or, to put it differently, [whether] the $22,000 cost of the *New York Times* rule might be paid by someone other than Leonard Damron.

My working postulate is that any rule of liability more stringent than that of *New York Times* would produce too much self-censorship by the *Star–Banner* and other publications, and my whole point would be lost were I to relax that assumption. The assumption, however, is one that is premised on the importance of a certain amount of *editorial* freedom, the idea being that editors and reporters should be able to do their jobs without having to peer over their shoulders at the specter of liability for anything other than intentional falsehoods. But if the goal is to liberate editors and reporters from the fear of liability, then one alternative to the actual state of affairs comes from recognition of the fact that the $22,000 would be paid not by the editorial department but by the publisher of the newspaper, and it is hardly necessary that the publisher would require that the editorial department change its practices in order to minimize publisher liability. If the rule of legal liability were negligence rather than actual malice, Damron would recover his $22,000. But if the publisher were to pay the award and at the same time make clear to the editorial staff that the publisher expected the editorial staff to operate *as if* the *New York Times* rule were in place, Damron would be compensated and the editorial staff would be no more chilled than it is now.

Plainly my original assumption—just the opposite of this possibility—is what drives existing law. *New York Times,* and indeed the entire constitutionalization of American defamation law, is based on the assumption that if the publisher is at financial risk, then this risk will filter down to the editorial department, with a consequent inhibiting effect on the content of the newspaper. And certainly this seems a plausible assumption, not only because the law generally assumes that businesses are undifferentiated economic units, but also because the trickling (or pouring) down of trouble above resonates so easily with what we know about how institutions operate.

Yet however plausible the assumption of trickle-down chilling appears, it turns out to be at odds with one of the pervasive tenets of the press itself—the separation of the advertising and editorial functions. Thus, although it is frequently the case that advertisers refrain from advertising in newspapers because of some aspect of the content of the paper, it is a central credo of American "elite" journalism that an advertiser's threat to do so, or act of doing so, will have no effect on editorial content. If an article critical of Mobil Oil or Chase Manhattan, or of oil companies or banks in general, will prompt Mobil or Chase to withdraw their ads, then that, it is commonly held, is the price to be paid for the editorial independence that defines the high-quality newspaper, magazine, or news broadcast. Thus, to put a number on all of this, if publishing an article critical of Mobil Oil were to lead Mobil to withdraw advertising for which it would have paid $22,000, then many American publishers would say that paying $22,000 for editorial freedom was well worth the price. Mobil's act, says the conventional journalistic wisdom, would occasion no changes in the newspaper's editorial practices. The loss would be absorbed outside of the editorial function, and the editorial staff would be under no pressure to change their behavior towards Mobil or other advertisers.

The parallel is as intriguing as it is obvious. If a publisher claims to be willing to spend $22,000 in order to save her editorial department from the chilling effect of worrying about whether editorial content will offend advertisers, why is she not willing to spend $22,000 in order to save her editorial department from the chilling effect of worrying about whether that content will produce legal liability for unintentional falsehood? From the publisher's perspective, the answer is obvious: assuming a publisher has selected her optimal degree of editorial independence from financial pressure, she will absorb the cost of editorial freedom from advertising pressures because if she does not, then no one else will; but there is no reason to absorb the cost of editorial freedom from defamation actions if she is able to have someone else, such as Leonard Damron, absorb those costs. She thus secures the benefits of editorial freedom without having to spend the $22,000 to obtain it. Accordingly, with respect to defamation, the publisher avoids costs that she bears with respect to advertising because she has successfully convinced the United States Supreme Court to get Leonard Damron to bear those costs for her.

Although publishers are thus no different from the rest of us in preferring that others pay for what we would pay for if we had to, we see now that there are two alternatives to a negligence rule with chilling side effects. One alternative is the rejection of the negligence rule, which is what the Court did in *New York Times;* the other alternative is a negligence rule the costs of which publishers absorb just as they supposedly absorb the costs of editorial independence from advertising. The choice of the former by the courts can thus be seen as contingent rather than necessary, even if a given amount of editorial freedom is desired. The choice of the *New York Times* approach is contingent because the choice is based on the unwillingness of publishers to pay for First Amendment benefits that publisher absorption would produce as easily as the actual malice rule.

* * *

This suggests that were *New York Times* to be reversed, or were the *New York Times* rule to be applied less stringently, it is by no means inevitable that the news and editorial functions of newspapers and magazines would be appreciably more constrained, for it is possible that one consequence of that reversal would be the same degree of editorial freedom but slightly lower after-suit profits for publishers. Of course, it is highly likely that many publishers would refuse to bear the costs of the First Amendment in this way. And if we as a society are concerned with the social benefit of editorial freedom more than the benefits to the press itself, then we must accede to this threat. But now we see that Leonard Damron has to bear the $22,000 cost for our First Amendment not because this is necessary in order to preserve the First Amendment, but because either Leonard Damron or the publishers of newspapers have to bear that cost in order to preserve the First Amendment, and publishers have refused and are likely to continue to refuse to do so. *New York Times* is thus the consequence of the Supreme Court's having been persuaded that the only alternative to less First Amendment protection was placing the cost on people like Damron, when in fact there was the alternative of placing the cost of the First Amendment on the newspaper itself.

But suppose the alternative of forcing publishers to bear the financial burden of the First Amendment is unrealistic. If, as appears increasingly the case, publishers are not willing to insulate their editorial departments from the pressures of advertising-revenue preservation, then publishers are probably not willing to insulate their editorial departments from the pressures of liability minimization. And there is little doubt that some publishers would be financially unable to do so even if they desired. Most publications simply do not have the resources presumably available to the *New York Times*.

Moreover, the economics of information are such that the production of most single items of new information brings, especially for a newspaper, small financial benefits (even though the publication of a single item can produce a large harm to, or a large benefit for, the object of that article). Because information cannot in general be monopolized once published, because published information can be used by others at virtually no cost, because each item of information published brings a minuscule economic benefit to the publisher, and because a single item of published information may nevertheless result in great liability, the production of any new piece of information brings for its publisher much greater risk of liability than potential for benefit. As a result, the extent to which the risk of liability might overdeter producers from producing new commodities is greater when information rather than some other newly produced good, especially one that can either be patented or that is difficult for others to reproduce, is the relevant commodity. Consequently, a publisher's commitment to insulating its editorial department from financial pressures would have to be greater than it would be in enterprises equally committed to production of new commodities but engaged in the production of commodities other than information. This may explain the seeming erosion of the ideal of editorial independence from advertising pressures, and much the same could be expected with respect to pressures from liability minimization.

In addition, if we are truly dealing with a social benefit, then there seems little more reason to pin the cost of it on the publishers of the *Ocala Star–Banner* than there is to pin it on Leonard Damron. And here we can again draw interesting comparisons between the press and other industries. Consider what happens when a federal agency requires automobile manufacturers to add airbags or a state or local agency requires landlords to provide fire protection equipment. Do landlords say that society will be better off if fewer tenants are burned, and thus absorb the costs of the improvements? Do automobile manufacturers say that society will be better off if there are fewer highway deaths, and thus diminish their profits by the cost of the airbags? Hardly. In tried and true American fashion, automobile manufacturers and landlords attempt to pass these costs along to the consumers, who then pay for safety whether they would have otherwise chosen to do so or not.

Following this pattern, we can imagine the same behavior in the case of newspapers and magazines. At least with respect to those publications that are sold to consumers (and here radio and television are relevantly different from newspapers and magazines, because the costs of radio and broadcast television are not levied directly by the broadcasters on listeners or viewers), one possibility is simply to increase the price of the newspaper to cover the $22,000. Or, a publisher could raise the price of the newspaper by an amount sufficient either to pay for libel insurance or to establish a reserve sufficient to satisfy judgments and defense costs consequent upon the existence of a negligence rule rather than the *New York Times* rule.

This approach requires assumptions about price elasticity that get a bit tricky. Although it is probably the case that, within the range sufficient to pay for the difference between the *New York Times* rule and a negligence rule, the demand for any given newspaper is comparatively price inelastic relative to many other consumer goods, it is unlikely to be totally price inelastic. And it turns out that the demand for advertising is quite sensitive to changes in circulation. So if a newspaper with a daily circulation of 100,000 raised its price five cents (from thirty to thirty-five cents) to create the just-described reserve, if it used the entire proceeds of the increase to fund the reserve, and if as a result of the price increase the circulation slipped to 95,000, the costs to be absorbed by the paper would not only be the $1500 per day caused by the loss of sales of 5000 newspapers at thirty cents. They would also include the loss of advertising revenue that followed from having a circulation of 95,000 rather than a circulation of 100,000.

Still, it is not inconceivable that the price increase would cover the advertising decrease as well. After all, a five-cent-per-day price increase for a daily newspaper with a circulation of 100,000 would generate additional circulation revenue of $1,186,250, assuming a reduction of circulation to 95,000. The question then would be whether this additional circulation revenue would be sufficient both to pay for the increased libel insurance as well as to compensate for lost advertising revenue, the amount of the latter being a function both of the elasticity of demand for advertising with respect to circulation, and the price elasticity of demand for advertising. But it does not seem unrealistic to suppose that it would be enough both to pay for a negligence rule and to offset any lost advertising revenues occasioned directly or indirectly by the price increase.

So although the foregoing discussion depends on a number of debatable assumptions about the nature of the market and price elasticity within it, it is not totally implausible to suppose that the costs of the First Amendment could be passed on to and spread out among readers. In implementation, this would mean that the prevailing rule would be a negligence rule, the effect of which would be that Leonard Damron would be able to recover his $22,000 and thus not have to shoulder the costs of the First Amendment alone. But because the price increase would pay for any expenditures under the negligence rule that would not have been incurred under an actual malice rule, there would be no reason (other than engaging in the hardly unheard-of practice of passing on to consumers additional "costs" not actually expended) for internal editorial practices to be any different than they now are under the actual malice rule. In other words, *New York Times* protection would be available even if its price were paid not by Leonard Damron but by the purchasers of the newspapers, in some sense a much more logically constituted group of First Amendment beneficiaries.

[Schauer goes on to explore other possibilities for reallocating the costs of free speech, including governmentally subsidized libel insurance and victim compensation schemes, both of which, according to him, might allow victim recovery without increasing publisher costs, and thus might allow victim compensation with no increase in the deterrence ("chilling") of speakers or publishers.]

A century ago Holmes declared that a central principle of the common law was the preference for letting injuries lie where they fell.

But even if Holmes was right then, that generalization hardly describes contemporary American law, where compensation for injuries, usually by the agent wrongfully causing them, is far more the rule than the exception. Were we operating under the Holmesian assumption, the general unwillingness to compensate those injured by communicative acts would be but an example of a more pervasive jurisprudential approach. [Yet to] the extent that compensation for injuries caused by others remains our baseline, and especially when a wide variety of nonphysical harms are compensated pursuant to that baseline, the exclusion of a host of harms in the name of the First Amendment represents an anomaly. This is most apparent with respect to defamation, [speech-induced] physical harm, and the intentional infliction of emotional distress, for here we are dealing not with creating new grounds for liability, but with claimants who would have valid tort actions were it not for the operation of existing First Amendment doctrine.

In those areas in which the First Amendment currently precludes compensation, it may be that the disproportionate cost of an undifferentiated social benefit is just a fact of life, to be put into the "life is unfair" category along with the way in which a small group of Olympic athletes in 1980 paid a disproportionate price for an undifferentiated foreign policy initiative and in which farmers and longshoremen disproportionately shouldered the burdens of the roughly contemporaneous wheat embargo. Or we may think [that] free speech itself benefits all of us roughly equally over the long run, even though it may benefit some people or some groups more, and burden some people and some groups more, in particular cases. Or it may be [that] we believe that over time the disproportionalities of all of our rights and all of our obligations even out, such that some pay more for some social goods, but benefit more from others. But even if all of these beliefs are sound, the immediate fact that the cost of a constitutional right is being borne disproportionately by victims of its exercise ought at least to occasion more thought, especially in the First Amendment area, than it has to date. [Even] if First Amendment doctrine emerged unchanged from such rethinking, and even if the costs of the First Amendment must thus remain borne overwhelmingly by its victims, then at least we could say that there was no alternative, rather than that it was the first approach that came to mind.

RONALD A. CASS, THE PERILS OF POSITIVE THINKING: CONSTITUTIONAL INTERPRETATION AND NEGATIVE FIRST AMENDMENT THEORY

34 UCLA L.Rev. 1405, 1411–1419, 1421–1422, 1438–1442, 1449–1451 (1987).

[First Amendment] theorists conform fairly well to a pattern. The usual style is, first, to identify a value that freedom of speech furthers. Most theoretical writings have suggested variants of four different values as critical to speech protection: individual development,[16] democratic government,[17] social stability,[18] and truth.[19] Having identified an important value, the theorist marshals evidence that this value has a long-recognized relation to freedom of speech. The theorist then explains why the value is more important or more closely connected to speech than are other values, emphasizing, for example, the peculiar utility of speech to democratic government or the special role of speech in forming individual beliefs and values. Often, this demonstration of linkage or importance is joined with exposition of deficiencies of other values as basis for speech theory. This theorist may argue that other values are not so integrally related to speech, detailing ways in which other values can be promoted as well through non-speech activities. Or the theorist may argue that his own chosen value necessarily is implicated in, and explanatory of, other values. Hence, individual liberty becomes an explanation of the desirability of democratic self-government, or truth an explanation for liberty. The point here is that the "deepest," most basic value should provide guidance. Next, the theorist marshals evidence that this value has long-recognized relation to freedom of speech. Then he explains why the value is more important or more closely connected to speech than are other values. Finally, the writer shows how the speech clause, thus interpreted, would operate to achieve desirable results. I will refer to this theoretical style variously as "positive," "affirmative," or "value-promoting."

Affirmative theories * * * differ from other theories in two respects. First, the affirmative theories rely on deduction. Each begins with a precept, usually a conception of ideal human endeavors, rooted either in a vision of individual or communal ends, and deduces from it the value that is served by speech. Second, the positive theories are reductionist. Many reduce the focus of inquiry to a single value served by speech. And all of these theories reduce the focus of First Amendment inquiry to the ways in which the particular identified value or values can be advanced by speech.[23]

* * *

16. *See* T. Emerson, The System of Freedom of Expression (1970) (speech advances individual self-fulfillment and other values); * * * Baker, *The Process of Change and the Liberty Theory of the First Amendment,* 55 S.Cal.L.Rev. 293 (1981) * * *; Richards, *Free Speech and Obscenity Law: Towards a Moral Theory of the First Amendment,* 123 U.Pa.L.Rev. 45 (1974) (moral self-development); Scanlon, *A Theory of Freedom of Expression,* 1 Phil. & Pub. Aff. 204 (1972) (liberty). * * *

17. *See, e.g.,* A. Meiklejohn, Free Speech and Its Relation to Self–Government (1948) (proposing self-government as the critical affirmative value); Bork, *Neutral Principles and Some First Amendment Problems,* 47 Ind.L.J. 1 (1971) (political process) * * *.

18. *See, e.g.,* Blum, *The Divisible First Amendment: A Critical Functionalist Approach to Freedom of Speech and Electoral Campaign Spending,* 58 N.Y.U.L.Rev. 1273 (1983) (political/social dissent).

19. *See, e.g.,* Barron, *Access to the Press—A New First Amendment Right,* 80 Harv.L.Rev. 1641 (1967) (diversity); Duval, *Free Communication of Ideas and the Quest for Truth: Towards a Teleological Approach to First Amendment Adjudication,* 41 Geo.Wash.L.Rev. 161 (1972).

23. These two characteristics exclude from the category defined here as affirmative, or positive, value promoting, some theories that share conceptual features with the works discussed here. Not all theories

Despite the popularity of this genre, the social returns from these efforts at theory to date have been meager. Some theories have picked up academic adherents, and many have prompted discussion among academicians. Some have been cited in court decisions, and may possibly even have affected judicial decisionmaking on occasion. But none of the theories has secured significant, much less sustained, support from the bench. * * *

The * * * theories, generally, share three defects. One may be a consequence, rather than a cause of the courts' aversion to the theories: the theoretical writings have not predicted judicial decisions very well. * * *

The theories' two other shortcomings are more telling. A second defect is that the theories do not accomplish what seems to be their principal goal: they rarely replace uncertainty with certainty. The theories provide few clear guidelines for decisionmakers and fewer clear rules for decision. Some of the theorists' elaborations and applications indicate the manner in which they intend the theory to govern particular situations. And some theories produce quite clear results in a wide range of cases, without need of elaboration by their creator.[30] In the main, however, the theories suggest (implicitly, if not explicitly) a continued need for accommodation of competing concerns, which produces a concomitant imprecision in many of the theories' applications. * * * The major thrust of most theoretical endeavors is [simply] to urge that, however the balance of incommensurable interests is struck, some particular interest should be given greater weight.

should be classed as positive because they reflect a generality of concern with speech (an effort to abstract from particular speech problems), a concern with the affirmative values served by speech, or even a focus that restricts the theories' apparent openness to sources of concern for speech value.

Professor Vince Blasi and Dean Lee Bollinger, for example, who have offered general theories of the First Amendment that might be viewed as similar in kind to those listed above, should be distinguished from the positive theorists. *See* L. Bollinger, The Tolerant Society: Freedom of Speech and Extremist Speech in America (1986); Blasi, *The Checking Value in First Amendment Theory,* 1977 Am.B.Found.Res.J. 521. Both Blasi and Bollinger develop theories of the First Amendment that emphasize one aspect. Blasi emphasizes the utility of speech, and especially of the institutional press, as a check on the operation of government. Bollinger emphasizes the role of tolerance as a central value in speech regulation.

While both of these approaches to the First Amendment produce strong theories built on an underlying value, Blasi and Bol-

linger each take pains to eschew an exclusive focus on the value with which he is especially concerned. Neither reduces his forces exclusively to *promotion* of the value. In part, this may reflect the fact that in both cases, the value identified is peculiarly bound up with *constraining* government speech regulation to a much greater extent than values supporting other strong theories. Blasi (and to a lesser degree Bollinger) places his theory clearly on reaction to the anticipated failures that accompany exercise of formal government power rather than seeing speech as an instrument to other ends. Moreover, Professor Blasi's work is nondeductive, as well as nonreductionist. His "checking value" theory is rooted in history, not ontology. * * * [T]he approaches taken by Blasi and Bollinger accord much more with the history of the First Amendment than do other theories. The references to positive or value-promoting theory, hence, do not encompass these two authors' work. * * *

30. *E.g.,* * * * Bork, *supra* note 17. Not coincidentally, these are the most aggressively deductive and reductionist of the speech theories.

The third criticism is somewhat at odds with the preceding objection: to the extent clear guidance is given, the solutions suggested by the theorists are unfortunate. * * * Nearly all of the affirmative theories lend themselves to outcomes that, to me, seem dramatic departures from the commonly understood and commonly accepted purposes of the First Amendment, that is, the understanding of ordinary citizens and the general view of academics not writing First Amendment theory. * * *

* * * The self-government thesis, the self-fulfillment/individual liberty argument, and the argument from truth all provide illustrations. Alexander Meiklejohn's work suggests that, while pornography is protected as inseparable from speech activities that advance the human understanding necessary for self-government, the speech of paid lobbyists, directly communicating with elected representatives about matters then pending before our representative institutions of government, may be outside the Amendment's purview.[34] Edwin Baker similarly has opined that, even though public displays of sexual activity might promote personal liberty and hence enjoy absolute protection against government regulation, speech by corporations (other than those classifiable as news media) cannot advance personal liberty and, therefore, must be entirely unprotected.[35] Jerome Barron and Thomas Emerson believe that in order to promote widespread access to diverse opinions, the government is obligated by the First Amendment to regulate speech in at least some instances.[36]

* * *

All three difficulties * * * are related. Each reflects the theorists' misperception of the core problem of First Amendment jurisprudence. The theorists have endeavored to cure the difficulties they see created by the courts' seemingly atheoretical decision process. The best theorists have sought to craft more orderly theses than they have discovered in judicial opinions; ideally, to create a strong, fully explanatory theory of free speech. The major problem for First Amendment decisionmaking, however, is not the courts' failure to articulate a truly coherent, comprehensive theory of free speech adjudication, but rather that no such strong theory is articulable. Absent agreement on a single value—whether it be utility, wealth, or freedom—to be maximized, we cannot achieve a truly coherent theoretical framework for decision. But the protection accorded speech has never represented a commitment to any single principle or value. * * *

* * *

[In place of positive theories of free speech I propose a "negative" theory.] It begins with identification of the concerns of the framers and subsequent judicial expositors of the First Amendment and of the

---

34. *See* A. Meiklejohn, Political Freedom 55–76, 160–63 (1960) * * *.

35. *See* * * * *Liberty Theory, supra* note 16. * * *

36. *See* Barron, *supra* note 19; Emerson, *The Affirmative Side of the First Amendment,* 15 Ga.L.Rev. 795 (1981).

situations that present these concerns most acutely or that implicate them only tangentially. This does not yield a basis for concrete resolution of most controversies over interpretation. But it does sort out speech problems into categories closer to or further away from the core of the Amendment's concerns.

* * *

If one grounds constitutional theory largely in the historical basis for substantive constitutional constraints, it is difficult to avoid focusing on problems rather than philosophic aspirations. The framers were not intent on promoting some well-defined conception of the good, whether individual or societal. They were responding to problems that already had arisen and that they feared might recur. The early discussions of the desirability of additional substantive constraints on government emphasize not the need to proscribe generally government interference with personal liberty—that was hardly the dominant mood after Shays' rebellion—but the need to curb *wrongful* interference with personal liberty.

* * * It is trite to observe that the anti-Federalists, with some Federalist support, were able to secure a Bill of Rights by the threat of non-support for the Constitution. The rhetoric that backed up this threat, and the fears that informed it, however, took the form of allegations that particular oppressive practices had been used in Europe or in the colonies, that freedom from these practices was a considerable portion of what the revolution had made possible, and that it was folly not to guard against the repetition of these practices. Substantive constraints on federal power were not the product of general beliefs in liberty, but of more focused fears about its unjustified infringement.

This limited, reactive, negative approach characterized the promulgation of all the substantive limitations on government, including freedom of speech. The positive theorists commonly look at the speech clause in isolation, but the same impetus is manifest throughout the eight substantive amendments in the Bill of Rights. One may wax eloquent over the conceptions of human potential that seem embedded in the speech clause; but similar flights of fancy are less easily undertaken with respect to prohibitions on quartering troops in private homes without consent in peacetime or without legal regulation in wartime, on issuance of search warrants not supported by oath or affirmation, or on trial other than in the district where a crime was committed.

In each instance, the limitations on government responded to specific perceived abuses of government power. The First Amendment's concerns over the establishment of a state religion, and over interference with free religious exercise, with speech and press, with assembly and petitions for redress of grievances all spring from the same ground that gave rise to the rest of the Bill of Rights. The phrasing of the amendments in the negative—as limitations on government rather than as self-contained guarantees of liberty—is emblematic of their genesis.

* * *

Because the conceptions of the framers were negatively oriented, the unifying, abstract concept of freedom of speech must be defined as freedom from the sorts of official speech restraints that seemed problematic. The concept that is most true to concerns that plainly supported speech and press protections (putting aside other concerns that arguably played supporting roles) focuses on the source of wrongful speech regulation: wrongful speech regulation responded to *personal* interests of official regulators. * * * Self-interest had prompted official suppression of speech by European and colonial governments, and a principal function of the First Amendment was to assuage fears that officials of the new federal government would do likewise. * * *

A second theme sounded during the constitutional debate also should find a place in the concept of freedom protected by the First Amendment, but its relation to the speech clause is less certain. In addition to self-interest narrowly conceived, past incidents of wrongful suppression or punishment of speech had been born of officials' intolerance: distaste for the message rather than realistic concern for its practical effects. This sort of intolerance for ideas accounted for much of the censorship that governments had effected. Although such censorship was directed against speech that today might be labelled political, religious, literary, or scientific, the impetus for it and basis for concern about it was largely linked to sectarian religious differences. Hence, to some extent, mention of intolerance in discussions of the suggested Bill of Rights might better be assimilated to the religion clauses of the First Amendment.

* * *

Still, the objection to intolerance can be separated from the concept of freedom of speech only with difficulty. Indeed, intolerance for ideas is closely associated with the sort of self-interest that fueled concern about official control of expression. Officials at times must be motivated by personal beliefs or by those of their constituents (even intolerant constituents), and the officials' tenure in office may be as much dependent on the currency of particular beliefs on other subjects as on information directly concerning the officials themselves.

If the concerns about wrongful speech regulation that animated adoption of the First Amendment's speech clause, then, are to be seen as different aspects of a broad, unifying, abstract concept of freedom of speech, that concept should encompass at least some protection against speech regulation from officials' self-interest and speech regulation from intolerance of ideas. The first of these concerns will be the stronger of the two, but both will play some part.

This concept of freedom of speech does not deny that speech has affirmative values. No one would have cared about speech regulations otherwise; the very notion of wrongful regulation implies that something is lost, in at least some cases, when speech is regulated. The concept of freedom of speech sketched here indeed is compatible in good measure with several different affirmative speech values. The abstraction on which constitutional consensus emerged—that sometimes speech regulation by government is undesirable and that it is imprudent to trust officials, even those accountable to the public through democratic-representative processes, to eschew such speech regulation—was not, however, a statement of any particular value served by any given speech.

BIBLIOGRAPHY

Lawrence A. Alexander & Paul Horton, *The Impossibility of a Free Speech Principle,* 78 Nw.U.L.Rev. 1319 (1983).

Robert Amdur, *Scanlon on Freedom of Expression,* 9 Phil. & Pub. Aff. 287 (1980).

Vincent Blasi, *Learned Hand and the Self–Government Theory of the First Amendment:* Masses Publishing Co. v. Patten, 61 Colo.L.Rev. 1 (1990).

Paul G. Chevigny, *Philosophy of Language and Free Expression,* 55 N.Y.U.L.Rev. 157 (1980).

Benjamin S. DuVal, Jr., *The Occasions of Secrecy,* 47 U.Pitt.L.Rev. 579 (1986).

Daniel A. Farber, *Free Speech Without Romance: Public Choice and the First Amendment,* 105 Harv.L.Rev. 554 (1991).

Kent Greenawalt, FIGHTING WORDS: INDIVIDUALS, COMMUNITIES, AND LIBERTIES OF SPEECH (1995).

R. Kent Greenawalt, *Free Speech Justifications,* 89 Colum.L.Rev. 119 (1989).

Peter J. Hammer, *Free Speech and the "Acid Bath": An Evaluation and Critique of Judge Richard Posner's Economic Interpretation of the First Amendment,* 87 Mich.L.Rev. 499 (1988).

Robert F. Nagel, *Teaching Tolerance,* 75 Calif.L.Rev. 1571 (1987).

Richard A. Posner, *Free Speech in an Economic Perspective,* 20 Suffolk U.L.Rev. 1 (1986).

Joseph Raz, *Free Expression and Personal Identification,* 11 Oxford J.Leg.Stud. 303 (1991).

Pierre Schlag, *Freedom of Speech as Therapy,* 34 UCLA L.Rev. 265 (1986).

Suzanna Sherry, *An Essay Concerning Toleration,* 71 Minn.L.Rev. 963 (1987).

Steven D. Smith, *Skepticism, Tolerance, and Truth in the Theory of Free Expression,* 60 S.Cal.L.Rev. 649 (1987).

David A. Strauss, *Persuasion, Autonomy, and Freedom of Expression,* 91 Colum.L.Rev. 334 (1991).

Harry H. Wellington, *On Freedom of Expression,* 88 Yale L.J. 1105 (1979).

Chapter III

PERVASIVE DOCTRINAL THEMES

A. INTRODUCTION

In this chapter and the next we turn from the history and theory behind free speech law to the doctrine itself. This chapter examines several themes that appear across the spectrum of free speech law. Chapter IV deals with discrete doctrinal issues: defamation, privacy, obscenity, commercial speech, racist speech, and sexual harassment.

The First Amendment appears to state a simple rule in plain language. It provides that "Congress shall make no law ... abridging the freedom of speech, or of the press[.]" This suggests that the Constitution envisions one rule for all kinds of speech (or at most two rules, one for speech and one for the press). It also implies that the rule is unqualified, or to put it in more positive terms, absolute. Justice Black was fond of saying the phrase " 'no law' means no law." [1] Constitutional law books would be much shorter if all this were so. The fact is that First Amendment law is far more complex than the Constitution's command. In this chapter we investigate the nature of the complexity, and ask whether it is necessary.

The word "freedom" in the First Amendment refers to a special kind of right. When we talk about a right to freedom (of speech, religion, or whatever) we are referring to a relation between two different actors (the claimant, the government) and two different actions (the claimant's speech, the government's constraint). There is much that the First Amendment does not say about these variables and the relation between them.

Consider first the claimant—the person whose freedom of speech the Constitution protects. The First Amendment says nothing about such a person. It only says that Congress can't interfere with "the freedom of speech." This, then, is one variable that the courts have to fill in. Can children claim freedom of speech? People who are mentally ill? Corpo-

1. *Justice Black and First Amendment "Absolutes": A Public Interview,* 37 N.Y.U.L.Rev. 549, 553 (1962).

rations? These are difficult questions, because speech has a different meaning and value for these persons than it does for you and me.

On the other side of the fence, the First Amendment speaks not about the government but about "Congress." This suggests that it speaks only to the legislature (a restriction which we should probably also carry over to the Fourteenth Amendment). The suggestion is reenforced by the phrase "shall make no law," since that is an enterprise only legislatures can engage in. But even those who claim to derive a so-called "absolutism" from a literal reading of the text of the First Amendment, like Justice Black, have wanted to apply the free speech clause to the judicial and executive branches. Black concurred in *New York Times Co. v. Sullivan*[2] and *The Pentagon Papers Case*.[3] The former dealt with the common law of defamation, the latter with executive efforts to enjoin disclosure of secret information. If we are going to extend the free speech rule beyond the legislature, however, we will also have to apply it to government activities besides lawmaking. Should it cover injunctions? Choice of law? Appellate review? We will return to this point shortly.

We said that freedom is a relation between two actors and two actions. First Amendment claimants want to engage in the act of speech. But it is not self-evident that "freedom of speech" embraces all and only those natural acts that non-lawyers would identify as speech. (Compare the phrase "festival of dance." Must such a festival exhibit all known varieties of dance? Might it include song and mime?) Perjury, bribery, extortion, and fraud are forms of speech, but they are not covered by the First Amendment. The Securities Act of 1933, which requires prior approval by a government agency (the Securities and Exchange Commission) of the public representations that can be made about many securities that are to be offered for sale, looks for all the world like the very kind of prior restraint that the First Amendment ordinarily prohibits, yet few have argued that in this respect the Securities Act of 1933 is even covered by the First Amendment.[4] Conversely, flags and armbands are not speech, but they are covered. One difficult question in this area has been how to define the category of acts that count as "speech" for First Amendment purposes.

But the issue of protected acts might be more complicated than this. We might want to subdivide the class of protected acts into smaller categories for the purpose of making rules. After all, different types of speech might have different values. (Compare political speech with advertising and pornography.) Or there might be historical paradigms that the law is especially sensitive about (loyalty oaths, seditious libel), and we may want to group speech acts around the paradigm that they most closely resemble. These decisions about the architecture of the First Amendment are controversial and difficult. The complexity of the

2. 376 U.S. 254 (1964).

3. New York Times Co. v. United States, 403 U.S. 713 (1971).

4. But see Aleta G. Estreicher, *Securities Regulation and the First Amendment*, 24 Ga.L.Rev. 223 (1990).

law affects our ability to understand it, and maybe our emotional attachment to its principles. Some also argue that categorization is more likely than other approaches to underprotect speech. Whether it is so or not depends not on language and logic but on a variety of empirical assumptions.

Freedom protects my act of speech against the government's act of interfering: the First Amendment says that Congress shall "make no law ... abridging" my freedom of speech. When we deal with the government's acts we encounter the same kinds of architectural questions we had in dealing with my acts of speech. Indeed, in some ways the structure is more complex: the law divides the class of government acts in several different directions. The great divide separates acts of content regulation from content-neutral acts. The former are viewed by the courts with the utmost suspicion. The latter are viewed more leniently.

This is not the only way of breaking down the act of "abridging." First Amendment doctrine also makes use of a number of functional categories, depending on the branch of government and the type of constraint it is imposing. Rules about overbreadth and vagueness limit the kinds of laws the legislature can enact. Executive officials are forbidden to impose prior restraints on speech; similar rules come into play when the courts issue injunctions. Executive and judicial behavior is also subject to rules of First Amendment due process. The free speech clause may even govern the choice of law rules available to courts.

Up to this point we have discussed only questions of coverage—what actors and what acts the First Amendment applies to. But the right to freedom also embodies a norm of protection—it requires that these variables stand in a certain relation to one another. Suppose that Congress passes a law forbidding people to advocate violent rebellion. The First Amendment undoubtedly covers content regulation of political speech. But how much protection does it afford? When Justice Black said that "'no law' means no law" he meant that within the area it covers, freedom of speech offers absolute protection. Others argue that we must sometimes (or always) balance the value of speech against the need for order (and other things), so that we get a kind of qualified protection.

Choosing among these ideals is not an easy job. One thing that makes it hard is that the decision about protection is related to the many decisions about coverage. We may enervate the First Amendment if we make it do too much work. Suppose that we decline to subdivide speech into categories, so that we must have the same rule for political speech as for commercial advertising. If we then impose a rule of absolute protection, cigarette manufacturers will be able to lie like politicians. Absolutism is more compatible with categorization.

Choosing the right degree of protection is also hard because it depends on empirical assumptions about individual and social psychology. In First Amendment jurisprudence we often hear arguments about slippery slopes. People who would read the speech clause expansively fear that if we start drawing lines we will not be able to stay behind them in future cases, not because our distinctions are arbitrary but because judges and lawmakers will yield to social pressures.

These are some of the issues we address in this chapter. We begin in Section B by looking at protected actors and actions, and at the structure of free speech doctrine: Who has speech rights? What acts are covered? How much protection does the clause afford? What empirical assumptions should the law make? In Sections C and D we turn to themes that concern the government and its actions. Section C examines the special rule against content regulation. Section D addresses the procedural rules that the First Amendment imposes on different branches of government: the rule against prior restraints, First Amendment due process, overbreadth, the scope of appellate review, and so on.

B. THE STRUCTURE OF THE DOCTRINE

In this section we begin by asking why the architecture of the First Amendment is so complicated. Law students are not the only ones who yearn for more simplicity. Courts who apply the law would make fewer mistakes if the law were less complex. And public and private actors would have an easier time conforming their behavior to the contours of the Constitution. Frederick Schauer's article on *Codifying the First Amendment* observes, however, that complexity is neither surprising nor undesirable in free speech law. The law would be simple only if freedom of speech had one central core. But as we saw in Chapter II, it more likely rests on a number of foundational principles, each of which generates its own rules. Daniel Farber and Philip Frickey put the same point metaphorically: we should not think of First Amendment law as a tower built on one foundation stone, but rather as part of a web of mutually reenforcing values. And spider webs are intricate.

We then turn to some of the variables that are implicit in the idea of freedom. Here we focus on two in particular: the claimants and the acts that it protects. (In Sections C and D we deal with the government and acts the First Amendment forbids.) John Garvey's article deals with the first. He explains why it is sometimes difficult to extend freedoms (but not other rights) to claimants like children, or corporations, who are not rational adult individuals. He concludes by offering a reason why we might nevertheless offer a modified variety of free speech to children and the mentally ill.

We then look in some detail at the kinds of speech-acts that the First Amendment protects. William Van Alstyne offers a graphic depiction of the ways in which the law has subdivided the freedom of speech. (His illustrations also show quite neatly how the questions of coverage and protection are interdependent.) Frederick Schauer's *Categories and the First Amendment* addresses the same theme more prosaically. He argues that it is impossible to do First Amendment law without using categories. "Speech" itself is a category, not a natural kind of act. (It excludes perjury, and includes oil paintings.) Nor can we escape making subcategories within the class of "speech"—there are differences between fact and opinion, product promotion and politics, that any sensible legal scheme must account for.

Like Van Alstyne, Schauer finds it difficult to talk about the scope of the term "speech" without also addressing the level of protection afforded by our freedom. His preference for categorization is driven in part by a desire to use strong and clear rules, and to minimize the balancing of interests in individual cases. The subsequent Note refers to several prominent articles that question whether this is possible. Pierre Schlag and Steven Shiffrin contend that balancing is something that courts always can and should do. Melville Nimmer's "definitional balancing" approach is an effort to split the baby. He praises the decision in *New York Times Company v. Sullivan* for holding that defamation of public officials could not be punished unless it was false and malicious. Implicit in that decision is an element of balancing (public officials' reputations get some protection). But it takes place at wholesale, not at retail: courts are not free in individual cases to ask whether *this* harm to reputation outweighs the value of *this* particular speech.

We conclude this section by trying to connect these doctrinal questions to the contexts of their application. We cannot answer questions about the scope of coverage or the risks of balancing simply by paying close attention to the language of the Constitution. Whether (and when) balancing *is* risky, for example, depends on how judges will behave under various conditions. We have to know something about the world to understand the First Amendment. Vincent Blasi argues that when we interpret the free speech clause we should take a pathological perspective on the world—we should make rules that will work in the worst of times. He offers a variety of reasons why we should do this, and then explains how such a perspective will affect the structure of free speech doctrine. It will lead, he says, to a lean, trim First Amendment. The Note following Blasi's article questions this conclusion. Perhaps the First Amendment would survive better in bad times if it looked more like the center for the Green Bay Packers. Frederick Schauer's final essay on *Slippery Slopes* points out that this familiar style of argument, like First Amendment doctrine generally, rests on empirical assumptions that we have to investigate before accepting.

FREDERICK SCHAUER, CODIFYING THE FIRST AMENDMENT: NEW YORK v. FERBER

1982 Sup.Ct.Rev. 285, 308–313, 315.

[In this article Schauer discusses *New York v. Ferber*,[a] a case in which the Supreme Court held that child pornography—including mate-

a. 458 U.S. 747 (1982).

rial that would not be obscene under *Miller* [b] standards—was a separate category of speech unprotected by the First Amendment.]

* * * The rules relating to child pornography now take their place alongside the equally distinct rules relating to obscenity, defamation, advocacy of illegal conduct, invasion of privacy, fighting words, symbolic speech, and offensive speech. Moreover, each of these areas contains its own corpus of subrules, principles, categories, qualifications, and exceptions. There are also special principles for particular contexts, such as government employment, the public forum, and electronic broadcasting, and in addition we have the pervasive tools of First Amendment analysis, such as chilling effect, prior restraint, vagueness, overbreadth, and the least restrictive alternative. Finally, there is the additional overlay of numerous broad approaches to a First Amendment issue. When we take all of this together it becomes clear that the First Amendment is becoming increasingly intricate, which has prompted one scholar to observe pejoratively that First Amendment doctrine is beginning to resemble the Internal Revenue Code.[133] The metaphor rings true, and maybe we are moving toward codification of the First Amendment. Whether this is cause for concern requires a closer look.

In talking about "codification," neither I nor anyone else is suggesting that the First Amendment itself should be codified. It is just fine as written—brief, elegant, and desirably vague, while still eloquently suggesting great strength and breadth. Nor would we want to organize the surrounding doctrine in a form that could be literally codified in a way that the Internal Revenue Code is. That approach would sacrifice too much flexibility for only a slight increase in precision.

It does not follow from the foregoing, however, that First Amendment doctrine should be as simple and vague as the Amendment itself. The arguments for textual simplicity do not apply with equal or even any force to doctrinal simplicity. A characteristic feature of American law is drafting simple textual instruments with the expectation that courts will use the open-ended text as the touchstone for creating, in modified common law style, a complex and comprehensive doctrinal structure. This feature pervades not only constitutional law but American statutory law as well.[135]

That tradition alone suggests that great complexity in First Amendment doctrine is no cause for surprise. Moreover, taking *Schenck* as the starting point,[136] we have now had sixty-four years' experience with First Amendment problems. As time goes on situations repeat themselves. We are then more able to discern patterns, and these patterns enable us to group recurring features into legal rules and categories. The more we

b. Miller v. California, 413 U.S. 15 (1973).

133. Conversation with William Van Alstyne.

135. Examples of simple and vague statutory language that have generated enormously complex doctrines include Section 1 of the Sherman Antitrust Act, 15 U.S.C. § 1 (1976), and the Securities and Exchange Commission's Rule 10b–5. 17 C.F.R. § 240.10b–5(a) (1981).

136. Schenck v. United States, 249 U.S. 47 (1919). * * *

have seen, the less likely we are to be surprised, and open-ended flexibility becomes progressively less important. In the face of this, we must shift the burden and ask whether there is any reason for treating the First Amendment specially in terms of doctrinal simplicity.

The desire for simplicity in First Amendment doctrine is often expressed in terms of a search for "coherence." [138] * * * But coherence need not produce simplicity. An intricate doctrinal structure might still fit together like a jigsaw puzzle, with each principle fitting neatly into the exceptions in another. But that approach requires enormous foresight to produce such precision in rules designed to govern the future. A coherent but complex doctrinal structure, devoid of gaps or inconsistencies, attempts to follow the model of a pure civil law system. Attempting to formulate such a doctrinal system suffers from the same deficiency that has led the pure civil law model to be only a futile dream; no matter how carefully we define our concepts, new situations will arise that just do not fit. First Amendment doctrine serves the normative function of guiding future action, and we cannot incorporate into our standards intended to guide the future every contingency because we just do not know what they will be. Because "we are men, not gods," we can at best imperfectly predict the future, and the uncertainty of the human condition places insurmountable obstacles in the way of formulating a coherent and complete system of highly specific norms that will cover every situation likely to arise. *Ferber* itself is a perfect example, because the phenomenon of child pornography is so new that it would have been impossible to predict even ten years ago. And there is no reason to believe that ten years from now we will not be presented with First Amendment issues that we have no way of foreseeing today.

[C]oherence is * * * commonly urged as a simple and unitary principle of the First Amendment,[143] with more specific rules and doctrines being no more than applications of the one unifying principle. If the First Amendment is taken "really" to mean x, and x is simple, we have a coherent principle by definition. But will any single principle help in deciding cases? One would think, after all, that that is a major purpose of the exercise.

A single principle, defined at a high level of abstraction, certainly assists in terms of flexibility. An abstract single principle will be able to accommodate almost any foreseeable and unforeseeable change in the nature of First Amendment problems. But that very flexibility is a crippling weakness, for unitary abstract principles can also accommodate any more particularized intuition of the designer or applier of the principle. Use of a single principle to deal with all of our problems produces application that is more likely to be conclusory than principled.

138. *E.g.,* * * * Redish, *The Value of Free Speech*, 130 U.Pa.L.Rev. 591, 592 (1982) * * *.

143. See note 138 *supra*. See also Baker, *Scope of the First Amendment Freedom of Speech*, 25 U.C.L.A.L.Rev. 964 (1978); Richards, *Free Speech and Obscenity Law: Toward a Moral Theory of the First Amendment*, 123 U.Pa.L.Rev. 45 (1974). * * *

As an example, let us take the single principle of "self-realization," which at the moment is enjoying a good run in the arena of First Amendment theory.[144] Faced with the problem in *First National Bank of Boston v. Bellotti*[145] whether to grant First Amendment protection to corporate speech, one self-realization theorist has argued against the result in that case because self-realization is a right of individuals and does not apply to corporations.[146] But another, starting from the same principle, has reached the opposite conclusion by emphasizing the self-realization goals served by the receipt of information.[147] Similarly, self-realization could produce opposite results in *Gertz*,[148] depending on whether we focused, on the one hand, on the effect on self-realization of being the subject of false statements or, on the other hand, on the self-realization of the defamer in being unfettered in his communicative acts. * * *

The problem of excess abstraction does not surround every single-principle theory. A sufficiently narrow principle could serve the function of influencing if not completely determining the decision of actual cases. Meiklejohn's original theory was both narrow and single-principled,[150] a feature shared by other political interpretations of the First Amendment.[151] But a precise single principle must be consequently narrow, and the problem then is that much seems to have been left out of the First Amendment.

But why must we assume that the First Amendment has a unitary essence? The First Amendment might instead be the simplifying rubric under which a number of different values are subsumed. We wish to prevent government from silencing its critics, but we wish as well to prevent an imposed uniformity in literary and artistic taste, to preserve open inquiry in the sciences and other academic fields, and to foster wide-ranging argument on moral, religious, and ethical questions. This list is representative rather than exhaustive, but it shows that the concept of freedom of speech may not have one central core. And each distinct but interrelated foundational principle may generate its own rules of application. * * *

* * *

Ferber reflects the Court's continuing recognition of the diversity of speech and the diversity of state interests. It is unrealistic to expect that one test, one category, or one analytical approach can reflect this diversity. As the First Amendment is broadened to include the hitherto

---

144. *E.g.*, Baker, note 143 *supra;* Redish, note 138 *supra;* Richards, note 143 *supra.* * * *

145. 435 U.S. 765 (1978).

146. Baker, *Realizing Self–Realization: Corporate Political Expenditures and Redish's The Value of Free Speech,* 130 U.Pa. L.Rev. 646 (1982).

147. Redish, *Self–Realization, Democracy, and Freedom of Expression: A Reply to Professor Baker,* 130 U.Pa.L.Rev. 678 (1982).

148. Gertz v. Robert Welch, Inc., 418 U.S. 323 (1974).

150. Meiklejohn, [Political Freedom (1960).]

151. See Bork, [*Neutral Principles and Some First Amendment Problems,* 47 Ind. L.J. 1 (1971).]

uncovered, diversity within the First Amendment increases. In addressing different problems separately, the Court is doing nothing more than following the common law model. Contract and tort are distinct because they address different concerns, and changes in the world and the broadening of the First Amendment make it likely that it will encompass problems as diverse as the difference between tort and contract. A unitary approach is likely to be both counterproductive and futile.

DANIEL A. FARBER & PHILIP P. FRICKEY, PRACTICAL REASON AND THE FIRST AMENDMENT

34 UCLA L.Rev. 1615, 1639–1643, 1645 (1987).

In purporting to answer first amendment questions by deductive reasoning from foundational principles, first amendment theorists are consistent with "the rationalist ethos of our times."[114] The pitfalls of this approach are aptly described by Robert Nozick:

> Philosophers often seek to deduce their total view from a few basic principles, showing how all follows from their intuitively based axioms. The rest of the philosophy then strikes readers as depending upon these principles. One brick is piled upon another to produce a tall philosophical tower, one brick wide. When the bottom brick crumbles or is removed, all topples, burying those insights that were independent of the starting point.[115]

* * * [T]he search for the foundational first-amendment "brick" has been unavailing so far. If so many thoughtful legal commentators have failed to identify *the* foundational value that can support unified first amendment theory, the prospects for future efforts seem dubious. The alternative * * * requires us to abandon the quest for a foundational brick. But without a foundation, is a viable first amendment possible?

We propose an alternative view of the first amendment's normative status. Rather than thinking of free speech as one level in a hierarchy of values, it may be better to think of it as part of a web of mutually reinforcing values. One value is "self-realization." Professor Redish is correct[a] that this value supports both democracy and free speech. But the converse is also true. Democracy and free speech also provide reasons to embrace self-realization: people who have freedom to develop their own unique lives will make better citizens of a democracy; and such people will produce a livelier, more exciting body of expression. Thus, democracy and free speech are both connected to self-realization, and the lines run in both directions. To complete the triangle, democracy and free speech are also connected directly. Democracy requires at

---

114. Kronman, *Alexander Bickel's Philosophy of Prudence,* 94 Yale L.J. 1567, 1571 (1985).

115. R. Nozick, Philosophical Explanations 3 (1981).

a. Farber and Frickey refer earlier to Martin Redish's book Freedom of Expression: A Critical Analysis (1984), which argues that self-realization is the ultimate value underlying the First Amendment.

least freedom for core political speech. On the other hand, one reason to support democracy is that democracies are much less likely to engage in widespread censorship than dictatorships.

Democracy, free speech, and self-realization all are supported in other ways by a host of other values. For example, free speech is helpful to scientific research—look at Galileo or at the Lysenko affair in the Soviet Union. One can support self-realization for psychiatric reasons (it makes for saner people), for social reasons (it is the foundation for a deeper, richer community life), or for the classical "liberal" reasons based on individual autonomy. In particular, free speech is itself a value with its own appeal. It can be considered good in and of itself. Other related values acquire additional strength because of their relationship to it.

In short, we don't have a tower of values, with free speech somewhere toward the middle, and more basic values underneath. Instead, we have a web of values, collectively comprising our understanding of how people should live. Foundationalism errs in seeking to reduce the complex relationships among our values to a linear arrangement in which a few values have privileged status as fundamental.

* * *

In our view, a strong social institution should not rest on a uniquely determined justification. If it does, it will gain the support of only those segments of society that agree with that justification. It is far stronger to have multiple justifications. [Consider, for example,] the foundation for our belief in democracy. [There are actually] a lot of unrelated reasons to support democracy. First, it spreads power in a more egalitarian way than any alternative. Second, in practice, it has proved less subject to horrible abuses than nondemocratic societies. No modern democracy has murdered millions of its own citizens; compare the leading nondemocratic alternatives: Hitler, Stalin, and the Maoist Cultural Revolution. Another possible utilitarian justification is that democracy fits best with market economies, which are more productive than state controlled economies. Furthermore, democracy fosters self-realization * * *. Quite a different kind of reason is that democracy is the kind of government we happen to have, and we should support our society's basic institutional practices as a way of affirming our group identity. Different individuals are likely to be attracted to these various justifications, although most of us will find at least several appealing. An institutional practice with this kind of diverse normative support is much more likely to gain widespread social allegiance. Analytical tidiness is less important than social robustness.

The first amendment illustrates the benefits of having diverse normative support for a legal principle. Some people may support it because they are concerned about political censorship, some because they are libertarians, some because they want vitality in the arts, some because it's the American thing to do * * *. Free speech is a powerful idea precisely because it appeals to so many diverse values. To demonstrate that commitment to free speech logically entailed adherence to some single value (like "self-realization") would actually weaken it. This is perhaps just another example of the web versus tower idea. Here, the importance of the web is that it provides a basis for broader social consensus. The tower is more vulnerable, not only to logical refutations of the kind Nozick is concerned about, but also to social dissension.

This preference for practical belief over grand deduction seems especially appropriate in legal theory. Lest it lose its vital human component, law must be concerned not only with the applicability of legal rules, but also their appropriateness in particular circumstances. Moreover, legal outcomes cannot survive if they are incompatible with the webs of belief of the community in general and the legal community in particular. * * *

* * *

* * * In place of [the] search[ ] for *the* right answer, we propose eclectic—but by no means unfamiliar—methodologies to construct the best answer available. A supportable answer may sometimes descend from deductive analysis alone. More often such an answer will ascend from a combination of arguments, none of which standing alone would constitute a sufficient justification. Such "supporting arguments" are "rather like the legs of a chair and unlike the links of a chain." [128]

JOHN H. GARVEY, FREEDOM AND CHOICE IN CONSTITUTIONAL LAW

94 Harv.L.Rev. 1756, 1757–1759, 1762, 1768–1776 (1981).

THE STRUCTURE OF CONSTITUTIONAL PROTECTIONS

There is a critical distinction between constitutional freedoms and other constitutional protections: A freedom protects from state-imposed constraint individual choices to perform or not to perform certain actions, and to pursue or not to pursue certain conditions of character. Freedom of speech protects both the choice to speak and the choice to be silent[.] [3] * * * By contrast, although other constitutional protections protect a certain action or condition against state interference, they may not permit a claimant to choose to pursue an opposite action or condition. For example, the seventh amendment protects common law suitors with twenty dollars at stake from governmental deprivation of the "right of trial by jury." The amendment does not guarantee suitors the option *not* to have a jury trial; it would permit the government to require jury trials in all cases. The fourth amendment "right to be secure ... against unreasonable searches and seizures" does not protect an eccentric interest in a condition of insecurity.

---

128. R. Summers, Instrumentalism and American Legal Theory 156 (1982).

3. *See* Wooley v. Maynard, 430 U.S. 705 (1977); West Va. State Bd. of Educ. v. Barnette, 319 U.S. 624 (1943).

Because they protect choice, freedoms produce by their very nature greater unpredictability than do other constitutional protections. For example, granting children the freedom to vote would entail the unique and unpredictable cost of introducing a largely irrational influence into the electoral process. By contrast, although extending the ban against unreasonable searches and seizures to incompetents would involve social costs, the incompetence of some of those thereby protected would not impose any *special* costs.

The elements of choice and unpredictability create obvious difficulties for the ascription of liberties to individuals incapable of making rational choices. The reason is that the rationales thought to justify protection of the various constitutional freedoms presuppose that the claimant can make rational decisions that will not result in significant social or individual harm. The Supreme Court has said that freedom of speech is guaranteed, in part, to achieve the goal of protecting "the free discussion of governmental affairs." [8] That protection in turn rests on two principles. First, the speaker has a right to participate in decisions that affect him. Second, the public deserves unrestricted access to information so that decisions arrived at democratically will be made intelligently. Both principles, however, make certain assumptions about the characteristics of the speaker. The first assumes a moral and rational being capable of self-government, an ability that voting laws do not attribute to children or to the mentally disabled. The second, though imposing no explicit limitations on the character of the speaker, at least supposes that his speech might possibly assist democratic decisionmaking; one who is severely retarded will only rarely offer such assistance.

The other principal reason for the guarantee of freedom of speech is its intrinsic value "as a means of self-expression, self-realization, and self-fulfillment." [13] It might seem contradictory for society to sanctify the speaker's autonomy while at the same time evaluating his competence in order to determine whether he has a right to speak. But I doubt that we really believe the two are incompatible. We let adults utter obscenities,[14] but we don't let children hear them,[15] however satisfying the exchange might be to both in their separate ways. The reason is that we recognize a right to autonomy only for persons within a certain range, a range defined by the ability to make rational choices about how one's self ought to be expressed, realized, and fulfilled. Thus, as the individual's capacity for moral and rational choice diminishes, state action restricting speech is less likely to be seen as a restraint on freedom.

* * *

8. First Nat'l Bank v. Bellotti, 435 U.S. 765, 776–77 (1978) (quoting Mills v. Alabama, 384 U.S. 214, 218 (1966)).

13. First Nat'l Bank v. Bellotti, 435 U.S. 765, 804 (1978) (White, J., dissenting). *See also id.* at 777 n. 12 (opinion of the Court).

14. Cohen v. California, 403 U.S. 15 (1971).

15. FCC v. Pacifica Foundation, 438 U.S. 726 (1978).

Any argument, then, that incompetents are entitled to claim constitutional freedoms encounters two serious obstacles, one practical and one theoretical. The first is the unpredictable social and individual consequences that may result from the exercise of irrational choice; the second is the difficulty of explaining why we should ascribe, to those unable to choose, liberties that are valued because of the protection they offer for choice. Despite these problems, I believe it is nonetheless possible to ascribe constitutional freedoms to persons with a diminished capacity for choice. * * *

* * *

AN INSTRUMENTAL CONCEPTION OF FREEDOM

If liberty involves the making of rational choices, its intelligent exercise demands practice. This idea is at the core of one way of justifying liberty for those [who are not rational adults.] According to this instrumental conception, the right to freedom may depend on the ability to choose, but acquiring the ability to choose also depends on the exercise of freedom. We can thus justify the ascription of freedoms to one presently without the capacity for choice because the individual's development into a mature and healthy person depends in large measure on the prior recognition of liberties. * * *

Over nearly the whole range of "speech" activities, the courts have imposed paternalistic restraints on the free speech of children in order to advance their health, education, and morals. A minor's freedom to peddle even religious ideas may be limited in order to avoid "emotional excitement and psychological or physical injury." [54] The child's right of access to ideas, at least those that are vulgar or pornographic, can be specially limited because a state might rationally conclude that such matter impairs the child's "ethical and moral development." [55] Such cases permit states to "protect" children by preventing them from doing things adults have a constitutional right to do. Perhaps the most severe imposition on the child's right of free expression is made in the interest of education: the requirement that youngsters hear what the state seeks to communicate through its compulsory school system. * * *

Parallel paternalistic limitations on freedom of expression exist in the institutional mental health system. Although the logistics of running a large institution obviously necessitate some restrictions, in many cases the restraint is justified primarily in terms of the patient's own interests. Statutes frequently permit censorship of incoming mail to promote the patient's welfare or to control the receipt of possibly harmful substances. Similarly paternalistic reasons are given for permitting qualification of visitation privileges, even when it is unnecessary to protect the interests of others. Even the availability of writing

54. Prince v. Massachusetts, 321 U.S. 158, 170 (1944). * * *

55. Ginsberg v. New York, 390 U.S. 629, 641 (1968) (quoting N.Y. Penal Law 484–e (current version at N.Y. Penal Law § 235.20–.22 (McKinney 1980))); see FCC v. Pacifica Foundation, 438 U.S. 726, 749–50 (1978) (vulgarity).

materials, though guaranteed in some states by statute, may be restricted to prevent injuries from pens or pencils.

Both courts and commentators often suggest that the interest of the state as parens patriae in restricting the freedom of incompetents is weighed against a right to free speech that is equal in scope whether the claimant is a child, a mentally ill person, or a healthy adult. That conception is misguided. Far from simply overriding an incompetent individual's freedom, we implicitly deny the freedom of incompetents when we impose paternalistic restraints upon them. * * * Paternalistic restrictions can be justified only on the assumption that the state is best able to choose on the individual's behalf, that is to say, only on the assumption that the individual's choice in the matter in question is not entitled to the same respect, and to the same constitutional protection, as the preference that the majority establishes for him.

If freedom of speech has to be justified in more restrictive terms for children and the mentally ill, what warrants attributing it to them at all, and what form would it take? * * *

1. *Self-Government.* One part of the instrumental justification of freedom of speech for children is that liberty assists their development into mature adults capable of democratic self-government. The Supreme Court has clearly endorsed this view in *Tinker v. Des Moines Independent Community School District.*[69] *Tinker* held that high school and junior high school students, aged thirteen to sixteen, were deprived of their freedom of speech when they were suspended for wearing black armbands to protest the Vietnam War. * * * [T]he Court thought free speech important not because Washington waited on the outcome of the school's foreign policy debate, but because free speech played a role in the students' own development: *"The Nation's future depends upon leaders trained through wide exposure* to that robust exchange of ideas which discovers truth 'out of a multitude of tongues, [rather] than through any kind of authoritative selection.'"

The primarily instrumental character of the child's free speech rights means that these rights need not be protected as zealously as those of adults. For example, prior restraints have long been seen as the cardinal sin against adult freedom of speech, in part because "[i]t is vital to the operation of democratic government that the citizens have facts and ideas on important issues before them. A delay of even a day or two may be of crucial importance in some instances."[73] Such restrictions are widely accepted when imposed on school newspapers, though; the justification demanded is nothing more compelling than a reasonable likelihood of disruption to school processes. The explanation is surely that the significance of student expression in ensuring the right outcome counts for far less than it would in the adult world, and the instrumental value of immediate publication—the educational benefits that are lost

---

69. 393 U.S. 503 (1969).

73. Carroll v. President & Comm'rs of Princess Anne, 393 U.S. 175, 182 (1968) [.]

when restraint or prepublication review is allowed—is outweighed by the significance of the pedagogical process that might be disrupted.

* * *

2. *Self-Realization.* The second significant value attributed to freedom of speech in the adult model is the key role it plays in the process by which an individual defines himself. This position is less plausible with regard to children, since they can hardly be expected to develop their natural capacities in a socially acceptable fashion when allowed to act without interference. Therefore, we are willing to impose significant limitations on the freedom of children to express themselves. We do not want to risk having too many people grow up to define themselves as liars or bigots; as a society we are not above bending the twig a little, though we won't tamper with the tree. But this does not mean that, for anyone not a fully competent adult, freedom of expression is completely subordinate to some social blueprint for the ideal citizen. Instead, we permit children to express themselves—within limits—with the instrumental hope that they will grow up able to appreciate the intrinsic satisfactions of self-expression. Society has an interest in encouraging autonomy and diversity, and freedom of speech for children serves several values important to that end. Courts often note the value of freedom in teaching children the satisfactions that can result from expression of their own individuality; in ensuring the development of skills used for rational discourse; in instilling an appreciation of how speech can affect, assist, and injure others; and in providing for the receipt of information important to the child's development.

An illustration of how these values are implemented is the treatment of racial insults in schools. Though face-to-face racial slurs could probably be forbidden for both adults and children, courts have tolerated restrictions even on wearing Confederate flags in the interest of avoiding racial disputes in the schools. Such control, greater than anything we would permit over adults, is prompted by the greater sensitivity of children to racial disparagement. But it can only be tolerated if we see the self-realization functions served by the speech of children as instrumental rather than intrinsic. Consider the first of those instrumental values: teaching children the satisfaction that can result from expressions of individuality. Expression of racial discrimination doubtless serves that end, in a perverse fashion, but precisely because it is perverse, we regulate children's speech, lest they develop into adults who define themselves as racists. With regard to the second and third of the functions served by the child's free speech right—the development of skills and of an appreciation of the impact of speech on others—it makes sense to conclude that those are lessons that may be learned another time when the consequences for the listener are not as severe.

As with children, recovery of a healthy personality in the case of the mentally ill does not necessarily occur without regulation. That being so, the individual's self-definition or realization through expression or receipt of information may play only an instrumental role in the patient's recovery, rather than be assigned an ultimate value as a good in itself. Thus, the statutes of most states provide that the communication and visitation rights of patients may be restricted "for the medical welfare of the patient."

Some of the instrumental purposes served by granting freedom of speech to children are already fulfilled in the case of the institutionalized mentally ill, whose language skills are more likely to be well developed. Free speech rights can nonetheless serve an important instrumental function in aiding the eventual readaptation of the mentally ill individual to society. The * * * total control exercised by an institution over its inmates fosters a dependence that is itself an obstacle to social readjustment. The surest means of avoiding such institutional dependence is to grant the patient the greatest possible autonomy consistent with the purposes of commitment.

WILLIAM VAN ALSTYNE, A GRAPHIC REVIEW OF THE FREE SPEECH CLAUSE

70 Calif.L.Rev. 107, 110–111, 113–115, 121–
125, 128–133, 136–137, 139–142 (1982).

I

THE LITERAL CONSTRUCTION

In respect to freedom of speech, the first amendment is exceptionally crisp and unambiguous. Thus, it provides: *Congress shall make no law abridging the freedom of speech.* Most of the principal affirmative restrictions on government power are far more ambiguous or equivocal. For instance, the fourth amendment protects "the right of the people to be secure in their persons, houses, papers, and effects" only against "*unreasonable* searches and seizures." The fifth amendment assures each person that he or she will not be deprived of life, liberty, or property, without "*due* process." The eighth amendment prohibits only such bail or such fines as are "*excessive*" and forbids only "*cruel and unusual* punishments."

* * *

The first amendment is strikingly different. On its face, it is both unequivocal and absolute. It requires no arcane learning to understand the clear and plain meaning of "Congress," "no law," "abridging," or "speech." To "abridge" means not merely to forbid altogether, but to curtail or to lessen. And the laws forbidden to Congress are not merely such as "unreasonably" abridge speech (*cf.,* the fourth amendment), nor are they laws that are "excessive" abridgements of speech. The imperative is simple, straightforward, complete, and absolute: *Congress shall make no law abridging the freedom of speech.*

* * *

* * * A suitable graphic of the first amendment might therefore look like this:

```
┌─────────────────────────┐
│                         │
│                         │
│                         │
│      100% Protected     │
│                         │
│   FREEDOM OF SPEECH     │
│                         │
│                         │
│                         │
│                         │
└─────────────────────────┘
```

Acts of
Congress

There are no lines, no intersecting points, no shaded areas of less protected or of unprotected speech.   The graphic, though singularly uninteresting, is also perfect and inviolate.

II

"THE" FREEDOM OF SPEECH

Despite the simplicity and logical force of a literal interpretation of the first amendment, it has never commanded a majority of the Supreme Court.   Primarily it has failed against the pressures of irresistible counterexamples [.]   * * *

Possibly the best known counterexample is a variation of an instance used by Mr. Justice Holmes: a person knowingly and falsely shouting "Fire!" in a crowded theater for the perverse joy of anticipating the spectacle of others being trampled to death as the panicked crowd surges toward the theater exit.   The counterexample could as well be: the mere oral statement of one person to another, offering to pay $5,000 for the murder of the offeror's spouse; a Congressman's bribe solicitation; an interstate manufacturer's deliberately false and misleading commercial advertisements; a witness committing perjury in the course of a trial; or a member of the public interrupting (by speaking) someone else already speaking at a city council meeting.   * * *

* * *

The objection of the irresistible counterexample thus upsets one's confidence in an absolute freedom of speech, despite the singular language of the first amendment itself.   And, on closer examination, even the language of the first amendment may provide *explicit* accommodation (*i.e.*, exclusion) of an indefinite number of these counterexamples. Specifically, it provides (merely) that: Congress shall make no law abridging *the* freedom of speech.

In complete fidelity to that language, a graphic depiction of the first amendment might look like this:

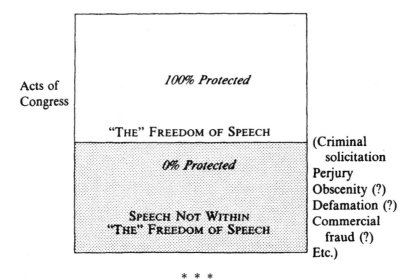

     *   *   *

IV

THE BOUNDED SCOPE OF "THE FREEDOM" OF SPEECH

The logical force of the second [graphic lies in its] accommodation of irresistible counterexamples and almost literal consistency with the complete language of the first amendment. However, there is an alternative equally responsive to both concerns.   *   *   *

This alternative falls back on the language of the first amendment to embrace the common-sense impression with which we started: *all* speech is protected from abridging laws made by Congress without exception. That the speech at issue is a fragment of perjured testimony does not make it any less speech nor remove it from the amendment. *   *   *

The instance of the irresistible counterexample is met [by a] more general definition of "the freedom of speech" that Congress may make no law abridging. [This] is a reference to some scope of freedom implied by the very term "the freedom" and, logically, therefore, a scope of freedom bounded. In short, it stands not as a synonym for complete freedom, but as a contrast with complete freedom. "The freedom" of speech that Congress may make no law abridging is therefore that degree, or that extent, of freedom of speech that Congress may make no law abridging.

     *   *   *

     *   *   * A graphic depiction of the first amendment thus described might look like this:

"THE FREEDOM" OF SPEECH	SPEECH BEYOND "THE FREEDOM"
100% Protected	*0% Protected*

All Kinds of Speech

Note, then, these several features. First, *all* speech is encompassed by the amendment, whether it be talk about the weather, one's choice of elected representatives, or procuring heroin. Second, "the freedom" of speech refers to a latitude, rather than to a subject or a kind of speech. Third, the exclusive question in each case is merely whether the utterances were within that latitude of freedom of speech comprising "the freedom" of speech that Congress may make no law abridging. And the irresistible counterexample is accounted for insofar as it may be expected to fall outside the latitude of "the freedom" of speech, albeit the referent for determining whether it does is not provided by the first amendment itself and necessarily, therefore, requires the judiciary to look elsewhere.

To a considerable extent, this view of the first amendment has not only characterized a substantial number of Supreme Court decisions, but also dominated the entire first amendment case law. Indeed, the main struggle has been among contending views respecting the appropriate test according to which speech is held to be either within *"the freedom"* of speech protected from abridging laws, or beyond that freedom and therefore unaffected by the first amendment. A leading example is the following formulation proposed by Judge Learned Hand and approved by a Supreme Court majority in 1951 in *Dennis v. United States:* "In each case [courts] must ask whether the gravity of the 'evil,' discounted by its improbability, justifies such invasion of free speech as is necessary to avoid the danger." [25] * * * The particular formulation looks like this:

25. 341 U.S. 494, 510 (1951).

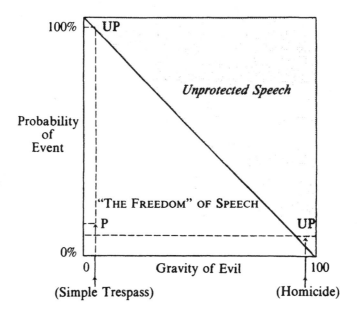

The vertical axis is graduated from zero probability to absolute certainty. The horizontal axis is graduated from evils of zero gravity to those of absolute gravity. The diagonal line cutting across the graphic marks the boundary of that scope of speech within "the freedom" of speech that Congress may make no law abridging. All cases to the left of the line are protected. All cases to the right of the line are unprotected.

[Suppose the] legislature adopted a law to discourage the inciden[ce] of trespass by making it a minor crime for any person to advocate, urge, counsel, incite, or teach to others the desirability of trespassing.

The law thus punishes speech. But it is not on that account either valid or invalid, for its validity requires that in each case we discount the gravity of the evil (which is not the speech but rather an act of trespass) by its improbability. Since the evil (simple trespass) is a comparatively trivial evil, nothing less than virtual certainty that it would occur unless the speech were forbidden will suffice to justify proceeding against the speaker. * * * Most such cases are thus "P" (protected) cases on the graph. Very few will be "UP" (unprotected).

The converse is true for homicide. The killing of people being a plain instance of what legislatures may rightly consider a grave evil, speech foreseeably engendering a bare possibility of that consequence becomes at once punishable. Virtually all such speech save, perhaps, utterances one may make aloud in his bedroom with no one about is thus "UP" (unprotected). * * *

* * *

V

THE CLEAR AND PRESENT DANGER THRESHOLD

There are nonetheless objectionable features to the Learned Hand formulation quite apart from the quintessential difficulty that it, too, compels even conscientious courts to look outside the first amendment to resolve such imponderables as what evils shall be deemed of more-or-less gravity than others in measuring the scope of "the freedom" of speech. For example, when the evil to be avoided is serious, then, as shown on the graphic, the test virtually dispenses with any probability requirement as a precondition of punishing or of preventing speech. Thus, a large (and uncertain) category of speech cases is treated not significantly differently than in the second graphic in which perjury, criminal solicitation, and obscenity were treated as kinds of speech *per se* not within "the" freedom of speech. While that apparent conformance is exceedingly helpful and comforting in one respect (*i.e.*, it reconciles those cases), in another respect it poses a severe problem.

According to that earlier graphic, "political" speech was not among the outcast kinds of speech. To the contrary, it was altogether within the 100% protected field. But the Hand approach precludes this easy (and protective?) definitional address to the first amendment. For the question according to the Hand test is not simply whether the speech in question involved politics or government in some generic, loose sense; rather, the focus is not on the speech at all, it is on the alleged evil to be avoided by outlawing the speech.

The *Dennis* case is itself an example of the resulting problem. Eugene Dennis was prosecuted under the Smith Act for "conspiring" to "organize" a group (the American Communist Party) whose purposes included teaching the doctrine of the propriety of force and violence as a means to "overthrow" the government of the United States. Since the deaths of any number of persons ranks as a very grave evil, and since Congress has the right to seek to prevent that grave evil, suppression of speech under the formula is permitted by the first amendment on the most meager probability that, unless suppressed, the speech *might* bring about that evil * * *.

[But] so long as there is no discernible prospect of serious harm actually occurring, the freedom to state grievances passionately and angrily, protesting not merely the existing government but expressing a desperate feeling that nothing but violence exists to modify that government, may be important speech. It raises the unspoken questions. It makes visible a despair that needs to be known. It demands answers from others that more genteel suggestions and less threatening discourse may fail to stimulate. It provokes to be sure. But the *Dennis* formulation ignores these central first amendment values because it permits such utterances to be treated like furtively made offers to hire a murder.
* * *

A formulation to cope with this complaint would set a minimum probability below which the alleged danger feared from this kind of speech would *never* be sufficient to justify punishing the speech. It might, for instance, look like this:

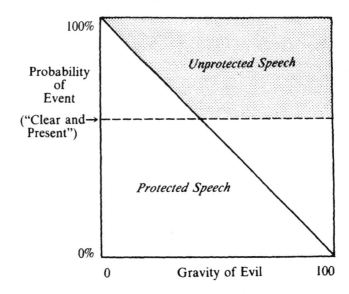

Under this view, although violence itself may be passionately advocated, when the feared danger lacks clarity and imminence, such speech remains within the latitude of speech that defines "the freedom" of speech. And this, of course, is the * * * substantially more protective formula [found in Justice Holmes's opinion in *Schenck v. United States* [41] and in *Brandenburg v. Ohio.*[42]]

* * *

Even the addition of "clear and present danger" to the formulation * * * leaves the graphic dramatically incomplete. There remains virtually unlimited elbowroom for legislatures to do in two steps what they might not do in one. If a given kind of detested speech does not generate a constitutionally sufficient danger of one kind of evil to rationalize its abridgment, the legislature may simply describe as an evil something the detested kind of speech *is* likely to bring about. The speech may then, constitutionally, be abridged. For instance, the street corner distribution of Communist handbills may be too remote from any likelihood of inducing violence against the government to suppress on that account. But their distribution under the circumstances is nonetheless very likely to produce litter. Litter in the public streets is assuredly something a legislature may deem an evil. A flat prohibition of any handbill distribution may, under the circumstances, be necessary to avoid the danger of that litter. The result would be no more handbills, Communist or otherwise.

---

41. 249 U.S. 47, 52 (1919) * * *.   **42.** 395 U.S. 444, 447 (1969) * * *.

The Holmes formulation, in its original terms, plainly embraces this outcome since it requires no determination of the gravity of the evil. [But the] first amendment forbids sanctions against speech except as necessary to avoid "serious" evils. The appropriate graphic looks like this:

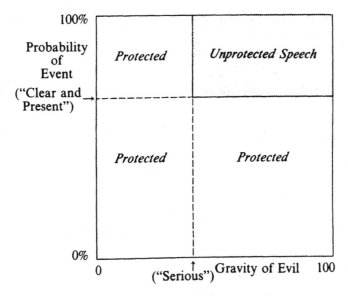

Thus, Mr. Justice Brandeis suggested in 1927: "Prohibition of free speech and assembly is a measure so stringent that it would be inappropriate as the means for averting a relatively trivial harm to society."[44] It followed that a certain degree of litter, unwelcome noise, mental perturbation, violated anonymity, and degraded reputation are withdrawn from the general police power to protect against that latitude of free speech contemplated by "the freedom" of speech.

* * *

VI

RECOMBINANT GRAPHICS

The conundrum of the irresistible counterexample is a difficult one, as we have seen. In fact, it is so powerful a device that it mocks virtually every effort, including the Holmes–Brandeis graphic, to render the first amendment foolproof against the risks of discretionary interpretation. That graphic demands that in *every* case there be a showing of an actual, clear, and present danger that a serious evil imminently lurks in an utterance punishable by law. * * * An offer of bribery to an honest official who testifies it never entered his mind to accept (and who, rather, at once reported the offer to the police) is not punishable, nor is the act of the lucky person who unwittingly solicits an undercover agent

44. Whitney v. California, 274 U.S. 357, 377 (1927).

to murder his spouse, rather than a gun-for-hire. No successful prosecution for criminal attempt in any of these cases? That must logically follow unless we cope with the counterexample by pretending that these are not instances of speech at all [.]

* * * By combining two graphics we have already set forth, * * * we can see how the problem might be met straightforwardly:

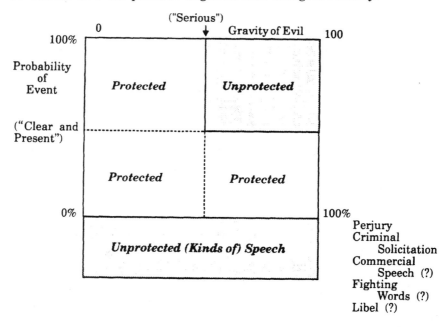

The description is a composite of the second graphic (certain *kinds* of speech are wholly unprotected), plus the developed Holmes–Brandeis graphic. It handles our problem, it has an administrable logic, and it fits the syntax of the first amendment. The language of "the freedom" of speech that Congress may make no law abridging, in this view, may be a qualifying phrase that communicates two considerations rather than a single distinction. It may mean both a delimitation of *kinds* of speech entitled to that latitude of speech constituting "the freedom" of speech and a certain latitude or *scope* of speech as reported in the *Dennis* formulation or as in the Holmes–Brandeis formulation. As a highly plausible matter, moreover, such an understanding of the first amendment is surely not unimaginable.

* * *

VII

CORRELATING PROTECTION TO KINDS OF SPEECH

Despite their evident difficulties, the last several graphics do tend to sum up the principal contending schools of first amendment interpretation during the past several decades. At the same time, there has gradually developed still another view that does not, as did these graphics, make quite so much depend upon which side of one-or-more fixed lines a given kind of case falls. To be sure, this view also does not escape problems of judicial discretion. But by introducing finer gradations of a particular sort, it may appear both more moderate and less rigid in the measuring of protected speech. Interestingly, it complements the graphic we examined in the *Dennis* case.

Dennis defined the principal task of the courts as graduating the kinds and degrees of evil to be balanced against the improbability of their occurrence resulting from particular speech to determine whether the degree of abridgment was unavoidable and therefore permissible. Correspondingly, an increasingly fashionable view holds that it is important to graduate the kind of speech to be invaded. If it is political speech (*e.g.*, rhetoric praising or abusing candidates for office, or rhetoric exaggerating the alleged effects, provisions, merits, or demerits of existing laws), the speech is deemed of such central importance to the functions of the first amendment that even the high probability of a reprehensible evil (*e.g.*, that a far more honest and intelligent candidate will lose to a dishonest, manipulative, selfish demagogue) will not justify any recourse against the wretched slanders of the victor. If it is commercial speech, on the other hand, the evil of consumer deception may be avoided on a lesser probability of fraud than in the political speech case, although commercial speech will not, on that account alone, be treated as 100% unprotected, as is obscenity or solicitation of homicide. Graphics carrying these additional views of first amendment priority may look like either of the following:

Protection of the First Amendment By Subject

Criminal
Punitive
Pornographic
Commercial
Aesthetic
Scientific
Philosophic
Economic
Social
Private
Religious
Issues
Candidates
Policies

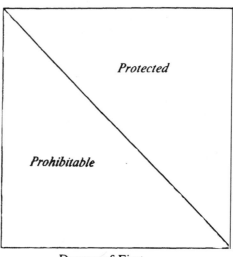

Political
Religious
Philosophic
Economic
Private
Social
Scientific
Aesthetic
Symbolic
Libel
Commercial
Obscene
Criminal

Protected

Prohibitable

Degree of First
Amendment Protection

These are unquestionably useful and interesting variations, and even our attempt to present them graphically is not quite adequate because it tends to understate their subtlety. The graphics imply a neat, concentric order of speech values, relating the proximity of speech categories to core values of political self-determination, with commensurate first amendment protection contingent upon the distance of an identifiable kind of speech from that first amendment center. Quite obviously, however, a particular speech may in fact cut across these artificial lines, readily embarrassing an attempt to say which kind of speech it was. The libelous may well be related to the political utterance, the aesthetic may be quite inseparable from the allegedly obscene.
* * *

In effect, then, these graphics illuminate an additional perspective, but they do not reduce the margins of uncertainty, instability, external reference, and elbowroom for judicial administration in the regime of the first amendment. Perhaps, moreover, the point illustrated by these variations is that there is no sure formula for reading the first amendment in any way that (a) copes with the irresistible counterexample, (b) fits with its syntax, *and* (c) enjoys even a plausible congruence with history, to make it foolproof. Which among these graphics seems better (or merely less poor) than the rest is assuredly debatable.

FREDERICK SCHAUER, CATEGORIES AND THE FIRST AMENDMENT: A PLAY IN THREE ACTS

34 Vand.L.Rev. 265, 267–268, 270, 272–277, 282–
283, 286–288, 296, 298–301, 303–305 (1981).

ACT ONE: THE QUESTION OF COVERAGE

* * *

The first amendment says that "Congress shall make no law ... abridging the freedom of speech ...." The substantive content marked off by this language is different from that which would be marked off by a first amendment that substituted, for the word "speech," the words "action," "travel," "property," or "contract." In this respect we can begin by saying that, in an important way, it is the category of "speech" that is set off by the first amendment for special protection. * * *

* * *

If we * * * define "speech" by reference to Webster's dictionary, then many distinctly discordant cases would be considered first amendment cases, a circumstance occasioned by the pervasiveness of language (speech) in almost every facet of human activity. * * * Not only do we fix prices with speech, but we also make contracts with speech, commit perjury with speech, discriminate with speech, extort with speech, threaten with speech, and place bets with speech. Is it possible to say that all of these cases and many more are covered by the first amendment?

* * *

The literalist is presented with a parallel problem in reference to those acts that are not speech in the ordinary language sense but are speech in the constitutional sense—armband wearing, communicative clothing, oil painting, political contributions, photography, and so on. If these activities count as speech because they share relevant similarities with speech, then some *attributes* of speech must serve to trigger the guarantees of the first amendment. If that is so, then some verbal acts may not share these attributes, and thus are not "speech" in the constitutional sense. What emerges from all of this is the conclusion that the constitutional definition of the word "speech" carves out a category that is not coextensive with the ordinary language meaning of the word "speech." When we define the word "speech," we are categorizing. This occurs regardless of the source of the definition, and in this sense categorization is implicit in *any* approach to the theory or structure of the first amendment.

* * * In setting the boundaries of the category of conduct encompassed by the first amendment, those approaches commonly referred to as "definitional" combine close attention to defining the boundaries of the category with a desire to grant absolute protection within those boundaries. The theories of Meiklejohn,[37] Frantz,[38] Emerson,[39] and Nimmer,[40] for example, all define "the freedom of speech" in their own purpose-oriented way (with which there is nothing wrong) and then argue that conduct falling within the contours of the category is absolutely protected.

These "definitional-absolutist" theories treat all nonprotected speech identically. They treat especially harmful political speech ("Go burn down the draft board—NOW!!," uttered in front of an angry mob of torchbearing antidraft protestors fifty yards from the draft board) the same way as extortion, contract law, and advice or encouragement in the commission of a nonpolitical bank robbery. If we look at the reasons for the exclusion of these utterances from first amendment protection, however, we see that especially harmful political speech is excluded because of the extent and the immediacy of the danger; discussing the wisdom of burning down draft boards at a peaceful teach-in is protected. Yet contract law, antitrust law, and the like are excluded for reasons having little if anything to do with the extent or the imminence of the danger. They are excluded, and properly so, because they have nothing to do with what the concept of free speech is all about.

In thus trying to preserve an enclave of absoluteness, the definers must then construct a theory that treats irrelevant (to the first amendment) speech like verbal betting in the same way as relevant but unprotected speech like incitement to burn down draft boards. Reductionism, the urge to reduce complex phenomena to overly simple formulae, has been a pitfall throughout legal theory, and no less so in relation to the first amendment. The efforts to create one formula that will generate an area of absolute protection have been heroic, but they have failed in one of two ways. Either they have, like Professor Emerson's distinction between expression and action, simplified things to such an extent that the resultant formula has little if any analytical or predictive value, or they have, like the Meiklejohn interpretation, achieved consistency and workability at the expense of excluding from coverage much that a full theory of freedom of speech ought to include.

The development of definitional-absolutist theories was encouraged largely by the desire to narrow the area of judicial discretion. In searching for absolutism, however, theories of this type have collapsed the important distinction between coverage and protection. This distinction is important in separating the question of the category of action to which the right (any right) applies from the question of whether the right should prevail in cases of conflict with other interests, or for that

37. [Meiklejohn, Free Speech and Its Relation to Self–Government (1948).]

38. [Frantz, *The First Amendment in the Balance,* 71 Yale L.J. 1424 (1962).]

39. [T. Emerson, The System of Freedom of Expression (1970); Emerson, *First Amendment Doctrine and the Burger Court,* 68 Calif.L.Rev. 422 (1980); Emerson, *Toward a General Theory of the First Amendment,* 72 Yale L.J. 877 (1963).]

40. [Nimmer, *The Right to Speak From Times to Time: First Amendment Theory Applied to Libel and Misapplied to Privacy,* 56 Calif.L.Rev. 935 (1968).]

matter other rights. No right can be unlimited in coverage, but it is at least plausible to imagine a right that is unlimited in protection (absolute) within the scope of coverage. As a matter more of political and sociological fact than of necessary logical correlation, rights can more plausibly be absolute when the range of coverage is narrow. Conversely, rights whose coverage is too broad are likely to offer little in the way of protection. One danger of definitional-absolutist theories, then, is that the criterion of absolutism exerts an inward pull on the boundaries of coverage. When a problematic case arises, it is tempting to pull in the boundaries so that the case is now totally outside the perimeter of the right, thereby eliminating the problem. The danger, however, is that the boundaries may eventually become far narrower than the underlying theory, resulting in a constriction of the right no less than if the protection within the boundaries of coverage had been defeasible within that range.

It is always easier to ask one question than two, and this in part explains the recurrent appeal of definitional-absolutist theories. The effectiveness of such a scheme, however, depends on whether that one question can be answered. In this context, then, the question is "What is the definition of the category of conduct to which we can grant absolute protection under the first amendment?" To answer this question we must in turn develop an underlying theory of the principle of freedom of speech, and, if the protection is to be absolute, build into that theory all of the conceivable exceptions to the principle. This seems an impossible task.

Defining an area of absolute protection is likely to be impossible for two main reasons. First, it is unlikely that any *one* theory can explain the concept of free speech, and no reason necessarily exists to suppose that it could. Freedom of speech need not have any one "essential" feature. It is much more likely a bundle of interrelated principles sharing no common set of necessary and sufficient defining characteristics. It is quite possible that the protection of political discussion and criticism, the aversion to censorship of art, and the desire to retain open inquiry in science and other academic disciplines, for example, are principles not reducible to any one common core. Any attempt to do so is likely to be both banal and to distort all of the principles involved. The standard jurisprudential and linguistic metaphor of the core and the fringe is useful in its place, but it is harmful if it leads us to search for only one core when there may in fact be several, or many.

The second difficulty in attempting to build all of the exceptions and qualifications into our definition of a right absolute in strength is that we simply do not know what all the exceptions and qualifications might be. Lacking omniscience, we can at best imperfectly predict the future. Rights whose shape incorporates all exceptions and qualifications would be extremely rough tools for dealing with the uncertainties of the future. Instead, we wisely achieve finer tools for future use by combining a relatively vague definition of the coverage of the right (for example, all speech of public importance or all discussion) with a relatively vague specification of the weight of the right (for example, that it prevails in all cases in which the justification for the restriction is not a clear and present danger of great magnitude). * * *

* * *

Act Two: The Varieties of Speech

Our first look at categorization and the first amendment focused on the first amendment as itself constituting a category. From this perspective the conclusion that categorization in this sense is unavoidable was inevitable. The question now is whether we can or should go further in the process of categorization; that is, does the category of conduct covered by the first amendment in turn contain further subcategories? Having concluded that the first amendment covers a particular set of circumstances, do we then apply a uniform test to determine whether the first amendment protects the act, or do we apply differing tests depending upon the subcategory within the first amendment into which the particular case falls?

Hostility toward the creation of subcategories within the first amendment has been a pervasive, albeit not invariably determinative, theme in contemporary free speech doctrine. This hostility can be embodied in a bipolar structure of no protection and full protection. "Full protection" refers not necessarily to absolute protection but only to the maximum level of protection that the first amendment provides, which may, for example, be only the use of some form of a "clear and present danger" standard. If we were to refuse to recognize any subcategories within the first amendment, we would determine first whether the facts of the case fell outside or inside the coverage of the first amendment. If they fell outside, there would be no protection, at least not by the first amendment. If they fell inside, the full protection of the first amendment, however much that might be, would attach to the conduct in question. Implicit in this all-or-nothing approach is an extreme reluctance to assign differing values to the speech that is covered by the first amendment. The works of Shakespeare have the same first amendment value as *Playboy,* which in turn has the same first amendment value as wearing a black armband or arguing for the virtues of Nazism.

* * *

Still, at least four arguments can be marshalled in favor of categorization within the first amendment. First, if we take the "full protection within" rule as the standard, there may be pressure to keep troublesome categories completely outside. When the choice is all or nothing, the difficulties of "all" may lead courts to choose "nothing." Thus, it may be that one of the reasons for the historical exclusion of commercial advertising was the potential for problems, especially in terms of truth and falsity, that would exist if commercial advertising were treated in the same manner as advocacy of adultery or the single tax. If the creation of a separate category within the first amendment is precluded, a tempting solution is merely to keep the speech that would constitute that category outside first amendment protection. Similar observations seem also applicable to the pre-*New York Times* exclusion of defamatory speech from the coverage of the first amendment.

Second, not all forms of speech are necessarily amenable to the same analytic approach. The tests and tools created to deal with the likes of *Brandenburg, Whitney, Schenck,* and *Debs,*[97] for example, may not be those most appropriate for dealing with problems of a quite different kind. Neither false advertising nor false attacks on private reputation fit easily into anything even close to a "clear and present danger" formula—nor, for that matter, does speech that offends rather than causes harm in a narrower sense. We are accustomed to thinking in terms of *levels* of protection, but it may be that different categories of speech should be treated *differently,* which does not necessarily entail more or less.

Third, and somewhat related to the second argument, most first amendment theory is formulated around the "advocacy" paradigm. When statements of fact are concerned, for example, many of the skeptical presuppositions of the first amendment are either irrelevant or highly attenuated. It is true that many statements of fact contain statements of opinion as well and that factual determinations are often erroneous, but the differences between "this car has a six-cylinder engine" and "socialism is wonderful" are apparent to all but the most resolute skeptic. * * *

Finally, the refusal to categorize is frightfully counter-intuitive. Many commentators have strongly criticized Justice Stevens' observation in *Young v. American Mini Theatres, Inc.*[102] that "few of us would march our sons and daughters off to war to preserve the citizen's right to see 'Specified Sexual Activities' exhibited in the theaters of our choice;" but he was right. We would not, if that were all we were protecting. The difficulty comes in describing the behavior, and therefore the category of behavior, at the appropriate level of generality, but most people do believe that there are "commonsense differences" between different categories of utterances. * * *

* * *

ACT THREE: RULES

Having determined that a set of facts lies within the coverage of the first amendment and having placed those facts within the appropriate subcategory of the first amendment, the question finally arises of just how we will decide the case, or, more accurately, how the judge will

---

97. Brandenburg v. Ohio, 395 U.S. 444 (1969); Whitney v. California, 274 U.S. 357, 375 (1927) (Brandeis, J., concurring); Debs v. United States, 249 U.S. 211 (1919); Schenck v. United States, 249 U.S. 47 (1919). These are generally considered to be the landmark cases in the development of first amendment doctrine relating to political advocacy.

102. 427 U.S. 50 (1976).

decide the case. It is at this stage that we can no longer escape facing up to the recurrent question of ad hoc balancing. The question at this stage is what the rules of guidance for the judge will look like within a given first amendment category.

* * *

The choice comes down to the amount of flexibility we wish to allow the judge to deal with a particular case whose existence we did not and quite possibly could not have foreseen. If we grant little or no flexibility, we increase the likelihood of anomalous results, the inevitable consequence of attempting to fit the unanticipated future into categories based on suppositions that did not include that event. We can, of course, accommodate the possibility of unanticipated future cases by granting greater flexibility to the judge, who can then look at how the interests are reflected in the particular case and reach what he perceives to be the proper accommodation of those interests.

This flexibility, though, entails two substantial costs. A problem of notice can occur because the more flexibility that the trial court has, the less certain anyone can be in advance of the likely result in a particular case. Lack of predictability in the law is always troublesome, and it is even more so when the inevitable caution that unpredictability yields will induce self-censorship ("chilling") of that which may very well be important. Moreover, the judge might just decide incorrectly. The greater the flexibility that is built into the governing standards, the less the judge is constrained by rules even for the type of case we *can* anticipate. The less the judge is constrained, the more likely there are to be errant results.

It is by now hardly a novel observation that particularized balancing of interests by the judge in respect to the case at hand (ad hoc balancing) is not a technique with a monopoly on the weighing of interests. We balance when we formulate rules for mechanical or categorical application. Nor is it a simple question of a choice between balancing at the rulemaking level or at the level of application. There is a spectrum rather than a dichotomy. The question is not *whether* to permit judges to balance in the particular case, but rather *how much* authority the governing rule should allocate to the judge to take account of the particular circumstances of the case at hand. Although this allocation could take place in the form of a specific grant of authority, it is much more common for it to exist implicitly in the degree of specificity of the governing rule.

When categorization is presented as a first amendment technique in opposition to balancing, what is in fact being advocated is the establishment of rules leaving little if any discretion to the judge in the particular case. The more a rule predetermines the outcome that flows from easily determinable facts, or the more a rule excludes certain facts from consideration by the judge, the less discretion is available to the judge and the more we can call the rule categorical. When a rule describes a category of facts with some specificity and when that rule mandates the results that flow from inclusion or exclusion from the specifically defined category, the judge has merely to place the case in the proper category in order to determine the correct result. Things will never be quite this simple, but it is possible to reduce or minimize the degree of discretion, although this comes at the cost of an increased proportion of potentially nonideal results in cases unforeseen at the time the rule was formulated. In formulating a categorical rule, we isolate what we in our best judgment determine to be the facts on which we wish and expect future cases to turn. In doing so we suppose that these facts will recur and that they will recur in substantially similar contexts—but we might be wrong.

Perhaps the most extreme form of a categorical rule in first amendment doctrine is in the law of defamation. The court has "merely" to determine whether the plaintiff was a public figure or a public official and then apply the appropriate standard of culpability. This is by no means an easy task, but the variability in what remains to be decided should not blind us to the extent to which issues have been removed from consideration in the particular case. All of the first amendment issues, for example, have been predetermined at the rulemaking level. It is not for the court in the particular case to determine whether the plaintiff has available adequate fora for a response, or if the particular words spoken are harmful or helpful to the process of public deliberation. Moreover, even the factual determinations are constrained by rule, at least to the extent that the concepts of "publicness" and "actual malice" have become more precise through a combination of rule language and interpretive case law.

At the opposite end of the spectrum are what have often been called content-neutral regulations of time, place, and manner, whose permissibility turns on factors such as the availability of alternative fora and the strength of the governmental interest. These determinations involve bringing first amendment considerations down to the level of application, a feature absent in the defamation cases, and they also involve a relatively unconstrained approach to the determination of the relevant facts.

* * *

In seeking answers to these questions pertaining to the appropriate blend of guidance and discretion, it is important to remember that there is no necessary correlation between the approach employed and the strength of the first amendment protection. Although ad hoc balancing has traditionally been associated with a puny first amendment and categorical rules with a powerful one, it could have been and still could be otherwise. It is possible, after all, to devise rigid rules that give little respect to free speech considerations. Consider, for example, a rule that said no first amendment protection was available when the speaker advocated violation of the law. * * *

[S]uch a rule is substantially more categorical than the *Brandenburg* rule, which requires a contextual and therefore ad hoc determination of likely effect as well. Similarly, it could have been the case that all judges with the power to balance the interests in the particular case had, even with little guidance or restriction of their discretion, found in favor of the speaker and against the restriction. If that had been our history, then the reflexive association of ad hoc balancing with limited first amendment protection might never have arisen. Ad hoc balancing gained its dismal first amendment reputation in large part because its chief proponent, Justice Frankfurter, held as well a theory of great deference to legislative determinations. The two need not necessarily be conjoined. * * *

It is thus behavioral observation and speculation far more than inexorable logic that dictates the extent to which categorical rules should narrow the range of judicial choice. That does not mean, however, that we have nothing on which to base the choice. Experience can guide us, and in this respect the virtues of particularized balancing are often quite hard to see. Freedom of speech is a long-term value not always fully appreciated in the case at hand. In order fully to accommodate this long-term interest, we must often make what at first sight appear to be discordant short-term decisions. Moreover, * * * freedom of speech is a value that runs counter to many of our intuitions. Psychological forces, if there are such things, run in favor of suppression. In a particular case the asserted governmental interest will often look far more appealing or even compelling than the first amendment interest. As a result, it is not at all surprising that discretion-limiting rules have traditionally provided far more in the way of first amendment protection than has particularized balancing. * * *

This is not to say that the same approach to the constraints on and particularity of balancing must necessarily be employed throughout the first amendment. If there are to be subcategories within the first amendment, as there now are, then the reasons that prompted the creation of distinct subcategories will also often lead to different approaches to adjudicative style for the different subcategories. This is most plain in reference to the subcategory of time, place, and manner regulations, in which the issues involved must almost of necessity be evaluated on a case-by-case basis. It seems true as well for commercial speech, in which the complexity of the factual issues involved compels greater deference to administrative fact finding than would be permissible for most other forms of covered speech.

The choice of the appropriate point between unguided judicial discretion and rigid verbal rules, then, must be influenced not only by the balance between predictability and flexibility for unforeseen cases, but also by the psychological factors relating to the likely outcome of that discretion. It is a decision that takes place *within* a given first amendment subcategory. In turn, the decision to create subcategories takes place *within* the process of delineating the category of coverage of the first amendment. Each categorization decision takes place within another, somewhat like those sets of Russian wooden dolls. Each categorization decision, like each doll, can stand alone if necessary, but the full impact is achieved in the way they all fit together.

———

Schauer argues that categorization is both necessary and useful in free speech law. For First Amendment purposes "speech" itself is a category, not a natural act; and it can be further divided into more (political speech) and less (pornography) valuable subcategories. There is not universal agreement on this point. Many theorists argue that categorization is incurably inexact, and so it produces rules that under-protect speech. (Such rules will sometimes over-protect speech too, but this is not a concern for most First Amendment writers.) The heroic solution to the problem of underprotective categories is to give all speech absolute protection. (One still needs to define the category "speech," but at least there are no *other* lines to draw.) "Definitional balancing" is an example of this approach. It is actually no more exact than all-out categorization—indeed it is less so, because it substitutes one big cookie cutter for a number of small ones. But it tends to err only on the side of over-protection and this, its proponents say, is a good thing.

The more labor-intensive solution is to try to reach the right result in each case without the aid of categories, neither under-protecting nor over-protecting speech. This is what is called "ad hoc balancing," and for obvious reasons it has its perennial adherents. Pierre Schlag is one, and he makes the negative case for balancing by showing the defects of categorization. In *An Attack on Categorical Approaches to Freedom of Speech,* 30 UCLA L.Rev. 671 (1983), Schlag points out the variance between what he calls the "normative" and the "operational" significance of categories. Consider Alexander Meiklejohn's defense of political speech. Meiklejohn defined that category in a normative way—it meant any speech that could improve the voters' "knowledge, intelligence, sensitivity to human values." [1] It would thus embrace science, art, drama, and poetry. But in operational terms, i.e. in the real world, these are not what we mean by political speech. Courts relying on normative categories like Meiklejohn's have to make judgments about how they apply to real life (judgments about how values relate to facts). But the whole point of a categorical approach is to keep the courts from making such discretionary judgments. It is not clear that we can achieve this goal.

Categories may, on the other hand, lure courts into a different kind of trap. If a case can be assigned to the appropriate category the rest of the judge's work is easy: the decision follows more or less mechanically from a set of predetermined rules. Categories then promise the judge relief from the responsibility of decision-making. Schlag argues that categorical systems tempt courts in this way to shape the facts to fit into some pigeonhole, without regard for what really happened.

---

1. Meiklejohn, *The First Amendment Is An Absolute,* 1961 Sup.Ct.Rev. 245.

Steven Shiffrin argues in *Defamatory Non–Media Speech and First Amendment Methodology,* 25 UCLA L.Rev. 915 (1978), that despite all outward appearances, balancing is and must be the Court's methodology in all First Amendment cases. Sometimes after balancing the relevant factors the Court will formulate a rule of general application for some specific context, like defamation. Here the Court, after weighing reputation against free speech values and other factors, has created a set of fairly exact rules. Sometimes it will rely upon ad hoc balancing, as it does for speech that advocates unlawful action. In cases like *Brandenburg* the Court is willing to tolerate more case-by-case decision-making because it assigns a lower value to the speech being abridged. But free speech doctrine is always the result of a complex balancing process. Here are some of the factors the Court considers: [2]

(1) the nature of the interest sought to be furthered by the state;

(2) the extent to which the state must abridge the particular speech in order to further that interest;

(3) the extent to which the abridgment will further the state interest;

(4) the impact of that abridgment on free speech values; i.e.,

(a) the extent to which the content involved can make a contribution to the marketplace of ideas;

(b) the extent to which government intervention can be tailored to prevent the arbitrary imposition of subjective values;

(c) the extent to which the speech is necessary to further values of self-expression or cathartic release; and

(d) the extent to which governmental abridgments can avoid substantial chilling effects on protected speech.

MELVILLE B. NIMMER, THE RIGHT TO SPEAK FROM TIMES TO TIME: FIRST AMENDMENT THEORY APPLIED TO LIBEL AND MISAPPLIED TO PRIVACY

56 Calif.L.Rev. 935, 941–947 (1968).

The absolutist interpretation of the first amendment whereby literally all speech is protected is both unrealistic and undesirable * * *. But if anything less than all speech is to be protected, then some selection must be made between that speech which is protected and that which is not. If such selection is to turn on rational rather than arbitrary considerations, it is obvious that the selection process requires a balancing of competing interests, and this returns us to the equally unacceptable alternative of ad hoc balancing.

2. 25 UCLA L.Rev. at 955.

Or does it? The Supreme Court decision in *New York Times Company v. Sullivan* [22] indicates a third approach which avoids the all or nothing implications of absolutism versus ad hoc balancing. *Times* points the way to the employment of the balancing process on the definitional rather than the litigation or ad hoc level. That is, the Court employs balancing not for the purpose of determining which litigant deserves to prevail in the particular case, but only for the purpose of defining which forms of speech are to be regarded as "speech" within the meaning of the first amendment. This at first blush may appear to be only a verbal distinction. Analysis suggests, however, that a good deal more is involved.

In *Times* the Court for the first time ruled on the question of whether libel laws constitute an abridgment of speech in violation of the first amendment. The New York Times had published an advertisement on behalf of the Committee to Defend Martin Luther King and the Struggle for Freedom in the South. The advertisement admittedly contained some false statements. In a subsequent libel action brought by L.B. Sullivan, a Montgomery city commissioner, against the Times and certain other defendants, an Alabama jury had awarded one-half million dollars in damages. In reversing the judgement and holding for the defendants, the Court in effect defined the kind of defamatory speech which is protected by the first amendment. The Court held that, at least where the defamatory speech is directed against a "public official," such speech is protected by the first amendment unless the speech is made "with knowledge that it was false or with reckless disregard of whether it was false or not."

Before considering whether the particular balance struck by the Court was correct, it should be made clear that there *was* balancing in *Times*, but that it was not ad hoc balancing. There was balancing in the sense that not all defamatory speech was held to be protected by the first amendment. The Court could not determine which segment of defamatory speech lies outside the umbrella of the first amendment purely on logical grounds, and no pretense of logical inexorability was made. By in effect holding that knowingly and recklessly false speech was not "speech" within the meaning of the first amendment, the Court must have implicitly (since no explicit explanation was offered) referred to certain competing policy considerations. This is surely a kind of balancing, but it is just as surely not ad hoc balancing.

If the Court had followed the ad hoc approach, it would have inquired whether "under the particular circumstances presented" the interest of the defendants in publishing their particular advertisement outweighed the interest of the plaintiff in the protection of his reputation. This in turn would have led to such imponderable issues as: How important was it to the defendants (or possibly to the public at large) that this particular advertisement be published? How "serious" was the injury to the plaintiff's reputation caused by the advertisement? * * *

22. 376 U.S. 255 (1964).

If *Times* had been decided on the ground that in the circumstances presented the importance of the publication of the particular advertisement outweighed the seriousness of the particular resulting injury to the plaintiff's reputation, what would that tell potential future advertisers and public officials as to their respective rights in connection with future advertisements? Not only would it tell them nothing; it might well serve as a serious deterrent to anyone who intends to criticize public officials, since it can hardly be predicted which way the scales will fall in the particular circumstances of a new case. The absence of a rule to which judges can turn could also result in decisions unduly influenced by prevailing public emotions. Suppose in the next case defamatory statements are made about a public official by reason of his conduct in connection with the Vietnam war. If the only referent available to the judges is the weight of the competing interests in speech and reputation, can anyone doubt that the speech is likely to have rough sledding, or at the very least, that a decision finding that speech outweighs reputation will require unusual judicial courage?

It has been argued that any objections which may be stated against ad hoc balancing are equally applicable to definitional balancing, since the same competing interests which are considered in the former will have to be considered in the latter. I would disagree with this for several reasons. First, it is not necessarily true that the same considerations are weighed in both definitional and ad hoc balancing. In the latter it is the interests presented in the particular circumstances of the case before the court which are weighed. For example, in a defamation case the court would weigh not the interest in speech generally but rather the interest (and hence the importance) of the particular speech which is the subject of the litigation. On the other side it would weigh not the interest in reputation generally, but the extent of the particular injury to reputation in the case before it. * * *

A more profound difference between the ad hoc and definitional lies in the fact that a rule emerges from definitional balancing which can be employed in future cases without the occasion for further weighing of interests. Moreover, such a rule should continue to be applicable notwithstanding the subsequent enactment of new legislation which in some different manner attempts to protect an interest inimical to speech. It is the first amendment which is being defined, not any particular legislation. Thus the *Times* rule which immunizes reputation-injuring speech other than that which is knowingly or recklessly false would presumably be equally applicable to new legislation which seeks to protect official reputations through novel means. The very existence of the rule makes it more likely that the balance originally struck will continue to be observed despite new and perhaps otherwise irresistible pressures. This in turn offers some measure of certainty, and minimizes speech deterrence.

Two concessions must be made, but neither constitutes a refutation of the thesis here offered. First, I would concede that neither definitional balancing nor any other technique can offer absolute assurance that a given court under sufficient internal or external pressure in some "hard" case will not depart from a definitional rule. Nevertheless, definitional balancing can insulate a judge from legally irrelevant pressures to a considerable degree if the judge wishes such insulation. How much easier it would be for a conscientious judge in a Southern community to explain to the members of the Lions Club that he found as he did because that was "the rule," rather than because upon a weighing of the interests involved he found weightier the side that public opinion opposed.

Second, I would make the concession that, *in vacuo,* ad hoc balancing is more likely to consider fine nuances and therefore produce a more just result. Like every line, the line drawn in definitional balancing has two edges, and speech which might be protected if the particular interests involved in a particular case were subject to the precision of the ad hoc scalpel might well lose protection by the cutting of the blunter definitional knife. But this likelihood may be offset by the fact that in ad hoc balancing weight is likely to be given only to the particular speech involved and not to "speech" generally, so that the speech side of the balance may be underweighed when compared with the immediate impact of a particular injury to a particular reputation. * * * Furthermore, such a likelihood would be present only in an ideal world where ad hoc balancing would not be subject to distortion from public and legislative pressures. We deal here only with speech cases; they in particular are not a part of such an ideal world. And even if the ideal could be achieved, the lack of a predictable line would still result in speech deterrence.

The point here is perhaps best illustrated in a nonspeech context but where pressures analogous to those found in speech cases might exist. Consider the unhappy history of the mythical state of Autophobia. The inhabitants of that state regarded the hazards of modern automotive travel as far more dangerous than any threat that might be posed by domestic or foreign communism. In some quarters hysteria ran rampant so that any driver of an automobile was suspect as probably a reckless driver, and even automobile passengers were regarded as fellow travellers. The more stable citizens, while recognizing the danger of reckless driving, also acknowledged the "competing interest" in expeditious transportation. When it came time for the state legislature to enact a speed law the more fearful members of the legislature argued that it would be dangerous to specify any specific maximum speed since this would constitute a green light for insidious drivers to proceed recklessly at just under the specified maximum. Their argument carried the day, and a law was enacted outlawing "excessive speeding," leaving it to the courts to determine in each case whether the driver's speed was in fact excessive.

The courts were thus required to engage in ad hoc balancing, weighing in each case the interest in safe driving against the interest in expeditious travel. This meant that drivers who wished to be sure of avoiding a brush with the law were deterred from driving at speeds which anyone might arguably contend were excessive. The absence of a rule as to what constituted excessive speed resulted in a traffic flow far slower than the interests of safety required. Still the law might have been found acceptable but for the further fact that whenever the courts were called upon to decide a case in which the defendant was charged with violating the speed law, they invariably found the defendant guilty. The popular hysteria against speeding made it very difficult for a judge in any given case to find that the defendant's interest in expeditious travel outweighed the community's interest in safe driving. The dissatisfaction of the more enlightened citizenry finally resulted in the enactment of a new speed law which specified given maximum rates in various areas with an overall maximum of 65 miles per hour. This maximum rate was determined by a kind of balancing of the interest in safety against the interest in expeditious travel, but the balancing occurred not on the ad hoc litigational level, but rather on the definitional level. The law now defined excessive speed and the courts were no longer called upon to weigh competing interests as presented by the facts in a given case. This was not without its disadvantages since, at least in theory, it meant that a particular driver who was proceeding at 67 miles per hour would be precluded from proving that in the given circumstances his speed was not excessive. But it was soon found that this lost privilege was more than compensated for by the fact that drivers who previously would have been deterred from safely driving at 55 miles per hour now were able to do so without fear of prosecution. It further meant that in speed case trials the courts were immunized from the pressures of the more hysterical or dogmatic segments of the community, since the rule to be applied required no further balancing, and hence no exercise of discretion which might be regarded as an undue coddling of subversive speeders.

The argument that ad hoc balancing is preferable to definitional balancing because the former permits a more sensitive appreciation of the equities in each particular case may be more easily made in non-speech areas where public passions do not generally ride as high. But even this may prove too much. It may be that if there were no legal rules but only beneficent judges, justice would be done more often. But if the ideal of a system of laws rather than men is not wholly attainable, that does not mean we should be ready to trade it for a system of men rather than laws.

VINCENT BLASI, THE PATHOLOGICAL PERSPECTIVE AND THE FIRST AMENDMENT

85 Colum.L.Rev. 449–461, 466, 469–474, 476–479 (1985).

THESIS

My thesis is that in adjudicating first amendment disputes and fashioning first amendment doctrines, courts ought to adopt what might be termed the pathological perspective. That is, the overriding objective at all times should be to equip the first amendment to do maximum service in those historical periods when intolerance of unorthodox ideas is most prevalent and when governments are most able and most likely to stifle dissent systematically. The first amendment, in other words, should be targeted for the worst of times.

I would not make that claim about all provisions of the federal Constitution. Certain clauses—the equal protection and cruel and unusual punishment clauses, for example—may be designed, or at least most wisely interpreted, to serve the society primarily in periods of unusual idealism or cohesion. Provisions of that sort may be more significant for their capacity to stimulate, channel, or institutionalize progressive social change than for any role they may play in preserving traditional arrangements. But the speech, press, and assembly clauses of the first amendment, as well as some other provisions of the Constitution—the religion clauses and the dormant commerce clause come to mind—are best viewed as having primarily a preservative function.[1] It is accordingly the pathological perspective that ought to inform the way those clauses are interpreted.

The central empirical proposition of my thesis is that certain segments of time are of special significance for the preservation of the basic liberties of expression and inquiry because the most serious threats to those liberties tend to be concentrated in abnormal periods. * * * At the outset, * * * it is necessary to address a few definitional considerations * * *.

First, the pathologies about which courts ought to be concerned are time-bound and exceptional. "Pathology" in the sense I use the term is a social phenomenon, characterized by a notable shift in attitudes regarding the tolerance of unorthodox ideas. What makes a period pathological is the existence of certain dynamics that radically increase the likelihood that people who hold unorthodox views will be punished for what they say or believe. * * *

Second, pathology need not be a nationwide phenomenon. Shifts in attitudes regarding the toleration of dissent that are confined to particular regions or localities should be of major concern in the formulation of first amendment doctrine. Boss Hague's antilabor reign of terror in Jersey City during the 1930s and the counterattacks against civil rights advocates mounted by numerous Southern communities in the 1960s

---

1. The crucial distinction is between provisions of the Constitution that establish the basic structure of the government and the most significant relationships of the political regime, and provisions that embody more discrete, and thus less "essential" though often no less important, normative commitments or aspirations. Because the basic structures and relationships are constitutive of the political community as an entity, preservation and continuity should be viewed as the first priority when those provisions are the subject of interpretation. In addition to the protection of free expression, the constitutive provisions of the American Constitution include the systems of federalism and separation of powers, the guaranty of a republican form of government, the separation of church and state, the legitimation of private property, the abolition of slavery and race-determined citizenship, and the requirement of due process of law.

figure in my analysis just as do the national Red Scare of 1919–1920 and the McCarthy Era.[2]

Third, I do not propose that the applicability of specific doctrines turn on a finding in a particular case that the situation in question is or is not pathological. That form of contingent doctrine is in fact antithetical to my thesis. I propose rather that continually applicable doctrines be formulated with emphasis on how well they would serve in the worst of times. In deciding first amendment cases, therefore, courts would always have to know roughly what evils they were guarding against as a general matter, but never precisely whether a particular situation amounted to such an evil.

* * *

THE ARGUMENT

The salient feature of my thesis is the overriding importance it attaches to the goal of preserving the theoretical integrity and practical effectiveness of a limited number of propositions that can be said to constitute the "core" of the speech, press, and assembly clauses of the first amendment. That goal is not lexically ordered in the sense that the slightest gain in nurturing the core necessarily outweighs substantial costs regarding the quality of first amendment adjudication outside the core. Nevertheless, short of extreme trade-offs, the strengthening of the core takes priority. I place such emphasis on that endeavor because of a view I hold regarding the nature of constitutional limitations generally.

The first task of any system of constitutional limitations is to guarantee that the truly fundamental features of the framework of government are maintained. The function of a "constitution" is to "constitute"—to "set up," "formally establish," "give form to," or "cause to become fixed" certain structures and principles of governance. * * *

* * *

* * * Stability and continuity are important primarily with regard to the central structural arrangements and basic norms of the constitutional regime. It is those provisions that purport to define the political community and embody the long-term commitments and aspirations of the populace. The manner by which secondary arrangements and norms should be extrapolated from the most basic provisions of the Constitution is, of course, an intriguing and important subject of consti-

---

2. The examples in the text are of twentieth century vintage, but pathologies have occurred intermittently throughout American history. Prominent instances include: the banishment of Ann Hutchinson from the Massachusetts Bay Colony in 1637, see E. Morgan, The Puritan Dilemma (1958); the Salem witchcraft trials, see J. Demos, Entertaining Satan (1982); the Alien and Sedition Acts, see J. Smith, Freedom's Fet-ters (1966); the antiMasonic hysteria that gripped the nation during the 1820s and early 1830s, see A. Tyler, Freedom's Ferment 351–58 (1944); the persecution of the Mormons during the 1840s and 1850s, see L. Arrington & D. Bitton, The Mormon Experience 44–64 (1979); and the repression of anarchists after the Haymarket Riot of 1886, see J. Garraty, The New Commonwealth 166–70 (1968).

tutional theory. But the prominence and vigor of disputation at that level should not lead us to ignore the importance of continuity and stability regarding the central norms of the constitutional tradition.

* * *

The conclusion that the constitutional tradition should build upon a limited number of relatively stable central norms does not help one to identify which norms occupy the central place and thus qualify for the special attention demanded by my thesis. * * * Whatever the measure adopted, however, it seems scarcely controversial to assert that at least some of the norms of the first amendment occupy such a central place in the American constitutional tradition.

The elaborate system of rights and structures set out in the text of the American Constitution makes sense only in the context of a commitment to limited government. That commitment necessarily entails some degree of conceptual separation between the state and its citizens and some practical capacity of citizens to challenge and check those who wield power in the name of the state. Certain norms regarding free expression and inquiry are integral to that conceptual separation and practical capacity. In this respect, the core commitments of the first amendment serve as one of the linchpins of the entire constitutional regime. Few other provisions have so central a role to play in constituting the American polity.

* * *

* * * Absent unusual social pressures, the central norms of a provision like the first amendment—that news reporting cannot be controlled by government, for example, or that citizens cannot be penalized for disagreeing with government policy—are taken for granted. The core commitments that derive from those norms are not regarded as burdensome or controversial. Normally, those core commitments need no special tending; the ordinary dynamics of adjudication provide more than sufficient protection.

The trouble is that this cheery description holds true only for most periods of time, not all. In pathological periods, at least some of the central norms of the constitutional regime are indeed scrutinized and challenged. The core commitments that derive from those norms are viewed by many as highly burdensome and controversial. In such periods the times seem so different, so out of joint, the threats from within or without seem so unprecedented, that the Constitution itself is perceived by many persons as anachronistic, or at least rigidly, unrealistically formalistic. In times when those misgivings take hold, the central norms of the constitutional regime are in jeopardy. The strength of the political community's commitment to those norms is tested, and it may matter a great deal how well the central norms were nurtured in the periods of calm that preceded the pathology.

There is reason to believe that susceptibility to pathological challenge is especially characteristic of the central constitutional norms regarding free expression and inquiry. Most constitutional commitments are fragile in the sense that they embody ideals that are easily abandoned or tempered in times of stress. Certain distinctive features of the commitment to free speech enhance that fragility.

The aggressive impulse to be intolerant of others resides within all of us. It is a powerful instinct. Only the most sustained socialization—one might even say indoctrination in the value of free speech—keeps the urge to suppress dissent under control. When the constraints imposed by that socialization lose their effectiveness, as most social constraints intermittently do, the power of the instinct toward intolerance usually generates a highly charged collective mentality. Because the instinct to suppress dissent is basic, primitive, and aggressive, it tends to have great momentum when it breaks loose from the shackles of social constraint. Aggression is contagious, and hatred of strangers for what they believe is one of the safest and most convenient forms of aggression. The problem is compounded by the fact that the suppression of dissent ordinarily is undertaken in the guise of political affirmation, of insisting that everyone stand up and be counted in favor of the supposed true values of the political community. As such, this particular type of challenge to constitutional liberties can take on the character of a mass movement; it can engage the imagination of the man on the street.

* * *

So far I have argued that the central norms of the constitutional tradition, which are normally immune from serious challenge both in political debate and adjudication, tend to be placed in jeopardy during pathological periods. That claim still does not establish that adjudication in ordinary times should be heavily influenced by the goal of strengthening the central norms of the first amendment tradition against the possibility of pathological challenges. Even if the most serious challenges to those norms tend to be concentrated in pathological periods, it may be that the best way to fortify a constitutional regime against pathological challenge is to develop a strong tradition of adjudication geared to normal times.

That possibility seems to me remote. Without some sort of consciously designed corrective, there is no reason to assume that adjudication in normal times will do a good job of nurturing the central norms of the constitutional regime. When those norms are not themselves under challenge, their main function is to serve as starting points for analogy or argumentation in disputes over the outer reaches of constitutional doctrine. That process may actually undercut the authority of the central norms. Grand ideas can come to be regarded as cliches when they are repeatedly invoked for partisan, rhetorical purposes in settings far removed from those that gave birth to the ideas. The very phenomenon of adversaries discerning radically different implications from a common norm can weaken the community's understanding of and devotion to the norm. The grist of everyday legal argumentation is the manipulation of ideas. That tradition of manipulation, though perfectly appropriate in adversarial discourse, may make it more difficult for the central norms of the constitutional regime to carry the authority they must—to evoke the reverence and deep conviction they must—if those norms are to withstand pathological pressures.

* * *

Given the major role played by history and tradition in my view of constitutionalism in the United States, it should come as no surprise that the value commitments I regard as most significant in determining the core of the first amendment are those that are forged in the foundry of political experience. * * *

Most of the value commitments that comprise the core of the first amendment are relatively specific in nature: Government cannot employ coercive measures to shape the content of news coverage.[15] Private citizens cannot be penalized for holding unpopular political opinions or for criticizing particular government policies.[16] The communication of a fact or value judgment relating to a matter of public concern cannot be prohibited solely on the ground that the communication is false, injures reputation, erodes moral standards, or stirs people to anger; some form of culpability on the part of the speaker must be established before any of these consequences can serve as a basis for regulating speech.[17] Publicly owned areas cannot be placed off limits to private speakers simply on the basis of the prerogatives of ownership; special justifications relating to competing public uses must be invoked.[18] A private citizen cannot be required to affirm any loyalties or beliefs unless he seeks to occupy a position of responsibility for which certain loyalties or beliefs are relevant.[19] Government cannot inquire into the private thoughts or political affiliations of any citizen except insofar as that information is important to an investigation of patterns of antisocial conduct or fitness for positions of special responsibility.[20] An individual cannot be held accountable for the beliefs, intentions, or actions of other persons or organizations simply on the basis of his political association or affiliation with those persons or organizations.[21]

15. See, e.g., Landmark Communications v. Virginia, 435 U.S. 829 (1978); Nebraska Press Ass'n v. Stuart, 427 U.S. 539 (1976); Miami Herald Publishing Co. v. Tornillo, 418 U.S. 241 (1974); Near v. Minnesota ex rel. Olson, 283 U.S. 697 (1931).

16. See, e.g., Brandenburg v. Ohio, 395 U.S. 444 (1969); Street v. New York, 394 U.S. 576 (1969); Yates v. United States, 354 U.S. 298 (1957).

17. See, e.g., Gertz v. Robert Welch, Inc., 418 U.S. 323, 347–48 (1974); Cohen v. California, 403 U.S. 15 (1971); New York Times Co. v. Sullivan, 376 U.S. 254 (1964); Terminiello v. Chicago, 337 U.S. 1 (1949).

18. See, e.g., United States v. Grace, 461 U.S. 171 (1983); Heffron v. International Soc'y for Krishna Consciousness, 452 U.S. 640 (1981); Edwards v. South Carolina, 372 U.S. 229 (1963); Hague v. CIO, 307 U.S. 496 (1939) (plurality opinion).

19. See, e.g., Wooley v. Maynard, 430 U.S. 705 (1977); Cole v. Richardson, 405 U.S. 676 (1972); West Virginia State Bd. of Educ. v. Barnette, 319 U.S. 624 (1943).

20. See, e.g., Gibson v. Florida Legislative Investigation Comm., 372 U.S. 539 (1963); Sweezy v. New Hampshire, 354 U.S. 234 (1957); Watkins v. United States, 354 U.S. 178 (1957).

21. See, e.g., United States v. Robel, 389 U.S. 258 (1967); Keyishian v. Board of Regents, 385 U.S. 589 (1967); Scales v. United States, 367 U.S. 203, 228–30 (1961).

A few propositions of a more general nature have received sufficient acceptance over time to qualify for inclusion in the core of the first amendment: A regulatory system that evaluates speech prior to its initial dissemination is especially problematic.[22] Courts should be highly reluctant to base their decisions regarding constitutional protection on ad hoc judgments regarding the truth or social worth of particular communications.[23] Arguments for regulation that depend on the claim that audiences will be injured or induced to injure others by the message conveyed by the speech must be treated with skepticism.[24] Harms that allegedly flow from speech not immediately but by a process that takes time to develop seldom provide a legitimate basis for suppressing the speech; whenever feasible the state must employ alternative means of preventing harms of that sort.[25]

* * *

IMPLICATIONS

* * *

Legal reasoning patterns would be affected in a myriad of ways, at many different levels, were the pathological perspective to become a dominant feature of first amendment analysis. * * *

1. *Sources of Justification.* A preference for the pathological perspective should lead lawyers and judges to analyze modern issues with reference to the central understandings of the constitutional framers and the teachings of classic, time-honored precedents. * * *

In pathological periods judicial authority is often threatened. The mysterious admixture of respect, self-interest, fear, and inertia that typically leads persons and institutions to obey the dictates of courts is disturbed. Under such conditions, courts need to be able to invoke sources of authority that carry weight with unsophisticated, resistant would-be regulators of speech. Rightly or wrongly, in our legal culture the appeal to history and tradition, even to the legendary wisdom of the Founding Fathers, seems to carry more weight than arguments from philosophical first principles or from the implications of dynamic lines of precedent. * * *

* * *

22. See, e.g., Nebraska Press Ass'n v. Stuart, 427 U.S. 539 (1976); Near v. Minnesota, ex rel. Olson, 283 U.S. 697 (1931); Blasi, [*Toward a Theory of Prior Restraint: The Central Linkage,* 66 Minn. L.Rev. 11 (1981)]; Emerson, *The Doctrine of Prior Restraint,* 20 Law & Contemp. Probs. 648 (1955).

23. See, e.g., Cohen v. California, 403 U.S. 15, 25 (1971); New York Times Co. v. Sullivan, 376 U.S. 254 (1964); Kingsley Int'l Pictures Corp. v. Regents, 360 U.S. 684 (1959).

24. See, e.g., Chicago Police Dep't v. Mosley, 408 U.S. 92, 99–101 (1972); Gitlow v. New York, 268 U.S. 652, 672–73 (1925) (Holmes, J., dissenting); Ely, *Flag Desecration: A Case Study in the Roles of Categorization and Balancing in First Amendment Analysis,* 88 Harv.L.Rev. 1482 (1975); Stone, *Content Regulation and the First Amendment,* 25 Wm. & Mary L.Rev. 189 (1983).

25. See, e.g., Brandenburg v. Ohio, 395 U.S. 444 (1969); Whitney v. California, 274 U.S. 357, 372–78 (1927) (Brandeis, J., concurring).

Simplicity of analysis has yet another function under the pathological perspective. Even when addressing issues for which the original understanding and the classic precedents provide little guidance, courts that adopt the pathological perspective should search for methods of justifying their judgments that appeal to the common, unsophisticated understanding of what law is. Complicated, subtle, imaginative legal arguments are not calculated to convince resistant officials and their constituencies that tolerance of threatening dissenters is a constitutional imperative. In overheated periods what is needed is a style of legal argumentation that appeals as little as possible to contemporary judgments of priority or efficacy that many persons will dispute. * * *

2. *Precepts and Principles.* * * *

* * *

By a legal "principle" I mean a value proposition of sufficient generality and thrust that for a fair number of particular cases acceptance or rejection of the proposition constitutes a major variable in determining how the case is resolved. Familiar first amendment principles include the prohibitions against content distinctions,[68] prior restraints,[69] restrictions analogous to seditious libel,[70] and regulatory justifications grounded in the paternalistic claim that audiences will act contrary to their own best interests if exposed to certain arguments or information.[71] Excepting perhaps the antiseditious libel principle, none of these principles is "absolute" in character in the sense that countervailing considerations cannot outweigh it. None is so precisely delimited that numerous, vexing definitional problems will not remain even after the principle has been fully embraced and repeatedly applied. But principles such as these have thrust: adoption of any one of them represents a notable value commitment that says much about how particular disputes will be adjudicated. In contrast, when first amendment doctrine is fashioned in a different idiom such as a multi-factor balancing test, a multi-stage analysis with a threshold level-of-scrutiny determination, or a standard that is highly dependent on particularistic assessments of motive, risk, or efficiency, adoption of the doctrinal scheme in question does not provide a strong indication of how a particular dispute will be resolved.

* * *

3. *Doctrinal Standards.* * * *

In crafting standards to govern specific areas of first amendment dispute, courts that adopt the pathological perspective should place a premium on confining the range of discretion left to future decisionmakers who will be called upon to make judgments when pathological

---

68. See Chicago Police Dep't v. Mosley, 408 U.S. 92 (1972).

69. See Near v. Minnesota ex rel. Olson, 283 U.S. 697 (1931).

70. See New York Times Co. v. Sullivan, 376 U.S. 254 (1964).

71. See Virginia State Bd. of Pharmacy v. Virginia Citizens Consumer Council, 425 U.S. 748 (1976).

pressures are most intense. Constitutional standards that are highly outcome-determinative of the cases to which they apply are thus to be preferred. This observation would counsel against standards such as the clear-and-present-danger test and its many variants that require in their application a contemporary assessment of social conditions.[72] More mechanistic measures for taking into account legitimate regulatory interests are preferable from the pathological perspective. Learned Hand's test in *Masses Publishing Co. v. Patten*,[73] which turns on the meaning of the speaker's words rather than the quality of the dangers they create, is one example.

* * *

[4.] *The Ambit of First Amendment Coverage.* * * * One strategy for combatting the stresses of pathological periods would be to extend first amendment protection as widely, fully, and creatively as possible in normal times so that the retrenchments that might be demanded in the worst of times would sacrifice only doctrinal fat. But since judicial credibility cannot be taken for granted in pathological periods, that strategy could be counterproductive. Better equipped for the storms of pathology might be a lean, trim first amendment that covered only activities most people would recognize as serious, time-honored forms of communication.

It is an intriguing and difficult question, well worth pausing over, whether adoption of the pathological perspective should lead courts to favor an expansive or a narrowly confined but heavily fortified set of first amendment principles. The question has implications for a wide variety of disputes. Should commercial advertising be included under the umbrella of the first amendment? Symbolic conduct? Is the expenditure of personal funds on a political campaign, one's own or another's, a first amendment activity? Are vivid depictions of genitalia in action instances of the expression about which the first amendment is concerned? What about the sale or rental of mechanisms such as video games that in the hands of users can stimulate a form of cognitive engagement?

An expansive first amendment that extended to all such activities would have certain advantages in periods of pathology. Most significant would be the absence of any tradition of courts making value-laden distinctions among acts of communication based on prescriptive notions of how communicators should influence their audiences. To exclude commercial speech and obscenity from the ambit of first amendment concern—even to accord such forms of expression a diminished level of protection—it is necessary to look beyond the form of the communication (words, pictures) and find something in its subject matter, type of impact on recipients, or the motivation of its disseminators, that distinguishes it from the communications that warrant full first amendment protection.

---

72. See, e.g., Dennis v. United States, 341 U.S. 494 (1951); Debs v. United States, 249 U.S. 211 (1919).

73. 244 F. 535 (S.D.N.Y.1917).

* * * Courts working within a first amendment tradition that authorized judicial inquiry into motivation, impact, and form would be tempted in pathological periods to find *something* distinctive in the speech of the most unpopular dissenters (concerted or surreptitious conduct, indoctrination, nihilistic motivation, coercive or selective impact) that would place it outside the ambit of first amendment protection. An expansive tradition regarding the reach of the first amendment would make it more difficult for judges to invoke such characteristics as a basis for suppressing speech.

Other considerations also favor an expansive conception of the first amendment as a preparation for pathology. The more universal a principle, the broader is the constituency of persons who gain from the principle. Political dissenters may benefit from finding themselves in the same boat with commercial advertisers, campaign contributors, and filmmakers interested in artistic freedom. There may also be a "muscle tone" argument for expanding the ambit of first amendment concern. In normal times, the bulk of disputes will not be over restrictions on speech growing out of political movements but over the conflicts that are endemic to everyday life, especially everyday economic life. A first amendment that figures in adjudication only rarely may not develop the doctrinal refinements, and the specialized bar, that may be needed in times of pathology.

The foregoing arguments, while not conclusive on the question, carry some weight. I am not impressed, however, by the argument that the first amendment should be construed expansively in normal times so as to provide judges with fodder for concessions that might be demanded by insistent political forces in pathological periods. Admittedly, doctrinal retrenchments can occasionally defuse demands to repress speech without seriously undermining the expressive liberties in dispute. The Supreme Court's 1973 reformulation of the test for obscenity appears to have had just such an effect, at least for a time. In pathological periods, however, concessions are more likely to stimulate than forestall demands for further repression. It is a shift in attitudes regarding the desirability of free speech that marks a period as pathological. Judicial retrenchments that authorize a break with tradition in the direction of permitting greater regulation of speech can only serve to legitimate such an attitude shift, no matter how insignificant in the grand scheme of things the particular speech in dispute may be.

In fact, a focus on the role of concessions suggests a stringent rather than expansive approach to the question of coverage. In pathological periods, courts need to present the forces of repression with strict, immutable legal constraints. That kind of implacable judicial posture is easier to assume when the basic reach of the first amendment is modest and compatible with widely shared intuitions regarding the natural ambit of the commitment to expressive liberty. If courts are ever to contribute to the stemming of destructive political tides, what judges say must ring true, at some level of consciousness, with the most influential shapers of public opinion. Just as history, simplicity, and a sense of conviction can enhance the intuitive appeal of judicial pronouncements, modesty of reach can be an important factor in the credibility calculus.

Probably the strongest argument for a lean first amendment derives from considerations more internal to the adjudicative process. There appears to be a close correlation between the ambit of coverage and the ability of courts to keep doctrine simple, informed by tradition, and dominated by principles. The wider the reach of first amendment coverage, the greater seems to be the judicial affinity for instrumental reasoning, balancing tests, differential levels of scrutiny, and pragmatic judgments.[90] For the reasons spelled out above, within any given area of doctrinal formulation courts that adopt the pathological perspective should strive to emphasize the role of tradition, simple precepts, and principles.

———

The empirical assumptions underlying Blasi's argument that we should adopt the pathological perspective on the First Amendment have been severely criticized by Martin Redish in *The Role of Pathology in First Amendment Theory: A Skeptical Examination,* 38 Case W.Res. L.Rev. 618 (1988). Redish contends that a preoccupation with core free speech values in ordinary times may actually lead to less, rather than more, protection during pathological periods:

"Blasi's analysis is amazing for its sweeping, totally unsupported assumptions about the nature of human reason and reaction in times of great political stress. Even if we were to engage in Blasi's practice of speculation about such matters, it is by no means intuitive that the stress placed on so-called first amendment "core" values during pathological periods will be ameliorated by adoption of a narrow reach of first amendment protection during less pressured times. Is it reasonable to surmise that individuals crazed with fear about the danger created by holders of a particular unorthodox political view (for example, anarchists, communists, or nazis) will be any less outraged at the judicial extension of first amendment protection to the speech of these groups, merely because during normal times the Supreme Court had chosen not to extend free speech protection to commercial speech, video games, or pornography? A more likely scenario, I believe, is that the level of public outrage during this period will be determined largely, if not exclusively, by the level of the public's fear of the groups in question, rather than on the basis of unrelated first amendment doctrine. Indeed, that no direct correlation exists between Supreme Court extension of constitutional protection to novel forms of expression on the one hand

---

90. For examples of these modes of analyses achieving prominence at the outer ambit of first amendment concern, see Clark v. Community for Creative Non–Violence, 104 S.Ct. 3065 (1984); Metromedia, Inc. v. San Diego, 453 U.S. 490 (1981); Central Hudson Gas & Elec. Corp. v. Public Serv. Comm'n, 447 U.S. 557 (1980); California Medical Ass'n v. Federal Election Comm'n, 453 U.S. 182 (1981). On the relationship between breadth of coverage and strength of protection for the principle of free speech, see F. Schauer, [Free Speech: A Philosophical Enquiry 134–35 (1982).]

and the intensity of negative public reaction to the first amendment's application to unpopular groups during pathological periods on the other is historically demonstrated by the two previous pathological periods to which Blasi points: the "Red Scare" of the 1920s and the anti-communist period of the 1950s. It can hardly be suggested that prior to either period, the Court had in any way extended constitutional protection to novel forms of speech. In the 1920s, the Court had barely extended the constitutional protection even to purely political speech, and on several occasions in the 1940s the Court had expressly rejected such arguably diluting extensions.[24] Obviously, the Court's refusal to make novel first amendment extensions did not prevent the development of first amendment pathology at its most intense. Why, then, is there any reason to suppose that current refusals to engage in such extensions will in any way prevent similar levels of severity during future pathological periods?

* * *

"Even if one were to accept Professor Blasi's asserted linkage, it is at least equally arguable that extension of the first amendment's scope to novel areas during normal times would actually have a beneficial effect during pathological periods. If we accept the view that the Supreme Court is engaged in a moral interchange with the public, as Professor Blasi apparently does, it is conceivable that reserving the essence of first amendment protection for major political battles could actually cause the first amendment to atrophy. The lives of most people are not directly affected by such cases. If the Court could, by means of decisions extending the first amendment's reach, articulate how the values fostered by the free speech right affect issues which most people face regularly, perhaps public understanding of and sympathy with these values will become more immediate and concrete.

"In certain situations, use of Professor Blasi's approach may even result in a form of *reverse* dilution: refusal to extend the first amendment's scope may logically imply reduced protection in more traditional areas of coverage. For example, the primary justification cited in support of the constitutionality of the proposed ban on cigarette advertising is that such advertising is aimed largely at those who are easily persuaded and incapable of making a valid judgment on their own. If such an argument were used to justify suppression of truthful speech receiving *full* first amendment protection, it would of course be summarily rejected; it is only because commercial speech is thought not to fall within the first amendment's "core" that such an argument could even be seriously suggested. Yet if we accept this logic in the cigarette advertising context, it is possible that we will have conceded more than we had thought. For once we accept the theory that individuals are incapable of evaluating truthful information in making life-affecting

---

24. *See, e.g.,* Valentine v. Chrestensen, 316 U.S. 52 (1942) (summarily rejecting protection of commercial speech); Chaplinsky v. New Hampshire, 315 U.S. 568 (1942) (rejection of protection for "fighting words"; establishment of "two-level" theory of first amendment coverage).

decisions as a justification for governmental suppression of such information, we may well have laid the groundwork for a process of reverse dilution: some may subsequently draw on the logic of the cigarette advertising ban as a justification for the suppression of truthful information in other contexts. Rejection of a reduced level of protection for commercial speech, however, would preclude acceptance of the asserted justification in the cigarette advertising context, just as it would today in the context of political speech, thus precluding the danger of future expansions of this precedent into other areas of first amendment protection."

FREDERICK SCHAUER, SLIPPERY SLOPES

99 Harv.L.Rev. 361, 363, 381–382 (1985).

Although the first amendment has no monopoly on slippery slope arguments, these arguments appear commonly in discussions about freedom of speech. The warning is frequently heard that permitting one restriction on communication, a restriction not by itself troubling and perhaps even desirable, will increase the likelihood that other, increasingly invidious restrictions will follow. The *Skokie* controversy [11] provides one of the most notorious modern examples of this type of argument in freedom of speech debates. The argument there was not that freedom of speech in theory *ought* to protect the Nazis, but rather that denying free speech protection to Nazis was likely to start us down a slippery slope, at the bottom of which would be the denial of protection even to those who should, in theory, be protected. * * *

* * *

[I]n virtually every case in which a slippery slope argument is made, the opposing party could with equal formal and linguistic logic also make a slippery slope claim. Imagine the following stylized dialogue, using the facts of [a different kind of First Amendment case—] *Lynch v. Donnelly*.[53] Objector: If you allow Pawtucket, Rhode Island, to erect a nativity scene on public property, then it is only one small step to allowing organized prayers and religious services on public property, and then the next step is involvement of public officials in those services, and then official endorsement of particular religious denominations, which is exactly what the establishment clause was originally designed to prevent. Defender: If you allow the courts to stop Pawtucket from erecting the nativity scene, then the next step is allowing the courts to prohibit any mention of religion at all, including studying the Bible as literature in schools and hanging Giotto paintings in publicly funded museums, and then the courts will prohibit any public official from mentioning religion,

---

11. National Socialist Party of Am. v. Village of Skokie, 432 U.S. 43 (1977) (per curiam); Collin v. Smith, 578 F.2d 1197 (7th Cir.), *stay denied*, 436 U.S. 953, *cert. denied*, 439 U.S. 916 (1978). * * *

53. 104 S.Ct. 1355 (1984).

and before long the courts will even prohibit fire and police protection of church buildings.

The example is meant to demonstrate that a persuasive slippery slope argument depends for its persuasiveness upon temporally and spatially contingent empirical facts rather than (or in addition to) simple logical inference. In the example just given, the logical structure of both arguments is equivalent. To some people, one argument will seem more persuasive than the other because the underlying empirical reality— partly behavioral, partly political, partly sociological, and partly everything else other than the comparatively noncontingent rules of logic and language—makes one equally logical possibility seem substantially more likely to occur than the other. In some situations people will fear the logically possible danger case [a] of excess government control. In others people will fear the logically possible danger case of excess judicial intervention. Commonly both of these dangers will be argued in the same case.[55] At that point the arguments ought to be channeled away from strict logical form and toward the underlying empirical reality. Unless this underlying empirical reality offers some persuasive reason why one danger case seems either more likely, or more dangerous, or both, then every argument of the form "if this, then that, and then that" can be met with an equally logical and equally plausible "if not this, then not that, and then not that." Thus the persuasive slippery slope argument must draw upon those largely empirical circumstances that might skew the otherwise equally likely danger cases systematically in one direction rather than another. For without empirical evidence of such systematic skewing, the slippery slope argument has nothing on which to stand.

Many slippery slope claims, whether in law or in popular discourse, are wildly exaggerated. As a result, it is possible for the cognoscenti to sneer at all slippery slope arguments, and to assume that all slippery slope assertions are vacuous. But things are not quite so simple. It is true that the phenomenon of the slippery slope is not strictly logical and that a slippery slope effect is always in logical and linguistic theory eliminable. But as long as law and life are inhabited by people with human weaknesses of bias and deficiencies of understanding, who govern with laws of limited complexity, then claims of slippery slope effect will not necessarily be invalid. Still, slippery slope claims deserve to be viewed skeptically, and the proponent of such a claim must be expected to provide the necessary empirical support. This empirical support

a. Schauer argues earlier that slippery slope arguments involve a common theme: the contrast between a tolerable solution to a problem now before us, and an intolerable result with respect to some currently hypothetical but potentially real future state of affairs. He refers to the first problem as the "instant case," and the latter as the "danger case."

55. In the context of criminal procedure it is indeed common for slippery slope argu-

ments to be made on both sides. Appeals to the danger cases of uncontrolled police power on the one hand, or of police shackled by procedural requirements on the other, are presented with some regularity. If they are presented in the same case, then they cancel each other unless one appeal seems more empirically plausible than the other.

provides the supplement necessary to complete the structure of a slippery slope argument. Any slippery slope argument relies at bottom on the empirical observation that rules alone cannot compel behavior. A perceptive decisionmaker will therefore be attuned to the dispositional environment in which linguistically articulated rules will be reevaluated by future decisionmakers, judicial or otherwise, whose actions today's rules are in some sense designed to constrain.

BIBLIOGRAPHY

Lawrence A. Alexander, *Low Value Speech,* 83 Nw.U.L.Rev. 547 (1989).

Hugo L. Black & Edmond Cahn, *Justice Black and First Amendment "Absolutes": A Public Interview,* 37 N.Y.U.L.Rev. 549 (1962).

Vincent Blasi, *The Role of Strategic Reasoning in Constitutional Interpretation: In Defense of the Pathological Perspective,* 1986 Duke L.J. 696.

David S. Bogen, *The Supreme Court's Interpretation of the Guarantee of Freedom of Speech,* 35 Md.L.Rev. 555 (1976).

George C. Christie, *Why the First Amendment Should Not Be Interpreted from the Pathological Perspective,* 1986 Duke L.J. 683.

William Cohen, *A Look Back at* Cohen v. California, 34 UCLA L.Rev. 1595 (1987).

David A. Diamond, *The First Amendment and Public Schools: The Case Against Judicial Intervention,* 59 Tex.L.Rev. 477 (1981).

Edward J. Eberle, *Practical Reason: The Commercial Speech Paradigm,* 42 Case West.Res.L.Rev. 411 (1992).

Thomas I. Emerson, *First Amendment Doctrine and the Burger Court,* 68 Calif.L.Rev. 422 (1980).

Daniel A. Farber & John E. Nowak, *Justice Harlan and the First Amendment,* 2 Const.Comm. 425 (1985).

Laurent B. Frantz, *The First Amendment in the Balance,* 71 Yale L.J. 1424 (1962).

Laurent B. Frantz, *Is the First Amendment Law?—A Reply to Professor Mendelson,* 51 Calif.L.Rev. 729 (1963).

Charles Fried, *Two Concepts of Interests: Some Reflections on the Supreme Court's Balancing Test,* 76 Harv.L.Rev. 755 (1963).

John H. Garvey, *Children and the First Amendment,* 57 Tex.L.Rev. 321 (1979).

Roger L. Goldman, *A Doctrine of Worthier Speech: Young v. American Mini Theatres, Inc.,* 21 St. Louis U.L.J. 281 (1977).

R. Kent Greenawalt, *Criminal Coercion and Freedom of Speech,* 78 Nw.U.L.Rev. 1081 (1983).

R. Kent Greenawalt, SPEECH, CRIME, AND THE USES OF LANGUAGE (1989).

Harry Kalven, Jr., *Upon Rereading Mr. Justice Black on the First Amendment*, 14 UCLA L.Rev. 428 (1962).

Kenneth Karst, *The First Amendment and Harry Kalven: An Appreciative Comment on the Advantages of Thinking Small*, 13 UCLA L.Rev. 1 (1965).

William T. Mayton, *"Buying up Speech": Active Government and the Terms of the First and Fourteenth Amendments*, 3 Wm. & Mary Bill of Rights J. 373 (1994).

Alexander Meiklejohn, *The Balancing of Self–Preservation Against Political Freedom*, 49 Calif.L.Rev. 4 (1961).

Wallace Mendelson, *The First Amendment and the Judicial Process: A Reply to Mr. Frantz*, 17 Vand.L.Rev. 479 (1964).

Wallace Mendelson, *On the Meaning of the First Amendment: Absolutes in the Balance*, 50 Calif.L.Rev. 821 (1962).

Robert F. Nagel, *How Useful Is Judicial Review in Free Speech Cases?*, 69 Cornell L.Rev. 302 (1984).

Melville B. Nimmer, *The Meaning of Symbolic Speech under the First Amendment*, 21 UCLA L.Rev. 29 (1973).

Mark C. Rutzick, *Offensive Language and the Evolution of First Amendment Protection*, 9 Harv. C.R.–C.L.L.Rev. 1 (1974).

Frederick Schauer, *Commercial Speech and the Architecture of the First Amendment*, 56 U.Cinc.L.Rev. 1181 (1988).

Frederick Schauer, *Exceptions*, 58 U.Chi.L.Rev. 871 (1991).

Jeffrey M. Shaman, *The Theory of Low–Value Speech*, 48 SMU L.Rev. 297 (1995).

Steven H. Shiffrin, *The First Amendment and Economic Regulation: Away From a General Theory of the First Amendment*, 78 Nw. U.L.Rev. 1212 (1983).

The Honorable John Paul Stevens, *The Freedom of Speech*, 102 Yale L.J. 1293 (1993).

Mark G. Yudof, *Library Book Selection and the Public Schools: The Quest for the Archimedean Point*, 59 Ind.L.J. 527 (1984).

Fred C. Zacharias, *Flowcharting the First Amendment*, 72 Cornell L.Rev. 936 (1987).

Freedom of the Press

Floyd Abrams, *The Press* Is *Different: Reflections on Justice Stewart and the Autonomous Press*, 7 Hof.L.Rev. 563 (1979).

C. Edwin Baker, *Press Rights and Government Power to Structure the Press*, 34 U.Miami L.Rev. 819 (1980).

Randall P. Bezanson, *Political Agnosticism, Editorial Freedom, and Government Neutrality Toward the Press,* 72 Iowa L.Rev. 1359 (1987).

Randall P. Bezanson, *The New Free Press Guarantee,* 63 Va.L.Rev. 731 (1977).

Lee C. Bollinger, IMAGES OF A FREE PRESS (1991).

Lee C. Bollinger, *Freedom of the Press and Public Access: Toward a Theory of Partial Regulation of the Mass Media,* 75 Mich.L.Rev. 1 (1978).

David Lange, *The Speech and Press Clauses,* 23 UCLA L.Rev. 77 (1975).

Pnina Lahav, ed., PRESS LAW IN MODERN DEMOCRACIES (1985).

Lili Levi, *Challenging the Autonomous Press,* 78 Cornell L.Rev. 665 (1993).

Anthony Lewis, *A Preferred Position for Journalism?,* 7 Hofstra L.Rev. 595 (1979).

Anthony Lewis, *A Public Right to Know about Public Institutions: The First Amendment as Sword,* 1980 Sup.Ct.Rev. 1.

Potter Stewart, *"Or of the Press",* 26 Hastings L.J. 631 (1975).

William W. Van Alstyne, *The First Amendment and the Free Press: A Comment on Some New Trends and Some Old Theories,* 9 Hofstra L.Rev. 1 (1980).

C. CONTENT REGULATION

We now turn our attention from speakers and the categories of speech to the government and its activities. We noted in the Introduction to this chapter that freedom of speech is a relation among all four of these variables. We have seen how the First Amendment rules vary for different speakers and different types of speech. In this section and the next we will look at how the rules change as we apply them to different government actors and different types of regulation.

The first article in this section observes that the First Amendment is addressed to Congress in particular. Its main concern is that legislators might suppress speech *by law,* not that executive officials will do so illegally. Hans Linde concludes that if this is so, the Court has gotten on the wrong track in its "clear and present danger" cases. When Congress passes a law against speech the Court should not ask whether the kind of speech it forbids threatens the requisite harm. It should simply strike the law down. Congress can pass laws against effects, but not against words. We should reserve the "clear and present danger" rule as a test of executive action under a valid statute.

Most of the articles in this section deal with the most important way of classifying the government's actions for purposes of the free speech clause—the distinction between acts that regulate the content of speech and acts that don't. In *Police Department v. Mosley* [1] the Court declared that "above all else, the First Amendment means that government has no power to restrict expression because of its message, its ideas, its subject matter, or its content." This is an overstatement. We saw in Section B that there are several categories of speech that are not covered by the First Amendment at all, and so not protected against government restriction. Perjury and bribery are examples. So too are obscenity, some kinds of defamation (malicious falsehoods about public figures), and perhaps some kinds of fighting words. There are several other categories of speech that, though covered by the freedom of speech, get less than full protection. We will deal in Chapter IV with commercial speech, which the government can regulate if it is misleading. Moreover, the law recognizes a difference between regulating speech because of its subject matter (it may treat political messages on busses worse than it treats commercial advertisements [2]) and regulating speech because of its viewpoint (it may not treat Republican political messages worse than Democratic political messages).[3]

Subject to these qualifications, however, there is a good deal of truth in the observation that content regulation is a cardinal sin against the First Amendment. Why should this be? Kenneth Karst asserts that it is because the right to freedom of speech subsumes an even more fundamental right to equality: the rule against content discrimination is the First Amendment counterpart to the Fourteenth Amendment rule against race discrimination. Karst would extend this rule to all corners of free speech law, even to categories (like obscenity and commercial speech) that are currently not covered or not fully protected.

Geoffrey Stone, like Karst, tries to explain what is so bad about content regulation. He focuses only on viewpoint-based restrictions, a more modest class of cases than Karst covers. And he does not subscribe wholeheartedly to Karst's suggestion that equality is at the heart of the matter. Stone argues that the rule is more likely designed to prevent government paternalism, intolerance, distortion of public debate, and improperly motivated actions.

Several of the articles in Section B observed that the level of First Amendment protection varies for different types of speakers and speech. The debate over absolutes and balancing is intertwined with the debate over categories. John Hart Ely makes the same point à propos the government's actions. He states that when the government engages in content regulation the courts will apply strict, nondiscretionary, categorical rules with the likely effect of holding its action unconstitutional. On the other hand when the government's action is content-neutral the courts will engage in balancing. This suggestion has proven quite influential. As Kent Greenawalt shows, that is how the Court ap-

---

1. 408 U.S. 92, 95 (1972).

2. Lehman v. City of Shaker Heights, 418 U.S. 298 (1974); CBS, Inc. v. Democratic National Committee, 412 U.S. 94 (1973).

3. See Stone, *Restrictions of Speech Because of its Content: The Peculiar Case of Subject–Matter Restrictions,* 46 U.Chi. L.Rev. 81 (1978).

proached the problem of flag-burning in *Texas v. Johnson.*[4] The outcome of the case was a foregone conclusion once it was decided that the state had engaged in a form of content regulation.

Susan Williams offers several refinements to Ely's treatment of content-neutral regulations. She explains that such cases really fall into two different groups: time, place, and manner (TPM) regulations, and regulations of symbolic speech. The Court has recently treated both groups alike but, Williams claims, this is a mistake. Restrictions on symbolic speech are more troublesome because, like content regulations, they affect the "communicative" aspects of speech (the symbols people use to communicate their messages). Larry Alexander accepts the problem that Williams sees, but is unsatisfied with her solution. Once we recognize that virtually all laws have incidental effects on speech, he argues, the only alternative is to give up the pretense of scrutiny altogether for incidental restrictions on speech, a strategy that would involve few changes in existing outcomes.

Issues of content regulation arise in many contexts, but nowhere more than in that doctrinally complex and messy domain known as public forum doctrine. In the concluding article in this section, Lillian BeVier tries to make sense out of existing public forum doctrine and argues, against the prevailing academic wisdom, that the existing approach is both explainable and defensible once we see that approach as representing a plausible vision of the role of categories and the role of judicial deference in the development of First Amendment doctrine.

HANS A. LINDE, "CLEAR AND PRESENT DANGER" REEXAMINED: DISSONANCE IN THE BRANDENBURG CONCERTO

22 Stan.L.Rev. 1163–1165, 1169–1172, 1174–1179 (1970).

THE BRANDENBURG CASE [a]

* * *

Brandenburg was a Ku Klux Klan organizer in Ohio. He was convicted on charges that he "did unlawfully by word of mouth advocate the necessity, or propriety of crime, violence, or unlawful methods of terrorism as a means of accomplishing political reform," and "assemble with a group or assemblage of persons formed to advocate the doctrines of criminal syndicalism." He had addressed an "organizers' meeting" of the Klan, conducted in the familiar style of that organization, after summoning a television reporter to make a film of the meeting that was broadcast and that later became the principal evidence for the prosecution.

* * *

---

4. 491 U.S. 397 (1989).   **a.** Brandenburg v. Ohio, 395 U.S. 444 (1969).

* * * The Court's brief per curiam opinion was not addressed to the constitutional immunity of Brandenburg's conduct under the particular circumstances. Rather, it declared the Ohio statute unconstitutional on its face. Specifically, the Court held that as written and applied, without any effort by the state courts to narrow it, the statute failed to distinguish between "mere advocacy" and "incitement to imminent lawless action." * * * In disposing of the Ohio statute on this ground, however, the per curiam opinion described the principle of the [Court's] recent decisions to be that advocacy of lawless action may be proscribed only when likely to lead to such action. The concurring Justices dissociated themselves from this apparent reference to the probability of danger as a first amendment test.

* * *

The Clear and Present Danger Test

The relevance of imminent public danger as a test of the validity of legislation, in distinction to the application of valid legislation to particular facts, has been an issue since *Gitlow v. New York*.[29] Justice Holmes had introduced the "clear and present danger" test for a unanimous Court in *Schenck v. United States*,[30] which sustained a conviction under provisions of the Espionage Act of 1917 written in "nonspeech" terms.[31] * * *

In *Schenck* the clear and present danger test was used to determine whether, under the circumstances, words alone might suffice to violate a concededly valid law. There was no claim that the law itself was invalid under the first amendment. "It seems to be admitted that if an actual obstruction of the recruiting service were proved, liability for words that produced that effect might be enforced," wrote Holmes. * * *

In *Gitlow*, 6 years later, a conviction for distributing another radical manifesto was founded on a law directed expressly against specified speech—a New York statute prohibiting the advocacy of "criminal anarchy."[35] The defense sought to invoke the constitutional criterion of

29. 268 U.S. 652, 670 (1925).

30. 249 U.S. 47 (1919).

31. The Espionage Act of 1917 made it criminal in wartime willfully to make "false statements with intent to interfere with" military operations, or to "cause insubordination, disloyalty, mutiny, or refusal of duty, in the military or naval forces of the United States," or to "obstruct the recruiting or enlistment service ...." * * * Schenck was indicted for conspiring to violate the latter two of these provisions. * * *

35. Law of Apr. 3, 1902, ch. 371, §§ 468a–b, [1902] N.Y.Laws 958, *as amended*, N.Y.Penal Law § 240.15 (McKinney 1957):

"§ 468a. *Criminal anarchy defined.* Criminal anarchy is the doctrine that organized government should be overthrown by force or violence, or by assassination of the executive head or of any of the executive officials of government, or by any unlawful means. The advocacy of such doctrine either by word of mouth or writing is a felony.

"§ 468b. *Advocacy of criminal anarchy.* Any person who:

"1. By word of mouth or writing advocates, advises or teaches the duty, necessity or propriety of overthrowing or overturning organized government by force or violence, or by assassination of the executive head or of any of the execu-

the *Schenck* opinion and contended that no actual danger of any concrete result of the manifesto had been shown. This effort to relate the "clear and present danger" test to a statute aimed expressly at the forbidden speech confronted the Court with a new question. In *Schenck* the "proximity and degree" of danger had served as a constitutional measure to test when words alone could be found to qualify as the act that Congress had intended to prohibit. How would the constitutional limits apply if government outlawed the words themselves?

Since New York's law itself defined the prohibited speech, the Court could choose among three positions. It could (1) accept this legislative judgment of the harmful potential of the proscribed words, subject to conventional judicial review; (2) independently scrutinize the facts to see whether a "danger," as stated in *Schenck,* justified suppression of the particular expression; or (3) hold that by legislating directly against the words rather than the effects, the lawmaker had gone beyond the leeway left to trial and proof by the holding in *Schenck* and had made a law forbidden by the first amendment.

The majority in *Gitlow* chose the first course. * * *

The dissenters chose the second position. "Clear and present danger" was constitutionally required to condemn Gitlow's manifesto under the New York Criminal Anarchy Act, just as it was to condemn Schenck's leaflet under the Espionage Act. * * *

FIRST AMENDMENT CONSTRAINTS ON LEGISLATION

"Clear and present danger" began as a test of the conditions under which speech or other expression may be subjected to some legal restraint directed in terms against something other than speech. It should be limited to its original meaning and function. "Clear and present danger" is of no use in judging the constitutionality of legislation that in terms restricts the permissible content of speech. Legislation directed in terms at expression, and particularly expression of political, social, or religious views, or against association for the purpose of such expression, should be found void on its face. The factual circumstances of the particular instance of expression cannot logically bear upon the constitutionality of the law. This follows, I believe, from the text of the first amendment and from the nature of legislation * * *.

* * *

* * * Other sections of the Bill of Rights are addressed to abuses that might characteristically come from executive or judicial officers in individual cases; of course, legislation that authorized such abuses would to that extent be unconstitutional. The first amendment, howev-

tive officials of government, or by any unlawful means; or,

"2. Prints, publishes, edits, issues or knowingly circulates, sells, distributes or publicly displays any book, paper, document, or written or printed matter in any

form, containing or advocating, advising or teaching the doctrine that organized government should be overthrown by force, violence or any unlawful means. . . .

"Is guilty of a felony . . . ." * * *

er, is addressed expressly to lawmakers.[46] It is not, in the first instance, an instruction to courts directing judges to protect freedom of speech, press, assembly, and petition. That judicial role indeed follows from judicial review. But the apprehension expressed in the first amendment is that legislators might decide to establish a religion, or prohibit the exercise of another, or suppress disfavored speech or publications *by law,* not that executive officers might do so illegally. So the first amendment forbade Congress to make such laws long before a judicial role in defining those freedoms was established.

It is not just a matter of fidelity to the text of the amendment. Attention to text earns only professional scorn in constitutional law. But when one among many constitutional limitations is literally directed against lawmaking, might the text perhaps embody a reason that even realists can respect? Might it make a difference whether legislators set out to make a law against acts, which may sometimes be accomplished by words, or a law against the words—a difference of constitutional dimension?

I believe that there is a constitutional difference, and that it is apparent when we focus on the legislative process, to which the first amendment was addressed, rather than on judicial defense of "protected" expression, which is a later development. The objective conditions under which the particular expression occurs * * *—whether stated as "clear and present danger" or some other formula—can be a factor at the time when suppression of that particular occurrence is before a court. It cannot easily be an element in the constitutionality of the decision to make a law proscribing a kind of speech or publication for the future. Yet the first amendment is addressed to that legislative decision, in the legislative forum, at that time. This intrinsic limitation on the rational use of "clear and present danger" is clearly illustrated by the Smith Act.

The Smith Act in 1940 wrote into federal law almost the exact terms of the New York Criminal Anarchy Act sustained in *Gitlow.* New York had enacted that law in 1902, soon after the assassination of President William McKinley. To the extent that this enactment represented a legislative diagnosis of a substantive evil, the evil was presumably the threat of assassination as an instrument of revolutionary politics, specifically the politics of anarchists. The legislative response was to outlaw not just actual or attempted assassination or conspiracies to assassinate, but the advocacy of anarchy. For nearly 20 years the Criminal Anarchy Act lay in repose. The legislators who had struck a blow against the bearded bomb-throwers of the 19th century went to their just rewards. The anarchists who hated organized government were succeeded by Marxists who preached the dictatorship of the proletariat; and with the triumph of Lenin's Bolsheviks in Russia, the radicalism of total freedom from government gave way to the most radically disciplined kind of

---

46. "Congress shall make no law ... abridging the freedom of speech, or of the press; or the right of the people peaceably to assemble, and to petition the Government for a redress of grievances." U.S. Const. amend. I. [Relocated footnote.]

organization. Whatever danger the new radicalism posed for New York in 1920, it was not the demonstrative assassinations that had been feared from the anarchists. Yet when Benjamin Gitlow, a former Socialist member of the New York Assembly, and his associates were prosecuted under the Criminal Anarchy Act for publishing their Left Wing Manifesto, the Supreme Court deferred to a supposed legislative judgment that their doctrines—separated from those of the anarchists by a history of bitter sectarian battles—carried with them enough substantive danger to justify their suppression.

Gitlow went to prison for 3 years. In the post-World War I patriotic reaction against a radicalism that had opposed the war as well as the nation's economic and political system, Attorney General A. Mitchell Palmer, whose own house had been bombed, demanded a federal peacetime sedition law. Another 20 years passed before a generation whose views on radicalism had been formed in 1919 achieved the seniority in Congress to enact such a law. Meanwhile Lenin's revolution gave way to Stalin's police state. While post-war economic collapse destroyed democratic regimes in continental Europe, the United States struggled through a disastrous depression without a revolution. The Government recognized the Soviet Union. That capital of Communism joined the League of Nations, and European Communist parties joined popular front coalitions against the threat from Hitler's Germany. Between the occupation of Czechoslovakia and the Ribbentrop–Molotov pact of 1939, the House of Representatives was working on a bill whose provenance was the fear of anarchist agitation in 1900 and the hatred of alien radicalism in 1919. It became law in 1940.

In the course of the following 5 years, the United States and the Soviet Union became allies in World War II. The American Communist Party transformed itself into the Communist Political Association to cooperate with the bourgeois establishment for the duration, and some of its leaders became war heroes. In 1945, while the Soviet Union and the United States were ushering in the brave new world at the San Francisco signing of the Charter of the United Nations, the Communist leadership, on instructions from Moscow by way of Paris, reorganized the party on the old model of a narrow, disciplined membership doctrinally committed to radical opposition to the existing order. In 1948 they were charged under the Smith Act with conspiring to carry out this act of reorganization for the purpose of advocating the overthrow of the Government of the United States by force and violence. * * *

Against this kaleidoscope of history, what was the legislative judgment that would deserve deference for its assessment of the danger from revolutionary speech? From conception to application, the Smith Act spans the whole spectrum of changing radicalism in this century. A prescription against internal revolutionary advocacy—designed as an answer to 19th-century anarchy, first applied locally against disciples of Leninism at the time of the Russian Revolution, transferred intact into federal law at the end of a bitter but largely peaceful economic crisis—

was found constitutional [in *Dennis v. United States* [b]] in punishing the organization of the Communist Party immediately after World War II, because of the exigencies of foreign policy in the years of the Cold War that followed. * * *

* * *

"Clear and present danger" is no help with the constitutionality of laws directed against words. *Was* the Smith Act constitutional in 1940, by the test of 1951? The better answer * * * is the third position that was possible in *Gitlow:* If you proscribe particular revolutionary acts, or attempts or conspiracies to commit them, then words inciting to such acts may perhaps be punishable if the evidence shows that they create imminent serious danger. But stick to such proscriptions; if your bill presumes the danger and directly outlaws the words themselves, it proposes a law "abridging the freedom of speech" forbidden you by the first amendment.

KENNETH L. KARST, EQUALITY AS A CENTRAL PRINCIPLE IN THE FIRST AMENDMENT

43 U.Chi.L.Rev. 20, 26–33, 35 (1975).

Although the principle of equal liberty of expression is inherent in the first amendment, it has only recently received full and explicit articulation in an opinion of the Supreme Court. Fleeting pronouncements are to be found in some opinions of a generation ago, and more recently the principle was the basis of an oft-cited concurring opinion.[34] But it was not until 1972, in *Police Department of the City of Chicago v. Mosely,*[35] that the Court enunciated the principle fully. In *Mosley,* a man who had been picketing peacefully near a school, carrying a sign protesting "black discrimination," sought to enjoin enforcement of a new city ordinance prohibiting picketing within 150 feet of a school during school hours; he had been advised by the police that he would be arrested if he continued to picket. The ordinance contained an exception for "peaceful picketing of any school involved in a labor dispute." The Seventh Circuit held the ordinance invalid as an overly broad restriction of first amendment rights. The Supreme Court affirmed but rested its decision on the ground that the ordinance violated the fourteenth amendment's guarantee of equal protection of the laws.

* * *

Adherence to the principle of equal liberty of expression will have far-reaching implications even though absolute equality is a practical impossibility. The principle requires courts to start from the assumption that all speakers and all points of view are entitled to a hearing, and permits deviation from this basic assumption only upon a showing of

b. 341 U.S. 494 (1951).

34. Cox v. Louisiana, 379 U.S. 536, 581 (1965) (Black, J., concurring).

35. 408 U.S. 92 (1972).

substantial necessity. The emergence of the equality principle compels a critical re-examination of several lines of first amendment decisions. We begin at the heart of the first amendment, with its prohibition on censorship of speech content.

* * *

The absence of a clear articulation of the principle of equal liberty of expression in Supreme Court decisions before *Mosley* may be attributable to a belief that the principle is so obviously central among first amendment values that it requires no explanation. In *Schacht v. United States,*[44] for example, a participant in an antiwar skit was prosecuted under a statute that prohibited wearing an Army uniform without authorization. The statute contained an exception allowing the uniform to be worn in a theatrical performance "if the portrayal does not tend to discredit" the armed forces. Justice Black, speaking for the Court, found it unnecessary to cite any authority or offer any explanation for holding that the statutory exception, "which leaves Americans free to praise the war in Vietnam but can send persons like Schacht to prison for opposing it, cannot survive in a country which has the First Amendment." There is a sense in which we have always known that "unless we protect [freedom of speech] for all, we will have it for none."

The equality principle, viewed as a barrier against content censorship, also implicitly underlies the elaborate first amendment doctrines that prohibit giving officials discretion to decide when speech shall be permitted and when it shall be punished or the speaker denied a license. The danger of delegating such discretionary authority is that a vague licensing[47] or criminal statute[48] would enable the prosecutor or censor to enforce the law selectively, tolerating orthodox views while suppressing unpopular ones.[49] The same concern underlies decisions imposing rigorous limits on the seizure of obscene literature.[50] It is not accidental that these first amendment doctrines serve equality not only at the level of principle but also at a practical level, defending nonconformists, dissenters, and the disadvantaged. The principle of equal liberty of expression, like the equal protection clause, has special relevance for protecting the downtrodden.

44. 398 U.S. 58 (1970).

47. *See, e.g.,* Shuttlesworth v. City of Birmingham, 394 U.S. 147 (1969); Joseph Burstyn, Inc. v. Wilson, 343 U.S. 495 (1952).

48. *See, e.g.,* Winters v. New York, 333 U.S. 507 (1948).

49. A similar concern is surely reflected in decisions like Cox v. Louisiana, 379 U.S. 536 (1965) and Edwards v. South Carolina, 372 U.S. 229 (1963), insofar as they involve the "hostile audience" problem. If the duty of the police in such a situation is to protect the speaker as long as they can, part of the reason must be to avoid letting the police decide to stop the speaker because of disagreement with his or her views. Feiner v. New York, 340 U.S. 315 (1951), decided the same day as Niemotko v. Maryland, 340 U.S. 268 (1951), is curiously insensitive to this concern. *Cf.* Gregory v. Chicago, 394 U.S. 111, 120 (1969) (Black, J., concurring): "[U]nder our democratic system of government, lawmaking is not entrusted to the moment-to-moment judgment of the policeman on his beat."

50. *E.g.,* Roaden v. Kentucky, 413 U.S. 496 (1973).

Given the centrality of the equality principle as a protection against content censorship, it seems likely that the Supreme Court will eventually complete the job of dismantling what Harry Kalven termed the "two-level" theory of speech.[52] According to this theory, which sprang from an unguarded dictum in *Chaplinsky v. New Hampshire*,[53] certain kinds of speech content, such as obscenity, libel, or "fighting words," lie outside the protection of the first amendment and may be banned without judicial scrutiny of the state's justification. Kalven destroyed the intellectual foundations of the two-level theory as early as 1960, in his classic analysis of the law of obscenity. He argued * * * that the two-level theory, by reading obscenity out of the first amendment because it lacks "redeeming social importance," violates the first amendment principle that prohibits weighing the social utility of speech.

The two-level theory is radically inconsistent with the principle of equal liberty of expression. While the equality principle in the first amendment does not prohibit all content regulation, it does require that courts start with a presumptive prohibition against governmental control of the content of speech. A showing of high probability of serious harm might justify regulation of a particular kind of speech content, but the two-level theory evades the question of justification by placing certain types of speech outside the scope of the first amendment. In other words, the two-level theory rejects the principle of equality in the marketplace of ideas.

In the field of defamation, the Court has already gone far toward abandoning the two-level theory. No one would suggest that *New York Times Co. v. Sullivan*[56] and its diverse offspring leave libel outside the boundaries of protected speech. And even the "fighting words" cases have fought their way out of the confines of the two-level theory, coming to rest on a variety of the clear-and-present-danger test.[59] * * *

In the obscenity cases, the Court continues to say that "obscene material is unprotected by the First Amendment."[61] Yet even in these cases the two-level theory is weakening. Justice Brennan, who fostered this child of the two-level theory, has now abandoned it.[62] * * *

In the long run the Court seems likely, in defining obscenity, to return to the guidelines it was beginning to develop before 1973 for *justifying* censorship: concern over the exposure of children or unwilling "captive audiences" to explicit sex-related material and concern over the commercial exploitation of sexual anxieties. Speech that is "obscene" will not be banished from all first amendment shelter, but will be subject to restriction upon a showing of serious harmful effects. The two-level theory is alive in the obscenity area, but it is not well.

---

52. Kalven, *The Metaphysics of the Law of Obscenity*, 1960 Sup.Ct.Rev. 1, 10.

53. 315 U.S. 568, 571–72 (1942).

56. 376 U.S. 254 (1964).

59. *See, e.g.,* Gooding v. Wilson, 405 U.S. 518 (1972); *cf.* Lewis v. New Orleans,

408 U.S. 913 (1972) (Powell, J., concurring). * * *

61. Miller v. California, 413 U.S. 15, 23 (1973).

62. Paris Adult Theatre I v. Slaton, 413 U.S. 49, 83–93 (1973) (dissenting opinion).

One last area where an offspring of the two-level theory survived longer than it deserved is the area of advertising and "commercial speech." *Valentine v. Chrestensen* [67] seemed to place commercial speech in general beyond constitutional protection. Despite occasional murmurs of discontent with such a categorical exclusion, the shadow of that decision darkened a corner of the first amendment until very recently.

Just last term, however, in *Bigelow v. Virginia*,[70] the Court invalidated a Virginia law that prohibited any advertisement encouraging the procuring of an abortion. * * * [T]he Court expressly laid to rest the notion that *Chrestensen* created a new branch of the two-level theory for commercial speech or advertising.

* * *

Just as the prohibition of government-imposed discrimination on the basis of race is central to equal protection analysis, protection against governmental discrimination on the basis of speech content is central among first amendment values.

GEOFFREY R. STONE, CONTENT REGULATION AND THE FIRST AMENDMENT

25 Wm. & Mary L.Rev. 189, 197–198, 200–202, 206–
207, 212–218, 225–228, 230–231 (1983).

It has been suggested that the "most puzzling aspect of the distinction between content-based and content-neutral restrictions is that either restriction reduces the sum total of information or opinion disseminated." [29] Indeed, in many instances a content-neutral restriction may more substantially reduce "the sum total of information or opinion disseminated" than a related content-based restriction. For example, a law banning all billboards restricts more speech than a law banning Nazi billboards, and a law limiting the political activities of public employees restricts more speech than a law limiting the Socialist political activities of public employees. Under current doctrine, however, the Court subjects the content-based restrictions to a more stringent standard of justification than the more suppressive content-neutral restrictions.

* * *

VIEWPOINT-BASED RESTRICTIONS

Consider two hypothetical statutes. First, suppose State X enacts a law prohibiting all billboards. Second, suppose State X enacts a law prohibiting all criticism of the antibillboard law. * * * The antibillboard law is content-neutral, * * * and thus will be tested by a relatively moderate standard of review; the anticriticism law is content-based, and thus will be tested by a more stringent standard of justification.

67. 316 U.S. 52 (1942).

70. 95 S.Ct. 2222 (1975).

29. Redish, [*The Content Distinction in First Amendment Analysis,* 34 Stan.L.Rev. 113, 128 (1981).]

The explanation is that the first amendment is concerned, not only with the extent to which a law reduces the total quantity of communication, but also—and perhaps even more fundamentally—with the extent to which the law distorts public debate. Although the anticriticism statute may produce only a small reduction in the total quantity of communication, the reduction falls entirely on one side of the debate. Moreover, the potential distorting effect of the statute is dramatic, for it subjects critics of the antibillboard law not to a mere marginal competitive disadvantage, but to an effective prohibition on the expression of their view. Any law that substantially prevents the communication of a particular idea, viewpoint, or item of information violates the first amendment except, perhaps, in the most extraordinary of circumstances. This is so, not because such a law restricts "a lot" of speech, but because by effectively excising a specific message from public debate, it mutilates "the thinking process of the community" and is thus incompatible with the central precepts of the first amendment.

* * *

Modest Viewpoint-Based Restrictions

The distorting effect, however, does not explain the distinction in its entirety, for not every law that restricts the communication of a particular idea, viewpoint, or item of information *substantially* prevents the message from being communicated. To the contrary, such restrictions are often limited in scope, restricting expression in only narrowly defined circumstances. For example, laws that prohibit the public destruction of a draft card as an expression of opposition to the draft, the display of the swastika within 100 feet of a synagogue on Yom Kippur, or the advocacy of homosexuality on any billboard are viewpoint-based, but restrict expression only in terms of time, place, or manner. They are thus unlikely to distort public debate to the same degree as viewpoint-based restrictions that more pervasively restrict the communication of particular messages. One might expect, therefore, that the Court would test these more modest viewpoint-based restrictions by less stringent standards, similar to the standards applied in the content-neutral context. The Court, however, has applied the content-based/content-neutral distinction, and the stringent standards of content-based analysis, even to these more modest viewpoint-based restrictions.

* * *

* * * Why? At least four possible explanations come to mind.

A. *Equality*

It has been suggested that the concept of equality "lies at the heart of the first amendment's protections against government regulation of the content of speech." [47] Indeed, it has been argued that, "[j]ust as the

---

47. Karst, *Equality as a Central Principle in the First Amendment,* 43 U.Chi.L.Rev. 20, 21 (1975). * * *

prohibition of government-imposed discrimination on the basis of race is central to equal protection analysis, protection against governmental discrimination on the basis of speech content is central among first amendment values." [48]   There is, indeed, a seemingly obvious connection between the content-based/content-neutral distinction and the concept of equality. When government restricts only certain ideas, viewpoints, or items of information, people wishing to express the restricted messages receive "unequal" treatment. When government restricts speech in a content-neutral manner, however, everyone is treated "equally." Moreover, an equality-based theory of the content-based/content-neutral distinction might explain the Court's use of the same standards of justification for *all* viewpoint-based restrictions, regardless of their potential to distort public debate. For just as we "strictly scrutinize" any law that discriminates on the basis of race, whether it denies an important or trivial benefit, so too must we "strictly scrutinize" any law that discriminates on the basis of content, whether it has a substantial or only a modest impact on public debate. It is the fact of discrimination, not the impact on public debate, that warrants "strict scrutiny."

* * *

Th[e] question remains whether the equality concept justifies the use of especially stringent standards of review to test the constitutionality of viewpoint-based restrictions that do not substantially prevent the communication of particular ideas, viewpoints, or items of information. In addressing this question, it is important to note that the Court's reliance on equality affects its analysis in two quite distinct ways.

First, recognition that a restriction is underinclusive may effectively undercut the asserted importance of the government interest said to support the restriction. In [*Police Department v.*] *Mosley*,[a] for example, the governmental interest in preventing the disruption of schools may be sufficient to justify a content-neutral restriction, but it loses force when the government creates an exemption. * * * In such circumstances, content-based restrictions may be unconstitutional, not because they are more "dangerous" than content-neutral restrictions, but because they are more difficult to justify. * * *

Second, the Court uses the equality concept to determine the appropriate standard of review. That is, once the Court characterizes the restriction as "content-based," it shifts immediately to the more stringent content-based standard of justification. This, of course, is the nub of the issue. Does the concern with equality explain this shift? The answer, I submit, is "no."

The problem, quite simply, is that restrictions on expression are rife with "inequalities," many of which have nothing whatever to do with

48. Karst, *supra* note 47, at 35.

a. 408 U.S. 92 (1972). In *Mosley* the Court held unconstitutional a Chicago ordinance that prohibited picketing or demonstrating on a public way within 150 feet of a school building while the school was in session. The ordinance expressly exempted "peaceful picketing of any school involved in a labor dispute."

content. The ordinance at issue in *Mosley,* for example, restricted picketing near schools, but left unrestricted picketing near hospitals, libraries, courthouses, and private homes. * * * Whatever the effect of these content-neutral inequalities on first amendment analysis, they are not scrutinized in the same way as content-based inequalities. Not all inequalities, in other words, are equal. And although the concern with equality may support the content-based/content-neutral distinction, it does not in itself have much explanatory power. To determine why some inequalities are more bothersome than others, we must look elsewhere.

B. *Communicative Impact*

A second possible explanation for the content-based/content-neutral distinction derives from the notion that the government ordinarily may not restrict speech because of its *communicative impact*—that is, because of "a fear of how people will react to what the speaker is saying."

* * *

In the most common communicative impact situation, the government attempts to restrict expression because the expression may persuade individuals to act in an undesirable or unlawful manner. For example, the government might prohibit any person from distributing antiwar leaflets within 100 feet of an enlistment center in order to prevent persons from being persuaded not to enlist in the armed forces. Is such a law, despite its modest suppressive effect, unconstitutional? May government legitimately restrict speech for this reason?

The Court has long embraced an "antipaternalistic" understanding of the first amendment. It has observed, for example, that the first amendment assumes that ideas and information are not in themselves "harmful, that people will perceive their own best interests if only they are well enough informed, and that the best means to that end is to open the channels of communication rather than to close them." * * *

* * *

This antipaternalistic understanding of the first amendment explains, at least in part, the Court's use of stringent standards of review to test the constitutionality of content-based restrictions that the government attempts to justify in paternalistic terms. Because paternalistic justifications are constitutionally disfavored, the government may restrict expression for paternalistic reasons in only the most compelling circumstances, if ever. And this is so even if the restriction does not substantially prevent the communication of a particular idea, viewpoint, or item of information, for the Court's use of stringent standards of review in such cases derives, not from a concern about the potential distorting effects of the restriction, but from the disfavored status of the government's justification.

In the second, and next most common, communicative impact situation, government attempts to restrict expression because the ideas or information communicated may offend others or may induce those who are offended to react in a hostile or disruptive manner. For example, to avoid offense to passersby and to prevent possible violent retaliation, a city might prohibit any person from displaying a swastika within 100 feet of a synagogue on Yom Kippur. Is such a law, despite its modest suppressive effect, unconstitutional? May government legitimately restrict speech for this reason?

The Court has long maintained that the first amendment does not permit government to prohibit the public expression of views merely because they are offensive or unpopular. * * *

The Court's reluctance to accept the "heckler's veto," and its refusal to permit one group of citizens effectively to "censor" the expression of others because they dislike or are prepared violently to oppose their ideas, seem well-grounded in the central precepts of the first amendment. Thus, "intolerance-based" justifications for restricting expression, like paternalistic justifications, are constitutionally disfavored, even if the restriction does not substantially prevent the communication of a particular idea, viewpoint, or item of information.

* * *

C. Distortion of Public Debate

A third possible explanation for the content-based/content-neutral distinction derives from the fact that content-based restrictions, by their very nature, restrict the communication of only some messages and thus affect public debate in a content-differential manner. Indeed, as we have seen, some content-based restrictions so substantially impair the communication of particular ideas, viewpoints, or items of information that, for that reason alone, they are presumptively invalid. We are concerned here, however, with viewpoint-based restrictions that do not *substantially* impair the communication of particular messages. Because these more modest viewpoint-based restrictions leave open alternative channels of communication, they do not as dramatically skew the thought processes of the community. The question, then, is whether the disparate effects of these more modest viewpoint-based restrictions can explain the content-based/content-neutral distinction.

* * *

[But] * * * there is in fact reason to doubt that we can confidently delineate a category of viewpoint-based restrictions that do not significantly distort public debate. As history teaches, judicial evaluations of viewpoint-based restrictions are especially likely to "become involved with the ideological predispositions of those doing the evaluating."[129] There is a danger, in other words, that judges and jurors may be influenced by conscious or unconscious biases that may undermine their ability to evaluate accurately and impartially the extent to which particular viewpoint-based restrictions actually impair the communication of

---

129. J. Ely, [Democracy and Distrust 112 (1980).]

specific, often disfavored, messages. Thus, the safest and most sensible course may be to test all viewpoint-based restrictions by the same stringent standards of review that we would apply to restrictions that substantially prevent the communication of particular ideas, viewpoints, or items of information.

* * *

D. *Motivation*

A fourth possible explanation for the content-based/content-neutral distinction derives from the notion, apparently embraced by the Court, that "when regulation is based on the content of speech, governmental action must be scrutinized more carefully to ensure that communication has not been prohibited 'merely because public officials disapprove the speaker's views.' " [130] This concern with ferreting out "improper" motivation reflects a general shift in constitutional jurisprudence, for although the Warren Court tended to shy away from motivation as a central feature of constitutional analysis,[131] the Burger Court has tended increasingly to emphasize motivation as a paramount constitutional concern.[132]

In the first amendment context, the concept of improper governmental motivation consists chiefly of the precept that the government may not restrict expression simply because it disagrees with the speaker's views. * * * This precept [is] central to our first amendment jurisprudence, for any effort of government to restrict speech because it conveys a "false" or "bad" idea is inconsistent with the three basic first amendment assumptions: in the long run, the best test of truth is "the power of the thought to get itself accepted in the competition of the market;" [136] in a self-governing system, the people, not the government "are entrusted with the responsibility for judging and evaluating the relative merits of conflicting arguments;" [137] and, in our constitutional system, the protection of free expression is designed to enhance personal growth, self-realization, and the development of individual autonomy.[138]

* * *

The problem, of course, is to devise some effective means to ferret out these improper motivations. It is at this point that the content-

---

130. Consolidated Edison Co. v. Public Serv. Comm'n, 447 U.S. 530, 536 (1980) (quoting Niemotko v. Maryland, 340 U.S. 268, 282 (1951) (Frankfurter, J., concurring)). *Accord* United States Postal Serv. v. Council of Greenburgh Civic Ass'ns, 453 U.S. 114, 132 (1981).

131. *See, e.g.,* O'Brien v. United States, 391 U.S. 367 (1968). * * *

132. *See* Rogers v. Lodge, 458 U.S. 613 (1982); Crawford v. Board of Educ., 458 U.S. 527 (1982); Washington v. Seattle School Dist. No. 1, 458 U.S. 457 (1982);

United States v. Goodwin, 457 U.S. 368 (1982); Larson v. Valente, 456 U.S. 228 (1982); Stone v. Graham, 449 U.S. 39 (1980); Bell v. Wolfish, 441 U.S. 520 (1979); Washington v. Davis, 426 U.S. 229 (1976).

136. Abrams v. United States, 250 U.S. 616, 630 (1919).

137. First Nat'l Bank v. Bellotti, 435 U.S. 765, 791 (1978).

138. Whitney v. California, 274 U.S. 357, 375 (1927) (Brandeis, J., concurring). * * *

based/content-neutral distinction enters the picture, for the probability that an improper motivation has tainted a decision to restrict expression is far greater when the restriction is directed at a particular idea, viewpoint, or item of information than when it is content-neutral. Indeed, in the content-neutral context the risk of improper motivation is quite low, for such restrictions necessarily apply to all ideas, viewpoints, and items of information, and are thus unlikely to reflect a specific intent on the part of those who adopted the restriction to suppress any particular message. In such circumstances, it seems sensible to presume the absence of improper motivation and to put the burden of proving such a motivation on the party challenging the restriction on motivational grounds.

When a restriction is directed at a particular idea, viewpoint, or item of information, however, the risk of improper motivation is quite high, for government officials considering the adoption of such a restriction will almost invariably have their own opinions about the merits of the restricted speech and there is thus a substantial risk that, in deciding whether to adopt the restriction, they will be affected, either consciously or unconsciously, by an improper motive.

JOHN HART ELY, FLAG DESECRATION: A CASE STUDY IN THE ROLES OF CATEGORIZATION AND BALANCING IN FIRST AMENDMENT ANALYSIS

88 Harv.L.Rev. 1482–1487, 1490–1491, 1496–1502 (1975).

[Ely begins his article with a discussion of *United States v. O'Brien,* [a] where the Supreme Court upheld a conviction for draft card burning.]

I

The "crux of the Court's opinion" in *O'Brien* was that:

[A] governmental regulation is sufficiently justified ... [1] if it furthers an important or substantial governmental interest; [2] if the governmental interest is unrelated to the suppression of free expression; and [3] if the incidental restriction on alleged First Amendment freedoms is no greater than is essential to the furtherance of that interest.

Whatever *O'Brien*'s other merits or demerits, the Court is surely to be commended for here attempting something it attempts too seldom, the statement of a coherent and applicable test. The test is not limited to cases involving so-called "symbolic speech." (One conclusion that should emerge from this Comment is that that is one of its virtues.) The test is, however, limited in the sense that it is incomplete. The fact that a regulation does not satisfy criterion [2] does not necessarily mean that it is unconstitutional. It means "only" that the case is switched onto another track and an approach other than that indicated in criteri-

a. 391 U.S. 367 (1968).

on [3] will be employed, a categorizing approach elaborated in other decisions of the late Warren period, which is in fact substantially more demanding than the approach indicated by criterion [3]. [Let us begin by looking at the latter approach.]

II

Criterion [3]'s requirement that the inhibition of expression be no greater than is essential to the furtherance of the state's interest strikes a familiar chord: "less restrictive alternative" analysis is common in constitutional law generally and in first amendment cases in particular. But there is always a latent ambiguity in the analysis, and *O'Brien* brought it to the surface. Weakly construed, it could require only that there be no less restrictive alternative capable of serving the state's interest *as efficiently as it is served by the regulation under attack.* But * * * in virtually every case involving real legislation, a more perfect fit involves some added cost. In effect, therefore, this weak formulation would reach only laws that engage in the gratuitous inhibition of expression, requiring only that a prohibition not outrun the interest it is designed to serve.

Further language in the *O'Brien* opinion, and the holding of the case, indicate that this is the strongest form of less restrictive alternative analysis in which, under the circumstances, the Court was prepared to engage. Coupled with the trivial functional significance the Court attached to criterion [1]'s critical word "substantial," however, this turned out to be no protection at all: legislatures simply do not enact wholly useless provisions. It is therefore no surprise to discover that earlier cases protecting more traditional forms of expression (such as the distribution of handbills [20]), although they too purported to apply a sort of less restrictive alternative test, gave it a significantly stronger meaning. The point of these cases, in contradistinction to *O'Brien,* was that the absence of gratuitous inhibition is *not* enough. For in banning the distribution of handbills, municipalities pursue a goal unconnected with the inhibition of expression, the reduction of litter, and they do so without placing any gratuitous limits on expression: the entirety of an anti-handbill ordinance serves the goal of reducing litter. Such cases thus suggest that the existence of possible alternative approaches—such as more trash cans and an anti-littering ordinance—triggers a serious balancing of interests: the question is whether the marginally greater effectiveness of an anti-handbill ordinance relative to alternative means of litter control justifies the greater burden on communication. In order to clear room for effective expression, the Court was saying, cities will simply have to put up with some litter, to be satisfied with less than optimal vindication of the interest they are pursuing, unconnected with expression though it is.

* * *

20. *See, e.g.,* Schneider v. State, 308 U.S. 147, 162 (1939). * * *

[It] seems likely that the Court will * * * distinguish between familiar and unorthodox modes of communication in deciding whether genuinely to balance in evaluating less restrictive alternatives or rather simply to assure itself, as it will always be able to, that no gratuitous inhibition of expression has been effected. In any event, the question of how to accommodate freedom of expression with the state's various expression-unconnected interests is, and will remain, an extremely difficult one. * * *

III

The two sorts of review we have been discussing—the "no gratuitous inhibition" approach that upheld the draft card burning law, and the balancing approach that has been employed in cases involving more familiar forms of expression—do differ significantly. That is not, however, because the latter is especially protective of expression (in fact it is notoriously unreliable) but rather because the former, honestly applied, will invalidate nothing. There was, of course, a time when balancing was sufficient to satisfy a majority of the Court as a general approach to the first amendment. But that was hardly the attitude of the Warren Court, at least in its later years. During the very period when *O'Brien* was decided, the Court was making clear its dissatisfaction with a general balancing approach, indicating that only expression fairly assignable to one of an increasingly limited set of narrowly defined categories could be denied constitutional protection. Thus in *Brandenburg v. Ohio,* [33] decided a year after *O'Brien,* a unanimous Court, invalidating the Ohio Criminal Syndicalism Act, indicated that:

> [T]he constitutional guarantees of free speech and free press do not permit a State to forbid or proscribe advocacy of the use of force or of law violation except where such advocacy is directed to inciting or producing imminent lawless action and is likely to incite or produce such action.

There is in *Brandenburg* no talk of balancing, let alone of a simple prohibition of gratuitous suppression: the expression involved in a given case either does or does not fall within the described category, and if it does not it is protected. * * * Quite obviously the Court of the late Warren period had two radically different first amendment approaches for what it saw as two significantly different sets of problems. Something about O'Brien's case caused the Court to adopt an approach much less protective of first amendment interests than that put forth in *Brandenburg.*

* * *

V

When the Court in *O'Brien* gets around to what is obviously intended as the definitive statement of its test—specifically in what I have

---

33. 395 U.S. 444 (1969) (per curiam).

designated criterion [2]—it [hints at the difference between these two approaches]:

> [A] governmental regulation is sufficiently justified ... if it furthers an important or substantial governmental *interest* [*that*] *is unrelated to the suppression of free expression....*

[This suggests that we should inquire] into whether the governmental interest or interests that support the regulation are related to the suppression of expression.

Obviously this approach is not self-defining: it can, for one thing, be interpreted in a way that will guarantee that its demand can always be satisfied. Restrictions on free expression are rarely defended on the ground that the state simply didn't like what the defendant was saying; reference will generally be made to some danger beyond the message, such as a danger of riot, unlawful action or violent overthrow of the government. Thus in *Brandenburg* the state's defense was not that the speech in question was distasteful, though it surely was, but rather that speeches of that sort were likely to induce people to take the law into their own hands. The reference of *O'Brien*'s second criterion is therefore not to the ultimate interest to which the state is able to point, for that will always be unrelated to expression, but rather to the causal connection the state asserts. If, for example, the state asserts an interest in discouraging riots, the Court will ask why that interest is implicated in the case at bar. If the answer is (as in such cases it will likely have to be) that the danger was created by what the defendant was saying, the state's interest is not unrelated to the suppression of free expression within the meaning of *O'Brien*'s criterion [2]. The categorization approach of cases like *Brandenburg* * * * rather than (either variant of) *O'Brien*'s criterion [3] is therefore in order, and the regulation will very likely be invalidated. The critical question would therefore seem to be whether the harm that the state is seeking to avert is one that grows out of the fact that the defendant is communicating, and more particularly out of the way people can be expected to react to his message, or rather would arise even if the defendant's conduct had no communicative significance whatever.

There may be a temptation to conclude that one has seen all this before, or at least its functional equivalent, in the shopworn distinction between "regulation of content" and "regulation of time, place and manner." That would be a mistaken equation, however, and one with severe costs for free expression. For the state obviously can move, and often does, "simply" to control the time, place or manner of communication out of a concern for the likely effect of the communication on its audience. Thus in *Tinker* [*v. Des Moines School District* [b]] the state regulated only the place and manner of expression—no armbands in school—but it did so, or at least this is the account most favorable to the state, because it feared the effect that the message those armbands conveyed would have on the other children. (Had the armbands lacked

b.   393 U.S. 503 (1969).

communicative significance, there would have been no way to defend or even account for the regulation.) * * *

O'Brien was different. The interests upon which the government relied were interests, having mainly to do with the preservation of selective service records, that would have been equally threatened had O'Brien's destruction of his draft card totally lacked communicative significance—had he, for example, used it to start a campfire for a solitary cookout or dropped it in his garbage disposal for a lark. (The law prohibited all knowing destructions, public or private.) Perhaps the Court should have engaged in some serious balancing, but its refusal even to consider the categorization approach appropriate to cases like *Brandenburg* * * * was quite correct. *O'Brien* is more like *Prince v. Massachusetts,* [67] in which the Court upheld the application of the state's child labor law to a child distributing Jehovah's Witness literature. Obviously the state was thereby regulating expressive activity, but the evil it was trying to avert was one that would have been equally implicated had the child been engaged in work with no communicative component whatever. Similarly, by employing what amounts to a balancing test to permit some municipal regulation of sound-trucks, the Court surely permits some restriction of expression. But again, the values the state seeks to promote by such regulation, values of quiet and repose, would be threatened as much by meaningless moans and static (which is usually how it comes out anyway) as by a political message. * * *

Sorting out free speech issues along these lines should have salutary consequences for freedom of expression. The debate on the first amendment has traditionally proceeded on the assumption that categorization and balancing—and I am using this as a generic term, to encompass all approaches (including "clear and present danger") that consider the likely effect of the communication—are mutually exclusive approaches to the various problems that arise under the first amendment. The categorizers, or "absolutists," were surely right that theirs was the approach more likely to protect expression in crisis times. But just as surely, an all-encompassing categorization approach could be made to look awfully silly, indeed to confess error, by demonstrations that there were contexts in which a refusal to admit the possibility of balancing was simply untenable. The sound-truck cases furnished a familiar example: "I understand that you would protect sound-trucks. But what about a hospital zone? What about the middle of the night? Surely you wouldn't let a mayoral candidate aim a bullhorn at your window at three in the morning. Surely you have to balance, or employ a clear and present danger test, at *some* point."

The argument is convincing—in context. But what the decisions of the late Warren era began to recognize is that categorization and balancing need not be regarded as competing general theories of the first amendment, but are more helpfully employed in tandem, each with its

67. 321 U.S. 158 (1944).

own legitimate and indispensable role in protecting expression. The fact that one would balance where the evil the state would avert does not grow out of the message being communicated—thereby balancing away the right to use a bullhorn at three in the morning, to shout "Boo!" at a cardiac patient, or to firebomb the induction center in protest against the draft—does not, the Court began to understand, commit him to a balancing approach to the constitutionality of a Criminal Syndicalism Law.

The categorizers were right: where messages are proscribed because they are dangerous, balancing tests inevitably become intertwined with the ideological predispositions of those doing the balancing—or if not that, at least with the relative confidence or paranoia of the age in which they are doing it—and we must build barriers as secure as words are able to make them. That means rigorous definition of the limited categories of expression that are unprotected by the first amendment. But in order thus to protect what really is in need of and amenable to such protection, we must first set to one side, by determinate principle rather than hunch, those situations to which such a categorization approach will inevitably prove unsuited. The Court has made a clear start in this direction, and it is a good one.

KENT GREENAWALT, O'ER THE LAND OF THE FREE: FLAG BURNING AS SPEECH

37 UCLA L.Rev. 925, 926, 930–937, 939 (1990).

I consider the soundness of the Supreme Court's decision last June in *Texas v. Johnson*[4] under general first amendment principles and ask whether the outcome should be different for the federal statute whose validity is now under review.[5] * * *

Last June the Supreme Court held, five to four, that Gregory Johnson's conviction under a Texas statute punishing flag desecration violated the first amendment guarantee of free speech. Johnson and other demonstrators during the 1984 Republican National Convention had protested Republican policies and dramatized the dangers of nuclear war. Johnson set a stolen American flag burning. He was convicted under a penal section entitled "Desecration of Venerated Object," which forbade intentionally or knowingly desecrating a state or national flag. To "desecrate" meant to "deface, damage, or otherwise physically mistreat in a way that the actor knows will seriously offend one or more persons likely to observe or discover his action."

* * *

THE CONSTITUTIONAL LEVEL OF SCRUTINY

* * * The critical question [in *Johnson* was whether the law was]

4. 109 S.Ct. 2533 (1989).

5. Flag Protection Act of 1989, Pub.L. No. 101–131, 103 Stat. 777 (Oct. 28, 1989) (amending 18 U.S.C. § 700 (1988)). [Short-

ly after this article was published the Supreme Court held the Flag Protection Act unconstitutional in United States v. Eichman, 110 S.Ct. 2404 (1990).]

governed by the formulation in *United States v. O'Brien*[19] or by some more demanding standard.

O'Brien was convicted for publicly burning his draft card. Congress had recently enacted a provision forbidding destruction of draft cards. * * *

Refusing to look beyond language to underlying purpose, * * * the Court treated the statute as not directed at communication. * * * [T]he Court then elaborated a test for such circumstances. A government regulation otherwise within constitutional power is sufficiently justified "if it furthers an important or substantial governmental interest; if the governmental interest is unrelated to the suppression of free expression; and if the incidental restriction on alleged First Amendment freedoms is no greater than is essential to the furtherance of that interest." * * *

In practice, the *O'Brien* test has [offered little First Amendment protection.] In *O'Brien* itself the Court accepted thin claims that granting a right to burn draft cards would interfere with the effective administration of the draft. In no later case has the Court actually held that a defendant's communicative activity was protected against application of a law not directed at communication. Since Johnson's prospects would have been poor had the Court used only the *O'Brien* test, the inquiry whether the Texas provision was directed at communication was of major importance. Thus, also, it is critically important whether the Court will determine that the new federal statute is directed at communication.

Some of what the Supreme Court says in *Johnson* on this subject * * * is a bit confusing. An initial effort at categorization may be clarifying. One way in which a law may be directed at communication is in distinguishing between good messages and bad ones. This is what is known as viewpoint discrimination. Since the government should not be in the business of preferring some messages to others, viewpoint discrimination rightly has been seen as highly threatening to free speech values and is considered to be invalid absent an extremely strong justification. Another way in which a law might be said to be directed at communication is by penalizing communicative acts that have harmful consequences, with harm judged independently of acceptance or rejection of the message. A law forbidding communications that are highly likely to cause deep emotional upset or to trigger violent responses is of this sort. We may call this harmful reaction regulation. A third way in which a law conceivably might be said to be directed at communication is when it protects the communicative value of something. We may call this symbol protection. It is incorrect to suppose that such a law inevitably must be aimed at acts which are themselves communicative. Suppose a country's flag is one solid color, bright red. To protect the symbolic force of that color, the state forbids any human use of bright red except in the flag. No walls or cars can be painted bright red, no clothes can be

19. 391 U.S. 367, 377 (1968).

dyed bright red. The law aims to protect the communicative force of a symbol, but it is not aimed particularly at communicative acts.

* * *

The Texas statute under which Johnson was convicted prohibited flag desecration, defined as damage or mistreatment of the flag "in a way that the actor knows will seriously offend" someone "likely to observe or discover his action." Since burning has been a recommended way to dispose of worn out flags, not every burning of the flag was offensive. In form, the statute was regulation to prevent harmful reaction, the offense to observers. What makes flag burning offensive? Almost always it is that the people burning the flag are intentionally showing some kind of disrespect for it. That need not be so. We can imagine someone lighting a campfire with a flag that happens to be near at hand, and the Court itself mentions a tired person dragging a flag through the mud. Either act might cause offense, and the actor might know that, yet he would have no message to communicate. But these are rare instances.

* * *

Assuming that the basis for people's taking offense is the message communicated, the Court does not immediately conclude that strict scrutiny of the statute is required. It asks instead whether the state has an interest behind its prohibition on flag burning that is unrelated to the suppression of expression. If the state had such an interest, it would apparently succeed in achieving the more relaxed scrutiny of *O'Brien*. One asserted state interest was the prevention of violence. The Court points out that offense is often not followed by violence and that first amendment decisions closely circumscribe when speech may be punished because of a likely violent reaction. Much controversial speech causes offense, and states cannot forbid all offensive speech because violence may occasionally result. This is standard first amendment doctrine, and the Court rightly eliminates prevention of violence as a basis for the Texas statute.

* * *

Having disposed of violence prevention as a possible basis for the statute, the *Johnson* Court turns to another asserted state justification, that of preserving the flag as a symbol of nationhood and national unity. The Court says that the state's interest is related to expression. It suggests that the state's concern is that flag desecration will cause people to stop believing that the flag stands for nationhood and national unity or that we enjoy unity as a nation. "These concerns blossom only when a person's treatment of the flag communicates some message...." Since Johnson's "political expression was restricted" because he expressed dissatisfaction with the country's policies, the "State's asserted interest in preserving the special symbolic character of the flag" must be subjected to the " 'most exacting scrutiny.' "

The Court's analysis on this point flows too smoothly. * * * Suppose people constantly dragged flags through the mud and used them to light campfires. The strength of the flag as a symbol might well diminish if people continually treated it shabbily. And its strength as a symbol could be damaged even if people mistreated it in demonstrations in favor of nationhood and national unity. Thus, the threat to the flag as a symbol of nationhood and national unity does not flow only from mistreatment that casts doubt on whether the flag represents national unity, whether national unity exists, or whether national unity of the sort we have is desirable. It is just this point that leads Justice Stevens to say in dissent that "[t]he content of respondent's message has no relevance whatsoever to the case." Nevertheless, the most offensive instances of shabby treatment are probably those that in some way attack the government, national unity, or the idea of the flag; and this type of attack was an aspect of Johnson's causing offense. Further, most people who wish to treat the flag shabbily knowing that what they do will offend others will be people with just such anti-establishment messages. In effect, the Texas law impinges much more heavily on people with these messages than on others. * * *

* * *

THE NEW FEDERAL STATUTE

* * *

The Flag Protection Act of 1989 provides that anyone who "knowingly mutilates, defaces, physically defiles, burns, maintains on the floor or ground, or tramples upon" a United States flag is guilty of a crime. The Act excepts actions to dispose of worn or soiled flags. Congress defeated efforts to amend the bill to cover only public acts; the law covers acts committed in private as well as in public. The idea underlying the statute is plain enough. The definition of the crime is removed as far as possible from focusing on communicative acts. The objective is to have this statute treated like the draft card statute in *O'Brien*. If it is treated as a statute not directed at communication that happens to interfere with some acts of symbolic speech, the *O'Brien* test will apply when communicative flag burning is punished. That standard of scrutiny is much more lenient than strict scrutiny. It is the drafters' aspiration that convictions will be upheld.

* * *

In *Johnson*, the Court assumes that only acts with a message could threaten the flag as a symbol of nationhood and national unity. * * * As I have noted, the *Johnson* Court is wrong on this point. Noncommunicative acts can tarnish the flag as a symbol. So the purpose of preserving the flag as a symbol does reach some defacing and destruction of the flag that is noncommunicative. But the correlation between forbidden acts that pose the threat and those meant to communicate is very high; moreover, the legislative history contains overwhelming evidence that Congress was concerned about those who intentionally show disrespect for the flag. Despite the absence of any surface reference to communicative acts, the purpose of the law is to inhibit expression. Although I shall not make the argument, I believe that purpose is so clearly establishable here that it should not be disregarded by the courts.[a]

SUSAN H. WILLIAMS, CONTENT DISCRIMINATION AND THE FIRST AMENDMENT

139 U.Pa.L.Rev. 615, 636–648, 650–654 (1991).

THE DEMISE OF DISTINCTIONS WITHIN CONTENT-NEUTRAL REGULATIONS

The meaning of content discrimination evolved alongside the development of different doctrinal lines designed to deal with the distinct problems of content-neutral regulations of speech. Two of the most important of these lines are the symbolic speech doctrine and the TPM doctrine. Unfortunately, the Supreme Court recently collapsed these two lines into a single, combined standard that apparently applies to almost all cases involving content-neutral regulations.

1. The Time, Place, or Manner Doctrine

The TPM doctrine had its genesis in and acquired its name from the early licensing cases. * * * The Court upheld a licensing scheme in *Cox v. New Hampshire*[93] after finding that it did not authorize discrimination on the basis of content, asserting that "[i]f a municipality has authority to control the use of its public streets for parades or processions, as it undoubtedly has, it cannot be denied authority to give consideration, without unfair discrimination, to time, place and manner in relation to the other proper uses of the streets."

The name of this category of regulations—TPM—might suggest that these restrictions are distinguished by the fact that they are not total bans on speech but merely regulations of the circumstances in which speech may occur. In other words, the "opposite" of a TPM regulation would be a complete ban or prohibition. The language in these early cases indicates, however, that a TPM regulation is distinguished primarily by its lack of content discrimination, either on its face or in its operation, rather than by the limited nature of its prohibition. It regulates the circumstances of speech rather than the content of the speech. The "opposite" of a TPM regulation is a content-based regulation.

The Court's approach to format bans confirms this understanding of TPM regulations. If any content-neutral rule ought to qualify as a

a. On June 28, 1995 the House of Representatives passed a proposed amendment to the Constitution which provides:

The Congress and the States shall have power to prohibit the physical desecration of the flag of the United States.

H.J. Res. 79, 104th Cong., 1st Sess. On June 29, 1995 the joint resolution was referred to the Senate Judiciary Committee. [Ed. note.]

93. 312 U.S. 569 (1941).

prohibition rather than a regulation of circumstances, a ban on an entire format of speech, such as handbilling or posting signs on public utility poles, would appear to be it. The Court, however, has consistently treated format bans as TPM regulations.[98] The Court has refused to do so only when the format bans are themselves content-based.[99]

It took some time and a couple of false starts, however, before the Court was able to specify the test to be applied to regulations of the time, place, or manner of speech. The first serious attempt to define a standard came with the "compatibility" approach in *Grayned v. City of Rockford*.[101] The majority in *Grayned* held that "[t]he nature of a place, 'the pattern of its normal activities, dictate the kinds of regulations of time, place, and manner that are reasonable.' ... The crucial question is whether the manner of expression is basically incompatible with the normal activity of a particular place at a particular time." The only specific doctrinal formula suggested by the Court to implement this approach was that "the regulation must be narrowly tailored to further the State's legitimate interest." * * *

The *Grayned* compatibility approach has, however, been overtaken by a more structured, and generally more lenient, test. The first statement of the modern TPM test appears * * * as a passing reference in a case creating new doctrine in a different area of first amendment jurisprudence. In *Virginia State Board of Pharmacy v. Virginia Citizens Consumer Council, Inc.*,[104] the Court announced a new approach to commercial speech. In the course of its analysis, however, it purported to summarize existing doctrine on TPM regulations, asserting that such regulations are constitutional "provided that they are justified without reference to the content of the regulated speech, that they serve a significant governmental interest, and that in doing so they leave open ample alternative channels for communication of the information."

The first two branches of the three part test do not raise any problems. The content neutrality requirement is a reasonable inference from the early licensing cases. The "significant" state interest requirement also has a foundation in precedent. A significant state interest represents a type of lowest common denominator: some of the earlier cases required a stronger state interest than that, but all required at least that much. The last branch of the test is, however, a substantial departure from precedent. * * *

---

98. *See* * * * Schad v. Mount Ephraim, 452 U.S. 61, 74–77 (1981) (ban on live entertainment); Schneider v. State, 308 U.S. 147, 155 (1939) (ban on handbilling); *cf.* Members of the City Council v. Taxpayers for Vincent, 466 U.S. 789, 803–06 (1984) (analyzing a ban on posting signs on public utility poles under the combined TPM and *O'Brien* standard that developed later).

99. *See, e.g.,* Metromedia Inc. v. San Diego, 453 U.S. 490, 515–17 (1981) (reject-ing ban on billboards that made exceptions for some commercial billboards); Carey v. Brown, 447 U.S. 455, 460–61, 470 (1980) (rejecting ban on residential picketing that made an exception for labor picketing) * * *.

101. 408 U.S. 104 (1972). * * *

104. 425 U.S. 748 (1976).

Although the names of the two tests sound similar, there is a substantial difference between a tailoring requirement, like the least restrictive means test, and an ample alternatives requirement. The tailoring requirement asks * * * whether there is a different method of achieving the government's goals that places fewer restrictions on first amendment freedom. The "least restrictive means" test is the strictest type of tailoring requirement: in theory the regulation will be struck down if there is any alternative method of achieving the government's goal that is less intrusive on speech. The "narrowly tailored" standard, as recently interpreted by the Court, is considerably weaker, requiring only that the means/end fit be good, reasonable, and not an unnecessary intrusion on speech. All tailoring requirements, however, are concerned with the fit between the government end served by the regulation and the means used.

The *Virginia Pharmacy* ample alternatives test, on the other hand, * * * asks not about the government's alternatives, but about the speaker's alternatives. The requirement exists because the Court believes that if adequate alternative channels of communication remain, then a regulation restricting a particular alternative will have no more than a minimal effect on speech. This test can also have degrees of strictness. The Court has sometimes described the requirement as one of ample alternative channels, which appears to set a high standard. In practice, however, the Court has often applied an "adequate" alternatives test, not an "ample" alternatives test. For example, in *Members of the City Council v. Taxpayers for Vincent*,[115] the Court upheld a ban on the posting of signs on public property, asserting that the remaining modes of communication were adequate without specifying what alternatives were available. * * *

* * *

Despite the test's questionable beginning, the Court reiterated its reliance on this three-part standard in several subsequent cases. The adequate alternatives branch became firmly established and, although applied rather differently by different members of the Court, it was relatively uncontroversial. * * * The major controversy * * * came to center around whether the test included a tailoring requirement, and if so, how stringent a requirement.

This issue was recently settled in the case of *Ward v. Rock Against Racism*.[120] The Court held that although a TPM regulation must be "narrowly tailored," it need not be the least restrictive means of serving the government's interest. Indeed, the tailoring requirement is satisfied as long as the " 'regulation promotes a substantial government interest that would be achieved less effectively absent the regulation' " and the regulation does not "burden substantially more speech than is necessary to further the government's legitimate interests."

115. 466 U.S. 789 (1984).   **120.** 109 S.Ct. 2746 (1989).

Thus, the TPM test has developed, from hazy and variable beginnings, into a fairly clear and fairly lenient standard. The government interest and tailoring requirements are quite close to the rational basis standard applied to regulations that do not affect fundamental rights at all. But the adequate alternatives branch of the test is unique and provides a foundation for a more protective approach towards speech.

2. The Symbolic Speech Doctrine

Symbolic speech occurs when the speaker attempts to communicate through non-verbal means. Such means include the simple presentation of recognized symbols, like the swastika or the *Marseillaise,* as well as the more active use of symbols, traditional or otherwise, such as the burning of a flag or of a draft card. In a true symbolic speech case—one in which it is crucial that the communication takes place through symbolic action—the regulation would have to be aimed at particular non-speech activities, rather than at certain content categories of speech, and the government's purpose would have to be to prevent some non-communicative harm caused by such activities. That is, the government action would have to be content-neutral in the ways that the Court has recognized. Only if these conditions are met could the government accurately say that the regulation impacts on speech only because of the speaker's choice to use that activity as a symbolic part of her message. Because the regulation will be content-neutral, a true symbolic speech case may look very much like a TPM case. Indeed, the regulation may be identical to a TPM regulation, differing only in that in a symbolic speech case it interferes with speech by preventing symbolic action rather than by restricting the time, place, or manner of verbal expression.

* * *

The Court first encountered a true symbolic speech case in *United States v. O'Brien.*[128] The Selective Service law at issue prohibited the knowing destruction of a draft registration card. O'Brien had burned his draft card on the steps of the Boston Courthouse as a protest against the Vietnam war. The Supreme Court upheld his conviction and provided a clear statement of the test to be used in a symbolic speech case. * * * Noting that "speech" and "nonspeech" elements were combined in O'Brien's expression, the Court held that "a sufficiently important governmental interest in regulating the nonspeech element can justify incidental limitations on First Amendment freedoms." The four-part test announced in *O'Brien* allows such incidental restriction if the regulation is

> within the constitutional power of the Government; if it furthers an important or substantial governmental interest; if the governmental interest is unrelated to the suppression of free expression; and if the

128. 391 U.S. 367 (1968).

incidental restriction on alleged First Amendment freedoms is no greater than is essential to the furtherance of that interest.

The language of this test seems to represent a fairly high standard of review. For example, it calls for an "important or substantial" state interest with the means "no greater than is essential" to serve the end. The Court's application of the test to *O'Brien*'s facts, though, presaged the lax and deferential way in which it has been used ever since. The Court found that the Selective Service law met all parts of the test. * * *

* * *

The *O'Brien* test differs from the traditional TPM standard in at least two ways. First, the TPM test's tailoring requirement is relatively weak. It certainly has never demanded that the restriction be "no greater than is essential to the furtherance of [the government] interest." On the other hand, the TPM standard includes an assessment of the adequacy of alternative avenues of speech. This prong is entirely absent from the *O'Brien* analysis * * *.

* * *

3.   The Collapse of the Two Lines of Doctrine

As this brief history of almost half a century demonstrates, the Court developed two distinct lines of doctrine to deal with TPM cases and symbolic speech cases. The Court, however, never carefully articulated the differences between the two types of cases that warranted this disparate treatment. It is unsurprising, then, that the two types of cases should come to look more alike under the pressure of a growing focus on content discrimination in the government's purpose. Disregarding the separate lines of development and different doctrinal standards for TPM and symbolic speech cases, the Court has, in the last decade, responded to this pressure by collapsing the two standards into a single test.

The process of consolidation began in *Members of the City Council v. Taxpayers for Vincent*,[146] in which the Court upheld a municipal ordinance prohibiting the posting of signs on public utility poles. The regulation represented a straightforward, indeed almost a classic, instance of a time, place, or manner restriction. The regulation was both facially and operatively content-neutral, and it was designed to combat the noncommunicative harms of distraction to motorists and visual clutter. Moreover, the would-be speakers never suggested that the use of the utility poles carried any symbolic or communicative significance for them; it was simply a cheap and efficient means of reaching a substantial audience.

Despite the obvious appropriateness of the TPM test, Justice Stevens, for the majority, stated that *O'Brien* "set forth the appropriate framework for reviewing a viewpoint-neutral regulation of this kind"

---

146.   466 U.S. 789 (1984).

and proceeded to apply the *O'Brien* standard to the case. The Court did not, however, completely ignore the TPM line of doctrine; the opinion is sprinkled with references to TPM cases and the TPM test. Indeed, the majority opinion devotes a separate section to discussing the adequacy of alternative methods of speech, despite the fact that the *O'Brien* test as quoted by the Court included no such inquiry. * * *

Six weeks later, the Court reaffirmed its combined test and addressed the issue somewhat more directly. In *Clark v. Community for Creative Non–Violence,*[154] the majority upheld a National Park Service regulation prohibiting sleeping in Lafayette Park in Washington, D.C. This rule had been challenged by a group wishing to sleep in tents in the winter as a symbolic protest of the plight of the homeless. The Court began its analysis by stating that expression, including symbolic expression, is subject to reasonable time, place, or manner regulations that are "justified without reference to the content of the regulated speech, ... narrowly tailored to serve a significant governmental interest, and ... leave open ample alternative channels for communication of the information." The Court [held] "that the Park Service regulation [was] sustainable under the four-factor standard of *United States v. O'Brien* for validating a regulation of expressive conduct, which, in the last analysis is little, if any, different from the standard applied to time, place, or manner restrictions." * * *

* * *

More recent cases have confirmed the demise of the TPM/symbolic speech distinction without providing substantially more by way of explanation. For example, in *Ward v. Rock Against Racism,* the Court, quoting from *Clark,* reasserted the similarity of the two tests and held that neither *O'Brien* nor the TPM standard required the government to use the least restrictive means of achieving its goal. The only explanation offered for the lower tailoring standard shared by the two tests was that they both concerned content-neutral, rather than content-based, regulations. * * *

* * *

Although the Court continues to refer to the *O'Brien* test, the unified standard that has evolved is really just a weak version of the TPM test. It includes the TPM test's adequate alternatives branch but leaves aside *O'Brien*'s explicit demand for heightened attention to both the strength of the government interest and the degree of means/end fit. Unlike some versions of the TPM test, the new standard does purport to include a tailoring requirement. That requirement, however, amounts to little more than the most minimal rational relation review as defined in *Ward.* In the absence of a meaningful tailoring requirement, the new test borrows nothing from *O'Brien* and is functionally identical to the TPM standard as described in *Virginia State Board of Pharmacy v. Virginia Citizens Consumer Council, Inc.* As a result, the range of

154. 468 U.S. 288 (1984).

doctrinal tools available to deal with complex first amendment problems has been reduced, and real first amendment protections have been lost.

[Williams goes on to argue that we should maintain the distinction between TPM and symbolic speech regulations. Other things being equal, the latter should be reviewed more strictly. They target the symbols that people like O'Brien wish to use to communicate their messages. Restrictions like these, on the "communicative" aspects of speech, are a form of content regulation. Though the government's intent is not malicious, Williams argues that they should be viewed with a kind of strict scrutiny. This is why the traditional symbolic speech test insists on an "important or substantial" government interest and on the least restrictive means.

[TPM regulations, by contrast, typically limit the "facilitative" aspects of speech. The loudness of a sound truck is not itself meaningful—it does not embody or represent a message. It is just a means of amplifying a message carried by other symbols (words). A TPM regulation does not, from the speaker's point of view, limit the content of speech. Hence the traditional test has been more lenient—a kind of rational basis requirement. Notice, though, that while TPM regulations do not control the speaker's message, they do limit her ability to transmit it. This is why we ask whether the speaker has adequate alternatives—not other messages, but other ways of getting this one to her audience.]

LARRY A. ALEXANDER, TROUBLE ON TRACK TWO: INCIDENTAL REGULATIONS OF SPEECH AND FREE SPEECH THEORY

44 Hastings L.J. 921–25, 931–36 (1993).

Standard First Amendment free speech analysis divides cases into two major groups. One group consists of those cases that Laurence Tribe has labeled "track one" cases.[1] In track one cases, the government's concern expressed in the challenged regulation is the communicative impact of speech, the messages that the audience for the speech will receive. Those messages may be objectionable from the government's standpoint for many reasons, some legitimate, others not. * * *

Track one analysis, inquiring what governmental purposes are legitimate bases for interdicting the receipt of messages, and what means the government may employ to accomplish those purposes, is difficult, complex, and controversial. It divides both courts and commentators along many lines. Yet despite its difficulty, complexity, and controversiality, track one analysis is relatively stable doctrinally if not theoretically. While courts and commentators may disagree over the outcomes of many of those cases that because of their difficulty actually get litigated or over the theoretical bases for the decisions, the courts and commentators do agree on the outcomes in the vast majority of *possible* cases. Moreover,

---

1. Laurence H. Tribe, American Constitutional Law § 12–2, at 791 (2d ed. 1988).

almost all observers would agree that track one analysis is extremely speech protective. The government is rarely successful in meeting track one's relatively settled tests for when it may legitimately interdict receipt of a message based upon a concern with the message's effect on the audience. * * *

The other major group of First Amendment free speech cases consists of Tribe's "track two" cases. Here, government is concerned with the noncommunicative impact of speech, not the message that is being conveyed.

Track two cases have traditionally been broken into two subcategories: the public forum cases and the symbolic speech cases. The former concern access of private speakers to governmental or quasi-governmental facilities, and in some cases to private facilities that the speaker seeks to have treated like governmental facilities. Current First Amendment jurisprudence distinguishes among traditional public fora, such as streets, sidewalks, and parks, public fora created by government designation, and nonpublic fora.[9] The conventional doctrine in public forum cases is that the government may impose narrowly drawn regulations of the time, place, and manner of speech in traditional public fora and designated public fora in order to serve significant governmental objectives unrelated to the speaker's message. The government may not, however, bar speech entirely from such public fora and must leave adequate alternative channels of communication available.[10] On the other hand, if a facility is a nonpublic forum, the government may bar speech entirely or selectively, so long as it does not discriminate according to viewpoint. * * *

The other subcategory of track two cases consists of the symbolic speech cases.[16] Here, the government forbids certain conduct irrespective of whether those who would otherwise engage in that conduct intend their engaging in it to symbolize and communicate some idea to others. The free speech issue arises when someone in fact wishes to engage in that conduct to symbolize and communicate an idea. The accepted doctrine is that government may regulate the symbol on the same grounds and with the same restrictions as it may regulate the time, place, and manner of speech in a public forum. That is, it may do so if it is advancing a significant interest unrelated to the communicative im-

---

9. Cornelius v. NAACP Legal Defense & Educ. Fund, Inc., 473 U.S. 788, 802 (1985); G. Sidney Buchanan, *The Case of the Vanishing Public Forum,* 1991 U.Ill.L.Rev. 949, 954. In International Society for Krishna Consciousness, Inc. v. Lee, 112 S.Ct. 2701 (1992), four Justices, Kennedy, Souter, Blackmun, and Stevens, would have held that airports, as well as other facilities, were public fora. *Id.* at 2715–20 (Kennedy, J., concurring in judgment); *id.* at 2724 (Souter, J., concurring in judgment and dissenting).

10. Ward v. Rock Against Racism, 491 U.S. 781, 796–802 (1989); Buchanan, *supra* note 9, at 954. It need not, however, choose the least restrictive means available. *See Ward,* 491 U.S. at 796–802; Buchanan, *supra* note 9, at 954.

16. Given that all speech employs symbols and is thus symbolic, the area should perhaps be redescribed.

pact of the conduct, if its statute is narrowly tailored, and if adequate alternative means exist for the speaker to convey his message.[17]

Unlike track one analysis, track two analysis has not proven to be speech protective, at least not as we normally think of speech protective doctrines. The government has always won track two cases, with two clear and two less clear exceptions. The clear exceptions are the decisions in *Schneider v. State*,[19] which struck down anti-littering ordinances as applied to the passing out of pamphlets, and *International Society for Krishna Consciousness, Inc. v. Lee*,[21] which upheld the right to distribute literature in an airport terminal. The less clear exceptions are the Court's decisions in *Hague v. CIO*,[23] which established the speech easement over public streets, sidewalks, and parks, and *Schad v. Borough of Mount Ephraim*,[25] which overturned a complete ban of live entertainment.

* * *

The Entire Corpus Juris as Track Two

* * *

[I] want to establish [that there should] be no distinction between track two laws directly regulating speech activities and all other laws. All track two laws regulate speech only indirectly in this sense: In a track two case, government's interest is not in what is being communicated but in the communication's effects on values unrelated to communication, such as noise, congestion, property, aesthetics, or privacy. Track two regulations are of First Amendment concern because they affect what gets said, by whom, to whom, and with what effect even though the regulations are not intended to affect such matters. Nevertheless, *all laws affect what gets said, by whom, to whom, and with what effect*. In short, all laws have information effects. Therefore, all laws, the entire corpus juris, should be subject to track two analysis.

Track two includes not only restrictions on obstructing traffic while speaking or demonstrating, using amplifying devices in residential neighborhoods, posting signs on utility poles, burning draft cards, or sleeping in parks, but also includes tort, contract, and property law, the tax code, and the multitude of criminal and regulatory laws and administrative regulations. For example, laws determining who owns what property under what restrictions or the price and availability of various resources will also determine what gets said, by whom, to whom, and with what effect—that is, the laws will have information effects. A change in the laws of any region of the corpus juris will have information effects. Laws equalizing income would surely have dramatic information effects. Elimination of the law against battery would produce a new form of

17. *See* United States v. O'Brien, 391 U.S. 367 (1968); Buchanan, *supra* note 9, at 953.

19. 308 U.S. 147 (1939).

21. 112 S.Ct. 2701 (1992).

23. 307 U.S. 496 (1939).

25. 452 U.S. 61 (1981).

symbolic speech as well as information—for example, what it is like to batter and be battered—and concerns that do not exist while the law against battery is on the books.

The ubiquity of potential track two cases has been noted. Susan Williams, for example, notes that "[t]here is * * * no clear dividing line between facilitative aspects of speech and other activities. Instead, there is a continuum * * *." Yet she believes that a line must be drawn.

> The task is required * * * because the alternatives are simply unacceptable. Some activities or resources that are not themselves a part of the act of speaking are, nonetheless, so closely related to speech that it would be absurd not to recognize that regulating them raises first amendment issues. Access to paper or typewriters might be a good example. On the other hand, without some limit, the free speech guarantee would be transformed into an invitation for all speakers to violate any generally applicable law if the violation contributes in any way, no matter how indirect, to their ability to speak. The constitutional solicitude for free speech demands that speakers receive special protection from regulations (even generally applicable ones) that affect either a communicative or a directly facilitative aspect of their speech activity. Nonetheless, at some point the connection to speech becomes so attenuated that the protection must disappear.[53]

Although Williams's concern is well-founded, the "direct-indirect" imagery on which she relies misses the fundamental point that the most profound information effects are produced by laws she would place on the indirect side of the divide. Cass Sunstein, on the other hand, is quite anxious to exploit precisely this point:

> [T]here may be no neutrality in use of the market status quo when the available opportunities are heavily dependent on wealth, on the common law framework of entitlements, and on the sorts of outlets for speech that are made available, and to whom. In other words, the very notions "content-neutral" and "content-based" seem to depend on taking the status quo as if it were preregulatory and unobjectionable.
>
> At least two things follow. The first is that many content-neutral laws have content-differential effects. They do so because they operate against a backdrop that is not prepolitical or just. In light of an unjust status quo, rules that are content-neutral can have severe adverse effects on some forms of speech. Greater scrutiny of content-neutral restrictions is therefore appropriate. Above all, courts should attend to the possibility that seemingly neutral restrictions will have content-based effects.[54]

53. [Susan H. Williams, *Content Dissemination and the First Amendment,* 139 U.Pa.L.Rev. 615, 724 (1991).]

54. [*Free Speech Now,* 59 U.Chi.L.Rev. 255, 296 (1992).]

As Williams recognizes, however, and Sunstein does not, the courts cannot apply the ordinary track two test to all laws, even though all laws are logically subject to track two analysis. For example, the setting of the marginal tax rate affects my income, which, if greater, I might devote to increased speaking. Under the current track two test, if the government's interest in the present rate is not significant, and the rate adversely affects my speech, the government would be required to abandon that rate in favor of another rate. But any other rate the government chooses will affect somebody's speech—it may result in lower transfer payments, adversely affecting the communication between poorer speakers and their audience—and, thus, *it* will have to serve a significant interest as well. Therefore, the track two test cannot be applied universally, unless the requirement of a significant government interest is trivialized either by finding almost any interest to be significant or by being made synonymous with "the entire corpus juris is what it should be." (The latter trivializes because it tautologizes: track two laws are constitutional if they are constitutional.)

This leaves the following problems. First, track two covers all laws since all laws have information effects—they affect what gets said, by whom, to whom, and with what effect. Second, a track two First Amendment challenge to a law or group of laws is a demand that the laws be changed; but every change in the laws will have information effects, so that track two First Amendment claims are always aligned against each other. Thus, testing challenged laws by the significant government interest test will entail testing all of their alternatives by that test. Finally, the universal application of track two analysis would result in the elimination of all sets of laws except those serving significant interests (as compared to all possible alternative sets). Because of this difficulty, the universal application of track two analysis would most likely result in complete abandonment of track two protection, with all asserted interests deemed "significant" so long as they are not concealing track one, message-related, governmental concerns.

THE INEVITABLE FAILURE OF TRACK TWO ANALYSIS

Track two laws have much greater information effects than track one laws (if the concept of greater effects is meaningful in this context). Yet, while track one analysis has been quite speech protective, at least superficially, track two analysis has been anything but speech protective.
* * *

What happens if instead of treating all speech interests as having a constant and significant weight, the particular value of the intended speech, given its intended audience, is weighed against the values the particular laws serve? This is the heart of my critique of track two analysis. In this Part, I propose that the value of speech cannot be balanced against the government's track two interests in any way that is principled and that respects the very freedom of thought that the First Amendment itself protects.

To make track two analysis work, we must assign a value to the audience's loss of information due to incidental restrictions on speech. That value in turn must be weighed against the values furthered by the incidental regulations at issue, values such as freedom from noise, litter, congestion, and taxes. Moreover, that value must also be weighed against the information lost to that and other audiences if the incidental regulations are struck down. (Each alternative set of regulations produces a different state of the world, which in turn makes available different information and/or different audiences for the same information. A trivial example: a world without an anti-litter law lacks the information "what a world with an anti-litter law is like." A less trivial example: a world in which extra police must be assigned to monitor and control street demonstrations and reroute traffic has less tax money available to hire teachers in public schools than a world in which street demonstrations are prohibited.)

In addition to the theoretical difficulties of the balancing process, the track two analysis also poses the theoretical problem of placing a value on the information at stake. On the one hand, if we evaluate the information at stake from the position of not knowing yet what it is, we face the theoretically impossible task of placing a specific value on unknown information. On the other hand, if we evaluate the information at stake from the position of knowing or imagining what it is, we risk imposing our evaluation on others through the striking down of the existing set of incidental regulations, and, thereby preempting the very freedom of evaluation of others that is central to the First Amendment. In the name of the First Amendment we are imposing an evaluative framework on others and arguably violating the First Amendment. Put differently, the First Amendment is supposed to protect a realm of pure process, the substantive results of which are legitimate only because that process is pure; once substantive results begin guiding the construction of the process itself, the legitimacy of the results of that process is compromised.

* * *

The entire corpus juris, from the general common law of contracts, property, and torts to the most particular tax regulation, affects what gets said, by whom, to whom, and to what effect. Speech and listening are costly activities. They use resources such as space, newsprint, radio frequencies, presses, and police protection, and impose other costs— noise, litter, and clutter. *Schneider,* for example, imposed the costs of litter or, alternatively, the costs in excess of the state's next best alternative for eliminating litter. (If a less restrictive alternative is on the order of a Pareto superior move—the alternative does all the good at no greater cost and without affecting speech—then less restrictive alternatives are unlikely to exist; all alternatives will have greater costs in some respects.)

Thus, the Court's decision in *Schneider* constitutionally mandated what can be viewed as a subsidy of pamphleteers. But why such a subsidy of pamphleteers?

Consider Jane, who complains about the high costs of *The New Republic,* cable television, books from Oxford Press, and a college education. Those costs result from laws—laws regarding property rights, laws conserving trees, laws affecting labor costs, laws regarding tax liability, and many other laws. Jane's receipt of speech—which is, after all, what the First Amendment is really about—is adversely affected by those laws. Why should her attempt to receive this speech not be subsidized? (Alternatively, if one resists the notion that listeners' rights are central to the First Amendment, why should *The New Republic* and Oxford Press, for example, not receive subsidies or relief from various laws in order to communicate with a wider audience?)

Next, consider John, who wishes to demonstrate on Main Street, which will tie up traffic and require police presence. If, against the city's wishes, a court mandates that he be allowed to demonstrate, then the decision can be viewed as a forced subsidy of John and correlatively a forced imposition of costs on others.

Next, consider Joan, who is denied several outlets for her message that, given her limited resources, would be the most effective: putting graffiti on the side of city hall, using a loudspeaker at night in a residential neighborhood, or putting up a pamphlet stand on land that, due to various zoning laws, is currently unaffordable for her. Why should *Schneider* but not Joan get a First Amendment subsidy here?

Finally, consider Jason, who wants the city to build an auditorium suitable for public lectures and rallies, but who is opposed by Jean, who would like the city to build more tennis courts because she and others prefer playing and discussing tennis to attending public lectures, and Jerry, who wants lower taxes so that he can afford to go to night school.

* * *

Without a theory of proper information effects, non-content-related regulations cannot be evaluated under the First Amendment, except in an arbitrary manner. *Schneider* did win, of course, and so did the Hare Krishnas in *Lee.* But why they and not O'Brien, the sleep-in protesters in *Clark v. Community for Creative Non–Violence,*[60] or the many other actual losers? And if *Schneider* and the Krishnas, why not my hypothetical Jane, John, Joan, and Jason?

As discussed above, assigning the speech value a constant weight in the calculus—for instance, equal to a significant governmental interest—does not help. Without a theory regarding information effects—what gets said, by whom, to whom, and with what effect—assigning any weight will be arbitrary. More importantly, because speech interests are affected regardless of what set of track two laws are chosen, the speech

---

60. 468 U.S. 288 (1984).

"constant" appears on both sides of the equation and does not produce a winner.

An alternative that might be considered would be straightforward balancing rather than assigning speech an arbitrary constant value. Under this approach, all of the information at stake under all alternative sets of laws would be examined, as well as all the non-speech values, and a determination would be made as to which set of laws is superior.

There are obvious practical and institutional objections to such a balancing proposal. Given that this approach would involve nothing less than a comparison of all possible entire sets of laws, both for their information effects and for their effects on all the non-speech values, the proposal is a practical impossibility for a legislature and surely for a court.

This practical objection should by itself be sufficient to undermine all track two judicial decisions and to dictate complete judicial withdrawal from track two. There remains, however, a theoretical objection to the enterprise as well. In principle, we cannot evaluate the information effects of track two laws: Either we assume the viewpoint of one who does not know what the information at issue will be, in which case we cannot evaluate it at all, or we assume the viewpoint of one who does know what the information will turn out to be, in which case we can evaluate it, but only from a partisan perspective inconsistent with the First Amendment itself.

LILLIAN R. BEVIER, REHABILITATING PUBLIC FORUM DOCTRINE: IN DEFENSE OF CATEGORIES

1992 Sup.Ct.Rev. 79–80, 102–13, 115–20.

In the companion cases of *International Society for Krishna Consciousness v. Lee* and *Lee v. International Society for Krishna Consciousness*,[1] the Supreme Court finessed an important opportunity to chart a clear future course for public forum doctrine. Instead of clarifying the law, shifting majorities of justices aligned themselves behind two seemingly inconsistent results, as the Court sustained an airport authority's ban on solicitation of money and invalidated its ban on distribution of literature. The opinions reveal that the Court is deeply divided and that it is mired in substantive and methodological confusion. A doctrinal consensus that once seemed to be emerging has now dissolved, and uncertainties abound on the crucial question of how intensively the Court will review regulations of speech on public property.

This disarray is exacerbated by the confusing set of opinions issued in two other recent decisions concerning the scope and content of First Amendment rights on public property. In *Forsyth County, Georgia v. Nationalist Movement*,[2] the Court invalidated a parade permit ordinance

1. 112 S.Ct. 2701 (1992); 112 S.Ct. 2709 (1992); 112 S.Ct. 2711 (1992).

2. 112 S.Ct. 2395 (1992).

because it authorized the county administrator to adjust the permit fee without prescribing adequate standards to guide his discretion in doing so. In *Burson v. Freeman*, the Court subjected a Tennessee law prohibiting electioneering within 100 feet of a polling place to exacting scrutiny, but sustained the law because it served the state's "compelling" interest in election integrity and in protecting citizens' rights "to vote freely for the candidates of their choice." [4]

Of these three cases, *Lee* is the most significant, in part because it addressed a long-simmering controversy over whether airports are traditional public fora. Unfortunately, *Lee* is also significant because, although it "answered" the question by holding that airports are not public fora, it cannot be said to have "settled" the issue. To the contrary, if anything, it unsettled it.

* * *

The cacophony of opinions in *Lee* testifies to deep division among the Justices about the underlying purpose of public forum doctrine. One way to understand the division is to see it as reflecting tension between two models of the First Amendment which have competed since *Hague* to supply the underlying premise of the public forum right.

First, there is the Enhancement model, which is concerned with how much speech takes place in society and with the overall quality of public debate. It is visionary in character. It envisions the First Amendment as embodying an ideal of democratic discourse in a self-governing society. The Enhancement model is committed to the view that First Amendment rules can and ought to be effective tools for augmenting both the quality and quantity of public debate, and accepts the corollary proposition that the Amendment sometimes imposes affirmative duties on government to maximize the opportunities for expression. It focuses almost exclusively on the substantive merits of particular claims. It takes as given that judicial review is an appropriate legal device for the realization of its ideals and seldom displays misgivings about the possibility that it might entail untoward institutional implications.

The Enhancement model derives in large part from the implications of Justice Brennan's opinion in *New York Times v. Sullivan*. In particular, it takes its cue from Brennan's affirmation of a "profound national commitment to the principle that debate on public issues should be uninhibited, robust and wide-open." According to the Enhancement model, this commitment has both substantive and strategic dimensions. Substantively, it presupposes that the core mission of the First Amendment is to promote an idealized vision of the democratic process by promoting speech about public and, in particular, political issues. Strategically, it presupposes a judicial mandate to interpret the First Amendment aggressively so as to promote and facilitate "uninhibited, robust and wide-open" debate. In its strategic dimension, this model assumes that "... the widest possible dissemination of information from diverse

4. 112 S.Ct. 1846, 1851 (1992).

and antagonistic sources is essential to the welfare of the public,'' [93] and that individuals have a constitutionally protected interest in *effective* self-expression. It ascribes to the Court the responsibility of devising legal rules that will make these assumptions a reality. The Enhancement model assumes that legal doctrine can transform public debate both qualitatively and quantitatively.

On the other hand is the Distortion model. This model shares with the Enhancement model the premise that the central mission of the First Amendment is to protect speech about government and political issues, broadly defined. The Distortion model differs from the Enhancement model, however, in its strategic dimension and its much less idealized vision of public debate. The Distortion model sets a less ambitious agenda for First Amendment doctrine. Instead of conceiving the Amendment as authorizing the Court affirmatively to enhance the quality of public debate or to prime the pump of quantity, the Distortion model portrays the First Amendment as embodying nothing more than a set of constraints upon government actors. It adopts no norm or idealized vision of quality or quantity of public debate except that which results from a rigidly enforced official government neutrality. This model regards the First Amendment as a source of negative rights (freedoms from) rather than as a source of positive entitlements (freedoms to). In contrast to the ambitious agenda of the Enhancement model, the Distortion model entails a modest notion of what First Amendment rules can and ought to do. According to the Distortion model, the essential task of First Amendment rules is to restrain government from deliberately manipulating the content or outcome of public debate and to prohibit it from censoring, punishing, or selectively denying speech opportunities to disfavored views.

The Enhancement and Distortion models have strikingly different implications for judicial review. Under the Enhancement model, the Court's responsibility is to ensure that speech is not unduly curtailed and to devise rules that will maximize the opportunities for expression. Under the Distortion model, the Court's responsibility is only to determine whether the challenged government practice reflects deliberate governmental discrimination against disfavored viewpoints. When the Court adopts a categorical approach under this model, it does so, not with a view to promoting "more speech," but with a view to minimizing the risk of governmental abuse.

* * *

[C]ritics on and off the Court have assumed implicitly that public forum doctrine must make sense in terms of the Enhancement model. Much of their criticism, accordingly, faults the doctrine for being insufficiently alert to First Amendment values and hence insufficiently generous in sustaining access claims. Justice Kennedy in *Lee,* for example, chided the Court for ignoring *"the fact* that the purpose of the public

---

93. *Associated Press v. United States,*
326 U.S. 1, 20 (1944).

forum doctrine is to give effect to the *broad command* of the First Amendment," and scolded it on the ground that its "failure to recognize the possibility that new types of government property may be appropriate forums for speech will lead to a serious curtailment of our expressive activity." In fact, however, although the Enhancement model has powerful rhetorical appeal, it has little explanatory power either with reference to public forum doctrine or to any other body of First Amendment law.

The Court itself has done little to rebut criticism like Justice Kennedy's or to join issue with its assumptions. To the contrary, [the] opinions in public forum cases that rejected First Amendment claims have offered almost no theoretical justifications either for the doctrines they embraced or for the applications of those doctrines in particular cases. [Close] scrutiny, however, supports a more sympathetic rendering of the merits of the Court's public forum categories, for these decisions can be seen, not as a half-hearted commitment to the Enhancement model, but as a whole-hearted rejection of that model in favor of the Distortion model's more restrained vision of the First Amendment's central mission. Indeed, once understood as well-designed embodiments of the Distortion model, the rules and categories that comprise modern public forum doctrine make considerable sense.

Consider, first, that beginning with *Hague,* the Court's public forum decisions display the Distortion model's central concern of preventing forum managers from deliberately skewing public debate by denying access to citizens because they want to express disfavored views. The *Hague* dictum rejected the view that the Constitution grants government the same power to control public property that private owners can exert over private property. Although, read broadly, the *Hague* dictum seems consistent with the Enhancement model's notion that government has a duty to maximize speech opportunities by making publicly owned property generally available for expressive activity, the Court actually invalidated the ordinance in *Hague* not because it denied access, but because it established a discretionary permit system. Thus, while the rhetoric of the *Hague* dictum is consistent with the Enhancement model, the actual principle of decision is consistent with the Distortion model. The holding in *Hague* did not require government to facilitate speech. It merely prohibited it from abusing its power by engaging in purposeful distortion of public debate.

Consider, second, the vagueness doctrine and the prohibition on viewpoint discrimination. These doctrines are designed not to achieve the Enhancement model's objective of promoting the quantity or quality of speech, but to achieve the Distortion model's goal of limiting the use of illegitimate criteria of decision by government agents.

Consider, third, the public forum categories themselves. As Justice Kennedy pointed out when he proposed his more accommodating test, the boundaries of these categories have not been drawn to maximize speech consistent with the Enhancement model. Rather, the boundaries have been drawn to accomplish the goals of the Distortion model by adjusting the standards of review to address the different systematic possibilities for abuse that the various categories of property present. This conclusion, which is critical to my analysis, is evident from a close review of the categories themselves.

1. *The traditional public forum.* The principal difficulty in viewing public forum doctrine as a manifestation of the Distortion model is the existence of a category of places—traditional public fora—to which the Court has guaranteed citizens a First Amendment right of access. Would the Distortion model, which is designed to forestall deliberate manipulation of public debate, prohibit even-handed government exclusion of speech from *any* publicly owned place? A negative answer to this question would significantly undermine the explanatory power of the Distortion model. In fact, however, at least with respect to streets and parks (and, now, public sidewalks), the Distortion model is consistent with such a rule. This is so because, as suggested by Justice Roberts in *Hague,* such places have historically been available for the public's exercise of the rights of speech and assembly. Historic openness supports a right of guaranteed access even under the Distortion model for a number of reasons. First, it forecloses any argument forum managers might make that expression is "incompatible" with the "primary use" of the property: these places have always, "time out of mind," accommodated not only a variety of uses, but a variety of uses *including speech and assembly.* Second, the long-standing availability of these places for First Amendment activity eliminates the need for courts to make their own assessment of compatibility. Third, because historic openness signals presumptive compatibility of speech and assembly with other uses of the property, it signals the possibility that illicit motives may lie behind the effort to exclude. * * *

2. *The designated public forum.* The Court has held that designated public fora are those properties that the government has voluntarily made available for expression. The government is not constitutionally required to keep such property open for expression, as it is with traditional public forums. So long as it does keep them open, however, its speech regulations are subject to review according to "the same standards as apply in a traditional public forum." Since *Cornelius,* the Court has effectively limited the designated public forum category to those properties that the government has intentionally, explicitly "opened for expressive activity by part or all of the public." This limitation has evoked the kind of concern expressed by Justice Kennedy in *Lee:*

> The requirements for such a designation are so stringent that I cannot be certain whether the category has any content left at all. In any event, it seem evident that ... few if any types of property other than those already recognized as public forums will be accorded that status.

Justice Kennedy's assessment is probably close to the mark, and this would indeed be a matter of concern if the Court were attempting to achieve the goals implicit in the Enhancement model. According to the Distortion model, however, it is not a matter of concern that few if any additional public forums will be created: according to the Distortion model, the creation of more public forums is not a goal of the First Amendment.

As a descriptive matter, in defining the criteria for determining when public property constitutes a designated public forum, the Court has not been pursuing the Enhancement model's goal of facilitating or maximizing speech. Rather, it has been serving the more limited objective of preventing deliberate viewpoint discrimination. The designated public forum category serves this purpose by calling on government to justify selective exclusions from property that it has deliberately opened to expressive activity. When the government itself intentionally designates public property as a forum, it announces its own judgment that speech is compatible with the property's other uses. Thus, a policy of selective exclusion would be presumptively suspect as the product, not of a legitimate concern with disruption, but of an illicit concern with the speaker's viewpoint. In other words, it is the intentional decision to designate property as a public forum, and not the decision to close it altogether to speech uses, that heightens the risk that the government will engage in deliberate viewpoint discrimination and explains the designated public forum category. If there is no systematic risk that a decision by government not to open public property to expressive activity reflects covert viewpoint discrimination, the Distortion model would not require the Court to expand the designated public forum category beyond its present boundaries. Whether such systematic risks exist is the principal issue in the analysis of the non-public forum category.

3. *The nonpublic forum.* [Before] *Lee,* the Court engaged in virtually no independent scrutiny of the access decisions of nonpublic forum managers, sustaining their content-neutral denials of access so long as they could be deemed "reasonable." Moreover, in making that determination, the Court accorded forum managers a very high level of deference. For this approach to be consistent with the Distortion model, such a level of deference must be justified in principle by the systematic absence in nonpublic fora of the kinds of First Amendment risks that the model is designed to prevent. The question, therefore, is whether decision making by the managers of nonpublic forum property presents such minimal risks of deliberate viewpoint discrimination that the Court is warranted in adopting a highly deferential stance.

In addressing this question, a useful point of departure is Robert Post's reformulation of public forum doctrine, in which he suggested that a "line between governance and management corresponds to the distinction between the public and nonpublic forum."[112] As I shall

112. Robert C. Post, *Between Governance and Management: The History and*   *Theory of the Public Forum,* 34 UCLA L Rev 1713, 1833 (1987).

demonstrate, this line also corresponds to the systematic presence or absence of the risk of deliberate government deck-stacking. Accordingly, a brief account of Post's analysis will be helpful.

At the outset, it is important to note that Post himself plainly ascribes to the Enhancement model. The First Amendment premises which he deems

> constitutionally congenial * * * [are] that the state should not suppress speech unless there is a good reason to do so, * * * [that the First Amendment] is designed to maximize the speech which the government is constitutionally required to tolerate * * * [and that] the first amendment's central objective * * * [is] ensuring "uninhibited, robust, and wide-open" public debate.

His analysis recognized, however, that the Court's conception of the public forum doctrine could not be squared with these premises without considerable sacrifice of descriptive accuracy. In particular, he acknowledged that the Court used the nonpublic forum category to "demarcate a class of government property in which the first amendment claims of the public are radically devalued and immune from independent judicial scrutiny." Accordingly, Post set himself the task of articulating a constitutional theory that could both explain and justify this unusual devaluation. Rather than attempting to forge a link between his First Amendment premises and the nonpublic forum category, however, he explained the nonpublic forum category and its concomitant judicial deference in terms of a complex "sociology of institutional authority, as well as a pervasive and important struggle between a public realm [where the First Amendment applies with full force] and an organizational domain of instrumental rationality [where the First Amendment is of only marginal importance]."

Some adherents of the Enhancement model argue that forum managers systematically undervalue speech and have significant incentives to overregulate it. They fear that deference permits forum managers to engage in gratuitous and unnecessary regulation. Rather than attempting to allay that concern, Post insisted that it is the wrong way to think about the issue. For him, the appropriate question is not the Enhancement adherent's query whether judicial deference results in too little speech, but whether deference is necessary

> *in order for a state organization to function effectively.* If the government decision at issue entails a kind of authority which requires flexibility and discretion to function effectively, or which is part of the creation of a specific organizational culture for the management of the affected institution, there are strong justifications for judicial deference.

[Post's] analysis supplies a crucial link in the effort to explain public forum doctrine in terms of the Distortion model. The line between government and management separates occasions where systematic First Amendment risks of deliberate government deck-stacking are present from those where they are not. Oddly enough, this is true because of the factors Post himself uses to separate governance from management.

Post's central insight is that government actions can be divided conceptually between those taken within government organizations in pursuit of organizational goals taken as given—the domain of management—and those taken in the public realm outside organizational boundaries—the domain of governance where "common values are forged through public discussion and exchange." When the state acts in the domain of governance, "the significance and force of all potential objectives are taken as a legitimate subject of inquiry." Because this is so, government officials face the systematic temptation deliberately to skew the debate in favor of the outcomes they prefer. The risk that they will succumb to this temptation thus justifies stringent judicial oversight when the state is "governing."

When, however, "the state acts internally to manage speech within its own institutions, public ends are taken as given and as socially embodied within the forms and objectives of a government organization." Within such government organizations, *precisely because public ends are taken as given,* the potential for deliberate government skewing of public debate is systematically irrelevant: by definition, the debate has run its course, its outcome is settled, and nothing remains to be skewed. Sometimes, the risk of deliberate skewing of public debate will in fact materialize even in a "management" context. Hence, the Court continues to prohibit deliberate viewpoint discrimination even in the nonpublic forum. The risk is not systematic, however, and judicial deference is therefore the appropriate norm in the absence of such deliberate discrimination.

* * *

A chasm separates the agenda of the Enhancement model from the more modest goals of the Distortion model. One way to characterize this chasm is as an artifact of the differing intensities of commitment of these models to core First Amendment values: adherents of the Enhancement model value expression more than adherents of the Distortion model, and they are less willing to tolerate regulation. Lapses from the ideal of "uninhibited, robust and wide-open" debate matter deeply to Enhancement adherents, but do not concern adherents of the Distortion model. If differing intensities of preference for speech in fact account for the principal disparities in the two models' doctrinal prescriptions, then the most significant normative question to ask about public forum doctrine is whether it accords sufficient weight to speech interests.

There may be a more complex explanation for this chasm, however, for it may be that it is due, not to differing intensities of preference for speech, but to differing (though unstated) assumptions about the practical limits of relying upon judicial review to transform the quality and quantity of public debate. The Enhancement model reflects, in addition to a preference for speech, an idealized conception of reality. The conception has an internal logic that, in its implicit faith in the transformative power of legal doctrine, may blind its adherents to real-world limitations that a practical perspective might require them to acknowledge. Adherents of the Distortion model, for example, might indeed share the Enhancement model's preference for speech, but might nonetheless entertain doubts, not shared by adherents of the Enhancement model, about the capacity of courts to make the kinds of comprehensive assessments of the effects of their decisions—on speakers, on forums, and on the quality and quantity of debate—that the Enhancement model contemplates. They may thus prefer brightline rules, where outcomes turn on fewer relevant variables and where the variables themselves reflect systematic risks of government abuse, to more ad hoc decision making that attempts to account for a multiplicity of factors. Adherents of the Distortion model might also be skeptical about the ability of legal doctrine to create a desired reality. For this reason alone, they might favor a First Amendment regime of negative constraints on government rather than one of affirmative duties. Indeed, one way to describe the pre-*Lee* public forum doctrine applied by Chief Justice Rehnquist in *Lee* is in terms of the Distortion model's relatively modest set of assumptions about the appropriate boundaries of the judicial task and the transformative power of judicial review. From this perspective, the doctrine appears as a rejection of the more ambitious assumptions of the Enhancement model that were so earnestly put forth by the *Lee* dissenters.

Thoroughly to explore these possibilities is beyond the scope of the present inquiry, for they raise fundamental issues about how to conceptualize the role of the Court, of legal doctrine, and of the complex relationship between substantive norms and judicial methodology. Nevertheless, it may be useful to focus briefly on the institutional component of the public forum debate, if only to cast a more revealing light on the full implications of the choice between the Enhancement model of Justices Kennedy and Souter and the Distortion model of Chief Justice Rehnquist.

One of the most salient aspects of Chief Justice Rehnquist's approach in *Lee* is that it is rule-based and categorical. It reposes considerable trust in the good faith and managerial judgment of forum administrators and credits their capacity to give appropriate weight to First Amendment values in their management decisions. Justice Kennedy and Justice Souter, on the other hand, claim to accept a categorical approach in principle, but actually reject the judicial deference that is implicit in the categorical approach and evince a strong inclination for case-by-case analysis. They prefer the individual judgment of judges in particular cases to the collective judgment of forum administrators. Moreover, they adopt analyses that, because of the uncertainty of their categorical boundaries and their subjectivism, assure a continuing flow of litigation on public forum issues. Implicit in their analyses is thus a commitment to a decisional strategy that dilutes or, like Justice Brennan, abandons altogether the categorical approach in favor of one that explicitly attempts to achieve its substantive goals by considering a multiplicity of variables in every case. * * *

[The] Kennedy–Souter approach rests on the assumption that it generates fewer errors in application than a more categorical approach. It proceeds on the premise that, in the course of litigation, the Court can accurately and precisely identify and assess every relevant factor. The animating idea is that in each case the Court knows the value to place on the speech interest; the extent to which that value is compromised by the challenged restriction; how much disruption the speech will cause; and the effect of its decision on the quality and quantity of public debate. Though it is left implicit, this assumption that accurate judicial assessment of all relevant factors is possible offers the only conceivable underpinning to the claim that intensive case-by-case judicial scrutiny of the decisions of forum managers is preferable in principle to the greater deference implicit in the categorical approach. In the public forum context, however, such an assumption is of questionable validity.

[Historically,] of course, close judicial review has been highly correlated with vindication of First Amendment claims. Such review has been thought to produce more speech at little cost, on the assumption that the cost consists exclusively of manageable increases in litigation and modest inconvenience to the normal operation of the forum. In fact, however, the costs of case-by-case review of forum managers' decisions are more worrisome. First, as Robert Post has argued, constant vulnerability to judicial second-guessing may "diminish the authority at issue to such an extent as to impair the ability of the bureaucracy to attain its legitimate ends." Second, although there is no evidence that this is so, the threat of judicial override may have the perverse effect of causing forum managers to decide that it is in their long-run strategic interest to make rules that are less rather than more accommodating to First Amendment activities, for a more restrictive posture might, by raising the cost, decrease the likelihood of access claims being made. Over time, such a strategy might require them to yield less of their managerial authority than a more permissive posture.

Third, the possibility of judicial intervention increases the risk that access claimants will engage in self-interested strategic behavior, for it encourages them to characterize their claims in terms that systematically exaggerate the benefits of their behavior to themselves and trivialize its costs to others. Conceptualize public property as a commons—owned by all, thus owned by none. Like all commons, it is susceptible to overexploitation or abuse by anyone who can require others to absorb the costs of her use while enjoying most of the gain herself. It is possibly true, though it has never been empirically verified, that public forum managers undervalue speech. Conversely, though, it is also plausible to argue that First Amendment claimants who have to internalize few of the costs of their activities at particular locales may tend both to overvalue their need to exercise their First Amendment rights at particular places and to underestimate the adequacy of alternative sites. The prospect of getting a sympathetic judicial hearing if they can convince a court that the costs are trivial and the alternatives unsatisfactory seems likely to exacerbate this tendency.

BIBLIOGRAPHY

Content Regulation

David S. Day, *The Hybridization of the Content–Neutral Standards for the Free Speech Clause,* 19 Ariz.St.L.J. 195 (1987).

Benjamin S. DuVal, Jr., *The Occasions of Secrecy,* 47 U.Pitt.L.Rev. 579 (1986).

Thomas I. Emerson, *Freedom of Expression in Wartime,* 116 U.Pa.L.Rev. 975 (1968).

Daniel A. Farber, *Content Regulation and the First Amendment: A Revisionist View,* 68 Geo.L.J. 727 (1980).

Stephen W. Gard, *Fighting Words As Free Speech,* 58 Wash.U.L.Q. 531 (1980).

John H. Garvey, *Black and White Images,* 56 Law & Contemp.Probs. 189 (1993).

Gerald Gunther, *Reflections on* Robel: *It's Not What the Court Did But the Way That It Did It,* 20 Stan.L.Rev. 1140 (1968).

Elena Kagan, *The Changing Faces of First Amendment Neutrality:* R.A.V. v. St. Paul, Rust v. Sullivan, *and the Problem of Content–Based Underinclusion,* 1992 Sup.Ct.Rev. 29.

Harry Kalven, Jr., *Ernst Freund and the First Amendment Tradition,* 40 U.Chi.L.Rev. 235 (1973).

Harry Kalven, Jr., A WORTHY TRADITION: FREEDOM OF SPEECH IN AMERICA (1988).

Donald E. Lively, *Fear and the Media: A First Amendment Horror Show,* 69 Minn.L.Rev. 1071 (1985).

Alexander Meiklejohn, *The First Amendment and Evils That Congress Has a Right to Prevent,* 26 Ind.L.J. 477 (1951).

Martin H. Redish, *Advocacy of Unlawful Conduct and the First Amendment: In Defense of Clear and Present Danger,* 70 Cal.L.Rev. 1159 (1982).

Martin H. Redish, *The Content Distinction in First Amendment Analysis,* 34 Stan.L.Rev. 113 (1981).

Amy Sabrin, *Thinking About Content: Can It Play An Appropriate Role in Government Funding of the Arts?,* 102 Yale L.J. 1209 (1993).

Paul B. Stephan III, *The First Amendment and Content Discrimination,* 68 Va.L.Rev. 103 (1982).

Geoffrey R. Stone, *Anti–Pornography Regulation as Viewpoint–Discrimination,* 9 Harv.J.L. & Pub.Pol. 461 (1986).

Geoffrey R. Stone, *Content–Neutral Restrictions,* 54 U.Chi.L.Rev. 46 (1987).

Geoffrey R. Stone, *Restrictions of Speech Because of its Content: The Peculiar Case of Subject–Matter Restrictions,* 46 U.Chi.L.Rev. 81 (1978).

Geoffrey R. Stone & William P. Marshall, Brown v. Socialist Workers: *Inequality as a Command of the First Amendment,* 1983 Sup.Ct.Rev. 583.

Frank R. Strong, *Fifty Years of "Clear and Present Danger": From* Schenck *to* Brandenburg, 1969 Sup.Ct.Rev. 41.

Public Forum

Ronald A. Cass, *First Amendment Access to Government Facilities,* 65 Va.L.Rev. 1287 (1979).

David S. Day, *The End of the Public Forum Doctrine,* 78 Iowa L.Rev. 143 (1992).

C. Thomas Dienes, *The Trashing of the Public Forum: Problems in First Amendment Analysis,* 55 Geo.Wash.L.Rev. 109 (1986).

Daniel A. Farber & John E. Nowak, *The Misleading Nature of Public Forum Analysis: Content and Context in First Amendment Adjudication,* 70 Va.L.Rev. 1219 (1984).

David Goldberger, *A Reconsideration of* Cox v. New Hampshire: *Can Demonstrators Be Required to Pay the Costs of Using America's Public Forums?,* 62 Tex.L.Rev. 403 (1983).

David Goldberger, *Judicial Scrutiny in Public Forum Cases: Misplaced Trust in the Judgment of Public Officials,* 32 Buffalo L.Rev. 175 (1983).

Harry Kalven, Jr., *The Concept of the Public Forum:* Cox v. Louisiana, 1965 Sup.Ct.Rev. 1.

Gary Leedes, *Pigeonholes in the Public Forum,* 20 U.Rich.L.Rev. 499 (1986).

Eric Neisser, *Charging for Free Speech: User Fees and Insurance in the Marketplace of Ideas,* 74 Geo.L.J. 257 (1985).

Robert C. Post, *Between Governance and Management: The History and Theory of the Public Forum,* 34 UCLA L.Rev. 1713 (1987).

Richard B. Saphire, *Reconsidering the Public Forum Doctrine,* 59 U.Cin. L.Rev. 739 (1991).

Matthew L. Spitzer, *The Constitutionality of Licensing Broadcasters,* 64 N.Y.U.L.Rev. 990 (1989).

Geoffrey R. Stone, *Fora Americana: Speech in Public Places,* 1974 Sup.Ct.Rev. 233.

Symbolic Speech

Dean Alfange, Jr., *Free Speech and Symbolic Conduct: The Draft–Card Burning Case,* 1968 Sup.Ct.Rev. 1.

David S. Day, *The Incidental Regulation of Free Speech,* 42 U.Miami L.Rev. 491 (1988).

Douglas W. Kmiec, *In the Aftermath of* Johnson *and* Eichman: *The Constitution Need Not Be Mutilated to Preserve the Government's Speech and Property Interests in the Flag,* 1990 B.Y.U.L.Rev. 577.

Arnold Loewy, *The Flag–Burning Case: Freedom of Speech When We Need It Most,* 68 N.C.L.Rev. 165 (1989).

Frank I. Michelman, *Saving Old Glory: On Constitutional Iconography,* 42 Stan.L.Rev. 1337 (1990).

Frederick Schauer, *Cuban Cigars, Cuban Books, and the Problem of Incidental Restrictions on Communication,* 26 Wm. & Mary L.Rev. 779 (1985).

Peter M. Shane, *Equal Protection, Free Speech, and the Selective Prosecution of Draft Nonregistrants,* 72 Iowa L.Rev. 359 (1987).

Geoffrey R. Stone, *Flag Burning and the Constitution,* 75 Iowa L.Rev. 111 (1989).

Geoffrey R. Stone, *Content–Neutral Restrictions,* 54 U.Chi.L.Rev. 46 (1987).

Peter Meijes Tiersma, *Nonverbal Communication and the Freedom of "Speech,"* 6 Wis.L.Rev. 1525 (1993).

Keith Werhane, *The O'Briening of Free Speech Methodology,* 19 Ariz.St. L.J. 635 (1987).

Time, Place, and Manner Regulations

C. Edwin Baker, *Unreasoned Reasonableness: Mandatory Parade Permits and Time, Place, and Manner Regulations,* 78 Nw.U.L.Rev. 937 (1983).

David S. Day, *The Hybridization of the Content–Neutral Standards for the Free Speech Clause,* 19 Ariz.St.L.J. 195 (1987).

Norman Dorsen & Joel M. Gora, *Free Speech, Property, and the Burger Court: Old Values, New Balances,* 1982 Sup.Ct.Rev. 195.

Franklyn S. Haiman, *Speech v. Privacy: Is There a Right Not to Be Spoken To?,* 67 Nw.U.L.Rev. 153 (1972).

Harry Kalven, Jr., THE NEGRO AND THE FIRST AMENDMENT (1965).

William E. Lee, *Lonely Pamphleteers, Little People, and the Supreme Court: The Doctrine of Time, Place, and Manner Regulations of Expression,* 54 Geo.Wash.L.Rev. 757 (1986).

D. PROCEDURAL COMPONENTS OF FREE SPEECH PROTECTION

In this section we continue our exploration of the free speech rules that focus on the nature of the government actor and the type of government act. We concentrate on the procedures used by legislatures, administrative officials, and courts to regulate speech. As a general proposition we may say that the First Amendment worries most about legislative and administrative actions, and sees the courts as a beneficent influence. There are obvious reasons for this view. In the case of federal judges the tenure and compensation protections in the Constitution provide some insulation from political pressure. Courts are also more institutionally detached than legislatures, prosecutors, and agencies from the problems they deal with: they don't control their own agenda, and they must decide according to legal rules. But this assumption of judicial beneficence does not always hold true; there are some kinds of free speech harm that courts alone can cause (the unsympathetic choice of law in defamation cases), and others that rival the worst abuses of the other branches (injunctions as a form of prior restraint).

We begin with First Amendment constraints on legislative procedures. That, Henry Monaghan says, is what the overbreadth doctrine amounts to. The popular belief is that overbreadth is a special standing rule for free speech cases. But Monaghan explains that it is simply a restriction on the means a legislature can use to regulate speech; it is the least restrictive alternative rule in First Amendment dress.

The besetting sin of administrators and judges is not overbreadth but over-eagerness. And the best known procedural requirement imposed by the First Amendment is the rule against jumping the gun and restricting speech in advance of publication. According to Blackstone, this was the essential meaning of freedom of the press. According to Holmes, it was all the framers had in mind.[1] There are two difficult questions in the law about prior restraints, and they are related to one another. The first is why the law takes such a dim view of this form of regulation. The question is not an easy one. Vincent Blasi suggests five possible answers, and Martin Redish disputes nearly all of them.

The second question is whether injunctions should be treated as a kind of prior restraint, whose classical form was the license. The Supreme Court held in *Near v. Minnesota*[2] that they should, but it did not give a very satisfactory explanation. Blasi offers one. He argues that when courts act by injunction they present most of the same dangers as licensing systems: adjudication in the abstract, overuse, delay, and so on. Redish, on the other hand, thinks that *Near* was a mistake. He asserts that we should trust the courts here as we do in other First Amendment venues to do the right thing.

---

1. Blackstone said that "The liberty of the press is indeed essential to the nature of a free state; but this consists in laying no *previous* restraints upon publications, and not in freedom from censure for criminal matter when published." 4 W. Blackstone, Commentaries *151–152. Justice Holmes opined that "the main purpose of [freedom of speech and freedom of the press] is 'to prevent all such *previous restraints* upon publications as had been practiced by other governments,' and they do not prevent the subsequent punishment of such as may be deemed contrary to the public welfare." Patterson v. Colorado, 205 U.S. 454, 462 (1907).

2. 283 U.S. 697 (1931).

There is certainly some truth in Redish's major premise. What Henry Monaghan calls "First Amendment due process" is by and large judicial process. In cases where administrative bodies are allowed to regulate speech—film censorship, parade permits, discipline of government employees, etc.—we generally rely on the courts to appraise the character of the speech, and insist that the courts act before or immediately after government intervention takes place.

Monaghan's article on *Constitutional Fact Review* illustrates another aspect of our reliance on the judicial process—here the appellate process. The Federal Rules of Civil Procedure generally require appellate courts to uphold trial courts' findings of fact unless they are clearly erroneous.[3] This is not true of First Amendment cases where the issue is the application of free speech law to facts. In these cases, Monaghan argues, more searching review helps appellate courts do a better job of developing constitutional norms case by case.

But it would be a mistake to draw from all this the lesson that the First Amendment is safe in the hands of the courts. There is always the possibility that they will misinterpret or misapply it. And more to the point here, there are occasions when the courts can *violate* it. Injunctions are one possibility (if we take Blasi's view of prior restraints). James Pielemeier points to another, which crops up in multistate defamation cases. The combination of long-arm jurisdiction and liberal choice of law rules can lead defamation plaintiffs to sue publishers in those few forums that are most hostile to the press. Pielemeier argues that this is cause for exercising some First Amendment control over choice of law decisions.

HENRY P. MONAGHAN, OVERBREADTH
1981 Sup.Ct.Rev. 1, 3–5, 8–9, 12, 37–39.

Overbreadth is * * * a label that has been utilized to cover not one but two doctrines. One is concerned with the content of the substantive constitutional standards for determining the validity of a statute affecting expression. This substantive dimension of overbreadth methodology is most frequently concerned with matters of regulatory precision; the means chosen by the legislature must be no broader than necessary to achieve legitimate governmental purposes. The other, more dramatic aspect of overbreadth analysis is the procedural dimension—a supposed special First Amendment standing rule permitting litigants to raise the rights of "third parties." In this essay, I propose to show that, for the Court at least, overbreadth doctrine does not in fact possess a distinctive standing component; it is, rather, the application of conventional standing concepts in the First Amendment context. Accordingly, overbreadth analysis is simply an examination of the merits of the substantive constitutional claim.

* * *

---

3. Fed.R.Civ.P. 52(a).

"Conventional" constitutional challenges are widely assumed to involve distinctive characteristics. Generally, a litigant may raise only his "own" rights, not those of others; thus he can challenge a statute only "as applied" to him. Formulations of this character can suggest that a conventional constitutional challenge can be completely reduced to a claim of substantive constitutional privilege; that is, the litigant must demonstrate that the conduct established by the evidence is, as a matter of substantive constitutional law, simply immune from regulation. * * * A litigant, of course, can always make such a challenge, and that contention can be framed either in privilege terms, or alternatively, as a challenge to the statute "as applied." However phrased, the challenge is wholly fact dependent: Do the determinative facts shown by the evidence fall on the protected side of the applicable rule of constitutional privilege?

In their efforts to identify the distinctive standing aspects of over-breadth methodology, many commentators assume that conventional constitutional challenges are invariably restricted to such fact-dependent claims of privilege. This conclusion seems to be entailed by the fact that courts can narrow the literal sweep of statutes to fit governing constitutional standards. In other words, in the process of applying a statute, courts can narrow the legislative prescription to a set of criteria which (a) are constitutionally permissible and (b) fit the general facts of the litigant's conduct as established by the evidence.

* * *

Quite plainly, the more a statute is cut down to state a permissible subrule general enough to cover the facts of the litigant's case, the more the substance of the litigant's claim becomes that of a fact-dependent claim of constitutional privilege. But this is not invariably so. A fundamental principle of our system of constitutional law lies behind the proclivity of courts to narrow the sweeping reach of statutory language. The operative rule, either as enacted or construed, must conform to the Constitution. Thus, in addition to a claim of privilege, a litigant has always been permitted to make another, equally "conventional" challenge: He can insist that his conduct be judged in accordance with a rule that is constitutionally valid. In sharp contrast to a fact-dependent privilege claim, a challenge to the content of the rule applied is independent of the specific facts of the litigant's predicament. Rather, it speaks to the relationship between the facial content of the rule being applied to the facts and the applicable constitutional law, and it insists that the rule itself be valid.

Considerable decisional law demonstrates that a sanction imposed under a facially invalid rule cannot be saved by fact-dependent references to the nonprivileged character of the litigant's conduct. * * * Vagueness cases illustrate the point. A litigant can challenge the terms of the rule applied without showing that his own conduct is privileged against conviction under a statute giving better notice of what constitutes the offense. Similarly, one could not be denied equal protection of the laws simply because the conduct at issue is not independently privileged.

* * *

* * * The doctrine is a general one, in no way limited to either First Amendment or criminal cases. In *Wuchter v. Pizzutti*,[48] for instance, the Court permitted a nonresident motorist to challenge a statutory scheme governing service of process on nonresidents. The statute imposed no requirement of notice, and the state court imposed none by way of construction. Even though the defendant had in fact received notice, the Court found a constitutional violation in these circumstances. "[Notice not] having been directed by the statute it can not, therefore, supply constitutional validity to the statute or to service under it."

* * *

[Hence,] overbreadth methodology simply applies the conventional principle that any litigant may insist on not being burdened by a constitutionally invalid rule. What is different from the conventional run-of-the-mill case is not standing but the substantive content of the applicable constitutional law.

As an expression of substantive constitutional principles, overbreadth is, of course, concerned with the weight of the governmental interest justifying any regulation. But the dominant idea it evokes is serious means scrutiny. Wherever that law mandates strict or intermediate scrutiny, a requirement of regulatory precision is involved; a substantial congruence must exist between the regulatory means (the statute, as construed) and valid legislative ends. Thus the Court has reacted interchangeably to "overbreadth" and "least restrictive alternative" challenges both inside and outside the First Amendment context. * * * [W]herever the Supreme Court is serious about judicial review— wherever, that is, the minimum rationality standard does not prevail— the Court will be concerned with the matter of least restrictive alternatives, with overbreadth.[157] By contrast, whenever the rational basis standard governs, substantive constitutional scrutiny is virtually nonexistent. Despite occasional judicial and academic protestations to the contrary, that review is essentially "toothless." In all cases subject to that standard, statutory "overbreadth" is not a meaningful objection as a matter of substantive constitutional doctrine. A central feature of rational basis review is that it accords wide latitude to the states to structure their social and economic programs as they see fit. As long as the legislative scheme can be perceived as designed to promote some

---

48. 276 U.S. 13 (1928).

157. We ordinarily do not consider the least restrictive alternative cases as presenting any departure from conventional standing principles. Nor should we when that same concept appears in the First Amendment context. Judicial conclusions of overbreadth or of the availability of less restrictive alternatives are equivalents. They are simply different statements that other, more finely tuned means exist to vindicate any presumably valid state policies. * * *

common good, the overbreadth of the statutory scheme does not render it constitutionally infirm.[159]

VINCENT BLASI, TOWARD A THEORY OF PRIOR RESTRAINT: THE CENTRAL LINKAGE

66 Minn.L.Rev. 11, 14, 20, 24–27, 49–51, 54–56, 58–64, 67–70, 84–85 (1981).

In this essay I revisit the issue introduced by *Near* [*v. Minnesota* [a]]: should the injunction, as a general matter, be regarded as a particularly repressive method of regulating speech, akin to the historically disfavored administrative licensing system? * * *

I build my inquiry around a search for features that modern licensing systems and injunctions have in common that might warrant grouping them together for similar treatment in first amendment analysis. Necessarily, I assess whether the common features that might differentiate licensing systems and injunctions from the standard "subsequent" punishments—criminal prohibitions and civil liability rules—are significant enough to warrant a special first amendment preference for the latter forms of speech regulation. * * *

* * *

My prototype for a licensing system is a procedure that requires a would-be speaker to obtain a permit from an administrative official before proceeding to speak; makes no provision for a formal hearing before that official; subjects permit denials to expeditious review by a court; and provides that persons who speak without a required permit can be criminally punished for that act alone, without regard to whether they would have been constitutionally entitled, had they pursued that course, to obtain a license for the speech that is the subject of the prosecution. The prototypical injunction I consider is * * * a judicial order, instituted after an adversary proceeding, that prohibits identified persons from engaging in specified communicative activities, on pain of being held in criminal or civil contempt by the judge who issued the injunction.

* * *

What then is it that licensing systems and injunctions have in common that unites them in the mind of the first amendment theorist? I can think of five potentially important features that appear on the surface to be shared by licensing systems and injunctions, and appear not to be shared, at least to the same extent, by criminal laws and civil liability rules: (1) the tendency, when the practical dynamics of the scheme are considered, to induce persons to engage in an unusually high

159. Williamson v. Lee Optical Co., 348 U.S. 483 (1955). See also, *e.g.,* Massachusetts Bd. of Retirement v. Murgia, 427 U.S. 307 (1976); New York City Transit Auth. v. Beazer, 440 U.S. 568 (1979); Minnesota v. Clover Leaf Creamery Co., 101 S.Ct. 715, 722–27 (1981); Schweiker v. Wilson, 101 S.Ct. 1074, 1080–85 (1981).

a. 283 U.S. 697 (1931).

degree of self-censorship of constitutionally protected expression; (2) the adjudication of constitutional claims at a time and in a manner that produces a formal, abstract quality of decision making; (3) the tendency to be used too readily; (4) an unusual capacity to distort the way audiences respond to communications; and (5) implicit premises that are antithetical to the philosophy of limited government. If any one or combination of these features turns out on close analysis to be notably more characteristic of both licensing systems and injunctions than of the standard "subsequent" sanctions on speech, and also significant in terms of first amendment values, we would have the beginnings of a theory of prior restraint.

SELF-CENSORSHIP

"Self-censorship" is an important phenomenon in first amendment analysis. Speakers, listeners, and society at large all suffer when the peculiar features of a regulatory scheme have a "chilling effect" on persons that causes them to forgo protected expression rather than get themselves enmeshed in the scheme. * * *

All laws regulating speech, criminal prohibitions and civil liability rules no less than other procedures, are designed to have one sort of "chilling effect": to deter persons from engaging in speech activities the ill effects of which are a legitimate basis for imposing regulatory restraints or sanctions. Moreover, even the most narrowly designed laws are bound to induce a measure of self-censorship of protected expression, at least so long as it takes some amount of time, effort and/or money to vindicate one's rights. The question to be examined is whether as a general matter the licensing system and the injunction induce significantly more self-censorship of speech that is protected under prevailing first amendment standards than the criminal prohibition and the civil liability rule. The proposition is stated vividly by Professor Bickel: "A criminal statute chills, prior restraint freezes." [57]

* * *

This * * * proposition is by no means self-evident. In some respects, licensing systems and injunctions seem preferable to criminal prohibitions and civil liability rules in terms of minimizing the deterrence of protected expression. Under a regime of criminal or civil sanctions, speakers ordinarily can test the limits of first amendment protection only by engaging in speech and risking sanctions should they guess wrong about the extent of their rights. Under a licensing procedure, in contrast, speakers can obtain a definitive ruling that their proposed acts of expression are constitutionally protected. Injunction procedures also provide for advance adjudication of speakers' rights. Although that adjudication will not invariably determine the extent of the state's power to impose subsequent sanctions for the speech in question, in most instances the speakers will learn a great deal from the

---

57. A. Bickel, [The Morality of Consent 61 (1975).]

injunction procedure regarding what acts of expression can be undertaken with impunity.

Under systems of subsequent punishment, the risk of self-censorship due to uncertainty is likely to be compounded by the potential severity of the sanctions that can be imposed against speakers. Except in the area of defamation, and there only in one limited respect, the Supreme Court has been unwilling to erect constitutional limitations on how severely persons can be sanctioned for engaging in unprotected expression. Long criminal sentences and enormous civil damage awards are not uncommon, even for speech at the margins of constitutional protection. Persons who violate permit requirements and injunctions can also be punished severely, but usually not for guessing wrong about the extent of their rights, only for failing to utilize available procedures for determining in advance the limits of those rights. Moreover, sanctions for the violation of injunctions and permit ordinances tend to be light in comparison with those commonly administered under the subsequent punishment regimes.

Thus, even if licensing systems and injunctions are found to share the quality of causing considerable self-censorship in distinctive (though not identical) ways, the case is not necessarily compelling for basing a theory of prior restraint on this particular common feature.   * * *

* * *

ADJUDICATION IN THE ABSTRACT

* * *

When adjudication precedes initial dissemination, the communication cannot be judged by its actual consequences or public reception. The adjudicative assessment of speech value versus social harm must be made in the abstract, based on speculation or generalizations embodied in presumptions. That decisional limitation can affect the substance of the judicial decision in at least four ways that might be detrimental to the claims put forth by speakers.

First, if the governing first amendment test for the speech at issue is one that turns on consequences (clear and present danger, for example), the necessity for speculation permits groundless fears to figure in the rationale for suppression. If the judgment were made at a later stage, the data from initial dissemination could on occasion serve to dispel such fears.   * * *

* * *

This objection to adjudication in the abstract does not apply when the first amendment test is based on the intrinsic character of the speech rather than its particular consequences (for example, the current doctrines regarding obscenity and fighting words). Even if the "intrinsic character" of speech categories is determined largely on the basis of generalizations about the normal consequences of the various communications that fall within each category, once the generalization is adopted there is no further assessment based on the consequences in individual cases. It should not matter, therefore, so far as the factor of groundless fears is concerned, whether adjudication under an intrinsic character standard precedes or follows the expressive event. * * *

Second, the dissemination of speech may create public opinion pressures that can exert a healthy influence on the formulation and application of first amendment standards. * * *

Third, once a communication is disseminated it becomes to some extent a *fait accompli*. The world is a slightly different place; perceptions regarding what is tolerable are altered. Not only can the effects of the speech not be undone, views regarding the desirability of those effects will be influenced by the common human tendency to find virtue in the status quo. This phenomenon too may influence the formulation and application of doctrine in the direction of permitting more speech.

Finally, a judge's determination whether speech is constitutionally protected is likely to be influenced by the fact that, in the case of adjudication before dissemination, a permissive decision can result in the judge being held responsible for any adverse consequences that ensue from the expressive activity. If a protest march disintegrates into a riot, the judge who ordered the issuance of the parade permit will be criticized. * * *

* * *

Overuse

So far we have examined how prior and subsequent systems of regulation compare in terms of their impact on potential speakers and on judges called upon to adjudicate the legal status of particular communications. Another dimension to consider is the impact of the various systems on the behavior of persons who seek to accomplish the suppression or sanctioning of speech. This is a diverse class of actors that includes legislators who work for speech-restrictive legislation, police officers who arrest speakers or try to deter speech by threats, licensing officials, prosecutors, and private persons who bring lawsuits against speakers. I shall refer to this group collectively as regulatory agents. It is possible that injunctive and licensing systems are undesirable simply because they tend in operation to be too fully utilized by regulatory agents—too often invoked to generate prohibitions that are too often enforced. * * *

The argument from overuse for preferring the subsequent punishment regimes is rather curious. It depends on the proposition that the frequency and effectiveness with which various regulatory powers are invoked is a proper matter to consider in determining which powers are constitutionally valid. If a power is valid when used sparingly, why should it become invalid when used systematically? If we want only a few exceptionally harmful communications to be regulated, should not that rationing be achieved by defining very narrowly what speech is unprotected against *any* form of regulation rather than by preferring the more inefficient and unsystematic methods of regulation?

Not necessarily. In one sense, all first amendment issues involve a tension between the gains to be expected from speech (transmission of knowledge, cathartic release, and so forth) and the social risks and costs associated with controversial communications (antisocial actions caused, misimpressions created, irritations engendered). The strength of the social interests supporting regulation depends to some extent on variables, such as the intensity preferences of persons who feel threatened by speech, that are more easily assessed by politically responsible or personally involved regulatory agents than by judges seeking to apply legal doctrines in a detached fashion. If the regulation of speech is made a costly, time consuming, even aggravating process, only the most highly motivated regulatory agents will persevere. The dedication of the regulatory agents who happen to be involved is by no means a perfect proxy for the severity of the harms caused by a particular communication. Nonetheless, a political culture that tends * * * to prefer too much regulation of speech probably can be relied upon to produce persevering regulatory agents whenever a speech causes or threatens to cause truly serious social harms. In this regard, a doctrinal preference for cumbersome procedures erects a filter which can supplement the effort to identify by means of substantive standards the occasions when the social interests in regulating speech outweigh the various interests served by unfettered expression.

* * *

* * * It remains to be shown, however, that injunctions and licensing systems share, in comparison with the subsequent punishment regimes, a tendency to be overused.

* * *

Injunctions are issued and permit applications are denied "by a stroke of the pen." In both cases, the process is expeditious. Certain procedures and evidentiary burdens limit how readily and pervasively those systems can be employed by regulatory agents, but checks of that sort do not fundamentally alter the essentially expeditious character of the prior regulatory regimes.

Under traditional principles of equity, regulatory agents who seek to enjoin speech normally must establish that "irreparable harm" is likely to ensue if the speech is not enjoined. They must convince the court that "legal" remedies (subsequent punishments, in the main) will not adequately protect the social interests threatened by the speech. But those are burdens of persuasion more than preparation; they are not likely to deter or seriously delay regulatory agents who desire to invoke legal authority to suppress speech. * * *

No special burden of persuasion, and in most cases not even a formal hearing, operates to check the suppressive stroke of the pen by a licensing official.   * * *

Not only are there no major burdens to force licensing officials to make priority judgments, there may be bureaucratic dynamics that encourage casual, routine invocation of the power to regulate expression. Licensing officials typically are selected because of their knowledge and concern about the social interests the regulatory system is designed to protect—crowd control, for example, or conventional mores regarding sexual depiction.   These officials can be expected to begin their chores with a predisposition to regulate expression.   The experience of ruling upon numerous permit applications, moreover, is hardly likely to heighten what little appreciation such persons may have for the value of free expression.   When the phenomenon of prospective accountability is added to the calculus, it seems inevitable that regulatory impulses of low or intermediate intensity would be pursued by most licensing officials absent some sort of doctrinal check deriving from a theory of prior restraint.

Under the subsequent punishment regimes, in contrast, the process by which regulatory impulses are implemented is far more complicated, drawn out, and interlaced with disincentives.   The passage of a criminal statute requires a majority vote in two separate representative bodies (except in Nebraska).   The traditional practice of committee deliberation slows down the process and often provides an opportunity for political minorities (including proponents of strong speech rights) to kill or modify proposed legislation.   The gubernatorial veto constitutes an additional obstacle.   The power to legislate against speech can certainly be abused, but usually only when the preferences of the political community run intensely in the direction of repression.   Even then, the cumbersome nature of the legislative process makes it difficult for the regulatory forces to keep up with innovative, adaptive speakers such as pornographers.   Injunctions and permit requirements, for which the basic substantive norms are formulated case by case, seem by comparison far more susceptible to both casual and comprehensive use.

* * *

So far as the formulation of prohibitory norms is concerned, it would seem that the procedures and traditions of the subsequent punishment regimes provide fairly effective safeguards against too casual or pervasive a use of the power to regulate speech.   By comparison, injunctive and licensing systems are particularly susceptible to being invoked in response to momentary public passions or political preferences that are not widely shared or deeply felt.

The various regulatory systems also exhibit differences in their enforcement procedures that can be expected to affect levels and patterns of use.   Several forces combine to generate a logic of full enforcement of injunctions.   Because of the personalized nature of the prohibition, the disobedience of an injunction takes on the character of defiance of the legal system itself. Symbolic considerations may dictate prosecution when material considerations alone would not. Even if officials might not regard a particular violation as serious, they may have difficulty pretending not to notice it because the personalized character of the proceedings at which injunctions are issued often places enjoinees in the public eye. In addition, the decision whether to charge speakers with contempt is often made by the judge who issued the injunction in the first place. * * * The fact that a conviction for contempt can be had within a short time after a violation takes place also should tend to encourage prosecutions. Finally, the existence of the collateral bar rule means that regulatory agents need not worry that the speaker's first amendment defenses will abort or complicate a contempt prosecution.[b] It is not surprising that there is no real tradition of prosecutorial discretion with regard to violations of injunctions.

Licensing systems are enforced by means of regular criminal prosecutions. Many of the forces that generate a logic of full enforcement of injunctions thus do not operate in the context of licensing: the promulgator of the legal norm does not make the enforcement decision, the lead time between violation and conviction is no shorter than for other types of criminal cases, and a tradition of prosecutorial discretion operates. Two factors suggest, however, that permit requirements are likely to be enforced more frequently than most other laws regulating speech.

First, the equivalent of a partial collateral bar rule governs prosecutions for speaking without a required permit. Defendants are permitted to contend that the licensing law is unconstitutional on its face, but not that the permit denial in their particular case was a violation of the first amendment.[113] So long as the licensing system as a whole is not invalid, the prosecution of persons who speak in the face of a permit denial or who ignore the permit process entirely is generally a pro forma matter. All the prosecutor must establish is that the activity engaged in by the defendants falls within the category of acts for which a permit is required. The prosecution of permit violations ordinarily requires little investigation or preparation by the district attorney's office. A high conviction rate can be anticipated. The prospect of success can function as a spur to prosecution.

Second, symbolic considerations should engender a propensity to prosecute permit violations. When a permit is actually sought and denied, a decision by the rejected applicant to proceed anyway with the

---

b. As a result of the Supreme Court's decision in Walker v. City of Birmingham, 388 U.S. 307 (1967), a speaker sometimes may not violate an injunction as a means of testing its constitutionality. Instead, the enjoined speaker is obligated to mount a constitutional challenge by moving to have the injunction vacated or modified, even if the claim is that the injunction is unconstitutional on its face. Under what is known as the collateral bar rule, failure to seek such anticipatory relief precludes the speaker from invoking a first amendment defense in a criminal contempt of court proceeding for violating the injunction. [Relocated text. Eds.]

113. Poulos v. New Hampshire, 345 U.S. 395 (1953).

proposed speech takes on the character of direct defiance, at least as much as does the violation of an injunction. * * *

* * *

IMPACT ON AUDIENCE RECEPTION

In addition to its impact on speakers, judges, and regulatory agents, a system should be evaluated also in terms of how its distinctive features affect the way audiences receive the communications that take place notwithstanding the regulatory constraints imposed by the system. Although speech can serve a function even when no one is influenced by what is said, all major first amendment theories place a high value on the social process by which persons are persuaded by communications to change their moral and empirical beliefs. It should be a matter of doctrinal concern if certain laws or methods of regulation cause audiences to shrink, or individual listeners to respond less intently (pro or con) to the speaker's message.

Licensing systems and injunctions governed by the collateral bar rule share the characteristic of providing an authoritative adjudication regarding the legality of a disputed communication before the moment of its initial dissemination. This phenomenon can have two effects that might be detrimental to audience reception of some communications that are determined to be constitutionally protected. First, the process of adjudication can delay dissemination of the speaker's message to a time when audience interest has waned or opportunities to act upon the speaker's advice have passed. * * *

* * *

The second major way in which the phenomenon of prior adjudication can affect audience reception is by influencing public expectations regarding a communication before the moment of its initial dissemination. Several distorting effects can be hypothesized.

First, audiences may wonder whether the communication that is transmitted represents the true message the speaker desired to convey. Did the speaker change a few passages in order to placate the censor or expedite the process of prior approval? Often there is no way to know, but doubts can infect the experience of reception. * * *

Second, the granting of a license or the lifting of an injunction constitutes an official seal of approval, the modern day equivalent of an imprimatur. In a curious way, speeches that have such a characterization may lose some of their impact for that reason alone. The element of excitement that is present when a speaker presses a protest to the edge of legality, accepting the risk of criminal or civil sanctions, is absent. * * *

* * *

In short, prior adjudication erects a filter between speaker and audience. Even for the messages that pass through the filter, the communicative process is detrimentally affected by the existence of such a barrier. The impact is difficult to document or predict, but under any theory that values speech largely for its capacity to influence listeners, this filtering phenomenon should be regarded as undesirable.

* * *

UNACCEPTABLE PREMISES

To this point, we have evaluated the various methods of speech regulation exclusively in terms of their impact on the behavior of speakers, adjudicators, regulatory agents, and audiences. Behavioral impact is not, however, the only dimension that needs to be considered in determining whether a regulatory method should be disfavored under the first amendment. One function of a constitution is to preserve certain institutional structures and public attitudes relating to the concept of political authority. In particular, the Bill of Rights should be interpreted not only with an eye to the actors who have a stake in the litigation at hand, but also with regard for the entire political community's stake in preserving a certain desired allocation of power between two vital abstract entities: the state and the individual citizen.

Regulatory procedures may distort that allocation if they are based on premises that are inconsistent with the philosophy of limited government that lies at the heart of the American constitutional tradition.
* * *

* * *

I conclude that whenever they are employed in a routine and comprehensive fashion, licensing and injunctive systems share three implicit premises that are unacceptable in a constitutional order that is founded on the principle of limited government and hence committed to maintaining a balance of authority between the state and the individual. First, the widespread use of licensing or enjoining implies a premise of comparative distrust, a belief that it is more dangerous to trust audiences with controversial communications than it is to trust the legal process with the power to suppress speech. Second, the invocation of such extraordinary regulatory procedures as permit requirements and injunctions implies that the activity of disseminating controversial communications is abnormally hazardous or disruptive, and hence represents a threat to, rather than an integral feature of, the social order. Third, licensing systems and injunctions coerce or induce speakers to relinquish full control over the details and timing of their communications. These regulatory systems must be premised, therefore, on the notion that either such control is not an essential attribute of the autonomy of speakers, or that such autonomy need not be respected. Either premise is objectionable.

MARTIN H. REDISH, THE PROPER ROLE OF THE PRIOR RESTRAINT DOCTRINE IN FIRST AMENDMENT THEORY

70 Va.L.Rev. 53, 59–62, 66–68, 70–73, 75–78 (1984).

I. THE TRADITIONAL JUSTIFICATIONS FOR THE PRIOR RESTRAINT DOCTRINE: RATIONALE AND CRITIQUE

Respected commentators, notably Professors Thomas Emerson[23] and Vincent Blasi,[24] have offered several arguments favoring the presumption against prior restraint, judicial or nonjudicial. * * * This section examines each of these proffered justifications and concludes that they are irrelevant to first amendment concerns, are equally true of subsequent punishment schemes, or are exclusively applicable to administrative rather than judicial restraints.

Inhibition of the Marketplace of Ideas

Commentators have argued that "[p]rior restraint limits public debate more severely" than does subsequent prosecution, because "[w]hile subsequent punishment may deter some speakers, at least the ideas or speech at issue can be placed before the public."[25] Prior restraint thus imposes a greater burden on the marketplace of ideas than does subsequent punishment.

This analysis contains a fundamental fallacy. The prior restraint doctrine as it traditionally has been formulated posits that expression which could be constitutionally subjected to subsequent punishment is immune from regulation by prior restraint. When the doctrine is cast in these terms, one can logically assume that the speech which the prior restraint keeps from the marketplace of ideas is speech which would not be found constitutionally protected in a subsequent prosecution. Therefore, the affected speech is presumably beneath first amendment protection. If this is the case, one may question whether any harm of constitutional magnitude occurs in preventing such speech from reaching the marketplace.

Professor Blasi * * * has argued that "once a communication is disseminated it becomes to some extent a *fait accompli*. The world is a slightly different place; perceptions regarding what is tolerable are altered. .... This phenomenon ... may influence the formulation and application of doctrine in the direction of permitting more speech." He is correct in suggesting that, at least in a technical sense, the world is in some way a "different place," but that difference is not necessarily of constitutional magnitude. Blasi's apparent assumption is that the pub-

---

23. See Emerson, [*The Doctrine of Prior Restraint,* 20 Law & Contemp.Probs. 648 (1955).]

24. See Blasi, [*Toward a Theory of Prior Restraint: The Central Linkage,* 66 Minn. L.Rev. 11 (1981).]

25. J. Nowak, R. Rotunda & J. Young, [Constitutional Law 887 (2d ed. 1983).]

lic availability of the challenged expression may somehow influence the substantive judicial first amendment analysis, leading speech that would otherwise be unprotected to be held protected. Yet Blasi fails to support this assumption with anything more than speculation, and the point is by no means intuitively clear. For Blasi's assumption to be correct, public reaction to the challenged expression must be favorable, the judiciary must somehow be made aware of this reaction, and the judiciary must be sufficiently influenced by this reaction to reverse its decision on constitutionality. Though all three of these events could conceivably occur in the same case, it is at least doubtful.

Initially, the public would not likely react to particular expression with sufficient fervor and unanimity that the reaction would be widely noticed. Secondly, given generally accepted first amendment jurisprudence, speech that is both subject to serious governmental challenge and likely to be found unprotected by the courts is invariably going to be speech that would be *rejected* by the majority, not accepted with wild enthusiasm. Thirdly, even if the public did express a coherent and favorable opinion, it is doubtful that that view would influence a court's substantive constitutional analysis. Moreover, it is arguable that it should not do so in any event because most would agree that generally a strong *negative* public reaction to challenged expression should have no influence on judicial constitutional analysis.

Overuse

Similarly unpersuasive is the argument that prior restraints threaten first amendment rights because they are likely to be employed more often than subsequent punishment schemes. The overuse theory is premised largely on the ground that prior restraints are inherently easier to obtain than criminal convictions and are therefore likely to be employed more frequently to stifle expression.   * * *

* * *

[But] those making the overuse argument fail to recognize the fundamental similarity [between criminal and injunctive] proceedings: in each, assuming no interim prior restraint, no penalty or restraint is imposed absent a full and fair judicial determination that the challenged expression is not protected by the first amendment. Thus, even if it were true that authorities are more likely to *attempt* to obtain judicial prior restraints than they are criminal convictions, a fact far from established, it does not follow that the former present greater threats to first amendment interests than do the latter. Regardless of how many attempts are made, those attempts will prove successful only after a judicial body has concluded that the speech in question is unprotected.[31]

One might respond that the relative number of attempts to impose penalties on expression remains an important consideration because the

---

31. To the extent [the] point is limited to *administrative* restraints, however, it is   valid.

assumed deterrent to the filing of criminal prosecutions will mean that certain expression will not be restrained even though a court might have found it unprotected. Requiring state authorities to employ solely criminal prosecutions to penalize speech thus will have the ultimate effect of leaving more expression unrestrained. If this expression would ultimately have been judicially determined to be unprotected, however, first amendment interests are unaffected by either the allowance or the restraint of that particular expression.

* * *

Abstract Determinations

Perhaps the strongest argument against judicial prior restraint is that because such a restraint is imposed prior to the actual dissemination of expression, a court's first amendment ruling will necessarily be made in the abstract without any knowledge of the actual effect of the challenged expression. Therefore the court will be forced to determine whether expression is so dangerous that it may be suppressed, without knowing whether harm will actually result—a problem that arguably does not plague subsequent punishment schemes.

Several answers can be made to this contention. First, even if substantive questions are decided more often in the abstract in prior restraint proceedings than in subsequent punishment proceedings, first amendment interests are not necessarily harmed as a result. The only way that the abstract nature of the determination could undermine first amendment interests is if the court were to assume the possibility of more harm than would actually have occurred. No firm basis exists for assuming such judicial behavior.[50] Because expression may be regulated only in the presence of a truly compelling governmental interest, courts will be slow to uphold any restriction on expression when the demonstration of harm flowing from the expression is purely speculative. Under properly applied first amendment standards, the harm's abstractness should actually aid free speech interests because the burden would always be on the government to demonstrate the existence of significant danger from the expression, not on the speaker to prove the opposite. A court could conceivably deny a prior restraint because harm is too speculative, but later allow a subsequent punishment because harm actually resulted from the speech.

* * * Second, even if abstractness were generally deemed a constitutional defect, the problem may plague subsequent punishment schemes, just as it does prior restraints. Both points may be illustrated by

---

50. See Jeffries, [*Rethinking Prior Restraint,* 92 Yale L.J. 409, 417 n. 57 (1983).] Professor Jeffries noted two reasons for trusting judicial behavior. First he observed that "with every passing decade—not excluding the 1970s and the advent of the Burger Court—there is increasingly widespread acceptance of First Amendment claims that would have been thought fanciful only a few years earlier." Next he suggested that judges hostile to first amendment claims in general will not be more hostile in prior restraint proceedings than they would be in subsequent prosecutions.

examining *Dennis v. United States*,[53] in which the Supreme Court upheld criminal convictions of Communist Party leaders for conspiring to advocate overthrow of the government. Under the terms of the indictment, the defendants had not even been accused of actually advocating overthrow; certainly, no evidence was presented that any harm had already occurred. On the contrary, the Court acknowledged that the government need not await any actual showing of damage before it could criminally prosecute. Although the decision has been heavily criticized for effectively dispensing with any requirement of temporal relation between expression and harm, such criticism does not imply that the only speech which could be punished is speech which has actually led to provable harm. In any event, such criticism underscores the point that abstractness, to the extent it is a constitutional problem, may plague subsequent punishment as well as prior restraint.

* * *

Impact on Audience Reception

* * *

Professor Blasi argued that "audiences may react less intently, perhaps less spontaneously, when they know that the speech has already passed through a regulatory filter." They may or they may not; Blasi provided no empirical or psychological basis on which to rest such a conclusion. The issue will likely turn on what we allow the regulatory filter to filter. In a totalitarian society that censors any statement critical of the government, an audience would likely be less than impressed with a speech staunchly endorsing the government.

* * *

Given the context of our constitutional system, prior approval of speech * * * would not amount to a government stamp of approval on speech; rather, it would mean only that nothing contained in the expression falls within any of the narrowly drawn categories of expression that are unprotected by the first amendment. Though an audience may be less receptive to expression when it knows that the expression has met constitutional standards, it is doubtful that we should defer to such an audience's prejudices. In any event, an audience just as plausibly could be *more* receptive to speech when it knows that the speech is constitutionally protected, because that protection may well increase the speaker's legitimacy in the audience's eyes.

Professor Blasi has argued that when prior restraint systems are employed "audiences may wonder whether the communication that is transmitted represents the true message the speaker desired to convey. Did the speaker change a few passages in order to placate the censor or expedite the process of prior approval?" Though some audience members might react in this manner to prior restraint systems, they could

---

53. 341 U.S. 494 (1951).

just as easily entertain similar doubts about the speaker's message if they knew that the speaker was subject to subsequent punishment. * * *

Improper Division of State and Individual Authority

* * *

[Blasi] incorrectly suggests that prior restraints, more than subsequent punishment systems, reflect the view "that speakers and audiences are to be trusted less than regulatory processes." A subsequent punishment system that is premised on the assumption that certain expression is not constitutionally protected and therefore is subject to punishment necessarily presumes that the speaker and audience are not to be "trusted." Otherwise, we would allow the speaker to communicate whatever she wished and trust the audience to reject any harmful or evil suggestions contained in the speech. Blasi's argument * * * confuses substance and procedure: to the extent that failure to accord first amendment protection improperly reflects a lack of faith in individual judgment, this lack of faith is a problem derived from the substantive scope of first amendment doctrine, not from the regulatory method chosen.

* * *

II. Determining the Proper Role of the Prior Restraint Doctrine

* * *

Although none of the traditional rationales supporting mistrust of prior restraint justifies a sharp dichotomy between all forms of prior restraints and subsequent punishment systems, an alternative theoretical basis supports a doctrine mistrustful of some forms of prior restraint. Such a doctrine specially disfavors prior restraint as a form of speech regulation when that restraint limits expression prior to a full and fair hearing in an independent judicial forum to determine whether the challenged expression is constitutionally protected. Such restraint is permissible only in the presence of a truly compelling interest.

In contexts other than the first amendment, the Supreme Court has long held that a person's constitutional rights are violated when she is subjected to the judgment of an individual or institution directly interested in the outcome of the case.[78] If the body or individual determining whether a governmental agency has violated a constitutional right is a

---

78. See, e.g., Gibson v. Berryhill, 411 U.S. 564, 578–79 (1973) (holding that state board of optometry was so biased by pecuniary interest that it could not constitutionally conduct hearings to revoke optometrists' licenses); Tumey v. Ohio, 273 U.S. 510, 531 (1927) (holding unconstitutional practice whereby adjudicator's financial benefit from conviction greater than from acquittal). Cf. United States v. United States Dist. Court, 407 U.S. 297, 316–17 (1972) (holding that executive officers do not meet fourth amendment neutral-and-detached-magistrate requirement for issuing warrants); Coolidge v. New Hampshire, 403 U.S. 443, 453 (1971) (holding that search warrant issued by chief investigator violates due process).

part of or directly controlled by the agency, that governmental agency is effectively determining the constitutionality of its own actions. * * *

Applied to the first amendment context, this principle gives rise to several conclusions. Nonjudicial administrative regulators of expression exist for the sole purpose of regulating; this is their raison d'être. They simultaneously perform the functions of prosecutor and adjudicator and, if only subconsciously, will likely feel the obligation to justify their existence by finding some expression constitutionally subject to regulation. Such a systemic danger does not plague the functioning of a judicial forum. In addition, the tradition of independence from external political pressure provides grounds for preferring judicial to administrative adjudication. Thus, if the constitutional right to freedom of expression can be abridged only in the presence of a truly compelling governmental interest and if only an independent judicial forum can adequately decide whether particular expression is unprotected by the first amendment, it follows that any restriction of expression by an agency of government other than such a judicial forum is an unconstitutional abridgment of that expression except in the most extreme circumstances. One must conclude, then, that nonjudicial restraint of expression prior to ultimate judicial review is the only form of prior restraint appropriately subjected to a special negative presumption.

HENRY P. MONAGHAN, FIRST AMENDMENT "DUE PROCESS"

83 Harv.L.Rev. 518, 520, 522–526, 532, 536–544 (1970).

I. THE REQUIREMENT OF A JUDICIAL DETERMINATION OF THE CHARACTER OF SPEECH

A. Obscenity

Central to first amendment due process is the notion that a judicial, rather than an administrative, determination of the character of the speech is necessary. Cases in the obscenity area first established the principle, but neither their reasoning nor their language implies that the principle is restricted to obscenity determinations. * * *

Freedman v. Maryland [16] [is the central obscenity case.] A Maryland motion picture censorship statute required an exhibitor to submit the film to an administrative board prior to its showing. If the board disapproved the film, the burden of instituting judicial review lay with the exhibitor. The statute put no time limits on either the administrative or the judicial determinations. Accepting the argument that under the statute "judicial review may be too little and too late," a unanimous Court invalidated the statute in an opinion by Mr. Justice Brennan. While unwilling to hold that a motion picture exhibitor had an absolute right to exhibit without a prior determination of obscenity, the Court

---

16. 380 U.S. 51 (1965) * * *.

ringed any such procedure with tight safeguards. Most important here was the Court's statement that

> [t]he teaching of our cases is that, because only a judicial determination in an adversary proceeding ensures the necessary sensitivity to freedom of expression, only a procedure requiring a judicial determination suffices to impose a valid final restraint.

Freedman's preference for judicial evaluation of first amendment claims rests upon the most fundamental considerations—the inherent institutional differences between courts and administrative agencies, no matter how judicial the administrative proceedings may be. First, long judicial tenure frees judges, in most cases, from direct political pressures. Judicial insulation encourages impartial decisionmaking; more importantly, it permits the courts to take the "long view" of issues. Administrative bodies, particularly at a state level, are rarely so insulated; indeed, they are often seen primarily as political organs. Second, the role of the administrator is not that of the impartial adjudicator but that of the expert—a role which necessarily gives an administrative agency a narrow and restricted viewpoint. This is particularly pernicious in the obscenity area; those constantly exposed to the perverse and the aberrational in literature are quick to find obscenity in all they see.[19] * * *

* * *

B. *Implications for Other Areas of Substantive Law*

Nothing in the rationale of *Freedman* and its predecessors suggests that their principles are confined to the obscenity area. In fact, when the subject matter of speech is political in character rather than bordering on the obscene, the need for a disinterested judicial judgment is even greater. One can, then, hypothesize as a general principle of first amendment due process that no procedure is valid which leaves the protected character of speech to the final determination of an administrative agency, no matter how "judicial" its procedure. This principle not only has a direct bearing on matters generally characterized by the label of "prior restraint," such as laws conditioning the exercise of first amendment rights on the issuing of a permit, but it also extends to matters affecting the internal operations of governmental institutions. For example, under *Freedman* it would seem plainly improper to discharge government employees or expel state university students where first amendment interests are involved unless provision is made for a timely judicial determination of the first amendment claims. * * *

* * *

---

19. One may well question what type of person will put himself forward as a judge of morality. * * * It has been observed, in the broader context of general censorship, that

[i]f he be of such worth as behooves him, there cannot be a more tedious and unpleasing journey-work, a greater loss of time levied upon his head, than to be made the perpetual reader of unchosen books and pamphlets ... we may easily foresee what kind of licensers we are to expect hereafter, either ignorant, imperious, and remiss, or basely pecuniary.

J. Milton, Areopagitica 20–21 (Everyman ed. 1927).

In applying *Freedman* to administrative determinations, however, one must recognize an important distinction. *Freedman* requires only that the court make a separate, independent judgment on the administrative record; it would push *Freedman* too far to require additionally that the court construct its own record. So far as the first amendment is concerned, the task of historical factfinding may be left to administrative agencies, at least if * * * the agencies' procedures appear reasonably capable of ensuring reliable findings. At a minimum, this would require an evidentiary proceeding, with the protections of counsel, confrontation and cross-examination. Moreover, even if these safeguards are present, a completely de novo proceeding would seem required unless there is a transcript or written summary of the administrative proceedings; without such an administrative record, a court cannot confidently determine either the dimensions of the first amendment claim or the exact posture in which it was evaluated. Of course, measured by these standards few administrative determinations, particularly those at the state and local level, will avoid a first amendment requirement of de novo judicial factfinding. * * *

* * *

II. Requirement that the Judicial Determination Precede or Immediately Follow Governmental Intervention

The other major teaching of the obscenity cases is that in the first amendment area judicial review must either precede final governmental action or expeditiously follow it. * * * *Freedman* * * * invalidated [a] statute[ ] which did not provide for immediate judicial review of the administrative determination. In part, this result seems predicated on the belief that delay in the availability of judicial relief differs only in degree, and sometimes not at all, from the complete absence of judicial review. The requirement of expeditious judicial review is an extension of the reasoning that underlies the *Thornhill* doctrine.[57] Under *Thornhill,* a defendant whose conduct could constitutionally be punished is permitted to challenge the constitutionality of the statute under which he is being prosecuted "on its face" at least in part because of the overriding first amendment interest in seeing that legislation which chills first amendment rights is struck down as soon as possible.

A. *Ex Parte Seizures and Restraining Orders*

The Court has consistently refused to sanction any attempt at wholesale seizure of materials or injunctive restraint of speech prior to an adversary proceeding before a court. * * *

* * *

In * * * *Carroll v. President and Commissioners of Princess Anne,*[75] decided last Term, the Court indicated that, like seizures, injunctions

---

57. The doctrine is derived from Thornhill v. Alabama, 310 U.S. 88 (1940).

75. 393 U.S. 175 (1968).

must follow adversary hearings, absent an overriding emergency. The Court held that no ex parte order is valid if an adversary hearing on the question of interim restraint is practicable, even though a procedure is available to dissolve the ex parte order. * * *

Despite the general undesirability of ex parte orders, they should not be invariably barred by the first amendment. The boundaries of any such rule would be unclear, particularly where speech is mixed with conduct, as in picketing and demonstrations. * * * *Carroll* should be read, therefore, as authorizing the issuance of brief ex parte restraining orders where there is a compelling justification for doing so, where it is not reasonably possible to have a prior adversary hearing, and where speedy methods are available to dissolve any erroneous order. This is consistent with generally accepted principles governing first amendment limitations: restrictions on free speech are valid where necessary to vindicate compelling governmental interests and where no less restrictive alternatives are available.

Since ex parte orders can have a drastic impact on first amendment interests, the limitations suggested above must be satisfied. The state ought to carry the burden of proof that an ex parte order is necessary, and unless the record affirmatively showed that the burden had been met any contempt finding should be invalidated. There is no justification, however, for permitting the parties to ignore an injunction simply because it is erroneous, whether or not they have unsuccessfully attempted to seek its dissolution. The first amendment cannot sensibly be read to require the impossible; some margin for good faith error is acceptable so long as reasonably adequate procedures are available to evaluate first amendment claims.

* * *

B. Permits

Although publication or distribution of a book cannot be conditioned on issuance of a permit or license,[88] most other first amendment activity—demonstrations, parades, public exhibition of a film—can. Licensing, which functionally has the impact of a specially tailored injunction with respect to the exercise of a first amendment right, has felt the impact of the principles announced in *Freedman*. The outstanding example of this impact is shown by *Shuttlesworth v. City of Birmingham*,[90] decided last Term.

In *Shuttlesworth*, the defendant was convicted for engaging in a march in violation of a local ordinance which required a permit. The ordinance authorized the denial of the permit if the local authorities concluded that "the public welfare, peace, safety, health, decency, good order, morals or convenience require that it be refused." Prior to the march city authorities had made it clear to defendant that under no

88. *See* Near v. Minnesota, 283 U.S. 697 (1931).

90. 394 U.S. 147 (1969).

circumstances would a permit be issued. On appeal, the conviction was reversed by the Supreme Court. The Court began by observing that peaceful demonstrations were unquestionably a form of expression. The Court, however, recognized that the municipality may "rightfully exercise a great deal of control in the interest of traffic regulation and public safety," and accordingly, permit ordinances narrowly directed to those ends could not be held invalid on their face. But "as written," this permit ordinance was not so confined; rather, it amounted to a grant of "extensive authority to issue or refuse to issue parade permits on the basis of broad criteria entirely unrelated to legitimate municipal regulation of the public streets and sidewalks." This is impermissible. Under the first amendment,

> a municipality may not empower its licensing officials to roam essentially at will, dispensing or withholding permission to speak, assemble, picket, or parade, according to their own opinions regarding the potential effect of the activity in question on the "welfare," "decency," or "morals" of the community.

The fact that the defendant had not applied for a license was irrelevant. Citing an almost unbroken line of decisions extending back to *Lovell v. City of Griffin*,[95] the Court held that a person faced with an unconstitutional licensing ordinance regulating free expression may ignore it with impunity and that in a criminal prosecution for violating such an ordinance, the defendant can raise the invalidity of the ordinance on its face.

* * *

Shuttlesworth did not explicitly delineate the relevance of *Freedman* to the permit granting process, but seemed to assume that, in general, *Freedman* would apply. The Court remarked in a footnote that whether [a narrow] interpretation [could] render[] the statute constitutional "would depend upon, among other things, the availability of expeditious judicial review of the Commission's refusal of a permit." * * *

All the reasons which justify the result in *Freedman* apply in the permit cases. And if the principles announced in the former case are applied to statutes and ordinances governing the issuance of permits for parades and demonstrations, virtually all will be held unconstitutional on their face—unless the state courts virtually rewrite them "to avoid constitutional doubt." Few, if any, of those statutes or ordinances contain any timetable whatever, or impose the burden of seeking judicial review upon the public authorities.

Freedman clearly should govern the permit cases, but the increased administrative burdens on the state are significant. The exhibitor can plan his operations so that questionable films will have sufficient time to clear the administrative-judicial procedure prescribed by *Freedman*. But there may be far less "lead time" in the case of demonstrations and protests. Some are planned well in advance; others are generated by

95. 303 U.S. 444 (1938). * * *

rapidly developing events. The premises implicit in a permit statute require recognition of the fact that the government may legitimately require some brief notice—for administrative processing and police protection—but the period must be of very short duration.

* * *

C. The Constitutional Preference for Criminal Proceedings and Anticipatory Relief

The Court has indicated a marked preference for the ordinary criminal prosecution as a judicial vehicle for determination of obscenity.[105] Several reasons for this preference are evident. The rigorous procedural safeguards which inhere in the criminal trial will "focus searchingly" on the first amendment claim. And in principle, at least, a criminal defendant is free to distribute the challenged materials during the period in which he is contesting the prosecution. (His willingness to do so will, of course, vary with a number of factors, including his judgment as to his chances of success and his fear of prosecution for interim distribution.) Additional and more subtle considerations also support the Court's preference. Use of the criminal process means that the burden of going forward rests with the government, and the force of inertia alone will discourage some prosecutions. Moreover, the action must be brought by a public prosecutor, who cannot be single-minded, as can an administrative agency, about the prosecution of first amendment cases; he has limited resources with which to enforce all the laws of the community, and concentration on one area will mean sacrificing enforcement in another.

A criminal prosecution may be an appropriate vehicle for protecting first amendment interests where the protected character of the speech involved can only be determined after the fact. However, where the speech is fixed (as in a movie) and its protected character can be determined prior to distribution and sale, an in rem procedure similar to that of Massachusetts may be superior. Massachusetts permits the Commonwealth to bring an in rem proceeding against any book to determine its status. Since the book distributor can appear to defend the book, this procedure permits him to obtain a penalty-free determination of the protected character of the book. Even if there is no constitutional obligation on the states to proceed by a penalty-free determination, where first amendment interests are at stake this Massachusetts in rem procedure is plainly desirable as a matter of policy.

HENRY P. MONAGHAN, CONSTITUTIONAL FACT REVIEW

85 Colum.L.Rev. 229–232, 234–240, 264, 267–273 (1985).

Bose Corp. v. Consumers Union of United States[1] held that the

---

105. *See, e.g.,* Bantam Books, Inc. v. Sullivan, 372 U.S. 58, 69–70 (1963).

1. 104 S.Ct. 1949 (1984).

clearly erroneous standard of Federal Rule of Civil Procedure 52(a)[2] does not prescribe the scope of appellate review of a finding of actual malice in defamation cases governed by *New York Times Co. v. Sullivan.*[3] Rather, as a matter of "federal constitutional law," appellate courts "*must* exercise independent judgment and determine whether the record establishes actual malice with convincing clarity." Thus, in addition to the familiar judicial duty to "say what the law is," the first amendment imposes a special duty with respect to law application: both trial and appellate judges must examine the evidence, marshal the relevant adjudicative facts, and then apply the controlling first amendment norms to those facts. Appellate judges may accept the historical facts found in the court below, but they may not defer to the first amendment law application conclusions of even inferior article III judges, no matter how "reasonable."

* * *

Bose began as a trade libel suit in a district court. Consumers Union had published a magazine article evaluating the qualities of numerous brands of loudspeaker systems, including one marketed by the Bose Corporation. While the plaintiff objected to several statements in the article, the case ultimately turned on only one: the path of the sound heard through the speakers. The article stated that the sound tended to wander "about the room"; but, sitting without a jury, the judge found that the sound tended to wander "along the wall" between the speakers. After concluding that the article contained a false and disparaging statement of "fact," and that for purposes of this litigation the Bose Corporation was a public figure, the judge found clear and convincing proof of actual malice. The crucial conclusion that the article writer, who had testified extensively, knew at the time of publication that the offending statement was false rested on a single premise: the article writer "is an intelligent person whose knowledge of the English language cannot be questioned. It is simply impossible . . . to believe that he interprets a commonplace word such as 'about' to mean anything other than its plain, ordinary meaning." The First Circuit reversed. Accepting dubitante that the offending comment was one of fact rather than opinion, the court concluded that Rule 52(a) does not govern the scope of appellate review of a finding of actual malice. And making its own independent determination, the court found nothing more than the use of "imprecise language."[a]

[The Supreme Court affirmed, three justices dissenting.] The fundamental disagreement between the Court and the three dissenting justices was how to characterize the question presented—whether the defendant acted with actual malice. The majority viewed the question

---

2. Fed.R.Civ.P. 52(a) ("Findings of fact shall not be set aside unless clearly erroneous, and due regard shall be given to the opportunity of the trial court to judge of the credibility of the witnesses.").

3. 376 U.S. 254 (1964) (Constitution forbids recovery of damages by public officials for defamation absent showing that statements were false and made with actual malice).

a. Relocated paragraph.

as one of first amendment law application, deserving of the Court's independent judgment. The dissenters viewed the question as simply one of historical fact governed by Rule 52(a). For both groups, the initial characterization determined the appropriate scope of appellate review.

It is not surprising that the justices in *Bose* were unable to agree on the proper characterization of the question presented. The difficulty has its origins in the "vexing" distinction between "questions of law" and "questions of fact." * * *

* * * [T]he two categories have been used to describe at least *three* distinct functions: law declaration, fact identification, and law application.

* * *

* * * Law declaration involves "formulating a proposition [that] affects not only the [immediate] case ... but all others that fall within its terms." In a strict sense, then, law declaration yields only what we commonly think of as "law"—conclusions about the existence and content of governing legal rules, standards, and principles. The important point about law is that it yields a proposition that is *general* in character.

Fact identification, by contrast, is a case-specific inquiry into *what happened here.* It is designed to yield only assertions that can be made without *significantly* implicating the governing legal principles. Such assertions, for example, generally respond to inquiries about who, when, what, and where—inquiries that can be made "by a person who is ignorant of the applicable law." * * *

Law application, the third function, is residual in character. It involves relating the legal standard of conduct to the facts established by the evidence. If all legal propositions could be formulated in great detail, this function would be rather mechanical and require no distinctive consideration. But such is not the case. Linking the rule to the conduct is a complex psychological process, one that often involves judgment. The more general the rule, the larger the domain for judgment. Thus, law application frequently entails some attempt to elaborate the governing norm. But in contrast to the generalizing feature of law declaration, law application is situation-specific; any ad hoc norm elaboration is, in theory, like a ticket good for a specific trip only. Moreover, in this kind of situation, specific norm elaboration is generally invisible. By definition, when law application occurs, further explicit norm elaboration ceases. And any implicit norm elaboration may be buried in a general verdict and in the decisionmaker's resolution of the controversy over the facts. The typical jury verdict in a negligence case provides a good example.

Quite plainly, anterior to law application a crucial policy decision must be made: should a further effort at norm elaboration be undertaken? For example, should the "recklessness" component of *Sullivan* 's actual malice standard be amplified to provide more detailed guidance on the frequently recurring question of whether a reporter must check his sources? Such policy decisions draw upon complex considerations that must be faced at each level of the proceeding. Law application decisions in the lower federal courts may lead the Supreme Court to believe that further norm elaboration is needed. Still, the important point for our purposes is that law declaration occurs only to the extent that further *general* norm elaboration occurs.

In light of the foregoing, it seems misguided to assume, as many courts apparently do, that all law application judgments can be dissolved into either law declaration or fact identification. Law application is a distinctive operation. The real issue is not analytic, but allocative: what decisionmaker should decide the issue? Our system has not proceeded on the premise that judges, to say nothing of appellate judges, must render independent judgment on all law application. Many such decisions are left in the hands of juries, masters, and administrative agencies. *Bose* confirms this point. The Court assumed that, but for the Constitution, no independent appellate review would be required. It did not hold that all questions of law application should be assimilated to law declaration so that Rule 52(a) has no applicability. A contrary holding would have rendered the independent judgment rule in constitutional cases simply a subset of law application in general, always to be viewed as essentially a "question of law."

* * *

Constitutional fact review presupposes that appellate courts will render independent judgment on any issues of constitutional "law" presented. Its distinctive feature is a requirement of similar independent judicial judgment on issues of constitutional law "application." That is, the courts must sort out the relevant facts and apply to them the controlling constitutional norms. Firmly embedded case law establishes that, absent limiting legislation, federal appellate courts, particularly the Supreme Court, possess that authority. This Article will argue, however, that constitutional fact review at the appellate level is a matter for judicial (and legislative) discretion, not a constitutional imperative. This discretion can be made responsive to important institutional needs. The most important of these are the danger of systemic bias of other actors in the judicial system and the need for continuous development of constitutional principles on a case-by-case basis. But appellate courts are under no inexorable compulsion to review every application of settled constitutional norms to the historical facts. * * *

* * *

A. APPELLATE DUTY

Bose insists that appellate courts must exercise independent judgment with respect to constitutional facts relevant to first amendment law application. [Why should this be so?]

1. All questions of constitutional law application could be viewed as demanding independent appellate review because of the "importance" of constitutional rights and immunities coupled with the central role of courts in preserving the constitutional order. This argument stresses the "importance" of constitutional values, rather than the danger of distorted factfinding or law application by a specific decisionmaker. While the argument has appeal, its ultimate conclusion seems to be simply asserted, rather than persuasively justified. It is, after all, not obvious that all constitutional rights are more valuable than other rights simply because they are mentioned in the Constitution. If the argument simply reflects a naked bias in favor of constitutional claims, one that seeks only to increase the likelihood that such claims will be vindicated, the bias does not appear to be constitutionally grounded. It is not a premise of our system that the courts are able to detect every violation of the constitutional order.

To my mind, the real center of this argument is a premise that additional intensive judicial review at the appellate level is needed to prevent an "intolerable" level of incorrectly decided cases—incorrect in the special sense that some court has improperly rejected a constitutional claim. The notion is that the greater the number of courts that look at an issue, the greater the possibility of a "correct" decision. But we have no clear idea of what it means to say that we face the danger of an "intolerable" level of incorrectly denied constitutional claims. *Neither the empirical nor the normative reference points for this argument are obvious.*

* * *

2. The general argument that all constitutional rights need the security of independent appellate review can be abandoned in favor of an argument that the first amendment is special. Two different forms of this argument can be distinguished. The first places stress on the importance of the right rather than upon the dangers of systemically distorted factfinding and law application. The familiar "chilling effect" rhetoric asserts that first amendment values are very fragile and especially vulnerable to an "intolerable" level of deterrence; and the danger of impermissible deterrence is real, as is evidenced by the high rate of appellate reversal in first amendment cases and by the specter of large damage awards in these suits. Even accepting the validity of these arguments, the necessity for a "several bites at the apple" approach again remains undemonstrated. *Freedman v. Maryland* [220] may be taken to establish that administrative action focusing on the content of speech cannot be final, and that the Constitution requires independent judicial judgment on whether the speech is protected. Perhaps, too, the first amendment guarantees a right to some appellate review. But it is a long way from accepting this set of propositions to a conclusion that we will end up with an "intolerable" degree of chilling effect unless all appellate

220. 380 U.S. 51 (1965) * * *.

courts are *required* to redetermine every instance of first amendment law application.

Bose attempts to recast the special nature of the first amendment in a way that places more emphasis on the dangers of distorted factfinding and law application: first amendment interests are especially vulnerable due to the general character of the first amendment rules themselves. The rules—such as the actual malice standard—are simply too indeterminate to be left for application by a trier of fact, even an article III district judge. Of course, this argument depends entirely upon the premises previously discussed: without independent appellate review on constitutional law application, there will be an intolerable level of mistakes in denial of first amendment defenses. Moreover, the argument indiscriminately lumps together all first amendment rules. Perhaps in defamation cases there is such an intractable problem of confusing falsity with malice that layers of de novo appellate review are warranted. But it is hard to believe that all first amendment rules suffer from indeterminacy defects that create comparable risks of misadministration. What is more, it is not apparent that first amendment rules are less precise than other rules of constitutional privilege. To my eye, therefore, the allegedly indeterminate nature of first amendment rules does not supply an adequate basis for a special constitutional duty of independent appellate review for first amendment claims.

* * *

B.   Appellate Discretion

Constitutional fact review at the appellate level is a potent doctrine even if viewed in discretionary rather than mandatory terms. When courts should exercise that discretion depends on a careful assessment of relevant policy considerations. Thus, even if, as I have argued, the "importance" of constitutional values does not yield a solid basis for constitutional fact review in the Supreme Court, *other* institutional concerns may do so. Two such concerns stand out: first, the danger of systemic bias of other actors in the judicial system; second, the perceived need for a case-by-case development of the law in a given area.

1. The need to guard against systemic bias brought about or threatened by other actors in the judicial system appears to be an important force behind the Supreme Court's exercise of constitutional fact review. It is no accident that the most salient modern examples of constitutional fact review are found in Supreme Court review of the state courts. [These cases] proceed on a premise of institutional distrust: constitutional fact review in the Supreme Court is necessary not because of the danger of occasional mistakes but because of the fear of systematic distortion of factfinding and law application. * * *

The premise that state courts are to be suspected of distorted factfinding and law application is disquieting. After all, the Constitution presupposes that the state courts will enforce declared federal law fairly. To be sure, the constitutional plan leaves to Congress the power to vary the normal presupposition, but absent clear legislative direction, it is not easy to see how any general distrust of the state courts can be a premise for judicial reasoning about the scope of the Supreme Court's appellate review. Still, reality has intruded here, and for nearly five decades the Court has, in substance, asserted a power to respond to perceived dangers of distorted factfinding and law application in the state courts. It is true that the rules announced governing the scope of review are now stated to be equally applicable to both state and federal courts. But the real bite of intensive review has been on the decisions of state courts. A discretionary, rather than a mandatory, conception of constitutional fact review seems more responsive to the felt need for such control. It permits the Court to recognize that not all constitutional adjudication in the state courts presents the same dangers of distortion, but that there may be appropriate occasions for intensive review. * * *

2. To my mind, the perceived need for case-by-case development of constitutional norms is likely to be the single most important trigger for constitutional fact review. Where such norms are in a process of development, the Court must examine enough factually similar situations to formulate an acceptable norm. The point is not that the line between law declaration and law application is so thin that the practical exigencies of the appellate process, both in screening cases and producing opinions, should be taken to permit constitutional fact review. Rather, the argument is an affirmative one: norm elaboration occurs best when the Court has power to consider fully a series of closely related situations involving a claim of constitutional privilege.

JAMES R. PIELEMEIER, CONSTITUTIONAL LIMITATIONS ON CHOICE OF LAW: THE SPECIAL CASE OF MULTISTATE DEFAMATION

133 U.Pa.L.Rev. 381, 408–409, 411–415, 419–420, 423 (1985).

Last year the Supreme Court held that nonresident plaintiffs may sue publishers for defamation in any state where the publisher regularly circulates materials. In *Keeton v. Hustler Magazine, Inc.* [1] the Court upheld the New Hampshire courts' assertion of jurisdiction over a claim for nationwide damages by a nonresident who had only inconsequential connections to the state, even though New Hampshire was the only state in which the statute of limitations had not run. This ruling potentially enables many defamation plaintiffs to forum shop and to file suit in states whose defamation laws are most favorable to their claims.

Although defamation defendants are now subject to the jurisdiction of the courts in any state in which they regularly distribute materials, the conclusion that they may also be subject to the defamation laws of any state with jurisdiction does not automatically follow. In *Keeton* the Court explicitly distinguished choice of law issues from its jurisdictional inquiry and declined to resolve them. The Court thereby left unsettled

[1]. 104 S.Ct. 1473 (1984). [Relocated footnote.]

whether the Constitution limits a state's ability to apply its defamation law. * * *

[Pielemeier explains that choice of law is an uncertain matter in defamation cases because of the non-physical nature of the tort, and because the steps leading up to the defamation (investigation, editing, printing, dissemination) may occur in several states. To make matters more difficult, modern courts use a great variety of choice of law approaches. These include the territorialist approach of the first *Restatement*, the "most significant relationship" approach of the second *Restatement*, an "interest analysis," a preference for the "better rule," and a simple preference for the law of the forum. Pielemeier points out that the last three approaches will frequently result in the application of forum law.

[When added to the jurisdictional rule announced in *Keeton*, these choice of law principles will have a significant effect on multistate media defendants. They will always be subject to suit in the forum whose law is most plaintiff-oriented. To make matters worse, the Supreme Court has shown no inclination to apply the Constitution to state choice of law decisions.[a] Pielemeier asks whether there are any special reasons for doing so in defamation cases.]

The Constraints of Federalism

* * *

[*Allstate Insurance Co. v. Hague* [b]] demonstrates the Court's willingness to permit a forum state to ignore other states' laws when it has an interest in applying its own. Notwithstanding this permissive approach to choice of law, however, the Court's decisions reflect two principles that mandate limits on state freedom in this area: (1) states are coequal sovereigns, and, accordingly, (2) no state's valid interests may be totally subordinated to the will of other states. The Court's choice of law decisions have assumed that in a given case the subordination of one state's interests to the interests of another, forum state will be offset by an equivalent subordination of the latter state's interests when a case is brought in the former state. Consequently, through this structure requiring the passive mutual accommodation by the states of their interests to the interests of forum states, all states are accorded roughly equal respect in that all have the ability to further their interests when they are forums—in the aggregate, the subordination of interests presumably "washes."

* * *

a. For example, in Allstate Insurance Co. v. Hague, 449 U.S. 302 (1981), the Court permitted Minnesota to apply its rule about "stacking" coverage of insurance policies to a case involving a Wisconsin resident who was killed in a Wisconsin car accident involving two uninsured Wisconsin drivers. Minnesota had a sufficient interest, the Court held, because the decedent had worked there and his widow had later moved there.

b. See note a, *supra*.

In the multistate defamation context, this [offsetting] will be thwarted by a constitutional choice of law rule that permits application of the law of any state of "injury" to the entirety of a plaintiff's claim. Defamation law primarily redresses damage to reputation, but such an injury, unlike injuries that give rise to other torts, is not localized. As Justice Rehnquist noted in *Keeton,* "The reputation of the libel victim may suffer harm even in a state in which he has hitherto been anonymous." Because the injury is not localized, reliance on its presence to justify application of forum defamation law potentially leaves other states with no power to apply their defamation laws to the multistate media operating within their borders. After *Keeton,* neither jurisdictional limitations nor requirements of distinctive contacts would ensure application of the state's laws to such entities at least some of the time. Any plaintiff could avoid those laws by suing in another state of circulation. Consequently, states with relatively speech-enhancing defamation laws would be placed in a state of vassalage to states with relatively speech-inhibiting defamation laws.

* * *

Two additional federalism-based concerns also mandate rejection of a permissive choice of law approach in this context. First, the combination of this choice of law approach with *Keeton*'s jurisdictional holding and the forum-shopping propensities of defamation plaintiffs may effectively federalize multistate defamation laws. To illustrate, suppose a state that is hostile to the press enacts defamation laws that grant publishers only those constitutional protections mandated by the Supreme Court. If that state's courts could and did apply those laws in all defamation cases against the national media that are brought before them, all plaintiffs suing the national media for defamation would bring their claims in that state's courts, unless the differences in the laws of another state are inconsequential. This would result, in effect, in the nationalization of defamation law as applied to multistate media, for in virtually all cases that state's law would control. And because that state's law would incorporate only those constitutional limits articulated by the Court, its application would be tantamount to federalization of defamation law.

* * *

The second federalism-based concern that requires rejection of a permissive choice of defamation law doctrine lies in its threat, to borrow the words of Justice Stevens in *Hague,* to "the federal interest in national unity." [204] Publishers may hesitate before distributing their product in a state if its relatively speech-inhibiting defamation laws may be applied to everything they print. A permissive choice of law doctrine therefore would discourage interstate communication. But national unity depends upon each state's ability to keep abreast—through multistate media—of the events, ideas, and trends in other states. The

---

204. *Hague,* 449 U.S. at 323 (Stevens, J., concurring).

"robust debate" encouraged by the Supreme Court in its defamation cases must be a national one. To discourage publishers from national distribution is to foster parochialism and isolationism; it is inimical to the federal interest in national unity.

* * *

FIRST AMENDMENT CONSTRAINTS

* * *

State action in the form of choice of law decisions ordinarily must comply with a minimal standard of rationality, an infrequently stressed constraint of the fourteenth amendment's due process clause. When state action impinges on first amendment freedoms, however, its validity is subject to heightened scrutiny. Thus, if the application of defamation laws impinges on these freedoms, the decision to apply them through a choice of law determination should be subject to these heightened standards.

* * *

[The Supreme Court's decisions] indicate that the Court judges the constitutionality of defamation laws by examining whether their application effectuates strong state interests without unnecessarily or unduly circumscribing protected speech. In *Gertz v. Robert Welch, Inc.,*[231] for example, the Court characterized the state interest in compensating private plaintiffs for actual damages as "legitimate" and "strong and legitimate" and invalidated awards of presumed damages because they furthered no "substantial" state interest. It limited the availability of presumed and punitive damages on the ground that state remedies for defamation could reach "no farther than is necessary to protect the legitimate [compensation] interest involved." Similarly, *New York Times* stressed that laws allowing truth alone as a defense would deter criticism, suggesting that laws of this nature are not sufficiently narrowly tailored and unduly limit protected expression.[236]

* * *

First amendment principles thus mandate that a state may apply its defamation rules only in a manner narrowly tailored to further strong state interests. In the multistate defamation context a court's decision to apply forum law to the entirety of a plaintiff's nationwide defamation claim would not meet this test if the plaintiff had only negligible connections to the state. Although the forum state may, according to *Keeton,* have a valid interest in redressing injuries *within* the state if the plaintiff's reputation suffered harm there, application of its law to redress injuries suffered in other states where the harm is not legally cognizable may result in compensation highly disproportionate to this interest. The forum state law's speech-inhibiting reach would extend

---

231. 418 U.S. 323 (1974).   **236.** [New York Times v. Sullivan, 376 U.S. 254 (1964).]

far beyond that necessary to further its underlying state interest, violating the first amendment requirement that it be narrowly tailored.

BIBLIOGRAPHY

In General

Vincent Blasi, *The Newsman's Privilege: An Empirical Study,* 70 Mich. L.Rev. 229 (1971).

David S. Bogen, *First Amendment Ancillary Doctrines,* 37 Md.L.Rev. 679 (1979).

Martin B. Louis, *Summary Judgment and the Actual Malice Controversy in Constitutional Defamation Cases,* 57 S.Cal.L.Rev. 707 (1984).

Scott M. Matheson, *Procedure in Public Person Defamation Cases: The Impact of the First Amendment,* 66 Tex.L.Rev. 215 (1987).

Jonathan C. Medow, *The First Amendment and the Secrecy State:* Snepp v. United States, 130 U.Pa.L.Rev. 775 (1982).

Robert C. Post, *The Management of Speech: Discretion and Rights,* 1984 Sup.Ct.Rev. 169.

Frederick Schauer, *The Role of the People in First Amendment Theory,* 74 Calif.L.Rev. 761 (1986).

Overbreadth

Lawrence A. Alexander, *Is There an Overbreadth Doctrine?,* 22 San Diego L.Rev. 541 (1985).

Richard H. Fallon, Jr., *Making Sense of Overbreadth,* 100 Yale L.J. 853 (1991).

Gerald Gunther, *Reflections on Robel: It's Not What the Court Did But the Way That It Did It,* 20 Stan.L.Rev. 1140 (1968).

Edward J. Imwinkelried & Donald N. Zillman, *An Evolution in the First Amendment: Overbreadth Analysis and Free Speech within the Military Community,* 54 Tex.L.Rev. 42 (1975).

William E. Lee, *The First Amendment Doctrine of Underbreadth,* 71 Wash.U.L.Q. 637 (1993).

Henry P. Monaghan, *Third Party Standing,* 84 Colum.L.Rev. 277 (1984).

Note, *Standing to Assert Constitutional Jus Tertii,* 88 Harv.L.Rev. 423 (1974).

Note, *The First Amendment Overbreadth Doctrine,* 83 Harv.L.Rev. 844 (1970).

Martin H. Redish, *The Warren Court, The Burger Court and the First Amendment Overbreadth Doctrine,* 78 Nw.U.L.Rev. 1031 (1983).

Robert A. Sedler, *The Assertion of Constitutional Jus Tertii: A Substantive Approach,* 70 Calif.L.Rev. 1308 (1982).

Prior Restraint

Vincent Blasi, *Prior Restraints on Demonstrations,* 68 Mich.L.Rev. 1481 (1970).

Stephen R. Barnett, *The Puzzle of Prior Restraint,* 29 Stan.L.Rev. 539 (1977).

David G. Barnum, *Freedom of Assembly and the Hostile Audience in Anglo–American Law,* 29 Am.J.Comp.L. 59 (1981).

Archibald Cox, *The Void Order and the Duty to Obey,* 16 U.Chi.L.Rev. 86 (1948).

Mark P. Denbeaux, *The First Word of the First Amendment,* 80 Nw. U.L.Rev. 1156 (1986).

Thomas I. Emerson, *The Doctrine of Prior Restraint,* 20 Law & Contemp.Probs. 648 (1955).

Monroe H. Freedman & Janet Starwood, *Prior Restraints on Freedom of Expression by Defendants and Defense Attorneys:* Ratio Decidendi v. Obiter Dictum, 29 Stan.L.Rev. 607 (1977).

Paul Freund, *The Supreme Court and Civil Liberties,* 4 Vand.L.Rev. 533 (1951).

Fred W. Friendly, MINNESOTA RAG (1981).

Stanley Godofsky & Howard M. Rogatnick, *Prior Restraints: The Pentagon Papers Case Revisited,* 18 Cum.L.Rev. 527 (1988).

James C. Goodale, *The Press Ungagged: The Practical Effect on Gag Order Litigation of* Nebraska Press Association v. Stuart, 29 Stan. L.Rev. 497 (1977).

Howard O. Hunter, *Toward a Better Understanding of the Prior Restraint Doctrine: A Reply to Professor Mayton,* 67 Cornell L.Rev. 283 (1982).

John Calvin Jeffries, Jr., *Rethinking Prior Restraint,* 92 Yale L.J. 409 (1982).

Harry Kalven, Jr., *Foreword: Even When a Nation Is at War,* 85 Harv.L.Rev. 3 (1971).

William T. Mayton, *Toward a Theory of First Amendment Process: Injunctions of Speech, Subsequent Punishment, and the Costs of the Prior Restraint Doctrine,* 67 Cornell L.Rev. 245 (1982).

William Murphy, *The Prior Restraint Doctrine in the Supreme Court: A Reevaluation,* 51 Notre Dame Law. 898 (1986).

L.A. Scot Powe, Jr., *The H–Bomb Injunction,* 61 U.Colo.L.Rev. 55 (1990).

Doug Rendleman, *Free Press–Fair Trial: Restrictive Orders after* Nebraska Press, 67 Ky.L.J. 867 (1979).

William H. Rodgers, Jr., *The Elusive Search for the Void Injunction: Res Judicata Principles in Criminal Contempt Proceedings,* 49 B.U.L.Rev. 251 (1969).

David Rudenstine, *The Pentagon Papers Case: Recovering Its Meaning Twenty–Five Years Later,* 12 Cardozo L.Rev. 1869 (1991).

Robert D. Sack, *Principle and* Nebraska Press Association v. Stuart, 29 Stan.L.Rev. 411 (1977).

Frederick Schauer, *Fear, Risk, and the First Amendment: Unraveling the "Chilling Effect",* 58 B.U.L.Rev. 685 (1978).

Benno C. Schmidt, Jr., Nebraska Press Association: *An Extension of Freedom and Contraction of Theory,* 29 Stan.L.Rev. 431 (1977).

Marin Scordato, *Distinction Without a Difference: A Reappraisal of the Doctrine of Prior Restraint,* 68 N.C.L.Rev. 1 (1989).

Joel L. Selig, *Regulation of Street Demonstrations by Injunction: Constitutional Limitations on the Collateral Bar Rule in Prosecutions for Contempt,* 4 Harv.Civ.Rts.—Civ.Lib.L.Rev. 135 (1968).

John Cary Sims, *Triangulating the Boundaries of* Pentagon Papers, 2 Wm. & Mary Bill of Rights J. 341 (1993).

Vagueness

Anthony G. Amsterdam, *The Void–For–Vagueness Doctrine in the Supreme Court,* 109 U.Pa.L.Rev. 67 (1960).

David S. Bogen, *First Amendment Ancillary Doctrines,* 37 Md.L.Rev. 679 (1978).

Meir Dan–Cohen, *Decision Rules and Conduct Rules: On Acoustic Separation in Criminal Law,* 97 Harv.L.Rev. 625 (1984).

John Calvin Jeffries, Jr., *Legality, Vagueness and the Construction of Statutes,* 71 Va.L.Rev. 189 (1985).

Note, *The Void for Vagueness Doctrine in the Supreme Court,* 109 U.Pa.L.Rev. 67 (1960).

Chapter IV

RECURRING ISSUES OF THE SPEECH AND PRESS CLAUSES

A. INTRODUCTION

The readings in the previous three chapters have dealt with history, theory, and method, but have not focused on the particular substantive contexts in which free speech questions are likely to arise. Although these contexts are numerous, it should come as no surprise that certain issues have recurred, in large part because the First Amendment exists as an overlay on patterns of understanding developed either in the common law or as part of a general social and political understanding only partially influenced by the First Amendment.

Space limitations prevent dealing here with all of the recurring doctrinal problems arising under the speech and press clauses of the First Amendment. Among those that have been omitted are the persistent questions about protection of the institutional press, including questions about whether the press clause grants it special protection (beyond what the speech clause gives it as just another speaker);[1] questions about press access and press privileges;[2] increasingly debated questions of campaign finance reform;[3] and a host of issues relating to the arguably special status of the electronic media.[4] Also unfortunately

---

1. Compare Randall Bezanson, *The New Free Press Guarantee,* 63 Va.L.Rev. 731 (1977), and Potter Stewart, *Or of the Press,* 26 Hastings L.J. 631 (1975), with David Lange, *The Speech and Press Clauses,* 23 UCLA L.Rev. 77 (1975), and William W. Van Alstyne, *The Hazards to the Press of Claiming a "Preferred Position",* 28 Hastings L.J. 761 (1977). And see also Chief Justice Burger's concurring opinion in First National Bank of Boston v. Bellotti, 435 U.S. 765 (1978).

2. Branzburg v. Hayes, 408 U.S. 665 (1972); Houchins v. KQED, Inc., 438 U.S. 1 (1978); Anthony Lewis, *A Public Right to Know About Public Institutions: The First Amendment as Sword,* 1980 Sup.Ct.Rev. 1.

3. See Lillian R. BeVier, *Money and Politics: A Perspective on the First Amendment and Campaign Finance Reform,* 73 Calif.L.Rev. 1045 (1985); Symposium, *Campaign Finance Reform,* 94 Colum.L.Rev. 1126 (1994).

4. Red Lion Broadcasting Co. v. FCC, 395 U.S. 367 (1969); Ithiel de Sola Pool, Technologies of Freedom (1983); Thomas G. Krattenmaker and Lucas A. Powe, Jr., Regulating Broadcast Programming (1994).

sacrificed are issues about the effect of the First Amendment in a range of government-operated facilities other than public fora, including, for example, primary and secondary schools, colleges and universities, government buildings, employees in the government workplace, prisons, and the military.[5] And some topics often treated as discrete, such as the problems of the public forum and of so-called "symbolic speech," are, we believe, better taken as parts of the general theme of content regulation.

Exclusions aside, we have elected to treat four recurring topics, and one new one, for special attention. Defamation and privacy is a topic that presents important questions about the intersection between the First Amendment and the common law, and about the role of the First Amendment in fostering public discussion about matters of political or social importance. In addition, it often falls between the cracks in law school courses. It is commonly treated only briefly in introductory Torts courses (the assumption being that the topic has become so thoroughly constitutionalized that it is better dealt with as part of a First Amendment or general Constitutional Law course). In these courses, however, defamation and privacy are again glossed over (on the assumption that they were covered extensively in Torts).

Questions about obscenity and pornography regulation have also recurred throughout the modern history of the First Amendment, in part because they raise hotly contested questions about the nature of the consequences of certain forms of communication, and in part because to many the persistence of obscenity regulation has seemed among the most anomalous aspects of modern First Amendment doctrine. More recently, however, the feminist anti-pornography movement has substantially transformed the way many people think about this issue, and the materials included here are designed to focus as much on what has changed as on what has remained the same in First Amendment decisionmaking.

Changing conceptions of what the First Amendment is all about also explain the inclusion here of materials on commercial speech, for the transformation from a topic totally outside the coverage of the First Amendment to one partially within it (and now possibly back again) provides a good case study of the more theoretical issues raised in Chapter II about the boundaries of the First Amendment. Moreover, current debates about regulation of cigarette and alcohol advertising demonstrate that the First Amendment is increasingly dominating the rhetoric of the debate, regardless of the trend in the decided cases.

Fourth, the regulation of racist speech (a matter of common concern in university communities) presents more clearly than most topics do the

---

5. Strong evidence of the growing importance of this topic, one where many standard First Amendment assumptions clash with the inevitability of governmentally sponsored content-control in numerous government institutions (selection of books for a public library, grading of exami-nations in state colleges and universities), is provided by the amount of space (nearly 300 pages) devoted to it in a new casebook devoted entirely to the First Amendment, William W. Van Alstyne, First Amendment: Cases and Materials (2d ed. 1995).

potential for conflicts between different constitutional values. To many people the question whether racist speech should be controlled is simultaneously the question whether equality should be considered as important as freedom of speech. In addition, the increased agreement about the harms of racist speech in general and racist epithets in particular makes clearer the questions about the extent of the sacrifices that existing First Amendment doctrine may impose, and about the identity of those who are commonly expected to make those sacrifices.

The new topic we treat is the emerging question of whether the First Amendment constrains the development of the law of sexual harassment, especially in the context of charges that a hostile and intimidating workplace has been created. Traditionally, the consideration of this topic has not been thought to raise First Amendment concerns at all, even though the activities complained of may be largely or only verbal or pictorial. Yet in recent years First Amendment defenses to such charges have become more common, a development that Kingsley Browne applauds and Catharine MacKinnon takes to indicate the problems with any conception of the First Amendment that refuses to acknowledge the inextricability of words and deeds.

B. DEFAMATION AND PRIVACY

Defamation law presents some of the hardest questions of free speech theory and doctrine, because the harms caused by factually false statements about identifiable individuals are hard to deny, and often hard to subjugate to the longer-term values protected by the speech and press clauses of the First Amendment. Nevertheless, *New York Times Co. v. Sullivan* [1] started a course towards strongly preferring recognition of the latter to recognition of the former, a course that has generally been continued in subsequent case law.

Still, the state of defamation law and commentary about it remains in turmoil. The articles excerpted here are designed to give some flavor of the current debates. It may be useful to begin by rereading Harry Kalven's article on *New York Times Co. v. Sullivan,* which appears in Chapter II.E. [2] The first piece in this chapter, by Rodney Smolla, recounts some more notorious recent libel cases. He concludes, as have many others, that the protections granted by *Sullivan* and subsequent cases may increasingly be more theoretical than real. Paul LeBel takes issue with this conclusion, however, and stresses the extent to which there remain valuable aspects in the traditional tort approach to libel and slander. He consequently wonders whether the thoroughgoing constitutionalization of defamation law has underrecognized both the virtues of the common law approach and the harms it was designed to redress.

---

1. 376 U.S. 254 (1964).

2. *The New York Times Case: A Note on "The Central Meaning of the First Amendment",* page 104 supra.

This tension between individual harms and First Amendment-protected social benefits is also the theme of Robert Post's analysis, and he sees in modern defamation law what is at best an uneasy reconciliation between the social goal of free public discourse and the value of reputation. Reconciling these interests has not been the exclusive concern of scholars, however; this is an area in which various law reform measures now compete for attention and support. Judge Pierre Leval's proposal simultaneously to eliminate the "chill" caused by excess exposure to financial liability and to provide redress for defamed individuals is particularly thoughtful. It bears some similarity to other proposals emanating from various individuals and organizations increasingly concerned to reform existing libel law.

RODNEY SMOLLA, LET THE AUTHOR BEWARE: THE REJUVENATION OF THE AMERICAN LAW OF LIBEL

132 U.Pa.L.Rev. 1–8, 11, 16–17, 19–21 (1983).

"A libeled American," Zechariah Chafee once wrote, "prefers to vindicate himself by steadily pushing forward his career and not by hiring a lawyer to talk in a courtroom." Americans have changed, Zechariah. America is in the midst of a rejuvenation of the law of libel. Only a decade ago, the law of defamation appeared headed for obsolescence. Yet an astonishing shift in cultural and legal conditions has caused a dramatic proliferation of highly publicized libel actions brought by well-known figures who seek, and often receive, staggering sums of money.

The reinvigoration of the modern law of defamation has been as pervasive as it has been sudden, radiating across the American culture. Defendants span a spectrum of size, wealth, power, and respectability, ranging from the mainstream orthodoxy of the national-news giants, to local news outlets, to the more sensational press.

Those who are now striking out against the media as defamation plaintiffs include many who have previously profited from media attention. People deeply involved in the political process, including elected officials and advocates of specific political positions, have not flinched from resort to the courts. Entertainers, writers, and others who have reaped the benefits of media attention also have not been hesitant to seek substantial damages when they believe that the media have begun to do their images more harm than good.

Among the public officials joining the litigation feast have been Philadelphia Mayor William J. Green, who sued a CBS television station for $5.1 million for reporting that he was under federal criminal investigation; former Governor Edward J. King of Massachusetts, who filed a $3.6 million suit against the *Boston Globe* for implications conveyed by articles, editorials, and political cartoons that King was "unfit and incapable of properly performing the duties of governor"; Governor

William J. Janklow of South Dakota, who filed a $10 million suit against *Newsweek* for an article allegedly implying that he had raped an Indian girl; former United States ambassador to Chile, Nathaniel Davis, and two of his ex-assistants, who filed a $150 million suit against the makers of *Missing,* alleging that the 1982 film implied that the American embassy was connected with the killing of an American free-lance writer during the 1973 coup d'etat in Chile; and General William Westmoreland, who has sued CBS for allegedly suggesting his complicity or incompetence in connection with the underestimation of enemy troop strength levels in Vietnam. Even former President Jimmy Carter was prepared to join the list by suing the *Washington Post* for a gossip column item relaying rumors that Blair House had been bugged during Ronald and Nancy Reagan's residence there before Reagan's inauguration. Carter chose not to take action after his public threat of suit was enough to force a retraction from the *Post* and a published letter of apology.

Public interest advocates who are prominent among the list of recent libel plaintiffs include Ralph Nader, who sued Ralph de Toledano for statements de Toledano made in a syndicated column about Nader's crusade against the lack of safety in General Motors' Corvair, and feminist attorney Gloria Allred, who filed a $10 million libel suit against a California State Senator because of a characterization in a press release.

Entertainers, writers, and other media figures have also contributed to the recent resurgence of the libel suit. Carol Burnett's $10 million libel action against the *National Enquirer,* and the $1.6 million verdict returned by the jury, although later reduced by the court, obviously added great impetus to the trend. There have, however, been many others. Wayne Newton sued NBC over a report linking him to organized crime, and Elizabeth Taylor filed a complicated action against ABC over a "docu-drama" that depicts Taylor's life.

* * *

More recent studies by the Libel Defense Resource Center (LDRC) vividly demonstrate significant changes in defamation cases. Although the LDRC studies have shown a continuing tendency for libel damage awards to be reduced or reversed on appeal, they reveal a dramatic increase in the size of damages awarded at trial. The most recent data from the LDRC indicate that the typical damage award is now in the millions of dollars, a sharp contrast to the Franklin survey which found only one case in the period from 1976 to 1980 in which a damage award was over a million dollars. Moreover, although data was not compiled on punitive damages in the Franklin studies, one LDRC study showed that thirty out of forty-seven damage awards included punitive damages, and seven of those punitive damage awards were for $1 million or more. More recent data from the LDRC indicate even more pervasive punitive damage awards, which have now reached a staggering average of "almost $8 million per punitive award."

The prospect of such lucrative awards is likely to entice more potential defamation plaintiffs to bring suit despite the fact that their claims do not meet the legal standards that appellate courts are struggling to impose.

* * *

I contend that there are four contributing causes to the recent rejuvenation of American libel law * * *. The first factor is a new legal and cultural seriousness about the inner self. Tort law has undergone a relaxation of rules that formerly prohibited recovery for purely emotional or psychic injury, a doctrinal evolution that parallels the growth of the "me-generation." A second factor is the infiltration into the law of defamation of many of the attitudes that have produced a trend in tort law over the past twenty years favoring compensation and risk-spreading goals over fault principles in the selection of liability rules. A third cause of the new era in libel is the increasing difficulty in distinguishing between the informing and entertaining functions of the media. The blurring of this line between entertainment and information has affected the method and substance of communications in important ways and highlights the inadequacies of the current legal standards governing defamation actions. The final factor is doctrinal confusion, caused in large part by a pervasive failure to accommodate constitutional and common law values in a coherent set of standards that is responsive to the realities of modern communications. That doctrinal confusion is particularly telling in an environment where cultural trends, such as a heightened concern for the inner self, and legal trends, such as the trend in tort law in favor of strict liability, both work against the ideals of free expression.

* * *

In William Shakespeare's *Othello,* the character Iago describes the sanctity of reputation in words that are well-known to the modern ear:

> Good name in man and woman, dear my lord,
> Is the immediate jewel of their souls:
> Who steals my purse steals trash—'tis something, nothing;
> 'Twas mine, 'tis his, and has been slave to thousands;
> But he that filches from me my good name
> Robs me of that which not enriches him
> And makes me poor indeed.

As often as these famous lines are held up as evidence of the highest regard for reputational values that runs through the Anglo–American cultural tradition, other less-famous words, also spoken by Iago, are usually ignored:

> As I am an honest man, I thought you had
> received some bodily wound; there is more sense in
> that than in reputation. Reputation is an idle and
> most false imposition; oft got without merit and lost

without deserving. You have lost no reputation at
all, unless you repute yourself such a loser.

Iago, of course, is a duplicitous character who does not hesitate to
utter contradictory sentiments in the same play. But the two conflicting
views that Iago voices about the importance of reputation are more than
merely the self-serving statements of a fickle Shakespearean antagonist;
they reflect a deeper dissonance in Anglo–American culture concerning
the value of reputation, a dissonance that has in turn manifested itself in
sharp contradictions within the law of defamation. Like Iago, American
courts have frequently been of two minds in their solicitude for reputation, at times permitting harsh penalties for defamatory speech well out
of proportion to the harm of the words or the culpability of the speaker,
and at times permitting obviously damaging speech uttered with trans-
parently dark motives to be spoken with complete impunity. Thus, any
attempt to account for changes in defamation law by looking only at the
current adjustment between first amendment and reputational values
ignores the importance of considering our contemporary attitude toward
the value of reputation which, in fact, underlies the whole of defamation
law. It is my contention that the rejuvenation of the law of defamation
is in part the result of strongly felt cultural attitudes about the importance of protecting psychic well-being, attitudes that have been able to
flourish largely because the contradictions in reigning doctrine provide
no coherent set of rules to hold them in check.

* * *

Developments in all areas of tort law *other than* defamation indicate
that courts are increasingly willing to recognize the legitimacy of protecting emotional and mental tranquility from injury. Courts have steadily
relaxed the rules restricting liability for the negligent and intentional
infliction of emotional distress and are more receptive to the maintenance of suits based on invasion of privacy. Across various categories of
tort law the concept of "injury" has been stretched outward to encompass new legal shelter for mental and emotional calm.

This trend in tort law has paralleled and has been responsive to a
corresponding trend in American culture. American culture from the
mid–1960's to the early 1970's was dominated by mass political action
advocating significant social change. Opposition to the Vietnam War
vulcanized disparate strands of countercultural energy into a united
movement of antiwar dissent. The antiestablishment energy generated
by the war protest subsequently dissipated into a range of less directed
fads and causes, many of them preoccupied with the discovery and
nourishment of various formulations of the individual self.

This shift has resulted in what is now widely perceived as the "me
generation." Contemporary America's attitude toward a defamed plaintiff is likely to reflect society's increased expenditure of money and effort
directed first to finding and then to nurturing the inner self. One does
not go to significant personal expense in an effort to define a self image,

and then sit idly by as that work is publicly undone by *60 Minutes* or the *National Enquirer.*

This conjecture is supported by the recognition that juries today are becoming notorious for their free and easy attitude in awarding stupendous sums in libel suits, an attitude that must be attributed to their sense of the rough equities of the issues litigated. As Henry Kaufman, General Counsel of the Libel Defense Resource Center, notes, "When a libel case gets to a jury, the First Amendment kind of drops to the wayside." This observation is consistent with the advice offered in a recent book on libel litigation which counselled defense attorneys not to "overuse the First Amendment theme" because "[j]udges and juries are not necessarily sympathetic to claims of the media that they have a special privilege to run roughshod over their fellow citizens."

The current reinvigoration of libel law, therefore, seems to be in part a grass roots response by jurors and the society they represent to the threat to psychic equanimity posed by the media.

PAUL A. LEBEL, REFORMING THE TORT OF DEFAMATION: AN ACCOMMODATION OF THE COMPETING INTERESTS WITHIN THE CURRENT CONSTITUTIONAL FRAMEWORK
66 Neb.L.Rev. 249–251, 292–94, 297–301 (1987).

As a result of a series of significant United States Supreme Court decisions over the last twenty-two years, the law of defamation has been wrenched from its common law moorings and cast adrift in search of a constitutional anchorage. Determining precisely what the contours of that First Amendment safe harbor are and what they should be, occupies the attention of courts, legal scholars, and media lawyers and their clients. Only recently has there emerged in counterpoint to the constitutional debates a more frequently expressed view that the solutions to the problems created by a defamation/free speech conflict are more appropriately sought through attempting to achieve reform in the arena of tort law instead of through a manipulation of constitutional doctrines.

The major premise of this Article is that a far more precise and flexible accommodation of the competing interests can be obtained in the context of tort analysis than is likely to result from a continuation of the constitutionalization/de-constitutionalization struggle currently under way. The law of torts consistently displays a capacity to produce a carefully tailored response to the important nuances of situations in which significant individual interests are adversely affected by socially worthwhile activities. Freed from the obligation of having to speak in the heavily freighted terms of constitutional adjudication, courts employing common law methods in developing and applying tort law concepts would be able to give careful attention to factors that might escape constitutional notice. To give one example, * * * consider the current attitude of some members of the Supreme Court that the first amendment does not permit the level of constitutional protection of defamatory communications to depend on a distinction between the media and the nonmedia status of different defamation defendants. One might initially suppose that the constitutional language itself would be capable of supporting such a distinction—the Court drawing on the press clause in the media case and the speech clause in the nonmedia case. Nevertheless, the significant point is that the distinction between media and nonmedia defendants is the kind of factor that fits well into tort law analyses that traditionally have been very concerned about such matters as why the defendant acted as it did, and what individual and social interests were being served by the defendant's conduct, even though that conduct produced injury to the plaintiff.

The last example should illustrate that the suggested shift in focus to the tort law opportunities for a restructuring of the law of defamation is not legitimately subject to dismissal on the ground that it is part of an "anti-media" development. The kind of interest analysis that is a standard part of modern tort law may in fact produce a body of decisions that recognizes a greater level of protection, based on the media status of the defamation defendant, than is likely to be obtained under the first amendment analysis the Court is now using. The enhanced attention to the tort law considerations in defamation analysis may thus result in "pro-media" effects as readily as it results in what are perceived to be "anti-media" consequences.

* * *

Two Substantive Reform Proposals

* * *

A. An Immunity for Speech About Government

* * *

The * * * *Sullivan* rules placing fault-as-to-falsity at the core of the defamation case are an inadequate response to the risk that government might use a defamation action as a means of deterring speech that is critical of government. In the first place, the critic of government who becomes a defamation defendant is still, under the *Sullivan* rules, subject to the risk of liability if the plaintiff is able to prove by clear and convincing evidence that the defendant knew the defamatory communication was false or published the communication with reckless disregard of its truth or falsity. Furthermore, should the public official plaintiff be able to make that showing, the defendant is liable not only for damages that compensate for the actual harm that the plaintiff can prove but for presumed and punitive damages as well. Even if the Court were to believe that the actual risk of liability under these circumstances was minimal, the risk is nevertheless real. The speech-deterrent effect of that risk is compounded by the potentially substantial cost that the defendant faces in order to resist the plaintiff's claim. Finally, the tension that is likely to be produced by an official stifling of criticism would not be relieved by the current constitutional rules that subject the critic to the risks of liability and the costs of defense that have just been described. Indeed, the frustration of being caught in a web of constitutional litigation rules that can be portrayed as arbitrary or ineffective may inject a further element of cynicism into the attitude displayed by the critic of government who becomes a defamation defendant.

* * *

The risk of government using defamation actions to suppress criticism may not be the most pressing social issue in today's society, but one ought to remember that less than a quarter-century ago this risk threatened to impede the progress of the most important social movement in this country's history. Whether offered as a means of avoiding the abuses of seditious libel or as a filter for constitutionally valueless falsehoods, the current panoply of constitutional rules offers insufficient protection for the critic of government.

The only truly adequate protection for criticism of government is an absolute privilege to say whatever one wishes about government without being called to account in any governmental forum. This privilege would consist of an absolute immunity from tort liability of any sort, whether asserted in an action for damages or in an action that seeks some other kind of non-monetary relief, and whether asserted in the context of a defamation claim or under the guise of some other tort such as invasion of privacy or the infliction of emotional distress.

This solution is simple, but it is not cost-free. The proposed immunity does provide a shield from behind which blatant falsehoods can be injected into the body politic. Nevertheless, even while recognizing that possibility, it can be argued that the immunity is still a valuable reform of the current state of affairs, and that its benefits do outweigh its costs. Political discourse may become more robust if the participants know in advance that the test of truth or falsity is really going to be administered in the public forum where individual citizens will make up their own minds, rather than being posed in some judicial setting, where an official winner and loser will be declared. In addition, perhaps there is reason to suspect that the body politic will become more resistant to falsehoods if the responsibility for reaching, and for acting on, judgments about the truth or falsity of claims rests squarely upon individual citizens.

What seems to be fairly clear from the survey of the current constitutional framework is that the proposed immunity faces a strong uphill fight if it is offered as a matter that is compelled by the constitutional guaranties of speech and press freedom. As stated earlier, however, there is no need to resort to the constitution to implement this reform, nor is there any need to persuade the Supreme Court to modify any of the existing constitutional rules developed over the last twenty-two years. The foundation upon which this reform can be built currently exists in the tort law of most of the states and is easily adopted as a matter of state law.

* * *

B. An Expansion of the Emotional Harm Component of the Defamation Claim

The historical function of a defamation action has been to vindicate and compensate for injury to the plaintiff's reputation. By raising the cost of conduct that poses a threat to reputation, the defamation action also deters the publication of harmful communications and forces the publisher to internalize the costs of the harm inflicted on the victim. It has probably always been realized that the emotional distress produced by the defamatory communication was an element of recovery to which a successful plaintiff was entitled. However, much of the contemporary literature on defamation either assumes or argues that the emotional harm component occupies a subsidiary or tangential place in the concept of defamation. It is that assumption which will be challenged in this section of the Article, on the basis that the assumption (1) is insufficiently protective of the victims of defamation, and (2) allows too great an opportunity for plaintiffs to characterize the claims they are asserting in ways that could place the defendants outside of the constitutional protections that have grown up around the defamation action. To overcome both of these shortcomings, a preferable alternative concept of defamation is one that recognizes that emotional harm should be placed on an equal footing with reputational injury.

The first perspective from which to demonstrate the inadequacy of an exclusive or primary focus on reputational injury is that of the person about whom defamatory statements are published. Assume that on a particular morning, you open your newspaper and read an article that includes statements about you that are false and that portray you in a way that is likely to make other people think less well of you. Whatever one might think about the historical roots of the defamation action and the advantages of adhering to ancient concepts of actionable wrongs, one ought nevertheless to recognize that the predominant initial response to that article is going to be *personal* reaction by the person about whom the statements are made, rather than a *reputation-injuring* reaction by other people who read the article or are subsequently told about its contents. The personal reaction may run a gamut of emotions, including anger, embarrassment, and helplessness. The intensity of the reaction may also vary, from minor annoyance to disabling withdrawal from contact with others.

A number of observations need to be made about this personal reaction. First, as the scenario illustrates, the plaintiff's reaction is not dependent on actual reputational injury. The personal reaction can occur before the victim is aware of what sort of response by others the defamatory publication has produced. Even if people whom the victim knows have a generally supportive response to the victim after they become aware of the publication, the initial personal reaction of the victim can be quite intense and may be aggravated by a concern about future responses to the publication. It may be reasonable to assume that there is a fairly close link between the intensity of some personal reaction and the reputational harm that is likely to be actually inflicted. However, a careful consideration of the distinct nature of the two types of harm reveals that there is no logical necessity that reputational harm occur in order for there to be a legitimate claim for the kind of personal reaction that can be characterized as emotional distress.

Second, the plaintiff's reaction is causally linked to conduct by the defendant that may be deemed wrongful. This is a crucial factor in light of the similarity between the reactions that the victim of a defamatory communication might suffer and the emotional reactions that a person might have to a wide variety of experiences that have absolutely nothing to do with defamation. Dismissing claims of emotional distress with an argument that the victim has to "learn to be tougher" or that "we can't provide a legal remedy every time a person gets upset" is much less compelling once the causal link between the harm and wrongful conduct by the defendant is recognized. What distinguishes the emotional distress caused by the defendant's wrongful conduct from other similar types of emotional distress is precisely the factor of the defendant's having exploited the plaintiff for some gain, pecuniary or otherwise, to the defendant. At the very least, a society is entitled to insist that such exploitation be very persuasively justified or that the gain be offset or neutralized by the transfer of compensatory damages from the defendant to the victim.

Third, the plaintiff's reaction is one that the legal system has always treated as a matter suitable for compensation and more recently has even treated as the basis of an independent claim for relief. The elements of an emotional distress claim may resemble some or all of the types of harm for which compensatory damages have traditionally been awarded in the case of intentional torts. In the last few decades, roughly paralleling the emergence of constitutional restrictions on defamation claims, courts have been recognizing that the infliction of emotional distress, without a finding of a more traditional tort category on which to append the emotional distress recovery, is conduct on which liability may be based. The publication of statements that have the potential for causing injury to the reputation of the victim is simply another, and highly foreseeable, way in which a defendant can be expected to cause harm of the emotional distress type.

Viewed from the perspective of the victim of defamatory communications, a focus on reputational injury is unreasonably narrow in its protection of, and compensation for injury to, legitimate personal interests. Recognition of an expanded role for the emotional harm component of the defamation claim would, therefore, appear to have as a likely effect an expansion of the damages for which defamation defendants might be liable. Such an effect is, however, *not* a probable result of the proposed reform. In the first place, once a plaintiff successfully surmounts the obstacles to establishing liability for defamation, the recovery that is allowed under the current set of legal rules almost certainly will include an opportunity for an award of substantial damages for what would be recognized as emotional harm. Second, the only cases in which the proposed reform offers relief to someone who would otherwise be barred from any recovery at all would be those instances in which proof of actual reputational injury is a prerequisite to liability for defamation. While it is true that there are such cases, and thus that the proposed reform would increase the incidence of liability, it is also likely that a substantial percentage of the plaintiffs who would be unable to prove actual injury to reputation would be able to base their claim for relief in different terms that do not require proof of injury of that sort. Thus, while the incidence of liability for defamation may undergo some marginal increase as a result of this reform, that increase may not be greater than the current incidence of liability for defamation and those similar tort claims that are now not subject to the full range of liability-limiting rules regarding defamation. The most likely outcome of the adoption of the proposed reform, from the perspective of the victim, is a more forthright recognition of the type of harm that the defendant's publication actually caused. At the same time, the proposed reform is unlikely to produce any significant increase in the amount or the extent of liability that defendants currently face.

ROBERT C. POST, THE SOCIAL FOUNDATIONS OF DEFAMATION LAW: REPUTATION AND THE CONSTITUTION

74 Calif.L.Rev. 691, 693, 695–96, 700–01, 708–10, 739–41 (1986).

THREE CONCEPTS OF REPUTATION

A. *Reputation as Property*

The concept of reputation that is most easily available to contemporary observers is that of reputation in the marketplace. This concept of reputation can be understood as a form of intangible property akin to goodwill. It is this concept of reputation that underlies our image of the merchant who works hard to become known as creditworthy or of the carpenter who strives to achieve a name for quality workmanship. Such a reputation is capable of being earned, in the sense that it can be acquired as a result of an individual's efforts and labor.

* * *

The concept of reputation as property presupposes that individuals are connected to each other through the institution of the market. The market provides the mechanism by which the value of property is determined. The purpose of the law of defamation is to protect individuals within the market by ensuring that their reputation is not wrongfully deprived of its proper market value. Defamation law should therefore not be concerned with purely private injuries which are independent of the market. Although individuals may attach importance to the way others regard them, a decline in this regard resulting merely in hurt feelings should not be the subject of redress.   * * *

Underlying the concept of reputation as property is an implicit image of a form of society that I shall call a "market society." Three distinctive features of this image should be emphasized. First, because the concept views a person as capable of creating his reputation, it presupposes that no matter what society's present estimation of an individual, he in theory always retains the capacity to work toward the production of a new reputation. In this sense individuals in a market society are understood to possess personal identities that are distinct from and anterior to their social identities. Individuals are not constituted by the social regard with which they are apprehended by others.

Second, because the concept of reputation as property requires defamation law to protect only those aspects of an individual's reputation that the market can measure, the concept assumes that the worth of a person's reputation will vary with market conditions. Reputation is thus not an absolute, a matter of either honor or dishonor. It is instead envisioned as a smooth and continuous curve of potential value. The legally protected interest in reputation will rise or fall depending upon an individual's productivity and upon fluctuations in market conditions.

Third, the concept of reputation as property presupposes that all persons are equal, in the sense of "the equal subordination of every individual to the laws of the market." No person has the right to a reputation other than that created by the evaluative processes of the market, and, conversely, every person enjoys an equal right to enter the market to attempt to achieve what reputation he can.

The concept of reputation as property, together with the image of the market society that it carries within it, can create a powerful and internally coherent account of defamation law. It can explain why the law protects reputation, and what kinds of social evaluation deserve the law's protection. There are aspects of modern defamation law that can be understood only by reference to the concept of reputation as property, as, for example, the fact that corporations and other inanimate entities can sue for defamation.

* * *

B. Reputation as Honor

There is an ancient tradition which views the worth of reputation as incommensurate with the values of the marketplace. The Bible, for example, tells us that "[a] good name is rather to be chosen than great riches." And Shakespeare observes that a "purse" is merely "trash" when compared to the value of a "good name." The concepts of reputation underlying this tradition are clearly incompatible with the notion of reputation as a form of property.

One strand of this tradition was influential in preindustrial England during the formative years of defamation law. This was the view that reputation was a form of honor. The concept of honor has many aspects, but the kind of honor that was most important for the development of defamation law may be defined as a form of reputation in which an individual personally identifies with the normative characteristics of a particular social role and in return personally receives from others the regard and estimation that society accords to that role. An individual does not earn or create this kind of honor through effort or labor; he claims a right to it by virtue of the status with which society endows his social role. For example a king does not work to attain the honor of his kingship, but rather benefits from the honor which society attributes to his position. The price of this benefit is that society expects him to aspire to "personify" these attributes and to make them part of his personal honor.

The anthropologist John Davis has observed that the "essential characteristics of honour are"

> first that it is a system of stratification: it describes the distribution of wealth in a social idiom, and prescribes appropriate behaviour for people at the various points in the hierarchy; it entails acceptance of superordination and subordination. Second, it is an absolute system .... Third, it does seem to be characteristic of honour that it is associated with integrity: the whole man is contemplated.[53]

Honor differs from the concept of reputation as property in each of these characteristics. Whereas reputation as property presupposes the equality of all individuals before the marketplace, honor presupposes that individuals are unequal. An individual's honor is but the personal reflection of the status which society ascribes to his social position. Individuals are therefore inherently unequal because they occupy different social roles. It is characteristic of honor that these social roles are hierarchically arranged. * * *

The concept of honor presupposes an image of society in which ascribed social roles are pervasive and well established, and in which such roles provide the point of reference both for the ascription of social status and for the normative standards of personal conduct.

* * *

C. Reputation as Dignity

When the United States Supreme Court attempts to characterize the nature of a state's interest in protecting reputation, it frequently relies upon a passage in Justice Stewart's concurring opinion in *Rosenblatt v. Baer:* [97]

---

53. J. Davis, People of the Mediterranean: An Essay in Comparative Social Anthropology 98 (1977).

97. 383 U.S. 75, 92 (1966) (Stewart, J., concurring).

The right of a man to the protection of his own reputation from unjustified invasion and wrongful hurt reflects no more than our basic concept of the essential dignity and worth of every human being—a concept at the root of any decent system of ordered liberty. The protection of private personality, like the protection of life itself, is left primarily to the individual States under the Ninth and Tenth Amendments. But this does not mean that the right is entitled to any less recognition by this Court as a basic of our constitutional system.

The rhetorical power of the passage is undeniable. It has proved enormously influential, and can fairly be characterized as an authentic contemporary expression of common law understanding of the law of defamation.

The passage, however, appears to rest on a paradox, for it is not immediately clear how reputation, which is social and public, and which resides in the "common or general estimate of a person," can possibly affect the "essential dignity" of a person's "private personality." The gulf that appears to separate reputation from dignity can be spanned only if defamation law contains an implicit theory of the relationship between the private and public aspects of the self.

*   *   *

Erving Goffman, the most influential modern writer in the symbolic interactionist tradition, has noted that the socialization process * * * should not be understood as having a definite terminus, a point at which an independent and mature self emerges as if from a chrysalis. Identity is rather continuously being constituted through social interactions.[102] For Goffman these interactions take the form of rules of "deference and demeanor." Rules of deference define conduct by which a person conveys appreciation "*to* a recipient *of* this recipient, or of something of which this recipient is taken as a symbol, extension, or agent." Rules of demeanor define conduct by which a person expresses "to those in his immediate presence that he is a person of certain desirable or undesirable qualities." Rules of deference and demeanor constitute "rules of conduct which bind the actor and the recipient together" and "are the bindings of society." By following these rules, individuals both confirm the social order in which they live and constitute "ritual" and "sacred" aspects of their own identity. The price of this process, however, is that each "individual must rely on others to complete the picture of him of which he himself is allowed to paint only certain parts."

Each individual is responsible for the demeanor image of himself and the deference image of others, so that for a complete man to be expressed, individuals must hold hands in a chain of ceremony, each giving deferentially with proper demeanor to the one on the right what will be received deferentially from the one on the left. While it

102. E. Goffman, Interaction Ritual 84–85 (1967).

may be true that the individual has a unique self all his own, evidence of this possession is thoroughly a product of joint ceremonial labor, the part expressed through the individual's demeanor being no more significant than the part conveyed by others through their deferential behavior toward him.

Goffman's account provides a theory for connecting the law of defamation to the concept of dignity. Dignity, after all, is a ritual and ceremonial aspect of the self that we associate with the self's integrity, which is to say with its completeness. Dignity can only be confirmed by the respect that is its due. Yet in Goffman's view dignity is always at risk, since in any social transaction the "chain of ceremony" may be broken, and hence a "complete man" may fail to be socially constituted. In this way our own sense of intrinsic self-worth, stored in the deepest recesses of our "private personality," is perpetually dependent upon the ceremonial observance by those around us of rules of deference and demeanor. The law of defamation can be conceived as a method by which society polices breaches of its rules of deference and demeanor, thereby protecting the dignity of its members. When rules of deference and demeanor are embodied in speech, and hence are subject to the law of defamation, I shall call them "rules of civility."

* * *

* * * [I]n *Dun & Bradstreet, Inc. v. Greenmoss Builders, Inc.*[247] * * * a credit reporting agency had issued an inaccurate report concerning a small corporation, Greenmoss Builders, which operated as a construction contractor. The credit report falsely stated that Greenmoss Builders had filed a voluntary petition for bankruptcy. The corporation sued for defamation, and the Vermont Supreme Court held that presumed and punitive damages could be awarded even in the absence of a showing of actual malice.

* * *

Most of the debate within the Court turned on questions of first amendment policy. Only Justice Powell attempted to craft a decision keyed to the nature of the state's interests in protecting reputation. Powell undertook to " * * * balance the State's interest in compensating private individuals for injury to their reputation against the First Amendment interest in protecting this type of expression." Justice Powell cited Stewart's *Rosenblatt* concurrence as authority for the view that the state's interest in protecting reputation is that of safeguarding "our basic concept of the essential dignity and worth of every human being." And Justice Powell deferred to the state's interest in maintaining a presumption of damages because of "the experience and judgment of history that 'proof of actual damage will be impossible in a great many cases.' "

247. 472 U.S. 749 (1985).

The root difficulty with Justice Powell's opinion is that it frames the issue to be resolved as an abstract conflict between the first amendment and something called "reputation." Although the issue is usually framed in exactly this way, the formulation is, as *Dun & Bradstreet* itself illustrates, deeply misleading. Reputation is not a single idea, but is instead a mélange of several different concepts. Each concept demands its own constitutional analysis. The failure to understand this seriously undercuts the force of Justice Powell's opinion. For example, although Justice Powell justifies defamation law in terms of the protection of human dignity, the plaintiff in *Dun & Bradstreet* was a corporation that could advance no conceivable claim to such dignity. It was clear from the outset that the harm suffered by the plaintiff, if any, was only to its corporate goodwill. In such a context the presumption of damages is anomalous at best. This is amply illustrated by the facts of *Dun & Bradstreet*: the defamatory "credit report was made available to only five subscribers, who, under the terms of the subscription agreement, could not disseminate it further." In effect, therefore, the reasons underlying Justice Powell's opinion had virtually no application to the facts of the case actually before him. * * *

Dun & Bradstreet perfectly illustrates the importance of separating reputation into its constituent concepts. Because he viewed reputation as a single, undifferentiated interest, Justice Powell was led to address an issue that was not present in the case before him, and to reach a judgment that was highly questionable in light of the specific facts of that case. Distinguishing among reputation as honor, property, and dignity will not magically dispel the serious dilemmas that reside in the constitutional regulation of common law defamation. Significant and intractable constitutional tensions will remain. But at least these tensions will be defined and their subtleties addressed, and they will no longer indiscriminately inflame all aspects of the relationship between the Constitution and defamation law.

Quite apart from its implications for constitutional law, the recognition of the distinct concepts of reputation underlying defamation law should be of some relevance to the development of common law doctrine. Instead of constructing rules and definitions that awkwardly attempt to span the gulf separating reputation as property from reputation as dignity, the two aspects of reputation can be distinguished and managed through different doctrinal structures. We need to reassess, for example, the relationship between the protection of reputation as property and the tort of injurious falsehood. In a similar way we must reevaluate the connections between the protection of reputation as dignity and the various torts protecting privacy and emotional well-being. The role of damages in protecting reputation as dignity requires reappraisal, as do the limitations and desirability of using courts to maintain community identity and cohesion through the enforcement of rules of civility.

PIERRE N. LEVAL,* THE NO–MONEY, NO–FAULT LIBEL SUIT: KEEPING *SULLIVAN* IN ITS PROPER PLACE

101 Harv.L.Rev. 1287–90, 1292–95, 1298–99 (1988).

Although the *Sullivan* rule is generally assumed to be a boon to press defendants, it also imposes significant costs on them. While protecting them from damage awards, it exposes their integrity to attack, forces them to reveal their investigative and editorial processes (often to their embarrassment), and requires them to expend significant sums in defending the issue. The high capacity of the post-*Sullivan* libel law to frustrate the interests of both sides has been noted by several commentators who have offered complex proposals for legislative changes.

I suggest that recognition of a no-damages libel suit, free of *Sullivan*'s actual malice requirement, would improve the efficiency of the cause of action, and reduce its costs and burdens for both defendants and plaintiffs. Such an action exists within the current legal framework without the need for legislation. I argue, first, that given a correct understanding of the *Sullivan* holding, a plaintiff who sues only for a judgment declaring the falsity of the libel and foregoes any claim for a monetary award is exempt from the obligation to prove that the defendant acted with malice. Second, I suggest that a no-money trial on the issue of truth or falsity may be advantageous in some cases to plaintiffs and defendants alike. The principal purpose of a libel suit is the restoration of a falsely damaged reputation; the plaintiff whose prime objective is to vindicate his reputation is more likely to succeed if relieved of the obligation to prove malice. The press defendant will be protected in such a trial from the risk of money liability as well as from the enormous pain, burden and cost that litigation of the *Sullivan* issue imposes on it. Finally, I suggest, regardless whether I have interpreted the *Sullivan* rule correctly, both plaintiff and defendant may find it advantageous in some cases to make an agreement that would relieve both sides of *Sullivan's* unwelcome burdens, while allocating other advantages as well.

* * *

The purpose of the malice requirement was not to protect falsity from exposure, but to protect the press from intimidation or annihilation by money judgments. Justice Brennan's opinion makes clear that the Court's sole concern was for the impact of money judgments on free speech. The opening sentence poses the question as "the extent to which the constitutional protections for speech and press limit a State's power *to award damages* in a libel action brought by a public official." The opinion concludes, "We hold today that the Constitution delimits a

---

* Judge, United States District Court for the Southern District of New York. Judge Leval presided at the trial of General William Westmoreland's libel suit against CBS.

State's power *to award damages* for libel ....'' The ruling was not addressed to and has no logical bearing on whether a court might declare a defamatory statement false. Nothing in it suggests that a falsely maligned plaintiff would need to prove malice if he sought no money damages, but only a judgment declaring falsity * * *.

* * *

Whether a plaintiff may bring a libel action for a declaration of falsity without money damages is a question of state law, not federal constitutional law. Permitting such an action advances the remedial objectives of the libel law. A libel action differs significantly from other tort actions in which a court redresses the loss only by an award of money damages. Where a plaintiff complains of a broken leg or of having been cheated, a jury's finding that the injury was caused by the defendant's negligence or fraud does nothing to undo the injury or compensate the plaintiff for it. In a libel case, by contrast, where the loss is an injury to reputation caused by the defendant's false statement, the court repairs the damaged reputation to some degree by the mere act of finding that the defamatory statement was false. In fact, were it not for the lapse of time between the publication of the libel and the finding of falsity (during which time plaintiff's reputation suffers) and the possible failure of the court's finding to reach all the people whose opinion was influenced by the false libel, the finding of falsity would undo the harm and render an award of money damages superfluous. One can well imagine a respectable legal system that would not award money damages for libel—unless, perhaps, a monetary loss was proven (such as a loss of employment)—but would restrict the plaintiff's available relief for intangible harm to a declaration of falsity of the libel.

The finding of falsity should be seen not merely as one of the elements that plaintiff must prove to make out his case but as part of the relief itself. We would be wrong to regard money as the sole—or even principal—objective of the libel action. At common law, because of the recognition that the correction of a false libel performed a valuable function, a plaintiff was permitted to sue for nominal damages. A plaintiff should be entitled to sue for the entry of a judgment embodying the verdict of falsity.

Important advantages would flow to plaintiffs and defendants from judicial recognition that a libel suit may be maintained solely for a judgment declaring falsity and that the *Sullivan/Gertz* fault rules have no application in such a trial. For the plaintiff concerned primarily with restoring a damaged reputation and willing to forego a claim for money, it permits a vastly cheaper lawsuit limited to the subject of the plaintiff's concern—the truth or falsity of the derogatory press account. It also offers him a far greater chance of successfully vindicating his reputation. If he proves the falsity of the libel to the jury's satisfaction, he wins; judgment is entered in his favor. In contrast, under *Sullivan,* even if he successfully proves falsity, he would in all likelihood emerge the loser because of his inability to prove "actual malice." Even plaintiffs who, given their druthers, would prefer to collect damages might find advantage in such a cause of action because of their recognition that *Sullivan* dooms them to failure.

There is reason to believe that a sizeable percentage of libel plaintiffs would be interested in pursuing an action for a judgment of falsity without a claim for damages if by doing so they could escape the requirements of *Sullivan*. In a survey conducted by the Iowa Libel Research Project, almost half of all libel plaintiffs cited either restoration of reputation or deterring further publication as the objective of their suit. Fewer than one in four plaintiffs—and even fewer of the public-figure plaintiffs—stated that they were suing to win damages.[25] Many public-figure plaintiffs declare publicly that they are not out for money.[26] Some, such as General William Westmoreland in his suit against CBS,[27] announce their intention to donate any winnings to charity.

* * *

The press too has much to gain from an action that permits the libel plaintiff to forego damages and avoid the *Sullivan* burdens. *Sullivan* was designed to save the press from the threat of crushing damage awards. Although the medicine has saved the patient, it has had serious side effects.

First, *Sullivan* diverts the focus of the trial to plaintiff's attack on the integrity of the press defendants. To be the subject of such an attack is at very least unpleasant. I have been told by press sources that several reporters, commentators, and editors who were the subject of such attacks in recent trials have been emotionally marked, sometimes to the point of illness, by the experience.

* * *

The *Sullivan* standards also expose the press to a high likelihood of public criticism, even when it is not merited. Any ambitious piece of journalism will likely contain some factual errors. Even if they are slight and insignificant, these will become a source of embarrassment at trial. It is also a rare piece of accusatory, investigative journalism that cannot, after the fact, be made to look slipshod or biased. The investigative reporter, searching for confirmation of her accusatory sources, will understandably have less interest in speaking to the cadre of loyalists who assure her of the probity of her subject. In an accusatory exposé, she may give little or no attention to denials. Also, pressures of time, money, and competition for priority place limits on how far an investigation will be taken before it is considered sufficiently confirmed to justify

25. *See* R. Bezanson, G. Cranberg & J. Soloski, Libel Law and the Press 122 (1987).

26. After she won a large libel award against the *National Enquirer*, actress Carol Burnett is reported to have stated, "If they'd given me one dollar plus car fare, I'd have been happy because it was the princi-

ple." R. Smolla, Suing The Press 111 (1986).

27. Westmoreland v. CBS, Inc., No. 82 Civ. 7913 (PNL) (S.D.N.Y.). The court's opinion denying summary judgment is reported at 596 F.Supp. 1170 (S.D.N.Y.1984).

publication. Whether the exposé was fair depends on the quality of judgment and evaluation employed by the investigative and editorial staffs. But even where fairness and good judgment prevailed, the reporter, editor, and publisher will be vulnerable to the charge that they sought and credited only incriminating sources, that their interpretation of ambiguous facts was biased, that they failed to interview or cite witnesses who would have confirmed the plaintiff's honesty, or that they rushed to publication before completing the investigation.

Finally, litigation of the *Sullivan* issues imposes great expense on the press at both the pretrial and trial stages. Discovery of the reporting and editing processes is likely to involve extensive document review and production as well as numerous and lengthy depositions.

* * *

Even if I am wrong in my belief that a plaintiff has the right under existing law to eliminate the *Sullivan* issues by foregoing his claim for money damages, it remains possible for plaintiff and defendant jointly to achieve the same result by agreement. Plaintiff's willingness to give up his claim for damages is valuable to the defendant; defendant's willingness to give up her *Sullivan* protection is valuable to the plaintiff. Because the *Sullivan* element was established solely for the defendant's protection, the defendant may agree to dispense with it. As noted above, many libel plaintiffs seek vindication rather than money, and many press defendants should be eager to be saved from the noxious side effects of *Sullivan*. Accordingly, there should be a strong shared incentive to agree to a no-money trial of truth or falsity that banishes the *Sullivan/Gertz* fault element.

* * *

Thus, the parties might reach a negotiated agreement to try a libel case, either in court or at arbitration, under the following principles, or any acceptable variation:

1. Plaintiff can win no money damages. He sues only for a verdict of falsity.

2. Plaintiff need not prove fault on defendant's part, only falsity.

3. Accordingly there will be neither discovery nor proof on the *Sullivan* issues of the defendant's good or bad faith.

Additional concessions might include:

4. Hearsay evidence will be admitted on the truth or falsity of the libel. (The judge may caution the jury on the possible dangers of reliance on hearsay, which is not subjected to cross-examination.)

5. Defendant guarantees that a finding in plaintiff's favor will be publicized in some manner. The agreement will specify the space (or time) and prominence of the publication.

INVASION OF PRIVACY

At common law the burden of proving truth in a defamation action was on the defendant, that being the logical corollary of the fact that at common law injury to reputation and not falsity was central to the nature of the action. As defamation has been constitutionalized, however, this no longer obtains, and it is now clear that the plaintiff, certainly in an action governed by *Sullivan* or *Gertz v. Welch*,[1] has the burden of proving that the statements made were false.

Such a view, however, neglects the fact that even the publication of truth may often injure the subject of that publication. Commonly we take the publication of truth to be valuable, injury to its subject notwithstanding. But on occasion many societies have recognized that the truth of a published proposition does not necessarily give the proposition so much social value that the publication should be encouraged.

Although this is the theory of part of the common law action of invasion of privacy, the tensions between the First Amendment and a tort action punishing the publication of truth should be apparent. In the selections that follow Stanley Ingber explores the interests that lie behind an action for invasion of privacy, and Diane Zimmerman concludes that, whatever the distinguished pedigree of actions for invasion of privacy, they cannot continue to exist consistently with strong protection of freedom of speech and press.

STANLEY INGBER, RETHINKING INTANGIBLE INJURIES: A FOCUS ON REMEDY

73 Calif.L.Rev. 772, 839–843 (1985).

1. THE ESSENCE OF PRIVACY

* * *

[A] * * * distinction must be made between disclosures the plaintiff finds objectionable because they detract from his stature in the community and disclosures objectionable because of the information's intimacy. While a false statement which detracts is justifiable grounds for a suit in defamation, publication of true information which detracts may be merely setting the record straight. Consequently, the plaintiff who wishes to sue because of such a disclosure, essentially, is hoping to continue to misrepresent himself to the public. Such an interest deserves little public sympathy or legal recognition.

Quite different is the plaintiff who suffers the publication of intimate facts. The essence of such injuries is the mass dissemination of facts not relevant to issues of public concern and thus not justifiably within the public domain. Professor Milton Konvitz writes of such a view of privacy:

---

1. 418 U.S. 323 (1974).

Its essence is the claim that there is a sphere of space that has not been dedicated to public use or control. It is a kind of space that a man may carry with him, into his bedroom or into the street. Even when public, ... it is a part of his "property" ... with respect to which its owner has delegated no power to the state.[336]

For example, when the press relates a man's emotional crisis upon being forced to leave his wife and children, the wrong is found in the fact that "a private life has been transformed into a public spectacle." This unjustified transformation attacks the essential core of the right to privacy.

To some extent the injury caused by a privacy invasion, much like defamation, is a specific type of emotional distress. * * * Compensation could be available for specific, pecuniary losses, such as the costs of psychological therapy, relocation to another community, or loss of wages following discharge from employment. General damages for intangible injuries would be unavailable unless the plaintiff could prove the injury was willfully inflicted.

However, the main impetus for an action for invasion of privacy is not the emotional distress the invasion causes. The focus is more on the protection of human dignity than on compensation for loss. Once an intimate fact has been publicly disclosed, others will know of it and the resulting injury—indignity and humiliation—cannot be rectified. In defamation the availability of declaratory judgments, retractions, and replies all serve to remedy the intangible damage caused by the reputational injury. No comparable remedies exist for invasions of privacy. Unlike virtually all other areas of communication, more speech or information can never rectify the wrong. Consequently, the justification for invasion of privacy actions is less to correct past wrongs than to discourage future transgressions. These suits serve primarily cost avoidance goals. Their main purpose is to deter or "chill" the media— precisely those purposes which the Supreme Court found most troubling in the context of defamation suits. Therefore, a careful constitutional analysis of a "right to privacy" is suggested.

2. CONSTITUTIONAL ANALYSIS

The theoretical justification for removing private issues from the robust debate encouraged by the first amendment can be stated fairly simply. Constitutional rules generally are rules to order and regulate group living. They are rules of the collectivity. The right of privacy, however, insulates a portion of individual life from the group, creating a domain excluded from collective life and thus not governed by the rules of collective living. Consequently, the rules safeguarding the right of privacy supersede those constitutional rules and rights, including first amendment rights, that focus on group dynamics.

---

336. Konvitz, [*Privacy and the Law: A*   Probs. 272, 297–80 (1966).]
Philosophical Prelude, 31 Law & Contemp.

The Supreme Court in *Griswold v. Connecticut*[345] and *Roe v. Wade*[346] recognized a constitutional right of privacy. *Griswold* insulated from governmental regulation an individual's decision whether to use contraceptive devices. *Roe* did the same for a woman's decision to abort a fetus during the first trimester. These decisions involve significant values of morality, life, and liberty. Democratic theory suggests that elected legislative bodies are generally best suited to make decisions requiring such a choice among values. In fact, before *Roe*, many state legislatures were in the process of considering the abortion issue. The Court in *Roe* halted this process, not by deciding whether abortion itself was right or wrong, but by determining that the choices involved in an abortion decision were within the province of the individual and not the public. Therefore, group deliberative processes were inappropriate.

Of course, all invasions of privacy do not constitute violations of constitutional rights justifying civil rights suits in addition to tort actions.[348] However, the force of the constitutional recognition that some areas of an individual's life fall outside of the group domain affects all issues in close proximity. It creates a force field that has an impact on cultural attitudes toward privacy generally. The result is that, unlike the value of reputation in the defamation context, the value of privacy may constitute a counterforce of perhaps equal symbolic and societal influence to the values embodied in the first amendment. Because the first amendment specifically protects freedom of speech and press while there is no comparable *constitutional* protection of reputation, a bias may justifiably exist when dealing with defamation favoring errors of too much rather than too little communication. In contrast, in privacy invasion cases there may be a more equal balance between the significance of first amendment and privacy values. Consequently, no preference may exist toward errors affecting one rather than the other interest. The danger of *chilling* the media may be no greater when privacy rather than reputation is at stake, but the societal price of insufficient *deterrence* may weigh more heavily in the privacy case.

DIANE L. ZIMMERMAN, REQUIEM FOR A HEAVY-WEIGHT: A FAREWELL TO WARREN AND BRANDEIS'S PRIVACY TORT

68 Cornell L.Rev. 291, 292–294, 343–356, 358–360, 362 (1983).

In 1890, Samuel Warren and Louis Brandeis stirred the American legal community with a ringing call to arms to protect the hapless citizenry against the truthful exposure of their personal affairs on the pages of the "yellow press."[1] Warren and Brandeis dubbed the protection they proposed a "right to privacy," and described it as the right "to

---

345. 381 U.S. 479 (1965).

346. 410 U.S. 113 (1973).

348. In any case, most civil rights statutes require that the violation be 'under the color of law.' *E.g.*, 42 U.S.C. § 1983 (1982).

1. Warren & Brandeis, *The Right to Privacy*, 4 Harv.L.Rev. 193 (1890).

be let alone." Their advocacy of this new tort created a minor revolution in the development of the common law.

Nonetheless, even after ninety years, the real impact of that revolution on legislatures and courts is hard to evaluate. Depending upon the biases of the viewer, the article's effect could be said to exemplify the power, the impotence, or even the perniciousness of legal scholarship. Those who assert that the impact of the article demonstrates the power of scholarship point out that the Warren–Brandeis argument led most states in this country to recognize a right to recover in tort for the wrongful public exposure of private information, as well as for a wide range of other invasions of privacy.

The impotence argument contends, however, that despite the ever-increasing number of claims under the Warren–Brandeis theory, plaintiffs rarely win. One frustrated judge exclaimed in an impassioned dissent that if a right to be protected against the publication of truthful information indeed existed within his state, his colleagues should honor it "by more than lip service." [5]

Finally, one can argue that the Warren–Brandeis contribution has actually had a pernicious influence on modern tort law because it created a cause of action that, however formulated, cannot coexist with constitutional protections for freedom of speech and press.

* * *

From the outset, advocates of privacy have * * * faced a dual, and sometimes internally inconsistent, task. On the one hand, they needed to develop a philosophical basis to support the right through an exploration of why a civilized and humane society should recognize and protect an interest in controlling public discussion of personal information. On the other hand, they had to protect free speech by creating numerous defenses and narrowing the scope of the privacy tort, so that much personal information could circulate without penalty.

* * *

Warren and Brandeis themselves conceded that their proposed tort was subject to some limitations and should not create a right to sue for any unauthorized publication. It is unclear whether they created these limitations to protect the free flow of information, to prevent the courts from sinking under an avalanche of litigation, or both. But, certainly, courts have recognized the free speech implications of the private-facts tort from the time of its adoption.

Whatever their motive, Warren and Brandeis proposed a test that they believed would distinguish cases where liability was justified from those where it was not. To be actionable, a revelation would have to

---

5. Bremmer v. Journal–Tribune Publishing Co., 247 Iowa 817, 829, 76 N.W.2d 762, 769 (1956) (Larson, C.J., dissenting). In a survey of state case law, the author found fewer than 18 cases in which a plaintiff was either awarded damages or found to have stated a cause of action sufficient to withstand a motion for summary judgment or a motion to dismiss.

involve "private" information, and not the sort of information in which the public maintained a "legitimate" interest.

A. PRIVATE INFORMATION: THE VARIOUS TESTS

1. *The Status of the Plaintiff as a Gauge of Private Information*

* * *

Warren and Brandeis believed that the classifications of "private" and "newsworthy" (that is, "public") were merely different points on a single continuum. They defined information as public or private based as much on the identity of the individual discussed as on the subject matter under discussion. Although courts continue to talk about its importance in privacy cases, the status approach as a way to distinguish privileged from tortious speech has proved unproductive. * * *

The Supreme Court has created a series of standards for libel which, very much like the distinction made by Warren and Brandeis, offer far greater protection to private than to public plaintiffs.[287] The Court has clearly indicated, however, that at least where opinions, ideas, nondefamatory falsehoods, and accurate factual speech are involved, the status of the plaintiff is constitutionally irrelevant.[288] * * * For example, the attitude of individual voters toward an administration's economic philosophy may be influenced by their knowledge of the latest government economic indicators and the President's policy speeches and life style. But the voters might be equally affected by a newspaper story describing the impact of that economic philosophy on an ordinary automobile worker who has just collected his last unemployment check and is unable to support his children or meet mortgage payments.

* * *

2. *Location Analysis as a Means of Defining Private Information*

To distinguish private facts from "public" information about an individual, courts often look either to the location of the action or to the nature of the subject matter. Courts using the "location" analysis commonly state that information individuals reveal about themselves in public places is by definition not private. Therefore, reports of such revelations are not actionable merely because the press has further publicized the information.

* * *

3. *The "Subject Matter" Test of Private Facts*

[C]ourts and commentators have also relied on a subject matter or "zone of privacy" test. Embarrassing events sometimes occur over

---

287. *See* Gertz v. Robert Welch, Inc., 418 U.S. 323 (1974) * * *.

288. The Court has thus far failed to distinguish between public and private figures in false-light privacy cases. *See, e.g.,* Cantrell v. Forest City Publishing Co., 419 U.S. 245 (1974); Time, Inc. v. Hill, 385 U.S. 374 (1967). Nor did the Court suggest that such a distinction is relevant in the only private-facts case it has decided, Cox Broadcasting Corp. v. Cohn, 420 U.S. 469 (1975). * * *

which the individuals involved have little control, but which are undisputably "public" under the location test. Courts in these cases sometimes rule that the subject matter is private even though the locus is not. For example, a woman's skirt was blown up around her waist as she stepped over an air vent as she emerged from a funhouse at a public fairground.[296] The Alabama Supreme Court affirmed an award of several thousand dollars against the newspaper that ran a picture of the unfortunate woman on subject matter grounds * * *.

Emerson supports a subject matter or "zone of privacy" test and argues that courts can remove some of the uncertainty surrounding the private-facts tort by identifying certain topics that are sufficiently intimate to establish in essence a prima facie case of liability.[298] Emerson considers as intimate "those activities, ideas or emotions which one does not share with others or shares only with those who are closest. This would include sexual relations, the performance of bodily functions, family relations, and the like." * * *

Like the location and status approaches, the subject matter approach has difficulties. It may be impossible to identify in advance appropriate categories that encompass the wide variety of possible fact patterns that can occur. Publishers would still face some uncertainty as to which subjects or facts invade privacy, and some chilling of free speech would remain. Moreover, categorical prohibitions may not take adequate account of variations in what is perceived as "private." For example, not all family relationships—even those rarely discussed—are necessarily intimate. Most importantly, it may be difficult to ascertain at any point in time, and certainly for any significant span of time, which subject matters are so personal as to justify tort protection. Public consensus is difficult to forge, hard to measure, and subject to rapid shifts. Differences of opinion over which subjects are offensive can be found at any moment in history among different geographical regions, or levels of social, economic, or educational status.

* * *

B. THE NEWSWORTHINESS DEFENSE

If the attempt to define "private" information has proved difficult the process of defining "newsworthy" information has practically destroyed the private-facts tort as a realistic source of a legal remedy. More than a decade and a half ago, Harry Kalven noted that the newsworthiness privilege was "so overpowering as virtually to swallow the tort."[308] All information is potentially useful in some way to the public in forming attitudes and values. Thus every communication is arguably privileged.

---

296. Daily Times Democrat v. Graham, 276 Ala. 380, 162 So.2d 474 (1964).

298. See Emerson, [The Right of Privacy and Freedom of the Press, 14 Harv.C.R.-C.L. L.Rev. 329, 343–44 (1979).]

308. See Kalven, [Privacy in Tort Law—Were Warren and Brandeis Wrong? 31 Law & Contemp.Probs. 326, 336 (1966).]

1. *Attempts to Define Newsworthiness: The Political Speech Model*

Because all information is arguably "newsworthy," the private-facts case law has been plagued by the same problem that has debilitated [Alexander] Meiklejohn['s] political-speech theory as a useful tool for rationalizing first amendment law. When Meiklejohn initially espoused the notion that the first amendment was designed to protect "political" speech as opposed to other kinds of speech, commentators criticized him for his substantially underinclusive definition. Does the first amendment leave unprotected most literature, art and learning not explicitly political in nature? Meiklejohn countered that speech relating to the process of self-governance need not be "about" politics. Meiklejohn claimed that people reach decisions based on many different kinds of information. "Political" speech, he said, is a very broad concept that includes "forms of thought and expression ... from which the voter derives the knowledge, intelligence, sensitivity to human values: the capacity for sane and objective judgment which, so far as possible, a ballot should express." [310] Thus, he created a new problem: instead of excluding too much important speech from first amendment coverage, Meiklejohn's redrafted political-speech theory threatened to provide no limits at all to the array of speech within the amendment's coverage.

The Supreme Court's experience with the political-speech doctrine in libel law illustrates some of the difficulty in applying the equally broad newsworthiness standard, and suggests that the Court may be reluctant to approve a body of tort law that employs such a nebulous standard to distinguish between constitutionally protected and unprotected speech.

Beginning with its decision in *New York Times Co. v. Sullivan,*[311] the Court held in a series of cases that to recover for libel, public officials and public figures must show that the defendant either knew that the speech was false or spoke in reckless disregard of its truth or falsity. In *Rosenbloom v. Metromedia, Inc.,*[312] a divided Court ruled that the *Sullivan* knowing-or-reckless standard applied to private plaintiffs as well. Justice Brennan, in his plurality opinion, relied on the political-speech theory to justify *Rosenbloom*. He reasoned that because the first amendment protects all speech that promotes "self-governance," the Court must extend the maximum protection to any material "of public or general interest" without regard to the "prior anonymity or notoriety" of the subjects of the discussion.

* * *

Only three years later, the Court in *Gertz v. Robert Welch, Inc.*[318] abandoned the *Rosenbloom* rule. The Court's opinion [seems to recognize] that no plaintiff could escape the restrictive *Sullivan* standard if the public interest remained the relevant criterion. The Court thus

---

310. Meiklejohn, [*The First Amendment Is An Absolute*, 1961 Sup.Ct.Rev. 245, 256.]

311. 376 U.S. 254 (1964).

312. 403 U.S. 29 (1971).

318. 418 U.S. 323 (1974) (opinion of Powell, J.).

abandoned the effort to distinguish libel cases based on the public interest in the subject matter and reverted to a focus on the status of the plaintiff.

* * *

2. *The Leave-it-to-the-Press Model*

If the case law is any gauge, most judges share the Supreme Court's reluctance to engage in line drawing over newsworthiness and simply accept the press's judgment about what is and is not newsworthy. Although courts will occasionally find that a particular story is not privileged, the vast majority of cases seem to hold that what is printed is by definition of legitimate public interest.

Although one could describe such deference to editorial judgment as capitulation, deference to the judgment of the press may actually be the appropriate and principled response to the newsworthiness inquiry. The press, after all, has a better mechanism for testing newsworthiness than do the courts. The economic survival of publishers and broadcasters depends upon their ability to provide a product that the public will buy. Unlike judges and jurors, the press must develop a responsiveness to what substantial segments of the population want (and perhaps even need) to know to cope with the society in which they live. To argue that the press merely "panders" to public taste at the lowest common denominator is to make a class-based judgment about the value of the information that people seek. The law cannot make such judgments consistent with the first amendment, and probably ought not to make them as a matter of policy.

* * *

3. *Passage of Time and the Erosion of Newsworthiness*

Although we might not wish to leave the determination of newsworthiness to the unregulated judgment of publishers, the absence of any other sensible test may dictate a continuation of the practice. Courts' efforts to devise a better standard have met with little success. Some courts have suggested that the passage of time erodes the newsworthiness of events. California stressed this factor in deciding two well-known cases in which the defendants revealed past criminal activities of the plaintiffs.[331] * * *

[But it] is difficult to imagine how the passage of time could constitute a serious consideration in determining newsworthiness. Such a standard would make the exploration of modern history a hazardous enterprise and endanger access to important information. The recollection and rethinking of past events often influences opinions on current issues. * * *

---

331. Briscoe v. Reader's Digest Ass'n, Inc., 4 Cal.3d 529, 483 P.2d 34, 93 Cal.Rptr. 866 (1971); Melvin v. Reid, 112 Cal.App. 285, 297 P. 91 (1931).

4. *Naming Names as a Gauge of Liability*

Courts have also occasionally relied on the defendant's use of the plaintiff's name or other identifying characteristics to distinguish newsworthy revelations from unnewsworthy. These courts concede that the facts themselves may be newsworthy, but argue that the public gains no additional "legitimate" knowledge by learning the identity of the party. * * *

A factual report that fails to name its sources or the persons it describes is properly subject to serious credibility problems. Consider, for example, the debate that erupted in 1981 over the practice of "disguising" subjects and quoting anonymous sources. A Pulitzer Prize was withdrawn from a Washington Post reporter when it was discovered that she made up, and not merely disguised, the characters in her story on juvenile drug addicts. * * *

* * *

5. *The Unconscionability Standard*

Although they have acknowledged that such tests as "newsworthiness" and "private nature of the information" may remain vague and may threaten fragile first amendment values, some courts and commentators have nevertheless argued that the Constitution permits private-facts liability in a small class of cases. These advocates would preserve a right of action when the revelations are so shocking, intimate and objectionable as to amount to unconscionable behavior on the part of the publisher. They claim that limiting recovery to cases that "shock the conscience" would minimize the chill on protected speech and would still redress the most serious abuses of privacy.

* * *

One illustration—drawn from a case that was not itself a private-facts action—should demonstrate why even the unconscionability standard will not (and should not) tame the newsworthiness privilege. In *Commonwealth v. Wiseman*,[357] the state of Massachusetts, acting as *parens patriae* on behalf of the inmates of a Massachusetts correctional institution, sought an injunction against further showings of the film "Titicut Follies." The footage was unquestionably shocking. The film showed identifiable naked patients futilely attempting to conceal their nudity; it depicted inmates who were incoherent and raving. It recorded some in the process of dying, and still others as they received treatments callously administered by staff psychiatrists. The reviewing court concluded that the movie constituted a "collective, indecent intrusion into the most private aspects of the lives of these unfortunate persons."

But the evidence cited by the court demonstrates that many viewers deemed the conditions in the institution, and not the film, to be unconscionable. The very brutality of the imagery gave the film its impact. One critic said that the movie's "repulsive reality" forced the

357. 356 Mass. 251, 249 N.E.2d 610, *cert. denied,* 398 U.S. 960 (1969). * * *

viewer "to contemplate our capacity for callousness. No one seeing this film can but believe that reform of the conditions it reports is urgent business."

* * *

In summary, the "shock-the-conscience" standard, which seeks to preserve some small measure of protection for private facts from the broad reach of the first amendment, probably is unworkable. Because "unconscionability" is ultimately a subjective determination, open to many different interpretations, this theoretical narrowing of the tort is not, as a practical matter, likely to discourage many potential litigants from suing, or to prevent courts from continuing to arrive at conceptually irreconcilable results. When we weigh the continued chilling effect of potential litigation and unpredictable liability against the benefits of allowing courts to retain the option of remedying some rare, genuinely offensive bits of publicity, we must question whether the preservation of even a small corner of the Warren–Brandeis tort is worth the risks. This observer answers in the negative.

BIBLIOGRAPHY

Defamation

David A. Anderson, *Is Libel Law Worth Reforming?*, 140 U.Pa.L.Rev. 487 (1991).

Randall P. Bezanson, *The Libel Suit in Retrospect: What Plaintiffs Want and What Plaintiffs Get*, 74 Calif.L.Rev. 789 (1986).

Randall P. Bezanson, *Libel Law and the Realities of Libel Litigation: Setting the Record Straight*, 71 Iowa L.Rev. 226 (1985).

Lee C. Bollinger, *The End of New York Times v. Sullivan: Reflections on Masson v. New Yorker Magazine*, 1991 Sup.Ct.Rev. 1.

Everette Dennis & Eli Noam, eds., THE COST OF LIBEL: ECONOMIC AND POLICY IMPLICATIONS (1989).

C. Thomas Dienes and Lee Levine, *Implied Libel, Defamatory Meaning, and State of Mind: The Promise of New York Times Co. v. Sullivan*, 78 Iowa L.Rev. 237 (1993).

Richard A. Epstein, *Was* New York Times v. Sullivan *Wrong?*, 53 U.Chi.L.Rev. 782 (1986).

Marc A. Franklin, *Good Names and Bad Law: A Critique of Libel Law and a Proposal*, 18 U.S.F.L.Rev. 1 (1983).

Martin F. Hansen, *Fact, Opinion, and Consensus: The Verifiability of Allegedly Defamatory Speech*, 62 Geo.Wash.L.Rev. 43 (1993).

Stanley Ingber, *Defamation: A Conflict Between Reason and Decency*, 65 Va.L.Rev. 785 (1979).

Paul LeBel, *Emotional Distress, the First Amendment, and "This Kind of Speech": A Heretical Perspective on* Hustler Magazine v. Falwell, 60 U.Colo.L.Rev. 315 (1989).

Anthony P. Lewis, New York Times v. Sullivan *Reconsidered: Time to Return to "The Central Meaning of the First Amendment,"* 83 Colum.L.Rev. 603 (1983).

Norman Rosenberg, PROTECTING THE BEST MEN: AN INTERPRETIVE HISTORY OF THE LAW OF LIBEL (1986).

Frederick Schauer, *Language, Truth, and the First Amendment: An Essay in Memory of Harry Canter,* 64 Va.L.Rev. 263 (1978).

Frederick Schauer, *Uncoupling Free Speech,* 92 Colum.L.Rev. 1321 (1992).

Steven H. Shiffrin, *Defamatory Non–Media Speech and First Amendment Methodology,* 25 UCLA L.Rev. 915 (1978).

Rodney Smolla, Dun & Bradstreet, Hepps, *and* Liberty Lobby: *A New Analytic Primer on the Future Course of Defamation,* 75 Geo.L.J. 1519 (1987).

Kathryn Dix Sowle, *A Matter of Opinion: Milkovich Four Years Later,* 3 Wm. & Mary Bill of Rights J. 467 (1994).

Symposium, *Defamation and the First Amendment: New Perspectives,* 25 Wm. & Mary L.Rev. 743 (1984).

Symposium, *Defamation in Fiction,* 51 Brooklyn L.Rev. 223 (1985).

Symposium, *New Perspectives on the Law of Defamation,* 74 Calif.L.Rev. 677 (1986).

Symposium, *Offensive and Libelous Speech,* 47 Wash. & Lee L.Rev. 1 (1990).

Privacy

Ruth Gavison, *Too Early for a Requiem: Warren and Brandeis Were Right on Prvacy vs. Free Speech,* 43 S.C.L.Rev. 437 (1992).

David A. Logan, *Tort Law and the Central Meaning of the First Amendment,* 51 U.Pitt.L.Rev. 493 (1990).

Robert C. Post, *The Social Foundations of Privacy: Community and Self in the Common Law Tort,* 77 Calif.L.Rev. 957 (1989).

Symposium, *The Right to Privacy One Hundred Years Later,* 41 Case West.Res.L.Rev. 643 (1991).

Samuel D. Warren & Louis D. Brandeis, *The Right to Privacy,* 4 Harv.L.Rev. 193 (1890).

Diane L. Zimmerman, *False Light Invasion of Privacy: The Light That Failed,* 64 N.Y.U.L.Rev. 364 (1989).

C. OBSCENITY AND PORNOGRAPHY

As many of the readings in Chapters II and III indicated, it is implausible to suppose that the First Amendment can be taken to cover the full range of human communicative activities, and the general irrelevance of the speech and press clauses to the law of evidence, to antitrust law, to perjury, to most of securities law, and to most of consumer protection law has occasioned little dispute. But this is not to say that all of the implicit or explicit exclusions from the coverage of the First Amendment have been as non-controversial, and there is little doubt that the most controversial of all is the Supreme Court's reaffirmation first in *Roth v. United States* [1] and then in *Paris Adult Theatre I v. Slaton* [2] of the long-standing exclusion of (judicially-defined) obscenity from the ambit of the speech clause. Among the most powerful and enduring attacks on the Supreme Court's "non-speech" approach has been that of Harry Kalven, who argued that this approach enabled the Court disingenuously to avoid difficult questions about the harms that obscenity is said to cause, and about the state's interest in regulating sexually explicit communication. Frederick Schauer, although maintaining that a legislature "should refrain from regulation," [3] attempts to justify the Court's approach to the constitutional question by situating the exclusion of obscenity from First Amendment coverage within a much larger range of less commonly discussed exclusions.

Although neither obscenity regulation nor debate about it has disappeared, current discussions have been dominated by the quite different issue of pornography regulation. Catharine MacKinnon, who (with Andrea Dworkin) has been at the forefront of the feminist anti-pornography movement, and has created the civil rights approach at issue in *American Booksellers Ass'n v. Hudnut, Inc.,* [1] explains and defends that approach in the article excerpted here. Cass Sunstein argues that pornography regulation is consistent with existing understandings of the central features of the First Amendment. Frank Michelman sees the First Amendment question in terms of two different conceptions of the First Amendment itself—one especially concerned with government regulation (including regulation of pornography), the other primarily concerned with fostering the kind of participatory public discourse that pornography is said to inhibit. Frederick Schauer attempts to clarify some of the definitional and empirical issues that undergird much of the pornography debate. Steven Gey, taking Schauer and MacKinnon as his primary targets, argues that both the historical non-speech approach to obscenity and the modern feminist attack on pornography share a willingness to distinguish forms of speech based on their value—a distinction he argues is fundamentally at odds with the central premises of the First Amendment.

HARRY KALVEN, JR., THE METAPHYSICS OF THE LAW OF OBSCENITY

1960 Sup.Ct.Rev. 1–4, 7–13.

The United States Supreme Court had no occasion to pass on the constitutionality of legislation making obscenity a crime for more than

1. 354 U.S. 476 (1957).

2. 413 U.S. 49 (1973).

3. 67 Geo.L.J. at 933.

4. 771 F.2d 323 (7th Cir.1985), aff'd without opinion, 475 U.S. 1001 (1986).

one hundred and fifty years after the adoption of the First Amendment. Within the last five years, however, the Court has been confronted with and decided most of the principal questions relating to the problem. * * *

* * *

The constitutional problems are primarily of two kinds. The first revolves around the ambiguity of the term "obscenity."

* * *

The second group of constitutional doubts derive[s] from the clear-and-present-danger test. Toward what dangers [is] obscenity legislation directed? Analysis reveals four possible evils: (1) the incitement to antisocial sexual conduct; (2) psychological excitement resulting from sexual imagery; (3) the arousing of feelings of disgust and revulsion; and (4) the advocacy of improper sexual values. All present difficulties. It is hard to see why the advocacy of improper sexual values should fare differently, as a constitutional matter, from any other exposition in the realm of ideas. Arousing disgust and revulsion in a voluntary audience seems an impossibly trivial base for making speech a crime. The incitement of antisocial conduct * * * evaporates in light of the absence of any evidence to show a connection between the written word and overt sexual behavior. There remains the evil of arousing sexual thoughts short of action. There is no doubt that the written word can excite the imagination. What [is puzzling is] that the law could be so solemnly concerned with the sexual fantasies of the adult population.

The Court finally reached the constitutional issue in 1956 in two cases which were heard and decided together: *People v. Alberts* and *United States v. Roth*.[31] In the *Alberts* case, a conviction was based on a California statute which made the distribution of obscene materials a crime. The *Roth* case involved a federal statute making criminal the transmission of obscene materials through the mails. The Court, agreeing that this was the first time the constitutional issue had been "squarely presented" to it under either the First or the Fourteenth Amendment, sustained the validity of both the federal and the state regulation.

* * *

The majority opinion, although it decisively and unequivocally disposed of doubts as to constitutionality, did so by a route which neatly bypassed all the perplexities raised [above]. Mr. Justice Brennan began by stating the question in a fashion that clearly foreshadowed the answer: "The dispositive question is whether obscenity is utterance within the area of protected speech and press." * * *

* * *

31. 354 U.S. 476 (1956).

Having thus stated the issue, Mr. Justice Brennan proceeded quickly to its disposition. He first noted that, although it had never passed on the question, the Court had several times previously appeared to assume its constitutionality in dicta. The First Amendment, in light of colonial history, cannot be read as intended to "protect every utterance." This argument is curious. Because thirteen of the fourteen states which ratified the Constitution had laws prohibiting libel, profanity, and blasphemy, he concluded that obscenity is without constitutional protection. There are at least two difficulties here. The Court seems to have assumed that the only argument against the constitutionality of obscenity regulation rests on the broad premise that under the First Amendment no utterances can be prohibited and that if this broad premise were destroyed the argument must collapse. Further, the Court's use of history was so casual as to be alarming in terms of what other propositions might be proved by the same technique. Is it clear, for example, that blasphemy can constitutionally be made a crime today? And what would the Court say to an argument along the same lines appealing to the Sedition Act of 1798 as justification for the truly liberty-defeating crime of seditious libel?

The opinion then proceeded to the crux of the matter. "All ideas having even the slightest redeeming social importance—unorthodox ideas, controversial ideas, even ideas hateful to the prevailing climate of opinion" are protected against governmental restraint. Obscenity on the other hand is "utterly without redeeming social importance." This is clear from the fact that over fifty nations have entered into international agreements for its regulation, and twenty obscenity laws have been enacted by Congress in the last century. The Court then quoted *Chaplinsky* [37] to the effect that "such utterances are no essential part of any exposition of ideas ..." and concluded: "We hold that obscenity is not within the area of constitutionally protected speech or press."

The opinion, however, was not yet finished. The most interesting part was to come. Mr. Justice Brennan turned to meet the challenge that there must be a clear and present danger of something to justify regulation of speech. * * * He disposed of th[is] with one quick thrust: since obscenity is not in the area of constitutionally protected speech, it is, quoting *Beauharnais v. Illinois*, [39] "unnecessary either for us or for the state courts to consider the issues behind the phrase 'clear and present danger.'" The Court thus found further use for the two-level free-speech theory which made its first appearance in *Chaplinsky* and was given status as doctrine in *Beauharnais*. The spectacular dilemma predicted for the Court when it confronted the perplexities of obscenity regulation turned out to have no horns at all. The perplexities may be puzzling but, the Court said, they are simply not relevant.

After putting obscenity so securely beyond the pale of constitutional concern, Mr. Justice Brennan hastened to add a good word on behalf of

---

37. Chaplinsky v. New Hampshire, 315 U.S. 568 (1942).

39. 343 U.S. 250 (1952).

sex: "Sex and obscenity are not synonymous." Then followed what must be the least controversial utterance in the Court's history: "Sex, a great and mysterious motive force in human life, has indisputably been a subject of absorbing interest to mankind through the ages." But obscene discussions of sex are not entitled to the protection afforded fundamental freedoms. "It is therefore vital that the standards for judging obscenity safeguard the protection of freedom of speech and press for material which does not treat sex in a manner appealing to prurient interests."

The Brennan opinion invites three lines of consideration. First, is the two-level theory of free speech tolerable as doctrine? Second, is there disclosed a weakness in the preoccupation of free-speech theory with competition in the market place of ideas when we turn to art and belles-lettres, which deal primarily with the imagination and not with ideas in any strict sense? Finally, will the tendency of the Court's decision be to relax or to make more restrictive the enforcement of the obscenity laws?

The two-level speech theory, although it afforded the Court a statesmanlike way around a dilemma, seems difficult to accept as doctrine. It is perhaps understandable in the context of *Chaplinsky,* where the speech in question is nothing more complex than the utterance "son of a bitch," said rapidly. In connection with libel, as in *Beauharnais,* or obscenity, as in *Roth,* however, it seems a strained effort to trap a problem. At one level there are communications which, even though odious to the majority opinion of the day, even though expressive of the thought we hate, are entitled to be measured against the clear-and-present-danger criterion. At another level are communications apparently so worthless as not to require any extensive judicial effort to determine whether they can be prohibited. There is to be freedom for the thought we hate, but not for the candor we deplore. The doctrinal apparatus is thus quite intricate. In determining the constitutionality of any ban on a communication, the first question is whether it belongs to a category that has any social utility. If it does not, it may be banned. If it does, there is a further question of measuring the clarity and proximity and gravity of any danger from it. It is thus apparent that the issue of social utility of a communication has become as crucial a part of our theory as the issue of its danger. * * * Neither in *Beauharnais* nor in *Roth* has the Court spoken at any length about the concept of social utility. It has confined itself on each occasion to the historical point that these categories—libel and obscenity—have long been regarded as worthless speech subject to prohibition. But, if history alone is to be the guide, the same inference might better be drawn about the utility of revolutionary speech.

It is at this point that Mr. Justice Brennan's phrasing of "the dispositive question" bears strange fruit. It seems hardly fair to ask: what is the social utility of obscenity? Rather the question is: what is the social utility of excessively candid and explicit discussions of sex? Here too there is the problem of the mixed utterance. The well-known sexual passages in *Lady Chatterley's Lover* are integral to the possibly strange but indubitably serious view of English postwar life that Lawrence wished to portray. And even if they were not a part of a complex whole—which will be destroyed with them if the novel is held obscene, just as the critical premises of the revolutionary would disappear—they would appear to have some value in their own right as a lyrical view of the potential for warmth, tenderness, and vitality of a fully satisfactory sexual experience. The Court's formula thus seems to have oversimplified the problem. The Court may understand obscenity, but it does not seem to understand sex.

The oversimplification is irritating because the Court appeared unaware, as it could not have been, of the distinguished items that have been held obscene. A legal term gets its meaning from the construction put on it by the courts, and the Court's logic thus appears to lead to the conclusion that, in its view, such books as *Lady Chatterley's Lover, Memoirs of Hecate County,* and *Strange Fruit,* all of which have been held obscene by distinguished courts, are in the category of speech which is "utterly without redeeming social importance."

I do not think the Court meant to say this—to say, for example, that *Memoirs of Hecate County* is worthless. There is an obvious way to avoid the apparent *reductio ad absurdum.* Presumably, in the future, the Court will take it. For everything now depends on what is meant by obscene. If the Court's formula is to make any sense, it must place a heavy burden on the definition of obscenity. Obscenity must be so defined as to save any serious, complex piece of writing or art, regardless of the unconventionality of its candor. If the obscene is constitutionally subject to ban because it is worthless, it must follow that the obscene can include only that which is worthless. This approach makes sense. So-called hard-core pornography involves discussions of sex which are not integral parts of anything else. In themselves, they are, at best, fantasies of sexual prowess and response unrelated to the serious human concern that moved Lawrence and, at worst, a degrading, hostile, alien view of the sexual experience. If the socially worthless criterion is taken seriously, the *Roth* opinion may have made a major advance in liberating literature and art from the shadow of the censor.

FREDERICK SCHAUER, SPEECH AND "SPEECH"— OBSCENITY AND "OBSCENITY": AN EXERCISE IN THE INTERPRETATION OF CONSTITUTIONAL LANGUAGE

67 Geo.L.J. 899, 922–923 (1979).

Th[e] refusal to treat pornography as speech is grounded in the assumption that the prototypical pornographic item on closer analysis shares more of the characteristics of sexual activity than of the communicative process. The pornographic item is in a real sense a sexual surrogate. It takes pictorial or linguistic form only because some individuals achieve sexual gratification by those means. Imagine a person going to a house of prostitution, and, in accord with his or her particular sexual preferences, requesting that two prostitutes engage in sexual activity with each other while he becomes aroused. Having achieved sexual satisfaction in this manner, he pays his money and leaves, never having touched either of the prostitutes. Imagine an individual who asks that a leather-clad prostitute crack a whip within an inch of his ear. Are these free speech cases? Hardly. Despite the fact that eyes and ears are used, these incidents are no more cognitive than any other experience with a prostitute. It is essentially a physical activity, the lack of actual contact notwithstanding. If the above examples are not free speech cases, is there any real difference between the same activity when presented on film rather than in the flesh? Consider further rubber, plastic, or leather sex aids. It is hard to find any free speech aspects in their sale or use. If pornography is viewed merely as a type of aid to sexual satisfaction, any distinction between pornography and so-called "rubber products" is meaningless. The mere fact that in pornography the stimulating experience is initiated by visual rather than tactile means is irrelevant if every other aspect of the experience is the same. Neither means constitutes communication in the cognitive sense. Pornography involves neither a communicator nor an object of the communication. The purveyor of the pornography is in the business solely of providing sexual pleasure; it is unrealistic to presume that he is anything but indifferent to the method by which pleasure is provided and profit secured. Similarly, there is no reason to believe that the recipient desires anything other than sexual stimulation. Hardcore pornography, then, is distinguished by its similarity in all relevant respects to a wide range of other sexual experiences.

The point is that the use of pornography may be treated conceptually as a purely physical rather than mental experience. This is of course an oversimplification. Physical sensations, including sexual arousal, have mental elements. Is pain physical or mental? Some of both, surely. The same is true of physical attributes of sexuality. A helpful illustration of this phenomenon is a spectrum, or a range—the intellectual predominates one extreme and the physical predominates the other. At the physical extreme of the spectrum the conduct possesses so few mental attributes that it has none of the characteristics of the intellectual process constituting the core of the constitutional definition of speech.

CATHARINE MACKINNON, PORNOGRAPHY, CIVIL RIGHTS AND SPEECH

20 Harv.Civ.Rts.—Civ.Lib.L.Rev. 1, 16–21, 24–26, 47–54, 65 (1985).

In pornography, there it is, in one place, all of the abuses that women had to struggle so long even to begin to articulate, all the *unspeakable* abuse: the rape, the battery, the sexual harassment, the prostitution, and the sexual abuse of children. Only in the pornography it is called something else: sex, sex, sex, sex, and sex, respectively. Pornography sexualizes rape, battery, sexual harassment, prostitution, and child sexual abuse; it thereby celebrates, promotes, authorizes, and legitimizes them. More generally, it eroticizes the dominance and submission that is the dynamic common to them all. It makes hierarchy sexy and calls that "the truth about sex" or just a mirror of reality. Through this process, pornography constructs what a woman is as what men want from sex. This is what the pornography means.   * * *

Pornography constructs what a woman is in terms of its view of what men want sexually, such that acts of rape, battery, sexual harassment, prostitution, and sexual abuse of children become acts of sexual equality. Pornography's world of equality is a harmonious and balanced place. Men and women are perfectly complementary and perfectly bipolar. Women's desire to be fucked by men is equal to men's desire to fuck women. All the ways men love to take and violate women, women love to be taken and violated. The women who most love this are most men's equals, the most liberated; the most participatory child is the most grown-up, the most equal to an adult. Their consent merely expresses or ratifies these preexisting facts.

The content of pornography is one thing. There, women substantively desire dispossession and cruelty. We desperately want to be bound, battered, tortured, humiliated, and killed. Or, to be fair to the soft core, merely taken and used. This is erotic to the male point of view. Subjection itself with self-determination ecstatically relinquished is the content of women's sexual desire and desirability. Women are there to be violated and possessed, men to violate and possess us either on screen or by camera or pen on behalf of the consumer. On a simple descriptive level, the inequality of hierarchy, of which gender is the primary one, seems necessary for the sexual arousal to work. Other added inequalities identify various pornographic genres or sub-themes, although they are always added through gender: age, disability, homosexuality, animals, objects, race (including anti-semitism), and so on. Gender is never irrelevant.

What pornography *does* goes beyond its content: It eroticizes hierarchy, it sexualizes inequality. It makes dominance and submission sex. Inequality is its central dynamic; the illusion of freedom coming together with the reality of force is central to its working. Perhaps because this is a bourgeois culture, the victim must look free, appear to be freely acting. Choice is how she got there. Willing is what she is when she is being equal. It seems equally important that then and there she actually be forced and that forcing be communicated on some level, even if only through still photos of her in postures of receptivity and access, available for penetration. Pornography in this view is a form of forced sex, a practice of sexual politics, an institution of gender inequality.

From this perspective, pornography is neither harmless fantasy nor a corrupt and confused misrepresentation of an otherwise natural and healthy sexual situation. It institutionalizes the sexuality of male supremacy, fusing the erotization of dominance and submission with the social construction of male and female. To the extent that gender is sexual, pornography is part of constituting the meaning of that sexuality. Men treat women as who they see women as being. Pornography constructs who that is. Men's power over women means that the way men see women defines who women can be. Pornography is that way. Pornography is not imagery in some relation to a reality elsewhere constructed. It is not a distortion, reflection, projection, expression, fantasy, representation, or symbol either. It is a sexual reality.

* * *

In this approach, the experience of the (overwhelmingly) male audiences who consume pornography is therefore not fantasy or simulation or catharsis but sexual reality, the level of reality on which sex itself largely operates. Understanding this dimension of the problem does not require noticing that pornography models are real women to whom, in most cases, something real is being done; nor does it even require inquiring into the systematic infliction of pornography and its sexuality upon women, although it helps. The way in which the pornography itself provides what those who consume it want matters. Pornography *participates* in its audience's eroticism through creating an accessible sexual object, the possession and consumption of which *is* male sexuality, as socially constructed; to be consumed and possessed as which, *is* female sexuality, as socially constructed; and pornography is a process that constructs it that way.

The object world is constructed according to how it looks with respect to its possible uses. Pornography defines women by how we look according to how we can be sexually used. Pornography codes how to look at women, so you know what you can do with one when you see one. Gender is an assignment made visually, both originally and in everyday life. A sex object is defined on the basis of its looks, in terms of its usability for sexual pleasure, such that both the looking—the quality of the gaze, including its point of view—and the definition according to use become eroticized as part of the sex itself. This is what the feminist concept "sex object" means. In this sense, sex in life is no less mediated than it is in art. One could say men have sex with *their image* of a woman. It is not that life and art imitate each other; in this sexuality, they *are* each other.

To give a set of rough epistemological translations, to defend pornography as consistent with the equality of the sexes is to defend the subordination of women to men as sexual equality. What in the pornographic view is love and romance looks a great deal like hatred and torture to the feminist. Pleasure and eroticism become violation. Desire appears as lust for dominance and submission. The vulnerability of women's projected sexual availability, that acting we are allowed (i.e. asking to be acted upon), is victimization. Play conforms to scripted roles. Fantasy expresses ideology, is not exempt from it. Admiration of natural physical beauty becomes objectification. Harmlessness becomes harm. Pornography is a harm of male supremacy made difficult to see because of its pervasiveness, potency, and, principally, because of its success in making the world a pornographic place. Specifically, its harm cannot be discerned, and will not be addressed, if viewed and approached neutrally, because it *is* so much of "what is." In other words, to the extent pornography succeeds in constructing social reality, it becomes invisible as harm. If we live in a world that pornography creates through the power of men in a male dominated situation the issue is not what the harm of pornography is, but how that harm is to become visible.

* * *

Obscenity, in this light, is a moral idea; an idea about judgments of good and bad. Pornography, by contrast, is a political practice, a practice of power and powerlessness. Obscenity is ideational and abstract; pornography is concrete and substantive. The two concepts represent two entirely different things. Nudity, excess of candor, arousal or excitement, prurient appeal, illegality of the acts depicted, and unnaturalness or perversion are all qualities that bother obscenity law when sex is depicted or portrayed. Sex forced on real women so that it can be sold at a profit to be forced on other real women; women's bodies trussed and maimed and raped and made into things to be hurt and obtained and accessed and this presented as the nature of women in a way that is acted on and acted out over and over; the coercion that is visible and the coercion that has become invisible—this and more bothers feminists about pornography. Obscenity as such probably does little harm. Pornography is integral to attitudes and behaviors of violence and discrimination which define the treatment and status of half the population.

* * *

At the request of the city of Minneapolis, Andrea Dworkin and I conceived and designed a local human rights ordinance in accordance with our approach to the pornography issue. We define pornography as a practice of sex discrimination, a violation of women's civil rights, the opposite of sexual equality. Its point is to hold accountable, to those who are injured, those who profit from and benefit from that injury. It means that women's injury—our damage, our pain, our enforced inferiority—should outweigh their pleasure and their profits, or sex equality is meaningless.

We define pornography as the graphic sexually explicit subordination of women through pictures or words that also includes women dehumanized as sexual objects, things, or commodities, enjoying pain or humiliation or rape, being tied up, cut up, mutilated, bruised, or physically hurt, in postures of sexual submission or servility or display, reduced to body parts, penetrated by objects or animals, or presented in scenarios of degradation, injury, torture, shown as filthy or inferior, bleeding, bruised, or hurt in a context that makes these conditions sexual. Erotica, defined by distinction as not this, might be sexually explicit materials premised on equality. We also provide that the use of men, children or transsexuals in the place of women is pornography. The definition is substantive in that it is sex-specific, but it covers everyone in a sex-specific way, so is gender neutral in overall design.

To define pornography as a practice of sex discrimination combines a mode of portrayal that has a legal history—the sexually explicit—with an active term central to the inequality of the sexes—subordination. Among other things, subordination means to be placed in a position of inferiority or loss of power, or to be demeaned or denigrated. To be someone's subordinate is the opposite of being their equal. The definition does not include all sexually explicit depictions *of* the subordination of women. That is not what it says. It says, this which *does* that: the sexually explicit which subordinates women. To these active terms to capture what the pornography *does,* the definition adds a list of what it must also contain. This list, from our analysis, is an exhaustive description of what must be in the pornography for it to do what it does behaviorally. Each item in the definition is supported by experimental, testimonial, social, and clinical evidence. We made a legislative choice to be exhaustive and specific and concrete rather than conceptual and general, to minimize problems of chilling effect, making it hard to guess wrong, thus making self-censorship less likely, but encouraging (to use a phrase from discrimination law) voluntary compliance, knowing that if something turns up that is not on the list, the law will not be expansively interpreted.

* * *

Although police have known it for years, reported cases are increasingly noting the causal role of pornography in some sexual abuse. In a recent Minnesota case, a fourteen-year-old girl on a bicycle was stopped with a knife and forced into a car. Her hands were tied with a belt, she was pushed to the floor and covered with a blanket. The knife was then used to cut off her clothes, and fingers and a knife were inserted into her vagina. Then the man had her dress, drove her to a gravel pit, ordered her to stick a safety pin into the nipple of her left breast, and forced her to ask him to hit her. After hitting her, he forced her to commit fellatio and to submit to anal penetration, and made her use a cigarette to burn herself on her breast and near her pubic area. Then he defecated and urinated on her face, forced her to ingest some of the excrement and urine and made her urinate into a cup and drink it. He took a string from her blouse and choked her to the point of unconsciousness, leaving burn marks on her neck, and after cutting her with his knife in a couple of places, drove her back to where he had gotten her and let her go. The books that were found with this man were: *Violent Stories of Kinky Humiliation, Violent Stories of Dominance and Submission*—you think feminists made up these words?—*Bizarre Sex Crimes, Shamed Victims,* and *Water Sports Fetish, Enemas and Golden Showers.* The Minnesota Supreme Court said "It appears that in committing these various acts, the defendant was giving life to some stories he had read in various pornographic books." [108]

* * *

Now I'm going to talk about causality in its narrowest sense.[115] Recent experimental research on pornography [116] shows that the materials covered by our definition cause measurable harm to women through increasing men's attitudes and behaviors of discrimination in both violent and nonviolent forms. Exposure to some of the pornography in our definition increases normal men's immediately subsequent willingness to aggress against women under laboratory conditions.[117] It makes normal men more closely resemble convicted rapists attitudinally, although as a group they don't look all that different from them to start with.[118] It also significantly increases attitudinal measures known to

108. State v. Herberg, 324 N.W.2d 346, 347 (Minn.1982).

115. Positivistic causality—linear, exclusive, unidirectional—has become the implicit standard for the validity of connection between pornography and harm. This standard requires the kind of control that can only be achieved, if at all, in laboratory settings. When it is then found there, as it has been, that pornography causes harm, *see infra* note 117, the objection is heard that laboratory settings are artificial. But their artificiality is what makes a conclusion about causality possible under this causal model. In real-world settings, a relation of linear consequentiality between pornography and harm is seldom sufficiently isolable or uncontaminated—indeed, seldom even sufficiently separable, the pornography and its impact being as pervasive and intertwined as they are—to satisfy this standard. I am suggesting that the positivistic model of causation may be inappropriate to the social reality of pornography. *See also* W. Heisenberg, The Physical Principles of the Quantum Theory 63 (1930); Horwitz, *The Doctrine of Objective Causation,* in The Politics of Law 201 (D. Kairys ed. 1982).

116. Major sources are: Pornography and Sexual Aggression, [113 (N. Malamuth and E. Donnerstein eds. 1984)]; D. Zillmann, Connections Between Sex and Aggression (1984); Donnerstein & Berkowitz, *Victim Reactions in Aggressive Erotic Films as a Factor in Violence Against Women,* 41 J. Personality & Soc. Psychology 710–24 (1981); Malamuth & Check, *The Effects of Mass Media Exposure on Acceptance of Violence Against Women: A Field Experiment,* 15 J. Research Personality 436–46 (1981); Malamuth & Donnerstein, *The Effects of Aggressive Pornographic Mass Media Sti-*

muli, 15 Advances Experimental Soc. Psychology 103 (1982); Russell, *Pornography and Violence: What Does the New Research Say?,* in Take Back the Night 216 (L. Lederer ed. 1983); Zillmann & Bryant, *Pornography, Sexual Callousness, and the Trivialization of Rape,* 32 J.Com. 16–18 (1982) * * *.

117. In addition to the references listed *supra* note 116, see: Donnerstein & Hallam, *The Facilitating Effects of Erotica on Aggression Toward Females,* J. Personality & Soc. Psychology 1270 (1978); Geen, Stonner & Shope, *The Facilitation of Aggression by Aggression: Evidences Against the Catharsis Hypothesis,* 31 J. Personality & Soc. Psychology 721 (1975); Zapolsky & Zillmann, *The Effect of Soft–Core and Hard–Core Erotica on Provoked and Unprovoked Hostile Behavior,* 17 J. Sex Research 319 (1981); Zillmann, Hoyt & Day, *Strength and Duration of the Effect of Aggressive, Violent, and Erotic Communications on Subsequent Aggressive Behavior,* 1 Com. Research 286 (1974). *See also* Malamuth, *Factors Associated with Rape as Predictors of Laboratory Aggression Against Women,* 45 J. Personality & Soc. Psychology 432 (1983) (valid relation between factors associated with real-world aggression against women and laboratory aggression).

118. Malamuth & Check, *Penile Tumescence and Perceptual Responses to Rape as a Function of Victim's Perceived Reactions,* 10 J. Applied Soc. Psychology 528 (1980); Malamuth, Haber & Feshbach, *Testing Hypotheses Regarding Rape: Exposure to Sexual Violence, Sex Difference, and the "Normality" of Rapists,* 14 J. Research Personality 121 (1980). The lack of distinction between convicted rapists and control groups may be the reason many people have concluded that pornography does not do any-

correlate with rape and self-reports of aggressive acts, measures such as hostility toward women, propensity to rape, condoning rape, and predicting that one would rape or force sex on a woman if one knew one would not get caught. This latter measure, by the way, begins with rape at about a third of all men and moves to half with "forced sex."

* * *

For those of you who still think pornography is only an idea, consider the possibility that obscenity law got one thing right. Pornography is more act-like than thought-like. The fact that pornography, in a feminist view, furthers the idea of the sexual inferiority of women, which is a political idea, doesn't make the pornography itself into a political idea. One can express the idea a practice embodies. That does not make that practice into an idea. Segregation expresses the idea of the inferiority of one group to another on the basis of race. That does not make segregation an idea. A sign that says "Whites Only" is only words. Is it therefore protected by the first amendment? Is it not an act, a practice, of segregation because of the inseparability of what it means from what it does? *Law* is only words.

The issue here is whether the fact that the central link in the cycle of abuse that I have connected is words and pictures will immunize that entire cycle, about which we cannot do anything without doing something about the pornography.

CASS R. SUNSTEIN, PORNOGRAPHY AND THE FIRST AMENDMENT

1986 Duke L.J. 589, 591–93, 595, 602–08.

Defining pornography is notoriously difficult; indeed, the difficulty of definition is a familiar problem in any attempt to design acceptable regulation. I will argue, however, that a definition can be framed so as to include only properly regulable materials. In short, regulable pornography must (a) be sexually explicit, (b) depict women as enjoying or deserving some form of physical abuse, and (c) have the purpose and effect of producing sexual arousal.

This definition draws on feminist approaches to the problem of pornography and represents a departure from current law, which is directed at "obscenity." Though built-in ambiguities are inevitable in light of the limitations of language, the basic concept should not be obscure. The central concern is that pornography both sexualizes vio-

thing. When all the unreported, undetected, not to mention unconscious or potential rapists in the control groups are considered, this conclusion stops being mysterious. * * * *See also* Abel, Becker & Skinner, *Aggressive Behavior and Sex,* 3 Psychiatric Clinics North America 133, 140 (1980) (fewer than 5% of rapists are psychotic while raping); Malamuth, *Rape Proclivity Among Males,* 37 J.Soc. Issues 4 (1981); Malamuth & Check, *The Effects of Mass Media Exposure on Acceptance of Violence Against Women: A Field Experiment,* 15 J. Research Personality 4 (1981); Malamuth, Heim & Feshbach, *Sexual Responsiveness of College Students to Rape Depictions: Inhibitory and Disinhibitory Effects,* 38 Soc. Psychology 399 (1980).

lence and defines women as sexually subordinate to men. Pornographic materials feature rape, explicitly or implicitly, as a fundamental theme. This definition differs from the approach urged by the Attorney General's Commission on Pornography, which operated within conventional obscenity law. The definition is somewhat narrower than the one suggested by the Indianapolis ordinance, which created liability for graphic, sexually explicit subordination of women as "sexual objects." The approach proposed here excludes sexually explicit materials that do not sexualize violence against women, and it ties the definition closely to the principal harms caused by pornography. The definition, therefore, excludes the vast range of materials that are not sexually explicit but that do contain implicit rape themes. The requirement of sexual explicitness is thus a means of confining the definition. Part of the definition, moreover, requires that the appeal of the materials be noncognitive—hence the requirement that the purpose and effect be to produce sexual arousal.

Examples of pornography as defined here can be found in such magazines as *Hustler* and numerous "adult" movies. It is difficult to capture the nature of genuine pornography without presenting examples. One such example is the "Beaver Hunters" advertisement in *Hustler,* which shows a nude woman strapped to the top of a car; the copy below the photograph states that the woman would be "stuffed and mounted" as soon as the "hunters" got her home. But pornographic materials cannot always be easily characterized as such. There is a continuum from the most violent forms of pornography to materials that to some degree sexualize violence but cause little harm and are not low-value speech. Many popular movies and novels that combine eroticism and domination should be protected under the first amendment. A common plot in both books and films involves a romantic encounter in which a woman initially resists a forcible sexual assault and then submits. Although harmful, such materials do not fall within the definition of pornography used here. Of course, there will be difficult intermediate cases; but as with other forms of expression not entitled to full first amendment protection, the fact that the relevant class is difficult to define is not itself a sufficient reason to proscribe government regulation.

An approach directed at pornography differs in important respects from one directed at obscenity. The term "obscenity" refers to indecency and filth; the term pornography—derived from the Greek word for "writing about whores"—refers to materials that treat women as prostitutes and that focus on the role of women in providing sexual pleasure to men. The underlying rationale for regulation therefore differs depending on the definition involved, and the coverage of regulation will differ somewhat as well. In contrast to the vague basis of the obscenity doctrine, the reasoning behind antipornography legislation is found in three categories of concrete, gender-related harms: harms to those who participate in the production of pornography, harms to the victims of sex crimes that would not have been committed in the absence of pornography, and harms to society through social conditioning that fosters discrimination and other unlawful activities.

* * *

Although the harms generated by pornography are serious, they are insufficient, standing alone, to justify regulation under the usual standards applied to political speech. After *Brandenburg v. Ohio*, speech— not including obscenity—cannot be regulated because of the harm it produces unless it is shown that the speech is directed to produce harm that is both imminent and extremely likely to occur. Moreover, the Court has rejected the notion that this showing can be made by linking a class of harm with a class of speech; it is necessary to connect particular harms to particular speech. These doctrinal conclusions will not be questioned here, although they do have powerful adverse implications for antipornography legislation. If current standards are applied, a particular pornographic film or magazine might be beyond regulation unless the harms that result from the particular material are imminent, intended, and likely to occur. Demonstrating this, of course, will be hard to do.

But acceptance of these doctrinal conclusions does not resolve the question of the constitutionality of antipornography regulation. The Court has drawn a distinction between speech that may be banned only on the basis of an extremely powerful showing of government interest, and speech that may be regulated on the basis of a far less powerful demonstration of harm. Commercial speech, labor speech, and possibly group libel, for example, fall within the category of "low-value" speech. Whether particular speech falls within the low-value category cannot be determined by a precise test, and under any standards there will be difficult intermediate cases. But in determining whether speech qualifies as low-value, the cases suggest that four factors are relevant.

First, the speech must be far afield from the central concern of the first amendment, which, broadly speaking, is effective popular control of public affairs. Speech that concerns governmental processes is entitled to the highest level of protection; speech that has little or nothing to do with public affairs may be accorded less protection. Second, a distinction is drawn between cognitive and noncognitive aspects of speech. Speech that has purely noncognitive appeal will be entitled to less constitutional protection. Third, the purpose of the speaker is relevant: if the speaker is seeking to communicate a message, he will be treated more favorably than if he is not. Fourth, the various classes of low-value speech reflect judgments that in certain areas, government is unlikely to be acting for constitutionally impermissible reasons or producing constitutionally troublesome harms. In the cases of commercial speech, private libel, and fighting words, for example, government regulation is particularly likely to be based on legitimate reasons. Judicial scrutiny is therefore more deferential in these areas.

The exclusion of obscene materials from first amendment protection, in contrast, stems largely from an act of definition. Obscene materials, to the Court, do not count as "speech" within the meaning of the first amendment. But this definitional distinction can be viewed as reflecting the same considerations that define the low-value speech category. If the materials are defined narrowly, only nonpolitical and noncognitive material will be prohibited. The limitation of obscenity law to speech not having "serious literary, artistic, political, or scientific value" fits comfortably with this understanding.

This four-factor analysis is, of course, controversial. The distinction between political and nonpolitical speech, for example, is often unclear and may ultimately depend on the political view of the decisionmaker. The difficulty inherent in such line drawing, moreover, may support abandoning any attempt to do so. Perhaps more importantly, distinctions between cognitive and emotive aspects of speech are thin and in some respects pernicious. Furthermore, approaches based on the purpose of the speaker are troublesome for familiar reasons. Finally, freedom of speech might be thought to promote self-realization and, on that ground, attempts to make distinctions among categories of speech might be questioned.

But it would be difficult to imagine a sensible system of free expression that did not distinguish among categories of speech in accordance with their importance to the underlying purposes of the free speech guarantee. A system that granted absolute protection to speech would be unduly mechanical, treading unjustifiably on important values and goals: consider laws forbidding threats, bribes, misleading commercial speech, and conspiracies. Any system that recognizes the need for some regulation but does not draw lines could be driven to deny full protection to speech that merits it—because the burden of justification imposed on the government would have to be lightened in order to allow regulation of, for example, commercial speech, conspiracies, and private libel. By hypothesis, that lighter burden would have to be extended across-the-board. The alternative would be to apply the standards for political speech to all speech, and thus to require the government to meet a test so stringent as to preclude most forms of regulation that are currently accepted. In these circumstances the most likely outcome would be that judgments about low-value would be made tacitly, and the articulated rationales for decisions would fail to reflect all the factors actually considered relevant by the court.

* * *

Under this approach, or any plausible variation, regulation of pornography need not be justified according to standards applicable to political speech. The effect and intent of pornography, as it is defined here, are to produce sexual arousal, not in any sense to affect the course of self-government. Though comprised of words and pictures, pornography does not have the special properties that single out speech for special protection; it is more akin to a sexual aid than a communicative expression. In terms of the distinctions made among classes of speech, pornography is low-value speech not entitled to the same degree of protection accorded other forms of speech.

* * *

These considerations suggest a conventional, two-stage argument for the regulation of pornography. First, pornography is entitled to only a lower level of first amendment solicitude. Under any standard, pornography is far afield from the kind of speech conventionally protected by the first amendment. Second, the harms produced by pornographic materials are sufficient to justify regulation. Admittedly, there will be difficult intermediate cases and analogies that test the persuasiveness and reach of the argument. The crucial point, however, is that traditional first amendment doctrine furnishes the basis for an argument in favor of restricting pornography[.]

FRANK I. MICHELMAN, CONCEPTIONS OF DEMOCRACY IN AMERICAN CONSTITUTIONAL ARGUMENT: THE CASE OF PORNOGRAPHY REGULATION

56 Tenn.L.Rev. 291, 302–304, 307, 309–310, 313–315, 318 (1989).

[In this article Michelman focuses on *American Booksellers Association v. Hudnut,*[a] where the Seventh Circuit held unconstitutional an Indianapolis ordinance that would have made production and distribution of pornography actionable as forms of sex discrimination. The opinion was written by Judge Frank Easterbrook.]

Fully unpacked, Judge Easterbrook's argument runs this way:

A good society is a free society. A free society is open to ideological challenge by cultural "outsiders." Political speech is a serviceable and (by comparison with alternatives) benign instrumentality of ideological challenge. Governments tend to act on behalf of the ideological powers that be. Hence, governmental restrictions on political speech are in general a social evil. Such restrictions are especially constitutionally indefensible when they select utterances for suppression on the basis of message content or viewpoint, because such selectivity can have no other justifying purpose than the illicit one of "thought control." Pornography is political expression in that it promulgates a certain view of women's natures and thus of women's appropriate relations and treatment in society; the Indianapolis ordinance is precisely designed to suppress that particular view by censoring pornography; therefore the Indianapolis ordinance is an instance of both the general social evil (governmental restrictions on political expression) and its particularly obnoxious manifestation (viewpoint-discriminatory suppression)[.]

* * *

a. 771 F.2d 323 (7th Cir.1985), aff'd without opinion, 475 U.S. 1001 (1986).

It is hard to quarrel with this reasoning as far as it goes. No doubt American constitutionalism is committed to the propositions that openness to ideological challenge is a good trait in a society and that governmental suppression of political speech is, for that reason (possibly among others), a prima facie social evil. But these propositions, without more, are insufficient to condemn the Indianapolis antipornography law on the ground of its bad consequences, because they do not yet deal with the possibility—a possibility with which all instrumentalist evaluations of social rules or practices are obliged to deal—of cost-justification. For it is always conceivable that the social evil consequent upon a given species or instance of regulation is outweighed or outranked by social evils consequent upon the absence of that same species or instance. Moreover, it is a highly plausible claim—this, after all, is the point of the Indianapolis ordinance's account, accepted by Judge Easterbrook for the purposes of his opinion, of pornography as a cause of women's subordination and silencing—that precisely this is true in the specific instance of pornography regulation. Yet Judge Easterbrook's opinion never undertakes a direct comparison of the magnitude or rank of the social evils consequent upon regulation with those consequent upon leaving pornography unregulated. Admitting that *privately* wrought suppression and manipulation of political views are not only possible in theory but are an actual consequence of the pornography that the Indianapolis ordinance would suppress, the opinion nevertheless contents itself with explaining how *governmentally* wrought suppression and manipulation are prima facie social evils by reason of their challenge-blocking consequences. At no point does the opinion suggest any reason for believing that the privately wrought suppression and manipulation that the ordinance would avert are, prima facie, fraught with any less potential blockage of critically inspired social change than are the suppression and manipulation that the ordinance would commit.

* * *

The state action idea may well play a crucial, if unspoken, part in leading Judge Easterbrook to conclude in favor of an absolute rule against governmental censorship of private publications, even of private publications that are causative—as pornography is causative, by Judge Easterbrook's own stipulation—of effects fairly describable in the ordinary English of the common-law tradition as deprivations of liberty and denials of equal protection of the laws. It is easily imaginable that Judge Easterbrook, if pressed, would point out that the pornographers whose communicative acts cause these effects are not states. He might say, pointing to the state action doctrine, that the Constitution places silencings and subordinations perpetrated by non-state persons—as opposed to those perpetrated by states—beneath its notice and concern. He might say that the reason why judges do not balance the evils of private subversions of liberty and equal protection against the evils of censorious governmental countermeasures is that the Constitution, through the state action doctrine, in effect tells them not to.

Perhaps all this seems to reflect a remarkably devil-may-care stance towards privately wrought subversions of liberty and equal protection. Just how clearly, you may wonder, does the Constitution dictate it? Doubtless one *can* trace the state action doctrine to the language of the fourteenth amendment, by emphasizing the amendment's grammar and vocabulary in designating the agents and the victims, respectively, of the deprivations and denials it names and prohibits. The prohibition does indeed run in terms against deprivations and denials whose perpetrators are "states" and whose sufferers are "persons." And yet if we start with the problem rather than with the text, we encounter uncertainty about extracting from the text a strict rule against judicial balancing of the evils of privately wrought deprivations of liberty against the deprivations of liberty wrought by state regulations designed to avert those privately wrought deprivations.

By "the problem" I mean the one typified by the *Booksellers* case. Given Judge Easterbrook's acceptance of the ordinance's stated grounds for condemning pornography, *Booksellers* is a case in which the practical alternative to direct regulatory infringement of the pornographers' interests in liberty and equal protection is infringement, by the unregulated creation and publication of pornography, of many women's claims to liberty and equal protection. Given such a case, it is anything but obvious that the state by choosing the regulatory alternative commits— much less commits without due process of law—the forbidden deprivation or denial. Quite to the contrary: so long as the state can fairly support a judgment that the infringements of liberty and equal protection consequent upon its choice for regulation of pornography are, in some appropriate sense, lesser than the infringements of liberty and equal protection consequent upon the opposite choice to leave pornography unregulated, that pro-regulation choice by the state would seem to come as close as humanly possible to good-faith compliance with the constitutional mandate.

Thus, by starting with the problem rather than with the text, we find that judicial rejection of balancing in favor of an absolute, blind rule against state regulation is as plausibly a defiance as it is a vindication of constitutional authority. We arrive at uncertainty. The only way to resolve the uncertainty seems to lie, as before, in resort by the judge to interpretive charity. The argument in favor of Judge Easterbrook's resolution must be that to read the Constitution as prescribing judicial balancing for a case like *Booksellers* would so plainly and grievously run against reason—substantive political-moral practical reason—that such a reading fairly ought to be rejected in favor of strict judicial enforcement of an absolute rule against governmental censorship. The argument, to be more specific, must be that it would have been unreasonable for our Constitution's authors not to notice that there is some crucial and drastic difference between the powers of states and the powers of persons (not states) to harm our interests in liberty and equal protection, such that subversions of liberty and equality interests by exercises of state power are much more to be feared by Americans—categorically more to be feared—than subversions of those interests by private power. For convenience, let us call this idea—that state power is categorically more dangerous to liberty and equal protection than private or market power—the public-power/private-power distinction (or public-private distinction for short). The public-private distinction therefore is an element required for the completion of Judge Easterbrook's argument in *Booksellers,* whether we approach that argument initially as one of reason or as one of authority.

* * *

The conclusion that I mean to suggest is a simple one. We are occupied here with such questions as: Which is worse—to let people silence pornographers (if they can succeed in doing so under the rules) by the public, state-based means of majoritarian lawmaking, or to let them do it (again, insofar as they can succeed by lawful means) by the private, market-based means of boycott? Or again: Which is worse—to leave pornographers subject to the vicissitudes of silencing by the lawmaking activities of political majorities, or to leave women subject to the vicissitudes of silencing by the private publishing activities of pornographers?

When we raise such questions, a categorical distinction between the dangers of private action and the dangers of state action cannot deliver reliable answers. It cannot do so because our actual experiences of political, economic, and social life are too messy, too mixed, and too ambiguous to support any such categorical, wholesale answer. Those experiences teach that there really is such a thing as the political tyranny of the majority; but they also teach that there really is such a thing as the despotism of so-called private, social, or market power. Competition in a market can be a good antidote or alternative to monolithic dictatorship by majoritarian law, but so can regulatory law be a good antidote or alternative to monopolistic or egoistic oppression in a market. We simply cannot say, a priori, that either avenue of social action—state or market—is categorically safer than the other.

* * *

A confirmed optimist about the deliberative character of popular political action would tend to see the regulatory alternative to private or market oppression as at least somewhat more likely to be considerate of all the interests involved, not least including people's interest in preventing the accretion of totalitarian, citizen-shaping power by any social agency—the government among others. In that respect, deliberative politics would compare favorably with the competitive and self-serving (not to say sometimes impulsive or vindictive) motivations that we must realistically expect of action in an unregulated market. Privately organized boycotts obviously are—however much obliged we may feel to respect them as exercises of liberty—potentially dangerous events, to be regarded with circumspection. So, no doubt, are the regulatory actions of governments. Yet a censorship decision arrived at by a truly deliberative democratic process would seem deserving of a more, not (as the actual state action doctrine has it) a less favorable reception, by virtue of its state-based provenance. The majoritarian political origins of the regulatory action would be treated as a validating factor, not (as under the actual state action doctrine) an invalidating one.

* * *

Taking my modest suggestion seriously would make a judge more receptive to the possibility that the Indianapolis antipornography ordinance just might be constitutional, after all. In order to decide, a judge would have to look. A judge would have to judge. That implication of my suggestion will, I expect, be to some a clear sign of the suggestion's merit and to others a conclusive demonstration of its vice.

FREDERICK SCHAUER, CAUSATION THEORY AND THE CAUSES OF SEXUAL VIOLENCE

1987 Am.B.Found.Res.J. 737, 740–42, 754, 763–770.

[I want to explain] the conclusion in the Report of the Attorney General's Commission on Pornography[3] that "substantial exposure to sexually violent materials as described here bears a causal relationship to antisocial acts of sexual violence and, for some subgroups, to unlawful acts of sexual violence."

* * *

[I will] focus on the category of written, printed, or photographic materials that clearly depict one of three themes: male sexual violence directed against women which is portrayed as desirable, acceptable, or appropriate; male sexual violence directed against women which is portrayed as consistent with the real if unexpressed desires of the women involved (the view that "no" means "yes"); and male violence against women, not necessarily sexual in the specific act of violence (shooting rather than rape, for example), but in which the violence is seen as spurred by sexual desires or seen as a source of male sexual satisfaction. With the exception of sado-masochistic material, which is somewhat more problematic, these three themes comprise the category referred to in the Report as sexually violent materials, or Class I materials.

Three points of clarification about this category are necessary. First, the category is not defined in terms of sexual explicitness, and sexual explicitness is not a necessary condition for inclusion in the category. The most sexually unexplicit version of the view that women "really" love being raped would be included, and the most sexually

3. United States Department of Justice, Final Report: Attorney General's Commission on Pornography (Washington: United States Government Printing Office, 1986) (hereinafter referred to as "Report"). * * *

I was one of the eleven commissioners of the Attorney General's Commission on Pornography.

explicit, unconventional but equal, and consensual sexual activities would be excluded. Second, artistic or political content or value cuts across the distinction between this category and others, and thus the presence of value—artistic, political, or otherwise—does not exclude an item from the category. An artistic and literary presentation of the view that women who are raped in fact come to love it, as in some scenes in *Dr. Zhivago,* is still included. Conversely, the absence of what would be considered by most people to be artistic value, as in many of the items commonly referred to as "loops," is insufficient to justify inclusion in the category. Third, sexual violence is defined to include any sexual activity, whether legally defined as "rape" or not, that is coercively committed by the use or threat of physical force. I find this definition a trifle narrow, because I would ideally want to include *coercive* sexuality that is not physically violent, as when a supervisor threatens firing or a teacher threatens a bad grade or a negative recommendation if the employee or student does not satisfy the sexual desires of the supervisor or teacher. Nevertheless, for my purposes here, I will minimize boundary problems by sticking to physical coercion and exclude coercion that is a consequence of economic or other non-physical power.

As a final preliminary clarification, I want to define the *acts* of sexual violence in a way that largely tracks the definition of *depictions* of sexual violence. Thus, sexual violence is here defined to include rape, attempted rape, sexual acts that are not rape but involve actual or threatened physical coercion, attempted sexual acts involving actual or threatened physical coercion, and actual or attempted acts of nonsexual physical violence inspired by a search for sexual fulfillment. Again, this definition sacrifices realistic breadth on the altar of precision. One could include not only various forms of economic coercion and various forms of non-physical use of institutional power such as that of teacher over student and supervisor over employee, but numerous other forms of sexual harassment and sex discrimination. But again, so that boundary disputes do not deflect from my central point, I will limit what I say to sexual violence as I have just defined it.

With these definitions and clarifications in place, we can then consider the central hypothesis. Do depictions of sexual violence, as here defined, bear a causal relationship to acts of sexual violence, as here defined? The answer to this question, in turn, hinges on what it means for a causal relationship to exist.

* * *

The conception * * * of causation * * * employed * * * in the Report of the Attorney General's Commission on Pornography [is that of *probabilistic causation.*] For people with some exposure to probability and statistics, and even for those who lack that exposure, probabilistic causation is straightforward and simple. Under a probabilistic account of causation, a causal relationship exists, *for types or classes,* insofar as the putative cause increases the incidence of the effect, and a causal relationship exists, in particular cases, insofar as the putative cause increases the probability of the effect.

* * *

Thus, the identification of a causal relationship under a probabilistic account does not entail the conclusion that the identified cause produces the effect in all, a majority, or even a very large proportion of cases. It only entails the conclusion that the identified cause increases the incidence of the effect for a population and increases the likelihood of the effect in an individual case. Moreover, the probabilistic identification of causation does not entail the conclusion that the identified cause is the greatest cause, and it certainly does not entail *anything* about what should be done about the cause. Indeed, its value is, in part, precisely in that it separates the causal inquiry from the policy inquiry in a way that attributive conceptions do not. It enables us to identify provable causal factors in a world of uncertainty and the unknown in a way that deterministic accounts do not.

Employing a probabilistic account of causation, therefore, we follow the account of causation central to the social sciences, and we can then recast the inquiry about sexually violent materials. The question now is whether, in a population in which every member was exposed to sexually violent materials (as here defined), there would be more instances of sexual violence than there would be in a population which had no exposure to such materials? If the answer to that question is in the affirmative, it still might and probably would be the case that sexual violence was produced in many cases in which no exposure to depictions of sexual violence occurred, that the presence of such exposure would produce sexual violence in only a small number of cases, and that such exposure would produce sexual violence only when combined with a myriad of other factors, some known and some unknown. Moreover, many of these other factors would likely be identifiable as even greater causes. But this does not make such a conclusion, if true, valueless, for much the same could be said about the relationship between cigarette smoking and heart disease. If we think about that relationship, we see that there may be value in identifying causal relationships even where the identified cause determines the effect only when combined with other factors, even when the effect follows the cause in only a small percentage of the total of cases, and even when the effect follows the absence of this cause but the presence of another cause in a much higher number of cases. In spite of all this, the value of this kind of inquiry comes from the fact that if the answer to the probabilistic inquiry is in the affirmative even in cases like this, then we can see that elimination of the cause, reduction of the cause, or counteraction of the cause will still reduce the incidence of the effect. That makes the inquiry fruitful, but it does not answer the question. To say that a causal relationship between exposure to depictions of sexual violence and acts of sexual violence will exist if such exposure increases the probability of sexual violence is only, finally, to formulate the question properly. It is not yet to answer it.

* * *

We are now in a position carefully to recast the question. As recast, the question the Report seeks to answer is, "Is there sufficient evidence for a governmental advisory commission without regulative powers to assert that there would be more acts of sexual violence committed by a population every member of which had been extensively exposed to favorable depictions of acts of sexual violence than there would be in a population no member of which had been exposed to favorable depictions of acts of sexual violence?" That is the question to which the Report answers "yes." When put in this fashion, it hardly seems an outrageous conclusion, but it might nevertheless be useful briefly to deal with the evidence in support of that answer.

In part, the evidence comes from controlled experiments of the variety performed by people such as Donnerstein, Malamuth, and others.[58] Of course these experiments [have their shortcomings]. Because they are performed, in general, on college-age males taking psychology courses, there are locality problems with respect to the group tested. Because the experiments measure aggression and attitude changes, sometimes only in the short term, there are also substantial locality problems in moving from the ethically limited results of the experiments to assertions about behavior. As the Report makes exquisitely clear, this move is based on non-scientific evidence, which is not to say it is based on no evidence whatsoever. Moreover, most of the experiments are themselves conducted on quite small samples, thus further lessening the level of confidence we can have in their results.

58. E.g., Edward Donnerstein, *Aggressive Erotica and Violence Against Women,* 39 J. Personality and Social Psychology 269 (1980); Neil Malamuth, *Maggie Heim, and Seymour Feshbach, Sexual Responsiveness of College Students to Rape Depictions: Inhibitory and Disinhibitory Effects,* 38 J. Personality and Social Psychology 399 (1980); Neil Malamuth and James Check, *Penile Tumescence and Perceptual Responses to Rape as a Function of Victim's Perceived Reactions,* 10 J. Applied Social Psychology 528 (1980); Neil Malamuth and James Check, *The Effects of Mass Media Exposure on Acceptance of Violence Against Women: A Field Experiment,* 15 J. Research in Personality 436 (1981); Neil Malamuth, *Rape Fantasies as a Function of Exposure to Violent Sexual Stimuli,* 10 Archives of Sexual Behavior 33 (1981); James Check and Neil Malamuth, *Sex–Role Stereotyping and Reactions to Depictions of Stranger Versus Acquaintance Rape,* 45 J. Personality and Social Psychology 344 (1983); Daniel Linz, Edward Donnerstein, and Steven Penrod, *The Effects of Multiple Exposures to Filmed Violence Against Women,* 34 J. Communication 130 (1984); Neil Malamuth and James Check, *The Effects of Aggressive Pornography on Beliefs in Rape Myths: Individual Differences,* J. Research in Personality (1985); Edward Donnerstein and Daniel Linz, Presentation Paper to the Attorney General's Commission on Pornography, September, 1985; Neil Malamuth, The Mass Media as an Indirect Cause of Sexual Aggression, Presentation Paper to the Attorney General's Commission on Pornography, September, 1985. There is no suggestion that all of the evidence inclines in exactly the same direction. Some experiments, even by the same researchers, would incline somewhat against the causal hypothesis when presented in undifferentiated form. E.g., Joseph Ceniti and Neil Malamuth, *Effects of Repeated Exposure to Sexually Violent or Non–Violent Stimuli on Sexual Arousal to Rape and Non–Rape Depictions,* 22 Behavioral Research Therapy 535 (1984). * * *

The conclusions of all of these experiments nevertheless provide strong evidence for the proposition that for college-age males in experimental settings, exposure to depictions of sexual violence bears a causal relationship to short-term increases in aggressive tendencies towards women and to short-term increases in the attitude of tolerance for sexual violence. This, in turn, provides *some* evidence for the proposition that exposure to depictions of sexual violence bears a causal relationship to acts of sexual violence within a population. Those who have claimed that it does not provide sufficient evidence in itself are, of course, correct, and neither I nor the Report claims otherwise. The scientific evidence provides one or a few bricks. No one I take seriously has claimed it provides the wall, and no one but a small minority of scientists has claimed that the universe of reliable evidence for a proposition is exhausted by the universe of evidence produced in scientific experimentation for that proposition.

Before turning to the question as to where the rest of the bricks come from, I must deal with the issue of spurious causal factors. By definition, the sexually violent materials in the hypothesis under discussion contain both sex and violence. There is, therefore, the risk that * * * either the sex or the violence is causally spurious. Fortunately, the best of the scientific evidence has tested for this possibility. The results of these experiments, which try to exclude the spurious by first isolating sex without the violence and then isolating violence without the sex, indicate most importantly that the violence is clearly not spurious. That is, if the violence disappears and we are testing only for the relationship between sex and sexual violence, there is *no* causal relationship, as the Report expressly announces. But if the sexualization (and not just the sexual explicitness) of the violence is eliminated, the evidence indicates that the strength of the causal relationship diminishes. Thus, although the studies indicate some relationship between nonsexualized violence and attitudes about sexual violence, or aggressive tendencies toward women, this relationship, in probabilistic terms, becomes stronger when the sexualization is added.

* * *

A brief recapitulation for purposes of emphasis and clarity might be useful here. I do not make the claim, nor does the Report, that the category of sexually explicit material bears a causal relationship to acts of sexual violence. I do not make the claim, nor does the Report, that the degree of explicitness is relevant in explaining the causal relationship between depictions of sexual violence and acts of sexual violence. The claim, put accurately, is that sexually violent material, some but not much of which happens to be sexually explicit and some but even less of which is legally obscene, bears a causal relationship, taken probabilistically, to the incidence of sexual violence in this society.

But if * * * the causal relationship is independent of the degree of sexual explicitness, then what does that say about the question of governmental regulation when the First Amendment therefore quite properly precludes regulation of almost the entire area of concern? Some media commentary by critics of the Report notwithstanding, the Report itself never even hints at expanding the area of permissible regulation beyond that permitted by *Miller* and its associated cases, and the Commission rejected a wide variety of specific urgings that it endorse regulation beyond that of *Miller*-tested legal obscenity. Thus, since regulation is properly constrained by existing First Amendment doctrine, it appears to be the case that governmental regulation within that area permitted by current First Amendment doctrine would involve not only strikingly underinclusive regulation but a false cut at the problem as well. * * * But it may be that explicit deregulation is politically implausible. * * *

* * *

As long as deregulation is politically impossible, as long as sexual violence and media endorsement of it remains a tragic problem in this society, and as long as even vastly underinclusive regulation may be a way for government to make an important symbolic statement about that problem, then the best solution within existing constitutional boundaries would be to stop regulating legally obscene material that was not violent, and regulate only legally obscene material that was sexually violent as well. There is no doubt that such a proposal, even as enacted law rather than prosecutorial policy, would be constitutionally permissible under *Miller*. *Miller*, after all, permits and indeed requires states (and the federal government) to specify the particular depictions that are proscribed. There is no reason why this specification could not and should not be limited to the sexually violent.[71] Such a law would probably result in few prosecutions, but that is also the case with current law. And such a law would also not touch the enormous universe of sexually violent materials that are not only not legally obscene but are also not even sexually explicit. Again, that is the case with current law as well. But such a guided constriction of current obscenity law would, entirely within existing constitutional limitations, transform the common conception of obscenity law as something about morality and decency and virtue into something about violence against women and about the sexual subordination of women in this society. This transformation of our understanding of obscenity law would help make a statement about the larger and constitutionally protected universe of sexually violent materials that are not legally obscene, and would help to focus concern on the extent to which sexually violent depictions, without regard to their explicitness, are a contributing factor in the appalling level of sexual violence in this society. And it is that message, about the relationship between sexual violence and the legiti-

---

71. I should add that I have no problem with the *idea* of a civil remedy nor with the real as well as symbolic functions of going after money. To this extent a version of the Indianapolis ordinance that incorporated the third prong of the Miller test might produce a law with exactly the same coverage as the guided construction of obscenity law I discuss here but with even greater symbolic (and real) effects.

mating images of sexual violence that are all around us, that the Report, in the final analysis, is all about.

STEVEN G. GEY, THE APOLOGETICS OF SUPPRESSION: THE REGULATION OF PORNOGRAPHY AS ACT AND IDEA

86 Mich.L.Rev. 1564, 1581, 1585–1587, 1593–1600, 1606–1607, 1610–1611 (1988).

THE CONSERVATIVE CENSORS

* * *

Pornography as Nonspeech

* * *

* * * This theory was originally propounded in a 1967 law review article by John Finnis.[100] More recently, the theory has been adopted and slightly modified by Frederick Schauer.[101] The latter version of the theory is also the conceptual centerpiece of the constitutional law section of the Report of the Attorney General's Commission on Pornography, part 2 of which apparently was written largely by Schauer. There is also some indication that the theory has influenced the Burger Court.

The basic outline of the theory is remarkably simple. The theory turns on the ancient distinction between "reason" and "passion." In the original statement of the theory, Finnis asserted that there was a constitutionally significant difference between "two often competing aspects of the human mind: the intellect or reason and the emotions or passions." * * * Obscenity lacks "redeeming social importance," Finnis writes, "precisely because it pertains, not to the realm of ideas, reason, intellectual content and truth-seeking, but to the realm of passion, desires, cravings and titillation. ... The two constitutional levels of speech, in effect, are defined in terms of two realms of the human mind."

* * *

Obscenity, says Schauer, should be viewed "as essentially a physical rather than a mental stimulus." "Physical stimulus" often entails some tactile element; something physically stimulates by actually touching the body. But Schauer declares that for first amendment purposes there is no difference between hard-core pornography and a rubber or plastic sex aid, because "[n]either means [of stimulation] constitutes communication in the cognitive sense." Thus, "the use of pornography may be treated conceptually as a purely physical rather than mental experience." But this simply does not describe human behavior in a way that

---

100. Finnis, *"Reason and Passion": The Constitutional Dialectic of Free Speech and Obscenity,* 116 U.Pa.L.Rev. 222 (1967).

101. Schauer [*Speech and "Speech"— Obscenity and "Obscenity": An Exercise in* the Interpretation of Constitutional Language, 67 Geo.L.J. 899 (1979).] *See also* F. Schauer, Free Speech: A Philosophical Enquiry 178–88 (1982) * * *.

anyone would recognize. Pornography must be seen by a conscious viewer; the viewer must read the prose (or watch the video) and translate the images into some mental diagram that then may well trigger some physical response. But the physical response cannot occur without the intercession of a series of mental processes. So how can this possibly be viewed as a "purely physical experience"? Furthermore, how can hardcore pornography possibly be viewed as more of a physical experience than wearing a jacket on which is sewn the phrase "Fuck the draft"?

In equating the reading or viewing of pornography with truly physical sexual experiences, Schauer also neglects a traditional distinction drawn between reading about a prohibited act and doing a prohibited act. It is permissible to purchase and possess the "Anarchists' Cookbook"; it is not permissible to follow the instructions in that book by buying the ingredients of a Molotov cocktail and mixing up a few incendiaries on the kitchen table. The first amendment permits many things to be experienced second-hand through print or videotape that cannot be done in person. It is not constitutionally significant that the vicarious experience may produce in the viewer the same emotions or responses as the act itself.

Despite his high-minded denials, Schauer ultimately fails to cloak the real justification for the interpretation of the first amendment he endorses. Schauer asserts that pornography may be suppressed because it lacks "a certain kind of value." Pornography can, he admits, have social value, but * * * some social value may also be found in "pollution, sex, political assassination, twelve-hour days, small children working at sewing machines, long hair, or short skirts." Presumably, then, the problem is that pornography has the wrong kind of social value. It is deleterious to the commonweal, like pollution and child labor. This analysis, however, is outside the realm of linguistic analysis and inside that dominated by the morality principle. The determination that "cognitive, emotive, aesthetic, informational, persuasive, or intellectual" expression is constitutionally protected while sexual expression is not involves an ordering of values, an assessment of moral worth, and a determination that some thoughts are bad thoughts, and therefore may be thwarted by any means available to the state.

* * *

The Feminist Censors

Mainstream academics such as Frederick Schauer recently have been joined by a group of *outré* theorists led by Catharine MacKinnon who search for a justification of censorship unrelated to the morality principle. In one sense, the groups are quite distinct. MacKinnon has pursued a different remedial route to the suppression of pornography than that typically taken by her compatriots. MacKinnon represents a branch of feminist analysis that has sought to define pornography as discrimination against women. MacKinnon, along with Andrea Dworkin, drafted an anti-pornography ordinance embodying this concept, and providing for civil remedies against violators. After an unsuccessful effort to pass such a statute in Minneapolis, a version of this ordinance was passed by the city of Indianapolis. The latter version was later held unconstitutional on first amendment grounds by the U.S. Court of Appeals for the Seventh Circuit.[151] * * *

* * *

The description of pornography as producing sexual inequality provides MacKinnon the opportunity to deny any allegiance to the morality principle. As the title of one of her articles asserts, pornography is "not a moral issue." [159] She attempts, instead, to justify the regulation of pornography on the basis of a harm principle. MacKinnon identifies three distinct categories of harm. The first two categories of harm are organized around a fairly traditional argument. This argument states that pornography commits violence against women. The two categories of harm refer to separate groups of women identified as subject to this violence. Category 1 includes women who participate in the making of pornography. Category 2 includes all other women in society who are harmed as a direct consequence of the distribution of pornography. Unfortunately, the evidence produced in support of the first two categories of harm fails to sustain MacKinnon's reliance on the harm principle. MacKinnon must therefore rely upon her third, and more esoteric, category. This category is based on her basic premise that pornography "constructs" reality. There are serious epistemological problems with this notion, as well as problems of political consistency. In the end, her difficulties lead MacKinnon to rely directly (if not avowedly) upon the morality principle.

A. *Pornography and the Identification of Harm*

MacKinnon's allegations concerning the first group of women injured by pornography can be answered relatively easily. MacKinnon makes the indisputable assertion that "[w]omen are known to be brutally coerced into pornographic performances." * * * But MacKinnon's response to this problem—to ban all pornography—does not necessarily follow from the existence of the problem itself. In the first place, MacKinnon does not consider the existence of other remedies for the violations that undoubtedly take place. A variety of other remedies may be applicable: criminal sanctions such as kidnapping, sexual battery, or contributing to the delinquency of a minor; traditional civil tort sanctions such as false imprisonment or battery; or new variations of remedies for invasion of privacy or the right of publicity. * * * [It] is also the case that MacKinnon's own preferred remedy does nothing at all to address the real problems of the women who tend to become involved in the making of pornography. The women who perform in pornogra-

---

151. American Booksellers Assn. v. Hudnut, 771 F.2d 323 (1985), *affd.*, 106 S.Ct. 1172 (1986).

159. MacKinnon, [*Not a Moral Issue*, 2 Yale L. & Poly.Rev. 321 (1984).]

phy tend to be young, poorly educated, and impoverished individuals who are often escaping from an abusive—if not life-threatening—family background. MacKinnon's solution would, at best, remove one opportunity for exploitation, only to leave the victims susceptible to virtually certain exploitation in another context. Her solution is therefore neither necessary nor sufficient to address the very real, pressing, and particularized harm she has identified.

The performers in pornography are not, however, the primary focus of MacKinnon's analysis regarding the direct violence done to women. She is more deeply concerned with the second group of victims. This group is composed of all women in society. MacKinnon asserts that women have suffered direct sexual subjugation resulting from the distribution of sexually explicit books and movies. The problem with this aspect of her analysis is that no one has been able to demonstrate that identifiable, physical harms result directly from pornography. * * *

* * *

B. *Pornography and the "Construction" of Reality*

[MacKinnon's main premise is] that pornography "constructs" reality. "Pornography," MacKinnon writes, "is not imagery in some relation to a reality elsewhere constructed. It is not a distortion, reflection, projection, expression, fantasy, representation or symbol either. It is sexual reality." For Frederick Schauer and the Meese Commission, pornography is something more than speech. For MacKinnon, pornography is reality. Both views ascribe extraordinary powers to expression. Words and images take on fearsome attributes. They can literally drive history, by "constructing" entire political, economic, and social structures.

* * * In MacKinnon's view, all social conditions are rooted in the expression that accompanies them. "Pornography can invent women because it has the power to make its vision into reality, which then passes, objectively, for truth." MacKinnon's theory proceeds only after removing pornography from its social context. Pornography does not service appetites produced by an unequal society, according to MacKinnon, it actually creates the unequal society. Pornography is the first cause, the prime mover, of all sexual inequality.

* * *

* * * [T]he feminist position is ultimately far more misguided than that of its conservative counterpart. The conservative censors are at least politically consistent; given the presently existing conditions, it is probable that enforcement of the morality principle will lead to a society largely to their liking. The same cannot be said of the feminist censors. Their support for the censorship of pornography is likely to lead to the further reinforcement of almost all the values they profess a desire to change. Feminist censors such as MacKinnon give courts the explicit

authority to define ideological values.[199]   Such authority presents no problem for conservative censors, since they presumably can expect to incorporate large portions of their social theory into law.   The feminist censors, however, are faced with the insurmountable dilemma presented by judicial demographics.   The judiciary is an overwhelmingly male enclave.   Moreover, the mores of judges are not likely to be very hospitable to the feminist critique of society in general.   Quite the contrary, permitting greater censorship of pornography reinforces paternalistic attitudes that have only recently been identified as constitutionally suspect in the equal protection area.[200]   The notion that women must be protected from visual or aural representations of male sexual dominance ironically allows the (usually male) judge to play the far more insidious role of father-figure, protecting his weak charge from the hostile environment of the outside world.   The institutionalization of the concept of judge-as-father-figure (and woman-as-victim) may be profoundly harmful to women seeking to obtain from the courts protection of equal opportunities historically denied on the basis of the male notion that women cannot withstand the pressure of the workaday world.

Permitting courts to serve an explicitly ideological function in the course of suppressing pornography also would have a more immediate effect on the feminist cause.   Feminism is justly concerned with protecting female sexuality from inordinate pressures exerted by a sexist society that views women from its own missionary-position perspective.   However, by making common cause with those who would outlaw pornography in order to preserve "traditional values" or some analog thereof, feminist censors are providing support for the further entrenchment of the same social institutions, arrangements, and mores that created the atmosphere in which pornography proliferates.

The pornographic perspective to which feminists object is the perspective of the unreconstructed heterosexual male, who defines society's sexual mores in light of his own limited point of view and absolutely proscribes any deviation from his rigid moral standards.   * * *   By relying so strongly upon the constitutive powers of ideas—and demanding the right to regulate such ideas through law—MacKinnon implicitly approves the very mechanism that has regularly been used against the interests of women (and all political outsiders) in the past.   The framework of absolute moral certainty employed by the present status quo is not fundamentally different from that articulated by feminist censors such as MacKinnon.   All such systems express a need to identify and

---

199. This is illustrated by MacKinnon's civil rights statute, which provides courts broad discretion to determine civil actions based upon the ad hoc definition of broad, value-laden terms such as "dehumanization" and "degradation." * * *

200. *See* Califano v. Goldfarb, 430 U.S. 199 (1977) (unconstitutional to assume widow, but not widower, dependent on de-

ceased spouse for purpose of Social Security survivor's benefits); Craig v. Boren, 429 U.S. 190 (1976) (sale of 3.2% beer to females, but not males, ages 18–20, discrimination violating Equal Protection Clause); Weinberger v. Wiesenfeld, 420 U.S. 636 (1975) (unconstitutional for Social Security to provide female wage earners less protection for survivors, than male wage earners).

eliminate the expression of deviant tendencies.[201] The enforcers of morality will always find some expression that "disgust[s] and sicken[s]."[202] The problem with systems based on the morality principle is that they can never justify judicial disgust on grounds that do not relate to the tenets of the judge's (or the dominant community's) own moral scheme.

BIBLIOGRAPHY

Paul Brest & Amy Vandenberg, *Politics, Feminism, and the Constitution: The Anti–Pornography Movement in Minneapolis,* 39 Stan.L.Rev. 607 (1987).

David Bryden, *Between Two Constitutions: Feminism and Pornography,* 2 Const.Comm. 147 (1985).

Harry Clor, OBSCENITY AND PUBLIC MORALITY (1969).

Daniel O. Conkle, *Harm, Morality, and Feminist Religion: Canada's New—But Not So New—Approach To Obscenity,* 10 Const. Commentary 105 (1993).

Anthony D'Amato, *A New Political Truth: Exposure to Sexually Violent Materials Causes Sexual Violence,* 31 Wm. & Mary L.Rev. 575 (1990).

Richard Delgado and Jean Stefancic, *Pornography and Harm to Women: "No Empirical Evidence?",* 53 Ohio St.L.J. 1037 (1992).

Andrea Dworkin, PORNOGRAPHY: MEN POSSESSING WOMEN (1981).

Andrea Dworkin, *Against the Male Flood: Censorship, Pornography, and Equality,* 8 Harv. Women's L.J. 1 (1985).

Ronald Dworkin, *Do We Have a Right to Pornography?,* 1 Ox.J.Leg.Stud. 177 (1981).

John Finnis, *"Reason and Passion": The Constitutional Dialectic of Free Speech and Obscenity,* 116 U.Pa.L.Rev. 222 (1967).

Dan Greenberg & Thomas H. Tobiason, *The New Legal Puritanism of Catharine MacKinnon,* 54 Ohio St.L.J. 1375 (1993).

Louis Henkin, *Morals and the Constitution: The Sin of Obscenity,* 63 Colum.L.Rev. 391 (1963).

Rae Langton, *Whose Right?: Ronald Dworkin, Women, and Pornographers,* 19 Phil. & Pub.Aff. 311 (1990).

Barry Lynn, *'Civil Rights' Ordinances and the Attorney General's Commission: New Developments in Pornography Regulation,* 21 Harv. Civ.Rts—Civ.Lib.L.Rev. 27 (1986).

201. This trait is clearly evident in the existing case law. *See* Bowers v. Hardwick, 106 S.Ct. 2841 (1986); Mishkin v. New York, 383 U.S. 502 (1966).

202. *Mishkin,* 383 U.S. at 508.

Catharine MacKinnon, FEMINISM UNMODIFIED: DISCOURSES ON LIFE AND LAW (1987).

Henry L. Monaghan, *Obscenity, 1966: The Marriage of Obscenity Per Se and Obscenity Per Quod*, 76 Yale L.J. 127 (1966).

Robert C. Post, *Cultural Heterogeneity and the Law: Pornography, Blasphemy, and the First Amendment*, 76 Calif.L.Rev. 297 (1988).

REPORT OF THE COMMISSION ON OBSCENITY AND PORNOGRAPHY (1970).

REPORT OF THE ATTORNEY GENERAL'S COMMISSION ON PORNOGRAPHY (1986).

David A.J. Richards, *Free Speech and Obscenity Law: Toward a Moral Theory of the First Amendment*, 123 U.Pa.L.Rev. 45 (1974).

David A.J. Richards, *Pornography Commissions and the First Amendment: On Constitutional Values and Constitutional Facts*, 39 Maine L.Rev. 275 (1987).

Kevin W. Saunders, *Media Violence and the Obscenity Exception to the First Amendment*, 3 Wm. & Mary Bill of Rights J. 107 (1994).

Frederick Schauer, THE LAW OF OBSCENITY (1976).

Robert Skipper, *Mill and Pornography*, 103 Ethics 726 (1993).

Geoffrey R. Stone, *Anti–Pornography Legislation as Viewpoint–Discrimination*, 9 Harv.J.L. & Pub.Pol. 461 (1986).

Nadine Strossen, *A Feminist Critique of "The" Feminist Critique of Pornography*, 79 Va.L.Rev. 1099 (1993).

Nadine Strossen, DEFENDING PORNOGRAPHY: FREE SPEECH, SEX, AND THE FIGHT FOR WOMEN'S RIGHTS (1995).

Symposium on the Attorney General's Commission on Pornography, 1987 Am.B.Found.Res.J. 641.

Melinda Vadas, *A First Look at the Pornography/Civil Rights Ordinance: Could Pornography Be the Subordination of Women?*, 84 J.Phil. 487 (1987).

D. COMMERCIAL SPEECH

For many years commercial speech, like libel and obscenity, was treated as simply outside the coverage of the First Amendment. In 1942 the Supreme Court gave its first clear expression to the two-level theory of speech—the idea that some categories of speech (in the ordinary sense of the term) did not count as "speech" for First Amendment purposes.[1] That same year the Court put commercial speech on the lower level. In

---

1. Chaplinsky v. New Hampshire, 315 U.S. 568, 571–572 (1942):

There are certain well-defined and narrowly limited classes of speech, the prevention and punishment of which have never been thought to raise any Constitutional problem. These include the lewd and obscene, the profane, the libelous, and the insulting or "fighting" words[.]

Valentine v. Chrestensen [2] it held that the First Amendment imposes "no ... restraint on government as respects purely commercial advertising."

In 1976 the Court changed its mind. It held in *Virginia Board of Pharmacy v. Virginia Citizens Consumer Council* [3] that commercial advertising was indeed "speech" within the meaning of the First Amendment, and struck down a state law that forbade price advertising by pharmacists. In some ways the decision was like opening Pandora's box. It was never really clear why commercial speech ought to be treated like other First Amendment activity. And it quickly became clear that it wouldn't be. Though the Court continues to maintain that commercial speech is *covered* by the First Amendment, it does not give it as much *protection* as other categories of speech get. [4] And to make matters more difficult we have found, after a few years of practice with the problem, that it is very hard to say just what "commercial speech" is: What about securities prospectuses? Labor picketing?

The articles in this section focus on these questions. Martin Redish, Daniel Farber, and Thomas Jackson and John Jeffries represent a spectrum of views about whether, why, and how much commercial speech should be protected. Redish argues that it is simply one more way to achieve the First Amendment goal of self-fulfillment, and so (presumably) it is entitled to the usual protection. Jackson and Jeffries claim that commercial speech has no more constitutional value than commercial products; that *Virginia Board of Pharmacy* was just *Lochner* in First Amendment dress; and that the right thing to do is to give it no protection. Farber is somewhere in the middle: commercial speech has a lot in common with more protected varieties, but it also has a contractual aspect that the government is entitled to regulate under *United States v. O'Brien*. [5]

Steven Shiffrin observes that to date the Court has seen only the tip of the iceberg. Commercial actors engage in lots of speech that is not advertising. What will we do when corporate executives assert that the Securities and Exchange Commission cannot regulate what they say about their companies' future?

MARTIN H. REDISH, THE FIRST AMENDMENT IN THE MARKETPLACE: COMMERCIAL SPEECH AND THE VALUES OF FREE EXPRESSION

39 Geo.Wash.L.Rev. 429, 443–447 (1971).

[C]ommercial speech furthers legitimate first amendment purposes. When the individual is presented with rational grounds for preferring

2. 316 U.S. 52, 54 (1942).

3. 425 U.S. 748 (1976).

4. In a series of recent cases the Court has tried to explain just how much less protection. Board of Trustees of SUNY v. Fox, 492 U.S. 469 (1989); Posadas De Puerto Rico Associates v. Tourism Co. of Puerto Rico, 478 U.S. 328 (1986); Metromedia, Inc. v. San Diego, 453 U.S. 490 (1981); Central Hudson Gas & Elec. Corp. v. Public Service Commission of New York, 447 U.S. 557 (1980).

5. 391 U.S. 367 (1968).

one product or brand over another, he is encouraged to consider the competing information, weigh it mentally in the light of the goals of personal satisfaction he has set for himself, counter-balance his conclusions with possible price differentials, and in so doing exercise his abilities to reason and think; this aids him towards the intangible goal of rational self-fulfillment.

It would be unreasonable to suggest that such mental exercise aids the process of rational development to anywhere near the extent that great literature, or perhaps some forms of political debate do. They are of a very different order. But it is important to recall that the courts have not limited substantial first amendment protection to great literature or to information central to the political process. The Supreme Court has recognized that magazines containing fictional crime-violence-lust stories are also within the scope of significant first amendment safeguards.[73] * * *

In any case, attempts by the courts to choose a vehicle for rational development are an unwarranted restriction of individual freedom. Some rational development is better than none, and given the current apathy on the part of many segments of the public towards issues of great political and social concern, it is arguable that for many, the only realistic means to stimulate use of the rational processes is to encourage the rational solution of problems that face individuals in their everyday life. Competing informational advertising in the commercial realm aids in the performance of this function.

* * *

Courts have, on occasion, reasoned that the legislative power to regulate the manufacture and sale of commercial products logically includes the lesser power to discourage purchase by prohibiting advertising. Though such an argument makes a superficially compelling case, it disregards the fact that by so acting, the legislature is prohibiting speech that advocates a purely lawful activity as long as the legislature has not, in fact, exercised the power of prohibiting sale. Such restriction has been generally frowned upon by the judiciary.

Government's power to restrict speech has never been equated with its power to restrict action. This is so partially because the nation favors a free exchange of ideas and information in the belief that the development of the mind is a value in and of itself. Perhaps more significant is the fact that we can never really presume to know the "truth"; many of our conceptions and understandings change, and therefore we desire a free and full exchange of opinion so that the citizenry may know all relevant considerations in choosing the best course of conduct.

73. *E.g.,* Winters v. New York, 333 U.S. 507, 510 (1948): "Though we can see nothing of any possible value to society in these magazines, they are as much entitled to the protection of free speech as the best of literature."

It may be generally true that much "[c]onsumer behavior in the marketplace is not rational and deliberate, but often impulsive and capricious," [83] and that much of advertising is directed not to appeal to the individual's intellectual, rational capacities, but rather to a consumer's subconscious, irrational desires or self-image. This situation, however, is not very different from the modern day political sphere, where voters often cast their ballots on the basis of totally uninformed, irrational grounds; the aim of politicians and their advisers is often to appeal more to the subconscious, irrational desires and beliefs of the voter than to his rational processes. Certainly no one would argue that these facts make the first amendment's role in the political area any less significant. Indeed, it may increase its importance, since the first amendment's basis is primarily normative rather than factual. Although the first amendment assumes that man has a will and an intellect, its concern is that he *should* use them; it does not turn on whether he *does* use them. The less he does use them, the greater is the need to encourage their use. The more non-rational appeals that are made, the more important it is to protect appeals with a rational basis.

To say on the one hand that the probability of individual rational development is greater for many in the commercial than in the political spheres, and on the other hand that many consumers at this time often do not act rationally in making their purchasing decisions is not necessarily inconsistent. The cause of this consumer irrationality is most likely the unfortunate lack of extensive rational informational advertising readily available. The function of the first amendment is limited to protection of the dissemination of legitimate information already in existence. The fact remains, however, that *some* advertising today does convey rational information, and to the extent that the modern individual is apprised of this information, in many cases he is more likely, for the reasons discussed earlier, to give it, rather than equally rational political appeals, serious, thoughtful consideration.

As a final point, it is important to recognize that first amendment interests continue into purely non-informational advertising. Dr. Meiklejohn to the contrary notwithstanding, the first amendment does recognize an interest existing in the speaker as well as the listener, and purely persuasive materials may serve that end. Much advertising which does not convey concrete information nevertheless represents the artistic creation of an individual, and as such deserves recognition as first amendment speech.

DANIEL A. FARBER, COMMERCIAL SPEECH AND FIRST AMENDMENT THEORY

74 Nw.U.L. 372, 381–384, 386–389 (1979).

A Reexamination of the First Amendment Status of Commercial Speech

The natural starting point for analyzing the constitutional status of commercial speech is to ask whether the subject matter of the speech

---

83. *Developments in the Law—Deceptive Advertising,* 80 Harv.L.Rev. 1005, 1010 (1967).

places it outside the boundaries of the first amendment. The subject matter of commercial speech is invariably some commercial product or service about whose existence, price, or qualities the speaker wishes to communicate. If product information were outside the pale of the first amendment, the consumer advocate as well as the commercial speaker would be left unprotected. General Motors could constitutionally enjoin Ralph Nader from revealing unfavorable facts about its cars, and magazines like *Consumer Reports* could be freely suppressed. These results are simply unacceptable. Millions of people may buy a single product, and the safety of that product is certainly a matter of public concern. Moreover, information about the quality and price of some products may relate to important political issues. For example, a belief that American cars are overpriced influences views on foreign car import restrictions, on inflationary price increases for domestic cars, and on the effects of oligopoly. Knowledge of product safety and reliability relates to consumer protection legislation. In short, product information is clearly entitled to constitutional protection in at least some contexts.

[Neither could economic] motivation * * * be made a disqualifying factor without enormous damage to the first amendment. Little purpose would be served by a first amendment which failed to protect newspapers, paid public speakers, political candidates with partially economic motives, and professional authors. Furthermore, the economically motivated speaker is often the most likely to raise important issues, since disinterestedness is less common than apathy.

Eliminating economic motive as a disqualifying factor seems to leave no basis for excluding commercial speech, as a class, from first amendment protection. There may, however, be an argument for denying first amendment protection to certain types of commercial speech. Advertisements frequently contain little information and instead are intended to create irrational product preferences. It might be tenable to treat commercial speech like pornography and require some minimal level of "redeeming social value" as a prerequisite for first amendment protection. Indeed, a social critic might suggest that the analogy is fairly close, that, in a sense, advertising is the pornography of capitalism, intended to arouse desire for objects rather than for persons. Several problems would arise, however, from adopting a requirement of redeeming social value for advertisements, the foremost being that such a scheme has not succeeded in the obscenity area. In addition, advertising may have social value other than its information content, such as its artistic significance. Moreover, pornography regulation derives from a unique historical tradition concerning sexual conduct and expression. Doctrines based on these traditions are unlikely to transplant well to unrelated areas. Finally, the practical effect of a "redeeming value" requirement would simply be to encourage an increase in the information content of advertising, which can be done more directly through affirmative disclosure requirements. In short, advertising enjoys constitutional protection because of its capacity to convey significant information, combined with the practical difficulty of excluding less useful advertising from the protected class. This is the basic significance of the holding in *Virginia Board.*[a] The critical question is how the protection given advertising differs or should differ from that afforded noncommercial speech.

* * *

A Proposed Analytic Framework

* * *

Economic motivation and subject matter have already been eliminated as distinguishing factors. How else does commercial speech differ from noncommercial speech? One obvious distinction is that the commercial speaker not only talks about a product, but also sells it. The sale itself is subject to broad state regulation. May such regulation include the attachment of liability to the use of language in connection with a sales transaction?

To ask this question is very nearly to answer it. Contract law consists almost entirely of rules attaching liability to various uses of language. For example, the constitutional status of an advertisement describing a product may be unclear, but a seller is obviously liable for damages for failure to deliver a product corresponding to the contract description. No first amendment problem exists. Yet contract liability is imposed under rules which would not be tolerated even in areas which traditionally have been subject to state regulation, such as libel. For instance, statements in the contract are frequently construed against the draftsman. In addition, liability may be imposed even though experts disagree about whether the product fits the description. The seller is usually held strictly liable, without any showing of malice, scienter, or even negligence. Despite all this, the state's power to impose liability is beyond any dispute. Not even the strongest partisan of content neutrality would argue that contractual liability cannot be validly imposed on the basis of the content of the language used in the contract. The reason appears to be that the use of language to form contracts is not the sort of "speech" to which the first amendment applies. Regulation aimed at this use of language does not demand the sort of justification which is required when the state regulates first amendment "speech."

Similar to the language of a written contract, the language in advertising can be seen as constituting part of the seller's commitment to the buyer. Thus, advertising can function as part of the contractual arrangement between the buyer and seller. Of course, in addition to serving this contractual function, advertisements also serve an informative function to which the first amendment applies. The critical factor seems to be whether a state rule is based on the informative function or

---

a. Virginia State Bd. of Pharmacy v. Virginia Citizens Consumer Council, Inc., 425 U.S. 748 (1976).

the contractual function of the language. So long as a regulation relates to the contractual function of the utterance, the regulation should not be subjected to the intensive scrutiny required when a regulation directly implicates the first amendment function of language. Thus, the problem is to devise a test which will distinguish between regulations involving the first amendment, informative aspect of advertising and those involving its non-first amendment, contractual aspect. The appropriate test would appear to be that articulated by the Supreme Court in *United States v. O'Brien* [71] for cases in which " 'speech' and 'nonspeech' elements are combined in the same course of conduct:"

> [a] government regulation is sufficiently justified if it ... furthers an important or substantial government interest; if the government interest is unrelated to the suppression of free expression; and if the incidental restriction on alleged First Amendment freedoms is no greater than is essential to the furtherance of that interest.

This line of analysis leads to a bifurcated approach to commercial speech cases, corresponding to the dual nature of the speech itself. If the interests asserted to justify a restriction relate to the contractual aspect of the speech, the validity of the restriction should be judged under the *O'Brien* test. On the other hand, if the asserted justifications do not relate to the distinctively contractual nature of commercial speech, there is no reason to deviate from the tests used for other kinds of speech, presumably including the principle of content neutrality. In practice, distinguishing between these two kinds of state interests is not difficult. A justification for regulating the seller's speech relates to the contractual function of the speech if, and only if, the state interest disappears when the same statements are made by a third person with no relation to the transaction. If the same interest is implicated by the third party's speech, the interest obviously cannot relate to any contractual aspect of the speech, since the third party is not involved in the contract.

Before considering how this approach can be applied to various situations, its general merits should be considered. First, it explains the intuitive belief that commercial speech is somehow more akin to conduct than are other forms of speech. The unique aspect of commercial speech is that it is a prelude to, and therefore becomes integrated into, a contract, the essence of which is the presence of a promise. Because a promise is an undertaking to ensure that a certain state of affairs takes place, promises obviously have a closer connection with conduct than with self-expression. Second, this approach focuses on the distinctive and powerful state interests implicated by the process of contract formation. In a fundamentally market economy, the government understandably is given particular deference in its enforcement of contractual expectations. Indeed, the Constitution itself gives special protection to contractual expectations in the contract clause. Finally, this approach

71. 391 U.S. 367 (1968).

connects a rather nebulous area of first amendment law with the commonplaces of contract law of which every lawyer has knowledge.

THOMAS H. JACKSON AND JOHN CALVIN JEFFRIES, JR., COMMERCIAL SPEECH: ECONOMIC DUE PROCESS AND THE FIRST AMENDMENT

65 Va.L.Rev. 1, 25–36 (1979).

[Jackson and Jeffries begin their article by arguing that the First Amendment is not concerned with commercial speech, because it has little or no bearing on the political process. "[S]peech which does 'no more than propose a commercial transaction' " [a] almost as a matter of definition has little to say about democratic self-government. They then turn to the justifications the Supreme Court offered in *Virginia Board of Pharmacy* for protecting commercial speech.]

Commercial Speech and Economic Liberty

In light of the irrelevance of traditional first amendment concerns to commercial advertising, it is not surprising that the Court in *Virginia Board of Pharmacy* spent relatively little effort trying to explain its decision in those terms. Instead, the opinion emphasized the adverse economic effects of Virginia's ban against drug price advertising. The Court saw this restriction as an invasion of two basic values of economic liberty. The first is the opportunity of the individual producer or consumer to maximize his own economic utility. The second is the aggregate economic efficiency of a free market economy. The Court correctly perceived that the suppression of drug price advertising is likely to impair both of these values.

In discussing maximization of individual utility, the Court began with the "assumption" that the advertiser's interest "is a purely economic one." While, as the Court noted, this factor does not disqualify the advertiser's claim to first amendment protection, neither does it provide a reason for giving such advertisements constitutional protection. A more potent consideration was the interest of the individual consumer. As the Court pointed out, a "consumer's interest in the free flow of commercial information . . . may be as keen, if not keener by far, than his interest in the day's most urgent political debate." The Court went on to describe with feeling and eloquence the impact of a price advertising ban on individual consumers:

> Those whom the suppression of prescription drug price information hits the hardest are the poor, the sick, and particularly the aged. A disproportionate amount of their income tends to be spent on prescription drugs; yet they are the least able to learn, by shopping from pharmacist to pharmacist, where their scarce dollars are best

a. Virginia State Bd. of Pharmacy v.   425 U.S. 748, 762 (1976).
Virginia Citizens Consumer Council, Inc.,

spent. When drug prices vary as strikingly as they do, information as to who is charging what becomes more than a convenience. It could mean the alleviation of physical pain or the enjoyment of basic necessities.

By voiding the legislative restriction on drug price advertising the Court hoped to enable individual consumers to spend their "scarce dollars" more effectively.

The Court's economic analysis is surely correct. In the competitive economic model, a seller advertises only if he believes it to be more efficient than an alternative expenditure of similar resources. A ban against price advertising increases the costs of obtaining price information and makes it less likely that the consumer's choices will be well informed. Because the marginal cost of acquiring more information at some point exceeds the marginal benefits of obtaining such information, the reduction of less costly sources of information means that a consumer (now more "uninformed" than would otherwise be the case) will pay more than is "necessary" (in a world of less costly information). On the evidence in this case, the consumer may pay as much as seven times more. The result is an unnecessary reduction in consumer purchasing power, and for the person of limited means, a decrease in the "alleviation of physical pain or the enjoyment of basic necessities." The ban, of course, may increase the welfare of pharmacists as a class but only by effecting a wealth transfer from consumers to pharmacists.

The Court also perceived that this impairment of individual economic opportunity has adverse implications for aggregate efficiency:

> So long as we preserve a predominantly free enterprise economy, the allocation of our resources in large measure will be made through numerous private economic decisions. It is a matter of public interest that those decisions, in the aggregate, be intelligent and well informed.

When consumers choose ignorantly, an inefficient allocation of societal resources is likely. While the ultimate results of legislative interference with the competitive market are difficult to predict, it seems plausible to assume that the consequence of a reduced flow of information will lead to some situational monopolies that would not exist if advertising were unrestricted. Most economists are willing to assume that the existence of some monopoly power likely will lead to a lower level of aggregate economic efficiency than would otherwise be the case.

As a matter of public policy, both of these considerations are significant. The opportunity of the individual consumer to maximize his own utility by making well-informed economic choices is important, particularly in the context of medical care. Moreover, the nation plainly has an interest in promoting allocative efficiency in the economy as a whole—that interest lies at the heart of the federal antitrust laws. Generally, one might regret any governmental action that invades these interests without some clearly offsetting benefit to the public good.

Virginia claimed such an offsetting benefit in the maintenance of professionalism among pharmacists. The state argued that unlimited advertising would lead to aggressive price competition in the preparation and sale of prescription drugs. Such competition, feared the state, would drive the conscientious pharmacist out of business and endanger the survival of the neighborhood pharmacy. * * *

While the state's arguments are not inherently implausible, one may well agree with the Court that Virginia's ban against drug price advertising contributed less to the professionalism of pharmacists than to their wealth. Certainly, the legislation benefited small, inefficient pharmacies that could not compete effectively with larger concerns if price advertising were allowed. In other words, the advertising ban operated to insulate certain sellers from the competitive marketplace and thus to achieve special advantage for the owners of small pharmacies. Whether this legislation also redounded to the benefit of the public at large seems more doubtful. The Court, at least, seems to have viewed Virginia's law as nothing more or less than a classic case of special interest legislation inconsistent with any disinterested understanding of the public good.

* * * It is surprising to discover, however, that these economic considerations add up to a *constitutional* impediment to legislative control of the marketplace. It is all the more startling to be told, as *Virginia Board of Pharmacy* announces, that the source of that constitutional restraint is the first amendment. One might have thought, as the Court has so often proclaimed, that demanding judicial review of economic legislation was a concern of the past. Even if that tradition were to be revived, one would expect to find the constitutional safeguards of economic liberty to be housed within the flexible contours of due process of law. Instead, economic due process is resurrected, clothed in the ill-fitting garb of the first amendment, and sent forth to battle the kind of special interest legislation that the Court has tolerated for more than forty years. In short, the Supreme Court has reconstituted the values of *Lochner v. New York* [108] as components of freedom of speech. * * *

Were it not for the first amendment trappings, this revivification of *Lochner* would no doubt excite substantial opposition. At the very least, it would be recognized as a contradiction of the heretofore settled idea that the Constitution tolerates extensive regulation of the economy. Various decisions have reiterated that proposition in a host of different contexts. For example, government constitutionally is free to restrict production of a good,[110] to determine the prices and conditions of sale,[111] and even to ban certain items from the marketplace.[112] Government also

---

108. 198 U.S. 45 (1905). * * *

110. *E.g.,* Wickard v. Filburn, 317 U.S. 111 (1942).

111. *E.g.,* Sunshine Anthracite Coal Co. v. Adkins, 310 U.S. 381 (1940); Townsend v. Yeomans, 301 U.S. 441 (1937); Old Dear-

born Distrib. Co. v. Seagram–Distillers Corp., 299 U.S. 183 (1936); Nebbia v. New York, 291 U.S. 502 (1934); Munn v. Illinois, 94 U.S. 113 (1877).

112. Nebbia v. New York, 291 U.S. 502, 527–28 (1934) * * *.

has the authority to limit access to a profession,[113] to prescribe wages and conditions of employment,[114] and even to outlaw certain lines of work.[115] Additionally, government may distort the free market economy by licensing a monopoly,[116] by creating other barriers to entry,[117] or by subsidizing public competition to private industry.[118]   In all of these ways, government may regulate and affect commercial transactions.   According to *Virginia Board of Pharmacy,* however, government may not suppress the solicitation of commercial transactions in the form of business advertising.   That kind of regulation is supposedly barred by the first amendment, even though it does not implicate the traditionally accepted meanings of freedom of speech.   The problem, says the Court, is that the ban against drug price advertising impairs the economic welfare of the individual consumer and contributes to aggregate economic inefficiency. These values are also implicated, however, by every one of the laws mentioned above.   Every kind of legislative restraint on the operation of the free market economy may be used to favor one group at the expense of the public at large and thus to further one or another social objective by encouraging an economically inefficient allocation of resources.

Indeed, such results are commonplace.   Price supports for farm products raise the price of bread and maintain an inefficient concentration of resources in food production.   Minimum wage laws add to unemployment, especially among young and unskilled workers, and distort the aggregate labor market.   Exactly the same values that are impaired by Virginia's ban against drug price advertising are also invaded by these and most other instances of governmental regulation of the economy.   Of course, countervailing social objectives often may justify governmental displacement of the free market, and we are very far from suggesting that regulation of the market is necessarily, or even presumptively, undesirable.   The point is, rather, that such judgments

---

113. *E.g.,* City of New Orleans v. Dukes, 427 U.S. 297 (1976) (per curiam); North Dakota State Bd. of Pharmacy v. Snyder's Drug Stores, Inc., 414 U.S. 156 (1973); Kotch v. Board of River Port Pilot Comm'rs, 330 U.S. 552 (1947).

114. *E.g.,* Massachusetts Bd. of Retirement v. Murgia, 427 U.S. 307 (1976) (mandatory retirement at age 50); Day–Brite Lighting, Inc. v. Missouri, 342 U.S. 421 (1952) (employees entitled to time off with pay to vote); NLRB v. Jones & Laughlin Steel Corp., 301 U.S. 1 (1937) (restraint of employers in selecting or discharging employees); West Coast Hotel Co. v. Parrish, 300 U.S. 379 (1937) (minimum wages); Erie R.R. v. Williams, 233 U.S. 685 (1914) (employers required to pay employees semimonthly and in cash); Knoxville Iron Co. v. Harbison, 183 U.S. 13 (1901) (employers required to redeem wages paid to employees, in form of merchandise, for cash).

115. Ah Sin v. Wittman, 198 U.S. 500 (1905) (legislation suppressing gambling).

116. This result is common in the licensing of utility companies, for example. *Cf.* Cantor v. Detroit Edison Co., 428 U.S. 579, 595–96 (1976) ("public utility regulation typically assumes that the private firm is a natural monopoly").

117. *E.g.,* Martin v. Walton, 368 U.S. 25 (1961) (per curiam); Semler v. Oregon State Bd. of Dental Examiners, 294 U.S. 608 (1935); McCloskey v. Tobin, 252 U.S. 107 (1920); Olsen v. Smith, 195 U.S. 332 (1904).

118. *E.g.,* 47 U.S.C. § 396 (1976) (establishing the Corporation for Public Broadcasting). *Cf.* American Commercial Lines v. Louisville & N.R.R., 392 U.S. 571, 593–94 (1968) (upholding ICC's position that railroads may not set prices below average price to attract business away from barge lines); Ashwander v. Tennessee Valley Auth., 297 U.S. 288, 338–39 (1936) (water power resulting from construction of federally owned dams may be converted to electricity and sold to private parties).

are properly left to popularly elected legislatures. In terms of constitutional values, price supports, minimum wage laws, and advertising bans are utterly indistinguishable. Constitutional objection to such laws stands or falls on precisely the ground asserted in *Lochner v. New York* and repeatedly repudiated in the decades since then.

Exactly the same point can be made in terms of the familiar notion that the greater power normally includes the lesser. Nothing in the federal Constitution bars a state from legislating prescription drug prices, even if the prices were set significantly higher than those that would prevail in a competitive market. Ancillary to such action, the state might also forbid commercial advertising of prescription drugs at any price other than that authorized by law. Given the authority to set prices in the first place, there is nothing remarkable in the extension of legislative control to price advertising. After all, if it is illegal to sell the X drug at the Y price, then no legitimate reason can be found to advertise such a sale. The typical business advertisement—speech that does "no more than solicit a commercial transaction"—serves no valid purpose when the underlying transaction is forbidden by law. The Supreme Court apparently has accepted this reasoning and has indicated its readiness to uphold legislative regulation of commercial advertising "incidental to a valid limitation on economic activity." [125]

The significance of this analysis lies in its application to the instance in which the legislature has not exercised its "greater power" over the underlying economic activity. Thus, for example, the legislature rationally might conclude that the sale of cigarettes should be allowed but that advertising should be banned to discourage new users. In such a case, according to the reasoning of *Virginia Board of Pharmacy,* governmental control over price advertising would offend the first amendment. This conclusion only makes sense if one assumes a first amendment value in the advertising of cigarettes independent of its role in encouraging or facilitating the sale of cigarettes. The latter transaction the government concededly has the power to forbid or control. If independent first amendment significance did exist in this instance, it would also exist when the state has declared the underlying transaction unlawful. So, for example, some legitimate function would arise for the advertisement, "I will sell you the X drug at the Y price," even where the sale is forbidden by law. That no such independent purpose in fact can be identified confirms the hypothesis that the significance of ordinary business advertising lies entirely in its relation to the contemplated economic transaction. It follows that such advertising should be subject to governmental regulation on the same terms as any other aspect of the marketplace.

125. Pittsburgh Press Co. v. Pittsburgh Comm'n on Human Relations, 413 U.S. 376, 389 (1973).

STEVEN SHIFFRIN, THE FIRST AMENDMENT AND ECONOMIC REGULATION: AWAY FROM A GENERAL THEORY OF THE FIRST AMENDMENT

78 Nw.U.L.Rev. 1212, 1213–1215, 1228–1232 (1984).

Each commercial speech case the Court has considered has involved advertising or the proposal of a commercial transaction,[5] and almost all of the commentators have looked at the "commercial speech" problem through the lens of commercial advertising. * * *

* * *

By looking at speech made pursuant to commercial transactions, however, we examine only the tip of the iceberg. Commercial actors such as corporations do not speak only to propose commercial transactions, to advertise, or even to influence the outcome of initiatives. Corporations speak to the press, for example, about their corporate future, regulated by the securities laws, to their shareholders about their future, regulated by still other aspects of the securities laws, to their employees, subject to the labor laws, to their competitors, subject to the antitrust laws, to government officials, with an eye on the lobbying laws, and to their lawyers, their accountants, their bankers, and their suppliers, subject to a host of government regulations. Some of these same corporations are banks, airlines, or public utilities subject to other layers of regulation. * * *

[Shiffrin concedes that Jackson and Jeffries are right when they argue that the First Amendment is not much concerned with price advertising.[a] Price advertising is not political speech. Nor does it deserve protection because it plays a role in fostering the efficient allocation of resources. "It was strange indeed," he says, "for the Court to suggest that the first amendment has been Chicago-school economics travelling incognito for all these years." But Shiffrin asserts that it is often very difficult to separate advertising and politics into discrete categories: what about a domestic producer advertising its product as an alternative to imports? This is not, however, the most serious problem facing commercial speech theory.]

* * * If it is difficult to fashion a neat dichotomy between commercial advertising and political speech, it is impossible to maintain a

---

5. Bolger v. Youngs Drug Prods. Corp., 103 S.Ct. 2875 (1983) (contraceptive advertising); Matter of R.M.J., 455 U.S. 191 (1982) (attorney advertising); Metromedia, Inc. v. San Diego, 453 U.S. 490 (1981) (commercial aspect of case involved advertising on billboards); Central Hudson Gas & Elec. Corp. v. Public Serv. Comm'n, 447 U.S. 557 (1980) (advertising electricity); Friedman v. Rogers, 440 U.S. 1 (1979) (use of trade name in optometry advertising); Ohralik v. Ohio State Bar Ass'n, 436 U.S. 447 (1978) (proposing sale of attorney's service); Bates v. State Bar of Ariz., 433 U.S. 350 (1977) (attorney advertising); Linmark Assocs., Inc. v. Willingboro, 431 U.S. 85 (1977) (advertising for sale of houses); Virginia State Bd. of Pharmacy v. Virginia Citizens Consumer Council, 425 U.S. 748 (1976) (drug advertising); Bigelow v. Virginia, 421 U.S. 809 (1975) (abortion advertising); Pittsburgh Press Co. v. Pittsburgh Comm'n on Human Relations, 413 U.S. 376 (1973) (advertising of jobs); Valentine v. Chrestensen, 316 U.S. 52 (1942) (advertising showing of a submarine).

a. Jackson & Jeffries, *Commercial Speech: Economic Due Process and the First Amendment,* 65 Va.L.Rev. 1 (1979).

commercial/political distinction when one moves beyond advertising to other categories of "commercial" speech. Let us first focus upon what most would regard as a sacred cow. Surely the first amendment has nothing to do with the securities laws, or at least so we have long assumed. In *Ohralik v. Ohio State Bar Association,* the Court went out of its way to explain that "[n]umerous examples could be cited of communications that are regulated without offending the First Amendment, such as the exchange of information about securities ... [or] corporate proxy statements. ..." [110] That is the Court's present bottom line, but it glosses over a significant doctrinal problem which makes the distinction between commercial and political speech impossible to maintain.

Suppose the chief executive of General Motors wants to give a speech at a press conference. He or she wants to talk about the future of the company, future production plans and expected sales, expected areas of difficult competition, and the potential for successes and failures in meeting that competition. Would such a speech be political or commercial? There are certainly commercial aspects to the speech. People will likely buy and sell General Motors stock in response to it. But the executive is not proposing a commercial transaction or advertising cars. Rather, the speech is about the economic future of General Motors.

Look * * * at the executive's speech through the lens of American libel law. In casting the decisive vote to extend the protection of *New York Times Co. v. Sullivan* to public figures, Chief Justice Warren recognized that "increasingly in this country, the distinctions between governmental and private sectors are blurred .... It is plain that although they are not subject to the restraints of the political process, 'public figures,' like 'public officials' often play an influential role in ordering society." [112] Even if the libel perspective were not available, it would be quite difficult to maintain that the remarks of a major auto executive are irrelevant to the political process. The fate of elected public officials often turns on the degree of inflation or unemployment, or more generally on economic conditions. The decisions of major corporate executives obviously affect economic conditions. Public officials have never been blind to this. They have tried to threaten, to subsidize, to regulate, and to persuade businesses to serve the public interest. They have talked of a partnership between business and government because there is one. If we shift our example from the auto industry to the defense industry, the point is even more obvious. The Lockheed executive's expectations for the future depend in large measure on his or her expectations about what government officials are likely to do in the future, and insights on that point are of political moment. The same is true of auto executives and many others. In short, if Jackson and Jeffries were to maintain that a first amendment

110. Ohralik v. Ohio State Bar Ass'n, 436 U.S. at 456. * * *

112. Curtis Publishing Co. v. Butts, 388 U.S. 130, 163–64 (1967) (Warren, C.J., concurring).

that covered only political speech would be irrelevant to the speech of corporate executives about the future of their companies, they would be forced to fall back on a simplistic model of politics.

Moreover, if the position would be a hard one for Jackson and Jeffries to take, it would be even harder for the Court to do so. Having opined that a pharmacist's public statements of drug prices are political because they serve to allocate resources in the economy, what room for maneuver could the Court find if it were confronted with the fact that bankers routinely examine the statements of corporate executives in deciding how productive resources shall be invested?

All this comes home to roost in the securities laws. For years the SEC has taken various positions as to what corporate executives could talk about without exposing their companies to crushing liability under the securities laws. Today the Commission purportedly encourages executives to make statements about the Company's future, but the form of the Commission's "encouragement" is such that a lawyer is likely to advise a corporate executive that serious risks attach to making future projections. Moreover, for many years the SEC discouraged executives from making projections. If the analysis so far is correct, for many years the SEC has been regulating speech that is important to the political process—*without any first amendment scrutiny.* On Jackson and Jeffries' own premises, even if they are right about *Virginia Pharmacy,* there are strong grounds for questioning the sagacity of the "commercial speech" doctrine.

The same set of questions arises when government regulates union or corporate elections. Here the regulations vary. The NLRB, for example, has vacillated for many years about the scope of its power to act when it finds that a representation election has been influenced significantly by the misleading statements of an employer. Similarly, the SEC regulates the content of proxy materials in corporate elections to screen out misleading statements. By contrast, a federal administrative agency surely could not screen out "misleading" statements made by a candidate for political office, or dictate other sanctions, even if it found the statements to be deceptive or misleading.

Even if one were prepared to cling to the idea that elections of those who command substantial productive resources are non-political, however, a separation between the political and the commercial could not be easily made here, either. For example, suppose a shareholder submits a proposal for the proxy materials suggesting that the corporation should not invest in South Africa, Israel, or the Middle East.   * * *

The union context is equally interesting. The debate over whether to unionize is a debate about the sources of power that should govern an important part of an employee's life. The debate often may turn on matters of general political interest. Moreover the union often works as lobbyist in the legislative process and as participant in the electoral process. At the same time, unions are bargaining to sell the services of their members at the highest price. In that sense they are "commercial" entities. Similarly, the content of the employers' speech often may involve statements that relate to matters of general political interest. When discussion focuses on how power ought to be distributed in the workplace, we might regard the discussion as inherently political. In any event, many union campaigns involve the most volatile of political issues. If those committed to a politically based conception of the first amendment were to consign labor law to a status beneath first amendment protection, they could not plausibly defend the consignment on the ground that such speech was irrelevant to the processes of political decisionmaking.

The approach that Jackson and Jeffries champion, then, is not well suited to support the conclusion that all economic regulation should be beneath first amendment protection. Even if one accepts their assumption that the first amendment is exclusively concerned with political speech, there is good reason to think that much so-called economic regulation touches speech of political importance. The case they marshal, however strong in the commercial advertising area, seems to cut the other way when one steps back to examine more of the territory than they and other commentators have typically examined.

BIBLIOGRAPHY

Lawrence A. Alexander, *Speech in the Local Marketplace: Implications of Virginia State Board of Pharmacy v. Virginia Citizens Consumer Council, Inc. for Local Regulatory Power,* 14 San Diego L.Rev. 357 (1977).

Alfred Aman, SEC v. Lowe: *Professional Regulation and the First Amendment,* 1985 Sup.Ct.Rev. 93.

C. Edwin Baker, *Commercial Speech: A Problem in the Theory of Freedom,* 62 Iowa L.Rev. 1 (1976).

Vincent Blasi & Henry Monaghan, *The First Amendment and Cigarette Advertising,* 256 J.A.M.A. 502 (1986).

Victor Brudney, *Business Corporations and Stockholders' Rights Under the First Amendment,* 91 Yale L.J. 235 (1981).

William C. Canby, Jr. & Ernest Gellhorn, *Physician Advertising: The First Amendment and the Sherman Act,* 1978 Duke L.J. 543.

Ronald A. Cass, *Commercial Speech, Constitutionalism, Collective Choice,* 56 U.Cinc.L.Rev. 1317 (1988).

Ronald Coase, *Advertising and Free Speech,* 6 J. Legal Stud. 1 (1977).

Colloquy, *The First Amendment in a Commercial Culture,* 71 Texas L.Rev. 697 (1993).

Comment, *First Amendment Protection for Commercial Advertising: The New Constitutional Doctrine,* 44 U.Chi.L.Rev. 205 (1976).

Edward J. Eberle, *Practical Reason: The Commercial Speech Paradigm,* 42 Case West.Res.L.Rev. 411 (1992).

Aleta G. Estreicher, *Securities Regulation and the First Amendment*, 24 Ga.L.Rev. 223 (1990).

Michael C. Harper, *The Consumer's Emerging Right to Boycott:* NAACP v. Claiborne Hardware *and Its Implications for American Labor Law,* 93 Yale L.J. 409 (1984).

Louise L. Hill, *Solicitation by Lawyers: Piercing the First Amendment Veil,* 42 Me.L.Rev. 369 (1990).

Alex Kozinski & Henry Banner, *Who's Afraid of Commercial Speech?*, 76 Va.L.Rev. 627 (1990).

Robert N. Kravitz, *Trademarks, Speech, and the* Gay Olympics *Case,* 69 B.U.L.Rev. 131 (1989).

Philip Kurland, *Posadas de Puerto Rico v. Tourism Company: " 'Twas Strange, 'Twas Passing Strange, 'Twas Pitiful, 'Twas Wondrous Pitiful,"* 1986 Sup.Ct.Rev. 1.

Donald Lively, *The Supreme Court and Commercial Speech: New Words with an Old Message,* 72 Minn.L.Rev. 289 (1987).

Fred S. McChesney, *Commercial Speech in the Professions: The Supreme Court's Question and Questionable Answers,* 134 U.Pa.L.Rev. 45 (1985).

Burt Neuborne, *The First Amendment and Government Regulation of Capital Markets,* 55 Brooklyn L.Rev. 5 (1989).

James G. Pope, *The Three–Systems Ladder of First Amendment Values: Two Rungs and a Black Hole,* 11 Hastings Const.L.Q. 189 (1984).

Martin H. Redish, *Product Health Claims and the First Amendment: Scientific Expression and the Twilight Zone of Commercial Speech,* 43 Vand.L.Rev. 1433 (1990).

Daniel Schiro, *Commercial Speech: The Demise of a Chimera,* 1976 Sup.Ct.Rev. 45.

Carl E. Schneider, *Free Speech and Corporate Freedom: A Comment on* First National Bank of Boston v. Bellotti, 59 S.Cal.L.Rev. 1227 (1986).

Symposium, *Commercial Speech and the First Amendment,* 56 U.Cinn. L.Rev. 1165 (1988).

Symposium on the First Amendment and Federal Securities Regulation, 20 Conn.L.Rev. 261 (1988).

Mark V. Tushnet, *Corporations and Free Speech,* in D. Kairys, ed., THE POLITICS OF LAW 253 (1982).

Charles D. Watts, Jr., *Corporate Legal Theory Under the First Amendment: Bellotti and Austin,* 46 U.Miami L.Rev. 317 (1991).

E. RACIST SPEECH

In 1952 the Supreme Court upheld an Illinois law that forbade portraying the "depravity, criminality, unchastity, or lack of virtue of a class of citizens, of any race, color, creed or religion[.]"[1] The Court's justification was that this was a kind of group libel, and libel was a category of speech that fell outside the protection of the First Amendment. That is no longer true since *New York Times v. Sullivan.*[2] One might also argue that a law like Illinois's only prohibits fighting words, though in recent years the Supreme Court has allowed people to call each other some surprising names.[3] It is thus uncertain whether the government today can regulate "racist" or "hate" speech. When the largely Jewish village of Skokie, Illinois enacted an ordinance in 1977 to prevent a group of Nazis from marching and displaying swastikas, the courts struck it down without hesitation.[4] But the issue is one that will not go away. Recent incidents on college campuses and elsewhere have reminded us that racism is not a thing of the past. Is there anything the government can do to protect its citizens from what Richard Delgado has called "words that wound?"[5]

Mari Matsuda argues that a rule against speech promoting racial hatred could be justified by the unique nature of such speech: it is universally condemned. She cites as evidence the International Convention on the Elimination of All Forms of Racial Discrimination, and the domestic law of all the major common-law countries except the United States. Richard Delgado argues that we prejudge the issue when we frame it in First Amendment terms. We might just as easily begin with the assumption that the government should protect the core value of equal personhood enshrined in the Thirteenth and Fourteenth Amendments. We will then find ourselves on a very different slope—one where the failure to protect the victims of racist speech looks like the beginning of a long slide. Charles Lawrence turns the First Amendment argument back on itself. He contends that racist speech undermines the free market of ideas by putting an end to discussion. The victims of such speech are injured and silenced, unable to respond.

Robert Post disagrees with all three of these justifications. Far from being universally condemned, as Matsuda claims, racism is omnipresent; indeed, that is the very reason we are so concerned about it.

1. Beauharnais v. Illinois, 343 U.S. 250 (1952).

2. 376 U.S. 254 (1964).

3. Gooding v. Wilson, 405 U.S. 518 (1972); Rosenfeld v. New Jersey, 408 U.S. 901 (1972); Lewis v. New Orleans, 408 U.S. 913 (1972); Brown v. Oklahoma, 408 U.S. 914 (1972).

4. Collin v. Smith, 578 F.2d 1197 (7th Cir.1978), aff'g, 477 F.Supp. 676 (N.D.Ill. 1978). The Supreme Court declined to stay the Seventh Circuit's decision. Smith v. Collin, 436 U.S. 953 (1978). The ordinance prohibited the "dissemination of any material ... which promotes and incites hatred against persons by reason of their race, national origin, or religion, and is intended to do so."

5. Delgado, *Words That Wound: A Tort Action for Racial Insults, Epithets, and Name–Calling,* 17 Harv.C.R.–C.L. L.Rev. 133 (1982).

As to Delgado's claim that we should begin with the assumption of equal personhood, Post responds that that assumption is itself the most basic reason for refusing to regulate public discourse. Lawrence's argument that racist speech silences its victims is one that Post finds troubling. But if that actually happens (and Post has his doubts), the real cause is not racist speech itself but the social conditions of racism, which a ban will do nothing to improve.

Finally, Akhil Reed Amar puts much of this debate into a textual and historical context, arguing that *R.A.V. v. City of St. Paul*,[1] and by implication much of the contemporary hate speech controversy, can usefully be viewed through the lens of the Reconstruction amendments to the Constitution. This argument is obviously of a piece with the arguments of MacKinnon, Lawrence, Matsuda, and Delgado about equality as a limitation on the reach of First Amendment protection, but Amar maintains that the Reconstruction amendments might usefully have been marshalled on *both* sides of the arguments in *R.A.V.*

MARI J. MATSUDA, PUBLIC RESPONSE TO RACIST SPEECH: CONSIDERING THE VICTIM'S STORY

87 Mich.L.Rev. 2320, 2341–2342, 2345–2348 (1989).

The international community has chosen to outlaw racist hate propaganda. Article 4 of the International Convention on the Elimination of All Forms of Racial Discrimination states:

Article 4

States Parties condemn all propaganda and all organizations which are based on ideas or theories of superiority of one race or group of persons of one colour or ethnic origin, or which attempt to justify or promote racial hatred and discrimination in any form, and undertake to adopt immediate and positive measures designed to eradicate all incitement to, or acts of, such discrimination and, to this end, with due regard to the principles embodied in the Universal Declaration of Human Rights and the rights expressly set forth in article 5 of this Convention, *inter alia:*

(a) Shall declare as an offence punishable by law all dissemination of ideas based on racial superiority or hatred, incitement to racial discrimination, as well as all acts of violence or incitement to such acts against any race or group of persons of another colour or ethnic origin, and also the provision of any assistance to racist activities, including the financing thereof;

(b) Shall declare illegal and prohibit organizations, and also organized and all other propaganda activities, which promote and incite racial discrimination, and shall recognize participation in such organization or activities as an offence punishable by law; [and]

---

1. 112 S.Ct. 2538 (1992).

(c) Shall not permit public authorities or public institutions, national or local, to promote or incite racial discrimination.

Under this treaty, states are required to criminalize racial hate messages. Prohibiting dissemination of ideas of racial superiority or hatred is not easily reconciled with American concepts of free speech. The Convention recognizes this conflict. Article 4 acknowledges the need for "due regard" for rights protected by the Universal Declaration of Human Rights and by article 5 of the Convention—including the rights of freedom of speech, association, and conscience.

Recognizing these conflicting values, and nonetheless concluding that the right to freedom from racist hate propaganda deserves affirmative recognition, represents the evolving international view. * * *

To those who struggled through early international attempts to deal with racist propaganda, the competing values had a sense of urgency. The imagery of both book burnings and swastikas was clear in their minds. Hitler had banned ideas. He had also murdered six million Jews in the culmination of a campaign that had as a major theme the idea of racial superiority. While the causes of fascism are complex, the knowledge that anti-Semitic hate propaganda and the rise of Nazism were clearly connected guided development of the emerging international law on incitement to racial hatred.

* * *

The Convention, including article 4, was unanimously adopted by the General Assembly on December 21, 1965. Under U.N. treaty procedure, it entered into force on January 4, 1969, and gathered an increasing number of state signatures over the years. The United States was an early signatory to the convention, consistent with its significant role in drafting and promoting the convention from the earliest stages. In 1978 President Carter submitted the convention to the Senate for ratification. The Senate has taken no significant steps toward ratification. Signature does not bind the United States to the treaty until the signing is ratified. Under the Vienna Convention on the Law of Treaties a state's signature does, however, bind it to refrain from defeating the object of the treaty.

* * *

Some commentators suggest that the United States should not ratify the Convention without explicit reservation to article 4, because the due regard clause is not "a sufficient safeguard for the rights set forth in the First Amendment." [131] In signing the Convention, the United States made a relatively short reservation, stating:

> The Constitution of the United States contains provisions for the protection of individual rights, such as the right of free speech, and nothing in the Convention shall be deemed to require or to

---

131. N. Nathanson & E. Schwelb, The United States and the United Nations Trea- ty on Racial Discrimination 8 (Studies in Transnational Legal Policy No. 9, 1975).

authorize legislation or other action by the United States of America incompatible with the provisions of the Constitution of the United States of America.

This limited reservation indicates the United States' basic position of support for the Convention. Such support is consistent with the American ideological commitment to equality and with the need to maintain international prestige. The reservation and the failure to ratify the convention separates the United States from an evolving world standard. * * *

The Convention is not the only expression of the emerging international view. * * *

[T]he existing domestic law of several nations—including states that accept the western notion of freedom of expression—has outlawed certain forms of racist speech.

The United Kingdom, for example, under the Race Relations Act, has criminalized incitement to discrimination and incitement to racial hatred. The Act criminalizes the publication or distribution of "threatening, abusive, or insulting" written matter or use of such language in a public place. The United Kingdom standard originally differed from the international standard in that it required proof of intent to incite to hatred. The intent requirement was later dropped. The Act is consistent with the international standard in that it recognizes that avoiding the spread of hatred is a legitimate object of the law, and that some forms of racist expression are properly criminalized. The legislative history of the Act suggests that the drafters were concerned with the spread of racist violence. Imminent violence, however, was not the only object of the Act. The Act recognized the inevitable connection between the general spread of race hatred and the spread of violence. While commentators have suggested that the Act is ineffective and capable of misuse, the existence of the Act supports the growing international movement toward outlawing racist hate propaganda.

Canada has similarly adopted a national statute governing hate propaganda. Sections 318 and 319 of the Canadian Criminal Code outlaw advocacy of genocide, defined as, *inter alia,* an act designed to kill a member of an identifiable group. They also outlaw communications inciting hatred against any identifiable group where a breach of peace is likely to follow. The law further outlaws the expression of ideas inciting hatred if such expression is tied to a probable threat to order.

The new Canadian Bill of Rights incorporates strong protections for freedom of speech and association. Conflict between the new bill of rights and the hate messages legislation has not prevented actions to limit hate speech.

Australia and New Zealand also have laws restricting racist speech, leaving the United States alone among the major common-law jurisdictions in its complete tolerance of such speech. What these laws and the United Nations Convention have in common is that they specify a particularly egregious form of expression for criminalization. All ideas about differences between races are not banned. The definitive elements are discrimination, connection to violence, and messages of inferiority, hatred, or persecution. Thus the entire spectrum of what could be called racist speech is not prohibited. A belief in intellectual differences between the races, for instance, is not subject to sanctions unless it is coupled with an element of hatred or persecution. What the emerging global standard prohibits is the kind of expression that most interferes with the rights of subordinated-group members to participate equally in society, maintaining their basic sense of security and worth as human beings.

RICHARD DELGADO, CAMPUS ANTIRACISM RULES: CONSTITUTIONAL NARRATIVES IN COLLISION

85 Nw.U.L.Rev. 343, 345–348 (1991).

Persons tend to react to the problem of racial insults in one of two ways. On hearing that a university has enacted rules forbidding certain forms of speech, some will frame the issue as a first amendment problem: the rules limit speech, and the Constitution forbids official regulation of speech without a very good reason. If one takes that starting point, several consequences follow. First, the burden shifts to the other side to show that the interest in protecting members of the campus community from insults and name-calling is compelling enough to overcome the presumption in favor of free speech. Further, there must be no less onerous way of accomplishing that objective. Moreover, some will worry whether the enforcer of the regulation will become a censor, imposing narrow-minded restraints on campus discussion. Some will also be concerned about slippery slopes and line-drawing problems: if a campus restricts this type of expression, might the temptation arise to do the same with classroom speech or political satire in the campus newspaper?

Others, however, will frame the problem as one of protection of equality. They will ask whether an educational institution does not have the power, to protect core values emanating from the thirteenth and fourteenth amendments, to enact reasonable regulations aimed at assuring equal personhood on campus. If one characterizes the issue *this* way, other consequences follow. Now, the defenders of racially scathing speech are required to show that the interest in its protection is compelling enough to overcome the preference for equal personhood; and we will want to be sure that this interest is advanced in the way least damaging to equality. There are again concerns about the decisionmaker who will enforce the rules, but from the opposite standpoint: the enforcer of the regulation must be attuned to the nuances of insult and racial supremacy at issue, for example by incorporating multi-ethnic representation into the hearing process. Finally, a different set of slopes will look slippery.   If we do *not* intervene to protect equality here, what will the next outrage be?

The legal analysis, therefore, leads to opposite conclusions depending on the starting point. But there is an even deeper indeterminacy: both sides invoke different narratives to rally support. Protectors of the first amendment see campus antiracism rules as parts of a much longer story: the centuries-old struggle of Western society to free itself from superstition and enforced ignorance. The tellers of this story invoke martyrs like Socrates, Galileo, and Peter Zenger, and heroes like Locke, Hobbes, Voltaire, and Hume who fought for the right of free expression. They conjure up struggles against official censorship, book burning, witch trials, and communist blacklists. Compared to that richly textured, deeply stirring account, the minority-protector's interest in freeing a few (supersensitive?) individuals from momentary discomfort looks thin. A textured, historical account is pitted against a particularized, slice-of-life, dignitary one.

Those on the minority-protection side invoke a different, and no less powerful, narrative. They see a nation's centuries-long struggle to free itself from racial and other forms of tyranny, including slavery, lynching, Jim Crow laws, and "separate-but-equal" schools. They conjure up different milestones—Lincoln's Emancipation Proclamation, *Brown v. Board of Education;* they look to different heroes—Martin Luther King, the early Abolitionists, Rosa Parks, and Cesar Chavez, civil rights protestors who put their lives on the line for racial justice. Arrayed against that richly textured historical account, the racist's interest in insulting a person of color face-to-face looks thin.

One often hears that the problem of campus antiracism rules is that of balancing free speech and equality. But more is at stake. Each side wants not merely to have the balance struck in its favor; each wants to impose its own understanding of what is at stake. Minority protectors see the injury of one who has been subject to a racial assault as not a mere isolated event, but as part of an interrelated series of acts, by which persons of color are subordinated, and which will follow the victim wherever she goes. First amendment defenders see the wrong of silencing the racist as much more than a momentary inconvenience: protection of his right to speak is part of the never-ending vigilance necessary to preserve freedom of expression in a society that is too prone to balance it away.

My view is that both stories are equally valid. Judges and university administrators have no easy, a priori way of choosing between them, of privileging one over the other. They could coin an exception to free speech, thus giving primacy to the equal protection values at stake. Or, they could carve an exception to equality, saying in effect that universities may protect minority populations except where this abridges speech. Nothing in constitutional or moral theory requires one answer rather than the other. Social science, case law, and the experience of other nations provide some illumination. But ultimately, judges and university administrators must *choose.*

CHARLES R. LAWRENCE, III, IF HE HOLLERS LET HIM GO: REGULATING RACIST SPEECH ON CAMPUS

1990 Duke L.J. 431, 452–455.

Face-to-face racial insults, like fighting words, are undeserving of first amendment protection for two reasons. The first reason is the immediacy of the injurious impact of racial insults. The experience of being called "nigger," "spic," "Jap," or "kike" is like receiving a slap in the face. The injury is instantaneous. There is neither an opportunity for intermediary reflection on the idea conveyed nor an opportunity for responsive speech. The harm to be avoided is both clear and present. The second reason that racial insults should not fall under protected speech relates to the purpose underlying the first amendment. If the purpose of the first amendment is to foster the greatest amount of speech, then racial insults disserve that purpose. Assaultive racist speech functions as a preemptive strike. The racial invective is experienced as a blow, not a proffered idea, and once the blow is struck, it is unlikely that dialogue will follow. Racial insults are undeserving of first amendment protection because the perpetrator's intention is not to discover truth or initiate dialogue but to injure the victim.

The fighting words doctrine anticipates that the verbal "slap in the face" of insulting words will provoke a violent response with a resulting breach of the peace. When racial insults are hurled at minorities, the response may be silence or flight rather than a fight, but the preemptive effect on further speech is just as complete as with fighting words. Women and minorities often report that they find themselves speechless in the face of discriminatory verbal attacks. This inability to respond is not the result of oversensitivity among these groups, as some individuals who oppose protective regulation have argued. Rather, it is the product of several factors, all of which reveal the non-speech character of the initial preemptive verbal assault. The first factor is that the visceral emotional response to personal attack precludes speech. Attack produces an instinctive, defensive psychological reaction. Fear, rage, shock, and flight all interfere with any reasoned response. Words like "nigger," "kike," and "faggot" produce physical symptoms that temporarily disable the victim, and the perpetrators often use these words with the intention of producing this effect. Many victims do not find words of response until well after the assault when the cowardly assaulter has departed.

A second factor that distinguishes racial insults from protected speech is the preemptive nature of such insults—the words by which to respond to such verbal attacks may never be forthcoming because speech is usually an inadequate response. When one is personally attacked with words that denote one's subhuman status and untouchability, there is little (if anything) that can be said to redress either the emotional or reputational injury. This is particularly true when the message and meaning of the epithet resonates with beliefs widely held in society. This preservation of widespread beliefs is what makes the face-to-face racial attack more likely to preempt speech than are other fighting words. The racist name-caller is accompanied by a cultural chorus of equally demeaning speech and symbols.

The subordinated victim of fighting words also is silenced by her relatively powerless position in society. Because of the significance of power and position, the categorization of racial epithets as "fighting words" provides an inadequate paradigm; instead one must speak of their "functional equivalent." The fighting words doctrine presupposes an encounter between two persons of relatively equal power who have been acculturated to respond to face-to-face insults with violence. The fighting words doctrine is a paradigm based on a white male point of view. In most situations, minorities correctly perceive that a violent response to fighting words will result in a risk to their own life and limb. Since minorities are likely to lose the fight, they are forced to remain silent and submissive. This response is most obvious when women submit to sexually assaultive speech or when the racist name-caller is in a more powerful position—the boss on the job or the mob. * * * Less obvious, but just as significant, is the effect of pervasive racial and sexual violence and coercion on individual members of subordinated groups who must learn the survival techniques of suppressing and disguising rage and anger at an early age.

ROBERT C. POST, RACIST SPEECH, DEMOCRACY, AND THE FIRST AMENDMENT

32 Wm. & Mary L.Rev. 267, 290–293, 302, 305–311 (1991).

PUBLIC DISCOURSE AND THE INTRINSIC HARM OF RACIST IDEAS

It is of course a commonplace of first amendment jurisprudence "that the government must remain neutral in the marketplace of ideas." The justification for this principle as applied to public discourse[a] is straightforward. Democracy serves the value of self-determination by establishing a communicative structure within which the varying perspectives of individuals can be reconciled through reason. If the state were to forbid the expression of a particular idea, the government would become, with respect to individuals holding that idea, heteronomous and nondemocratic. This is incompatible with a form of government predicated upon treating its citizens "in ways consistent with their being viewed as free and equal persons."

For this reason the value of self-determination requires that public discourse be open to the opinions of all. "[S]ilence coerced by law—the

a. Post defines "public discourse" as encompassing the communicative processes necessary for the formation of public opinion, whether or not that opinion is directed toward specific government personnel, decisions, or policies.

argument of force in its worst form" [120] is constitutionally forbidden. In a democracy, as Piaget notes, "there are no more crimes of opinion, but only breaches of procedure. All opinions are tolerated so long as their protagonists urge their acceptance by legal methods." [121] The notion that racist ideas ought to be forbidden within public discourse because of their "elemental wrongness" is thus fundamentally irreconcilable with the rationale for first amendment freedoms.

The contemporary debate nevertheless contains [several] distinct arguments that racist ideas ought to be proscribed because of their "deontic" harm.[b] The first is that the idea of racism is *"sui generis"* because it is "universally condemned." [123] The same authors who make this claim, however, also stress "the structural reality of racism in America," a reality manifested not merely in an "epidemic of racist incidents," but also in the widespread racist beliefs characteristic of "upper-class whites" and important social "institutions." In fact it is probably fair to characterize these authors as proponents of regulating racist speech precisely because of their urgent sense of the *prevalence* of racist practices. Although the nightmare of these practices ought to occasion strong public response, their prevalence substantially undermines the conclusion that racism is "universally condemned" in any sense relevant for first amendment analysis. Such practices can be understood only as manifestations of strongly held but otherwise unarticulated racist ideas.

* * *

A [second] argument is that the free expression of racist ideas is inconsistent with our commitment to the egalitarian ideals of the fourteenth amendment. At root this argument rejects autonomy as the principal value of democracy and substitutes instead what Kenneth Karst has eloquently argued is "the substantive center of the fourteenth amendment: the principle of equal citizenship." [130] Although some political theorists have endorsed this position, it runs against the overwhelming American commitment to the importance of "self-rule," to the fundamental belief "that the American people are politically free insomuch as they are governed by themselves collectively."

Of course the principle of self-rule contains its own commitment to the value of equal citizenship, to the notion that, as a formal matter, citizens must be "viewed as free and equal persons." But the meaning of this commitment is measured by the purpose of enabling the processes of self-determination. The appeal to the fourteenth amendment, on the other hand, is meant to signify commitment to a substantive value of

---

120. Whitney v. California, 274 U.S. 357, 375–76 (1927) (Brandeis, J., concurring).

121. J. Piaget, [The Moral Judgment of the Child 57 (M. Gabain trans. 1948)].

b. The phrase "deontic harm" refers to what Post elsewhere calls the "elemental wrongness" of racist expression, regardless of the presence or absence of particular empirical consequences.

123. Matsuda, [*Public Response to Racist Speech: Considering the Victim's Story,* 87 Mich.L.Rev. 2320, 2359 (1989).]

130. Karst, *Citizenship, Race, and Marginality,* 30 Wm. & Mary L.Rev. 1, 1 (1988).

equality that is not defined by reference to this purpose, so that the implementation of the value may adversely affect processes of self-determination. The argument thus envisions the possibility of "balancing" fourteenth amendment values against first amendment principles.

In balancing the value of equal citizenship against the principle of self-determination, however, we must ask who is empowered to interpret the meaning of the highly contestable value of equal citizenship. To the extent that the value of equal citizenship is used to justify limiting public discourse, the interpreter of the value cannot be the people, because the very function of the appeal to the fourteenth amendment is to truncate the communicative processes by which the people clarify their collective will. In such circumstances the Ultimate Interpreter, whoever or whatever it may finally turn out to be, must impose its will without popular accountability. Our government currently contains no such Interpreter, not even the Supreme Court, whose constitutional decisions are always shadowed by the potential of constitutional amendment or political reconstruction through subsequent appointments. The impossibility of locating such an Interpreter suggests the difficulties that attend the argument from the fourteenth amendment.

* * *

PUBLIC DISCOURSE AND HARM TO THE MARKETPLACE OF IDEAS

The most effective arguments for regulating racist speech are those that double back on the concept of public discourse itself and contend that such regulation is necessary for public discourse truly to instantiate the principle of self-determination. * * *

* * *

[Some argue] that the concentrated effect of [racist] speech on members of victim groups is to foreclose public discourse as an effective avenue of collective self-determination. In the contemporary debate this effect has been addressed under the rubric of "silencing."

The literature on silencing has burgeoned. So far as I can make out the literature presents three distinct arguments to support the concept of silencing: victim groups are silenced because their perspectives are systematically excluded from the dominant discourse; victim groups are silenced because the pervasive stigma of racism systematically undermines and devalues their speech; and victim groups are silenced because the visceral "fear, rage, [and] shock" of racist speech systematically preempts response.[189] * * *

The first argument, more developed in the context of recent feminist literature than in that of racist speech, is that the language of public discourse, although seemingly neutral and objective, has a built-in bias that prevents the articulation of minority positions. Thus racism in the

---

189. Lawrence, [*If He Hollers Let Him Go: Regulating Racist Speech on Campus,*   1990 Duke L.J. 431, 452.]

dominant discourse is compressed into "the neutralized word 'discrimination,'" in which "the role of power, domination, and oppression as the source of the evil" is effaced, and "[m]uch of the political, historical, and moral content of 'equality' has been dropped." Similarly, the understanding of whites that racism is an "intentional belief in white supremacy"—the perpetrators' perspective—has been folded into the very language of public debate, whereas the understanding of minorities that racism " 'refers *solely* to minority subordination'"—the victims' perspective—is banished from the language.

Although the premise of this argument seems to me true, it does not by itself support the conclusion that racist speech ought to be regulated. All communication rests on foundations of unarticulated assumptions. The very function of dialogue is often to move toward enlightenment by uncovering and exposing these assumptions. Enlightenment can be gradual and progressive, or it can result from the shock of intense political struggle. That our language always encompasses both more and less than our intentions is thus not an argument for the suppression of racist speech, but rather for the encouragement of further public debate.

The point might be made, however, that public debate fails to achieve such enlightenment because the pervasive racism of American society devalues and stigmatizes minority contributions to this debate. The voice of the victims goes unheard. There is thus a call for an "outsider jurisprudence" which will legitimate that voice and enable "[l]egal insiders . . . [to] imagine a life disabled in a significant way by hate propaganda."

Once again, the premise of this argument appears sound, but its conclusion does not. Audiences always evaluate communication on the basis of their understanding of its social context. This is not a deformity of public discourse, but one of its generic characteristics. It poses the question of how an audience's prepolitical understanding of social context may be altered, a question that confronts all participants in public dialogue. The urgency of the question does not justify restricting public discourse; it is rather a call for more articulate and persuasive speech, for more intense and effective political engagement.

* * *

The third argument for restraining racist speech does not turn on the characterization of public discourse as irrational, but rather as coercive. Recent literature contains searing documentation of the profound personal injury of racist speech, and this injury may in particular circumstances be so shocking as to literally preempt responsive speech. Although the analogous harm of uncivil speech is randomly scattered throughout the population, the disabilities attendant upon racist speech are concentrated upon members of victim groups. Hence, where members of dominant groups perceive "isolated incidents," members of victim groups perceive instead a suffocating and inescapable "racism that is a persistent and constituent part of the social order, woven into the fabric of society and everyday life."

Under such conditions it is to be expected that members of dominant and victim groups may well come to conflicting judgments about whether racist speech shocks significant segments of victim group population into silence. The recent literature proposing restraints on racist speech is eloquent on the need to "listen[ ] to the real victims" of such speech and to display "empathy or understanding for their injury." [200] And of course any fair and just determination about the regulation of public discourse would require exactly this kind of sensitivity. But there is also a tendency in recent literature to move from the proposition that a fair determination cannot be made unless "the victims of racist speech are heard," to the very different proposition that such a determination ought to use "the experience of victim-group members [as] a guide." [202] The latter proposition seems to me plainly false.

The issue on the table is whether irrationality and coercion have so tainted the medium of public discourse as to require shrinking the scope of self-government. That issue significantly affects every citizen, and its resolution therefore cannot be ceded to the control of any particular group. In fact I do not see how the issue can be adequately resolved at all unless some notion of civic membership is invoked that transcends mere group identification. Unless we can strive to deliberate together as citizens, distancing ourselves from (but not abandoning) our specific cultural backgrounds, the issue can be resolved only through the exercise of naked group power, a solution not at all advantageous to the marginalized and oppressed.

Paradoxically, therefore, the question of whether public discourse is irretrievably damaged by racist speech must itself ultimately be addressed through the medium of public discourse. Because those participating in public discourse will not themselves have been silenced (almost by definition), a heavy, frustrating burden is de facto placed on those who would truncate public discourse in order to save it. They must represent themselves as "speaking for" those who have been deprived of their voice. But the negative space of that silence reigns inscrutable, neither confirming nor denying this claim. And the more eloquent the appeal, the less compelling the claim, for the more accessible public discourse will then appear to exactly the perspectives racist speech is said to repress.

Even if this burden is lifted, however, and it is simply accepted that members of victim groups are intimidated into silence, it would still not follow that restraints on racist speech within public discourse are justified. One might believe, for example, that such silencing occurs chiefly

---

200. Lawrence, *supra* note [189], at 436.

202. * * * This tendency is explicitly thematized in Iris Marion Young's artless proposal that "a democratic public" should cede to "constituent groups that are oppressed or disadvantaged" a "veto power regarding specific policies that affect a group directly." Young, *Polity and Group Difference,* 99 Ethics 250, 261–62 (1989).

through the structural conditions of racism, rather than specifically through the shock of racist speech. "The problem," as the Chairman of the Black Studies Department of New York's City College recently remarked apropos of the racist comments of an academic colleague, does not lie with specific communicative acts, but rather with "racism" itself, "insidious in our society and built into our culture." [204] If that were true, restraints on racist speech would impair public discourse without at the same time repairing the silence of victim groups.

* * *

My own conclusion * * * is that the case has not yet been made for circumscribing public discourse to prevent the kind of preemptive silencing that occurs when members of victim groups experience "fear, rage, [and] shock." I say this with some hesitation, and with considerable ambivalence. But even if the empirical claim of systematic preemptive silencing were accepted (and I am not sure that I do accept it), it is in my view most directly the result of the social and structural conditions of racism, rather than specifically of racist speech. Because the logic of the argument from preemptive silencing does not impeach the necessity of preserving the free expression of ideas, public discourse could at most be regulated in a largely symbolic manner so as to purge it of outrageous racist epithets and names. It seems to me highly implausible to claim that such symbolic regulation will eliminate the preemptive silencing that is said to justify restraints on public discourse.

AKHIL REED AMAR, THE CASE OF THE MISSING AMENDMENTS: R.A.V. v. CITY OF ST. PAUL

106 Harv.L.Rev. 124–25, 146–48, 151–60 (1992).

In *R.A.V. v. City of St. Paul*,[1] the Justices claimed to disagree about a good many things, but they seemed to stand unanimous on at least two points. First, the 1989 flag burning case, *Texas v. Johnson*[2]—itself an extraordinarily controversial decision—remains good law and indeed serves as an important font of First Amendment first principles. Second, the First Amendment furnishes a self-contained and sufficient framework for analyzing government regulation of racial hate speech such as cross burning.

* * *

[*R.A.V.*'s] first point of apparent consensus—*Johnson* lives!—is nothing less than an "occasion for dancing in the streets."[13] *R.A.V.*'s second point of seeming unanimity, however, is more sobering. All nine

---

204. Berger, *Professors' Theories on Race Stir Turmoil at City College*, N.Y. Times, Apr. 20, 1990, at B1, col. 2.

1. 112 S.Ct. 2538 (1992).

2. 491 U.S. 397 (1989).

13. This, of course, echoes Alexander Meiklejohn's celebrated and celebratory reaction to New York Times Co. v. Sullivan, 376 U.S. 254 (1964). *See* Harry Kalven, Jr., *The* New York Times *Case: A Note on "The Central Meaning of the First Amendment,"* 1964 Sup.Ct.Rev. 191, 221 n. 125.

Justices analyzed cross burning and other forms of racial hate speech by focusing almost exclusively on the First Amendment. They all seemed to have forgotten that it is a *Constitution* they are expounding, and that the Constitution contains not just the First Amendment, but the Thirteenth and Fourteenth Amendments as well.

* * *

The particular 5–4 split in *R.A.V.* may help us locate the true fault lines of dispute. First we should note that the *R.A.V.* line up parallels, in many ways, the Court's 5–4 split in *Johnson.* A nose counter might thus have predicted that the Scalia Five's opinion would reflect an especially strong commitment to *Johnson,* a prediction confirmed by a close reading of the opinion—though * * * even the minority accepted *Johnson.*

The line up was interesting in a second way. The majority featured the four most junior Associate Justices joined by the Chief Justice, while the four most senior Associate Justices comprised the minority. Here is a small sign—again, confirmed by a close reading of the opinions—that the majority opinion was not simply a restatement, but a remodeling, of past case law. This remodeling was most evident in the majority's insistence that the Court's prior descriptions of fighting words and libel as wholly unprotected were not "literally true."

Finally, and most importantly, we should note that three of the four Justices in the minority have in the past voted to uphold government schemes specially targeted to benefit racial minorities, whereas no member of the Court majority has (yet) done so. This fault line also left strong traces in the opinions, with Justice White expressing open approval of laws specially tailored to protect "groups that have long been the targets of discrimination" and Justice Blackmun speaking of the need to protect "minorities" from "racial threats," "race-based fighting words" and "prejudice."

Yet when we closely examine the opinions themselves, it seems that there were other intertwining and more complicated issues also lurking just beneath the surface of the case. Let us begin by noting that some of the claimed grounds for disagreement did not in fact exist. For example, contrary to the rhetorical excess of the minority, the majority did *not* place "fighting words" on a par with core political speech; it explicitly acknowledged that some (suitably defined) category of fighting words may be banned altogether. Moreover through its examples, it repeatedly affirmed the centrality of anti-government political expression. Similarly, even though Justice White insisted at times that "fighting words" and other categories of speech are entirely unprotected, the minority— no less than the majority—was unwilling to allow gross viewpoint-based discrimination even in those categories.

Why, then, all the *sturm und drang* in *R.A.V.* ? In large part, because, as already noted, the White Four may simply have more tolerance for minority-protective laws, especially when no "innocent whites" are made to pay the price, but only those who engage in "evil and worthless" harassment of racial outgroups. Yet if this is so, the debate is misframed: the real issues here are *Reconstruction Amendment* issues, which were not openly defined and engaged because the case was packaged as a "First Amendment" case.

The caustic debate was misframed in other respects, with the various opinions at times sliding past each other and sliding over some of the big issues posed by the case. And this misframing—combined with subtle differences in focus—may indeed account for some of the remaining disagreement among the Justices. The White Four's opinion tended to focus on the particular alleged facts before the Court. The Scalia Five's opinion, by contrast, focused on the words of the ordinance as applied to the category of fighting words, properly defined. This difference led to two much larger differences in perspective that again implicate attitudes about racial minorities. First, Justice White seemed to see *R.A.V.* as a case about *race;* Justice Scalia, by contrast, saw the case as *equally* implicating concerns about religion and gender. Again and again, Justice Scalia used examples involving those topics. Second, Justice White appeared to assume the case was about protecting *vulnerable* social groups (for example, blacks) from *dominant* social groups (for example, whites). Thus, Justice White spoke of protecting "groups that have long been the targets of discrimination." Nowhere did he openly address the possibility that the St. Paul ordinance might apply against a black-power group hurling racial epithets at whites—"Cracker!"—or radical feminists proclaiming that "all men are scum." Justice Scalia, on the other hand, used language and examples that suggest he would read the ordinance to apply symmetrically—against blacks as well as whites, women as well as men.

Was the ordinance symmetric or asymmetric? Its formal words "on the basis of" suggest symmetry, but its explicit examples—burning crosses and swastikas—suggest special concern with white power (or more generally, abuse of power by historically dominant social forces). Would the ordinance have been more or less constitutionally troubling if symmetric? *These* are the most vexing issues underlying *R.A.V.,* yet they were not sharply identified by the Court, much less analyzed. And they are not purely First Amendment issues, but Reconstruction Amendment issues as well.

* * *

How might the Justices have profitably integrated the Reconstruction Amendments into their opinions in *R.A.V.*? Begin with Justice Scalia. Ironically, the Court's most dedicated textualist failed to even make mention of the constitutional words that were, strictly speaking, at issue in the case. For every textualist should know that the First Amendment's text explicitly restrains only *Congress,* but the plain words of the Fourteenth Amendment do govern action by the states (and, derivatively, cities such as St. Paul). The Reconstruction Congress expressly designed the Fourteenth Amendment to make applicable against states various personal rights, freedoms, privileges and immunities declared in the original Bill of Rights—most definitely including freedom of speech and of the press. Indeed, a careful textualist might note how the First Amendment's phrasing—"Congress *shall make no law . . . abridging* "—was carefully echoed by the Privileges or Immunities Clause of the Fourteenth—"*[n]o* state *shall make . . . any law* which shall *abridge.*"

In light of the general acceptance of the incorporation doctrine, (at least when speech and press rights are concerned), my point may seem a mere pedantic quibble. Lawyers, judges, and scholars commonly refer to state and local censorship cases as "First Amendment" cases. *Texas v. Johnson,* for example, was, strictly speaking, a Fourteenth Amendment case involving a state flag protection law; yet every Justice in the case described it as a "First Amendment" case—as did I in [my discussion above.]

But the Fourteenth Amendment's general invisibility in "First Amendment" discourse has blinded us to the myriad ways in which the Reconstruction experience has colored the way we think about and apply the First Amendment of the Founding. The Reconstruction Amendment was more than a global word processing change to the original Bill of Rights, replacing the original ban on the "federal" government with an identical ban on "state or federal" government. As I have explained in more detail elsewhere, the original First Amendment reflected, first and foremost, a desire to protect relatively popular speech critical of unpopular government policies—the kind of speech, for example, that the 1798 Sedition Act sought to stifle. The Fourteenth Amendment shifted this center of gravity toward protection of even unpopular, eccentric, "offensive" speech, and of speech critical not simply of government policies, but also of prevailing social norms. Whereas the paradigm speaker under the First Amendment was someone like John Peter Zenger in colonial New York—a popular publisher who wanted to get to a local jury likely to be sympathetic to his anti-government message—the paradigm speaker under the Fourteenth Amendment was someone more like Harriet Beecher Stowe in the antebellum South—a cultural outsider whose writings challenged head on the social order and general orthodoxy of dominant public opinion.

With our eyes fixed on the subtle differences between Founding and Reconstruction visions of free speech, we can now chart the distinct evolution of our First Amendment Tradition. First came the Sedition Act crisis, dramatizing the need to protect popular antigovernment speech—a pure First Amendment paradigm. Next came *New York Times v. Sullivan,* which protected locally unpopular, but nationally acceptable criticism of both government and society. Thus, *Sullivan* was a mixed First and Fourteenth Amendment case, with a dash of *McCulloch v. Maryland* thrown in (because a retrograde state was trying to shut down a national civil rights movement). Then came *Johnson,* with judges bravely protecting antigovernment speech that was antisocial and unpopular at both the local and national level. No doubt,

Gregory Johnson, unlike the popular John Peter Zenger, would not have been content to place his fate in the hands of a jury of ordinary citizens. This, too, implicated both First and Fourteenth Amendment patterns. Finally came *R.A.V.*, in which the speech fit a pure Fourteenth Amendment mold: plainly provocative and outrageous to widely shared cultural norms of proper behavior, but (unlike speech under the Sedition Act, *Sullivan, O'Brien,* and *Johnson*) less obviously directed against government policy as such. In attempting to suppress such speech, the St. Paul government may well have been acting not as a self-interested cadre of officials seeking to immunize themselves from criticism and entrench themselves in office (the original First Amendment's primary concern), but as an honest agent of dominant community morality (whose censorial excesses the Fourteenth Amendment was designed to curb).

Of course, the alleged cross-burning in *R.A.V.* was directed against African–Americans, whom the Fourteenth Amendment was specially drafted to protect. But it is precisely at this point that Justice Scalia could and should have stressed his symmetric reading of the St. Paul ordinance. For as he apparently read it, the ordinance would also have targeted for special punishment certain black-power epithets aimed at whites. Had a similar ordinance been applied *against* blacks by Southern whites in the 1960s, Justice Scalia might have asked, would not its selective censorship of racial speech have been troubling?

If Justice Stevens had responded at this point by stressing that the ordinance was truly "evenhanded," barring "low blows" all around, Justice Scalia might profitably have drawn on the history behind the Fourteenth Amendment to stress the possible danger of ostensibly "evenhanded" bans. (Although generally open to historical arguments, Justice Scalia in *R.A.V.* made little use of history beyond a throwaway reference to 1791, the date of the First Amendment's ratification.) Had Justice Scalia kept his eye on the Fourteenth Amendment, he might have pointed to a famous event in the 1830s that catalyzed the anti-slavery movement—the so-called gag rule in Congress that "evenhandedly" prevented any member from raising the slavery issue. In practice of course, the ban worked to disadvantage the anti-slavery critics of the pro-slavery status quo.

Justice Scalia might also have reminded his audience about the importance of a vigorous conception of free speech to the black-led civil rights movement of the 1960s. For example, the landmark "First Amendment" case of the modern era, *New York Times v. Sullivan* was, on its facts, a case protecting vigorous criticism by blacks of widespread ideas and social practices—and so were many other of the key "First Amendment" cases of the era, as Harry Kalven reminds us in his book, *The Negro and the First Amendment.*

Had Justice Scalia presented these Fourteenth Amendment arguments, he would have added considerable strength to an already strong rhetorical performance. The opinion of the Court might have picked up additional votes—including perhaps that of Justice Blackmun, whose separate opinion suggests that he may not have been fully aware of the ordinance's threat to minorities if construed symmetrically. But even more important, the Court's opinion would have helped African–Americans and other minorities look beyond the alleged facts of *R.A.V.* to understand that the ordinance posed a threat to *their* freedom as well. They too—indeed, they *especially,* Justice Scalia might have said—should be wary of government censorship, and all the more so when that censorship is selective.

Missing the Thirteenth Amendment

For Justices White and Stevens, the key Reconstruction Amendment to have emphasized was not the Fourteenth, but the Thirteenth. The Thirteenth Amendment's abolition of slavery and involuntary servitude speaks directly to private, as well as governmental, misconduct; indeed, it authorizes governmental regulation in order to abolish all of the vestiges, "badges[,] and incidents" of the slavery system. The White Four could well have argued that the burning cross erected by R.A.V. was such a badge.

Although the Thirteenth Amendment's second section explicitly empowers only Congress to enforce its anti-slavery vision, states are not powerless to act. Without Section 2, Congress might have lacked the specific enumerated power to eliminate the vestiges of slavery, but states generally need no such specific enumeration before they can act. Rather, state lawmakers typically may support the Constitution's mandates using their general police power under their state constitution, and in keeping with a specific invitation in Article VI's Supremacy Clause and Supremacy Oath.

Might not the kind of harassment alleged in *R.A.V.* be deemed an obvious legacy of slavery—the Klan rising again to terrorize free blacks? Consider the following evocative sentence from Justice Stevens's opinion: "The cross-burning in this case—directed as it was to a single African–American family trapped in their home—was nothing more than a crude form of physical intimidation." If cast as a First Amendment argument, this imagery suggests why the speech at issue should not have been protected—it threatened violence and involved an unwilling private audience, unable to avoid an unwanted message, thereby violating the autonomy principle. Furthermore, it was not directed in any way at a larger political audience as part of a legitimate exercise of political persuasion and thereby fails the Meiklejohn-popular sovereignty test. The incident was, in short, a classic example of the fighting words category of unprotected expression.

But the First Amendment packaging fails to explain why race-based fighting words directed at African–Americans should be treated differently from *other* fighting words. Consider how Stevens's evocative sentence takes on a new color if placed in a Thirteenth Amendment frame. The threat of white racist violence against blacks calls to mind an especially vivid set of historical images—slavery—and the otherwise stale First Amendment metaphor of a *"captive* audience" suddenly springs to life, poetic and ominous. Now we have a focused *constitutional* response to questions about why race might be different, and why a burning cross—or the word "nigger"—might be different. *These,* Justice Stevens might have argued, are badges—symbols—of servitude, and the Constitution allows legislatures to treat them differently from other kinds of speech.

Two important qualifications are in order. First, Section I of the Thirteenth Amendment is not logically tied to race; it protects persons of all races against slavery and involuntary servitude. However, the Supreme Court has long recognized—both before the Thirteenth Amendment in the infamous *Dred Scott* case and thereafter—the important connections between slavery and race in America. And from the Civil Rights Act of 1866 to the present, Congress has treated *race-based* oppression as a unique badge and incident of slavery that may be specially targeted and punished. The Act of 1866—the precursor of section 1982—is especially significant here, as it was purposely drafted pursuant to the Thirteenth Amendment, and yet it prohibited *race-based* misconduct even in formerly free states (such as Minnesota).

Second, the argument sketched out thus far in no way authorizes states to betray the basic principles of the Fourteenth Amendment—including its protection of free speech—simply by purporting to enforce the Thirteenth. Laws that regulate only fighting words, properly defined, may present no realistic threat to the hard core of free speech. But perhaps the Thirteenth Amendment might allow word regulation beyond the fighting words category. For example, the Court has upheld legislation under the Thirteenth Amendment that bars, among other things, the use of words such as "For Whites Only" on a residential "For Sale" sign. As noted earlier, Justice Scalia seemed to allow for such restrictions if the words are "swept up incidentally within the reach of a statute directed at conduct rather than speech," such as the private racial discrimination in housing prohibited by section 1982, which Justice Scalia cited on this point. But if mere refusal to deal with another on the basis of race can constitute a badge of servitude, surely the intentional racial harassment of blacks can constitute a badge of servitude as well. Under this theory, the intentional trapping of a captive audience of blacks, in order to subject them to face-to-face degradation and dehumanization on the basis of their race, might be proscribed as "incidental" to a general statute designed to eliminate all "badges and incidents" of the legacy of slavery. Intentional trapping—temporary involuntary servitude, a sliver of slavery—is arguably more like conduct than like speech, akin to (and arguably much worse than) refusal to deal on the basis of race. * * *

Had the Justices focused on the Reconstruction Amendments, they would have been forced to think more clearly about whether gender-based and religion-based hate speech warranted similar treatment to race-based hate speech and whether, within each category, symmetry or asymmetry should obtain. On the first issue, they would have had to consider that American slavery was originally rooted in religious discrimination—only non-Christians were enslaved—and that like blacks, women have suffered deeply entrenched and systematic status-based subordination based on physical traits fixed at birth. On the other hand, they could have noted that by the time of the Thirteenth Amendment's adoption, American slavery had lost its connection to discrimination against non-Christians and that, thus far, the Court and Congress have both linked slavery only to race, not to gender or religion. Section 1982, for example, prohibits only race-based residential discrimination.

On the symmetry issue, the Justices would have had to deal squarely with a question they slid past all too quickly: could the ordinance be applied *against* racial minorities? If so, why were the anti–Scalia Justices so unconcerned, and why did Justice White's and Justice Blackmun's opinions use language focused only on racial hate speech directed at—rather than spoken by—racial minorities? If, on the other hand, Justices White, Blackmun, and O'Connor were willing to uphold an ordinance they read as asymmetric, that too required explanation. Perhaps they might have emphasized that this form of "affirmative action" for racial minorities did not threaten any "innocent whites" and possibly would not involve courts in the tricky task of administering rules based on the percentages of racial blood in a person's veins. In other affirmative action contexts, the government must decide who counts as sufficiently "black," for example, to qualify for race-based benefits. Under the St. Paul ordinance, however, perhaps prosecution might well lie even if the trapped family was not black, as long as R.A.V. *thought* they were, or even if a light-skinned mulatto sought to denigrate a darker Jamaican as "black scum." In any event, the Thirteenth Amendment approach raises an interesting possibility not easily visible through a conventional First Amendment lens: openly asymmetric regulation of racial hate speech may be less, rather than more, constitutionally troubling.

There is, of course, no guarantee that the Scalia Five would have embraced the Thirteenth Amendment approach had it been vigorously pressed in *R.A.V.* But the Court, one hopes, would at least have been obliged to speak with much greater clarity than it did about the differences it saw between the St. Paul ordinance and section 1982. In the process, it might have clarified exactly how far legislation under the Thirteenth Amendment can go without running afoul of freedom of speech under the First and Fourteenth Amendments.

In any event, my purpose here has not been to resolve definitively the issues raised by *R.A.V.,* but to show how more careful attention to Reconstruction might have enabled all the Justices in *R.A.V.* to write sharper and more persuasive opinions.

BIBLIOGRAPHY

Hadley Arkes, *Civility and the Regulation of Speech: Rediscovering the Defamation of Groups,* 1974 Sup.Ct.Rev. 281.

Katharine T. Bartlett & Jean O'Barr, *The Chilly Climate on College Campuses: An Expansion of the "Hate Speech" Debate,* 1990 Duke L.J. 574.

Alan E. Brownstein, *Hate Speech and Harassment: The Constitutionality of Campus Codes that Prohibit Racial Insults,* 3 Wm. & Mary Bill of Rights J. 179 (1994).

J. Peter Byrne, *Racial Insults and Free Speech Within the University,* 79 Geo.L.J. 399 (1991).

Joshua Cohen, *Freedom of Expression,* 22 Phil. & Pub. Aff. 207 (1993).

Richard Delgado, *Words That Wound: A Tort Action for Racial Insults, Epithets, and Name–Calling,* 17 Harv.C.R.–C.L.L.Rev. 133 (1982).

Donald Downs, NAZIS IN SKOKIE: FREEDOM, COMMUNITY, AND THE FIRST AMENDMENT (1985).

Edward J. Eberle, *Hate Speech, Offensive Speech, and Public Discourse in America,* 29 Wake Forest L.Rev. 1135 (1994).

Mary Ellen Gale, *Reimaging the First Amendment: Racist Speech and Equal Liberty,* 65 St. John's L.Rev. 119 (1991).

John H. Garvey, *Book Review,* 3 Const. Comm. 462 (1986) (of Downs).

Marvin Glass, *Anti–Racism and Unlimited Freedom of Speech: An Untenable Dualism,* 8 Can.J.Phil. 559 (1978).

R. Kent Greenawalt, *Insults and Epithets: Are They Protected Speech?,* 42 Rutgers L.Rev. 298 (1991).

Graham Hughes, *Prohibiting Incitement to Racial Discrimination,* 16 U. Toronto L.J. 361 (1966).

Henry H. Hyde & George M. Fishman, *The Collegiate Speech Protection Act of 1991: A Response to the New Intolerance in the Academy,* 37 Wayne L.Rev. 1469 (1991).

Thomas David Jones, *Article 4 of the International Convention on the Elimination of All Forms of Racial Discrimination and the First Amendment,* 23 How.L.J. 429 (1980).

Elena Kagen, *Regulation of Hate Speech and Pornography After R.A.V.,* 60 U.Chi.L.Rev. 873 (1993).

Kenneth Karst, *Boundaries and Reasons: Freedom of Expression and the Subordination of Groups,* 1990 U.Ill.L.Rev. 95.

David Kretzmer, *Freedom of Speech and Racism,* 8 Cardozo L.Rev. 445 (1987).

Kenneth Lasson, *Racial Defamation as Free Speech: Abusing the First Amendment,* 17 Colum.Hum.Rts.L.Rev. 11 (1985).

Kenneth Lasson, *Group Libel Versus Free Speech: When Big Brother Should Butt In,* 23 Duq.L.Rev. 77 (1984).

Frederick M. Lawrence, *Resolving the Hate Crimes/Hate Speech Paradox: Punishing Bias Crimes and Protecting Racist Speech,* 68 Notre Dame L.Rev. 673 (1993).

Frederick M. Lawrence, *The Punishment of Hate: Toward a Normative Theory of Bias–Motivated Crimes,* 93 Mich.L.Rev. 320 (1994).

Jean C. Love, *Discriminatory Speech and the Tort of Intentional Infliction of Emotional Distress,* 47 Wash. & Lee L.Rev. 123 (1990).

Toni M. Massaro, *Equality and Freedom of Expression: The Hate Speech Dilemma,* 32 Wm. & Mary L.Rev. 211 (1991).

Calvin R. Massey, *Hate Speech, Cultural Diversity, and the Foundational Paradigms of Free Expression,* 40 UCLA L.Rev. 103 (1992).

Note, *A Communitarian Defense of Group Libel Laws,* 101 Harv.L.Rev. 682 (1988).

Offensive and Libelous Speech Symposium, 47 Wash. & Lee L.Rev. 1 (1990).

David Reisman, *Democracy and Defamation: Control of Group Libel,* 42 Colum.L.Rev. 727 (1942).

Dean M. Richardson, *Racism: A Tort of Outrage,* 61 Or.L.Rev. 267 (1982).

Deborah R. Schwartz, *A First Amendment Justification for Regulating Racist Speech on Campus,* 40 Case W.Res.L.Rev. 733 (1990).

Robert A. Sedler, *The Unconstitutionality of Campus Bans on "Racist Speech:" The View From Without and Within,* 53 U.Pitt.L.Rev. 631 (1992).

Suzanna Sherry, *Speaking of Virtue: A Republican Approach to University Regulation of Hate Speech,* 75 Minn.L.Rev. 933 (1991).

Steven H. Shiffrin, *Racist Speech, Outsider Jurisprudence, and the Meaning of America,* 80 Cornell L.Rev. 43 (1994).

Rodney Smolla, *Rethinking First Amendment Assumptions About Racist and Sexist Speech,* 47 Wash. & Lee L.Rev. 171 (1990).

Nadine Strossen, *Regulating Racist Speech on Campus: A Modest Proposal?,* 1990 Duke L.J. 484.

Symposium, *Hate Speech After* R.A.V.: *More Conflict Between Free Speech and Equality?,* 18 Wm.Mitchell L.Rev. 889 (1992).

Nicholas Wolfson, *Free Speech Theory and Hateful Words,* 60 U.Cin. L.Rev. 1 (1991).

F. SEXUAL HARASSMENT

Chapter II opened by characterizing a central issue in free speech theory as one of demarcating the *coverage* of the principle of freedom of speech, and also of the First Amendment. Once we look at the law of securities regulation, antitrust, contract, commercial law, perjury, and the like, it is no longer plausible to suppose that the First Amendment is even relevant to the full universe of linguistic conduct. Now we conclude our materials on freedom of speech by returning to the same topic, here in the context of sexual harassment.

Various federal, state, and local civil rights laws prohibit sexual harassment, and much of the law fits into two categories. One is commonly called "quid pro quo" sexual harassment, with the prototypical example being the employer or teacher who offers a promotion, a raise, or a good grade in exchange for sex. The other is "hostile environment" sexual harassment, where a prototypical example would be a workplace environment in which male employers and co-workers routinely physically molest female employees or direct gender-based insults at them. In both varieties the unlawful conduct is commonly substantially verbal, and in both varieties until recently the free speech claims of the harassers were either non-existent or not taken seriously. Within the past several years, however, it has become more common for people to argue, and to be taken seriously when they argue, that the verbal conduct that some say is harassing is in fact protected, or at least covered, by the First Amendment, and so immunized by the First Amendment from the reach of various civil rights laws.[1] In the selections that follow Kingsley Browne argues that much that we think of as sexual harassment is in fact protected by the First Amendment, and Catharine MacKinnon uses sexual harassment in the workplace as a way of showing both that speech can be equality-denying and that the central questions of free speech theory may still be the ones of whether, when, and why consequential speech will be included within the reach of the First Amendment and when it will be excluded.

KINGSLEY R. BROWNE, TITLE VII AS CENSORSHIP: HOSTILE–ENVIRONMENT HARASSMENT AND THE FIRST AMENDMENT

52 Ohio St.L.J. 481–82, 491–93, 512–15, 542–50 (1991).

"Women do not belong in the medical profession; they should stay home and make babies!" Is such a statement occurring in the workplace a constitutionally protected expression of a currently unfashionable social view, or is it sexual harassment in violation of Title VII of the Civil Rights Act of 1964? If it violates Title VII, is Title VII to that extent inconsistent with the first amendment? Many courts and commentators have addressed the first question—that is, the contours of "hostile environment" harassment—but few have acknowledged the possibility of constitutional protection for such statements. The purpose of this

---

1. Such First Amendment arguments were made in Robinson v. Jacksonville Shipyards, Inc., 760 F.Supp. 1486 (M.D.Fla. 1991), but were rejected by the court. They again surfaced in the opinions in R.A.V. v. City of St. Paul, 112 S.Ct. 2538 (1992), and in the briefs and oral arguments in Harris v. Forklift Systems, Inc., 114 S.Ct. 367 (1993), although in this latter case the opinion of the Supreme Court, upholding the sanctions, made no mention of the First Amendment claims.

Article is to examine the extent to which the broad definition of "hostile work environment" adopted by the courts in harassment cases establishes a content-based—even viewpoint-based—restriction of expression that is inconsistent with contemporary first amendment jurisprudence. To the extent that it does establish such a restriction Title VII must be given a narrowing construction in order to avoid a finding of invalidity.

* * *

Regulation of speech in the workplace that is deemed "harassing" is pervasive. The Guidelines of the Equal Employment Opportunity Commission provide the most commonly accepted definition of "sexual harassment," a definition that courts have adapted to fit cases of racial harassment as well: "verbal or physical conduct of a sexual nature [that] has the purpose or effect of unreasonably interfering with an individual's work performance or creating an intimidating, hostile, or offensive work environment." [8] Although the Guidelines purport to regulate only "verbal or physical *conduct*," the concept of "verbal conduct" has no obvious meaning, and courts have consistently interpreted it to mean "verbal expression." [9] Relying on the EEOC's definition of hostile-environment harassment, courts, both state and federal, have found employers liable for "conduct" ranging from clearly unprotected forcible sexual assault and other unwanted sexual touching to "obscene propositions," sexual vulgarity (including "off color" jokes) and "sexist" remarks, some of which are almost certainly protected by the first amendment. Similarly, racial jokes, slurs, and other statements deemed derogatory to minorities have served as the basis for claims of racial harassment.

* * *

Title VII expressly prohibits neither sexual nor racial harassment. Instead, it generally provides that it is an unlawful employment practice for an employer "to discriminate against any individual with respect to his compensation, terms, conditions, or privileges of employment because of such individual's race, color, religion, sex, or national origin." Nonetheless, courts have identified two forms of sexual harassment that violate Title VII—"*quid pro quo* " and "hostile work environment" harassment. "*Quid pro quo* " harassment typically involves a claim that an employee, usually female, was required to submit to sexual advances as a condition of receiving job benefits or that her failure to submit to such advances resulted in a tangible job detriment, such as discharge or failure to receive a promotion. "Hostile work environment" harassment

---

8. 29 C.F.R. § 1604.11(a)(3). Because the EEOC lacks the authority to promulgate substantive regulations, the Guidelines lack the force of law. However, federal courts, including the Supreme Court, have uniformly relied upon them, *see, e.g.,* Meritor Sav. Bank, F.S.B. v. Vinson, 477 U.S. 57, 65 (1986), and many state statutes and regulations have adopted the EEOC language, *see, e.g.,* Ill.Rev.Stat. ch. 68, § 2–101(E); Mich.Comp.Laws § 37.2103(h).

9. *See* Rabidue v. Osceola Ref. Co., 584 F.Supp. 419, 432 (E.D.Mich.1984), *aff'd,* 805 F.2d 611 (6th Cir.1986), *cert. denied,* 481 U.S. 1041 (1987) (the term " 'verbal conduct of a sexual nature' * * * seems to be directed toward profane words and pictures that deal with sex").

involves the claim that the workplace is so "polluted" with sexual hostility toward women—or racial hostility to other races—that it discriminatorily alters the "terms and conditions of employment" within the meaning of the statute. The hostility may be expressed either through conduct or through speech. The focus of this Article is limited to hostile-environment harassment and then only to the extent that the hostile environment is created in whole or in part by expression.

* * *

Expression contributing to harassment claims comes in a variety of forms. While much of it is exceedingly crude and probably outside the protection of the first amendment, some is merely uncivil, some at most insensitive, and some perhaps wholly harmless. As the description of the cases below reveals, speech that is only arguably sexist, sexual, or racist may form the basis for a claim of harassment. Central to a finding of unlawful harassment is often a conclusion by the court that the message is "offensive," "inappropriate," or even "morally wrong." Even if the employer ultimately prevails in such cases, it must incur a high cost in litigation fees for declining to regulate the speech of employees. * * *

There are two primary messages conveyed by the expression that leads to sexual harassment complaints. The first is a message of unwelcomeness or hostility; expressions that women do not belong in the workplace or scornful or derisive statements about women would fall in this class. The second is a message that the harasser views the plaintiff in particular or women in general in a sexual light. For sake of discussion, the former will be called the "hostility message," while the latter will be called the "sexuality message."

Many sexual harassment cases have involved the use of "bad words" of a sexual nature. Crude or otherwise inappropriate language referring to or addressing women is commonly present in hostile-environment cases, though it is not generally by itself enough to establish a claim of harassment. The terms complained of are primarily of two kinds, and they convey both of the above-described messages: (1) the "hostility message" is conveyed by terms of derision, such as "broad," "bitch," and "cunt;" and (2) the "sexuality message" is conveyed by terms of "endearment," such as "honey," "sweetie," and "tiger." The complained-of terms may refer to women in general, particular women other than the plaintiff, or they may refer to the plaintiff herself and be addressed either to her or to others while referring to her.

At least with respect to the most vulgar expressions, arguably it is just the use of "indecent" words—words that are "beyond the pale" of what can be spoken in polite society—that is being regulated. That, of course, would justify viewing the most vulgar terms as contributing to a hostile environment, but it would not justify reliance on milder terms, such as "broad." But Title VII is not a "clean language act," and bad language conveying no idea is not the target of the harassment cases.

Thus, the court in *State v. Human Rights Commission,*[70] distinguished between "gender-specific" terms, such as "cunt," "bitch," "twat," and "raggin' it"—which constitute "conduct of a sexual nature"—and "general sexual" terms, such as "fuck" and "motherfucker" used as expletives, which do not. The court held that a supervisor's reference to women's physical appearance and his reference to women by "gender-specific" derogatory terms constituted sexual harassment because it was an "expression of animosity" toward women. The finding of harassment was not based primarily on one-to-one expressions of hostility by the supervisor toward the employee, but instead on the general disrespect he showed women in his conversations with others.

* * *

Plaintiffs in sexual harassment cases also frequently challenge the exhibition of written or pictorial material that they believe is demeaning or mocking toward women. Pin-ups or "girlie magazines" in the workplace have been the subject of innumerable sexual harassment claims. The conflicting approaches to the problem of sexually oriented displays are revealed by the majority and dissenting opinions in *Rabidue v. Osceola Refining Co.* The majority rejected a claim that was based upon anti-female language and pin-ups, stating:

> The sexually oriented poster displays had a *de minimis* effect on the plaintiff's work environment when considered in the context of a society that condones and publicly features and commercially exploits open displays of written and pictorial erotica at the newsstands, on prime-time television, at the cinema, and in other public places.

On the other hand, Judge Keith's frequently cited dissent would have found that the alleged harasser's "misogynous language" combined with the pin-ups constituted a Title VII violation because they "evoke and confirm the debilitating norms by which women are primarily and contemptuously valued as objects of male sexual fantasy." In the dissent's view, the "precise purpose" of Title VII was to prevent sexual jokes, conversations, and literature from "poisoning the work environment." Two of the displays that Judge Keith seemed to find particularly reprehensible were a poster showing a woman in a supine position with a golf ball on her breasts and a man standing over her, golf club in hand, yelling "Fore" and a supervisor's desk plaque declaring "Even male chauvinist pigs need love."

Had courts squarely faced the first amendment issue in hostile-environment cases, they could not have employed the EEOC Guidelines as they did without creating a new exception to the first amendment. The standard for hostile-environment harassment cases is strongly viewpoint-based and can be upheld only by a showing of a government

---

70. 178 Ill.App.3d 1033, 534 N.E.2d 161 (1989).

interest of the highest order. No currently recognized first amendment doctrine can explain the analysis in these cases.

* * *

If [the] current interpretation of Title VII cannot withstand scrutiny under current first amendment doctrine, one obvious response would be to modify the doctrine to permit restriction of sexist and racist speech. A number of recent commentators have suggested that such modifications be adopted. However, the case for modification is a weak one that is fundamentally hostile to first amendment values. Moreover, it assumes something that has yet to be demonstrated—that offensive speech totally lacks value under the first amendment. * * *

The fact that the preceding discussion has focused on the more extreme and vicious epithets that may be hurled at blacks and women should not obscure the fact that harassment doctrine under Title VII is not so limited. Even if the word "nigger" may be prohibited consistent with the first amendment, what about other words applied to blacks, such as "nigra," "Negro," "colored," and, with the advent of the now-preferred "African American," perhaps even the term "black" itself? All of the above words were at one time thought to be the "civil" alternative to more demeaning references. They may now be considered to be insulting to varying degrees. Moreover, not all offensive speech consists of discrete epithets; it may also include ideas that are viewed as offensive but expressed without use of offensive words. Many harassment claims have been based upon racial, ethnic, or sexual jokes. Although some may find such jokes categorically offensive, most would acknowledge a broad range of meaning for such jokes. Although some are hateful, others are more gentle, even affectionate. Courts in harassment cases, however, almost never describe the jokes for which they are imposing liability, instead simply describing them as "racial and ethnic jokes" or "dirty jokes" and assuming that is the end of the inquiry.

Similarly, in the sexual context, assuming that the most offensive vulgarities are regulable, other terms, such as "broads," "girls," or even "ladies," or such terms of address as "honey," "babe," and "tiger" are less obviously so, even though they are often considered "degrading" of the female sex. Moreover, if sexual terms limited to women are prohibited, that suggests that equivalent terms relating to men should likewise be prohibited. A rule that prohibited anti-female statements but permitted anti-male statements would be inconsistent with the viewpoint neutrality required by the first amendment.

A mighty conviction that "women should not be sex objects" or that "bigotry is bad" is an insufficient basis for attempting to outlaw expressions of those views. In the first place, the first amendment requires an official agnosticism on questions of social policy. Government may legitimately advocate and implement one policy over another, but it may not stifle debate simply by labelling certain social views "wrong." * * *

The considerations discussed above counsel hesitation even if we are convinced that offensive speech lacks first amendment value. The problem of the "slippery slope" suggests that regulating speech that we assume valueless may lead to regulation of speech that does have value. Moreover, there is a substantial difficulty in establishing an acceptable mechanism for determining on an ad hoc basis which speech is protected and which is not. These concerns assume even greater proportions, however, if it is acknowledged that some of these statements are not wholly without first amendment value.

Scholars over the years have identified a number of reasons that we protect speech. A detailed discussion of these reasons is beyond the scope of this Article, but under almost any rationale, at least some of the speech involved in harassment cases has some value. The most obvious traditional first amendment value of racist and sexist speech is that it constitutes an expression of views on important issues of social policy. Political speech is often said to be at the "core" of first amendment protection. It cannot be doubted that the general subject of relations between the sexes and the races is an important matter of public concern. Everyone would agree that statements such as "blacks are entitled to the same respect as whites" or "women have as much right to participate in the economic life of our country as men" have significant value under the first amendment; indeed those sentiments have been enshrined in many of our laws. For purposes of political debate, the converse of those statements must also be seen as having first amendment value because of the government's "paramount obligation of neutrality." Although we may personally believe that the former statements have greater merit, in the sense that they are morally correct and reflect contemporary values, under the first amendment both statements are entitled to equal legal protection. That we as a society no longer accept the truth of the statements arguing for inequality does not make them any less worthy of protection. Under almost everyone's view of the first amendment, the statements would have been protected in the nineteenth century, when they reflected prevailing social norms; they cannot be banned now simply because conceptions of sound policy have changed.

In addition to whatever value it might have in contributing to political discourse, sexist and racist speech also may serve a valuable function by acting as a "safety valve," which has been recognized by some as a reason to protect speech. A similar value has been identified in ethnic jokes. One of the commonly cited functions of the first amendment is to encourage expression of feelings of frustration and thereby decrease resort to violence. In a number of harassment cases, it appears that some of the offensive language is a product of resentment of affirmative action or even of prohibitions against discrimination. If so, that resentment can only be exacerbated by insulating women and minorities from offense and requiring a modification of employee behavior upon entry of women or minorities into the workplace. Expressions of hostility may be superior to the manifestations of hostility that might result if the expression is prohibited.

Modification of first amendment doctrine should not even be contemplated to accommodate harassment claims without a clear vision of the benefits of doing so. Yet, it is far from obvious that regulation of offensive speech achieves the goals of eliminating prejudice. In fact, expressions of sexist and racist views may actually have a *beneficial* impact on social views, because hearing such statements in their baldest form may have the effect of demonstrating the poverty of the beliefs expressed. As John Stuart Mill recognized, even obviously false statements are worthy of protection:

> [E]ven if the received opinion be not only true, but the whole truth; unless it is suffered to be, and actually is, vigorously and earnestly contested, it will, by most of those who receive it, be held in the manner of a prejudice, with little comprehension or feeling of its rational grounds.

The creators of *All in the Family* understood this. Archie Bunker was not created as a television character for the purpose of persuading viewers of the correctness of his ideas. Rather, his character was an attempt to demonstrate the ugliness of prejudice by exposing viewers to its expression. Stifling that expression could have the unwanted effect of reducing the extent to which persons having unarticulated prejudices examine them. * * *

The impulse to censor is a powerful one, and it has been given free rein under Title VII. Not only has "targeted vilification" been regulated, but much less harmful and less invidiously motivated expression has been restricted as well. That so much speech has been stifled without substantial outcry is in large measure a reflection of the powerful current consensus against racism and sexism. But it is precisely when a powerful consensus exists that the censorial impulse is most dangerous and, ironically, least necessary. The primary risk of censorship in our society today is not from a government fearful of challenge, but from majorities seeking to establish an orthodoxy for all society. When the orthodoxy is one of "equality," that risk is at its highest.

The definition of "harassment" contained in the EEOC Guidelines and applied by the courts, combined with vicarious employer liability, creates a substantial chilling effect on discussion in the workplace of matters even tangentially dealing with sex and race. Acting pursuant to those Guidelines, courts have displayed remarkably little discernment among examples of expression. Once they have been labelled as racist or sexist, all such expression has been deemed regulable. Although much of the speech that has been described in this Article arguably may be regulated through appropriately narrow and specific legislation that is viewpoint neutral, the Guidelines are not the appropriate vehicle, and, in fact, are so vague and so overbroad that they may not be applied even to unprotected speech consistent with the Constitution.

The current approach to regulation of offensive speech is directly contrary to the traditional notion that noxious ideas should be countered through juxtaposition with good ideas in the hope that the bad ideas will lose out in the marketplace of ideas. To a degree perhaps unprecedented, the current attempt to stifle offensive speech can be viewed as an attempt to achieve not only an egalitarian orthodoxy of speech and action but an orthodoxy of thought itself. Consider, for example, prohibitions against employees' having sexually explicit pictures on the inside of their lockers or their reading *Playboy* (or worse) in the workplace. The justification for such regulation is not that women of delicate sensibilities might see the material and be shocked by it. Rather, the basis for the prohibition is that some people, mostly women, are offended by what the employee is thinking while he is looking at the pictures; they are offended by the way he "views"—that is, "thinks about"—women.

[In] addition to its Orwellian overtones, the assumption that beliefs can be altered by forbidding expression is probably wrong. [The] only effective method of altering a world view that is deemed pernicious is to provide a persuasive response—that is, "more speech." "Shut up!" is not a persuasive response.

Although the contrary is sometimes asserted, challenging censorship is not to cast one's lot with those censored or to minimize the substance of the opinions of those urging censorship. Instead it is to accept the fundamental *constitutional* truth that the government may not establish a fundamental *moral* truth through suppression of expression. Probably everyone reading this Article would agree that the world would be a better place without much of the expression that is described in the harassment cases. It does not follow, however, that the world would be a better place if elimination of such expression is compelled by the threat of governmental sanctions. Persuasion that the offensive views are wrong or that they not be expressed where they are unwelcome is a far better solution than "silence coerced by law—the argument of force in its worst form."[408]

CATHARINE MACKINNON, ONLY WORDS

45–48, 54, 58–64 (1993).

If ever words have been understood as acts, it has been when they are sexual harassment. For fifteen years, unremitting pressure for dates, unwelcome sexual comments, authoritative offers to exchange sex for benefits, and environments permeated with sexual vilification and abuse have been legally actionable in employment and education. Only words—yet they have not been seen as conveying ideas, although, like all social practices, they do: ideas like what men think of women, what men

408. Whitney v. California, 274 U.S. 357, 375–76 (1927) (Brandeis, J., concurring).

want to do to women, what women should do for men, where women belong. Sexualized racism and visual pornography have been integral to sexual harassment all along. In a not uncommon example, a Black woman worker was shown "a pornographic photograph depicting an interracial act of sodomy" by a white male co-worker who "told her that the photograph showed the 'talent' of a black woman" and "stated that she was hired for the purpose indicated in the photograph."

Until recently, sexual harassment has never been imagined to raise expressive concerns, although all sexual harassment is words, pictures, meaningful acts and gestures. Yet it has been legally understood in terms of what it does: discriminate on the basis of sex. Unwelcome sex talk is an unwelcome sex act. When threatening, severe, or pervasive enough, it works to exclude and segregate and denigrate and subordinate and dehumanize, violating human dignity and denying equality of opportunity. The First Amendment has not come up, even in a case in which a court issued an injunction prohibiting saying things like "Did you get any over the weekend?" First Amendment issues have not often been raised against racial harassment claims either, even one in which the court found that the law requires employers to "take prompt action to prevent bigots from expressing their opinions in a way that abuses or offends their co-workers."

With a fine sense of reality, courts have not taken chanting "cunt" at a working woman as conveying the idea "you have a vagina," or as expressing eroticism, but rather as pure abuse. When told such profanity was a simple expletive, one judge was not fooled. If you stubbed your toe, he asked, would you yell, "oh, cunt"? For cultures in which the answer is affirmative, one might ask why women's genitals are a negative expletive. In a similar spirit, neither a shipyard dartboard with a drawing of a woman's breast with a nipple as the bull's eye, nor items like a construction site urinal with a woman's vulva painted on it, has been considered art. A drawing of a nude segmented female torso with "USDA Choice" stamped on it has not been defended as political satire. The workplace comment "Black women taste like sardines" has not been construed as a possible advertisement for fish, hence protected commercial speech. "It doesn't hurt women to have sex right after childbirth," in the same workplace, has not been seen as an idea of scientific value, however misguided. Graffiti stating, "The more you lick it, the harder it gets" has not been construed as sex education, nor "do you spit or swallow?" as a query expressing concern for oral hygiene.

One Black woman, the only one working in a particular soap factory, reported that soap carved in the shape of a penis was periodically sent down her assembly line. In one restaurant, male management shaped hamburger meat in the form of a penis and asked a woman worker, "Is this big enough?" Another woman who worked in a warehouse charged that male co-workers would expose their buttocks to her. When considering legal action against this type of activity, no one has argued that the soap or hamburger may be artistic expression, the flashing symbolic speech or guerrilla theater, or a male equivalent to nude dancing. When a man slips a woman's paycheck into his pants and requires her to "go for it," nobody suggests he is making a militant display of dissent against the economic system.

Construing these events as "speech"—in terms of their form as expression and their content as ideas—apparently looks like what it is: a transparent ploy to continue the bigoted abuse and avoid liability. The misogynist meaning and exclusionary impact of such expression have not been contested by most defendants, either. The harm done by this behavior is importantly contextual, certainly, but it is implicitly recognized that social life occurs only in social context, and this is a social harm. That these experiences differ for harasser and harassed is not denied either; this difference seems only to support the fact of their unequal positions in a single shared system of social meaning, further supporting the act as one of inequality. One court rejected the defendant's argument that because racial slurs were common parlance, they did not have racial overtones. Many have rejected defenses that the abuse being litigated was only a joke. The postmodern pose of creative misinterpretation—acting as though words do not mean what they mean or do what they do—has seldom been tried, and even then not to protect the abuse as speech. * * *

[For] fifteen years courts have shown real comprehension that what might be called speech, if forced into an abstract First Amendment mold, are in fact acts of inequality, hence actionable as discrimination. Although sexual harassment might be characterized as "sexual expression," it has never been suggested that its regulation must meet obscenity standards. Actions against racial harassment at work have not been held to constitutional standards for group defamation or incitement either. Under discrimination laws, courts have taken legal action against group-based invective, no matter that it contains ideas or seeks to express or further a political position. Indeed, its role in furthering the politics—that is, the reality—of inequality has been understood as integral to its injuriousness. "KKK" on workplace walls has not been protected as political advocacy, and whether or not violence is imminently incited by it has not mattered. The term "nigger-rigged" has not been protected as merely offensive or satire or hyperbole. A noose hanging over an African–American's work station has not been construed as symbolic speech or protected as discussion of a disfavored subject. Scrawled notes of "African monkeys, why don't you go back to the jungle?" have not been regarded as nonlibelous proposals for a nice tropical vacation.

Beyond simply not being regarded as a problem, the very same terms of group threat and denigration that form the basis of sexual and racial harassment suits have also routinely provided the required evidence of the mental state called "discriminatory intent" for suits against other forms of discrimination. The fact that such verbal behavior serves as a vehicle for a bigoted ideology has not made it protected expression; it has identified the behavior, and other acts surrounding it, as discrimination. Under discrimination law, such expression is not a political opinion; it is a smoking gun.

For expressive purposes, the distinction that matters, in my view, is not between harassment based on race and harassment based on gender, which are often inseparable in any case, but between speech that is sex and speech that is not. Harassment that is sexual is a sex act, like pornography. Harassment that is not sexual works more through its content, as the traditional model of group defamation envisions, however hateful and irrational, however viscerally it plays on prejudice, however damaging to equality rights.

By harassment that is not explicitly sexual, I mean teachers' saying that women students are no good at this subject or calling on only men, or scholarship purporting to document the superiority of some racial groups over others, or statements in a workplace like, "There's nothing worse than having to work around women." It is amazing how few examples there are in this category, and how much of what might be simply gender or racial harassment proves on deeper examination to be sexual, like "Women are only fit company for something that howls."

Sexuality is a central dynamic in gender; sexuality and gender converge in the world. Consider the man who placed an explicitly sexual picture on the desk of a woman co-worker "with a note saying something like, 'You should be doing this instead of a man's job.'" All sexual harassment, including that against women and men of color specifically, is gendered. A great deal of harassment that is sexual is expressly racist. Examples include: "Jew faggot," "Black bitches suck cock," "Niggers are a living example that the Indians screwed buffalo," and the endless references to the penis size of African–American men. Laws against defamation often prohibit publications that "portray * * * unchastity * * * of a class of citizens, of any race, color, creed, or religion * * *" specifically. This refers to the men as well as the women in these groups. The fact that these laws have never been applied to racist pornography, in which women of color are routinely presented as "unchaste," suggests that portrayal of "unchastity" in women is regarded as just life, or perhaps that only unchastity in men is a racial insult. But it has not been applied to the pornography using men of color either.

Sexual words and pictures, delivered in context, work the way pornography works: they do not merely describe sexuality or represent it. In a sense, they have sex. When a man sends a note ending, "I'm going to fuck you even if I have to *rape* you," he is getting off on writing and sending the note and envisioning the recipient reading it. The recipient feels sexually violated as well as terrified of rape. (Need I add, this has nothing to do with the use of the term "fuck" as such.) When male workers say, "Hey pussycat, come here and give me a whiff," it is a sexual invasion, an act of sexual aggression, a violation of sexual boundaries, a sex act in itself.

I am not ultimately sure why this is the case, but it has something to do with the positioning of sex words in sexual abuse, in abuse as sex, in sex as abuse, in sex. Words of sexual abuse are integral to acts of sexual abuse from birth to after death. As incantations while sexual abuse is occurring, they carry that world with them, such that to utter them is to let loose in the body the feeling of doing it, and sex is done largely for the purpose of creating that feeling. The more pornography invades the sexuality of a population, the more widespread this dynamic becomes. It is not so much that the sexual terms reference a reality as that they reaccess and restimulate body memory of it for both aggressor and victim. The aggressor gets an erection; the victim screams and struggles and bleeds and blisters and becomes five years old. "Being offended" is the closest the First Amendment tradition comes to grasping this effect.

This process of empowerment of the perpetrator and traumatization of the victim occurs not because of the content of the words in the usual sense but because of the experiences they embody and convey. For this function of words carrying lived reality from one place to another, it matters that the physical tortures that accompany the words are being inflicted on a mass scale on women as a group. It matters that children are being sexually abused as the words of abuse are spoken and pictures taken. It matters that electrodes are being applied to the genitals of women being called "cunt" in photography studios in Los Angeles and the results mass-marketed. In Argentina under the junta, when people were rounded up and tortured and disappeared because they were Jewish, "Jew" used as a taunt and term of torture had such a meaning.

This is only to say the obvious: just as language shapes social reality, the social reality of language in use determines what it conveys and means and does, such that to say that these words do not have this meaning or do these things is to say that this social reality does not exist. Were there no such thing as male supremacy, and were it not sexualized, there would be no such injury as sexual harassment. Words do not do it alone, of course, but what sexual harassment does, only words can do—or, rather, the harm of sexual harassment can be done only through expressive means.

The social coding of sexuality as intimate and pleasurable also contributes to the distinctive sting and intrusiveness of harassment that is sexual. Sexuality is defined as intimacy as such; nothing else goes onto you or into you in the same way. One is socially called to participate in sexuality with one's most intimate self. Sexual abuse is further unique in that the victim is expected to enjoy it. Perpetrators of racial abuse experience pleasure that may be said to be sexual in the sense of the thrill of dominance, whether or not it becomes literally orgasmic; the victims are not expected to enjoy it. Sex as a form of abuse demands and exacts pleasure from the victim as well, both fake and at times tragically real. It probably still needs to be said that this does not mean that the victims want the abuse. The forced complicity of the manipulated response of the victim's body is part of the injury and attaches both to the abusive relation and to the words that go with it.

Because of its location in intimacy, harassment that is sexual peculiarly leaves nothing between you and it: it begins in your family, your primary connections, those through which the self is developed. Sexual abuse occurs most often within one's own family and community. With harassment that is not sexual, for example religious or ethnic, the target has a family, a community reviled together, an "us" that defies being defined by this treatment by "them." Someone is on your side, someone to go home to, rather than to run away from home from. This does not keep the shame from burning, the self-revulsion from attacking your body, or the despair from cannibalizing your future, just as with sexual abuse. It does provide a separation that says this is not just you, this is not all there is to you.

For at least these reasons, speech that is sex has a different relation to reality than speech that is not sex has. Sexual harassment, because it is sexual, and because of the place of words and images in sex, and the place of sex in life, manipulates the perpetrator's socialized body relatively primitively and directly, as pornography does, and often because pornography already has. This is men's beloved "hard-wiring," giving them that exculpatory sense that the sexual desires so programmed are natural and so operate before and beyond their minds—got there before they did, as it were. But it is nothing more than social conditioning. Put another way, if First Amendment protected thought is what men are doing while masturbating to pornography, raping employees while saying, "Just like I could hire you, I could fire you," and shouting "cunt" in a crowded shipyard, every mental blip short of a flat EEG is First Amendment protected speech. Whatever mental process is imagined to be involved in consuming pornography, it has not stopped obscenity from being placed beyond First Amendment protection, either.

Moreover, there is no evidence that consumers of racist propaganda aggress against the target of the literature whether or not they agree with the positions it takes. This is not to say that such material works wholly on the conscious level, but rather that it does not primarily work by circumventing conscious processes. The same can be said for nonsexually explicit misogynist literature. With pornography, by contrast, consumers see women as less than human, and even rape them, without being aware that an "idea" promoting that content, far less a political position in favor of the sexualized inequality of the sexes, is being advanced. Rape myth acceptance scale scores soar without conscious awareness that attitudes on women and rape are being manipulated through manipulating sexual responses. Nothing analogous to the sexual response has been located as the mechanism of racism, or as the mechanism of response to sexist material that is not sexual.

One way to think about issues of expressive freedom here is to ask whether something works through thought or not through thought. An argument that some races or genders or sexual persuasions are inferior to others is an argument—an antiegalitarian argument, a false argument, a pernicious argument, an argument for hate and for hierarchy, but an argument nonetheless. It is an act of inequality of a particular kind, whose consequences for social inequality need to be confronted on constitutional terrain where equality and speech converge, in a context as sensitive to the need for equality guarantees in the law of speech as for speech guarantees in the law of equality. So-called speech that works as a sex act is not an argument. An orgasm is not an argument and cannot be argued with. Compared with a thought, it raises far less difficult speech issues, if it raises any at all.

Considering the dynamics of racism is complicated by the difficulty of knowing what drives it. Given all the damage it has done, and its persistence and adaptability across time and space, there can be no doubt that it is deep and strong and explosive. Perhaps sexuality is a dynamic in racism and ethnic prejudice as well as in gender bias. Upon examination, much racist behavior is sexual. Consider the pure enjoyment of dominance that makes power its own reward, reports of the look of pleasure on the face of racist torturers, accounts of the adrenalin high of hatred and excitement that survivors of lynchings describe having seen, the sexual atrocities always involved. Recall the elaborate use of race, ethnicity, and religion for sexual excitement in pornography and in much racist harassment. Remember the racially coded sex and marriage taboos and titillations and targetings in white supremacist societies, the sexual denigration pervasive in anti-Semitism. Once the benefits and functions of much racial murder, torture, hatred, and dominance, perhaps even economic supremacy, are exposed as sexual, its rationalizations as natural, converging with gender on the idealogical level, what of racism is left to explain? Something, but what?

Chapter V

THE ESTABLISHMENT CLAUSE: GENERAL

A. INTRODUCTION

At a distance of 200 years we tend to lose sight of the novelty of the establishment clause. In the 18th century, however, the idea of creating a system of government that neither supported nor depended upon religion was a radical one. That idea was already implicit in the Constitution of 1787, which made no mention of God. Those who drafted it thought that explicit protection against a religious establishment was unnecessary because the federal government had a limited number of enumerated powers, and control over theological affairs was not among them. As Hamilton said in Federalist No. 84, "why declare that things shall not be done which there is no power to do?" Several of the ratifying states wanted more assurance, though, and the first Congress proposed an amendment disclaiming authority to make any "law respecting an establishment of religion[.]" It was ratified in 1791.

Americans in the late 20th century almost unanimously agree that this is a good idea. In one way this is not surprising. We are an increasingly secular society, and fairly accustomed to the notion that religion and government occupy different, nonintersecting spheres of influence. But Americans did not think that way in 1791. How can we explain their willingness to accept such a novel idea? To put it in other words, why, as an historical matter, do we have an establishment clause? This is the focus of Section B.

That question—why we have an establishment clause—is important today for more than antiquarian reasons. Though we all agree that the clause embodies a good idea, we hold a surprising variety of theories about what the idea is. Some say the clause forbids coercion. Others also object to special treatment. Still others would forbid any aid to religion. Which of these is the proper interpretation? Even more fundamentally, why do we object to some of these practices? Many people even today think that religion is a very good thing. If so, why should the government not promote it the way it does democracy and racial equality? These questions are addressed in Section C.

Section D examines the rules the courts apply in establishment clause cases. At this moment they are in flux. Until fairly recently the Supreme Court followed the three-part test of *Lemon v. Kurtzman*.[1] Today there are several other options. One is the "no endorsement" test proposed by Justice O'Connor in *Lynch v. Donnelly*.[2] Another is the coercion test accepted (in several forms) by a majority of the Court in *Lee v. Weisman*.[3]

B. HISTORY

In *Everson v. Board of Education*[4] the Supreme Court for the first time applied the establishment clause to a state law. Justice Black's opinion has had enormous influence over later interpretations of the clause. He concluded that the First Amendment had the same objective, and provided the same protection, as the Virginia Bill for Religious Liberty enacted in 1786. That bill was written by Thomas Jefferson. Its enactment was managed by James Madison, who also played an influential role in drafting the First Amendment.

Justice Black's version of history contains important elements of truth, but there is also much that it omits. To begin with the most obvious point, Jefferson and Madison, though good friends and allies in the fight against the Virginia establishment, did not think alike on matters of religion. Jefferson typified the Enlightenment view of religion. Walter Berns argues that he opposed revealed religion because it was inconsistent with his belief in democracy and natural right. Revelation is a politically dangerous idea because it attributes special insight to the godly. Democratic government, by contrast, requires an assumption "that all men are created equal." The point of the establishment clause, for one who thinks like this, is to protect government against the subversive effects of religion.

Edmund Cahn suggests that Madison had different reasons for wanting an establishment clause. Madison believed that religion is intrinsically valuable, and that institutional religion is good for its members. It therefore behooves us to protect religious groups against persecution. The free exercise clause forbids it outright. But the establishment clause may be a more effective guarantee against the oppressive practices of a religious monopoly.

A more serious problem with the Court's version of history is that it omits influences of an entirely different order. Mark DeWolfe Howe argues that we might want separation of church and state for theological rather than political reasons. He points in particular to the evangelical principles of people like Roger Williams, who believed that a "wall of separation" was necessary to protect the churches against the worldly corruptions that accompanied government influence. Jefferson's En-

---

1.   403 U.S. 602 (1971).

2.   465 U.S. 668, 687 (1984) (O'Connor, J., concurring).

3.   112 S.Ct. 2649 (1992).

4.   330 U.S. 1 (1947).

lightenment argument against establishment (that religion causes harm) makes it difficult to explain why the First Amendment in the same breath protects religious freedom. The beauty of the evangelical explanation is that it offers a single theory to justify both the establishment and the free exercise clauses.

Gerard Bradley reminds us of still another force at work among the framers. The establishment clause states that "Congress shall make no law respecting an establishment of religion[.]" One natural way of interpreting this injunction is that it forbids Congress to interfere with state religious establishments. It is, in other words, a rule of federalism (like the Tenth Amendment). Bradley points out that the forces of establishment were far from spent at the time we adopted the Bill of Rights. We should not overlook the possibility that some people favored the First Amendment because it protected state arrangements against national interference.

WALTER BERNS, THE FIRST AMENDMENT AND THE FUTURE OF AMERICAN DEMOCRACY

20–24 (1976).

"All eyes are opened, or opening, to the rights of man," Jefferson said. "The general spread of the light of science has already laid open to every view the palpable truth, that the mass of mankind has not been born with saddles on their backs, nor a favored few booted and spurred, ready to ride them legitimately, by the grace of God." This "palpable truth" is a scientific truth, not a religious truth or opinion but a truth discovered by the new political science; and the United States was the first country to organize itself on it. It was the first country to recognize the self-evident truth of the natural freedom and equality of all men and, therefore, that legitimate government can arise only out of consent. It was, as the motto on its Great Seal proclaims, a *novus ordo seclorum,* a new order of the ages. In this decisive respect, it was the first "new nation," and its newness consisted in large part in the nonreligious character of its founding principle. The uniqueness of this fact is emphasized in the thought of John Locke, the Englishman frequently called "America's philosopher," whom Jefferson, referring to him as one of the three greatest men who ever lived, accepted as one of his teachers. In the first of his *Two Treatises of Government,* Locke goes to what today are regarded as extraordinary lengths to show what we would regard as self-evident—namely, that kings do not rule by virtue of any donation from God to Adam and his heirs. This having been shown, he says at the outset of the *Second Treatise,* it is necessary "to find out another rise of government, another original of political power," and by saying this, he suggests that the only alternative to government based on the religious doctrine of divine donation is, as it turns out, government based on the nonreligious doctrine of the rights of man and the contract men make with each other. To secure these rights, governments are instituted among men.

Such a government was not established with the settling of the American colonies[.] * * * It had not been fully established in Virginia even by the end of 1781, when Jefferson wrote his *Notes on the State of Virginia*. As he saw it, the people of Virginia had not yet been sufficiently instructed in these principles, even after they had declared their independence. "The convention of May 1776, in their declaration of rights, declared it to be a truth, and a natural right, that the exercise of religion should be free; but when they proceeded to form on that declaration the ordinance of government, instead of taking up every principle declared in the bill of rights, and guarding it by legislative sanction, they passed over that which asserted our religious rights, leaving them as they found them." Heresy was, in principle, still punishable under the laws of Virginia; a Christian could deny the doctrine of the Trinity only at the price of his right to hold "any office or employment ecclesiastical, civil, or military" and, if he should persist in his denial, at the price of his liberty, his right to sue or inherit property, and even his "right to the custody of his own children." This, Jefferson complained, "is a summary view of that religious slavery under which a people have been willing to remain, who have lavished their lives and fortunes for the establishment of their civil freedom." Men are endowed with natural rights, and rulers have no authority over these rights except as men, in the compact forming civil society, have submitted to them. But it was Jefferson's view—and he was sustained in this by the existence of the Virginia law, as well as by the strength of the opposition he and Madison had to overcome in order to establish religious freedom in the state—that too many Virginians persisted in the error of regarding it as proper for the rights of conscience to be submitted to government.

This Virginia law and the religious establishments that continued to exist in some other states were vestiges of the orthodox Christianity that had come under attack in the seventeenth century from the new political science. It had to be attacked or somehow displaced, because, as Professor Mansfield has said, any revealed religion is incompatible with modern natural right. A revealed religion is revealed only to the godly, and the godly are only too likely "to take advantage of the favor of revelation to demand political power for themselves or their allies." [44] In a limited way—limited when compared with the claims staked out by the priests and princes against whom Hobbes, Spinoza, and Locke had to contend—this is what the nominally pious Virginians were doing. To destroy the political power of revealed religion, it was first necessary to destroy or displace the authority of revealed religion, which, in the Europe of the seventeenth century, meant the authority of Scripture and, especially, of the New Testament, wherein the proof of Jesus' authority is supplied by "the multitude of miracles he did before all sorts of people." This is necessary because "where the miracle is admitted,

44. [Harvey C. Mansfield, Jr., "Thomas Jefferson," in American Political Thought: The Philosophic Dimensions of American Statesmanship, ed. Morton J. Frisch and Richard G. Stevens (New York: Scribner's, 1971),] p. 28.

the doctrine cannot be rejected." Thus Hobbes wrote a critique of "miracles, and their use"; Locke wrote a *Discourse of Miracles,* from which the passage quoted above is taken; and Spinoza attempted to demonstrate that "God cannot be known from miracles." Christianity had to be made reasonable, which is why Locke, in addition to writing *Some Considerations of the Consequences of the Lowering of Interest and Raising the Value of Money* and helping to found the Bank of England, found it necessary to write *The Reasonableness of Christianity.*

Jefferson, of course, was a statesman, not a philosopher, but his statesmanship was informed by what he had learned from the natural rights philosophers who preceded him. From them he had learned that Christianity had to be made reasonable, and he was willing, albeit in words that he was careful to keep from the public, to commit his thoughts to paper. He denied the divinity of Christ. He nevertheless described himself as a Christian—not the sort of Christian that any of the Christian churches could have recognized, but a Christian "in the only sense [Jesus] wished anyone to be." He was perfectly willing to attribute to Jesus "every *human* excellence," which, he insisted against the churches, was all Jesus ever claimed for himself. The so-called Christians think otherwise, said Jefferson, because they had been corrupted, taught to believe in the Bible and that the Bible is a record of God's self-revelation to man. This doctrine, wholly false in his judgment, Jefferson traced to the fact that Jesus, like Socrates, "wrote nothing himself," thereby making it possible for "the most unlettered & ignorant men [writing] from memory & not till long after the transactions had passed [to commit] to writing his life and doctrines ...." Hence, the doctrines "he really delivered ... have come to us mutilated, misstated, & often unintelligible," and they were further "disfigured by the corruptions of schismatising followers, who have found an interest in sophisticating & perverting the simple doctrines he taught by engrafting on them the mysticisms of a Grecian sophist, frittering them into subtleties, & obscuring them with jargon, until they have caused good men to reject the whole in disgust, & to view Jesus himself as an imposter." His moral doctrines, Jefferson went on, are in fact "pure & perfect" and inculcate a "universal philanthropy, not only to kindred and friends, to neighbors and countrymen, gathering all into one family, under the bonds of love, charity, peace, common wants and common aids."

To say that Jefferson advocated religious freedom and the separation of church and state, and to leave it at that, is to miss what was then the radical character of his views on religion. Americans, no more than the immediate addressees of Locke's writings, would not accept a policy of freedom and separation, or of toleration (and Jefferson made copious notes and significant use of Locke's *Letter Concerning Toleration*), until or unless they were persuaded of the ground of this toleration, and the ground of this toleration is the opinion that traditional Christian doctrine is false. When it is shown to be false and, more practically, when the truth of this falseness is "by the light of science" spread among and accepted by the mass of mankind, it will be possible for men to attach themselves more firmly to the God of the Declaration of Independence— "Nature's God"—and the religious problem will be solved and free government secured.

EDMOND CAHN, THE "ESTABLISHMENT OF RELIGION" PUZZLE

36 N.Y.U.L.Rev. 1274, 1277–1279, 1287–1290 (1961).

In 1776, * * * George Mason headed a committee to frame the Virginia Declaration of Rights and Madison rendered decisive service on the committee. Mason drafted a clause which went no farther than to reflect John Locke's ideal of "toleration" for those who did not belong to the Established Church. Madison succeeded in converting this into a guarantee of freedom of religion, to which "all men are equally entitled . . . according to the dictates of conscience." He also attempted but did not succeed in inserting an explicit condemnation of "peculiar emoluments or privileges" for those who belonged to a particular church.

An unremitting debate ensued between the supporters of establishment, led from time to time by Patrick Henry and Edmund Pendleton, and the disestablishmentarians, led by Mason, Jefferson, and Madison. At almost every session of the Virginia Legislature the former proposed to extend the legal and economic privileges of the church, the latter to remove the remaining vestiges of its special position. In 1779, Jefferson drafted and submitted his celebrated "Bill for Religious Freedom," which at that time failed even to reach a third reading in the Assembly.
* * *

In 1784 the sponsors of establishment pressed for enactment of their bill, which would require all persons to pay an annual contribution for the support of the Christian religion or of some Christian church or denomination which the taxpayer might designate. The bill contended, in its preamble, that since organized religion was beneficial to the general welfare, all citizens should be required to participate in supporting it. Thus, the contention which would be put forward in the twentieth century in support of school bus assistance and general Sunday laws (that is, that sectarian education and the sectarian sabbath possessed a strictly secular utility) was advanced, considered, and—as we shall see—rejected in the struggle that led to the First Amendment.

At this stage, George Mason, George Nicholas, and others asked Madison to prepare a statement of the full case for separation of church and state. He produced the epochal "Memorial and Remonstrance Against Religious Assessments" * * * * which was circulated in 1785 and evoked a mighty wave of support for disestablishment. Taking advantage of the tide, Madison called up Jefferson's Bill for Religious Freedom and in 1786 obtained its enactment. * * *

* * *

* * * Madison matched Jefferson perfectly in a lifelong devotion to the religious freedom of the individual and what he repeatedly called "the rights of conscience." The first five paragraphs of the Memorial offer little more than a vigorous paraphrase of Jefferson's statements in the Bill for Religious Freedom. They leave the purport of the Bill entirely intact. Madison's distinctive achievement consisted in superimposing an *institutional* [approach to] "religion" on Jefferson's [individualism.]

* * * Since like other educated men of the epoch, Madison was conversant with the writings of the *philosphes,* he undoubtedly learned a good deal from them. Madison followed Voltaire in insisting, as he frequently did, that the best possible safeguard of religious freedom was not in legal guarantees but in the sheer multiplicity of religious sects. This conviction Madison retained from early youth to the end of his life; even in old age, he saw fit to regard separation of church and state as a pertinent topic in an essay on the general theme of monopolies!

Though he may have come across the reliance on multiplicity of sects in Voltaire [35] or, for that matter, in the manuscript of Jefferson's *Notes on Virginia,* [36] Madison made it wholly his own, fitting it with skill into his pluralistic philosophy of society. He saw that the religious sphere had attributes of its own that made it essentially unlike the spheres of economics and of political structure. Granted that in any sphere of human activity the processes of competition, rivalry, and reciprocal checks and balances would serve to restrain monopoly and preserve liberty; nevertheless, when an activity was religious in nature, the government possessed no jurisdiction or warrantable power over it. It had no more right to aid than to hinder the competing sects.

In America, Madison submitted most astutely, the rights of conscience must be kept not only free but *equal* as well. And in view of the endless variations—not only among the numerous sects, but also among the organized activities they pursued and the relative emotional values they attached to their activities—how could any species of government assistance be considered genuinely equal from sect to sect? If, for example, a state should attempt to subsidize all sectarian schools without discrimination, it would necessarily violate the principle of equality because certain sects felt impelled to conduct a large number of such schools, others few, others none. How could the officers of government begin to measure the intangible factors that a true equality of treatment would involve, *i.e.,* the relative intensity of religious attachment to parochial education that the respective groups required of their lay and

---

35. In 1764, Voltaire (addressing the Christian world tactfully as "Insensés ... Malheureux .... Monstres ...!") summarized the matter succinctly, "On vous l'a déjà dit, et on n'a autre chose à vous dire: si vous avez deux religions chez vous, elles se couperont la gorge; si vous en avez trente, elles vivront en paix." Voltaire, Dictionnaire Philosophique, verb. Tolérance II, at 269 (J. Benda ed., Paris).

36. The Political Writings of Thomas Jefferson 36–38 (Edward Dumbauld ed. 1955). For understandable reasons, the multiplicity-of-sects analysis was not thought appropriate for mention in either Jefferson's Bill or Madison's Memorial.

clerical members? It would be presumptuous even to inquire. Thus, just as in matters of race our belated recognition of intangible factors has finally led us to the maxim "separate therefore unequal," so in matters of religion Madison's immediate recognition of intangible factors led us promptly to the maxim "equal therefore separate." Equality was out of the question without total separation. * * *

* * * Reading the text of the Memorial, one catches echoes of many noble voices—John Knox and Andrew Melville in Scotland, Peter Wentworth and John Lilburne in England, not to mention the Hebrew prophets who were their common source and inspiration. During the Virginia contest, the Presbyterians of the state were among those who provided significant support for Madison's efforts. All of these would have rejected a narrow or circumscribed notion of religion's role.

Yet, after we have awarded due credit to the general climate of American thought and Madison's own libertarian genius, there is still much in the particular history of the Baptists that confers depth on the 1785 Memorial and poignancy on the role of religious associations. One understands nothing about so-called "voluntary" associations or their human significance unless one grasps what they mean to the members of a persecuted group. Often, to such a group, church-affiliation is "voluntary" only in the sense that life itself is, or if not life, then the keeping of self-respect. In Revolutionary Virginia, the Baptists were the ones to whom persecution had disclosed not merely the personal but also the corporate value of religion, not merely its individual function as a search but also its group function as a refuge.

The keynote of seventeenth and eighteenth century Baptist experience was sounded at the start. Significantly enough, the first English Baptist Church was organized not by free men in England but by religious exiles in Amsterdam. Their initial confession of faith contained a splendid article on religious liberty and separation of church and state, declaring that "the magistrate is not to meddle with religion, or matters of conscience nor to compel men to this or that form of religion." This, be it noted, as early as the year 1611! The subsequent ordeal of almost unremitting persecution, both in England and in America, only served to reinforce these sound principles and increase the number of adherents. When Madison wrote in his Memorial about the rise of the Christian Church, its independence of government support, and its growth in the face of official persecution, other readers probably recalled the events of the first and second centuries; the Baptists probably recalled those of the seventeenth and eighteenth. Thus the Memorial evoked ideals and loyalties that were not monadic but explicitly social and institutional.

* * *

* * * Recognizing organized religion as an ongoing social institution, Madison was much too realistic to overlook the influence it can exert on the general welfare. He proceeded to argue an excellent secular case, proving that here too the establishmentarians were completely mistaken. Religion in a society could indeed serve the general welfare,

but government support of religion could serve only the forces of resentment and hatred. Religion could be solidary, but government assistance could be only divisive. These hardheaded considerations, set forth in paragraphs 9 to 15 of the Memorial, have had a massive impact; in fact, they may constitute the main cause why religious liberty has survived in America. Madison warned that anything resembling an establishment would (a) deter persons oppressed in other countries from coming to America, (b) banish some of our citizens from their own land, (c) destroy the harmony we have endeavored to build among highly diverse groups, (d) provoke bitter inter-group hostilities, and (e) weaken the general enforcement of the laws and "slacken the bands of Society."

The argument he concluded with was overwhelming. How could Americans yield on establishment without impairing all the rest of their fundamental rights? Having insisted earlier in the Memorial that even "three pence" for support of an establishment would imperil the people's religious liberty, he now drew the full register of consequences. Since all of our basic rights were held by the self-same constitutional title as freedom of conscience, a compromise on the issue of establishment must jeopardize the entire "basis and foundation of Government."

MARK DeWOLFE HOWE, THE GARDEN AND THE WILDERNESS

1–2, 5–10 (1965).

MR. JUSTICE REED of the Supreme Court once warned his associates that "a rule of law should not be drawn from a figure of speech."[1] The Court did not heed the admonition, and as a result, much judicial energy has been devoted to the task of defining the constitutional significance of "the wall of separation between church and state." The figure, when it appeared upon the scene of constitutional law, was clothed in Jeffersonian garb, for the metaphor to which the justices made reference was found in a letter which Thomas Jefferson had written to the Baptists of Danbury, Connecticut. If you remember his use of the metaphor, you will recall that it was made explicitly relevant to the prohibitions of the First Amendment. "I contemplate with sovereign reverence," wrote Jefferson, "that act of the whole American people which declared that their legislature should 'make no law respecting an establishment of religion or prohibiting the free exercise thereof,' thus building a wall of separation between church and state."

Though this message to the Baptists could easily, perhaps even properly, be read as an ingratiating effort to echo a Baptist orthodoxy— as an insistence, that is, that the spiritual freedom of churches is jeopardized when they forget the principle of separation—it is not surprising that it was taken to reflect a more familiar, though possibly exaggerated, aspect of Jefferson's philosophy—the aspect, that is, which made him the child of Europe's Enlightenment and the father of Amer-

---

1. McCollum v. Board of Education, 333 U.S. 203, 247 (1948).

ica's.　When one interprets the metaphor of separation in the context of Jefferson's effusive preamble to Virginia's Act for Establishing Religious Freedom, it is not at all surprising that it has been taken to reflect the bias of eighteenth-century rationalism.　That preamble sparkles with the anticlerical presuppositions of the Enlightenment.　It explicitly bespeaks the fear that "the impious presumption" of ecclesiastical rulers would, if not confined, establish and maintain false religion throughout the land. The same mistrust of clerics is revealed in the preamble's pronouncement that "forcing [a man] to support this or that teacher of his own persuasion, is depriving him of the comfortable liberty of giving his contributions to the particular pastor, whose morals he would make his pattern, or whose powers he feels most persuasive to righteousness." [3] Surely it is not surprising that one who had expressed these convictions, and came later to speak his metaphorical words, should have been taken to regard the First Amendment as the safeguard of public and private interests against ecclesiastical depredations and excursions.　＊　＊　＊

＊　＊　＊

The phrase which I have chosen as a title for this series of lectures I have taken from a piece of writing by Roger Williams entitled "Mr. Cotton's Letter Lately Printed, Examined and Answered."　I should like to quote the entire paragraph in which Williams spoke of the garden and the wilderness.

> ... The faithful labors of many witnesses of Jesus Christ, extant to the world, abundantly proving that the church of the Jews under the Old Testament in the type, and the church of the Christians under the New Testament in the antitype, were both separate from the world; and that when they have opened a gap in the hedge or wall of separation between the garden of the church and the wilderness of the world, God hath ever broke down the wall itself, removed the candlestick, and made His garden a wilderness, as at this day.　And that therefore if He will ever please to restore His garden and paradise again, it must of necessity be walled in peculiarly unto Himself from the world; and that all that shall be saved out of the world are to be transplanted out of the wilderness of the world, and added unto his church or garden.

You see, of course, where this passage leads us—back to the metaphor from which a majority of the Court drew a rule of constitutional law.　The extraction of law from Jefferson's metaphor, we have seen, carried an unmistakably Jeffersonian flavor—the tang, that is, of enlightened rationalism.　If, instead of taking the metaphor from Jefferson, the Court had taken it from Roger Williams, what flavor would imbue the derivative rule of law?　Of one thing we may be sure; it would not be Jeffersonian.　When the imagination of Roger Williams built the wall of separation, it was not because he was fearful that without such a barrier the arm of the church would extend its reach.　It

---

3.　12 Hening, Statutes at Large, 84–85 (1823).

was, rather, the dread of the worldly corruptions which might consume the churches if sturdy fences against the wilderness were not maintained. Jefferson's total concern obviously included a deep anxiety that the liberties of individuals would be endangered if a wall of separation did not stand between them and the state. His concern may even have included some uneasiness about the fate of churches if they were not safeguarded from the authority of the government. Yet it is wholly clear, I take it, that the metaphor as it came from the pen of Jefferson carried a very different overtone of conviction from that which it bore in the message of Williams. The principle of separation epitomized in Williams' metaphor was predominantly theological. The principle summarized in the same figure when used by Jefferson was primarily political.

Several factors have combined, I think, to make the Jeffersonian rather than the evangelical version of the metaphor the Court's starting place. As I have already pointed out, the figure, when it came from the pen of Jefferson, seemed to express both the skepticism and the confidence of the Enlightenment. Our century is also an age of emancipation—an era, that is, in which the intellectual is apt to take his doubts as seriously as he does his convictions and to make of his faith, if he have it, an exercise in symbolism. It is an age, accordingly, in which a necessarily hurried reading of history will quickly persuade the enlightened reader that the prohibition against the enactment of law respecting an establishment of religion effected the transformation of Jeffersonian suspicion into a rule of constitutional law. Today's Court has found it easy, therefore, to assume that the framers of the First Amendment intended to keep alive that bias of the Enlightenment which asserted that government must not give its aid in any form to religion lest impious clerks tighten their grip upon the purses and the minds of men.

Another consideration of a rather different order has played a part in leading today's Court to give the metaphor a Jeffersonian rather than an evangelical interpretation. A frank acknowledgment that, in making the wall of separation a constitutional barrier, the faith of Roger Williams played a more important part than the doubts of Jefferson probably seemed to the present Court to carry unhappy implications. Such an acknowledgment might suggest that the First Amendment was designed not merely to codify a political principle but to implant a somewhat special principle of theology in the Constitution—a principle, by no means uncontested, which asserts that a church dependent on governmental favor cannot be true to its better self. I have already suggested that it is not a distorting exaggeration to say that Williams' principle of separation was primarily a principle of theology and Jefferson's predominantly a principle of politics. If that suggestion is accepted, it may seem that the Court pursued the natural course when it read the First Amendment as the translation of Jefferson's rather than Williams' figure of speech. It is hard for the present generation of emancipated Americans to conceive the possibility that the framers of the Constitution were willing to incorporate some theological presuppositions in the framework of federal government. * * *

* * *

From everything which I have so far said, you will rightly gather that I am persuaded that if the First Amendment codified a figure of speech it embraced the believing affirmations of Roger Williams and his heirs no less firmly than it did the questioning doubts of Thomas Jefferson and the Enlightenment. The fact that there is a theological theory of disestablishment, traceable to Roger Williams, is recognized by all those historians who insist that the American principle became a political reality only because it was sustained by the fervor of Jonathan Edwards and the Great Awakening. The forces let loose by that revival still operated in 1790 to give the sanctities of the garden priority in many minds over the prerogatives of the wilderness. We may legitimately regret the facts of history, but I do not suppose that the regretting and the denying of reality are identical processes.

Though it seems to me that today's liberals have not sufficiently recognized the complexities of motive which fashioned the policy of separation, the justices have been compelled by the very structure of the First Amendment's prohibitions to acknowledge that it sought to do something more than secure the people from ecclesiastical depredations. For the prohibition is not only against the enactment of laws respecting an establishment of religion; it is against the making of laws prohibiting its free exercise. The specificity of this second assurance makes it clear beyond controversy that the framers could not have intended the policy of separation, enunciated in the prohibition of establishment, to frustrate or inhibit the religious experience. The Court's endeavor in recent years, accordingly, has been to discover some means by which it may vigorously enforce a Jeffersonian principle of separation while, at the same time, it protects the conscience of the individual. In seeking to have it both ways—to safeguard the conscience of individuals and to prevent aid to religion—the Court's tendency has been to look upon its task as that of blending a secularist's rule of separation, derived from Jefferson, with a believer's rule of freedom, derived from Roger Williams. It has failed sufficiently to recognize, I think, that the rule of separation was no less a postulate of faith than it was an axiom of doubt. If one is to respect the realities of history in formulating rules of constitutional law, it is not as easy as the Court has pretended it to be to cast out the theology of the First Amendment.

GERARD V. BRADLEY, CHURCH–STATE RELATIONSHIPS IN AMERICA
20–26 (1987).

NEW ENGLAND COVENANT POLITICS: MASSACHUSETTS, NEW HAMPSHIRE, CONNECTICUT, AND VERMONT

* * *

There is certainly some basis for assigning the New England states a place apart from their southern neighbors. This was the land founded upon Calvinist theology, where social organization was rooted in a covenant theory that taught that the people's unity was religious before it was political. The Puritan settlers modeled their government on the Israelite theocracy of the Old Testament, including the views that civilian officials should enforce religious conformity and that the Ten Commandments were a starting point for political order. During the seventeenth century, the laws of Massachusetts and New Haven, for instance, even specified that the word of God governed in cases not comprehended by colonial statutes. More generally, during the colonial era, distinctions among civil and spiritual, political and religious were, at best, embryonic in New Englanders' thought.

The historical inseparability of church and state is evident in the constitutions and laws enacted by the states soon after the Declaration of Independence from Britain obliged them to fashion new legal orders. The Vermont Constitution of 1777 illustrated the pattern by describing the disputed territorial claims of New York and New Hampshire to it as a "violation of the tenth command," a matter of envying thy neighbor's goods. The people of Massachusetts "covenanted" with each other in their 1780 constitution and acknowledged the goodness and providence of the "great Legislator of the Universe." The preamble to the Connecticut Constitution of 1776 (which did little more than affirm the 1662 charter) looked forward to the "Tranquility and Stability of Churches and Commonwealths."

These pious generalities had practical bite. The constitution of each state required individual public worship, and irregular church attendance cost 3 shillings in Connecticut and 10 shillings in Massachusetts. Each also specified a duty to support and maintain religious teachers and institutions, if only of the Protestant variety. New Hampshire limited elected office to Protestants; Vermont required of its public officials a declaration of Protestant belief, as well as a renunciation of all allegiance, "civil or ecclesiastical," to all foreign princes and prelates. Besides thereby disqualifying Catholics from public office, Vermont guaranteed religious liberty to Protestants only, New Hampshire and Massachusetts extended religious freedom to all "Christians," and Connecticut granted ecclesiastical corporate privileges only to Protestant sects.

More remarkably puritanical in social theory than these constitutional provisions were the statutes that fleshed them out. Publicly maintained, supported, sponsored, and encouraged religious orthodoxy was the legal rule. Provisions governing the Lord's day involved much more than obligatory church attendance and fully warrant Mencken's definition of a Puritan as one whose sneaking suspicion is that somewhere, somebody is having a good time. No one enjoyed themselves on Sunday in New England. Beside the expected prohibition of all servile work, amusements, and gaiety, Massachusetts forbade "unnecessary walking" and empowered wardens "forcibly to stop and detain any person ... he shall suspect of unnecessarily travelling ... [and] take into custody ... those who do not give satisfactory answers." Refusing to give "direct answers" to the warden cost the taciturn traveler a 5 pound fine. Connecticut's Sabbath police—grand jury men, constables, and tithing men—were enjoined to "carefully inspect the behavior of all Persons on the Sabbath or Lord's day; and especially between the Meetings for divine worship on said Day". The regulators were specifically authorized to make warrantless arrests of Sabbath breakers, and anyone "neglecting to afford his utmost Assistance to apprehend and secure" such offenders suffered the same penalty as for failure to assist the sheriff in his other law enforcement duties.

Criminal prohibitions of blasphemy were just as pervasive, even more colorful, and amounted to nothing less than an official declaration of the truth of Christianity. In Connecticut "whipping on the naked body" (as many as forty stripes) along with an hour in the pillory attended "cursing or reproaching the true God or his government of the World." * * *

Further promotion of religion, piety, and morality took a variety of forms, and Connecticut was especially notable for its efforts here. It required every household to keep a Bible and denied copyright protection to anything injurious to religion and morals. "Mountebanks" and medicine shows were suppressed because they too were a "detriment of good Order and Religion." Connecticut, as did the other New England states, exempted church property from taxation. Each taxed its inhabitants specifically for the maintenance of Protestant ministers and houses of worship.

The systems of taxation for religion rested on the basic New England theme of local town autonomy. Article III of the Massachusetts Declaration of Rights was produced by a committee that included future President John Adams and Caleb Strong, a member of the First U.S. Senate, which passed the Establishment Clause. Article III, apparently drafted by revolutionary firebrand Sam Adams on behalf of the committee, authorized the legislature to require towns and parishes (parishes were geographical units) to provide at community expense for "public worship" and for the "support and maintenance of public Protestant teachers of piety, religion and morality," where such provision was not made "voluntarily." ("Voluntarily" referred to Boston where a non-coercive system of support for religion prevailed throughout the colonial era.) The New Hampshire Constitution of 1784 empowered the legislature to "authorize" the same undertaking, which meant that towns could not be forced to settle and maintain ministers. Vermont's 1777 constitution did not specifically authorize the legislature to implement its declaration in favor of public worship, but in 1783 the legislature adopted essentially the prevailing town system. There was no effective change since prior to that Vermont towns had been governed by New Hampshire church laws. In Connecticut "ecclesiastical societies" were geographically defined and empowered to settle and maintain ministers. The societies were Congregational, but by 1784 all other Protestant sects were extended the same powers and privileges for maintenance of public worship.

* * *

The mechanics of these systems developed over time in varying bits of legislation and differed some from state to state, but a composite profile of them is available. First, a majority of those legally qualified to vote in a geographically defined town, parish, or society decided which Protestant ministry to settle in the town and voted a tax on all inhabitants to raise funds for church construction and a ministerial stipend. The sect most often selected was Congregational, but (especially in New Hampshire) other sects could and did achieve local hegemony. In Holderness, for example, Samuel Livermore, an active participant in the House of Representatives debate over the Establishment Clause, was a pillar of the settled Episcopal church. Throughout New England, the tax was assessed solely and specifically for these purposes, was locally collected and administered, and the entire process was codified in local rules, or bylaws.

Perhaps the most notable feature of the system was its treatment of those Protestants outside the publicly maintained denomination, known as dissenters. (In New England as elsewhere, non-Protestants occupied an unfortunate category of their own and were not dissenters as contemporaries used that term.) As early as 1693 in New Hampshire, and by the 1780s in Massachusetts, Connecticut, and Vermont, no one was required to support the minister of a sect other than one's own. The aspiring dissenter secured a certificate from his congregation, stating that he was a regular attendee and supporter of it. When lodged with the clerk of the publicly maintained society, the certificate exempted the holder from the general assessment. To qualify for this relief, one had to subscribe to some Protestant church, and each of those churches was required by law to maintain itself through public levy. One result was that a single town might have two or more congregations publicly supported; certainly more than one denomination was so maintained somewhere in each state. These public props persisted into the nineteenth century. Vermont was the first to abandon them in 1807, Massachusetts the last in 1833.

[Paradoxical as it may seem to modern minds,] the constitutions of these states * * * not only enshrined conscience as an inviolable, unalienable right but also forbade religious establishments. Massachusetts and New Hampshire expressed nonestablishment in precisely the same terms: "no subordination of any one sect or denomination to another shall ever be established by law." No other reference to the subject of establishments appears in either constitution. Vermont's constitutions of 1777 and 1786 track the New Hampshire and Massachusetts provisions, forswearing "partiality for, or prejudice against, any particular class, sect, or denomination of men whatever." The preamble to the Connecticut organic act of 1784 read: "so ... that Christians of every denomination, demeaning themselves peaceably, and as good Subjects of the State, may be equally under the Protection of the Laws." Each state guaranteed freedom of conscience to "all men" in Vermont, to every individual in New Hampshire, to all "subjects" in Massachusetts and Connecticut. * * *

The point is not [that] everybody in New England agreed with the full range of church-state regulations, although the regimes noted undoubtedly received the enthusiastic support of an overwhelming majority. It is that nonestablishment indisputably meant no sect preference and that no sect preference was obviously consistent in the minds of these founders with aid and encouragement of religion. It is more than that, for even the attacks of critics like Isaac Backus and William Plume reveal agreement on the definition of establishment as legally enforced sectarian superiority. Their disagreement was primarily over whether the regimes actually comported with the standard definition. The attack on the systems of public worship and tax support along establishment lines was little more than a claim that Congregationalism was still legally favored and that dissenting sects were still subordinated. One claim of the dissenting (that is, non-Congregational) sects was that the certificate system implied sect subordination by requiring dissenters to secure credentials satisfactory to the majority church before they were permitted to withdraw from its support. The challenge was quite accurate; dissenters had to go to a lot of trouble to achieve what Congregationalists enjoyed simply by being in the majority. This problem was largely de facto and not de jure, however, for only Connecticut deviated from facially sect-neutral laws and then only by recognizing the sociological reality of Congregational hegemony.

A second claim of subordination stemmed from this practicality of numbers. To qualify for relief, dissenters had to show attendance and support of another church. Where the dissenters were separate handfuls of Baptists, Quakers, and Universalists, however, each might be unable to erect and support a ministry of its own. A variety of practices grew up to sustain dissenters in this situation. In Connecticut, Baptists frequently crossed the border to worship in Rhode Island, and Connecticut recognized certification by Rhode Island congregations. More commonly dissenters joined a magnet congregation whose sole purpose was to provide certificates, while the separate parcels of dissenters actually worshipped apart.

A third establishment tendency resided in the laws themselves and constituted a kind of residual preference. For the taxes of newcomers, those who failed to designate a recipient, and dissenters who could not secure certificates from an operating congregation, usually the money went to the majority congregation, usually the Congregationalists.

Fourth, this elaborate minuet had to be administered, and was frequently litigated, in what was for dissenters hostile territory. Litigation meant judges and juries composed primarily of hostile Congregationalists, and contested issues included whether a minister who preached universal salvation was a "Protestant teacher of religion, piety, and morality" and whether a Presbyterian could be compelled to support a Congregational minister because they were really the same sect.

A final preference arose from the Baptist disavowal of professional clergy. Instead they chose ministers from their own congregation to serve without compensation. Baptists therefore did not need the system at all, and its burdens fell on them with no immediate tangible benefit. Baptist leader Isaac Backus claimed that his sect's ministers could not in good conscience accept money involuntarily acquired, so Baptists' taxes usually went to the town's ministers. For these reasons, Backus complained to the Massachusetts delegation of the 1776 Continental Congress about the discrimination suffered by dissenters. The delegates replied that the certificate provisions granted sufficient liberty, and John Adams added that he doubted they could be called an "Establishment" at all.

These arguments from sect discrimination exhausted the establishment critique on the compulsory finance provisions during the pre–First Amendment period. Literally no one suggested an establishment existed simply because religion was aided. As Baptist minister Samuel Stillman remarked in 1779, "There are many ways that the magistrate can encourage religion" while respecting rights of conscience in a nonestablishment regime, which, Stillman noted, Massachusetts was. Indeed the criticisms noted were not of the system as a whole but of discrete features of it. The frontal attack on the idea of compulsory worship and taxation came much later (in the nineteenth century) and was primarily rooted in an elaborate argument derived from freedom of conscience. What the New England dissenters highlighted instead was a potential, if not actual, establishment tendency in systems of compulsory support of the clergy, a flaw detected almost wherever such systems were proposed or enacted. But that flaw was one of preference among sects and simply confirmed that nondiscriminatory aid to religion complied with the nonestablishment norm.

It is perhaps inevitable that historians should focus on the critics who ultimately dismantled the New England church-state regime and who in the process made arguments about religious liberty pleasing to modern ears. It is not inevitable that we forget—and we should not forget—that during the 1780s theirs was not the popular view. The essentials of the New England church-state arrangement were before the people and their representatives repeatedly during the last part of the eighteenth century and every time received their hearty approval.

C. THEORY

Given the variety of historical influences behind the establishment clause, it should not be surprising that modern readers interpret the clause in various ways. We might find, for example, that the heirs of the Enlightenment are less willing than evangelicals to adjust the demands of the government to the needs of religion. Of course none of these eighteenth century traditions survives unmodified. Each of them has adapted its understanding of the First Amendment in response to the great changes in religion, society, and thought that have occurred during the past two centuries. This Section looks at modern ways of reading the establishment clause. Each of them shows the imprint of history. But we take the modern theories as they are, rather than try to identify them by their geneology. There has been a good deal of intermarriage among them.

We divide this Section into three parts: Strict Separation, Neutrality, and Accommodation. This taxonomy is a very rough cut. Our objective is to show a spectrum of views about the meaning of disestablishment. It ranges from the "strict," or "secularist" interpretation (on the left, as it were) to the "accommodationist," or "religious" interpretation (on the right). We do not try to cover all the points in between.

1. STRICT SEPARATION

Ira Lupu explains that for a period of nearly 35 years—from 1947, when the Establishment Clause was first applied to the states, until 1980, when Ronald Reagan was elected President—separation was the prevailing theory of church-state relations. Lupu catalogues the various aspects of First Amendment doctrine that supported this theory. He also reviews a number of justifications for it. The most important is the idea that religion is and ought to be a private matter. It is, Lupu says, a "special" practice, "apart from ordinary culture, tending its special garden." Another is the popular fear of political division along religious lines, leading in the worst case to "a religious war of all against all." Lupu goes on to explain how separation has waned in importance during the past 15 years. It is a change that he obviously views with some regret, though he is by no means nostalgic for the old order.

Alan Schwarz finds the justifications relied on by most separationists to be unconvincing. He argues that religion is not—at least not exclusively—a private matter. It performs functions of vital public concern, like sustaining the moral sense that democratic government requires of its citizens. As to the idea that religion causes strife, Schwarz notes that the same is true of racial integration. But that is not a reason for holding fair housing laws unconstitutional. Schwarz proposes that we read the establishment clause as a rule against government action that influences the outcome of religious choices. Government aid that simply helps people carry out decisions independently made (Sunday closing laws, bus rides, even draft exemptions) is constitutional.

IRA C. LUPU, THE LINGERING DEATH OF SEPARATIONISM

62 Geo.Wash.L.Rev. 230–242, 278–279 (1994).

For the generations that came of age between World War II and the election of Ronald Reagan to the Presidency, the separation of church and state was a stock phrase, an almost-hyphenated way of encapsulating an attitude toward a particular aspect of constitutional culture. Two linchpin propositions constituted the major components of this attitude. First, serious religion was not the business of government and its institutions; religion should be private rather than public. This proposition had its most constitutional force in the setting of public elementary and secondary schools, in which students are present by governmental compulsion. Separation of church and state thus had its most concrete, operational meaning in the oft-repeated notion that the public schools should be kept free of religion. Second, separationism required the state to tolerate but not assist those persons—in separationism's heyday, predominantly persons belonging to the Roman Catholic Church—who chose parochial over public education.

* * *

Separationism thrived best when white Anglo–Saxon Protestants of low-level religious intensity constituted the bulk of our cultural elite. For members of this group, separationism reflected an attractive mix of privatized (hence unobtrusive) religion, opposition to a public subsidy of the educational mission of the Roman Catholic Church, and support for the mission of socializing Americans in what this elite perceived as the common American culture. Hence, separationism required reduction in public celebration of sectarian religion, stringent limits on public aid to parochial schools, and religiously "neutral" public schools.

Many of the cultural and political conditions that sustained the concept of separationism have eroded considerably in the past twenty years. Our cultural elite has grown far more diverse. America has experienced a religious awakening, in which high-intensity, publicly oriented religion has expanded dramatically. The public schools have declined in their capacity to deliver a good education and are no longer considered the uncontroversial home of common culture. These phenomena have resulted in the rise of private parochial schools among many sects and denominations and have produced intensified combat about the propriety of religious thought and practice in both public schools and public life generally.

Predictably, the Supreme Court has both led and followed these trends. As in the political culture itself, a set of themes compete within the Court for recognition as the successor to separationism. Chief among these themes are neutrality and accommodation, although it is increasingly evident that some version of neutrality is winning out. As one would expect from an institution committed in some strong yet incomplete respect to stare decisis, however, the law of the Religion Clauses remains encrusted with significant aspects of the separationist motif. Like Captain Ahab at the climactic moment in Moby Dick, separationism beckons as it perishes.

* * *

The Dominant Era of Separationism, 1947–1980

Any thematic account of a thirty-five year period in constitutional law necessarily runs a substantial risk of oversimplification. Nevertheless, of all the judgments one might make about interpretation of the Religion Clauses by the Supreme Court, the most supportable is that from 1947–1980 the roots of separationism grew and spread.

Five primary elements constituted the decisional-law backbone of separationism. The first of these is the version of Establishment Clause history articulated in 1947 in *Everson v. Board of Education.*[13] In *Everson,* the Court considered the constitutionality of a local community's decision to subsidize the costs of public transportation to and from parochial as well as public schools. Although a narrow majority upheld the scheme, *Everson* is best and most importantly remembered for its broad separationist dicta and for the Court's unanimous adoption of the Virginia history of religious liberty as the key to the meaning of the First Amendment's Establishment Clause. Indeed, on the latter point, the dissent by Justice Rutledge went one better than Justice Black's opinion for the Court; the dissent emphasized the Virginia history and insisted that Ewing Township unconstitutionally aided the parochial schools. This historical account, which placed James Madison and his justly famed (and staunchly separationist) Memorial and Remonstrance Against Religious Assessments at the heart of the meaning of the Establishment Clause, became the "official" history of the clause until challenged by scholars and Justices in the early 1980s.

The second crucial gesture in the Court's embrace of the separationist ethos occurred in *The School Prayer Cases.*[21] These decisions were far more important than the abstract history-building efforts in *Everson* because they injected separationism powerfully into the political culture. Unlike *Everson,* which dealt only with subsidizing public transportation to and from parochial schools (and upheld the subsidy), *The School Prayer Cases* particularized the doctrine of church-state separation by applying it to the widespread, highly symbolic, often popular, and crisply defined practice of school prayer. These decisions made church-state questions the stuff of widespread public protests and congressional politics.

Third, separationism helped make sense of some important features of existing relations between government and organized religion. Just as *The School Prayer Cases* sharpened the meaning and scope of separationism by invalidating a common practice, *Walz v. Tax Commission*[24] provided a reciprocal boost to the separationist regime by legitimating an equally common practice, namely, the exemption from taxation of real property devoted to religious use. In *Walz,* that practice was attacked as

---

13. 330 U.S. 1 (1947).

21. School Dist. v. Schempp, 374 U.S. 203 (1963); Engel v. Vitale, 370 U.S. 421 (1962).

24. 397 U.S. 664 (1970).

an impermissible state assistance to religion. The Supreme Court's near-unanimous rejection of that attack drew powerfully on the image of separation: "The exemption creates only a minimal and remote involvement between church and state. . . . It restricts the fiscal relationship between church and state, and tends to complement and reinforce the desired separation insulating each from the other." Tax exemptions for organized religion thus helped religious associations to do what *The School Prayer Cases* forbade the state from doing, namely, to develop and maintain the citizenry's spiritual life.

Fourth, the decision in *Flast v. Cohen*,[29] upholding federal taxpayer standing to challenge federal expenditures as violative of the Establishment Clause, reinforced the character of the clause as representing a polity principle rather than a rights principle. A regime of rights quite sensibly limits party status to those persons and institutions whose own interests are sharply implicated by governmental action. In contrast, enforcement of polity principles through adjudication requires assignment of enforcement rights to private attorneys general, i.e., to those who lack a strong personal stake but nevertheless are sufficiently committed to the cause that they will litigate aggressively on behalf of structural concerns. *Flast*'s creation of a special exception to the rule barring federal taxpayer standing is thus perfectly consistent with an interpretation of the clause that implicates concerns of structure and relationship rather than concerns of coercion, loss of liberty, or other individualized interests.

Finally, as an essential step in the maintenance of separationism, in 1971 the Court in *Lemon v. Kurtzman*[33] erected a general doctrinal framework for implementing the separationist vision. By purporting to capture the Establishment Clause in a three-part test for all seasons— including a prohibition not only on governmental practices that advance religion but also on practices that interact significantly with religious institutions—*Lemon* promised that separationism would be the guiding force of Religion Clause adjudication. Indeed, for the rest of the 1970s, a separationist majority kept that promise.

* * *

The Attack on Separationism, 1980–1992

Understood institutionally, development of the Religion Clauses during the Reagan–Bush years reflected a retreat from judicial policing of the boundaries between religion and government. This, of course, was part of the overall program of putting an end to "judicial activism." Understood thematically, these developments constituted an assault on separationism in every respect: in its history, its doctrinal structure, and its core premises concerning the role of religion in public life.

29. 392 U.S. 83 (1968).   **33.** 403 U.S. 602 (1971).

A. Establishment Clause Counterhistory

In *Wallace v. Jaffree,*[49] the Court invalidated an Alabama statute requiring that public schools open the day with a moment of silence for prayer or meditation. In dissent, Justice Rehnquist used the case as an opportunity to attack directly the separationist history at the center of *Everson v. Board of Education.* Justice Rehnquist strenuously contended that the Court in *Everson* had unjustifiably interpreted the First Amendment in the provincial light of the history of church-state battles in Virginia. He also argued that the correct history of the Establishment Clause supported bans on state churches and sectarian discrimination but did not support a ban on nonpreferential aid programs that included religion or a ban on programs that preferred religion generally. Justice Rehnquist did not persuade a majority in *Wallace,* but he did succeed in casting doubt on what had been the official history of the Establishment Clause and in suggesting that an alternative possessed a respectable claim to historical legitimacy as well.

B. The Justiciability Retreat

Even before a majority of the Court began to alter substantive Establishment Clause principles, it signalled a new attitude toward their underpinnings. In *Valley Forge Christian College v. Americans United for Separation of Church and State,*[55] the Court denied standing to a separationist organization and its members (who included federal taxpayers) to challenge a transfer of real property from the federal government to a pervasively Christian school for the ministry. The Court's opinion distinguished *Flast v. Cohen* on the ground that *Flast* involved expenditure of monies while *Valley Forge* involved a land transfer under a different grant of congressional power. This was true enough but entirely irrelevant to *Flast*'s theory that expansive standing rules were a necessary, effective, and constitutionally appropriate mechanism for enforcing the Establishment Clause. If federal taxpayers could not challenge the property transfer, then no one could, because no other "injury" could be located. Although *Flast* remained good law within its boundaries, *Valley Forge* strongly signalled that the law was moving away from the structural premises of separationism.

C. Governmental Sponsorship of Religious Exercises and Symbols

In the years in which separationism represented the dominant ethos, the Supreme Court decided no cases involving government-sponsored religious displays or government-sponsored prayer outside the school context. In 1983, however, the Court signalled the beginning of a new regime in *Marsh v. Chambers,*[60] which upheld Nebraska's practice of opening its legislative sessions with prayer. * * *

Following soon upon *Marsh,* in what now seems a true turning point, the Court in *Lynch v. Donnelly*[64] upheld the publicly sponsored

49. 472 U.S. 38 (1985).

55. 454 U.S. 464 (1982).

60. 463 U.S. 783 (1983).

64. 465 U.S. 668 (1984).

display of a Nativity scene at Christmastime. Without relying on any specific constitutional history of the sort that had influenced the outcome in *Marsh, Lynch* simply shoved *Lemon* aside. The *Lynch* opinion relied heavily on the notion that Christmas was a cultural as well as a religious holiday and that a Nativity scene could be absorbed within the cultural dimensions of the holiday. In what has become a focal point for emerging Establishment Clause principles, Justice O'Connor's concurring opinion suggested that the key question was one of governmental endorsement of religion but concluded that the scene in question did not constitute such endorsement.

* * *

[T]he nonendorsement principle rests on a foundation profoundly different from that of separationism. The nonendorsement principle is concerned with the individual alienation, or feelings of exclusion, that an observer of a government-sponsored religious symbol might experience; separationism focuses upon the social, rather than individual, harms that a church-state merger may create. Similarly, the attention paid in nonendorsement writing to "insiders" and "outsiders" rings with equal protection considerations. Though separationism achieves minority-protecting functions, it reflects the broader social purpose of secularizing the public arena and discouraging sectarian rivalries. These rivalries are more likely to occur as separationism wanes and the new regime emerges.

D. *Religious Exercises in Schools*

Separationism has survived best in the context in which it has always had the most persuasive power, namely, the permissibility of religious exercises in the public schools. This setting combines many of separationism's core concerns, including the privatization of religion, the dangers of a divisive local politics of religion, the role of common schools as unifying carriers of shared aspirations and culture, and the threat to individual religious liberty created by the compulsory character of education of the young.

In the light of the presence of these features, judicial results in cases of this character are sobering. In * * * *Lee v. Weisman*,[79] a narrow majority struck down the graduation prayer at issue, but that result came about only because Justice Kennedy took an expansive view of his otherwise quite narrow theory that coercion is a necessary element of an Establishment Clause violation.

Significantly for the story of separationism, Justice Kennedy's view requiring coercion in Establishment Clause cases resonates with Justice O'Connor's nonendorsement principle. Both approaches treat the Establishment Clause as a source of individuated entitlements—that is, claims by individuals to be free of a certain class of state-created harms (whether psychic, social, or other). Moreover, this approach is in significant tension with separationism, within which Establishment Clause

---

79. 112 S.Ct. 2649 (1992).

claimants are not individuals advancing atomistic rights but rather are surrogates seeking to defend a constitutionally specified social order. The moves to nonendorsement and noncoercion are thus quite consistent with the related move in the standing cases from *Flast* to *Valley Forge*.

E.   *The Retreat from Lemon in Cases Involving Religious Institutions*

* * *

General developments in the 1980s set the stage for a process of repudiation of *Lemon* in the very aid-to-parochial-schools context in which it originated.   In *Mueller v. Allen*,[85] the Court narrowly upheld a neutrally worded Minnesota income tax deduction for tuition and other expenses associated with private elementary and secondary education. * * *

From *Mueller* it was but a short step to *Witters v. Washington Department of Services for the Blind*,[91] in which the Court ruled that Washington State was free to pay an educational grant to Mr. Witters, who was blind, notwithstanding Mr. Witters's choice to use the grant at a Christian college for education in the ministry.   Once again, [as it had in *Mueller*,] the Court relied upon the private and independent choice of Mr. Witters—not the state—to use state assistance for a religious purpose.   In this case, however, unlike in *Mueller*, the Court was unanimous as to the result[.]

* * *

CONCLUSION

* * *

If it turns out that the constitutional culture is rejecting the regime of church-state separation once and for all, what will be forsaken?   First, separationism has a side, rarely evident in the case law, that is quite protective of religion and its institutions.   The image of religion apart from ordinary culture, tending its special garden, represents a positive spin on the theme of privatization.   The emerging regime of religious pluralism and equality, with religious institutions seen as full and equal partners with other intermediate associations in the nurturing of public life, is attractive in its own way; in such a regime, however, religion will no longer bear the marks of constitutional "specialness" that it once had.   Moreover, if the political culture turns against association more generally, religion will fall with the rest.

Of course, strong separationism itself may well have favored irreligion, because it lined up state power with secular rationality.   One of the powerful lessons of the past twenty years of American law and history is that an ideology of secular rationality is not objective or neutral but is partial to a particular set of institutions (most notably science and the

85.   463 U.S. 388 (1983).   **91.**   474 U.S. 481 (1986).

markets). Nor is secular rationality particularly conducive to the life of the spirit, without which it may not be possible for a nation to thrive.

The challenge in the postseparationist period is for state and society to harness the forces that lead to religious awakening and pluralism without (re)kindling a religious war of all against all. Whether the Idea of America retains enough shared content to hold the center against the tendency of our many pluralisms to pull us apart remains an open question; whether a judicially enforced church-state separation might contribute to the maintenance of that Idea seems, for now, to be almost entirely an academic inquiry. Though it may linger in the political and legal culture of constitutionalism, the image of separation of church and state is fading out.

ALAN SCHWARZ, NO IMPOSITION OF RELIGION: THE ESTABLISHMENT CLAUSE VALUE

77 Yale L.J. 692, 708–716, 719–723, 728 (1968).

A. OTHER ESTABLISHMENT VALUES

* * *

It is agreed that the establishment clause prohibits government from intentionally creating an official or preferred religion; at this point agreement ends. Some contend that the clause does not prohibit anything except an official or preferred religion; others that the clause effects a wall of separation, to be breached only by a secular or religious value weightier than the separation principle.[61] The latter position is subsumed under the phrase "no aid to religion." The validity of the "no-aid" principle is the essential controversy arising under the establishment clause, and the various attempts to create devices to soften the impact of that principle without abandoning it are responsible for the confusion in the area. The question then arises: why shouldn't government aid religion? Several reasons, purportedly of constitutional dimension, have been given.

1. *Aid Impairs Religious Liberty*

The first argument is that aid justifies regulation and regulation impairs free exercise.[62] The argument is neither historically nor juridically correct. Government has always aided religion, nonpreferentially as in fire and police protection, and preferentially as in tax and draft exemptions. These aids have not in fact been accompanied by regulations which impaired free exercise. Moreover, if aid presented a constitutionally significant danger of infringing upon free exercise, nonpreferential as well as preferential aid should be invalid. To the extent that aid authorizes regulation, that regulation could as easily be affixed to

61. L. Pfeffer, Church, State and Freedom 727 (1967) * * *.

62. Everson v. Board of Educ., 330 U.S. 1, 53 (1947) (dissenting opinion of Rutledge, J.); *id.* at 26–27 (dissenting opinion of Jackson, J.) * * *.

one form as the other; yet even the most militant separationists would allow some forms of nonpreferential aid. * * * This consideration is relevant to the question of whether a religious institution should apply for aid; it is not relevant to whether the aid may be constitutionally granted.

2. *Aid Causes Strife*

The Court and commentators sometimes refer to avoidance of strife as an establishment clause value from which the no-aid principle is derived. The strife to be avoided is apparently supposed to be caused by the antagonism of religious or irreligious groups who are not aided or who feel that others have received a disproportionate share.[70] * * *

To state this proposition is to ridicule it. If avoidance of strife were an independent constitutional value, no legislation could be adopted on any subject which aroused strong and divided feelings. Nor could a constitutional doctrine of strife avoidance be limited in application to legislation which exacerbates religious differences on the ground that those differences are more upsetting than any others. Patently, racial differences are today a far greater cause of strife than differences in religious belief. Would, then, the possibility of exacerbated racial controversy in and of itself invalidate open housing legislation?

Moreover, prohibiting aid to religion does not avoid strife, it merely alters its source. Aid to parochial schools may exacerbate strife by antagonizing Protestants who for the most part would not derive advantages from such an aid program. Failure to aid, however, antagonizes Catholics who pay taxes to support public school education and pay separately to educate their own children at parochial schools. * * *

3. *Aid Costs Money*

Most governmental aids to religion involve an expense which is borne in part by the nonbeliever and the other-believer, either indirectly through their tax bill, as in a subsidy to religion, or directly as in exemption of Sabbatarians from Sunday closing laws. The supposed inequity of this burden often is stated as the reason for the no-aid principle. Justice Black, for instance, writes for the Court in *Everson*, "No tax in any amount, large or small, can be levied to support any religious activities or institutions . . . ," and he cites the Virginia Bill For Religious Liberty for the proposition " 'that to compel a man to furnish contributions of money for the propagation of opinions which he disbelieves, is sinful and tyrannical.' "

Emphasis upon pocketbook injury suffered by the nonbeliever or other-believer suggests that the value being invoked is that public moneys cannot be used to support private purposes. Religion, it is

---

70. "Public money devoted to payment of religious costs, educational or other, brings the quest for more. It brings too the struggle of sect against sect for the larger share or for any. Here one by numbers alone will benefit most, there another." Everson v. Board of Educ., 330 U.S. 1, 53 (1947) (dissenting opinion of Rutledge, J.).

assumed, is exclusively a private affair. Ergo, the government may not use public funds to aid religion. The minor premise of this syllogism, however, is false. Religion has significance to an individual in areas which may fairly be called private; it also has significance in areas which are of vital public concern. Successful government in the United States depends upon popular participation in the affairs of government and in a thousand other affairs which are private only because individual and associational participation have made government intervention unnecessary. Some of this vitally necessary participation results from unalloyed self-interest (vote your pocketbook). Much of it, however, requires a sense of the rightness and wrongness of things—a sense indispensable to involvement where immediate self-interest is absent. One need not accept Kant's argument that God exists because true morality cannot exist without God in order to recognize that religion is important if not indispensable to a moral sense, that a moral sense is important to involvement, and that involvement is necessary to democracy. * * *

* * *

In any event, does the public purpose doctrine necessarily require a benefit to the state? Why may not satisfaction of a "private" need or desire be a public purpose, when that need or desire will be frustrated without government aid and when the public considers it to be worthy (as it arguably considers religion)? Before the government can supply food stamps to starving Americans, must it first be shown that the economy will thereby benefit or that crime will be avoided or contagious disease prevented? Or isn't giving food to hungry people a sufficient public purpose?

* * *

4. *Aid Impairs Secular Unity*

Every level of government has an interest in the unity of its citizens. A shared system of values minimizes dissension and facilitates joint action toward a common goal. The best means of achieving unity is to reserve for government operation those institutions which exert the greatest influence on shaping the values of the population. Perhaps the most important of all such institutions is the educational system. Justice Frankfurter, concurring in *Illinois ex rel. McCollum v. Board of Education,*[89] describes the public school as "[d]esigned to serve as perhaps the most powerful agency for promoting cohesion among a heterogeneous democratic people" and as "a symbol of our secular unity."

Not all aids to religion meaningfully affect secular unity. Some—like exempting Mrs. Sherbert from unemployment compensation requirements—are not relevant to the unity goal. Others—like exempting conscientious objectors from military service and providing army chaplains—may conceivably weaken the unifying tendencies of a secular institution. But the essential purposes of the military as an institution

---

89. 333 U.S. 203[, 216–17] (1948).

do not include the promotion of unity. Therefore, even complete acceptance of secular unity as a constitutional value need not yield a rigid no-aid standard. Some aids to religion, however, contravene the unity value by weakening secular institutions which significantly promote that value. Aid to parochial schools, for instance, will decrease the enrollment of Catholic children in the public schools and thus impair the unifying tendencies of that institution. And released time, while probably having the effect of increasing attendance of Catholic children at public schools and thus strengthening the institution, impairs its unifying effect.

On what basis, however, is it assumed that secular unity is a constitutional requirement? The state, to be sure, has a corporate interest in unity, but in no other context is a state corporate interest converted into a constitutional requirement. The state has an interest in an educated population. Is compulsory education, then, a constitutional mandate; and is a government program to employ school dropouts, then, unconstitutional? The Constitution defines permissible governmental interests; it does not require that permissible interests be effectuated nor prohibit a legislature from impairing one in order to serve another permissible interest. The function of choosing between permissible but inconsistent interests, at least in every other context, is assigned to the legislature and ultimately, through the political process, to the people.

* * *

5. *Aid Impairs Equality Among Religions and Between Religion and Irreligion*

Whatever additional content the establishment clause may have, it clearly prohibits discrimination among religions and between religion and irreligion.[103] To the extent, however, that the agreed principle of no preference is analogous to the equal protection clause, it does not yield a derivative principle of no aid. It merely requires that if aid is granted, the aided category must include all religions and irreligions. So read, the establishment clause requires that aid be granted atheists and agnostics if Protestants and Catholics are aided. * * *

To substitute an equal-aid for a no-aid principle would not result in identical, and perhaps not even in equal, benefits. Legislators, judges and administrators may, improperly, define religion and irreligion according to their own beliefs, thus discriminating against irreligion and the minority, odd-ball sect. More importantly, identical benefits are often impossible to achieve. To allow each schoolchild in turn to recite a prayer or antireligious statement of his choosing, for instance, while satisfying the value of equal opportunity, would most benefit the majority belief since that belief would realize the most prayer time. Or, to

---

103. Abington School Dist. v. Schempp, 374 U.S. 203, 216–17 (1963); Torcaso v. Watkins, 367 U.S. 488, 495 (1961); Zorach v. Clauson, 343 U.S. 306, 314 (1951); Everson v. Board of Educ., 330 U.S. 1, 15–16 (1946).

grant financial aid to all religious and irreligious institutions will provide a lesser benefit to the minority sect which may not have the members, finances, organization, or even the desire to utilize the grant. The equality principle, however, does not demand identical benefit. Disparity in resultant benefits is an unavoidable characteristic of any aid program, and the equality principle, as conventionally understood, requires only that all members of the same class (*i.e.,* all religions and irreligions) receive the same opportunities. Indeed, the conventional equality value demands that a religion with a large number of adherents receive a greater share of a government program intended to aid individuals than a minor sect. It is thus apparent that if the establishment clause did no more than incorporate a conventional equal protection value, it would not invalidate equitably allocated aid which produced disparities in benefit.

B. The No-Imposition Value

The no-preference principle incorporated within the establishment clause is not, however, merely an application of the conventional equality value. It seeks to prevent inequality not only as an independent, ultimate goal, but as a protection against a possible consequence of inequality: an imposition of religion. Failure to divide an aid-to-religion pie into identical segments is not unconstitutional because it results in *A* eating more than *B;* that result may be fair and practicable. The danger lies in the fact that *A* may, and historically has, thrown its pie at *B,* or more accurately, at *B* 's child. If only the equality value were involved, *B,* not wishing pie or not being able to digest it, should not begrudge *A* his piece so long as *B* had the opportunity of participating. But in a pie-throwing contest, keeping ammunition from your opponent is as important as having some yourself.

There are two aspects of the imposition danger—one institutional, the other individual. In both cases, the ultimate fear is that government aid will, directly or indirectly, be used to influence choice of religion, not merely to enhance another's exercise. And it is this fear which causes strife and which makes use of the nonbeliever's or other-believer's taxes so galling. To the individual, the essential danger is that the family's right to determine the religious beliefs of its members, especially its children, will be undermined, either directly by government imposition of religion or indirectly by government aid to the imposition efforts of religious institutions. Regarding religious choice as exclusively a family affair, the no-imposition value, in its individual aspect, resolves into a standard prohibiting all aid which presents a substantial danger of imposition of religion. To the religious or irreligious institution, the essential danger is that government aid will, by intention or otherwise, favor the proselytizing efforts of a competitor. From the institutional point of view, the battle for adherents could, theoretically, be staged under a no-aid standard or under a standard of identical aid. But since it is impossible to aid all proselytization identically, the institutional interest also resolves into a standard which prohibits all aid presenting a substantial imposition danger.

* * *

As already discussed, it has been asserted that aid to religion imperils the religious liberty of members of the aided institution. Although this assertion is not persuasive, more substantial questions are raised by the related claim that aid imperils the liberties of nonbelievers and other-believers. That claim relies upon the historical fact that the ascendancy of a religious group has often been associated with the denial of civil liberties to nonbelievers and other-believers. Nor is that association of only historical validity. Despite the ecumenical movement, it remains true that the supposedly divine source of most religious dogma gives each dogma a claim to exclusive validity which is basically inconsistent with toleration of other beliefs. * * *

The threat to civil liberties presented by a dominant religious group was clearly a substantial consideration in the adoption of the establishment clause and it fully supports the accepted view that the clause prohibits establishing or preferring a religion. The issue, however, is not exclusive or preferential aid, but any aid. But if equal aid results in unequal benefits and if equal benefits cannot in practice be realized then any aid will increase the power of some churches more than others, and often the church that benefits most is the one which is already closest to dominance. It seems to follow that the best means of avoiding the dangers of dominance is to adopt a no-aid rather than an equal-aid standard. In this context, the real danger of aid to Catholic parochial schools seems to be not that it impairs unity, considered as a state interest, or defeats the Protestant's associational claim, but that it increases the power of the Catholic church, both in absolute terms and in relation to the power of other churches; it is not the Catholic child's absence from a public school that raises constitutional dangers; it is his presence at a parochial school.

The trouble with this position is that it proves too much. The free exercise clause of the first amendment makes religion a constitutional value. Hence, the position must conceive of religion simultaneously as a value and as a threat, the separation principle which includes a no-aid doctrine being necessary to maintain equilibrium between them. But what precisely is this supposed equilibrium? Assume that the now only incipient dangers of religion come closer to fruition as a result of the emergence of a dominant and militant religious group in the United States. In these circumstances, would retention of equilibrium require regulation of the threat? The answer is unquestionably that the free exercise clause forbids any state action against the dominant religious group, at least until first amendment rights of nonbelievers are actually violated. But if equipoise does not require or allow regulation when the threat is imminent, why does equipoise forbid aid at a time when the threat is wholly inchoate? This is not to deny that religion constitutes an incipient danger to the rights of other-believers or that a no-aid principle would do more to mitigate that danger than a principle of equal aid, just as a constitutional prohibition upon religion would be more effective than either. It is to say, however, that in the light of the private and public value of religion, it is better to partially neutralize its incipient dangers by an equal-aid standard than to neutralize them more effectively by a no-aid standard.

The foregoing paragraph seeks to demonstrate that if, in appraising the value of religion against its incipient dangers, a choice had to be made between unrefined no-aid and equal-aid standards, the latter would be preferable. In fact, however, no such choice need be made. * * * Any aid—equal or unequal—which has the effect of inducing religious belief * * * offends the value of exclusive parental choice of religion and is consequently invalid under a no-imposition standard. Conversely, aid which does not have the effect of inducing religious belief, but merely accommodates or implements an independent religious choice, does not increase the danger of religion and, since it does not offend the value of parental choice, does not violate the no-imposition standard. * * *

* * *

To be distinguished from imposition is state action which does not influence choice but helps implement a religious or irreligious choice independently made. In rendering such aid the state is expressing a judgment that religion is a worthy activity, and it may be argued that in recognizing worthiness, the state is by design or otherwise encouraging belief and hence influencing religious choice. As a practical matter, however, recognition of worth will not have a substantial imposition effect and will have no effect at all where the religion aided is a minority sect. Exemption of Mrs. Sherbert from South Carolina's unemployment compensation requirement represents a judgment that the exercise of Seventh-day Adventism is more worthy than bowling on Saturdays, but the exemption has no significant effect and arguably no effect at all upon whether someone becomes a Seventh-day Adventist. Similarly, the Sabbatarian exemption from Sunday closing laws does not induce one to become a Jew; draft exemption to conscientious objectors does not normally induce one to become a Quaker; closing the public schools on all religious holidays or on every Wednesday at 2 P.M. does not induce the adoption of religion; and compulsory Sunday closing, while implementing an independent desire to attend church services, has no substantial effect upon the creation of such desire. The availability of preferential aid to religious exercise may, to be sure, induce false claims of religious belief, but the establishment clause is not concerned with false claims of belief, only with induced belief.

Some aids to religion, whether preferential or nonpreferential, may have the effect of intensifying an independently made religious belief. While a parochial school bus subsidy does not induce adoption of Catholicism, it may result in a more intense belief. But * * * action which has the effect of intensifying belief is qualitatively different from action which induces belief; the former supplements while the latter contradicts the establishment values of individual and family determination of religious choice. Perfect neutrality is impossible: implementation of a desire to attend parochial school may intensify belief, but failure to implement defeats religious choice; and since freedom of religious choice, not neutrality per se, is the fundamental establishment value, the neutrality tool is useful only insofar as it promotes that choice.

2. NEUTRALITY

"Neutrality," like "equality," is a word that means different things to different people. In the debate over affirmative action some people maintain that the equal protection clause requires equal opportunity—a process that treats everyone alike. (A written examination given to candidates for the police force is an example of such a process.) Others say that the real meaning of equality is equal results—the outcome is what counts, not the process. (A written examination might yield a disproportionate number of white police officers.)

Neutrality is an establishment clause principle that appeals to nearly everyone because it is ambiguous in this way. Douglas Laycock distinguishes several different ways in which the term is used in First Amendment jurisprudence. Neutrality in the *formal* sense requires that the government be "religion-blind" (just as some people say that the government should be color-blind). It is much like the equal opportunity side of the equal protection debate. This is an argument made by Philip Kurland in an influential early article on the religion clauses.[1] Formal neutrality would forbid the government to exempt religious believers from the effect of general laws. But it would also require the government to give aid to religious schools if it aided other private schools. Laycock rejects this principle in favor of *substantive* neutrality. He argues that our objective should be to exert as little influence as possible on the outcome of religious choices—a principle that sometimes necessitates special treatment of religion. This is a rule akin to the equal results side of the equal protection debate. Laycock notes that the Supreme Court often uses the term neutrality in a third sense—what he calls *disaggregated* neutrality. It asks whether government action advances religion, while ignoring the inhibiting effects of alternative courses of action.

Laycock's principle of substantive neutrality holds that we should try to minimize the effect of government action on religious choices. Government should not advance or inhibit religion. But where is the starting point from which to measure advances and retreats? Is fire protection for churches an advance, or should we take it for granted as something that everyone starts out with? Donald Giannella argues that the starting point for neutral government action moves as the business of government expands. In a society where the government owned all

---

1. Kurland, *Of Church and State and* (1961).
the Supreme Court, 29 U.Chi.L.Rev. 1

the land, giving property to churches (along with other voluntary associations) might not count as aid to religion.

DOUGLAS LAYCOCK, FORMAL, SUBSTANTIVE, AND DISAGGREGATED NEUTRALITY TOWARD RELIGION

39 DePaul L.Rev. 993, 999–1010 (1990).

FORMAL NEUTRALITY

By far the best known definition of religious neutrality is Philip Kurland's. In 1961, he tendered the following principle:

> The [free exercise and establishment] clauses should be read as stating a single precept: that government cannot utilize religion as a standard for action or inaction because these clauses, read together as they should be, prohibit classification in terms of religion either to confer a benefit or to impose a burden.[21]

This standard of no religious classifications is closely akin to the equal treatment and equal opportunity side of the affirmative action debate. But the shift of context has enough implications so that a different label is required. I will call this standard formal neutrality.
* * *

* * *

[Formal neutrality has been almost universally rejected, because it produces surprising results that are inconsistent with strong intuitions.]

The most striking example is historical. The National Prohibition Act forbad the sale or consumption of alcoholic beverages in the United States, but it exempted the use of sacramental wine. Under formal neutrality, the exemption was unconstitutional. The exemption undeniably classified on the basis of religion. It was lawful to consume alcohol in religious ceremonies, but not otherwise.

Now consider Prohibition without the exemption. There would be no violation of formal neutrality; religion would not even be mentioned in the statute. But it would be a crime to celebrate the Eucharist or the Seder. If the free exercise of religion includes anything beyond bare belief, it must be the right to perform the sacred rituals of the faith. A law enacted largely at the behest of Protestants that barred the sacred rites of Catholics and Jews, a law that changed the way these rites had been performed for millennia, could not be reconciled with any concept of religious liberty worthy of the name. That the law was formally neutral and enacted for a secular purpose would be no comfort to the victims.

---

21. Kurland, *Of Church and State and*   (1961).
the Supreme Court, 29 U.Chi.L.Rev. 1, 96

But facial neutrality would be dispositive to the Supreme Court of the United States. In a stunning opinion handed down after this lecture was delivered, the Court said that government may regulate the Mass for good reasons, bad reasons, or no reasons at all, so long as the regulation is facially neutral and does not single out religion.[25] The Court held that criminal punishment of the central religious ritual of an ancient faith raises no issue under the free exercise clause and requires no governmental justification whatever! The example that I chose because I thought it was beyond reasonable argument has now been decided the other way.

* * *

In the Prohibition example, formal neutrality seems to trample religion. But formal neutrality also produces results that many Americans find unacceptably favorable to religion. Consider the case of financial aid to private education. Under formal neutrality, government can give unlimited amounts of unrestricted aid to religious schools, so long as the aid goes to all schools and not to religious schools alone. But formal neutrality does not stop there. Any aid to secular private schools *must* be given to religious schools, on exactly the same terms. To exclude religious schools from the aid program, or to impose restrictions on religious uses of the money, would be to classify on the basis of religion. That would violate formal neutrality.

* * *

As these two examples make clear, formal neutrality has something to offend everybody. As a general standard, it appeals to none of the competing factions in religion clause litigation. But it has had disproportionate influence on our understanding of what it means to be neutral.

Substantive Neutrality

My understanding of neutrality is quite different. Again because we need a label, I will call my proposal "substantive neutrality."

My basic formulation of substantive neutrality is this: the religion clauses require government to minimize the extent to which it either encourages or discourages religious belief or disbelief, practice or nonpractice, observance or nonobservance. If I have to stand or fall on a single formulation of neutrality, I will stand or fall on that one. But I must elaborate on what I mean by minimizing encouragement and discouragement. I mean that religion is to be left as wholly to private choice as anything can be. It should proceed as unaffected by government as possible. Government should not interfere with our beliefs about religion either by coercion or by persuasion. Religion may flourish or wither; it may change or stay the same. What happens to

25. Employment Div. v. Smith, 110 S.Ct. 1595 (1990). * * *

religion is up to the people acting severally and voluntarily; it is not up to the people acting collectively through government.

* * *

My conception of religious neutrality includes a neutral conception of religion. That is, any belief about God, the supernatural, or the transcendent, is a religious belief. For constitutional purposes, the belief that there is no God, or no afterlife, is as much a religious belief as the belief that there is a God or an afterlife. It is a belief about the traditional subject matter of religion, and it is a belief that must be accepted on faith, because it is not subject to empirical investigation. Serious believers and serious disbelievers are sometimes troubled by this equation of their belief systems, but we cannot make sense of the religion clauses without it. This constitutional conception of religious belief as any belief about religion explains why atheists are protected from persecution, and why the government cannot establish atheism.

* * *

That is a bare sketch of substantive neutrality. The next step is to compare and contrast formal and substantive neutrality. Sometimes the two types of neutrality produce the same result. That is, sometimes we can minimize encouragement or discouragement to religion by ignoring the religious aspects of some behavior and treating it just like some analogous secular behavior.

But often the two understandings of neutrality diverge. Government routinely encourages and discourages all sorts of private behavior. Under substantive neutrality, these encouragements and discouragements are not to be applied to religion. Thus, a standard of minimizing both encouragement and discouragement will often require that religion be singled out for special treatment.

Consider [the example I mentioned above.] To prohibit the consumption of alcohol, without an exception for religious rituals, is to flatly prohibit important religious practices. Such a prohibition would discourage religious practice in the most coercive possible way—by criminalizing it. Many believers would abandon their religious practice; some would defy the law; some of those would go to jail. Such a law would be a massive departure from substantive neutrality.

To *exempt* sacramental wine is not perfectly neutral either. Religious observers would get to do something that is forbidden to the rest of the population, but that observation goes to formal neutrality. Would this special treatment encourage religion? It is conceivable that the prospect of a tiny nip would encourage some desperate folks to join a church that uses real wine, or to attend Mass daily instead of weekly or only at Easter. It is conceivable, but only to a law professor or an economist. Such an exemption would have only an infinitesimal tendency to encourage religious activity. In contrast, withholding the exemption would severely discourage religious activity. The course that most nearly approaches substantive neutrality—the course that minimizes both encouragement and discouragement—is to single out religious uses for an exemption. In this and similar applications, substantive neutrality is akin to the equal impact, equal outcome side of the affirmative action debate.

* * *

Most obviously, substantive neutrality is harder to apply than formal neutrality. It requires judgments about the relative significance of various encouragements and discouragements to religion. Absolute zero is no more attainable in encouragement and discouragement than in temperature. We can aspire only to minimize encouragement and discouragement. Because substantive neutrality requires more judgment than formal neutrality, substantive neutrality is more subject to manipulation by advocates and result-oriented judges and law professors.

More important, substantive neutrality requires a baseline from which to measure encouragement and discouragement. What state of affairs is the background norm from which to judge whether religion has been encouraged or discouraged? This question also requires judgment; there is no simple test that can be mechanically applied to yield sensible answers.

A conceivable mechanical standard is to treat religion as though government did not exist. If religion is better off than if government did not exist, it has been encouraged; if it is worse off, it has been discouraged. The only thing to recommend this standard is its intellectual purity; I doubt that it appeals to anyone in the real world.

To take the most obvious example, no one suggests that churches be denied police and fire protection. Police and fire protection are sometimes explained as merely incidental benefits. But to what are they incidental? I am not at all sure that police and fire protection arise as an incident of something else. These services are not incidental; they are provided outright and for their own sake. One might say that police and fire protection for churches is incidental to police and fire protection for everybody else, or for all property in the community. But it is easy to imagine either isolated or concentrated religious properties that would strain that rationale to the breaking point. That rationale also fails to explain why we protect churches against vandalism, embezzlement, and other property crimes that pose no threat to the neighbors.

One of the Supreme Court's better opinions on incidental benefits answers the question I have posed. A permissible benefit is one that is incidental to a larger policy of neutrality.[35] The benefits of police and fire protection are such an incident of neutrality. Police and fire protection are such a universal part of our lives that they have become part of the baseline. To deny police and fire protection would be to outlaw religion in the original sense of that word—to put religion outside the protection of the law. To demand that churches provide their own police and fire protection in a modern society would be to place an

35. [Roemer v. Board of Public Works, 426 U.S. 736,] 746–47 [(1976)].

extraordinary obstacle in their way—a discouragement that would make religion a hazardous enterprise indeed. To provide such services does not make religion attractive to anyone who is not attracted on the merits. As a practical matter, any encouragement is tiny. The discouraging effect of cutting off basic services greatly exceeds the encouraging effect of providing them.

* * *

Unless we carefully think through such issues, we will tend to select our baselines by intuition, and we will give free rein to our political preferences and our prejudices. Our preferences can operate freely because the principle of neutrality by itself is insufficient to define the baseline. Judgments about the state of the world must be brought to bear. We must keep in mind what neutrality is supposed to accomplish. Our goal is not to leave religion in a Hobbesian state of nature, nor to leave it regulated exactly to the extent that commercial businesses are regulated, with no extra burdens and no exemptions. Our goal is to maximize the religious liberty of both believers and nonbelievers.

* * *

DISAGGREGATED NEUTRALITY

The Supreme Court is rarely content with a broad principle if it can substitute a three-part test. Its most famous formulation of the neutrality requirement is the second part of the *Lemon* test, which says that a law violates the establishment clause if one of its substantial effects is either to advance or inhibit religion.[42] This formulation began simply as an elaboration of neutrality, but is often disaggregated into a test of no advancement and a separate test of no inhibition. If a law has some substantial effect that advances religion, that may be the end of the case. And there is sometimes a very low threshold for finding effects to be substantial.

In the extreme case of *Aguilar v. Felton*,[44] the Supreme Court invalidated a federal program to provide remedial instruction in math and reading to low income children in private schools. Congress enacted this program in pursuit of neutrality—to provide the same remedial program to disadvantaged children without regard to their religious choices. Why did the Court strike it down? Because the public employees who provided the remedial instruction might be influenced by the religious environment of parochial schools, and under that hypnotic influence, might encourage the children to religious belief. That possibility created a risk of a substantial effect of advancing religion; that risk could be avoided only by close supervision that would excessively entangle church and state. That was the end of the case.

I call this disaggregated neutrality, because it looks only at one side of the balance of advancing or inhibiting. Because absolute zero is not

42. Lemon v. Kurtzman, 403 U.S. 602,   **44.** 473 U.S. 402 (1985).
612 (1971) * * *.

achievable, it is always possible to find some effect of advancing or inhibiting religion. Thus, if you look only at one side of the balance, you can always find a constitutional violation. Some of those who would have government sponsor their faith play the same game on the inhibits side of the balance: if government does not lead school children in prayer, or display religious symbols on major holidays, the public may infer that government is hostile to religion. Therefore, these critics conclude, silence is not neutral.

Substantive neutrality always requires that the encouragement of one policy be compared to the discouragement of alternative policies. The principal effect of *Aguilar* was to greatly increase the cost of providing remedial programs to children in private schools. After *Aguilar,* the government or the school must provide separate off-campus facilities and the children must travel to those facilities and back again. The effect of increasing the cost was to reduce the number of children who could be served. So thousands of our least advantaged citizens are now forced to choose: forfeit their right to remedial instruction in math and reading, or forfeit their right to education in a religious environment. That effect discourages religion, and dwarfs the risk that the government's remedial math or reading teacher might suddenly start proselytizing. By disaggregating neutrality, the Court has lost sight of its original objective.

Another way to disaggregate neutrality is to shift back and forth among different versions of neutrality without explanation. If you think that neutrality with respect to government-imposed burdens means that churches and believers never get an exemption (formal neutrality), but that neutrality with respect to government benefits means that churches can never participate (disaggregated substantive neutrality), you had better have a good explanation. The most obvious explanation is simply hostility to religion. If you have the opposite preferences, you are equally in need of a good explanation.

* * *

In the [current] Term * * * the Court has dramatically embraced formal neutrality to uphold taxation and regulation of churches and believers.[56] In *Jimmy Swaggart Ministries,* the Court unanimously held that churches can be taxed, so long as the tax laws do not single out churches for discriminatory rates or incidents of taxation. The Court in dictum suggested that it would apply the same standard to regulation of churches, except where compliance with the regulation would require the church to violate its "sincere religious beliefs." In *Employment Division v. Smith,* the exception for sincere religious belief disappeared by a vote of five to four. The free exercise of religion now means that churches cannot be taxed or regulated any more heavily than General Motors. The only remaining protection is that provided by formal neutrality;

56. Employment Div. v. Smith, 110 S.Ct. 1595 (1990); Jimmy Swaggart Minis- tries v. Board of Equalization, 110 S.Ct. 688 (1990).

religious conduct cannot be singled out for facially discriminatory regulation.

* * *

This conception of neutrality is irreconcilable with *Aguilar* and the other cases striking down government payments to religiously affiliated schools. In *Aguilar,* the federally-funded instruction in remedial math and reading was directed on equal terms to poor children in all schools, public and private, secular and religious. But the Court did not say that this "neutral and nondiscriminatory" instruction "neither advances nor inhibits religion." Instead, it found that the government money conferred obvious benefits on religion, and did not say that those benefits were of no constitutional significance.

The Court's current position comes to this: when government demands money or obedience *from* churches, neutrality consists of treating churches just like other subjects of taxation or regulation, and it is irrelevant that the church is worse off than it would be without the tax or the regulation. But when government pays money *to* churches, neutrality consists of not making the churches any better off than they would be without the payment, and it is irrelevant that the churches are treated just like other beneficiaries of the same program.

DONALD A. GIANNELLA, RELIGIOUS LIBERTY, NONESTABLISHMENT, AND DOCTRINAL DEVELOPMENT PART II. THE NONESTAB-LISHMENT PRINCIPLE

81 Harv.L.Rev. 513, 516–520, 522–526 (1968).

I. THE VALUES UNDERLYING NONESTABLISHMENT

It is impossible to find substantial agreement among scholars as to what political principles are embodied in the establishment clause. At one extreme are those who would severely limit its thrust to no more than a guarantee that the federal government would not interfere with state policies and prerogatives in this area. Under this interpretation the establishment clause is so tied to early notions of federalism that it is irrelevant to the substance of "due process"; accordingly, it should not be applied against the states by incorporation into the fourteenth amendment. At the other extreme are those who agree with Madison that the clause was meant to express an ideal principle of democratic government, which forbids all official acts of the state that recognize or support religion.[10] Between these extremes are a number of intermediate views. Some would limit the scope of the clause to the support of institutional religion, forbidding direct aid to churches and church agencies; others would perhaps substantially broaden the scope of the clause

---

10. Everson v. Board of Educ., 330 U.S. 1, 39 (1947) (Rutledge, J., dissenting). For a discussion sympathetic to a view of nonestablishment that requires the state to avoid any official recognition or support of religion see L. Pfeffer [Church, State, and Freedom 128–80 (rev. ed. 1967).]

by forbidding aid to religion, whether direct or indirect, but narrow it to apply only when one religious faith is preferred over another, or where religion is favored over irreligion.

All of these views, except perhaps the first, have a personal and social value in common—that of voluntarism. Religious voluntarism, of course, is an important aspect of the freedom of conscience guaranteed by the free exercise clause. But a broad interpretation of the establishment clause also gives vent to the social dimension of this value by restricting the use of political power in shaping the ideological and sociological forces which give social form to religion. The growth and advancement of a religious sect must come from the voluntary support of its membership. Religious voluntarism thus conforms to that abiding part of the American credo which assumes that both religion and society will be strengthened if spiritual and ideological claims seek recognition on the basis of their intrinsic merit. Institutional independence of churches is thought to guarantee the purity and vigor of their role in society, and the free competition of faiths and ideas is expected to guarantee their excellence and vitality to the benefit of the entire society. The practical achievement of religious voluntarism in our pluralistic society calls for substantial insulation of the political process from religious pressures and interfaith dissension. The kind of interfaith dissension caused by involvement of religion with politics was in large part the historic evil against which the nonestablishment clause was directed as "an article of peace."

The twin values of voluntarism and political noninvolvement with religion suggest three propositions defining the proper scope of the establishment clause. First, governmental preference of a particular religion, or even of religion in general over irreligion, gives rise to an advantage which is clearly inconsistent with voluntarism and will surely breed political dissension. Second, application of government funds to religious purposes suffers from these twin evils because each citizen is taxed to support the religions of others; but this proposition of fiscal noninvolvement with religion is subject to exceptions. The state may undertake to subsidize certain programs to which religious interests bear a socially recognized relationship. When this occurs, to insist on exclusion of all religious elements from the benefits of a program can hinder rather than preserve religious voluntarism and can curb the program's effectiveness; this is especially true where participation by religious groups is relevant to the social goals of the programs involved or is merely the consequence of equalizing the position of religious associations vis-à-vis other private ones.[18] The third proposition, which would forbid any governmental action that in fact aids religion, is open to the greatest qualification. Where the state does no more than extend to

---

18. Governmental subsidies to religiously operated schools on Indian reservations and to military chaplains provide examples of public expenditures that are justified because of legitimate overall regulatory responsibilities in these areas. * * * Partic- ipation by religiously affiliated associations in state-financed welfare programs serves both to advance such programs and to extend political equality to such organizations. * * *

religion the benefits of the prevailing social order, it does not lend the kind of support forbidden by the principle of voluntarism. Indeed, to deny religion such benefits would place it at a handicap inconsistent with values of free self-development. Moreover, failure to extend benefits generally available only because religion will somehow be advanced in a particular case can effect such an invidious discrimination in favor of nonreligion as to engender the political dissension which the establishment clause sought to avoid.

Governmental neutrality in religious matters therefore justifies, and may compel, governmental aid to religion under certain circumstances. One aspect of this neutrality, * * * which I shall refer to as free exercise neutrality, permits, and sometimes requires, the state to make special provision for religious interests in order to relieve them from both direct and indirect burdens placed on the free exercise of religion by increased governmental regulation. This view of neutrality was adopted by the Supreme Court in *Sherbert v. Verner*,[20] which held that a state must exempt unemployment compensation claimants from the requirement of accepting available work if compliance interferes with their observance of the Sabbath. * * *

While the principle of free exercise neutrality explains religious exemptions from governmental restrictions on behavior, it does not seem to justify governmental action that tends to structure a secular order in which religion is given an apparently preferred status, such as in the zoning of land where churches are usually treated more favorably than other places of public assembly. That principle is particularly weak as a justification for public expenditures that support welfare programs under religious auspices; this is true even if one concedes that working for the welfare of others is a traditional form of religious exercise, because governmental support of thoroughly secular welfare programs does not directly burden anyone's ability to engage in good works. Consequently, free exercise neutrality would permit the government to support the welfare activities of religious associations financially only when the total tax burden on the community is so crushing that private ability to engage in welfare programs is severely undercut.

Thus, to justify aid to religious interests and associations when it flows from the secular order established by the state, we must turn to a second aspect of neutrality. This aspect, which I will call political neutrality, can be completely separated from free exercise neutrality. Its aim is not to remove governmental burdens on the practice of religion but rather to assure that the establishment clause does not force the categorical exclusion of religious activities and associations from a scheme of governmental regulation whose secular purposes justify their inclusion. The principle of political neutrality recognizes that religious associations operate in the temporal realm and accordingly can be legitimately included among the beneficiaries of the prevailing order established and sustained by the state. If religious groups are to be

20.   374 U.S. 398 (1963).

effectively organized bodies rather than loose associations of mendicants, they must be able to own property, enter into contracts, hire employees, and engage in a host of activities with secular dimensions and consequences. In short, making religious voluntarism a reality requires that religious associations be treated with political equality and accorded civil opportunities for self-development on a par with other voluntary associations. For instance, to deprive churches of police and fire protection—because the state would be aiding religion in violation of the establishment clause—would be insupportable doctrine. The extremely serious disadvantage to religious associations would mark governmental hostility toward their development, not neutrality, and such invidious discrimination could lead only to bitterness and strife in the political arena, not insulation of politics from religion.

* * *

II. Political Neutrality and Expanding Government

The importance of the principle of political neutrality increases with the expanding role of government. Even Madison might have changed some of his absolutist notions of separation to accord with twentieth century realities. For example, his veto of the congressional act incorporating the Protestant Episcopal Church in the town of Alexandria in the District of Columbia was a natural outgrowth of his view that absolute separation prohibits any official act which recognizes or supports religion. At the time, refusal to allow incorporation was not as serious as it would be today; indeed, incorporation then conferred special recognition and status on associations so favored. Charters were rarely granted to business institutions and often corporate status had carried with it the power to tax. But with incorporation now a legal status available with equal liberality to corner service stations and mammoth business enterprises, as well as to substantial philanthropic foundations that influence the shape and direction of modern educational and social thought, it is doubtful that the author of *The Federalist Number 10,* with his bias in favor of vigorous social pluralism, would want to place religious interests and ideologies at a material handicap in their confrontation with secular interests and ideologies. In any event, those of his disciples who regard him as the leading prophet of the religion clauses have not treated his views on incorporation as a binding fundamentalist tenet of the constitutional gospel according to Madison. To this extent even the doctrinaire theory of strict separation has yielded to changing circumstances.

That the no-aid aspects of the separation principle should be relaxed in direct proportion to the extent of governmental regulation can most easily be demonstrated by examination of a hypothetical situation. Assume a state which is entirely collectivized, like the Soviet Union, but which subscribes to the principle of church-state separation modeled on the establishment clause of the Constitution. Adherence to the nonestablishment principle would require such a government to grant autonomy to church officials in purely ecclesiastical matters and to avoid governmental preference among religions. But would it also prohibit direct economic aids to religion by the state? Clearly not, unless the non-establishment principle were to be perverted and used to destroy voluntarism rather than preserve it.

Assuming that such a collectivized society were to permit all kinds of voluntary associations to operate with a significant amount of freedom and effectiveness, it would have to devise some scheme by which to make state-owned resources, like land, available to these groups. The principle of political neutrality would justify comparable treatment of religious organizations in order that they might have appropriate and substantially equal opportunities for self-development. Of course, one could turn to the free exercise principle to rescue religious organizations from the emasculation that an absolute no-aid theory of nonestablishment would entail in such a society. But specific religious guarantees would not be necessary to protect against such a result. Political neutrality justifies the "aid" involved because it is up to the state to allocate all the land in the society to all the various social uses freely desired by the citizenry. Although such governmental support of religion would violate the principle of separation in a society characterized by private ownership of property, it is as basic as fire and police protection in a thoroughly collectivized one.

This example is not as far-fetched as it seems for purposes of illuminating American establishment problems. It supplies perspective for the disturbing case of *Quick Bear v. Leupp*,[27] in which the Supreme Court upheld congressional appropriations to support religious schools on Indian reservations. Once Washington had decided to treat the Indians as wards of the state and a substantial number evinced an interest in the Christian religion, such aid was a natural and appropriate part of the assistance given to them. The governmental action here involved was comparable to the allocation of land to the use of religious groups in a collectivized society. In both cases the government has taken over the total responsibility of allocating certain economic resources. In discharging its responsibility it takes into account the wishes of the citizenry who would make such decisions for themselves in our contemporary society. Here again the value of voluntarism is preserved rather than impaired if the state takes the religious factor into account to bring about the result the citizens would have achieved if they were making the decisions.

* * *

Of more significance than these isolated cases of government collectivization are the situations presented by an American economy which, though far removed from that of a communistic society, is equally remote from the agrarian, frontier society of our founding fathers. Increasing socialization in two areas of American life creates a conflict between the strict neutrality and no-aid principles comparable to that

---

27. 210 U.S. 50 (1908).

created in my hypothetical collectivized society. The first area embraces those fields of regulation in which the state plays an important and often decisive role in the allocation of economic uses or resources. In this area, which includes zoning of land or allocation of radio and television licenses, the analogy to a collectivized society is clear. The second area encompasses the entire field of the government's fiscal operations. In this area the continually expanding public sector acquires many of the attributes of a collectivized society, so that unqualified adherence to the no-aid principle will tend to have a destructive impact on voluntarism. The strict no-aid principle would deny religious societies any role in the government's pervasive public welfare programs. Since these programs would divert resources to the public sector from the private one—where they would have been available for religious, charitable, and other philanthropic uses—and a strict no-aid interpretation of the establishment clause would deny tax exemptions for religious uses, at some point the resulting squeeze on religious institutions would sap the social and economic vitality that they would have possessed if private decisions had more fully determined the allocation of resources. Application of the principle of political neutrality, on the other hand, at least would allow religious institutions to enjoy the same treatment as secular ones in government programs.

---

3. ACCOMMODATION

Michael McConnell rejects both strict separation and neutrality as ways of understanding the establishment clause, because neither one offers enough protection for religious liberty. He argues that religion is a welcome element in a pluralist society, and should be encouraged. A government where the people are sovereign depends on the virtue of its citizens, and religion does much to cultivate that quality. Of course when we encourage religion we run the risk that a religious faction might become too strong and tyrannize nonadherents. Though it seems paradoxical, McConnell says, accommodation actually reduces this risk. If we encourage a multiplicity of sects, the competition among them will keep any one from getting too strong (much as competition in the economic market prevents the acquisition of monopoly power).

Mark Tushnet points out two weaknesses in McConnell's argument. One concerns the claim that religion is good because it helps maintain public virtue. Tushnet notes that there are other ways of doing that, so there is no reason to give special consideration to religion. A rule of neutrality will suffice. The other concerns McConnell's multiplicity-of-sects argument. Tushnet points out that some of the insights of public choice theory should make us wary about accepting without question the legislative bargains struck by coalitions of groups.

Dallin Oaks offers an intriguing concluding suggestion: he argues that both separation and accommodation approaches to the establishment clause tend to get carried over to the free exercise clause, with surprising consequences. When government gives little support to religion, the law gives it little room to regulate or tax religion either. The rules of non-establishment and free exercise are both strict. (This is the "separation" solution.) When government gives more support to religion, it will also increase the level of regulation and taxation. The rules of non-establishment and free exercise are both relaxed. (This is the "accommodation" solution.) Oaks says that over the last half century we have shifted in emphasis from separation to accommodation.

MICHAEL W. McCONNELL, ACCOMMODATION OF RELIGION

1985 Sup.Ct.Rev. 1, 3, 8, 10–14, 16–23.

My thesis is that between the accommodations compelled by the Free Exercise Clause and the benefits to religion prohibited by the Establishment Clause there exists a class of permissible government actions toward religion, which have as their purpose and effect the facilitation of religious liberty. Neither strict neutrality nor separationism can account for the idea of accommodation or define its limits. Only an interpretation of the Religion Clauses based on religious liberty—an interpretation grounded in the political theory underlying the Constitution—satisfactorily distinguishes permissible accommodations from impermissible establishments.

* * *

A. STRICT NEUTRALITY

An attractively simple [First Amendment principle] might be that religion has no special status—that the government may not make any distinction on the basis of the religious or nonreligious character of the activities involved. * * *

* * *

[But] * * * strict neutrality cannot be a full explanation for the Religion Clauses. Let us consider the three forms in which the question of neutrality between religion and nonreligion arises: (1) neutrality between religion and unbelief; (2) neutrality between religious and nonreligious moral convictions; and (3) neutrality between religion and various activities or beliefs wholly unrelated to religion or conscience.

Religious liberty demands some degree of neutrality between religion and unbelief. Unbelief is, after all, a system of opinions regarding the existence of God and thus regarding ultimate religious questions of life and value. If "[t]he Religion then of every man must be left to the conviction and conscience of every man," [28] each person must be as free to disbelieve as he is to believe. Moreover, insofar as unbelief leads the

---

28. Madison, Memorial and Remonstrance Against Religious Assessments, ¶ 1, reprinted in an appendix to Everson v. Board of Education, 330 U.S. [1,] 64 [(1947).]

unbeliever to certain actions, not dissimilar to religious practice—for example the calling to preach, proselytize, or attend meetings—these actions are entitled to no less protection from the state than traditional religious actions of a similar nature.

When moving from belief (and communication of belief) to religious observance, however, there is no strict parallel—no coherent requirement of neutrality—between religion and unbelief. It is a commonplace that free exercise protects not just belief but also some action. Beyond a limited number of communicative and associational actions that may, for some unbelievers, be an integral part of their system of unbelief, unbelief entails no obligations and no observances. Unbelief may be coupled with various sorts of moral conviction, which will be considered below. But these convictions must necessarily be derived from some source other than unbelief itself; belief in the nonexistence of God does not in itself generate a moral code. Accordingly, to the extent that religious *actions* are protected under the Religion Clauses, there will be an asymmetry in the treatment of religion and unbelief. The protection of religious opinion will equally benefit religion and unbelief; the protection of religious action will primarily benefit religion.

Neutrality between religiously and nonreligiously motivated moral convictions presents a more difficult question. To some extent, nonreligiously based moral conviction is accorded special respect in our legal system, frequently (if not altogether satisfactorily) under the Free Speech Clause. The right not to proclaim the motto "Live Free or Die" on one's license plate,[31] to opt out of the flag salute in public school,[32] and to refuse financial support for union political activities under a union shop[33] are well known examples. In large part, however, the legal tradition is otherwise: an act of disobedience to the law, however sincerely motivated by moral scruple, is ordinarily thought to be punishable. "The concept of ordered liberty," the Court has said, "precludes allowing every person to make his own standards on matters of conduct in which society as a whole has important interests."[35]

* * *

The Court has consistently treated religiously grounded moral objections as worthy of greater consideration.[37] * * * In *Wisconsin v. Yoder,* the Court stated that "[a] way of life, however virtucus and admirable, may not be interposed as a barrier to reasonable state regulation ... if it

---

31. Wooley v. Maynard, 430 U.S. 705 (1977).

32. West Virginia Department of Education v. Barnette, 319 U.S. 624 (1943).

33. Abood v. Detroit Board of Education, 431 U.S. 209 (1977).

35. Wisconsin v. Yoder, 406 U.S. 205, 215–16 (1972); see, *e.g.,* United States v. O'Brien, 391 U.S. 367 (1968).

37. *E.g.,* Thomas v. Review Board, 450 U.S. 707 (1981) (religious objection to nature of work); Wisconsin v. Yoder, 406 U.S.

205 (1972) (religious objection to compulsory schooling); Gillette v. United States, 401 U.S. 437 (1971) (religious objection to military service); Sherbert v. Verner, 374 U.S. 398 (1963) (religious objection to work schedule); Zorach v. Clauson, 343 U.S. [306, 313 (1952)] (religious conflicts with school schedules). As *Gillette* and *Zorach* indicate, the Court's special solicitude for religious conflicts extends beyond free exercise cases.

is based on purely secular considerations; to have the protection of the Religion Clauses, the claims must be rooted in religious belief." The Court has not articulated any rationale for this difference in treatment; but it seems plausible in light of the fact that there is no explicit textual basis, parallel to the Free Exercise Clause, for requiring governmental toleration of secular moral systems. * * *

Neutrality between religion and activities wholly unrelated to religion or conscience—tennis, for example, or the study of history—is a much clearer matter. Government may regulate, support, or require such activities without constraint under the Religion Clauses. They are not like religion in any significant respect and need not be treated as if they were. The government can exempt churches from taxation without exempting tennis clubs. Conversely, government schools are prohibited from teaching the tenets of a religion as fact, but they can teach the tenets of history as fact. Most importantly for present purposes, government may show respect for religious conviction and facilitate the practice of an individual's freely chosen religion, without being forced to accord the same respect to the myriad nonreligious preferences of the people. There is, in short, no requirement of neutrality between religion and nonreligion in this sense. Any constitutional constraint must arise because the special treatment of religion would have a deleterious effect on religious liberty—not because other activities or systems of thought are of equal constitutional dignity.

B. STRICT SEPARATION

A second common view of the constitutional status of religion is that of strict separation between church and state. Under this view, the government may not aid religion in any way, direct or indirect, large or small. Since the government's assistance generally arises from its coercion of others (through taxation or otherwise), any government aid to religion forces some persons to support a religious exercise against their will. Accordingly, it has been said that the government is "stripped of all power to tax, to support, or otherwise to assist any or all religions." [41]

This "no-aid" view, too, while it had considerable support on the Court at one time, has now been rejected by even the most separationist Justices.[43] The principal support for this view was a mistaken reading of the history of the Religion Clauses by the Court and, more conspicuously, by the dissent in *Everson v. Board of Education*. In light of the purposes of the Religion Clauses, it has little to commend it. Excluding religious institutions and individuals from government benefits to which they would be entitled under neutral and secular criteria, merely because they are religious, advances secularism, not liberty. In the extreme case—denial of access to basic public services such as sewage hookup or

---

41. Everson v. Board of Education, 330 U.S. at 11.

43. McDaniel v. Paty, 435 U.S. [618,] 638–43 [(1978)] (Brennan, J., concurring);

see Mueller v. Allen, 463 U.S. 388, 393 (1983).

fire and police protection—denial of "aid" would be tantamount to prohibition. Thus the Court recognized, even in *Everson,* that "we must be careful, in protecting ... against state-established churches, to be sure that we do not inadvertently prohibit [the state] from extending its general state law benefits to all its citizens without regard to their religious belief."

C. RELIGIOUS PLURALISM

An alternative view is that religion is a welcome element in the mix of beliefs and associations present in the community. Under this view, the emphasis is placed on freedom of choice and diversity among religious opinion. The nation is understood not as secular but as pluralistic. Religion is under no special disability in public life; indeed, it is at least as protected and encouraged as any other form of belief and association—in some ways more so. The idea of accommodation of religion, which is foreign to interpretations of the Religion Clauses based on strict neutrality or separation, follows naturally from the pluralist understanding. * * *

* * *

[A]ny form of civil society must depend, in part, on the citizens' commitment to order and morality. Coercion is an insufficient basis for civil order, except perhaps in the more ruthless despotisms. And any democratic form of society must inevitably reflect the values of its people. The need for internalized constraints and natural sentiments of justice is thus particularly acute for citizens of a republic, in which rule by force is replaced by self-rule. As the Founders understood it, the republic was peculiarly dependent on public virtue to maintain the mutual respect and harmony on which republican liberty rests.[53] If the people are corrupt, how can a republican government—in which sovereignty resides in the people—be just?

* * *

A source of public virtue outside of government was therefore necessary to the ultimate success of the republican experiment. Private associations—families, civic groups, colleges and universities, above all, churches—supply the need. They are the principal means by which the citizens in a liberal polity learn to transcend their individual interests and opinions and to develop civic responsibility. These associations bear the brunt of the responsibility for articulating and inculcating values of morality and justice in the liberal republic. Frequently denominated "mediating" structures or institutions,[57] these associations "have played

53. See, *e.g.,* The Federalist Papers, No. 55 (Madison), at 346 (1787) (New American Library ed. 1961) ("[T]here are other qualities in human nature which justify a certain portion of esteem and confidence. Republican government presupposes the existence of these qualities in a higher degree than any other form"). * * *

57. See, *e.g.,* Berger & Neuhaus, To Empower People: The Role of Mediating Structures in Public Policy (1977); Kerrine & Neuhaus, *Mediating Structures: A Paradigm for Democratic Pluralism,* 446 Annals 10 (1970).

a critical role in the culture and traditions of the Nation by cultivating and transmitting shared ideals and beliefs." It is in the context of these communal associations that individual citizens commonly derive their system of values, even their sense of personal identity and integrity. If the liberal community ultimately has worth in the classical sense of promoting the good for its citizens—that is, the virtuous life—that end is met not by the government but by the free associations of the people.

* * * Historically and to the present day, however, no such institutions are as important to the process of developing, transmitting, communicating, and enforcing concepts of morality and justice as are the churches. It is in this sense that Tocqueville described religion as "the first of [America's] political institutions." [65] The role of the churches has been especially notable in connection with public morality and justice, as recent public controversies over matters such as racial discrimination, nuclear disarmament, abortion, and immigration illustrate. The special status of religion under the Constitution—both the individual's choice of faith and the institution's autonomy—derives in large part from these considerations.

The "political" effects of religion must be distinguished, in this sense, from individual morality. Unlike individual moral thought, religion is communal and institutional. It is poised between the individual and the state; it is social but not universal. Religious thought is not the product solely of individual reason but is rooted in history and tradition. It commands veneration and not mere assent. It carries with it a system of internalized discipline (most pronounced in traditional theistic religions with their belief in divine punishments and rewards) far stronger than mere opinion of right and wrong. It was accordingly widely thought by the Founders that republican self-government could not succeed unless religion continued to foster a moral sense in the people.[68]

The problem for liberal theory was how to realize the benefits of religion in public life without suffering the dangers. The typically Madisonian solution was to rely on the number and diversity of religious views to foster strong and vigorous religion and at the same time guarantee against religious tyranny. Madison wrote in *Federalist* 51: [69]

> In a free government the security for civil rights must be the same as that for religious rights. It consists in the one case in the multiplicity of interests, and in the other in the multiplicity of sects. The degree of security in both cases will depend on the number of

---

65. Tocqueville, Democracy in America 292 (Anchor Books ed. 1969).

68. Each of the early Presidents spoke on the theme. John Adams, for example, stated that "[w]e have no government armed with power capable of contending with human passions unbridled by morality and religion. Our constitution was made only for a moral and a religious people. It is wholly inadequate for the government of any other." Hauerwas, A Community of Character 79 (1981). See also Washington, Farewell Address, in 1 Messages and Papers of the Presidents 212 (1897); Jefferson, Notes on the State of Virginia 163 (1787). * * *

69. The Federalist Papers, No. 51, at 324.

interests and sects; and this may be presumed to depend on the extent of country and number of people comprehended under the same government.

Liberal political theory thus favored religion, but it did not favor any one religion. It guaranteed religious freedom in the hope and expectation that religious observance would flourish, and with it morality and self-restraint among the people. But it feared monopoly in religion, especially at the national level. This is the theory that best explains the Religion Clauses of the First Amendment. * * *

* * *

This pluralist understanding of the First Amendment was dominant in early interpretation * * * Beginning in the very session that framed the Bill of Rights, Congress openly signaled its approval and endorsement of religion in general through such diverse actions as calling on the President to recommend to the people a day of prayer, appointing House and Senate chaplains, and making land grants for schools in the territories on the theory that "[r]eligion, morality, and knowledge [are] necessary to good government." This evidence has recently been rehearsed in other places and need not be elaborated here.[81] In brief, the principal objects of the Religion Clauses were consistent with the liberal political theory summarized above. They were to prevent coercion (and lesser forms of governmental pressure) in matters of religion and to encourage a multiplicity of religious sects. Government respect for, and encouragement of, religion in general—in ways that do not compel religious exercise or invade the religious liberty of others—was considered appropriate and even necessary.

An incident during debate over what is now the Second Amendment casts light on the specific issue of accommodation. The committee draft of the Amendment included a clause that "no person religiously scrupulous shall be compelled to bear arms." [83] Interestingly, no House member opposed the clause on the ground that it favored religion. Even Representative Jackson, who thought it was "unjust" to require "one part [of the country] to defend the other in case of invasion" was willing to permit the religious exemption "upon paying an equivalent, to be established by law." [84] Nonetheless, Representative Benson moved to strike the clause, stating,[85]

> No man can claim this indulgence of right. It may be a religious persuasion, but it is no natural right, and therefore ought to be left to the discretion of the Government .... I have no reason to believe but the Legislature will always possess humanity enough to indulge this class of citizens in a matter they are so desirous of; but they ought to be left to their discretion.

81. See Wallace v. Jaffree, [472 U.S. 38, 91–106 (1985)] (Rehnquist, J., dissenting). * * * Malbin, [Religion and Politics (1978).]

83. 1 Annals [of Congress 778 (J. Gales ed. 1834).]

84. *Id.* at 779.

85. *Id.* at 780.

Benson's motion was defeated by a vote of 24–22. The Senate, however, rejected inclusion of the military religious exemption clause and it was deleted in conference.

This incident, while of course not dispositive in itself of the meaning of the Religion Clauses, establishes a link between the understanding of religious liberty reflected in the First Amendment and the idea of accommodation of religion. Two important points that remain central to the argument for accommodation today emerge from the debate: that preferential treatment for religion in some matters is desirable (and perhaps sometimes mandatory), and that the government is not limited in making religious accommodations to those required under the Constitution. While the state must retain authority to protect the vital collective interests of the people, it will "possess humanity enough" to recognize the higher claims of religion when it can.

MARK TUSHNET, THE EMERGING PRINCIPLE OF ACCOMMODATION OF RELIGION (DUBITANTE)

76 Geo.L.J. 1691, 1695–1697, 1699–1701 (1988).

A. ORIGINAL INTENT

The specific intent of the drafters and ratifiers of the religion clauses is a matter of substantial controversy, the details of which need not engage us here. Professor Michael McConnell's defense of the accommodation principle properly moves back from those details to consider whether the principle is consistent with the general theory of government held by the framers' generation.[39] Unfortunately, McConnell's discussion truncates that theory in a way that makes the accommodation principle appear to be more consistent with the framers' theory than it actually is.

McConnell stresses what has come to be called the republican strand in the framers' political theory. The concept of virtue was central in republicanism. A virtuous citizenry was necessary to ensure that public policy be guided by considerations of general welfare rather than private interest, and to guard against the corruption of government by vicious public officials. A well-designed government would have the power to promote the acquisition and perpetuation of civic virtue among the citizenry. One source of civic virtue was religion. This aspect of republican theory was expressed in the Northwest Ordinance: "Religion, morality, and knowledge being necessary to good government, ... schools and the means of education shall forever be encouraged." The accommodation principle similarly authorizes government to act in ways that "encourage" the development of civic virtue through individual exercises of religion.

The republican pedigree of the accommodation principle is weakened somewhat by the effects of social change, the usual nemesis of original

---

39. McConnell, [*Accommodation of Religion,* 1985 Sup.Ct.Rev. 1.]

intent theories. To some degree, republican theory regarded religious belief as an empirically necessary predicate to civic virtue. That claim can no longer be accepted, for secularism has produced some secularists who are virtuous in a republican sense. Religion may now be one among several methods of inculcating civic virtue, rather than a necessary method as assumed in the Northwest Ordinance. The existence of several methods thus seems to support not the accommodation principle but rather a principle akin to one of nondiscrimination—a principle that the government may encourage all of the methods of inculcating civic virtue but may not single out one of them, that is, religion, for special accommodation. * * *

* * *

B. POLITICAL PLURALISM

When James Madison sought to defend the proposition that the extended republic created by the Constitution would preserve liberty by encompassing many political groups, he expressly drew an analogy between political pluralism and religious pluralism.[57] The political argument was that the new government would be able to act only when its actions satisfied a wide range of political groups that were often in conflict. When the condition of satisfying that range of groups is met, the resulting legislation is unlikely to threaten fundamental values.

Madison's argument can be qualified and elaborated in many ways, but its core insight remains powerful. The accommodation principle can be seen as a straightforward application of the pluralist argument to questions arising out of political contention over religious issues in a religiously pluralistic society. People are members of religious groups and of other groups as well. These crosscutting group memberships indicate that legislation on issues affecting religion is likely to be of a "least common denominator" sort. Such legislation might, for example, aid "religion in general" in a way that does not discriminate against denominations. In addition, and more important here, laws that benefit one segment of the community at the expense of the majority of the community are difficult to question. Public aid to nonpublic education provides a good illustration. It is well-known that such aid flows primarily to Roman Catholic schools, which serve a minority of the population. Yet, if a majority is willing to increase its own taxes to

57. The Federalist No. 10, at 136 (J. Madison) (B. Wright ed. 1961):

> The influence of factious leaders may kindle a flame within their particular states, but will be unable to spread a general conflagration through the other states. A religious sect may degenerate into a political faction in a part of the Confederacy, but the variety of sects dispersed over the entire face of it must secure the national councils from that source.

Id.; The Federalist No. 51, at 358 (J. Madison) (B. Wright ed. 1961):

> In a free government the security for civil rights must be the same as that for religious rights.... The degree of security in both cases will depend on the number of interests and sects; and this may be presumed to depend on the extent of country and number of people comprehended under the same government.

Id.

provide that aid, one is hard-pressed to see what is objectionable about their choice. * * *

Two important qualifications are implicit in this analysis. First, it is unrealistic to think of legislation as the product of an undifferentiated majority placing burdens on itself. More accurately, a coalition of groups, including the beneficiaries of the accommodation, constitutes a majority that imposes burdens on itself to some degree and on the minority coalition to some degree. We might be concerned about situations in which the burdens assumed by the nonbeneficiary members of the majority coalition were substantially less than those imposed on the minority losers. * * *

The second qualification is that sometimes the majority is not a coalition at all, but a group unified around its own religious commitments. The statutes affecting religion enacted by such a majority might provide benefits to the majority at the expense of the religious minority. [School prayer statutes may be an example.] * * *

Pluralist arguments, like original intent ones, thus provide some support for the accommodation principle. In particular cases, though, that support may be undermined by the exact array of pluralist forces that produced the statute in question.

DALLIN H. OAKS, SEPARATION, ACCOM-MODATION AND THE FUTURE OF CHURCH AND STATE

35 DePaul L.Rev. 1, 3–10 (1985).

America is passing a critical intersection and taking a new direction in the law of church and state. This article describes the nature and causes of that new direction and where it is leading us.

SEPARATION AND ACCOMMODATION

To use the familiar vernacular, "separation" is giving way to "accommodation." The dividing line between church and state, once a "wall ... high and impregnable," [14] is now a hedge low-lying and penetrable.

The current transition to accommodation has two aspects, which correspond to the two commands in the religion clause of the first amendment. Not surprisingly, courts are softening both commands. The judicial prohibition against an establishment of religion is relaxing. This allows an increase in the extent of permissible government support of religion. Courts are also weakening the guarantee of free exercise of religion. Religious organizations are subject to more regulation and taxation, and religious-based exemptions from laws of general application are on the decline.

14. Everson v. Board of Educ., 330 U.S. 1, 16, 18 (1947).

For purposes of this analysis, one may visualize the relationship between the divergent commands of non-establishment and free exercise in terms of a beam scale, as portrayed in the familiar scales of justice. The two scale pans receive the force of the countervailing commands of non-establishment and free exercise. This article suggests that forces in law or public policy tend to balance this scale in equilibrium. When some force increases the weight on one side of the scale, a state of equilibrium will be restored by a corresponding increase on the other side. Therefore, when non-establishment law permits an increase in government support of religion, free exercise law soon restores the equilibrium by permitting an increase in government regulation and taxation of religion. A similar result occurs when the sequence is reversed.

Under this metaphor, "separation" and "accommodation" represent the total weight on the scales, although these labels are logically related to the establishment side. Thus, "separation" signifies a minimum quantity of government support of religion, and a corresponding minimum amount of government regulation and taxation. Non-establishment and free exercise are in their most rigorous state. The scales are in balance, and the relationship is in equilibrium.

"Accommodation" signifies a condition where the weight of government support has been increased. Such an increase is followed by, or follows, a comparable increase in the extent of government regulation and/or taxation. The accommodation equilibrium represents increased weight on both sides of the scales: government support on one side and regulation and taxation on the other. Stated otherwise, accommodation represents a relaxation of both the non-establishment and free exercise commands of the religion clause.

There are many unanswered questions regarding the transition from separation to accommodation. Which side of the scales is affected first, and what accounts for the equilibrium in the hypothesis? Do changes in the level of government support cause comparable changes in the level of regulation or taxation, as the sequence seems to suggest? Or is the relationship the reverse? Or are both changes produced by some third force?

Even when changes in legal rules or results move sequentially, it is difficult to identify the causes of change. In fact, it is not certain what produces the equilibrium in this hypothesis. It may be as simple as the common-sense operation of accountability and fairness: what government supports it regulates or taxes, and, on the other hand, what government regulates or taxes it will also support, directly or indirectly. Perhaps the most likely explanation is that the movement from separation to accommodation between church and state is produced by forces outside that relationship.

* * *

The change in emphasis from separation to accommodation seems to be a consequence of two interrelated developments of the last half-century: the expansion in the role of government, and the changing definition of religion.

1. The Role of Government

During our lifetimes we have seen increased government regulation of relationships and activities in which churches engage in approximately the same way as other organizations and individuals. These relationships and activities include employment relations, commercial exchanges, financing, and the use of land or other property. The vision of those who devise and administer such regulations is shaped to their subject matter. For this purpose the regulatory vision detects little or no difference in whether the regulated activity involves a religious institution or not. Thus, those who regulate employment relationships tend to look at a church employer like any other employer. It is difficult to persuade regulators that religious institutions should have special exemptions. As a result, the regulatory burden on churches has tended to increase along with the regulatory burden on others.

We have also seen increased regulation of the unique activities of all non-profit organizations, such as charitable solicitation and financial disclosure. Laws restricting tax exemptions for non-profit organizations have also affected churches. Although these kinds of changes typically are not aimed at churches as such, they inevitably enlarge the area of the tender interface between church and state.

Finally, as the scope of government has increased, federal, state, and local governments more and more have become a competitor of churches. This has increased church-state conflicts in such areas as education, hospitalization, adoption, counseling, and other social services.

The expanding interface of religion and government has increased the practical difficulty of what may be termed the "separation equilibrium" and also has enhanced the relative attractiveness of what may be called the "accommodation equilibrium."

2. "Religion" Defined

* * *

The definition of religion is a crucial factor in the law of church and state. The area of confrontation between church and state grows as the number of organizations and types of activities included within the definition of religion increases. Increased confrontation between church and state will intensify pressure to relax the prohibition against government support of religion. Thus, the more inclusive the definition of religion, the greater the pressure for accommodation. A larger area of confrontation will also tend to weaken the guarantee against government regulation and taxation of religion.

a. "Religion" and the Guarantee of Free Exercise

For purposes of the guarantee of free exercise, the definition of religion has moved from theism to "ultimate-concern" philosophy. In 1890 the Supreme Court defined religion as "one's views of his relations to his Creator, and to the obligations they impose of reverence for his being and character, and of obedience to his will." [28] In 1931 Chief Justice Hughes wrote for himself and Justices Stone, Holmes, and Brandeis that "the essence of religion is belief in a relation to God involving duties superior to those arising from any human relation." [29] In the famous 1947 *Everson* opinion,[30] however, Justice Black included "non-believers" in his listing of various denominations and categories of religion.

* * *

The problem with a definition of religion that includes almost everything is that the practical effect of inclusion comes to mean almost nothing. Free exercise protections become diluted as their scope becomes more diffuse. When religion has no more right to free exercise than irreligion or any other secular philosophy, the whole newly expanded category of "religion" is likely to diminish in significance. This has already happened.

b. "Religion" and the Prohibition Against Establishment

In contrast, for purposes of the prohibition against government establishment, religion has retained its traditional theistic connotations of worship and belief in God. The legal gatekeeper for this part of the wall between church and state has blocked any government traffic that would not pass the three-prong test for establishment: a secular legislative purpose, a primary effect that neither advances nor inhibits religion, and an administration that does not foster excessive government "entanglement" with religion.[40] The irony of this three-prong test is that, as applied, it has screened out government support for only that form of religion which fits under the traditional theistic definition. No other philosophy or value system among those enjoying the expanded guarantee of free exercise has had to pass this test. Notwithstanding the comprehensive belief systems and the religious fervor of those who have promoted secular humanism, environmentalism, behaviorism, or other theories of value or human behavior, their causes have received government support without having to pass the three-prong test. Only traditional theistic religion has been banished from the "public square."

The Supreme Court has never explained why religion has a broad non-theistic meaning for purposes of free exercise and a narrow theistic meaning for purposes of non-establishment. There are many scholarly

28. Davis v. Beason, 133 U.S. 333, 342 (1890).

29. United States v. Macintosh, 283 U.S. 605, 633–34 (1931) (Hughes, C.J., dissenting).

30. 330 U.S. 1, 16 (1947).

40. Committee for Pub. Educ. & Religious Liberty v. Nyquist, 413 U.S. 756 (1973).

works on the definition of religion under the first amendment, but most deal with religion for purposes of free exercise and gloss over the awkward fact that the same definition does not apply to establishment.

In the long run we have a right to expect that the United States Supreme Court will formulate a definition of religion that can be applied to both the guarantee of free exercise and the prohibition of non-establishment. The language of the religion clause dictates a common definition, and fairness and practicality demand it.

Theoretically, a common definition could be achieved if the Court would return to its original theistic definition. A return to the original definition would limit the number of organizations and beliefs to which the religion clause applies. The consensus of knowledgeable commentary considers this alternative unlikely, since it would be unacceptable to exclude non-theistic eastern religions and emerging systems of philosophical belief from the protections of the first amendment. This consensus has undeniable force.

The more likely alternative for uniformity is for the Supreme Court to formulate a comprehensive definition of religion analogous to the broad non-theistic definition it has applied in free exercise cases. There is, however, a problem with this non-theistic alternative. A broad definition of religion when applied to the current rules prohibiting the "establishment" of religion would drive government out of some areas of activity where its sponsorship, support, and influence are now pervasive. Under a broad definition of religion, the traditional rules against establishment might bar the government not only from sponsoring educational activity involving religious or philosophical values, but also from taking actions overtly based on such values.

If applied to anti-establishment, a broad definition of religion would so enlarge the area of interface between church and state that the current rules against government support of religion might lead to a paralyzing tangle of litigation that could put a host of government programs in jeopardy. The obvious corrective for this unacceptable prospect is for the substantive rules against the establishment of religion to relax to the point that both religion and government can co-exist along the enlarged border of interface.

D. RULES

Translating the general principles reviewed in the last section into rules of law is a difficult task. (It is not made any easier by the Supreme Court's inability to decide which principles count.) Legal rules ideally should provide clear direction for new cases, so that private actors and public officials can conform their conduct to the requirements of law. Until recently the most important rule in establishment clause jurisprudence was the three-part test of *Lemon v. Kurtzman:* (1) a law must have a secular purpose; (2) its primary effect must be one that neither advances nor inhibits religion; (3) it must not foster an excessive

entanglement of government and religion.[1] During the past few terms
the Court has cast doubt on the continued vitality of *Lemon* by studious-
ly ignoring it in its decisions in *Rosenberger v. Rector and Visitors of the
University of Virginia*[2] and *Lee v. Weisman*.[3] The articles in this section
deal with the *Lemon* test and some alternatives to it that the Supreme
Court has been experimenting with lately.

Gary Simson believes that the *Lemon* test has its points. He argues
that the Court could improve it in three ways. First, it should take the
purpose requirement more seriously, and strike down any law enacted
with the help of a nonsecular purpose. Second, it should enforce the
effects requirement more strictly. A law should not give any significant
aid to religion unless doing so is necessary to serve a substantial
government interest. Under this rule it would be unconstitutional to
loan books to parochial schools. Third, Simson would drop the entanglement part of the test, and deal with its concerns under the first two
prongs.

Phillip Johnson responds that the *Lemon* test is conceptually incoherent. It is difficult to distinguish between religious and secular
purposes. (Doesn't the government have a "secular" reason for supporting sects that encourage their members to obey the laws and promote
racial equality?) And if we could identify strictly religious purposes and
effects, why should the Constitution forbid the government to aid its
citizens in the enjoyment of a right (free exercise) which the First
Amendment protects? The rule against entanglement, Johnson says, is
chiefly designed to prevent divisiveness along religious lines. But he
suggests that courts exacerbate religious controversy when they prevent
voters and legislators from resolving disputes democratically.

Criticisms like Johnson's have obviously had some effect on the
Court, which has been trying out alternatives to the *Lemon* test in
recent years. One early contender was the "no endorsement" test
proposed by Justice O'Connor in *Lynch v. Donnelly*.[4] O'Connor actually
described her test as a gloss on *Lemon,* not an alternative. The purpose
prong, she said, should forbid the government to act with the intent of
endorsing (or disapproving of) religion. The effect prong would forbid
laws that create a perception of endorsement (or disapproval). O'Connor's proposal was initially received quite favorably both on and off the
Court. But Steven Smith contends that it has serious flaws. The
notion of endorsement itself is fatally ambiguous. And the rules against
intentional and perceived endorsement strike at the wrong kinds of
conduct.

A more radical proposal is the coercion test first offered by Justice
Kennedy in a dissent in *County of Allegheny v. ACLU*[5] and later used (in
a modified form) in his opinion for the Court in *Lee v. Weisman*. The

1. 403 U.S. 602 (1971).

2. 115 S.Ct. 2510 (1995).

3. 112 S.Ct. 2649 (1992).

4. 465 U.S. 668, 687 (1984) (O'Connor,
J., concurring).

5. 492 U.S. 573, 659–660 (1989) (Kennedy, J., dissenting).

Supreme Court held in the first school prayer case that the establishment clause, unlike the free exercise clause, did not require proof of coercion as an essential part of any violation.[6] Justice Kennedy would change all that (though the modified test used in *Lee* requires only "indirect" coercion). Michael Paulsen explains how the law would look if we carried through on this reform.

GARY J. SIMSON, THE ESTABLISHMENT CLAUSE IN THE SUPREME COURT: RETHINKING THE COURT'S APPROACH

72 Cornell L.Rev. 905–906, 908–910, 915–917, 922–925, 931–934 (1987).

Writing for the Supreme Court in 1971 in *Lemon v. Kurtzman*,[1] Chief Justice Burger acknowledged that, in deciding what is permitted and what is forbidden by the first amendment's prohibition on laws "respecting an establishment of religion," the Court could "only dimly perceive the lines of demarcation." According to the Chief Justice, in interpreting the "at best opaque" language of this clause, the Court was obliged to "draw lines with reference to the three main evils against which the Establishment Clause was intended to afford protection: 'sponsorship, financial support, and active involvement of the sovereign in religious activity.' " In a passage that the Court and other courts would quote repeatedly in later establishment clause decisions, he then went on to explain:

> Every analysis in this area must begin with consideration of the cumulative criteria developed by the Court over many years. Three such tests may be gleaned from our cases. First, the statute must have a secular legislative purpose; second, its principal or primary effect must be one that neither advances nor inhibits religion; finally, the statute must not foster "an excessive government entanglement with religion."

* * *

I

THE SECULAR PURPOSE REQUIREMENT

* * *

The first prong of the *Lemon* test sets forth as a necessary condition for constitutionality that the law under review have a "secular legislative purpose." The Court has made clear that this requirement focuses on the actual purpose or purposes that motivated adoption of the law. Although the Court has varied somewhat in its statements elaborating on this requirement, it seems clear that, unless a law is proven to be predicated entirely or almost entirely on nonsecular purposes, this requirement is met.

---

6. *Engel v. Vitale,* 370 U.S. 421, 430 (1962).

1. 403 U.S. 602 (1971).

This requirement is defensible to the extent that it recognizes that a law adopted for reasons incompatible with the establishment clause should be struck down even though the law would be unassailable if adopted for valid reasons. As several commentators have argued convincingly at length,[25] the various provisions of the Constitution are most reasonably interpreted to afford protection against laws predicated on purposes implicitly prohibited by those provisions. * * *

The first prong's secular purpose requirement is not defensible, however, to the extent that it limits the protection afforded by the establishment clause against illicitly motivated laws to laws predicated entirely or almost entirely on nonsecular purposes. This limitation is inconsistent with the basic rationale for invalidating illicitly motivated laws—a rationale described by Professor Brest as follows:

> 1. Governments are constitutionally prohibited from pursuing certain objectives—for example, the disadvantaging of a racial group, the suppression of a religion, or the deterring of interstate migration.

> 2. The fact that a decisionmaker gives weight to an illicit objective may determine the outcome of the decision. The decision-making process consists of weighing the foreseeable and desirable consequences of the proposed decision against its foreseeable costs. Considerations of distributive fairness play an important role. To the extent that the decisionmaker is illicitly motivated, he treats as a desirable consequence one to which the lawfully motivated decisionmaker would be indifferent or which he would view as undesirable.

> 3. Assuming that a person has no legitimate complaint against a particular decision merely because it affects him adversely, he does have a legitimate complaint if it would not have been adopted but for the decisionmaker's consideration of illicit objectives. If in fact the rule adopted is useful and fair, the adversely affected party might have no legitimate grievance, whatever considerations went into its adoption. In our governmental system, however, only the political decisionmaker—and not the judiciary—has general authority to assess the utility and fairness of a decision. And, since the decisionmaker has (by hypothesis) assigned an incorrect value to a relevant factor, the party has been deprived of his only opportunity for a full, proper assessment.[28]

In keeping with the above rationale, the Court should revise the first prong of the *Lemon* test to require the invalidation of any law that would not have been adopted if a nonsecular purpose had not been considered. The fact that such a purpose may not have been the

---

25. *See, e.g.,* Brest, Palmer v. Thompson: *An Approach to the Problem of Unconstitutional Legislative Motive,* 1971 Sup.Ct. Rev. 95 * * *.

28. Brest, *supra* note 25, at 116–17.

exclusive or even the primary one motivating adoption should be seen as beside the point. * * *

* * *

II

IMPERMISSIBLE EFFECTS

A. The Range of Effects Adverse to the Clause

Under the second prong of the *Lemon* test, a law fails to survive establishment clause review unless its "principal or primary effect ... neither advances nor inhibits religion." * * * [E]ffects adverse to the clause * * * should be identified in terms of the "three main evils" that the clause was designed to prevent. The Court therefore should expressly limit the scope of the second prong to effects of sponsoring religion, supporting religion with public funds, or involving the state actively in religious activity.

To help ensure consistent and objective decisionmaking and the degree of protection against the "three main evils" that the clause was intended to afford, I * * * suggest that the Court announce criteria along the following lines for deciding the existence of any of these effects adverse to the clause. First, a law has an effect of sponsoring religion if it either: communicates to nonadherents of religion a preference on the part of the state that they adhere to some religion; communicates to nonadherents of a particular religion, religious belief, or religious practice a preference on the part of the state that they adhere to such religion, religious belief, or religious practice; or communicates to adherents of a particular religion, religious belief, or religious practice a preference on the part of the state that they abandon such religion, religious belief, or religious practice. Second, a law has an effect of supporting religion with public funds if it authorizes an expenditure of public funds that benefits the operations of a religious institution or that increases the likelihood that an individual will exercise freedom of choice in favor of a religious alternative. Third, a law has an effect of involving the state actively in religious activity if it interferes with the authority of a religious group or organization to decide a matter of religious doctrine.

The first of the above criteria focuses on the reasonable perception of persons who would feel pressured and alienated by the allegedly sponsored message. In doing so, it builds on the assumption that the framers' objection to laws sponsoring religion was aimed at the pressure to conform and the sense of second-class citizenship generated by such laws. If people are to be protected from these harms, the existence of sponsorship must be measured by the reasonable perception of the persons who would experience them. To determine the existence of sponsorship based on the reasonable perception of "an objective observer" [50]—someone apt to be less sensitive to it—would insulate from

50. *See* Wallace v. Jaffree, 472 U.S. 38, 76 (1985) (O'Connor, J., concurring) * * *.

constitutional scrutiny at least some laws inflicting harms of the sort that the framers wished to prevent.

The second criterion recognizes two types of effects as effects of supporting religion with public funds: an effect of benefiting religious institutions, and an effect of encouraging individuals to pursue a religious course of action. In doing so, it implements the assumption that the framers' objection to laws supporting religion with public funds was based on a principle that it is wrong to exact contributions from one person to support another's religion. Both of the effects recognized by this criterion are offensive in terms of this principle.

The third criterion focuses on one type of state involvement in religious activity—state involvement that to some extent displaces the authority of a religious group or organization to decide which doctrines it holds true. * * * The history that provides the backdrop for the adoption of the establishment clause includes extreme examples of involvement of the sort identified by this criterion. Perhaps the most notable is the British government's introduction of the Book of Common Prayer, which described in detail for use in the established Church of England the proper form and content of religious ceremonies. Governmental action today, however, rarely implicates this criterion. Basically, the criterion comes into play as a constraint on the manner in which courts may resolve internal church disputes brought before them: To the extent that the resolution of such disputes depends upon a matter of religious doctrine, this criterion casts doubt on the validity of any attempt by the judiciary to inject its own notions of proper doctrine. * * *

B. The Primary Effect Distinction

In providing that laws may be invalidated for effects adverse to the clause, the Court in *Lemon* was careful to indicate that courts should not strike down every law having such an effect. It limited invalidation for adverse effects to laws having such an effect as their "principal" or "primary" one.

* * *

Basically, I suggest that the primary effect distinction is best understood as stating a requirement relevant to laws having a substantial effect adverse to the clause: A law must not have a substantial effect adverse to the clause unless the effect is obviously unintended. * * * According to the Court in *Lemon*, the establishment clause's prohibition on laws "respecting an establishment of religion" encompasses any law that constitutes a "step that could lead" to an established religion. I suggest that the Court at least intuitively is operating on a theory of the establishment clause that assumes that the only type of law that constitutes a tangible "step that could lead" to an established religion is one predicated on an intent to bring about one of the evils that the clause was designed to prevent. If the Court indeed is operating under this theory of the clause, it makes a great deal of sense for it to go beyond the requirements of the first prong in taking illicit intent into account. * * * [T]he first prong only requires the invalidation of laws that challengers have borne the difficult burden of proving rest on an intent to achieve an effect adverse to the clause. It leaves standing laws that, though not proven to rest on illicit intent, in fact were motivated by such intent. A reasonable way of weeding out these less apparent but tangible "step[s] that could lead" to an established religion is to attach a presumption of unconstitutionality to laws that there is good reason to suspect are based on illicit motives. If one may assume that a law that achieves a *substantial* effect of a certain kind probably was intended to achieve that effect, laws having a substantial effect adverse to the clause are plainly laws of this description. Unless the suspicion of illicit intent aroused by their substantial adverse effect is dispelled by evidence negating such intent—that is, unless the substantial effect is obviously unintended—these laws therefore should be struck down.

Although an exception for "obviously unintended" substantial effects may reflect a sound interpretation of the establishment clause, it undoubtedly leaves something to be desired as a basis for objective and consistent application. With this in mind, I suggest that a substantial effect adverse to the clause should be regarded as "obviously unintended" if the law having such effect is necessary to serve a substantial governmental interest. * * * This suggestion reflects the assumption that there is no good reason to suspect that a law is designed to serve an unlawful objective if it is the best available means of serving a lawful objective worthy of serious attention.

* * *

There can be little question that this alternative formulation of the second prong generally requires less tolerance for laws having an effect adverse to the clause than the Court has displayed in the past. * * *

The state law sustained in *Board of Education v. Allen* [c] requires local school boards to purchase and loan to parochial school students nonreligious books for use in their courses. The law has a substantial effect of supporting religion with public funds regardless of whether the parochial school in which the books are used previously purchased the books for the students or required the students' parents to purchase them. On the one hand, if the school previously purchased the books, the law materially benefits the school by relieving it of a nontrivial operating expense. On the other hand, if the parents previously purchased the books, the law, by relieving the parents of a nontrivial expense of educating their children outside the public schools, materially increases the likelihood that parents contemplating sending their children to parochial schools will opt to do so.

Under the proposed approach, the law is therefore unconstitutional unless it is necessary to serve a substantial state interest. The state's interest in ensuring that the children of the state are educated in secular

---

c. 392 U.S. 236 (1968).

subjects with books of good quality is undoubtedly substantial: The state's interest in providing the children of the state with a good secular education is an interest of the highest order, and few persons would deny that a basic prerequisite to a good secular education is good textbooks. The textbook loan program is not necessary to serve this substantial interest, however—and therefore must fall—because the state need not be the one to supply the books. The interest is served with equal precision by the less drastic means of requiring parochial schools, as a condition for licensing by the state, to purchase or require parents to purchase secular textbooks that are conducive to quality education.

* * *

State funding of basic health care in parochial schools * * * offers an interesting example of governmental action that falls neither entirely within nor entirely without the category of laws having a substantial adverse effect but necessary to serve a substantial state interest. * * * [T]his funding of health care of the sort made available in the state's public schools has a substantial effect of supporting religion with public funds. It also plainly serves the state's substantial interest in ensuring a certain minimum level of health care for all children. Whether it serves this interest with the requisite necessary relationship, however, depends upon the type of health care that it purchases.

On the one hand, to the extent that the funding goes to provide for the type of nursing care that sensibly must be readily available on premises in an institution housing large numbers of children for much of the day, this necessary nexus does not exist. The state's interest is served equally well by requiring the schools to furnish such care, and this alternative is available to the state because the provision of this care is properly seen as a natural burden of operating the schools.

On the other hand, to the extent that the funding goes to provide health care not designed simply to respond to the events of the day at the school, the requisite necessary relationship appears to exist. First, it is dubious that all or even almost all children will actually receive the care unless it is brought to them at the school. Second, although a requirement that the parochial schools fund such care themselves would serve the state's interest equally well, this alternative is not open to the state. Such care is plainly not mandated by the nature of the parochial school endeavor. For the state to impose this requirement therefore would unreasonably burden the schools' operation.

III

EXCESSIVE ENTANGLEMENT

The third and final prong of the *Lemon* test provides that the law under review "must not foster 'an excessive government entanglement with religion.'" The Court's understanding of this requirement is illustrated by the way in which the Court applied it in *Lemon* to a state law funding salary supplements for teachers of secular subjects in parochial schools. In invalidating the law under the *Lemon* test's third prong, the Court began with the assumption that the aid would be impermissible if used to fund religious education. The Court then reasoned that there was a very real danger that the aid allocated by this law would be misused because "a dedicated religious person, teaching in a school affiliated with his or her faith and operated to inculcate its tenets, will inevitably experience great difficulty in remaining religiously neutral." In the Court's view, a "comprehensive, discriminating, and continuing state surveillance" therefore would be essential to ensure that the teachers receiving salary supplements under this law teach their secular subjects in a religiously neutral way. According to the Court, however, these "prophylactic contacts" would involve "excessive and enduring entanglement between state and church," and the law therefore must fall.

* * *

* * * According to the Court in *Aguilar v. Felton*,[118] the third prong's prohibition on excessive entanglement is "rooted in two concerns":

> When the state becomes enmeshed with a given denomination in matters of religious significance, the freedom of religious belief of those who are not adherents of that denomination suffers, even when the governmental purpose underlying the involvement is largely secular. In addition, the freedom of even the adherents of the denomination is limited by the governmental intrusion into sacred matters.

The first of the "two concerns" identified by the Court is the acknowledged evil of sponsoring religion; the second is the one of active state involvement in religious activity. By the Court's own admission, entanglement is therefore not an independent evil that the clause was designed to prevent. Rather, it has significance for establishment clause purposes only insofar as it implicates two of the "three main evils" that the clause was designed to prevent.

[Simson concludes that the entanglement test is superfluous, because it regulates government action that the courts can already reach under the first two prongs of the *Lemon* test.]

PHILLIP E. JOHNSON, CONCEPTS AND COMPROMISE IN FIRST AMENDMENT RELIGIOUS DOCTRINE

72 Calif.L.Rev. 817, 826–831 (1984).

[Government action challenged under the Establishment Clause must] pass a three-part test formulated by the Supreme Court in *Lemon v. Kurtzman*:[36] it must have a secular purpose, its principal or primary

---

118. 473 U.S. 402 (1985).   **36.** 403 U.S. 602 (1971).

effect must be one that neither advances nor inhibits religion, and it must not foster " 'an excessive government entanglement with religion.' "

* * *

The *Lemon* test has been ridiculed because of the seemingly absurd lines that the Supreme Court has drawn in its name, especially in the area of public aid to religious schools. One example is particularly notorious: the Supreme Court has permitted states to provide free secular textbooks to parochial school students, but has forbidden as an establishment of religion the furnishing of "instructional materials," such as maps.[41] There is nothing about the *Lemon* test itself, however, that required the Supreme Court to draw the line where it did rather than somewhere else. The problem with the *Lemon* test is not that it requires drawing lines, but rather that its three concepts—religious purpose, religious effect, and entanglement—do not help us to decide where the lines should be drawn. [Indeed,] it is not clear why these concepts are even relevant.

A. Religious Purpose or Effect

Consider, for example, the difficulty of making sense out of the crucial distinction between *religious* purpose or effect and *secular* purpose or effect. Governments usually act out of secular motives, even when they are directly aiding a particular religious sect. An atheistic ruler might well create an established church because he thinks it a useful way of raising money, or of ensuring that the clergy do not preach seditious doctrines.[42] In democratic societies, elected officials have an excellent secular reason to accommodate (or at least to avoid offending) groups and individuals who are religious, as well as groups and individuals who are not. They wish to be re-elected, and they do not want important groups to feel that the community does not honor their values.

Moreover, it is generally acknowledged that religious belief influences behavior, whether for better or for worse. A government might have excellent secular reasons for opposing sects that forbid their members to perform military service or that require racial segregation. For similar reasons, the state might want to support sects that teach their adherents to obey the laws or respect the equality of all races. If establishing a religion had no secular purpose, secular rulers would rarely be attracted to the idea.

Clearly, then, it is difficult to tell religious and secular purpose apart, or to say which effect is primary and which secondary. But beyond that, it is difficult to understand why it is necessarily unconstitutional for legislation to have the purpose or effect of assisting religious

41. *See generally* Wolman v. Walter, 433 U.S. 229 (1977).

42. King Henry VIII disestablished the Church of Rome and established the Church of England because he wanted to divorce his wife and seize the property of the monasteries. * * *

practice generally, when the Constitution itself gives a special status to religion. The free exercise clause itself can be said to have the purpose and effect of allowing the citizenry to practice their religion freely. Can it be unconstitutional for government to assist the citizens to exercise their constitutional rights under the free exercise clause? But such assistance seems to have the purpose and effect of aiding religion!

The perennial problem of public financial assistance to religious schools can once again be used to illustrate the point. Suppose that a state legislature appropriates money which is to be transferred directly to religious schools to subsidize their operations, complete with a preamble announcing that the statutory purpose is to assist parents to exercise their constitutional rights under the free exercise clause, specifically to ensure that their own children receive a religious education.[43] Whether that purpose is termed "religious" or "secular" is entirely a matter of semantic choice. The legislation purposely assists religious activity, but it also purposely assists people to exercise a right guaranteed by that secular document, the Constitution. One effect of this assistance might be that more youngsters will have religious beliefs than would otherwise be the case. But that is also a likely effect of the free exercise clause itself. Perhaps there are excellent reasons for limiting the permissible forms of state aid to religious educational institutions. The point here is that discussing "religious purpose" and "religious effect" is not a useful way of identifying those reasons or deciding what the limitations ought to be.

The notion that it is wrong for legislation to have the purpose or effect of assisting religion only makes sense in terms of an assumed "neutral" starting point that defines what advantages or disadvantages religion ought to have. When the federal government supplies chaplains for the armed services, it clearly means to assist the military personnel to practice their various religions. Even Justices who take a strict "wall of separation" approach to most establishment issues find the military chaplain program acceptable, because they see it as compensation for the difficulties the government creates by removing military personnel from their former environments. Provision of routine public services like sewers and fire protection to church-related structures is also rarely questioned, and nobody proposes to deny the use of subsidized public transportation to people who are going to church. Even very substantial aid in the form of tax exemptions for churches and other religious institutions like hospitals and schools is acceptable to most of the Justices, because it can be viewed as treating them like other similar charitable and educational institutions.

Measures that have the effect of aiding religious practices or institutions—as all the stated examples do—become controversial only when people perceive them as going beyond a conventionally accepted norm.

---

43. A state would be much more likely to justify such a subsidy on the ground that it compensated the schools for the purely secular societal benefit of education in secu-lar academic subjects. * * * The hypothetical in the text is meant to state a more difficult example.

Until we know where that norm is located, the test of religious purpose or effect is meaningless. Once we have set that norm, *it* measures the appropriate level and forms of public aid for religion, and we can dispense with the *Lemon* criteria altogether. The constitutionality of subsidies to religious schools or employment of either legislative or military chaplains must turn on the nature of the subsidized activity rather than the subjective purpose of the legislators who voted for the appropriation. Clearly, then, the tests that look to religious purpose or effect do not explain the distinctions that the Court has drawn.

B. ENTANGLEMENT

There are equally difficult problems with "entanglement," the third branch of the *Lemon* test. Entanglement in this context seems to have at least two distinct connotations. In the more literal sense, it means simply "excessive involvement." It is undesirable for the state to become deeply involved in the government or regulation of religious institutions, because such involvement itself may curtail religious freedom or involve the state in controversies with which it is not competent to deal. For this reason, the Supreme Court has insisted that states permit religious organizations a greater degree of self-government than would be required in the case of secular organizations such as corporations, labor unions, or charities.

A second and more important meaning of entanglement seems to be "divisiveness." Religious issues are considered to be particularly likely to arouse strong passions and enmities, especially when one faction or another sees the possibility of enlisting the state to further its cause. To avoid bitter controversies over what the state's role should be, the state should avoid matters touching on religion to the greatest extent possible. It is in this sense of divisiveness that entanglement is most often used in the cases.

Justification of an active judicial role overseeing state involvement with religion on the basis of a policy of avoiding divisive entanglements rests upon two problematic factual assumptions. One is that religious disputes and religious people are particularly contentious, so that state involvement in religious matters is more likely to breed bitter conflicts than state involvement in such matters as the distribution of wealth or civil rights. Undoubtedly, religious conflicts have led to wars and persecutions, as have conflicts over secular ideologies like fascism and communism. What is problematic is whether, in conditions of contemporary American society, matters such as school prayers, legislative chaplains, and Christmas displays are more hotly disputed than many secular matters with which state legislatures deal routinely.

The second problematic assumption is that courts alleviate divisiveness when they take an issue away from the voters and legislators and decide it on the basis of a constitutional principle. This is a most implausible idea, and such evidence as exists seems to be against it. Many of us find it easier to accept being outvoted by a majority of our fellow citizens or their representatives than by a handful of judges.

Legislative battles over the issue of legalized abortion seem to have become *more* bitter and divisive since the Supreme Court attempted to preempt the issue in *Roe v. Wade.* The very act of deciding a dispute on the basis of some abstract legal principle rather than on the give-and-take of legislative compromise tends to identify more clearly one side as the winner and the other side as the loser, with the result of increasing the bitterness of the loser.

One sure way to encourage conflict on any subject is to encourage people to think that what seem to be minor irritations are in reality violations of some sacred principle for which they have a duty to fight. The Supreme Court's decision in *Lynch v. Donnelly,*[53] involving the constitutionality of a community's tradition of including a crèche or nativity scene in its otherwise secular Christmas display, illustrates the tendency of expansive judicial remedies to generate conflict that might not otherwise occur. The crèche had been part of the annual display for at least forty years. The district court found that no controversy existed over it, until local members of the American Civil Liberties Union brought a lawsuit to enjoin its display. Nonetheless, the district court, and the dissenting opinion in the Supreme Court by Justice Brennan, found the divisiveness engendered by the lawsuit itself to be evidence that the Christmas display posed a danger of divisive entanglement, noting that the calm that had prevailed prior to the lawsuit might merely have reflected a feeling on the part of dissatisfied individuals that it would be futile to oppose the majority.

No doubt a sense of futility is a possible explanation for the absence of recorded complaint, but that fact also demonstrates that, by encouraging persons who are easily offended by religious symbolism to believe that the courts stand open to remedy their complaints, the courts foster divisive conflicts over religion. Similarly, by encouraging citizens and legislators to believe that aid to religious schools is a matter to be decided on the basis of abstract constitutional principles rather than by compromise and accommodation, the Supreme Court may well have made such disputes more bitter than they otherwise would be.

STEVEN D. SMITH, SYMBOLS, PERCEPTIONS, AND DOCTRINAL ILLUSIONS: ESTABLISHMENT NEUTRALITY AND THE "NO ENDORSEMENT" TEST

86 Mich.L.Rev. 266, 268–278, 280–284, 286–288, 291–295 (1987).

I. The Emergence of the "No Endorsement" Test

The Supreme Court's modern efforts to give doctrinal content to the establishment clause began in 1947; but it was not until 1971 that the Court settled upon the test that dominates current establishment doctrine. In *Lemon v. Kurtzman,*[7] the Court declared that in order to

---

53. [465 U.S. 668] (1984).   **7.** 403 U.S. 602 (1971).

survive an establishment challenge a law must meet three requirements: "First, the statute must have a secular legislative purpose; second, its principal or primary effect must be one that neither advances nor inhibits religion . . .; finally, the statute must not foster 'an excessive government entanglement with religion.' "

Although the *Lemon* test has survived for over a decade and a half, few have found the formulation satisfactory. * * *

* * *

[In *Lynch v. Donnelly*[a] Justice O'Connor proposed] a "clarification" of the *Lemon* test. Her proposal focuses on the factor of governmental "endorsement" of religion.[20] In O'Connor's approach, the secular purpose prong of the *Lemon* test would mean that government may not act with the *intent* of endorsing, or disapproving of, religion. *Lemon's* requirement of a primarily secular effect would be modified to mean that laws or governmental practices are invalid if they create a *perception* that government is endorsing or disapproving of religion. A law which avoids creating a perception of endorsement could be sustained even though "it in fact causes, even as a primary effect, advancement or inhibition of religion." Conversely, a law which appears to endorse religion would presumably be unconstitutional even though religion in reality derived no significant benefit from the law.

Justice O'Connor's *Lynch* opinion offered two justifications for the "no endorsement" test. One was practical in character; the "no endorsement" test, O'Connor contended, "clarifies the *Lemon* test as an analytical device." The other justification was more theoretical. O'Connor started from the fundamental premise that "[t]he Establishment Clause prohibits government from making adherence to a religion relevant in any way to a person's standing in the political community." She then argued that government might transgress that prohibition either by "excessive entanglement with religious institutions" or by endorsing or disapproving of religion. "Endorsement," she explained, "sends a message to nonadherents that they are outsiders, not full members of the political community, and an accompanying message to adherents that they are insiders, favored members of the political community. Disapproval sends the opposite message."

[In *Wallace v. Jaffree*[b] Justice O'Connor] gave further analytical content to the "no endorsement" test. She emphasized that the review of legislative intent under the test's first prong should be "deferential

---

a. 465 U.S. 668 (1984). *Lynch* approved the use of a creche in the Christmas display put on by the city of Pawtucket, Rhode Island.

20. O'Connor's choice of the creche case to announce this "endorsement" rationale seems ironic; opponents of the decision might well reply that far from rationalizing the result, an "endorsement" analysis in fact identifies precisely what was objection-able in the case. The creche, after all, provided little or no material assistance to religion, but it did "endorse" Christianity, or at least create perceptions of endorsement. * * * Thus, the circumstances of the test's own nativity did not bode well for its prospects of rescuing establishment doctrine from confusion and incoherence.

b. 472 U.S. 38, 67 (1985) (O'Connor, J., concurring).

and limited." [C]ontrary to her language in *Lynch,* which had suggested that the relevant perceptions were those of real human beings who are the recipients of messages from government, O'Connor now made clear that the dispositive question is whether the law would be perceived as endorsement by an "objective observer" who is familiar with the text, legislative history, and implementation of the law in question. In addition, the "objective observer" should be understood to be familiar with the values recognized in the free exercise clause. This qualification represents an attempt to justify limited government accommodation of religion, and to escape the oft-noted tension between the free exercise and establishment clauses. Government sometimes confers special privileges upon some persons because of their religious beliefs. Some privileges, such as the right to receive unemployment compensation while refusing for religious reasons to work on Saturdays, may even be required by the free exercise clause.[33] If similar privileges are denied to nonbelievers, an untutored observer might well perceive the conferral of such special privileges as an endorsement of religion and thus, under O'Connor's test, as a violation of the establishment clause. Justice O'Connor's more sophisticated "objective observer," however, would draw no such conclusion, but instead would understand that the privilege was intended to further free exercise values.

This qualification of the "no endorsement" principle was underscored in *Estate of Thornton v. Caldor, Inc.,*[35] a decision striking down a Connecticut statute requiring employers to excuse employees from work on whatever day of the week employees might regard as their Sabbath. Justice O'Connor concurred because she believed that the unqualified accommodation required by the statute would be perceived as an endorsement of religion. * * *

* * *

Thus, after initially proposing the "no endorsement" test in *Lynch,* Justice O'Connor has continued to advocate and refine the test. Her efforts seem to be having an effect. Numerous academic commentators have written approvingly of the test. Lower courts have begun to treat the proposed prohibition on endorsement as established law. And Supreme Court majority opinions have invoked the "no endorsement" idea with approval. Recently, in *Edwards v. Aguillard,*[47] the Supreme Court quoted from O'Connor's *Lynch* concurrence, and invalidated a Louisiana statute requiring "balanced treatment" of evolution and creationism in public schools because "the primary purpose of the Creationism Act is to endorse a particular religious doctrine."

33. *See* Hobbie v. Unemployment Appeals Commn., 480 U.S. 136 (1987); Thomas v. Review Bd., 450 U.S. 707 (1981); Sherbert v. Verner, 374 U.S. 398 (1963).

35. 472 U.S. 703 (1985).

47. 482 U.S. 578 (1987).

II. Flawed Doctrine: Analytical Defects in the "No Endorsement" Test

* * *

A. *Endorsement*

Although the central concept in Justice O'Connor's test—"endorsement"—may at first glance seem straightforward, this appearance is misleading. Endorsement connotes approval; but approval may take various forms, and it is far from certain that O'Connor's test is intended, or can sensibly be understood, to prohibit all forms of governmental approval of religion. Upon examination, therefore, the concept of endorsement seems both elusive and elastic.

* * *

Consider, for instance, the following varieties of approval or endorsement.

(1) Historically, proponents of different faiths have often assumed that since religions differ in their doctrines, practices, and claims to divine authority, not all of them could be correct; among diverse religions, rather, only one could fully enjoy God's favor and approval. Thus, disputes have raged over the issue of which religion is true or divinely preferred. If government took a position in a sectarian dispute by indicating that it accepted a particular religion as the true or divinely sanctioned faith, it would thereby endorse or approve that religion. This form of approval might be described as "exclusive preferment."

(2) Government might express a judgment that important doctrines of a religion are true without indicating that it believes the religion is exclusively true or divinely preferred. This form of approval might be described as an "endorsement of truthfulness."

(3) Without indicating any view on the truthfulness of religious doctrine, government might express a judgment that a religion, or religion generally, is valuable or good by suggesting, perhaps, that religion instills qualities of good citizenship or helps to maintain civil peace.

(4) Without indicating any view either as to religion's truthfulness or as to its value to society generally, government might acknowledge that many individual citizens care deeply about religion and that the religious concerns of such citizens merit respect and accommodation by government. This limited form of implicit approval or support might be described as "accommodation endorsement."

Though not exhaustive, this list shows that the concept of "endorsement" may be understood in various senses. Intuitively, exclusive preferment seems the strongest form of endorsement and, presumably, the form most offensive to Justice O'Connor's test. At the other extreme, when one considers endorsements of value or accommodation endorsements, the issue is less clear. Except for her suggestion that some accommodations of religion should be permitted, however, O'Connor has failed to specify which senses of endorsement fall within her test's prohibition. As currently formulated, therefore, the test threatens to aggravate existing doctrinal confusion.

* * *

B. *Intent to Endorse*

Even if the meaning of endorsement could be adequately clarified, the question of whether government officials "intend" to endorse religion would present difficulties. Some of these are difficulties that inhere in any constitutional "intent" inquiry, while others specially afflict the "no endorsement" test.

* * *

In the past, the Supreme Court has been understandably reluctant to authorize judicial inquiries into governmental intent.[76] On a purely factual level, inquiries into the intent of governmental officials are inherently treacherous; indeed, when the governmental body in question is a legislature composed of many members with complex and conflicting motives and aims, it is difficult to say whether such an inquiry is even meaningful. Moreover, by making intent dispositive of a measure's constitutionality, the Supreme Court would create powerful incentives for government officials to dissemble or disguise their motives. Finally, a court undertaking a motive inquiry risks showing disrespect for the officials of other bodies or branches of government.

* * *

Beyond these frequently noted difficulties that inhere in any "intent" inquiry, the "no endorsement" test creates further complications because it does not ask simply what government *intended*; it asks what government *intended to communicate*. But many governmental measures may not have been intended to communicate anything at all. Sending messages is no doubt an important part of what government does; but it is hardly *all*—or even the most important part—of what government does. Indeed, it seems more plausible to think of legislators and executive officers as wielders of power than as mere senders of messages, and thus as primarily concerned with the substantive consequences of their acts rather than with the messages which such acts may happen to communicate. Hence, it is possible that measures challenged under the establishment clause may have been intended to give material assistance to religious interests but not specifically to "endorse" religion. The application of O'Connor's "intent" inquiry to such measures becomes particularly problematic.

* * *

76. *E.g.,* Palmer v. Thompson, 403 U.S. 217, 224–25 (1971); United States v. O'Brien, 391 U.S. 367, 383–85 (1968); Fletcher v. Peck, 10 U.S. (6 Cranch) 87, 130–31 (1810). Under the fourteenth and fifteenth amendments, however, the Court does occasionally look to intent in determining the constitutionality of laws or practices. *E.g.,* Mobile v. Bolden, 446 U.S. 55 (1980); Washington v. Davis, 426 U.S. 229 (1976).

* * * To be sure, some politicians *do* seek to attract the votes of religious persons by sending messages endorsing religion. But other supporters of governmental assistance to religious interests or institutions may often attempt, if only for tactical reasons, to provide such assistance in disguised forms carefully crafted to *avoid* endorsing religion: The Minnesota school aid program,[92] and the preparation of "creation science" textbooks carefully cleansed of explicit biblical references, may be cases in point. In many instances, it would be disingenuous for the supporters of such measures to deny that they hope to help, or to advance, religion. But their concern—and their intent in backing such measures—is apparently to extend material assistance to religion, not to send messages endorsing religion. Asking whether such measures are intended to communicate a message of endorsement seems nonsensical; they are not intended to communicate at all.

* * *

C. *Perceptions of Endorsement*

The second prong of Justice O'Connor's test, which forbids laws or practices that create a perception that government has endorsed or disapproved of religion, generates further analytical problems. By making perceptions an independent ground for invalidating a law, the second prong raises a critical question: Whose perceptions count?

Justice O'Connor has suggested two different answers to that question. In *Lynch,* she implied that the relevant perceptions would be those of real human beings—the actual flesh-and-blood citizens of Pawtucket, or perhaps of the nation as a whole. This answer, however, raises insuperable problems. If *any* citizen's perception that a governmental action endorses or disapproves of religion were sufficient to invalidate the action, then the result would be governmental paralysis; religious diversity in this country is sufficiently broad to ensure that almost anything government does will likely be seen by someone as endorsing or disapproving of a religious viewpoint or value. On the other hand, to say that the perception must be that of a majority, or of some designated group of citizens, seems unacceptable. Such a standard, besides creating additional factual questions about what a majority perceives, would offend the central principle of Justice O'Connor's own test by establishing as definitive, and thereby endorsing, the religious viewpoint of a majority or other designated group while discounting the religious perspective of minorities or outsiders.

The other general kind of answer to the question of whose perceptions count would reject the perceptions of actual citizens as a controlling standard, and instead would adopt the perceptions of a fictitious, judicially created observer. Since *Wallace,* Justice O'Connor has adopted this course. The dispositive question, in her view, is not factual but legal; the question is whether a law or practice would be perceived as endorsement by a hypothetical "objective observer."

---

92. The program is described in Mueller v. Allen, 463 U.S. 388 (1983).

However, in avoiding one set of problems, O'Connor encounters another. In the first place, a purely fictitious character will perceive precisely as much, and only as much, as its author wants it to perceive; and there is no empirical touchstone or outside referent upon which a critic could rely to show that the author was wrong. The most that could be said in a given case is that the "objective observer's" perceptions are remarkably unlike those of most real human beings. But that criticism is of doubtful force, because the adoption of a fictitious observer as the standard represents a deliberate decision that the perceptions of real human beings should not control. Thus, O'Connor's adoption of a fictitious perceiver drains the test's perception prong of whatever truly objective content it otherwise might have; and it thereby reduces the test's capacity to provide guidance to governmental officials or to lower courts, as well as the possibility for critical evaluation of a court's application of the test.

Furthermore, the adoption of an "objective observer" standard logically tends to bring about the collapse of O'Connor's second prong into her first prong. Though disembodied, Justice O'Connor's observer hardly operates behind a veil of ignorance. A principal advantage of a fictitious observer, rather, is that its perceptions need not be subject to the limitations which afflict mere mortals. Thus, unlike most ordinary citizens, the "objective observer" is said to be familiar with the text, legislative history, and implementation of the statute under review.[109] All of this comes very close to saying that the observer knows the legislators' objectives in adopting the law—or, in other words, that the observer knows what the legislators intended. Indeed, this conclusion seems inescapable. In applying the test's first prong, after all, judges must determine whether legislators intended to endorse religion; and surely the "objective observer," who is privy to the same information, can ascertain at least as much. Thus, the judge who examines the text, background, and implementation of a law and concludes that the law was not intended to endorse religion should rule that an "objective observer" examining the same factors would draw the same conclusion. To rule otherwise would be to confess that the judge is not being "objective."

But if the "objective observer" knows what the legislators intended, then the observer will perceive endorsement in all those instances, and only in those instances, in which the judge believes an intent to endorse exists. Of course, the observer might recognize that other perceivers— real human beings not blessed with the observer's knowledge of text, legislative history, and implementation—will sometimes perceive an intent to endorse even when none exists. But the perceptions of such other mortal perceivers no longer control; that, after all, is why the "objective observer" was created. To the "objective observer," intent and perception will inevitably coincide. Thus, the two prongs of the test cease to operate independently, but instead dissolve into each other.

109. *See * * * Wallace,* 472 U.S. at 76 (O'Connor., J., concurring). * * *

Far from being a flaw in the test, such a reduction, at least if it were acknowledged, might seem to be a victory for simplicity. The problem is that a focus either upon legislative intent or upon the fictitious perceptions of a disembodied observer diverges from the purpose which Justice O'Connor attributes to the "no endorsement" test. As noted, O'Connor has explained that the "no endorsement" test seeks to prevent government from sending messages which lead some citizens to believe that they are "outsiders" because of their religious beliefs. If that is the purpose of the test, however, then the pertinent fact controlling the application of the test should be neither the perhaps indiscernible intent of government officials nor the imagined perceptions of a fictitious observer; the controlling standard, rather, should be the actual perceptions of real citizens. If citizens in fact perceive that government is endorsing or disapproving of religion, then they may feel like "outsiders," even though the legislators intended no such consequence (and even though a hypothetical "objective observer" would suffer no similar sense of exclusion). Conversely, if citizens do not in fact perceive an endorsement of religion, then they are not made to feel like "outsiders" because of their religion regardless of what legislators may have intended, or what an "objective observer" might perceive. Thus, the content of Justice O'Connor's test does not correspond to its ostensible purpose.

MICHAEL STOKES PAULSEN, LEMON IS DEAD

43 Case W.Res.L.Rev. 795, 846–848, 852–854, 857–859 (1993).

The advantage the coercion standard has over *Lemon* (in addition to being a more faithful and principled understanding of the Establishment Clause as a matter of text and history) is that it creates far fewer unnecessarily hard cases within the broad middle range of actual practice. * * * I will focus on applications of the coercion test in two related, important, and representative areas of repeated Establishment Clause controversy: religious activities in public schools and government aid to private, including religious, schools.

The public school context supplies several important examples. Ironically (and probably contrary to the expectations of some of its backers), the coercion test is not necessarily more sympathetic to religious activity in public schools than *Lemon,* and may even be less so.

School prayer violates either test, if "school prayer" means government-sponsored religious exercises as part of the school program in a context where the practical ability of students to absent themselves from the proceedings, or the costs visited on them for doing so, render such an opt-out a constitutionally defective alternative. Importantly, however, it is not "peer pressure" that makes an opt-out insufficient. Private pressure to conform does not constitute state action, absent government's deliberate creation or encouragement of social pressure as a means of coercion. Rather, it is the fact that individuals are required by the government to identify and publicly declare their religious beliefs or lack thereof that is problematic, under a "First Amendment privacy" rationale. Individuals have the right to maintain the privacy of their political and religious opinions and affiliations; they may not be required to publicly identify, by word or deed, their positions. In essence, an opt-out scheme asks individuals to "raise their hands" and publicly identify themselves not only as dissenters, but as lacking religious belief. The cost of refusing to so identify oneself is attendance at a religious exercise. The practice, as the school prayer and Bible reading cases themselves recognized, is inescapably coercive.[178]

There is a group of easy cases on the other side. Once it is recognized that the forbidden compulsion is *government* compulsion, it becomes clear that the Establishment Clause does not authorize—and, indeed, the Free Speech and Free Exercise Clauses do not permit—suppression of religious activity by private persons simply because their religious activity makes use of public school facilities and the public school setting. Thus, while "school prayer" or devotional exercises of the type involved in *Engel* and *Schempp* involve government coercion, voluntary extracurricular religious student group meetings involve no such coercion. Such meetings are not rendered suspect under the Establishment Clause by virtue of peer pressure from students or the fact that the meetings occur on school grounds.

That is the holding of *Board of Education v. Mergens*,[180] upholding the constitutionality of the federal Equal Access Act. * * *

* * *

The line sometimes drawn between on-campus and off-campus religious activity is by and large irrelevant under a coercion standard, so long as students are not a "captive audience" for the religious activity at issue. The most important consequence is in the released-time context. It is but a short step from recognizing the correctness of the Supreme Court's decision upholding the Equal Access Act in *Mergens* to recognizing the incorrectness of *Illinois ex rel. McCollum v. Board of Education*, a 45–year–old precedent in which the Court struck down a program of on-premises released-time religious instruction at public schools conducted by denominational instructors and not regular classroom teachers.[193] If coercion is the standard, a genuinely *elective* course—even if it be a course in the doctrines and tenets of a particular religion—does not violate it. While the particular facts of *McCollum* may be suspect in that religious courses were the only electives offered during the released-time period (so that students' only alternative was a study hall), the principle that religious instruction may be offered as a public school elective should not be questionable. So long as a student has alternatives, the choice is not coerced. So long as students (or their parents) must *affirmatively* exercise such choice to attend religious instruction (an "opt-*in*") and so long as the administration of the opt-in does not authorize teachers to direct or influence student choice, there is none of

178. *See* Engel v. Vitale, 370 U.S. 421, 430–31 (1962); School Dist. of Abington v. Schempp, 374 U.S. 203, 223 (1963).

180. 496 U.S. 226 (1990).

193. 333 U.S. 203, 209–12 (1948)[.]

the subtle, "raise-your-hand-and-identify-yourself" coercion involved in the school prayer context. The fact that instruction occurs on school premises does not itself make attendance coerced; it is an *elective* course. The fact that the state accords credit toward graduation does not make attendance at that *elective* "compulsory" (a "compulsory elective" is an oxymoron); similar credit would be given regardless of the choice made. The fact that the instruction is conducted by non-school personnel eliminates even the "role model coercion" hypothesis. In short, *McCollum* is wrong in principle and unsustainable under any fair conception of the coercion test.

So far, the examples I have discussed have concerned the question of when religious activity in public schools is attributable to government compulsion rather than the choices of private actors that the government tolerates or accommodates on the same basis as other choices. A different question is presented where the activity in question is plainly that of the government, but either its coercive tendency or its "religious" nature is disputed. Government speech and public education presents a classic problem because virtually the whole enterprise consists of government speech. May the government engage in religious speech on the same basis as other speech, in the context of public schools?

The paradigmatic case in the school context is *Stone v. Graham.*[196] Decided by the Court under the "purpose" prong of *Lemon, Stone* invalidated a Kentucky statute mandating the posting of the Ten Commandments in public classrooms. Two things make the case troubling. First, the Court has long conceded that public school teaching "about" religion is perfectly appropriate. Why teaching the Ten Commandments does not fit this category is unclear. The problem lies in the incoherence of the Court's concession: It is hard to know where "neutral" teaching "about" religion (is there such a thing?) leaves off and inculcative teaching "of" religion begins.

Second, if schoolchildren are deemed "coerced" in matters of religious exercise by the posting of the Ten Commandments—in the sense of being an indoctrinated, captive audience—it is difficult to avoid the conclusion that they are coerced in their belief structures by everything they are taught in school. It may well be that both propositions are true—that public schools are coercive in *all* that they teach, religious or not—but that the Establishment Clause permits government indoctrination that is "secular" in character and not government indoctrination that is "religious" in character. It does seem strange, however, to think that the First Amendment itself entails a *requirement* of content-discrimination in government's own speech. * * *

* * *

Importantly, if (as increasingly appears the case) the nature of public schools' instructional program is such that maintenance of religious principles for many requires opting-out of the public school system

---

196. 449 U.S. 39 (1980) (per curiam).

entirely, the combination of compulsory attendance laws and the huge financial penalty placed on attendance at non-government-run schools places a strong coercive burden on religious exercise. An understanding of the coercion concept sufficiently broad to invalidate commencement prayer (because it makes attendance at a religious worship ceremony the price of attendance at one's own or one's child's graduation) also renders suspect the present system of public education (because it makes either "mere exposure" to anti-religious indoctrination or the paying of private school tuition the price of a "free" public education). The unconstitutional conditions doctrine requires the conclusion, in the one case as in the other, that governmental imposition of such a cost on religious liberty can be highly coercive in its effects, especially on those not in a position to pay.

Short of the bracing conclusion that coercion in the free exercise context *requires* equivalent governmental funding of private religious schools, the coercion standard in the establishment context makes clear that government funding for religious schools is at least constitutionally permitted. Indeed, at any level of funding below the level at which public schools are supported, the coercion standard makes the constitutionality of such aid an easy case. As with the Equal Access Act or a *McCollum*-type forum, *equal* treatment of religion—neutral inclusion on equal terms with non-religious institutions in a general benefit program—cannot conceivably be regarded as coercive of religious choice so long as one uses a fair baseline for measuring the effects of government action on religion. Providing parents who wish to choose religious education for their children with the same level of "free" education in the form of government support "coerces" religious exercise only in the perverse sense that *absence* of such equal treatment really does involve government compulsion directed *against* such a choice.

Under the coercion standard, *Lemon,* and the whole line of cases restricting government aid to religious elementary and secondary schools—aid invariably falling far short of the level of government financial support for public schools—were all wrongly decided.[210] And that is an important and desirable implication of *Lemon*'s passing and the ascent of a coercion test. The death of *Lemon* means the removal of the primary legal barrier to correcting the serious financial penalty imposed on religious education.[211]

210. *See* Aguilar v. Felton, 473 U.S. 402, 406–07 (1985); School Dist. of Grand Rapids v. Ball, 473 U.S. 373, 375–78 (1985); Wolman v. Walter, 433 U.S. 229, 233 (1977); Meek v. Pittenger, 421 U.S. 349, 352–55 (1975); Committee for Public Educ. & Religious Liberty v. Nyquist, 413 U.S. 756, 762–67 (1973); Lemon v. Kurtzman, 403 U.S. 602, 607–11 (1971); Tilton v. Richardson, 403 U.S. 672, 675 (1971).

211. It is sometimes argued that the use of public funds for religious purposes, even if resulting from the individual choices of persons who receive such funds as part of a generally available social welfare program, constitutes compulsion of nonbelievers in the form of taxation. Such an argument is flawed on a number of scores. First, the logic of the argument suggests that the use of public *facilities,* no less than public funds, for religious purposes (by private beneficiaries) "coerces" dissenting taxpayers. The argument, of course, has been rejected in the public facilities context. *See, e.g.,* Board of Educ. v. Mergens, 496 U.S. 226 (1990)[;] Widmar v. Vincent, 454

BIBLIOGRAPHY

History

Arlin M. Adams & Charles J. Emmerich, *A Heritage of Religious Liberty,* 137 U.Pa.L.Rev. 1559 (1989).

Sydney E. Ahlstrom, A RELIGIOUS HISTORY OF THE AMERICAN PEOPLE (1972).

Robert S. Alley, JAMES MADISON ON RELIGIOUS LIBERTY (1985).

Harold Berman, *Religion and Law: The First Amendment in Historical Perspective,* 35 Emory L.J. 777 (1987).

Irving Brant, JAMES MADISON: FATHER OF THE CONSTITUTION, 1787–1800 (1950).

Thomas E. Buckley, CHURCH AND STATE IN REVOLUTIONARY VIRGINIA 1776–1787 (1977).

Robert L. Cord, SEPARATION OF CHURCH AND STATE (1982).

Robert L. Cord, *Founding Intentions and the Establishment Clause: Harmonizing Accommodation and Separation,* 10 Harv.J.Law & Pub.Pol. 47 (1987).

Edward S. Corwin, A CONSTITUTION OF POWERS IN A SECULAR STATE (1951).

Patricia E. Curry, *James Madison and the Burger Court: Converging Views of Separation,* 56 Ind.L.J. 615 (1981).

Thomas J. Curry, THE FIRST FREEDOMS (1986).

Donald L. Drakeman, *Religion and the Republic: James Madison and the First Amendment,* 25 J. Church & St. 427 (1983).

Edwin Scott Gaustad, *A Disestablished Society: Origins of the First Amendment,* 11 J. Church & St. 409 (1969).

U.S. 263 (1981)[.] There is no principled basis for distinguishing the two situations. In one instance the benefit is access to a government-created forum available on an equal basis for specified purposes; in the other, the benefit is access to a government-created pool of financial resources available on an equal basis for specified purposes. The financial value of the benefit—and cost to taxpayers—might even be equivalent in some cases. There is no difference in principle between a benefit that consists of dollars and one that consists of use of a physical resource that has a monetary value.

Second, the argument that use of tax dollars to support religion constitutes coercion of taxpayers cannot be squared with the Court's free exercise cases requiring that a monetary benefit—unemployment compensation—be provided to individuals who are forced to leave their jobs because of conflicts with religious principle or practice. * * *

The open forum cases suggest the general conclusion that the use of general revenues, or of a benefit (financial or otherwise) made generally available on a religion-neutral basis, does not constitute "coerced support" of religion in the sense in which the framers understood coerced financial support—that is, unique, earmarked taxes (tithes, really) by government for the special support of churches in particular. * * * In short, while taxation is a form of coercion, it does not amount to coerced support for religion in the framers' sense of the term where religion is simply permitted to benefit from a neutral government program of general applicability on the same terms as secular beneficiaries[.]

Timothy L. Hall, *Roger Williams and the Foundations of Religious Liberty*, 71 B.U.L.Rev. 455 (1991).

John R. Howe, THE CHANGING POLITICAL THOUGHT OF JOHN ADAMS (1966).

Philip Kurland, *The Irrelevance of the Constitution: The Religion Clauses of the First Amendment and the Supreme Court*, 24 Vill.L.Rev. 3 (1978).

Philip Kurland, *The Origins of the Religion Clauses of the Constitution*, 27 Wm. & Mary L.Rev. 839 (1986).

Kurt T. Lash, *The Second Adoption of the Free Exercise Clause: Religious Exemptions Under the Fourteenth Amendment*, 88 Nw. U.L.Rev. 1106 (1994).

Douglas Laycock, *"Nonpreferential" Aid to Religion: A False Claim About Original Intent*, 27 Wm. & Mary L.Rev. 875 (1986).

David Little, *The Origins of Perplexity: Civil Religion and Moral Belief in the Thought of Thomas Jefferson*, in Russell E. Richey & Donald G. Jones, eds., AMERICAN CIVIL RELIGION (1974).

Martin E. Marty, PILGRIMS IN THEIR OWN LAND: 500 YEARS OF RELIGION IN AMERICA (1984).

Robert G. McCloskey, *Principles, Powers, and Values: The Establishment Clause and the Supreme Court*, 1964 Religion and the Public Order 3.

Alfred W. Meyer, *The Blaine Amendment and the Bill of Rights*, 64 Harv.L.Rev. 939 (1951).

William Lee Miller, THE FIRST LIBERTY: RELIGION AND THE AMERICAN REPUBLIC (1985).

Edmund S. Morgan, ROGER WILLIAMS: THE CHURCH AND THE STATE (1967).

William C. Porth & Robert P. George, *Trimming the Ivy: A Bicentennial Reexamination of the Establishment Clause*, 90 W.Va.L.Rev. 109 (1987).

Rodney K. Smith, *Nonpreferentialism in Establishment Clause Analysis: A Response to Professor Laycock*, 65 St. John's L.Rev. 245 (1991).

Joseph M. Snee, S.J., *Religious Disestablishment and the Fourteenth Amendment*, 1954 Wash.U.L.Q. 371.

Anson Phelps Stokes, CHURCH AND STATE IN THE UNITED STATES (1950).

Carol Weisbrod, *On Evidences and Intentions: "The More Proof, the More Doubt"*, 18 Conn.L.Rev. 803 (1986).

Theory

Arlin M. Adams & Sarah Barringer Gordon, *The Doctrine of Accommodation in the Jurisprudence of the Religion Clauses*, 37 DePaul L.Rev. 317 (1988).

Wendell R. Bird, *Freedom from Establishment and Unneutrality in Public School Instruction and Religious School Regulation,* 2 Harv. J.L. & Pub.Poly. 125 (1979).

Gerard V. Bradley, *Dogmatomachy—A "Privatization" Theory of the Religious Clause Cases,* 30 St. Louis U.L.J. 275 (1986).

Kelly C. Crabb, *Religious Symbols, American Traditions and the Constitution,* 1984 B.Y.U.L.Rev. 509.

David K. DeWolf, *State Action Under the Religion Clauses: Neutral in Result or Neutral in Treatment?,* 24 Richmond L.Rev. 253 (1990).

Carl H. Esbeck, *A Restatement of the Supreme Court's Law of Religious Freedom: Coherence, Conflict, or Chaos?,* 70 N.D.Law. 581 (1995).

Carl H. Esbeck, *Toward a General Theory of Church–State Relations and the First Amendment,* 4 Pub.L. Forum 325 (1985).

Carl H. Esbeck, *Five Views of Church–State Relations in Contemporary American Thought,* 1986 B.Y.U.L.Rev. 371.

Timothy L. Hall, *Religion, Equality, and Difference,* 65 Temp.L.Rev. 1 (1992).

Wilber G. Katz, RELIGION AND AMERICAN CONSTITUTIONS (1964).

Paul G. Kauper, RELIGION AND THE CONSTITUTION (1964).

Douglas Laycock, *"Noncoercive" Support for Religion: Another False Claim About the Establishment Clause,* 26 Val.U.L.Rev. 37 (1991).

Ira C. Lupu, *Keeping the Faith: Religion, Equality and Speech in the U.S. Constitution,* 18 Conn.L.Rev. 739 (1986).

Ira C. Lupu, *Reconstructing the Establishment Clause: The Case Against Discretionary Accommodation of Religion,* 140 U.Pa.L.Rev. 555 (1991).

John H. Mansfield, *The Religion Clauses of the First Amendment and the Philosophy of the Constitution,* 74 Cal.L.Rev. 847 (1984).

Michael W. McConnell, *Accommodation of Religion: An Update and a Response to the Critics,* 60 Geo.Wash.L.Rev. 685 (1992).

Michael W. McConnell, *Neutrality Under the Religion Clauses,* 81 Nw. U.L.Rev. 146 (1986).

Michael W. McConnell, *You Can't Tell the Players in Church–State Disputes Without a Scorecard,* 10 Harv.J.Law & Pub.Pol. 27 (1987).

Robert T. Miller & Ronald B. Flowers, TOWARD BENEVOLENT NEUTRALITY: CHURCH, STATE, AND THE SUPREME COURT (1982).

Richard E. Morgan, THE SUPREME COURT AND RELIGION (1972).

Dallin Oaks, ed., THE WALL BETWEEN CHURCH AND STATE (1963).

Michael Paulsen, *Religion, Equality, and the Constitution: An Equal Protection Approach to Establishment Clause Adjudication,* 61 Notre Dame L.Rev. 311 (1986).

Michael J. Perry, MORALITY, POLITICS & LAW (1988).

Leo Pfeffer, *Freedom and/or Separation: The Constitutional Dilemma of the First Amendment,* 64 Minn.L.Rev. 561 (1980).

Alan Schwarz, *The Nonestablishment Principle: A Reply to Professor Giannella,* 81 Harv.L.Rev. 1465 (1968).

Frank J. Sorauf, THE WALL OF SEPARATION: THE CONSTITUTIONAL POLITICS OF CHURCH AND STATE (1976).

John M. Swomley, RELIGIOUS LIBERTY AND THE SECULAR STATE (1987).

Symposium, *Confronting the Wall of Separation: A New Dialogue Between Law and Religion on the Meaning of the First Amendment,* 42 DePaul L.Rev. 1 (1992).

Laurence Tribe, *Seven Deadly Sins of Straining the Constitution Through a Pseudo–Scientific Sieve,* 36 Hastings L.J. 155 (1984).

Mark V. Tushnet, *The Constitution of Religion,* 18 Conn.L.Rev. 701 (1986).

John Valauri, *The Concept of Neutrality in Establishment Clause Doctrine,* 48 U.Pitt.L.Rev. 83 (1986).

William W. Van Alstyne, *Trends in the Supreme Court: Mr. Jefferson's Crumbling Wall,* 1984 Duke L.J. 770.

William W. Van Alstyne, *What Is "An Establishment of Religion"?,* 65 N.C.L.Rev. 909 (1987).

Jonathan Weiss, *Privilege, Posture, and Protection: "Religion" in the Law,* 73 Yale L.J. 593 (1964).

David E. Wheeler, *Establishment Clause Neutrality and the Reasonable Accommodation Requirement,* 4 Hastings Const.L.Q. 901 (1977).

Rules

Daan Braveman, *The Establishment Clause and the Course of Religious Neutrality,* 45 Md.L.Rev. 352 (1986).

Jesse H. Choper, *Religion and Race Under the Constitution: Similarities and Differences,* 79 Cornell L.Rev. 491 (1994).

Jesse H. Choper, SECURING RELIGIOUS LIBERTY (1995).

Comment, *"A Picture Held Us Captive:" Conceptual Confusion and the Lemon Test,* 137 U.Pa.L.Rev. 1827 (1989).

Daniel O. Conkle, *Religious Purpose, Inerrancy, and the Establishment Clause,* 67 Ind.L.J. 1 (1991).

Daniel O. Conkle, *Toward a General Theory of the Establishment Clause,* 82 Nw.U.L.Rev. 1113 (1988).

Edward Gaffney, *Political Divisiveness Along Religious Lines: The Entanglement of the Court in Sloppy History and Bad Public Policy*, 24 St. Louis U.L.J. 205 (1980).

Frederick Mark Gedicks, *Motivation, Rationality, and Secular Purpose in Establishment Clause Review*, 1985 Ariz.St.L.J. 677.

Philip Kurland, *The Religion Clauses and the Burger Court*, 34 Cath. U.L.Rev. 1 (1984).

Douglas Laycock, *A Survey of Religious Liberty in the United States*, 47 Ohio St.L.J. 409 (1986).

Arnold Loewy, *Rethinking Government Neutrality Towards Religion Under the Establishment Clause: The Untapped Potential of Justice O'Connor's Insight*, 64 N.C.L.Rev. 1049 (1986).

William P. Marshall, *"We Know It When We See It": The Supreme Court and Establishment*, 59 S.Cal.L.Rev. 495 (1986).

Michael W. McConnell, *Coercion: The Lost Element of Establishment*, 27 Wm. and Mary L.Rev. 933 (1986).

Note, *Developments in the Law: Religion and State*, 100 Harv.L.Rev. 1606 (1987).

Note, *Permissible Accommodations of Religion: Reconsidering the New York Get Statute*, 90 Yale L.J. 1147 (1987).

Note, *Political Entanglement as an Independent Test of Constitutionality Under the Establishment Clause*, 52 Fordham L.Rev. 1209 (1984).

Norman Redlich, *Separation of Church and State: The Burger Court's Tortuous Journey*, 60 Notre Dame L.Rev. 1094 (1985).

Peter M. Schotten, *The Establishment Clause and Excessive Governmental–Religious Entanglement: The Constitutional Status of Aid to Nonpublic Elementary and Secondary Schools*, 15 Wake Forest L.Rev. 207 (1979).

Mark V. Tushnet, *Reflections on the Role of Purpose in the Jurisprudence of the Religion Clauses*, 27 Wm. & Mary L.Rev. 997 (1986).

Chapter VI

THE ESTABLISHMENT CLAUSE: PARTICULAR PROBLEMS

A. Introduction

In this chapter we look at a variety of particular problems arising under the establishment clause. It is often said that in the modern world we think of religion as a private affair, to be walled off from the public sphere. This idea can be misleading, and it may be mistaken, but it provides a useful way of categorizing the kinds of controversies courts have to deal with.

One set of problems arises when religion crosses the line into public life. This can occur when citizens or public officials take account of religious belief in playing their appointed roles in a democratic system. Repeated individual actions also beget social patterns of behavior. The language, symbols, and customs of our political life have, over time, become impregnated with religious thought. To what extent should we try to secularize (purify) that process?

Another set of cases within this category deals with the role of religion in the public schools. Most people believe that the public schools exist, not just to teach children literary, mathematical, and scientific skills, but to train them in the values of good citizenship. But what are those values? Because adults have different feelings about the role of religion in their own public lives, they cannot agree about the place of religion in the public education of their children. It is fairly well settled that schools should not *conduct* religious rituals. But to what extent should prayer, for example, be *tolerated* or even *encouraged?* And how should religious belief enter into the curriculum in biology, geology, history, and the social sciences?

The other large category of problems concerns government poaching in the religious sphere. (Notice how this classification presumes a certain point of view. If religion is not a private matter then religion and government occupy the same sphere, and it makes no sense to distinguish government-in-religion from religion-in-government.) Consider the case of government aid to parochial schools. There are two dangers here. One is that the government will be captured, or worse enlisted, in the religious enterprise. This is the problem we discussed above, but in a new setting. The other danger is quite different: secular ideas could (like a computer virus) take over the religious realm.

For organizational purposes we have separated the discussion of history and principles in Chapter V from the specific problems in this chapter. But one cannot see these issues except against that background.

B. RELIGION IN PUBLIC LIFE

We begin our consideration of religion in public life by stepping back from the First Amendment per se. We ask whether a public place for religion is inconsistent with the very idea of a liberal democratic society. We then look at our own twentieth century American society. Whatever our theory might tell us, the reality is that religion plays a visible role in civil affairs. How can we explain this? And how square it with the establishment clause?

1. RELIGION IN A LIBERAL DEMOCRACY

Let us first consider whether there can be a public role for religion in any society that is liberal and democratic. There are those who say there cannot. A "liberal" society, by some accounts, is one that takes no position on how its members should live—i.e. it has no official view of the good. Most religions have strong opinions on that subject. Perhaps it is inconsistent with liberal citizenship to inject these views into public deliberations. There may also be something undemocratic about doing so. John Rawls argues in *A Theory of Justice* that a democratic government should base its actions "on evidence and ways of reasoning acceptable to all. * * * [A] departure from generally recognized ways of reasoning would involve a privileged place for the views of some over others[.]"[1] Appeals to metaphysical principles tend to inhibit public debate. They may also, as Rawls says, privilege certain citizens over others, and that seems inconsistent with democratic equality.

Kent Greenawalt opens this discussion with the suggestion that we can't rule religion either entirely in or entirely out of bounds in political decision-making. He finds that it has a place when we are dealing with issues that call for some nonrational commitment or judgment of value. Examples might include the morality of abortion and the need for environmental protection.

Kathleen Sullivan takes a more separationist view than Greenawalt. She contends that "public moral disputes" (and here she means to include abortion as well as other disagreements) "may be resolved only on grounds articulable in secular terms." She fears that any relaxation of this strict rule would lead again to the kind of religious wars we ended with the establishment clause. Sullivan acknowledges that the culture

---

1. A Theory of Justice 213 (1971).

of liberal democracy has its own substantive content, and that this content may conflict with some people's religious beliefs. By giving it a favored position we actually favor one world view over others. But that is the political and constitutional deal we have made in America.

Frederick Gedicks takes a more accommodationist view than Greenawalt. He argues that the distinction between public and private life that is central to this debate is itself a human construct. There is no area that is inherently or really public. (On this point he has the agreement of post-modern critics of constitutional law.) Nor is there any convincing epistemological distinction between secular and religious thought. Political campaigns are in fact not carried out in rational, empirical terms; religious debate is not as irrational and chaotic as its critics say. Thus there is no ideologically neutral justification for the exclusion of religion from public life.

John Garvey offers an entirely different perspective on this debate. Rather than asking whether religion is consistent with the premises of liberal democracy, he asks whether liberal democracy can get in the way of religious belief. Not surprisingly, he concludes, it can—at least sometimes. For purposes of illustration he uses the case of Mario Cuomo, a Catholic and former governor of New York. Cuomo adhered in his private life to his church's teaching on the subject of abortion; but he claimed that he was obliged to take a different position in his public duties. Garvey argues that some element of separation is possible, but that it cannot be done (consistent with Catholic teaching) to the degree Cuomo believes.

KENT GREENAWALT, RELIGIOUS CONVICTIONS AND LAWMAKING

84 Mich.L.Rev. 352, 356–358, 360, 368–370, 372, 379–380 (1985).*

[W]e may begin with three major competing positions about the responsibilities of citizens. One is that in a liberal democracy citizens are free [in making political judgments] to rely on any grounds they please, including religious grounds. The second position is that citizens should not rely on religious grounds for their political actions. A position of this sort may also exclude some other grounds besides religious ones. The third, intermediate, position, the one I take, is that reliance on certain kinds of religious grounds is appropriate but that reliance on other kinds of religious grounds is not.

* * *

* * * The first position boils down to the view that liberal democracy is a set of procedures for making political decisions, with some understood limits on what the majority can do to the minority. In this

---

* The lectures from which this excerpt is taken were expanded into a book, Religious Convictions and Political Choice (New York, Oxford Univ. Press 1988), in which Greenawalt no longer uses a distinction among rational, irrational, and nonrational bases of decision.

view, which we might call an interest accommodation view, the premises of liberal democracy have nothing to say about why people support the political positions they do.

Stated so absolutely, the view is clearly wrong. Within a liberal democracy people are permitted to support illiberal outcomes, such as the legal subjugation of one race by another, but a model liberal citizen does not support illiberal outcomes. So much is obvious. Suppose two alternative outcomes are both within the range of liberal positions and each is supported by substantial liberal arguments. I believe this is true about the present debate over preferential treatment of minorities. Opposing preferences because one thinks any racial classifications are unjust or reinforce racist attitudes is not illiberal. But opposing preferences because one hopes to perpetuate the social inferiority of racial minorities is illiberal. The premises of liberal democracy do have *something* to say about acceptable bases for political positions, as well as about acceptable political outcomes.

But if we put aside motivations that are themselves at odds with liberal premises, are not people free to decide on any other bases? Isn't liberal democracy *otherwise* indifferent about the bases of personal preferences? This is a more troublesome question, and all I shall do is state my own view succinctly. Some issues properly turn on personal preferences. Were a vote taken, for example, on whether a bear or a snake were to become the state symbol, people could rightly vote in terms of pure preference. For such issues, any mode of deriving a preference is appropriate, including a religiously based view that the bear is a loftier creature. On some other issues, however, a good citizen has a responsibility to decide what is right, not simply to vote his preference. I assume that a model citizen should decide in this way about such matters as abortion, treatment of animals, capital punishment, and foreign affairs. A person would not be justified in voting for capital punishment just because executions give him an emotional kick or increase the sales of his sensational newspaper. We expect something more of the good citizen than these inadequate reasons. As to issues of this sort, the appropriateness of relying on religious convictions needs to be defended. Such reliance cannot simply be lumped together with other bases of personal preference, and justified on the theory that people can vote their preferences.

I turn now to the second major position, that citizens and officials in a liberal democracy should not rely on religious bases for judgment. This position finds fairly frequent expression and occasional systematic defense. In a recent introduction to ethics and law, David Lyons suggests that political morality should be governed by principles and arguments "accessible to all persons." He says that to reject the idea of "a naturalistic and public conception of political morality ... is to deny the essential spirit of democracy." [1] Under this view, citizens should not publicly press political objectives on religious grounds, nor, we may infer,

---

1. D. Lyons, Ethics and the Rule of Law 190–91 (1984).

should they use such grounds to make up their own minds about public issues. * * *

* * *

The thesis that political decisions should be made on secular rational grounds is a claim about the ethical import of liberal democracy, about what "good citizenship" in that polity entails. My rejection of substantial aspects of that thesis derives from a different view about the ethical import of liberal democratic premises. * * *

* * *

[Consider, for purposes of illustration, the question of] environmental protection. As I shall use the term, an environmental ethic concerns itself with safeguarding more inclusive categories of being, such as species, the land, the natural setting, ecosystems, or the biosphere. The worry is not the death or pain of individual entities, but human destruction of, or failure to preserve, the environment. Should the life of one nearly extinct snail darter count for more than the life of one salmon? * * *

* * *

[T]he claim that people should respect nature in its own right is not one that can be successfully grounded in rational argument. People have radically different reactions to what nature in some larger sense is owed by human beings, and neither analogies to ordinary moral constraints nor other forms of rational analysis provide much assistance in settling who is right. Attaching inherent value to the preservation of species, and even to maintenance of the physical environment, is not contrary to reason; but such views do require some nonrational commitment or judgment of value.

I want to pause here to say a little bit more about this distinction between rational and nonrational bases of judgment and where I place religious convictions. I roughly categorize convictions that bear on ethical judgments as rational, irrational, and nonrational. I confess to considerable uncertainty about where rationality ends; but among rational convictions I include those that are apparent to anyone with ordinary rational faculties or that can be demonstrated or persuasively argued on rational grounds. Beliefs that humans have greater ethical capacities than leaves, and that love is more productive of happiness than hate, can be rationally established. An irrational conviction is contrary to what can be established on rational grounds. A nonrational conviction, in my sense, is a conviction that is not irrational but that reaches beyond what rational grounds can settle.

There is much disagreement about what rational thought can establish about religious truth, but few particular religions are claimed to be establishable on rational grounds alone. Most Christians, for example, do not believe that rational argument can persuasively show the special place of Jesus Christ. Something more is needed, a commitment through faith or a personal sense that a special place for Jesus fits with how one apprehends human existence and its meaning.

I must be careful here to avoid misunderstandings. I do not say that rationality *plays no part* in religious conviction. A large number of conceivable religious premises do appear offensive to reason; reason helps us decide what lies within the range of plausible religious positions. Moreover, highly refined rationality is used in the development of particular religious positions and their implications. Belief in the Trinity may be nonrational, but an elaboration of the concept of the Trinity can be highly rational. When I say that ethical judgments based on religious convictions are founded on nonrational premises, I mean only that a critical nonrational element is present.

* * *

I have suggested that with respect to * * * environmental protection, the place of convincing interpersonal argument is decidedly limited. On critical questions, a person must resort to his own sense of life and a reflective view that makes him comfortable. If I am right, people must inevitably rely to a large extent on nonrational judgments in assessing proper legal protections.

If people must rely on nonrational judgments, should not religious believers be able to rely on their religiously informed view of humanity's place in the world as they struggle with moral questions and their political implications? If rational secular morality provides no correct resolutions, or a limited range of possible resolutions, a liberal democrat need not disavow his deeply held religious premises in favor of alternative nonrational assumptions that could yield a starting point.

* * *

[Consider, as a second illustration, the problem of abortion.] The nub of the question whether a restrictive abortion law can be justified turns on the point at which a fetus warrants significant protection from society. The issue is so intractable because of the sharp divergence over the fetus' moral status. Those who think, for example, that at the moment after conception a fetus, or more strictly at this early stage a zygote, has moral rights as full as those of a newborn baby tend to regard abortion very differently from those who think that moral rights arise only at a late stage of pregnancy or at birth. * * *

* * *

[But] the moral status of the fetus and desirable legal policy are not resolvable on rational grounds[. I]ndividuals must decide these questions on some nonrational basis. For many persons, the basis for judgment is supplied in whole or part by religious perspectives, which either indicate the fetus' moral status or gravely influence one's mode of thinking about it.

* * *

Most religious believers will be hard put to evaluate the status of the fetus or animals in purely secular terms. The matter is not one of weighing evidence pro and con, but of adopting one of a number of debatable perspectives about how to look at a problem. If one believes he already has a clear answer or an overarching perspective on the relevant question of value that is derived from his religion, he may find it impossible to decide what perspective he would otherwise adopt.

Even when the religious believer consciously relies mainly on naturalistic arguments, important religious premises may lurk in the background. For example, the idea that God gives people souls at some point in development may influence someone to look for one critical point, a point where a shift occurs from virtually no moral status to full moral status. When this approach is combined with an emphasis on strict duty, and in particular the strict duty not to take innocent life, reflected in traditional Christianity and Judaism, the approach is highly unfavorable to any claim that the pregnant woman's interests override those of the fetus when the two conflict.

The inability of most people to perceive the distinctive import of their religious views certainly makes one skeptical that their influence could be eradicated. The proponent of secular bases of judgment may respond that his point is only that citizens should try to decide on secular grounds alone. But asking that people pluck out their religious convictions and take a fresh look, disregarding what they presently take as basic premises of moral thought, is not only unrealistic. It is positively objectionable, because it demands that people try to compartmentalize beliefs that constitute some kind of unity in their approach to life.

We hear frequently that reliance on religious convictions to oppose permissive abortion laws violates the liberal principle that the religious convictions of one segment of society should not be imposed on the rest. But in respect to abortion, the religious perspective informs a judgment of who counts as a member of the community, a judgment that I claim each citizen must make in a nonrational way. Once that judgment is made, a restriction on abortion may be thought to protect life, the most obvious and vital interest that members of the community have. Such restrictions do not violate premises of liberal democracy.

KATHLEEN M. SULLIVAN, RELIGION AND LIBERAL DEMOCRACY

59 U.Chi.L.Rev. 195, 197–201 (1992).

Just as the affirmative right to practice a specific religion implies the negative right to practice none, so the negative bar against establishment of religion implies the affirmative "establishment" of a civil order for the resolution of public moral disputes. Agreement on such a secular mechanism was the price of ending the war of all sects against all. Establishment of a civil public order was the social contract produced by religious truce. Religious teachings as expressed in public debate may influence the civil public order but public moral disputes may be resolved only on grounds articulable in secular terms. Religious grounds for resolving public moral disputes would rekindle inter-denominational strife that the Establishment Clause extinguished.

* * *

* * * The bar against an establishment of religion entails the establishment of a civil order—the culture of liberal democracy—for resolving public moral disputes. * * * The social contract to end the war of all sects against all necessarily, by its very existence, [distorts] the outcomes that would have obtained had that war continued. Public affairs may no longer be conducted as the strongest faith would dictate. Minority religions gain from the truce not in the sense that their faiths now may be translated into public policy, but in the sense that no faith may be. Neither Bible nor Talmud may directly settle, for example, public controversy over whether abortion preserves liberty or ends life.

The correct baseline [for measuring Religion Clause violations] is not unfettered religious liberty, but rather religious liberty insofar as it is consistent with the establishment of the secular public moral order. [T]he exclusion of religion from public programs is not * * * an invidious "preference for the secular in public affairs." [14] Secular governance of public affairs is simply an entailment of the settlement by the Establishment Clause of the war of all sects against all. From the perspective of the prepolitical war of all sects against all, the exclusion of any religion from public affairs looks like "discrimination." But from the perspective of the settlement worked by the Establishment Clause, it looks like proper treatment.

What is this civil moral order that the religious truce established? Is it itself a countervailing faith or civil religion? * * *

The culture of liberal democracy may well function as a belief system with substantive content, rather than a neutral and transcendent arbiter among other belief systems. Various versions of this argument have been expressed not only by liberalism's critics, but by contemporary liberal theorists themselves. On one such view, liberalism's purported procedural neutrality conceals implicit but unstated substantive ends that ought to be flushed out so that people can accept or criticize them. [18] For example, toleration of competing visions of the good is itself a vision of the good; and the idea of equal dignity and respect is itself a substantive rejection of social hierarchy. Another view, developed in the recent work of Professor John Rawls, sees the culture of liberal democracy less as an imperial third force overriding the embedded norms of social subcommunities than as a historically emergent statement of the

---

14. [Michael W. McConnell, *Religious Freedom at a Crossroads*, 59 U Chi L Rev 115, 169 (1992).]

18. See, for example, Michael Sandel, *Liberalism and the Limits of Justice* (Cambridge, 1982).

"overlapping consensus" among them.[19] This view sees the commitment to religious tolerance that ends the war of all sects against all not as a neutral *modus vivendi,* but rather as a substantive recognition that there is more than one path to heaven and not so many as once thought to hell.

Under either of these views, the culture of liberal democracy might well look like a faith to those who disagree with it. For example, suppose a required public school reading text depicts Jane as a wage-earning construction worker and Dick as an unremunerated child-tending househusband. And suppose that a religious community views this a perversion of the sexual division of labor set forth in the book of Genesis. To the religionist, the text undoubtedly looks like an expression of a countervailing faith at odds with her own.

But [e]ven if the culture of liberal democracy is a belief system comparable to a religious faith in the way it structures knowledge, it simply does not follow that it is the equivalent of a religion for political and constitutional purposes. Neither the Bill of Rights, the Republican Party platform, nor the American Civil Liberties Union Policy Guide is the constitutional equivalent of the Ten Commandments, whatever devotion they enjoy from their adherents. The Supreme Court has long drawn a distinction between religion and philosophy for purposes of limiting free exercise exemptions: secular pacifists do not get the same breaks from the military draft as pacifist Quakers,[21] and high school dropouts who march to the beat of Henry David Thoreau do not get the same breaks as those who follow the path of their Amish elders.[22] Similarly, a reading text depicting counter-traditional gender roles, while it does inculcate values, does not amount to the establishment of a "religion" of feminism. For constitutional purposes, feminism may be a "faith," but it is not a religion.

The culture of liberal democracy is the overarching belief system for politics, if not for knowledge. Numerous self-limiting features ought to keep at bay any concern that liberal democracy could be a totalistic orthodoxy as threatening as any papal edict. First, the content of the culture of liberal democracy is subject to continual revision in the crucible of pluralistic politics. Liberal democracy may have traditions, but it has no fixed canon or creed. Consider, for example, the vigorous debate now being waged over whether history textbooks in the public schools should shift from a "eurocentric" to a "multicultural" account in light of the rapidly changing demographics of the nation's major cities. Second, the guarantee of free speech ensures that no one may be forced to swear adherence to the culture of liberal democracy any more than to swear oaths of fealty to the Pope. Third, the guarantee of free speech also ensures that religious points of view can participate in the public

19. [John Rawls, *The Idea of an Overlapping Consensus,* 7 Oxford J Legal Stud 1 (1987).]

21. See *Gillette v. United States,* 401 U.S. 437 (1971).

22. *Wisconsin v. Yoder,* 407 U.S. 205, 215–16 (1972).

debate; it is not clear that the public culture of liberal democracy can ever deviate too far from the "overlapping consensus" among social subcultures, including religious subcultures.

FREDERICK MARK GEDICKS, PUBLIC LIFE AND HOSTILITY TO RELIGION

78 Va.L.Rev. 671, 674–675, 678–681, 693–696 (1992).

The impulse to divide society into mutually exclusive public and private spheres derives from the Lockean tradition of natural rights. In that tradition, citizens are thought to have inalienable rights against government that are held independently of the state. Under a Lockean political regime, the reach of permissible government action (public life) depends on the boundaries of the inviolable sphere of individual rights (private life).

[The] division of society into public and private spheres thus mirrors the fundamental division in Western thought between subject and object. In private life, subjectivity and passion hold sway. Individuals are free to do whatever they please for any reason (or for no reason) as long as they do not harm anyone else. Value choices need not be defended by publicly accessible reasons because private behavior is assumed to be the result of desire, which is beyond rational or empirical analysis.

Public life, on the other hand, is the realm of objectivity and reason. In this realm, government and individuals must serve the collective "public interest" rather than the idiosyncratic tastes and preferences of any individual. Value choices must be rationally defended in public life, for unlike private actions, public actions cannot be justified by mere appeal to an individual's tastes or preferences. Indeed, once positivism eclipsed natural rights in American jurisprudence, public life constrained the pursuit of these tastes and preferences, constituting the objective limitation of the social world imposed upon the subjective freedom of the individual. As a consequence, actions in public life must be justified empirically or rationally, by reference to the observable and explainable phenomena of the exterior world.

* * *

Religion has long been placed in American private life. Religious belief in the Western tradition centers on a transcendent force or belief—that is, a force or belief beyond the material, phenomenal world. As such, religious belief is not subject to verification or falsification according to the objectivist conventions of public life. Secularism constitutes the test of residency in American public life, and religion by its nature cannot pass the test.

Keeping religion and religious belief confined to private life enables the liberal state to marginalize religion without eliminating it. "Religion, rather than being abolished, becomes a private whim, an expression of purely subjective, individualized values." [46]   As one of the purest contemporary expressions of subjective, impossible-to-confirm values, religious belief need not (and, indeed, cannot) be considered by those who act in public life.   Liberal government thus treats religious belief neutrally—as a subjective value preference restricted to private life, rather than as objective knowledge proper to public life.   This position can be genuinely neutral, however, only if the boundary between the private world of subjective preference and the public world of objective fact is natural, fixed, and inevitable.

Judges during the liberty-of-contract era did believe that the boundary between public and private life was stable and discoverable by objective means.   The natural-law premises of that age suggested that human activities were inherently public or private.   It followed that all aspects of human life could be identified as properly belonging to one sphere or to the other by uncovering the essential nature embedded within any particular human activity.

Few would defend this position today.   In the first place, the modern eclipse of natural law by positivism dealt a serious theoretical blow to the notion that the line between public and private life can be drawn objectively.   More fundamentally, recent developments in postmodern philosophy and literary criticism have fatally undermined the epistemological premises of the proposition that substantive meaning like "public" or "private" resides in the phenomenal world independent of an act of interpretation.

Prior to these developments, Western intellectual thought from the time of Descartes had been founded upon a radical distinction between mind and world.   Under this theory, not only do things exist in the world independent of the human mind, but they are possessed of an essential character.   Because these essential characteristics reside in the things themselves, the true nature of something is never a function of human perception; to the contrary, the truth of human perception is a function of the true nature of the things.   Thus, under the classical Western conception of truth and knowledge, a proposition is true only to the extent that it corresponds to the world "as-it-really-is," and one can know something only by understanding the essential characteristics of that world.

Philosophers and literary critics have largely abandoned the correspondence theory of truth in favor of theories that do not separate the observer and the observed.   But without the correspondence theory, or something like it, it is impossible to determine whether an activity has been "properly" classified as public or private.   The public or private character of an activity depends not on the discovered attributes of a self-existent world but on the classifier's subjective perception of that world.

46. [Alan Freeman & Elizabeth Mensch, The Public–Private Distinction in American   Law   and   Life,   36   Buff.L.Rev.   237,   241 (1987).]

Thus, far from reflecting the world as-it-really-is, the division of society into public and private life is merely a socially contingent metaphor used to ascribe meaning to the world as-we-experience-it. Any human activity arguably possesses both a public and a private dimension. As Louis Seidman has observed, the boundary between public and private life is not drawn by nature but is instead "a human construct that must be fought for and quarrelled over." [58]

Secularism, then, does not mark any natural or inevitable distinction between private and public life. The confinement of religion to private life reflects the exercise of contingent social power, not the disinterested discovery of essential meaning of self-existent reality.

* * *

The hallmark of contemporary liberal political theory is neutrality between competing conceptions of the good. This means that the liberal state cannot take a position regarding any claim that cannot be rationally or empirically demonstrated to be true. Thus, those who claim that liberalism is hostile to religion simply have made a category mistake. The liberal argument is that because the claims of religion are not amenable to empirical or rational proof, they are fundamentally different from the claims of secular ideologies and disciplines that can be proven rationally or empirically and thus need not be dealt with the same way. Secular enterprises yield knowledge, which the liberal state is bound to accept; religion only yields unprovable beliefs about the good, as to which the liberal state must remain neutral.

Completely captured by the association of secularism with public life and the confinement of religion to private life, liberals fail to see how thin the distinction is between knowledge and belief. It never occurs to them that religious claims might be rational or that secular claims would be irrational. For example, liberal theorists repeatedly argue that political deliberations in a liberal democracy must be governed by critical rationality—that is, citizens in a liberal state should act only pursuant to empirically plausible reasons. As conceived by liberals, religion entails unchallengeable commitments born of faith and extra-rational appeals to transcendent authority. Accordingly, liberals generally disqualify religion from full and uncontroversial participation in politics because it lacks the participational prerequisites to liberal political dialogue.

It seems fair to ask where in the United States such rational deliberative politics are practiced. At the heart of every successful elective campaign these days lies the creation of photo opportunities and soundbites. Attractive visual images of the candidate and pithy, stylized quotations from campaign speeches are hardly the stuff of rational deliberation; on the contrary, they are designed to attract votes by appealing to the noncognitive, affective aspect of human consciousness. At best, it is unclear that politics as usually practiced in the United

58. [Louis M. Seidman, Public Principle and Private Choice: The Uneasy Case for a Boundary Maintenance Theory of Constitutional Law, 96 Yale L.J. 1006 (1987).]

States is any more critical and rational than religion. The liberal belief that reason mediates political conflict is no less a matter of faith than religious belief in God.

Liberals argue, of course, that rational deliberation is a political ideal that actual practice only approximates. The presence of uncritical or extra-rational appeals to the noncognitive hardly proves that the ideal is an inappropriate goal of politics, even though it may be a difficult one to achieve. But religion possesses substantial elements of criticism and rationality and has for centuries. If politics as actually practiced falls well short of the ideal of critical rationality, and if religious belief is partially based on reason, on what basis is religion disfavored in political life?

The hostility to religion that I have described here entails epistemological and political preferences for secularism that have no ideologically neutral justification. Liberalism privileges secular ways of knowing and marginalizes religious ones by manipulating the boundary between public and private life. Liberalism politically privileges secularism over religion by naming public life (the realm of secularism) rational and orderly and private life (the realm of religion) irrational and chaotic.

JOHN H. GARVEY, THE POPE'S SUBMARINE

30 San Diego L.Rev. 849–851, 859–871 (1993).

[When Kent Greenawalt discusses] the place of religious arguments about public policy in a liberal democracy, [he looks] at the problem [as a liberal democrat would]. I want to approach it from the opposite direction—to look at how liberal politics might get in the way of a [person's] religious obligations, and how the conscientious politician can deal with this dilemma. Religious obligations differ across denominations, so I will confine my observations to the Catholic politician. I focus on Catholics for several reasons. I myself am one, so the issue has some personal interest. And Catholics are the largest denomination in the United States, so the question matters for a lot of people. The Catholic Church also asserts more authority over its members (a stricter obligation on their part to obey) than most American sects do. In addition, the American Catholic bishops in recent years have exercised their teaching authority across a range of publicly salient issues—the economy, nuclear war, abortion, medical care, and so on. These facts, taken together, multiply and intensify the occasions when Catholic politicians are forced to reconcile their religious and political loyalties. Sometimes the drama is compelling enough to capture the attention of the newspapers.

Consider the case of Mario Cuomo. He is the Governor of New York and a liberal Democrat. In September 1984, he gave an address at the University of Notre Dame entitled *Religious Belief and Public Morality: A Catholic Governor's Perspective*. He began by explaining that he accepted the Church's teaching about abortion as the rule for his own life. But as a public official he could not approve a legal prohibition of abortion. Most of New York's citizens were not Catholics, and many of them (indeed many Catholics) disagreed with what the Church said. An anti-abortion law would be unfair to them, and ineffective in the way Prohibition was. Cuomo added that he also favored Medicaid funding of abortions for the poor.

A month later Archbishop (now Cardinal) John J. O'Connor of New York said that, although he would not urge voters to choose any particular candidate in the upcoming elections, the most important question they faced was the need to "protect the rights of the unborn." O'Connor may have had several politicians in mind. Geraldine Ferraro, another New York Catholic whose views mirrored Cuomo's, was then running for Vice President. Two years later O'Connor's Vicar General, Bishop Joseph T. O'Keefe, announced that parishes within O'Connor's archdiocese should not provide a platform to speakers "whose public position is contrary to [the] teaching of the Church." O'Keefe said the policy was not aimed at Cuomo, though it would of course apply to him.

* * *

[My] ultimate concern is to explain the kind of deference Governor Cuomo (as a practicing Catholic) should give to the Church's teaching. But it turns out that we cannot state that explanation in a simple formula. [I will first] examine the claims of authority that the Catholic Church makes over all its members in their daily lives. [Then] I will look at the special case of public officials.

A. ORDINARY CATHOLICS

The authoritativeness of the Church's teaching for ordinary Catholics depends in part on who the teacher is. Vatican II states that the highest authority resides in the college of bishops with the pope at their head. In the modern Church this is a lot of bishops, and they do not often get together. When they do (in an ecumenical council like Vatican II), they exercise their authority in a particularly "solemn way." Even when not gathered together the bishops can sometimes teach with the same authority, provided "they concur in a single viewpoint as the one which must be held conclusively." The pope can also act alone with an authority equivalent to that of an ecumenical council. He is, Vatican II observes, "the supreme teacher of the universal Church." [31] Each of these actors (ecumenical council, the dispersed college of bishops, the pope) is thought to be capable of acting infallibly, though they seldom do so, and such action depends on other factors.

These are not the only Church officials capable of acting authoritatively. Individual bishops have jurisdiction over Church members within their territory. Their pronouncements are obligatory (though not infallible) in a sense which I will explore below. Groups of bishops may

---

31. [*Dogmatic Constitution on the Church* (*Lumen Gentium*), in The Documents of Vatican II §§ 22, 25, 30–38 (Wal- ter M. Abbott ed. & Joseph Gallagher trans. ed., 1966).]

also gather together on a national or territorial basis to form episcopal conferences, a practice encouraged by Vatican II. The National Conference of Catholic Bishops is a fairly active example. These groups, like their members, can act authoritatively but not infallibly. Then there is a whole host of congregations, commissions, offices, and so on that make up the Vatican bureaucracy, and that function in ways not unlike the modern administrative state.

I need not detail the positions of all the various actors within the Church hierarchy to make my first point, which is simply that the authoritativeness of Church teaching varies with (among other things) the identity of the speaker. It also varies with the speaker's intention. The pope teaches infallibly only when "he proclaims by a definitive act some doctrine of faith or morals." The bishops do so only when "they concur in a single viewpoint as the one which must be held conclusively." [36] The principle is like the clear statement rule that we sometimes use in interpreting statutes: Y [a church official or institution] is understood to have acted with infallible authority only when it has made perfectly clear its intention to do so. And the significance of intentions is not confined to the question of infallibility. None of the many documents produced by Vatican II was meant to be definitive in that way. But they bear various titles intended to indicate the degree of authoritativeness attached to each: "dogmatic constitution," "pastoral constitution," "constitution," "decree," "declaration."

The authoritativeness of Church teaching thus varies with the speaker's office and intentions. It also varies with the subject matter. The idea is a familiar one to lawyers. The United States Supreme Court is often said to have ultimate authority to interpret the federal constitution, but it has no such authority with regard to state law. We sometimes express this by talking about the scope of its jurisdiction. So it is with the Church, whose jurisdiction is limited to matters of "faith or morals." [38] Though it has sometimes pretended otherwise, for example, it has no brief explaining to us the proper form (monarchical, democratic) that civil government ought to take.

Even within the domain of faith and morals there is a great variety of issues, and the Church speaks with more authority on some of them than on others. There are, in the first place, those things said to be revealed in the gospel message (for example, that Jesus is God). Theologians say that these are the primary object of the Church's magisterium, things about which it can speak with most authority—at times infallibly. Then there is a range of other matters, more or less closely related to these, to which the Church can speak with diminishing degrees of authority (recognition of a Church council as ecumenical; canonization of saints; etc.). I do not want to dwell on these details, but only mention them to indicate how highly refined and variable is the notion of authority, and because they bear on my main interest, which is the

36. [*Id.* § 25.]   **38.** [*Id.*]

deference due from observant Catholics to the Church's instructions on moral questions—abortion in particular. That is a subject on which various authorities within the Church have taught with a fairly consistent voice for a long time. The Second Vatican Council condemned the practice in the *Pastoral Constitution on the Church in the Modern World.* Pope Paul VI repeated this condemnation in his encyclical *Humanae Vitae.* The National Conference of Catholic Bishops has done the same on numerous occasions. So has the Congregation for the Doctrine of the Faith. Cardinal O'Connor and the bishop of Brooklyn have echoed these positions. What obligations do these teachings impose on Mr. Cuomo?

As a matter of Church law, Cuomo's obligations depend in part on whether the teachings of the pope and the council are supposed to be infallible, and that is an uncertain point. Neither the *Pastoral Constitution* nor the encyclical displays the kind of clear intention that accompanies infallible pronouncements. It may nonetheless be that papal and episcopal opinion on the subject merits that status because it has been so unanimous and so longstanding. I will assume that it does not, for the sake of making a point that can be applied more widely. Here is what Vatican II said about the appropriate response to noninfallible moral teachings:

> Bishops, teaching in communion with the Roman Pontiff, are to be respected by all as witnesses to divine and Catholic truth. In matters of faith and morals, the bishops speak in the name of Christ and *the faithful are to accept their teaching and adhere to it with a religious assent of soul.* This *religious submission of will and of mind* must be shown in a special way to the authentic teaching authority of the Roman Pontiff, even when he is not speaking ex cathedra.[46]

I understand the two italicized phrases to be essentially equivalent, and for simplicity's sake I will focus on the phrase "religious submission of will and of mind." This claims two kinds of authority. One is practical, over how *X* acts ("submission of will"). The other is epistemic, over how *X* thinks (submission "of mind"). Political authority, by contrast, is strictly practical. It requires obedience but not agreement. Indeed, the First Amendment protects our freedom to disagree with the law. But the Church, because it is concerned with the formation of consciences, pays as much attention to mental states as it does to behavior.

There is a scene in Peter Pan where Peter is instructing the Darling children how to fly. The secret is to think lovely thoughts, but that is something he cannot get them to do. Like Peter, the Church cannot always get me to think lovely thoughts. Even when I am willing I may not be able. Suppose that I am a pregnant woman considering whether to have an abortion. I can conform my behavior (submission of will) to Church teaching by just refusing to abort. But how can I get myself to think that abortion is wrong (submission of mind) if, notwithstanding

46. [*Id.*]

what the Church tells me, my mind will not go along with that proposition? Learning about morals is like learning geometry. I do not learn geometry by committing propositions to memory. Unless I work out the proofs, I cannot apply them and will not remember them—in a word, I do not understand them. So it is with the proposition that abortion is wrong. This will fit with some of my convictions (how I feel toward the life growing inside me; how I think I should behave toward my father who is on a respirator) and not with others (what I think about incest, rape, and pregnant teenagers), and I cannot affirm or deny it until I have worked it through.

What then does submission of mind mean for this process? It means, in the first place, that I should recheck my proof if I get a different answer than the Church did. The Church's teaching counts for something if it gives me reason to think that my own convictions may be wrong. Submission of mind might also mean that I should try reasoning backward through my proof, beginning with the authoritative answer. This sometimes works in mathematics, where knowing the answer helps me to figure out the other steps in the problem. And if none of this gets me to the orthodox conclusion, I think I should remain willing to hear new arguments and new evidence, i.e. make my judgment interlocutory rather than final. Finally, there will be cases where after long reflection I find the balance of moral reasons uncertain. (Suppose I simply cannot decide whether I think that human life begins at conception.) Here the Church's teaching could change the outcome of my thinking because it is an additional piece of evidence—a kind of morally expert testimony that changes the balance of proof.

These observations explain an important difference between epistemic and practical authority. [Joseph Raz has remarked [a]] how we give some authorities preemptive effect. My broker has this kind of authority over my account. I do not weigh his advice along with other reasons and sometimes reject it. I follow his direction even when I think it is wrong. Consider another example. A court decision rests on reasons (stated in an opinion); but once the decision becomes final it is itself a reason for X to act as directed. X cannot impeach the decision by showing that the reasons supporting it are weak; that is what it means for a matter to be res judicata. The decision preempts the reasons that led to it.

Epistemic authority, unlike practical authority, cannot have this preemptive effect. It can influence, and in uncertain cases determine, the direction of my thought. But if I think it is wrong, it ipso facto fails.

I now want to say a few words about the submission of will. Suppose I am pregnant and cannot bring myself to think—though I have tried—that abortion would be wrong in my case. (I am in frail health.) Must I nonetheless carry my pregnancy to term? In a word, yes. The Church's practical authority is preemptive, like a conscription law whose

a. Joseph Raz, The Morality of Freedom 57–62 (1986).

morality I might dispute. An observant Catholic can and should comply with it notwithstanding her disagreement.

But is this not asking me to behave irrationally, and maybe at times immorally? (Think again about conscription laws.) In general I think not. * * * This case is formally like the preemptive authority of my broker: I know that I will get a better return by following his advice than I will by making my own decisions in cases where I think he is wrong. This is true even though he sometimes is wrong, because his error rate is lower than mine. Of course I have different reasons for [trusting my broker's judgment than I have for trusting the Church's judgment], but that cuts in the Church's favor. I think that it has a low error rate because I believe that Jesus is God, and that Jesus remains with the Church in various ways (in its sacraments, its scripture, its tradition, etc.)—in a word, for reasons that are fairly fundamental.

The second kind of justification has nothing to do with whether the Church is right or wrong in its teaching in this case. It is that in at least some cases orthopraxis, like orthodoxy, is a way of expressing the principle of unity that has an independent religious value in the life of the Church. We see parallel examples in the affairs of unions (solidarity), political parties (party loyalty), families ("blood is thicker than water"), armies ("ours is not to reason why"), and nations ("my country right or wrong"). In many of these cases the principle is not a strong one. Indeed, the standard example is a caricature of the individual who gives this principle too much weight when it collides with another moral imperative. But the weight it deserves varies from one case to another depending on the justification for collective action, and Church unity may be more important than some other kinds.

I do not want to overstate this point. I have been picturing a case where X thinks that abortion is not immoral and favors that course because it would promote her own medical health. But imagine another case (make it compelling) where X has given her most conscientious attention to the Church's epistemic authority, and yet concludes that the course prescribed by the Church would be actually immoral. Under these circumstances it is hard to justify giving the Church's practical authority preemptive effect. The [analogy of the broker suggests] that X can reduce her error rate by obedience in all cases. But it cannot justify immoral action as a means to that end. Nor should we urge immoral action as a way of achieving Church unity. In this case I think that X is morally obliged to deviate from the Church's teaching, even though the Church might impose sanctions on her for doing so.

B. Public Officials

All this talk so far, you might say, is beside the point, because Governor Cuomo concedes his obligation to conform (in mind and will) to the Church's teaching in his own life. He quarrels only with the Cardinal's assertion that he should make that teaching the law of the state of New York. What state officials must do in their official capacity, he contends, is a matter that is beyond the Church's jurisdiction.

Not quite. The Church acknowledges (though it has not always) that "Christ [gave it] no proper mission in the political, economic, or social order." [50] But this does not mean everything that strict separationists might hope. The Church also rejects "the outmoded notion that 'religion is a purely private affair' or that 'the Church belongs in the sacristy.' Religion is relevant to the life and action of society." [51] In particular it maintains that it "has the right to pass moral judgments, even on matters touching the political order, whenever basic personal rights or the salvation of souls make such judgments necessary." [52] This of course entails that it should speak out on the issue of abortion, which it sees as involving both "personal rights" (of the fetus) and "salvation" (of those who procure and perform abortions). But there are several reasons why its teachings in this forum might be less authoritative than the model I have discussed above.

To begin with, of course, most citizens of the state are not members of the Church. Over them the Church has no authority at all, only such influence as the force of its arguments deserves. Cuomo is not exempt on that account, but it is a fact that bears on his obligations in a second way. It is no less true for Catholics than it is for others that duty is limited by possibility. Compromise is an unpleasant but necessary feature of political life. If the Governor finds it impossible to secure enactment of the Church's agenda, he can hardly be condemned for doing only what he can.

The need to compromise with nonmembers is not the only limit facing the observant Catholic politician. It is not self-evident that the full resources of the state should be used to enforce moral norms even in cases where a majority of the voters would stand for it. No one argues that Cuomo should work for passage of laws to enforce the moral norms (binding within the Church) against contraception and divorce. * * *

The * * * moral law is a command of perfection that would land us all in jail were the state to enforce it to the letter. That would have disastrous implications for the Corrections budget. And it might mean that none of us would show up for work on Monday. [There are also] any number of institutional problems connected with efforts by one legal authority to assimilate the regulatory law of another. It would be hard for the secular legal system to be sure that it correctly understood the corpus of Catholic moral rules. The borrowed norms might clash with existing New York law in ways too numerous to anticipate. The borrowed offenses might involve elements (e.g. questions about a sinner's mental state) that the existing secular law system (adversary procedure, rules of discovery, evidence, methods of trial and review) was incompetent to prove. (Remember that in the Catholic Church penitents confess their sins.) The burden of enforcing a supplementary set

---

50. [*Pastoral Constitution on the Church in the Modern World (Gaudium et Spes)* § 42, in The Documents of Vatican II.]

51. [*Declaration on Religious Freedom (Dignitatis Humanae)* § 4 n. 11, in The Documents of Vatican II.]

52. *Gaudium et Spes* [§ 76].

of norms might overload a justice system designed to do other work. And so on.

All of the reasons I have given so far are jurisdictional (the problem of nonmembers) or prudential (the need for compromise; the danger of pursuing perfection; the costs of assimilation). They do not go to the merits. By that I mean that they are consistent with saying that the Church rules would be best if we could have them. But that is not necessarily so. Consider the rules about economic due process. Although the Supreme Court asserts authority over constitutional questions, it gives great leeway to other branches on matters of business regulation. One common justification is that it knows little about business and economics, and the legislature (or the agency), so long as it stays within wide limits, is more likely to reach the right answer. Conservative Catholics make precisely the same point about the Catholic bishops' efforts in the economic realm. Though they say they are in complete agreement with the bishops' ultimate aims, they argue that we can get there faster by concentrating on production rather than (as the bishops naively do) distribution. I do not necessarily endorse this conclusion, but the method of argument is perfectly sensible. Moral questions arise in contexts that Church authorities will know little about, and in such cases other people might get to the right answer first.

The Church's authority over observant Catholic public officials is, then, qualified in a number of important ways. Let us consider what this might mean for the question of abortion. I should rather say questions, because there are many, and the answers differ. Consider first the precise issue for which *Roe v. Wade* is taken to stand: whether abortion is a fundamental human right protected by the Due Process Clause. That is a fairly abstract ethical proposition, unmixed with the kinds of contingencies that lead bishops astray. It is also obviously inconsistent with the Church's teaching that abortion is an "unspeakable crime." [57] If we confine our attention to the simple question whether to recognize the right, there are few prudential reasons that would move one in sympathy with the Church's position to do so. It is difficult for me to see how Cuomo, if he accepts the Church's teaching about abortion, could agree with the Supreme Court's decision in *Roe*. But this is also an issue that he has no influence over. It can only be determined by the Supreme Court or by a constitutional amendment.

On the other hand, accepting the Church's teaching would not, I think, commit Cuomo to the proposition that New York should make procuring or performing an abortion a criminal offense. This is an issue, unlike the last, where enforcing the Church's position would control the behavior of nonmembers. That is not inherently improper; Cuomo routinely enforces the position of the Democratic Party against nonmembers. But it would lead non-Catholics to vote against him, and to undo any successes he had along this line. I am not convinced that Cuomo is morally obliged to pursue pyrrhic victories.

---

57. *Gaudium et Spes* [§ 51].

Quite apart from its effect on nonmembers, a criminal abortion law might entail very high enforcement costs. Proponents of abortion usually cite the example of Prohibition. The offense there is trivial but the point is not. If we had a high rate of illegal abortions and prosecuted violations vigorously we could put a lot of young women and doctors in jail. If doctors complied (I assume they would) and women continued to abort, they would run a new set of health risks. If juries balked at convicting (and they often would), we would encourage disrespect for the law and waste enforcement resources that we could employ elsewhere with more success (drunk drivers and drug dealers also kill people).

This is not to say that anti-abortion laws are, absolutely speaking, a bad idea—only that the government cannot successfully get too far out ahead of public opinion. I hasten to add that that has not been Cuomo's problem. I suspect that the people of New York are, if anything, more willing than he to accept some limitation on abortion rights. If that is so, the Governor could find common ground with Church nonmembers for doing something about the problem. And a law that had popular support would not entail the enforcement costs I have hypothesized. In short, I see no prudential reason that Cuomo can cite for declining to stand with at least one foot on his principles.

The third abortion question involved in Cuomo's case is the issue of government funding, which he supports. On this issue it is harder for the observant Catholic official to depart from the Church's teaching. It is not just a matter of declining for prudential reasons to enforce the moral law. Funding abortions actually promotes (what Cuomo concedes is) evil. And taxing Church members to raise the funds implicates them too. Cuomo argues that it is unjust to withhold funds because doing so leaves poor women worse off than rich ones. But if he is concerned about equalizing standards of living this is hardly the place to start.

I want to conclude this section with a few observations about the enforcement of Church authority. Suppose that the Governor publicly contradicts some authoritative teaching of the Church, or like Cuomo, affirms that he will obey in his personal life but takes an inconsistent political position. What sanctions are (from the Church's point of view) proper?

Under canon law, one who procures an abortion is subject to automatic excommunication.[62] This means that she is unable to receive the sacraments, to participate in certain ways at mass and other public worship, and to hold any Church office or perform any official ecclesiastical function. The excommunication becomes effective without any trial, though this cannot happen inadvertently. The offender must know in advance not only about the gravity of the offense but also about the Church's punishment.

---

62. 1983 Code of Canon Law c. 1398.

But that is not the offense that Catholic politicians are typically concerned with. Cuomo, for example, has rejected abortion as a possibility in his own life. His offense (if it is one) has been to support the actions of women who want to have abortions, by a course of official conduct (failure to promote regulation; approval of Medicaid funding) and public statements (his speech at Notre Dame). I have suggested that some, at least, of these activities are inconsistent with the Church's teaching on abortion, which Catholics are expected to heed. Canon 752 of the Code of Canon Law codifies the obligation to heed Church teaching and "to avoid whatever is not in harmony with that teaching." Canon 1371 deals with sanctions for violation of these obligations:

> The following are to be punished with a just penalty:

> 1 . . . a person who teaches a doctrine condemned by the Roman Pontiff or by an ecumenical council or who pertinaciously rejects the doctrine mentioned in can. 752. . . .

What counts as a "just penalty" can vary. The local bishop seems to have considerable discretion, and the Code encourages him to proceed cautiously. Cardinal O'Connor [once] suggested that excommunication was a possibility, but no American bishop has tried it. Bishop Maher in San Diego withheld communion (a less severe sanction) from Lucy Killea, a state senator who advocated abortion rights. O'Connor's Vicar and Bishop Daily of Brooklyn have barred Cuomo from speaking at parish churches.

These sanctions are intended to be coercive in the way that civil contempt is coercive: they aim at reformation of the offender's conduct. But they are effective only against religious believers. If I had no interest in participating in the religious life of the Catholic community, excommunication would not concern me. (It would be like being thrown out of the Book of the Month Club.) And once I was willing to sever my religious ties, the Church would have no independent source of leverage.

2. CIVIL RELIGION

The pledge of allegiance to the flag speaks of the United States as "one nation, under God." The pledge is a political statement but it incorporates religious ideas. (It was used to great effect by George Bush during the 1988 presidential campaign for both these reasons.) And it is not unique. Our currency speaks of our trust in God. Our legislatures invoke his aid. Even the Supreme Court begins its day with the prayer that God will "save the United States and this honorable Court." Is it not hypocritical to engage in these theist practices while speaking about the separation of church and state? They may not amount to the kind of establishment we had in New England in the eighteenth century, but they certainly are a ringing endorsement of some kind of religion. What is their place in the system regulated by our First Amendment?

Robert Bellah asserts that these practices are part of an American civil religion. Though it has a language in common with private religion, civil religion exists alongside it and serves a different function.

It is a way of explaining and sanctifying our past and future, and calling the nation to a sense of transcendent values. It is not specifically Christian (it speaks of "God" rather than "Jesus"), nor even Judeo–Christian. But it is, Bellah says, genuinely religious. At its best it has had "incisive relevance to the American scene" and offered a "level of religious insight" that rivals the churches'.

The Yale Note acknowledges the reality of Bellah's civil religion, but argues that it undermines the aims—both political and theological—of the establishment clause. It suggests that when we want to call the people to moral reflection, or to foster a cohesive social identity, we should substitute other, more inclusive, practices.

ROBERT N. BELLAH, CIVIL RELIGION IN AMERICA

96 Daedalus 1, 3–14, 18–21 (1967).

The * * * separation of church and state has not denied the political realm a religious dimension. Although matters of personal religious belief, worship, and association are considered to be strictly private affairs, there are, at the same time, certain common elements of religious orientation that the great majority of Americans share. These have played a crucial role in the development of American institutions and still provide a religious dimension for the whole fabric of American life, including the political sphere. This public religious dimension is expressed in a set of beliefs, symbols, and rituals that I am calling the American civil religion. * * *

* * *

THE IDEA OF A CIVIL RELIGION

The phrase *civil religion* is, of course, Rousseau's. In Chapter 8, Book 4, of *The Social Contract,* he outlines the simple dogmas of the civil religion: the existence of God, the life to come, the reward of virtue and the punishment of vice, and the exclusion of religious intolerance. All other religious opinions are outside the cognizance of the state and may be freely held by citizens. While the phrase *civil religion* was not used, to the best of my knowledge, by the founding fathers, and I am certainly not arguing for the particular influence of Rousseau, it is clear that similar ideas, as part of the cultural climate of the late-eighteenth century, were to be found among the Americans. * * *

[Consider, for example, the Declaration of Independence.] There are four references to God. The first speaks of the "Laws of Nature and of Nature's God" which entitle any people to be independent. The second is the famous statement that all men "are endowed by their Creator with certain inalienable Rights." Here Jefferson is locating the fundamental legitimacy of the new nation in a conception of "higher law" that is itself based on both classical natural law and Biblical religion. The third is an appeal to "the Supreme Judge of the world for the rectitude of our intentions," and the last indicates "a firm reliance on the protection of divine Providence." In these last two references, a Biblical God of history who stands in judgment over the world is indicated.

* * *

The words and acts of the founding fathers, especially the first few presidents, shaped the form and tone of the civil religion as it has been maintained ever since. Though much is selectively derived from Christianity, this religion is clearly not itself Christianity. For one thing, neither Washington nor Adams nor Jefferson mentions Christ in his inaugural address; nor do any of the subsequent presidents, although not one of them fails to mention God. The God of the civil religion is not only rather "unitarian," he is also on the austere side, much more related to order, law, and right than to salvation and love. Even though he is somewhat deist in cast, he is by no means simply a watchmaker God. He is actively interested and involved in history, with a special concern for America. Here the analogy has much less to do with natural law than with ancient Israel; the equation of America with Israel in the idea of the "American Israel" is not infrequent. [This] becomes explicit in Jefferson's second inaugural when he said: "I shall need, too, the favor of that Being in whose hands we are, who led our fathers, as Israel of old, from their native land and planted them in a country flowing with all the necessaries and comforts of life." Europe is Egypt; America, the promised land. God has led his people to establish a new sort of social order that shall be a light unto all the nations.

* * *

What we have, then, from the earliest years of the republic is a collection of beliefs, symbols, and rituals with respect to sacred things and institutionalized in a collectivity. This religion—there seems no other word for it—while not antithetical to and indeed sharing much in common with Christianity, was neither sectarian nor in any specific sense Christian. At a time when the society was overwhelmingly Christian, it seems unlikely that this lack of Christian reference was meant to spare the feelings of the tiny non-Christian minority. Rather, the civil religion expressed what those who set the precedents felt was appropriate under the circumstances. It reflected their private as well as public views. Nor was the civil religion simply "religion in general." While generality was undoubtedly seen as a virtue by some, * * * the civil religion was specific enough when it came to the topic of America. Precisely because of this specificity, the civil religion was saved from empty formalism and served as a genuine vehicle of national religious self-understanding.

* * *

CIVIL WAR AND CIVIL RELIGION

Until the Civil War, the American civil religion focused above all on the event of the Revolution, which was seen as the final act of the

Exodus from the old lands across the waters. The Declaration of Independence and the Constitution were the sacred scriptures and Washington the divinely appointed Moses who led his people out of the hands of tyranny. The Civil War, which Sidney Mead calls "the center of American history," [6] was the second great event that involved the national self-understanding so deeply as to require expression in the civil religion. In 1835, de Tocqueville wrote that the American republic had never really been tried, that victory in the Revolutionary War was more the result of British preoccupation elsewhere and the presence of a powerful ally than of any great military success of the Americans. But in 1861 the time of testing had indeed come. Not only did the Civil War have the tragic intensity of fratricidal strife, but it was one of the bloodiest wars of the nineteenth century; the loss of life was far greater than any previously suffered by Americans.

The Civil War raised the deepest questions of national meaning. The man who not only formulated but in his own person embodied its meaning for Americans was Abraham Lincoln. For him the issue was not in the first instance slavery but "whether that nation, or any nation so conceived, and so dedicated, can long endure."   * * *

But inevitably the issue of slavery as the deeper cause of the conflict had to be faced. In the second inaugural, Lincoln related slavery and the war in an ultimate perspective:

> If we shall suppose that American slavery is one of those offenses which, in the providence of God, must needs come, but which, having continued through His appointed time, He now wills to remove, and that He gives to both North and South this terrible war as the woe due to those by whom the offense came, shall we discern therein any departure from those divine attributes which the believers in a living God always ascribe to Him? Fondly do we hope, fervently do we pray, that this mighty scourge of war may speedily pass away. Yet, if God wills that it continue until all the wealth piled by the bondsman's two hundred and fifty years of unrequited toil shall be sunk, and until every drop of blood drawn with the lash shall be paid by another drawn with the sword, as was said three thousand years ago, so still it must be said "the judgments of the Lord are true and righteous altogether."

But he closes on a note if not of redemption then of reconciliation— "With malice toward none, with charity for all."

With the Civil War, a new theme of death, sacrifice, and rebirth enters the civil religion. It is symbolized in the life and death of Lincoln. Nowhere is it stated more vividly than in the Gettysburg Address, itself part of the Lincolnian "New Testament" among the civil scriptures. Robert Lowell has recently pointed out the "insistent use of birth images" in this speech explicitly devoted to "these honored dead":

6. Sidney Mead, The Lively Experiment (New York, 1963), p. 12.

"brought forth," "conceived," "created," "a new birth of freedom." He goes on to say:

> The Gettysburg Address is a symbolic and sacramental act. Its verbal quality is resonance combined with a logical, matter of fact, prosaic brevity.... In his words, Lincoln symbolically died, just as the Union soldiers really died—and as he himself was soon really to die. By his words, he gave the field of battle a symbolic significance that it had lacked. For us and our country, he left Jefferson's ideals of freedom and equality joined to the Christian sacrificial act of death and rebirth. I believe this is a meaning that goes beyond sect or religion and beyond peace and war, and is now part of our lives as a challenge, obstacle and hope.[8]

Lowell is certainly right in pointing out the Christian quality of the symbolism here, but he is also right in quickly disavowing any sectarian implication. The earlier symbolism of the civil religion had been Hebraic without being in any specific sense Jewish. The Gettysburg symbolism ("... those who here gave their lives, that that nation might live") is Christian without having anything to do with the Christian church.

* * *

Memorial Day, which grew out of the Civil War, gave ritual expression to the themes we have been discussing. As Lloyd Warner has so brilliantly analyzed it, the Memorial Day observance, especially in the towns and smaller cities of America, is a major event for the whole community involving a rededication to the martyred dead, to the spirit of sacrifice, and to the American vision.[11] Just as Thanksgiving Day, which incidentally was securely institutionalized as an annual national holiday only under the presidency of Lincoln, serves to integrate the family into the civil religion, so Memorial Day has acted to integrate the local community into the national cult. Together with the less overtly religious Fourth of July and the more minor celebrations of Veterans Day and the birthdays of Washington and Lincoln, these two holidays provide an annual ritual calendar for the civil religion. The public-school system serves as a particularly important context for the cultic celebration of the civil rituals.

The Civil Religion Today

In reifying and giving a name to something that, though pervasive enough when you look at it, has gone on only semiconsciously, there is risk of severely distorting the data. But the reification and the naming have already begun. The religious critics of "religion in general," or of the "religion of the 'American Way of Life,'" or of "American Shinto" have really been talking about the civil religion. As usual in religious polemic, they take as criteria the best in their own religious tradition

---

8. "On the Gettysburg Address," [in Allan Nevins (ed.), Lincoln and the Gettysburg Address (Urbana, Ill., 1964),] pp. 88–89.

11. * * * W. Lloyd Warner, American Life (Chicago, 1962), pp. 8–9.

and as typical the worst in the tradition of the civil religion. Against these critics, I would argue that the civil religion at its best is a genuine apprehension of universal and transcendent religious reality as seen in or, one could almost say, as revealed through the experience of the American people. Like all religions, it has suffered various deformations and demonic distortions. At its best, it has neither been so general that it has lacked incisive relevance to the American scene nor so particular that it has placed American society above universal human values. I am not at all convinced that the leaders of the churches have consistently represented a higher level of religious insight than the spokesmen of the civil religion. Reinhold Niebuhr has this to say of Lincoln, who never joined a church and who certainly represents civil religion at its best:

> An analysis of the religion of Abraham Lincoln in the context of the traditional religion of his time and place and of its polemical use on the slavery issue, which corrupted religious life in the days before and during the Civil War, must lead to the conclusion that Lincoln's religious convictions were superior in depth and purity to those, not only of the political leaders of his day, but of the religious leaders of the era.[12]

Perhaps the real animus of the religious critics has been not so much against the civil religion in itself but against its pervasive and dominating influence within the sphere of church religion. * * *

It is certainly true that the relation between religion and politics in America has been singularly smooth. This is in large part due to the dominant tradition. As de Tocqueville wrote:

> The greatest part of British America was peopled by men who, after having shaken off the authority of the Pope, acknowledged no other religious supremacy: they brought with them into the New World a form of Christianity which I cannot better describe than by styling it a democratic and republican religion.[16]

The churches opposed neither the Revolution nor the establishment of democratic institutions. Even when some of them opposed the full institutionalization of religious liberty, they accepted the final outcome with good grace and without nostalgia for an *ancien régime*. The American civil religion was never anticlerical or militantly secular. On the contrary, it borrowed selectively from the religious tradition in such a way that the average American saw no conflict between the two. In this way, the civil religion was able to build up without any bitter struggle with the church powerful symbols of national solidarity and to mobilize deep levels of personal motivation for the attainment of national goals.

Such an achievement is by no means to be taken for granted. It would seem that the problem of a civil religion is quite general in

---

12. Reinhold Niebuhr, "The Religion of Abraham Lincoln," in Nevins (ed.), *op. cit.,* p. 72. * * *

16. [Alexis de Tocqueville, Democracy in America, Vol. 1 (New York, 1954),] p. 311. * * *

modern societies and that the way it is solved or not solved will have repercussions in many spheres. One needs only to think of France to see how differently things can go. The French Revolution was anticlerical to the core and attempted to set up an anti-Christian civil religion. Throughout modern French history, the chasm between traditional Catholic symbols and the symbolism of 1789 has been immense.

American civil religion is still very much alive. Just three years ago we participated in a vivid re-enactment of the sacrifice theme in connection with the funeral of our assassinated president. The American Israel theme is clearly behind both Kennedy's New Frontier and Johnson's Great Society. Let me give just one recent illustration of how the civil religion serves to mobilize support for the attainment of national goals. On 15 March 1965 President Johnson went before Congress to ask for a strong voting-rights bill. Early in the speech he said:

> Rarely are we met with the challenge, not to our growth or abundance, or our welfare or our security—but rather to the values and the purposes and the meaning of our beloved nation.

> The issue of equal rights for American Negroes is such an issue. And should we defeat every enemy, and should we double our wealth and conquer the stars and still be unequal to this issue, then we will have failed as a people and as a nation.

> For with a country as with a person, "What is a man profited, if he shall gain the whole world, and lose his own soul?"

* * *

The civil religion has not always been invoked in favor of worthy causes. On the domestic scene, an American–Legion type of ideology that fuses God, country, and flag has been used to attack nonconformist and liberal ideas and groups of all kinds. Still, it has been difficult to use the words of Jefferson and Lincoln to support special interests and undermine personal freedom. The defenders of slavery before the Civil War came to reject the thinking of the Declaration of Independence. Some of the most consistent of them turned against not only Jeffersonian democracy but Reformation religion; they dreamed of a South dominated by medieval chivalry and divine-right monarchy. For all the overt religiosity of the radical right today, their relation to the civil religious consensus is tenuous, as when the John Birch Society attacks the central American symbol of Democracy itself.

With respect to America's role in the world, the dangers of distortion are greater and the built-in safeguards of the tradition weaker. The theme of the American Israel was used, almost from the beginning, as a justification for the shameful treatment of the Indians so characteristic of our history. It can be overtly or implicitly linked to the idea of manifest destiny which has been used to legitimate several adventures in imperialism since the early-nineteenth century. Never has the danger been greater than today. * * *

* * *

Behind the civil religion at every point lie Biblical archetypes: Exodus, Chosen People, Promised Land, New Jerusalem, Sacrificial Death and Rebirth. But it is also genuinely American and genuinely new. It has its own prophets and its own martyrs, its own sacred events and sacred places, its own solemn rituals and symbols. It is concerned that America be a society as perfectly in accord with the will of God as men can make it, and a light to all the nations.

It has often been used and is being used today as a cloak for petty interests and ugly passions. It is in need—as is any living faith—of continual reformation, of being measured by universal standards. But it is not evident that it is incapable of growth and new insight.

It does not make any decision for us. It does not remove us from moral ambiguity, from being, in Lincoln's fine phrase, an "almost chosen people." But it is a heritage of moral and religious experience from which we still have much to learn as we formulate the decisions that lie ahead.

NOTE, CIVIL RELIGION AND THE ESTABLISHMENT CLAUSE

95 Yale L.J. 1237, 1253–1257 (1986).

In order to consider how to apply civil religion in an interpretation of the establishment clause, it must be evaluated in terms of the concerns lying at the heart of the clause, namely Jeffersonian fears of clericalism, Madisonian desires for pluralism and Williams' concern for the purity of the ecclesia. While some scholars have seen civil religion as a valuable response to an important need of disestablished societies, others have severely criticized both the phenomenon itself and the particular way in which it has been characterized. These criticisms have been of two sorts—one theological, the other political—and both implicate establishment clause values of pluralism, freedom from clerical tyranny and respect for the purity of religious beliefs and institutions.

The theological critiques run roughly as follows: Civil religion is the product of deep tensions and confusions, and not at all a step in the direction of their resolution. It is the episodic, un-systematic expression of confused societies, caught up in wrenching processes of religious and social change far beyond their comprehension and control. It is, in the words of one scholar, "a somewhat schizoid blend of Puritanism and the Enlightenment, of coercion and persuasion, of Jehova the god of battles and the mild and tolerant god of nature." [79] This inchoate jumble of millenarianism coupled with American nationalism, these critics would say, can hardly be viewed as a source of communal strength and inspiration. The most charitable thing we could say about civil religion is that Americans have picked through some of the ruins of the great

---

79. Hughes, *Civil Religion, the Theology of the Republic and the Free Church Tradi-* tion, 22 J. of Church & State 75, 77 (1980).

medieval cathedrals, taken a rafter here, a pew there and the shards of a stained-glass window, thrown them all together and called it a house. Moreover, the very thought of a religion of the republic as a substitute for a lost, pre-modern faith is downright idolatrous, or, in Roger Williams' terms, a fantastic degradation and parody of religion.

The various critiques of civil religion that can be grouped under the rubric of political criticism take as their starting point the fact that when talking about civil religion we are, at bottom, talking about myths. More to the point, we are talking about a political mythology, a cluster of myths that reinforce one another and constitute the historical or quasi-historical elements of a political order. Political myths, civil religion among them, are not only inclusive, binding the members of a polity around a common core of memory and observance; they are exclusive as well, identifying insiders and outsiders according to the predilections of those who generate society's myths and values. The relative cultural and spiritual homogeneity of our myths runs counter to Madison's ideal of disestablishment.

And myths can deceive. The tone of American civil religion is more often than not celebratory and there is never a hint that the martyrs might have died in vain. America's moral failings, as a democracy and as a nation ostensibly under God, are glossed over. The exclusion of any memory of the fate of this continent's natives, or of the miseries inflicted on women, immigrants and racial and ethnic minorities from the collective memory embodied in civil religion is indeed disturbing, not least from a Jeffersonian perspective. To the extent that civil religion allows us to forget or perpetuate past injustices, it corrupts the polity and its government's ability to function wisely. It is worth noting that this sort of selective reading of history is itself not infrequently characteristic of traditional, sacral religions.[84]

* * *

[The Note goes on to acknowledge that, despite these criticisms, civil religion is a reality that the law cannot simply wish away. Indeed, it is possible that a "critically reflective civil religion can play a positive role in cementing the communal symbolic life of American society." The important thing is not to confuse civil religion with "its sacral, traditional counterpart." The Note then suggests, by reference to several recent cases, how the courts might express "shared and constitutive values" without drifting over into an impermissible establishment.]

* * *

84. One particularly subtle (though well-intentioned) form of this obfuscation is the emergence in recent years of the locution "Judeo–Christian tradition" which, while it has some rough descriptive weight, papers over the literally and figuratively tortuous relations that have generally obtained between Jews and Christians over the past twenty centuries. *See* A. Cohen,

In *Marsh* [*v. Chambers* [a]] a consideration of civil religion would have provided the Court with the following insights: Although prayer is, of course, an eminently religious activity, it is also a manifestation of * * * the sense of responsibility to a transcendent principle of morality. If the Court had recognized that valuable civil goal of moral reflection, it could identify means of effectuating that goal without recourse to sacral religious prayer. What seems important to us about legislative prayer can be preserved without offense to the Constitution by having, say, an elder member of the house open the session with a reading of the Declaration of Independence or Learned Hand's famous "Spirit of Liberty" speech, or simply with the very evocative ritual of a moment of silence. Given the existence of these alternatives, which could of course be suggested in dicta, a court could find legislative prayer as presented in *Marsh* unconstitutional without striking down a treasured vestige of the American heritage.

In *Lynch* [*v. Donnelly* [b]] the Court could have recognized that while Nativity scenes have long been a part of American religious folkways, they are traditional, sacral symbols that have no place in front of City Hall. The idea of civil religion could have been successfully employed as a way of distinguishing the Nativity of Christ from the pledge of allegiance and other practices of civil religion that we are willing to accept by pointing to the essentially political character of the pledge, couched in religious terminology though it may be. Moreover, the concerns to which civil religion addresses itself, the fostering of a unified, cohesive sense of social identity for all members of the polity, militate against the erection of a Nativity scene, a religious representation that is meaningful only to some (even if to many) citizens and *not* to others.

To think of other examples: A court could comfortably find a Martin Luther King memorial constitutional, because the significance of his life and words derives not from his stature as a religious leader but as a major participant in one of the great political struggles of American history. A consideration of the values we nurture through our civil religion helps us understand just why it is that we are commemorating Martin Luther King. A constitutional challenge to National Prayer Day could be met by suggesting a National Day of Reflection that would preserve the essentially transcendental character of the day without casting it in traditional, sacral terms. A challenge to the motto "In God We Trust" could be met with the recognition of the importance of a unified national expression of faith, and a suggestion for a less sacral alternative.

The Myth of the Judeo–Christian Tradition (1971).

a. 463 U.S. 783 (1983). In *Marsh* the Court held that a state legislature did not violate the Establishment Clause when it opened its session with an ecumenical prayer by a Christian minister.

b. 465 U.S. 668 (1984). In *Lynch* the Court allowed the City of Pawtucket to erect a nativity scene as part of its annual holiday display.

By familiarizing themselves with the notion of civil religion, courts can develop the tools with which to consider public rituals and symbols within the social and political contexts in which they arise. They could then evaluate them on that basis and, if they concluded that serious establishment clause concerns were implicated by any given practice, could offer creative suggestions that captured the social and political value of the rejected practice, thus taking the sting out of what are, understandably, very politically unpalatable decisions.

C. RELIGION IN PUBLIC SCHOOLS

The role of religion in the public schools is an issue the Supreme Court has had to deal with repeatedly. The Court first applied the establishment clause to the states in 1947.[1] The very next year it took up religious instruction in the public schools. It forbade released-time programs (though it later allowed them off premises).[2] In the 1960's it forbade public schools to compose[3] or recite[4] prayers. The Court also looked at religious influences on the curriculum: it held that states could not prevent the teaching of evolution for religious reasons.[5]

There is some lingering discontent over these decisions, though the rules they announced have proven fairly stable. Religious parents may still desire the same things for their children, but the terms of the debate have changed. Special treatment for religion is now out of the question. The issue is whether religious practices and beliefs are entitled to equal recognition in the public arena, or whether they must be confined entirely to the private sphere.

This is the theme running through all the pieces in this section. We first take up moment-of-silence laws—the modern counterpart to school prayer. We then address the Equal Access Act—an issue that has much in common with released time programs. We conclude with a consideration of the "balanced treatment" of creation science and evolution.

1. A MOMENT OF SILENCE

In *Wallace v. Jaffree*[6] the Supreme Court struck down a moment-of-silence law enacted by the state of Alabama. The Court indicated that it might be willing to uphold some such laws. The problem with Alabama's was that it endorsed prayer during the silent period. But this seems to be an area where the campaign for "equal" or "neutral" treatment of religion will have some future successes.

Walter Dellinger explains how the Alabama law differs from a truly neutral silence law. He adds his own thought that even neutral silence

1. Everson v. Board of Education, 330 U.S. 1 (1947).

2. McCollum v. Board of Education, 333 U.S. 203 (1948); Zorach v. Clauson, 343 U.S. 306 (1952).

3. Engel v. Vitale, 370 U.S. 421 (1962).

4. Abington School District v. Schempp, 374 U.S. 203 (1963).

5. Epperson v. Arkansas, 393 U.S. 97 (1968).

6. 472 U.S. 38 (1985).

laws have an objective religious meaning. Given the cultural context in which they are adopted, communities will understand them as endorsements of religion.

Rodney Smith discusses a number of objections, like Dellinger's, to silence laws. Some say they are unnecessary because students are in any case free to pray whenever they like. Others argue that the benefit of the accommodation (a "moment" for reflection) is too trivial to justify the costs it entails for church-state relations. Smith concedes that there is force to these and other concerns, but he sees still more merit in silence laws. He is particularly impatient with the idea that religion must be kept wholly separate from public education.

WALTER DELLINGER, THE SOUND OF SILENCE: AN EPISTLE ON PRAYER AND THE CONSTITUTION

95 Yale L.J. 1631, 1634–1637 (1986).

Three separate Alabama statutes were originally challenged in *Wallace v. Jaffree*.[a] One provided that teachers could lead all "willing students" in group oral recital of a specified prayer that was set out in the statute. The Supreme Court summarily upheld the invalidation of this statute, thus unanimously reaffirming its original school prayer decision. A second Alabama statute, adopted in 1978, authorized a one-minute period for silent meditation in all public schools. The district court upheld this statute, and the plaintiffs did not challenge it on appeal. The third Alabama statute, adopted in 1981, differed from the preexisting moment-of-silence statute in that it added the words "or voluntary prayer." It was this statute that the Court considered and invalidated in *Jaffree*.

Justice Stevens noted in his Opinion of the Court that the unchallenged 1978 statute fully accomplished the goal of setting aside a moment of silence in which students who chose to pray could do so. Thus the only thing the 1981 silent prayer statute at issue in *Jaffree* added to the earlier moment of silence law was "the State's endorsement and promotion of religion and a particular religious practice." Justice Stevens' opinion, joined by Justices Brennan, Marshall, Blackmun, and Powell, suggests that it is a permissible purpose for a state to adopt legislation "protecting every student's right to engage in voluntary prayer during an appropriate moment of silence during the school day"—a right that the Court said was protected by the earlier, neutral moment-of-silence statute. Such a purpose was, in the Court's view, "quite different from" the "legislative intent to return prayer to the public schools." The thrust of Justice Stevens' opinion for the Court—that the flaw in the statute before the Court was the state's explicit endorsement of "prayer" as an officially approved use of a moment of silence—appears to be fully consistent with the idea that a statute like

a. 472 U.S. 38 (1985).

Alabama's earlier, neutral "moment of silence" law is constitutionally permissible.

* * *

Jaffree's invalidation of a silence law "merely" because it added to pre-existing law the words "or voluntary prayer" has been criticized by those who would have sustained it as unduly fastidious. Justice White, dissenting, read the Alabama legislature's addition of the word "prayer" not as a state suggestion or endorsement of prayer, but rather as an informational device that merely let students know that prayer is one acceptable activity. So read, White suggests, the statute should no more be unconstitutional than would be a teacher answering in the affirmative if a student were to ask if it is permissible to pray during a moment of silence.

The notion that explicit designation of "prayer" in a state statute does not constitute state endorsement or encouragement seems disingenuous. Imagine a state statute providing that a moment of silence be conducted at the beginning of each school day for "meditation or erotic fantasy." Could one plausibly say in that case that the state is being wholly "neutral" with regard to "erotic fantasy," that the statute merely reflects the fact that students can (and some no doubt will) use any period of silence for that purpose? In my view, the seemingly trivial fact of the addition of the word "prayer" crosses the line of constitutionality precisely because it is utterly unnecessary to the goal of creating a formal opportunity for reflection in which students can, if they wish, choose to pray. That purpose is wholly accomplished by a statute or policy that simply provides that a moment of silence be set aside. If a simple moment of silence is created, parents, priests, rabbis, and ministers can, if they wish, suggest to their children or parishioners that they use the moment of silence for prayer. Providing in the state's Code of Laws that "prayer" is a designated activity takes the state itself across a thin line and into the improper business of official endorsement of a religious exercise.

The other apparent conclusion of *Jaffree*—that moment-of-silence statutes not specifically mentioning prayer are constitutionally permissible—is somewhat more problematic. As I continue to reflect on this problem, I become less certain that such laws should be upheld, (even though I remain convinced that the Supreme Court will in fact sustain such statutes). Silence can be a powerful message. Since a normal school day ordinarily includes any number of occasions during which an individual student acting on her own initiative can engage in a moment of silent prayer or reflection, the formal creation in public school classrooms of an organized, teacher-supervised moment of silence is an event that has no readily apparent purpose—unless the government is attempting to convey a message. Even where no textual mention is made of prayer, a community of observers may well perceive that the "meaning" of a school-organized moment of silence is that the government is endorsing something, and that something might be seen as religion.

RODNEY K. SMITH, NOW IS THE TIME FOR REFLECTION: WALLACE v. JAFFREE AND ITS LEGISLATIVE AFTERMATH

37 Ala.L.Rev. 345, 385–388 (1986).

Those who argue against reflection, meditation, or prayer statutes typically raise the following arguments: (1) a moment of meditation is unnecessary because students already may silently pray or meditate whenever they so desire; (2) a moment of reflection or prayer is at best a trivial accommodation of free exercise rights in the public sector, and would carry substantial costs to our system of church-state relations; (3) minority religions and nonreligionists will suffer by virtue of application of a meditation or prayer statute; (4) such statutes reinforce the unfortunate tendency toward government involvement in religious matters; and (5) reflection, meditation, and prayer tend to disrupt the school day and the learning process.

Opponents of meditation or prayer statutes argue that students already may pray silently. To this, Professor Rees has responded:

> The statement is both correct and trivial. One can do anything anywhere so long as one is careful to do it in such a way that nobody notices. The use of the term "right" to denote the fact that one can pray with impunity so long as one prays silently would entail a radical reappraisal of the extent to which human rights should be said to exist in totalitarian and authoritative regimes around the world. In this sense of the word, students have the right to pray in school not only in the United States but also in the Soviet Union. Citizens of South Africa and Cambodia have the right to call for the overthrow of the government as long as they do so silently.[169]

Although Professor Rees's criticism appears at first to be valid, closer examination reveals its flaws. The right to pray silently is different from the right to call for the overthrow of one's government, because one cannot overthrow one's government without some type of overt action. One can engage fully in silent prayer without governmental permission. Nevertheless, providing a period for reflection would facilitate the exercise of the right during a busy school day. * * * The question, then, is whether the government should facilitate individual reflection, meditation, or prayer, or whether it should leave a student to her own devices to fulfill her desire to pray during the school day.

Opponents of reflection or prayer statutes also argue that the right is itself trivial. They note that a minute or moment of meditation, like that provided under the Alabama statute [in *Wallace v. Jaffree* [a]], hardly provides the student with a meaningful opportunity to meditate, pray, or

---

169. [See S.Rep. No. 99–165, 99th   **a.** 472 U.S. 38 (1985).
Cong., 1st Sess. 34–35 (1985).]

reflect on any matter of significance. Proponents, however, reply that any time set aside for serious reflection, meditation, or prayer is at least a symbolic boon to students who desire to reflect upon matters of conscience. While proponents concede that five minutes would be preferable to one, they argue that even an organized minute serves two purposes: it gives the students a structured period in which to reflect, and it shows students that such moments are of value and are a legitimate part of education. Opponents counter that schools should not place even a limited imprimatur on such practices, because those practices may have religious overtones.

In a related sense, opponents argue that organized practices would harm minorities, who find moments of reflection, meditation, or prayer to be offensive. To this, proponents respond that the moments are voluntary in the purest sense of the word, and that the student need not use the time period for religious reflection. Those who argue against such practices generally add that they find the practices particularly offensive when foisted upon young and impressionable children. Young children, in their view, are peculiarly susceptible to institutional pressure and are less capable than adults of ignoring the religious overtones related to such practices. Proponents of reflection must concede that such criticism is not without some substance, and that school officials must be very careful in administering the practices.

Opponents are also concerned that such practices may open the door to increasing government involvement in religious matters. Adherents of this view typically advocate a strict separation of church and state. For advocates of such a position, any modification of the wall of separation between church and state has the potential of bringing the wall down. They feel that the establishment clause should predominate over the free exercise clause because the dangers of establishment are greater than the benefits of free exercise. Proponents of free exercise counter that the proper relationship between church and state, particularly in a society characterized by a pervasive public sector, is one of cautious accommodation, not one of strict separation. They add that principles can be developed to guard against excesses, thereby effectuating the establishment clause without limiting free exercise.

Finally, Senator Mathias, an opponent of moments of silent reflection or prayer, has argued, "Today, our public school classrooms are supposed to be dedicated to learning. But [if moments of silence are upheld,] they could be given over, once or twice or ten times a day, to devotional exercises." [173] This is really a version of what may be termed the "hocus-pocus" argument. In this regard, some opponents of all religious or potentially religious activities or exercises in the public schools argue that religion or matters of conscience are and must be kept wholly separate from the learning or educational process. For them, schools are organized to teach "facts," not to dwell on religious material,

---

173. *See* [Senate Comm. on the Judiciary, 99th Cong., 1st Sess., Transcript of the Proceedings on S.J.Res. 2, at 58 (Comm. Print 1985).]

doctrine, or related "hocus-pocus." The "hocus-pocus" view lurks behind some of the opposition to recognizing any role for individual religious exercise in public education, because for those who hold this view, religion is anathema to education. Those who favor some role for religious exercise or matters of conscience in the public sector rarely have to counter this argument. Although some opponents of religious exercise are at heart antireligious and may adhere to the view that religion is "hocus-pocus," such a view is intolerant and demeans the individual's right of choice. It belies an intolerance on the part of the antireligionist that rivals the intolerance of some religionists who have persecuted unacceptable sects throughout history.

2. EQUAL ACCESS

In *Board of Education v. Mergens*[1] the Supreme Court upheld the federal Equal Access Act, which requires secondary schools receiving federal aid to let religious student groups use school premises on the same terms as other student groups. This includes religious groups, like the one in *Mergens*, that want to read the Bible and pray together. This is, like moment-of-silence laws, an area where the appeal for equal treatment of religion has proven persuasive.

Geoffrey Stone says that equal access is *permitted* by the establishment clause. He is chiefly concerned with responding to those who argue that it is *required* by the free speech and free exercise clauses. Stone explains that there is a difference between laws that disadvantage a particular denomination (something our First Amendment freedoms strictly forbid) and laws that disadvantage religion in general (something our freedoms allow, but only where there is a substantial government interest). Equal access is a question of the latter type.

Ruti Teitel takes a third position on equal access: she thinks that it is *forbidden* by the establishment clause. Teitel argues that when the government lets religious groups meet on school property during school hours, it confers a number of benefits on religion. These include not only tangible aid (like rent-free space), but also the imprimatur of government approval. Such aid, she claims, is forbidden by the "effects" prong of the test in *Lemon v. Kurtzman*.[2] (You should ask yourself whether this argument retains much force after the Court's decision to approve monetary aid in *Rosenberger v. Rector and Visitors of the University of Virginia*.[3])

GEOFFREY R. STONE, THE EQUAL ACCESS CONTROVERSY: THE RELIGION CLAUSES AND THE MEANING OF "NEUTRALITY"
81 Nw.U.L.Rev. 168–173 (1986).

There are three basic positions in the controversy over equal access of student religious groups to public school facilities: (1) The free speech

1. 496 U.S. 226 (1990).
2. 403 U.S. 602, 612 (1971).
3. 115 S.Ct. 2510 (1995).

and free exercise clauses require public schools to grant religious groups the same access that they grant nonreligious groups; (2) the establishment clause requires public schools to deny access to religious groups even if they grant access to nonreligious groups; and (3) the Constitution does not dictate a result, thus permitting public schools to decide for themselves whether to grant religious groups equal access to school facilities. * * * In my view, the third position best accommodates the conflicting constitutional interests. The Constitution requires public schools neither to exclude religious groups from public school facilities nor to grant such groups equal access.

[Those who adopt the first position rely on the principle that] "the Constitution requires the government to be neutral toward religion." Thus, if a public school permits nonreligious groups to meet in school facilities, the premise of neutrality requires the school to grant access to religious groups as well. Neutrality, however, is not a self-defining concept. Its meaning may vary depending on the context and nature of the issue. Consider, for example, the fourteenth amendment's guarantee that no state shall deny any person the equal protection of the laws. Under this guarantee, a state must grant equal protection to opticians and optometrists, to men and women, to blacks and whites. But the meaning of equal protection will vary depending on the nature of the classification. Different classifications threaten the values underlying the guarantee of equal protection in different ways. Accordingly, different classifications must be tested by different standards of review. The same is true of neutrality.

* * *

The Supreme Court's analysis of political expression provides a useful analogy. The protection of political speech, like religious speech, lies at the very core of the first amendment. The Court often has recognized, however, that government may grant special benefits to nonpolitical speech without extending those benefits to political speech, so long as it does not expressly favor any particular political viewpoint. In *Lehman v. City of Shaker Heights,*[6] the Court upheld the constitutionality of a city's policy permitting the interior of its transit vehicles to be leased for the display of commercial messages, while excluding all political messages. In *Greer v. Spock,*[7] the Court upheld the constitutionality of a military base's policy permitting civilian speakers to address military personnel on subjects ranging from business management to drug abuse, while prohibiting speech of a partisan political nature. And in *Cornelius v. NAACP Legal Defense and Educational Fund,*[8] the Court upheld the constitutionality of an Executive Order permitting charitable organizations to solicit contributions from federal employees through the Combined Federal Campaign, while excluding political advocacy organizations from the campaign.

6. 418 U.S. 298 (1974).   **8.** 473 U.S. 788 (1985).

7. 424 U.S. 828 (1976).

As these decisions illustrate, governmental policies that disadvantage political speech as a class trigger standards of review that are less stringent than those appropriate for policies that expressly disadvantage specific political viewpoints. This is because policies that disadvantage political speech as a class are less threatening to first amendment values than laws that expressly disadvantage specific points of view.

A similar principle governs religious expression. As the Supreme Court has long recognized, the "clearest command" of the religion clauses is that "one religious denomination cannot be officially preferred over another." [11] Any law that expressly grants "a denominational preference" is "suspect" and must be tested by "strict scrutiny in adjudging its constitutionality." Denominational discrimination in the religious context is the analog of viewpoint discrimination in the political context. Governmental policies that expressly discriminate against specific religious denominations are therefore appropriately tested by the same stringent standards of review that the Court uses to test the constitutionality of governmental policies that expressly discriminate against specific political viewpoints. The corollary is also true, however. Governmental policies that grant special benefits to nonreligious expression as a class should be tested by the same—less demanding—standards that the Court uses to test the constitutionality of governmental policies that grant special benefits to nonpolitical expression as a class. In the religious, as in the political, realm the broader subject-matter classification is less threatening to core first amendment values.

The equal access controversy does not pose an issue of denominational discrimination. The decision not to grant equal access to religious groups distinguishes not between Jews and Christians or Buddhists and Mormons, but between religious and nonreligious expression. The demands of neutrality must be defined against this backdrop.

* * *

I do not mean to suggest that classifications between religious and nonreligious expression are unproblematic. To the contrary, governmental policies that grant special benefits to nonreligious over religious expression pose serious first amendment questions. Such policies should be upheld only when they serve substantial governmental interests. Nevertheless, they do not violate the "clearest command" of the first amendment, and it is important to кeep denomination-based restrictions distinct from those that deal with religious expression as a class.

Two decisions—*Tinker v. Des Moines Independent School District* [17] and *Widmar v. Vincent* [18]—are generally cited in support of the proposition that the first amendment requires public schools to grant religious groups the same access to public school facilities that they grant to nonreligious groups. In *Tinker,* several students were suspended from school for wearing black armbands to protest the war in Vietnam.

---

11. Larson v. Valente, 456 U.S. 228, 244 (1982)[.]

17. 393 U.S. 503 (1969).

18. 454 U.S. 263 (1981).

School officials defended this action on the ground that the armbands would generate controversy and distract students from their schoolwork. The Supreme Court held that the suspensions violated the first amendment. The Court observed that students do not "shed their constitutional rights to freedom of speech or expression at the schoolhouse gate" and that the challenged restriction could not be sustained without proof that the prohibited expression would " 'materially and substantially interfere with ... the operation of the school.' "

Tinker does not govern the equal access controversy. The rule held unconstitutional in *Tinker* was expressly viewpoint-based. As the Court emphasized, the "school authorities did not purport to prohibit the wearing of all symbols of political or controversial significance." Rather, "a particular symbol—black armbands worn to exhibit opposition to this Nation's involvement in Vietnam—was singled out for prohibition." This fact—that the challenged restriction involved the "prohibition of expression of one particular opinion"—was central to the Court's analysis. The analogy in the religion context would be a school rule permitting students to wear all religious symbols except the Star of David. While that rule would be barred by *Tinker,* the equal access controversy poses no such issue.

In *Widmar,* the Supreme Court held that "a state university, which makes its facilities generally available for the activities of registered student groups," cannot constitutionally "close its facilities to a registered student group desiring to use the facilities for religious worship and religious discussion." The Court explained that, by making its facilities available to more than 100 student organizations, the university voluntarily had created a public forum and that, in order to justify a content-based exclusion from a public forum, the university would have to show that the exclusion was "necessary to serve a compelling state interest."

The decision in *Widmar* was premised on the doctrine that even subject-matter exclusions from a public forum are unconstitutional unless necessary to serve a compelling state interest. Thus, in *Widmar* the exclusion of religious expression as a class was tested by stringent standards of review. But public high schools, junior high schools, and elementary schools are not universities, and courts should resist declaring them public forums. Unlike universities, public schools pose special problems of compelled attendance, they are expressly dedicated to the inculcation and "preservation of ... values," and, as the Supreme Court itself noted in *Widmar,* they deal with students who are more "impressionable" than university students and less able to appreciate that a school's equal access policy reflects neutrality toward, rather than endorsement of, religion. None of these considerations is sufficient to justify a denomination-based exclusion from public school facilities. A denial of equal access to all religious groups is less threatening to first amendment values, however, and, at least in the public school context, should be tested by a less demanding standard of justification.

Public school officials should be free to decide for themselves—free of constitutional compulsion—whether to grant religious groups equal access to school facilities. The denial of equal access to religious groups need not be necessary to serve a compelling state interest in order to be constitutionally valid. The more appropriate standard is whether the exclusion serves a substantial state interest. Under that standard, the outcome seems clear. Just as government often has a substantial interest in accommodating free exercise values, even when a decision not to accommodate would not violate the free exercise clause, so too the government may accommodate establishment values even when a decision not to accommodate would not violate the establishment clause. Thus, although a school's decision to grant equal access to religious groups may not violate the establishment clause, this access clearly poses a serious threat to core establishment clause concerns, such as implied endorsement, entanglement, and potential conflict along religious lines. In these circumstances, the decision to deny equal access does not violate the Constitution.[30]

RUTI TEITEL, THE UNCONSTITUTIONALITY OF EQUAL ACCESS POLICIES AND LEGISLATION ALLOWING ORGANIZED STUDENT–INITIATED RELIGIOUS ACTIVITIES IN THE PUBLIC HIGH SCHOOLS: A PROPOSAL FOR A UNITARY FIRST AMENDMENT FORUM ANALYSIS

12 Hastings Const.L.Q. 529, 559, 562–564, 566–567, 571–572 (1985).

The second prong of the *Lemon* establishment test proscribes any government sponsorship of activities and policies that have the effect of advancing religion, regardless of the government's otherwise secular intent.[142] * * *

* * *

Government confers a number of benefits on religion when religious meetings are organized in the public schools: the provision of the free use of tax-financed classrooms, heat and light, free monitoring by teachers or government authorities, and the use of state compulsory attendance laws to gather an audience all combine to promote religious practice and education. In considering the constitutionality of outside religious instructors coming into the public schools to teach, the Court in *McCollum* [*v. Board of Education*] held that use of rent-free classrooms, together with the benefit derived from the state compulsory attendance

---

30. The understanding of neutrality set forth in this Article has implications for issues beyond the equal access controversy. Consider, for example, a law granting a full tuition tax credit for attendance at all private, nonparochial schools. Although such a law is not neutral with respect to religion, it is consistent with the core command of denominational equality. In light of the state's substantial interest in not supporting religious education, such a law might well pass constitutional muster. * * *

142. Lemon v. Kurtzman, 403 U.S. 602, 612 (1971).

laws, constituted an unconstitutional establishment.[170] The attendance laws provided the benefit of gathering a student audience for proselytizing purposes. In *Abington School District v. Schempp,* the Court reaffirmed the *McCollum* holding and recognized the additional benefit posed by free teacher supervision of religious activities.[172]

The Equal Access Act, by allowing religious clubs to meet on classroom public school premises, under teacher supervision and at times associated with the school day, extends to school religious clubs that government aid deemed to be impermissible in *McCollum* and *Abington,* including classroom space, heat and light, free teacher monitoring, and the benefit of state compulsory school attendance laws.

Whether equal access would be similarly unconstitutional if restricted to times *not* contiguous with the public school day—and thus not benefitting from state attendance laws—is unclear. At issue is whether the financial benefit attendant to the rent-free use of the public school premises is itself sufficient to render government aid to religion unconstitutional. In *McCollum,* unconstitutional benefit derived from both the rent-free use of the school premises and the compulsory attendance machinery. In *Widmar* [*v. Vincent*], on the other hand, no state law compelled university classroom attendance and the Court permitted the equal access club the use of the classrooms. Other nonclassroom costs related to student clubs were borne not by taxpayers but rather were paid for out of student fees.[177]

The chief distinction appears to be the purpose and function of the forum. In *Widmar,* where the government property at issue was a public forum, the benefit derived from its use was held to be per se incidental. In contrast, as concerns the public schools, which are not public forums, the rent-free use of the premises may be enough to constitute unconstitutional government aid. Thus, although the Court has not yet ruled on this point, even weekend use of the public schools on a rent-free or artificially low rent basis may afford an unconstitutional benefit to religion.

* * *

The Establishment Clause bars not only government benefit to religion in the tangible forms discussed above, but also bars "imprimatur," or government endorsement or the appearance of an endorsement which will unconstitutionally advance religion. * * * The inquiry is twofold. It measures objective indicia of government approval of a religious activity; and it encompasses a subjective component—the perception of government endorsement.

* * *

170.   333 U.S. 203, 209–10 (1948).
172.   374 U.S. at 223.
177.   454 U.S. [263,] 274 (1981). [In *Widmar* the Court held that a state university which made its facilities generally available for the activities of student groups could not exclude student religious groups.]

Numerous objective factors constitute government endorsement when equal access clubs are organized in the schools: school approval of the club, allotment of club time during the school day, the benefit of state compulsory attendance, teacher supervision of the clubs, and use of school media.

* * *

Central to the presumption of sponsorship in the public schools is the youth and impressionability of school children. This subjective factor compounds the objective government sponsorship to create an even greater appearance of government endorsement of religious activities organized in the public schools.

The Supreme Court has discussed this perception of government sponsorship in its decisions striking religious activities in the public schools, and in its decisions sustaining organized prayer in other forums. The Court held in *Widmar* that a university equal access policy "does not confer any imprimatur of State approval on religious sects or practices." In the university, the absence of imprimatur of state approval is due to both the absence of objective imprimatur indicia, such as university recognition of the clubs, state compulsory attendance, and teacher supervision, and to the absence of what might be termed "subjective imprimatur." Subjective imprimatur is missing because university students are "young adults" and therefore "less impressionable" than younger students, who might view the extent of state action or sponsorship as approval.

3. CREATION SCIENCE

The science curriculum is one area where the argument for equal treatment of religion has not fared well. After the Court held that states could not forbid the teaching of evolution, Louisiana passed a law requiring schools to give "balanced treatment" to evolution and so-called creation science. In *Edwards v. Aguillard*[1] the Court held that this law violated the establishment clause because it had no secular purpose.

Why do appeals to equality, neutrality, and "balance" fail here? Steven Goldberg suggests it is because of the special place we give to science in First Amendment law. Louisiana's law had a religious basis, but there is nothing unique about that. Sodomy laws do too, and they don't violate the establishment clause. The difference, Goldberg claims, lies in the force that each law collides with. Science is the darling of the First Amendment, whose purpose (in part) is to prevent a repeat of Galileo's case. Science should not be frustrated in the name of religion.

Stephen Carter finds this a curious reading of the First Amendment which, after all, mentions religion and not science. Carter acknowledges that creationism is bad science. But that has no bearing on whether it is constitutional. Indeed, it does not even show that creationism is false. The Christian fundamentalist theory of knowledge begins with herme-

1. 482 U.S. 578 (1987).

neutics, not science. We cannot dismiss it as irrational for that reason
alone. And when we require children raised in that tradition to adopt
another point of view in school, we seem to be engaged in the very sort
of indoctrination that the liberal tradition forbids.

STEVEN GOLDBERG, THE CONSTITUTIONAL STATUS OF AMERICAN SCIENCE

1979 U.Ill.L.F. 1–10.

Because the United States Constitution says little about science
explicitly, analysis of the role of science in American society is not
perceived as having an important constitutional dimension. Yet numerous provisions of the Constitution have the intent and effect of shaping
the relationship between government and science. The result is that the
Constitution contains an *implied* science clause: Congress may legislate
the establishment of science, but shall not prohibit the free exercise of
scientific speech.

* * *

A. HISTORICAL PERSPECTIVE

Veneration of science was a central tenet of eighteenth century
Enlightenment thinking, for science was believed to illuminate not
merely natural phenomena but political and theological matters as well.
Isaac Newton was not simply revered; he was nearly deified. Leading
Americans of the Revolutionary Era shared this Enlightenment view.
Science and public affairs were so closely related that any distinction
between scientific and political leaders is difficult to maintain. Ritten-
house and Rush, the leading astronomer and physician of the day, were
important office holders and political figures. Both were close friends of
Jefferson, whose scientific interests, particularly in the field of natural
history, are well known. Madison too was intrigued with natural
history, while Hamilton studied medicine, enjoyed mathematics, and
urged friends to learn chemistry to improve their thinking. With Ben
Franklin, the boundary between scientist and statesman dissolves altogether. One of the world's leading physicists and America's foremost
Ambassador, Franklin was, to many European *philosophes,* the Enlightenment incarnate.

The science that so appealed to America's founders, and that continues to be valued today, was an outgrowth of the revolutionary advances
in astronomy and physics associated with Galileo and Newton. It was
characterized by reliance on empirical data as opposed to sacred texts or
royal pronouncements, and by an effort to use man's knowledge of
nature to improve the human condition. Scholars have devoted considerable attention to the way in which infatuation with this type of science
affected the building of political institutions; the way, for example, in

which Newton's laws of motion may have inspired the constitutional system of checks and balances. But the building of a clockwork Constitution accounts for only half of the science-government relationship. The Constitution that results has an impact on the further development of science.

* * *

The establishment clause was designed for many purposes, some of them conflicting. One purpose was to prevent the suppression of enlightened science by the Church. Thus, in his "Memorial and Remonstrance Against Religious Assessments," Madison argues that fifteen centuries of establishment Christianity resulted in "superstition" on the part of clergy and laity alike. The centerpiece of Jefferson's attack on established religion in *Notes on the State of Virginia* is a pointed history of science and religion: "Galileo was sent to the Inquisition for affirming that the earth was a sphere; the government had declared it to be as flat as a trencher, and Galileo was obliged to abjure his error. This error, however, at length prevailed, the earth became a globe ...."

The Jeffersonian wall between church and state was designed in part to protect American Galileos. In this respect, the free exercise and establishment clauses are complementary. Some religions may rely on dogma to the detriment of science while others believe scientific inquiry enhances God's glory. Thus nonestablishment combined with free exercise encourages people * * * to pursue their researches. Throughout American history, the religious tolerance built into the first amendment has bolstered American science. American Quakers, for example, whose faith encourages scientific endeavor, made major contributions to American science beginning in the eighteenth century.

The speech and press clauses were also designed in part to further progress in science. Milton, the leading influence on colonial ideas of free speech, was influenced greatly by a visit he made to the exiled Galileo. The *Areopagitica,* a basic source to this day on the evils of licensing speech, describes Milton's trip to Italy where he "found and visited the famous Galileo, grown old, a prisoner to the Inquisition, for thinking in astronomy otherwise than the Franciscan and Dominican licensers thought."

* * *

B. THE MODERN ESTABLISHMENT CLAUSE

Modern judicial interpretations of the establishment, speech, and press clauses accord science the protected status envisioned by the framers of the Constitution. The establishment clause played a decisive role in the twentieth century successor to the dispute between Galileo and the church. Just as astronomy displaced man from the center of the universe, the theory of evolution displaced man from his special status among the earth's inhabitants. In the case of evolution, the establishment clause resolved the resulting religion-science dispute in favor of science.

The evolution controversy came before the Supreme Court in *Epperson v. Arkansas*,[37] a 1968 challenge to the constitutionality of an Arkansas statute prohibiting the teaching of evolution. The challenge was successful because the case was a dispute between religion and science. An amicus brief demonstrated to the Court that science was in fact at stake by including a statement signed by 179 biologists asserting that evolution "is firmly established even as the rotundity of the earth is firmly established." The brief for the appellants, in a passage with roots in the eighteenth century, argued that the uninformed use "all forms of physical and mental torture, to maintain the status quo of their unenlightenment and their accepted beliefs." During oral argument, counsel for the State was asked, "What if Arkansas would forbid the theory that the world is round?" And the Court's opinion, in striking down the statute under the establishment clause, featured excerpts from arguments against fundamentalist religion generally.

Commentary on *Epperson* has tended to focus on the doctrinal point that the Court found the statute unconstitutional because it had been enacted for a religious purpose. Such inquiries into purpose or motive are quite rare in religion cases, and *Epperson* hardly seemed a likely candidate. The Court's proof of an illegal purpose consisted merely of citation to newspaper advertisements, letters to the editor, and law review articles. No statement of any legislator was included. In other cases where a religious purpose seems likely, the Court has declined to find one or even to look very hard for one. Academic emphasis on purpose or motive in the usual sense is misplaced here. The Court's scrutiny of the statute was more intense than in the usual establishment case because the competing value at stake was science. Indeed, the Court said as much: "The State's undoubted right to prescribe the curriculum for its public schools does not carry with it the right to prohibit, on pain of criminal penalty, the teaching of a scientific theory or doctrine where that prohibition is based upon reasons that violate the First Amendment." The Arkansas statute's improper purpose was not to aid religion, but rather to aid religion at the expense of science.

Subsequent decisions have made this point more clear. Disputes about evolution continue in part because of the resurgence in recent years of American fundamentalism, including a "creationist" movement which has leveled continuing attacks on the theory of evolution. * * *

* * *

To analyze these decisions as religion cases, without reference to the role of science, is misleading. Consider, by comparison, application of the establishment clause to state laws against homosexuality. Those laws, at least as much as evolution laws, are religious in origin in every meaningful sense. They derive directly from specific Biblical passages,

---

37.   393 U.S. 97 (1968).

and the offense in question was defined traditionally as "the abominable sin not fit to be named among Christians." Furthermore, homosexuality laws cannot be analogized for constitutional purposes to criminal laws, like those against murder, which have religious roots but have taken on a secular purpose. Unlike laws against murder, laws against homosexuality are retained in larger measure because of religious pressure, and many homosexual crimes affect only consenting adults. Yet establishment clause challenges to the laws against homosexuality have failed uniformly. Moreover, in decisions involving homosexuality, courts often go out of their way to *rely* on the Biblical origins of the laws. Citations to Leviticus are routine; sodomy cases are replete with references to Sodom and Gomorrah.

If a teacher were fired for teaching that homosexuality is acceptable, the establishment clause would not protect him in court. Similarly, if a textbook presents slanted arguments against homosexuality, establishment clause challenges would fail. The establishment clause cannot be understood solely as a statement about religion; its content depends upon the context in which religion is operating. When religion shapes our moral standards, constitutional scrutiny is more lax than when religion shapes our scientific standards. Analyzing the evolution decisions without reference to the constitutional status of science is like analyzing a steam engine without reference to the steam.

STEPHEN L. CARTER, EVOLUTIONISM, CREATIONISM, AND TREATING RELIGION AS A HOBBY

1987 Duke L.J. 977, 979–984, 992–994.

THE CREATION SCIENCE CONUNDRUM

* * *

Although creationists are quick to point out that many of those who support their view of the origin of earth and of life hold advanced degrees in the sciences, it would, I suspect, be an error to suppose that many creationists came to their views by a careful study of scientific evidence. The liberal critic may be right to say that creationism is bad science. But why should that issue be the crucial one? Creationists are not irrational merely because they are unscientific. Creationism was not created from thin air; creation theory developed as a consequence of the preferred hermeneutical method of many Christian fundamentalists for understanding the world. This hermeneutical approach is best expressed by the combination of the following propositions drawn from the Articles of Affirmation and Denial adopted in 1982 by the International Council on Biblical Inerrancy: (1) "the normative authority of Holy Scripture is the authority of God Himself"; (2) "the Bible expresses God's truth in propositional statements, and . . . biblical truth is both objective and absolute"; (3) "since God is the author of all truth, all truths, biblical and extrabiblical, are consistent and cohere, and . . . the

Bible speaks truth when it touches on matters pertaining to nature, history, or anything else"; and (4) "Genesis 1–11 is factual, as is the rest of the book." [8]

Critics of scientific creationism may doubt the validity of these propositions, but there is hardly any room for doubt that those who profess them are sincere. And once the adherent of this literalist hermeneutic states these propositions, what chance is there that the theory of evolution is correct? Virtually none. Evolution is just a theory, scientific creationists insist, and must, as a theory, be open to challenge. And challenge it they do, pointing to mountains of exceptions and inexplicable transitions. To the Biblical literalist, however, the most important evidence against evolution theory is not the complexity of the fossil record or the troubling matter of falsification, but the beginning of the Book of Genesis, comprising, as one creationist has written, "eleven chapters of straightforward Bible history which cannot be reinterpreted in any satisfactory way."

I emphasize these points because I believe that critics often overlook that there is a nontrivial hermeneutic and a rational application of it behind the creationist rejection of evolutionary theory. The creationist position is no mindless assault on modernism in general or on secular science in particular, although obviously it contains elements of hostility to both. Nor do the "equal time" statutes necessarily represent officially authorized proselytizing. It is something of a commonplace in liberal theory to treat the parental attempts to control the school curriculum as though the parents are trying to impose their own religious beliefs on others, but I very much doubt that this vision is a realistic one. More likely, the parents are frightened of the conflict between religious authority on the one hand, and the authority of secular society—as represented by the schools—on the other.

These parents, very devout and very worried, are trying to protect the core of their own beliefs. It is not that the parents want the public schools to proselytize in their favor; it is rather that they do not want the schools to press their own children to reject what the parents believe by calling into question a central article of their faith. The response of the Christian fundamentalist to evolutionary theory may thus be more consistently viewed as a reaction to a fear of indoctrination: religion demands one intellectual position, and the state seeks to command another. Liberalism is curiously intolerant of what certainly may be viewed as a classic case of conscience interposed before the authority of the state. Nor have the consciences of the protestors been formed without any thought. They understand quite well that the hermeneutic they have chosen has interpretive implications, not just for the Bible, but for the entire natural world, and devout literalists understand and accept them. The creationist parents are not a superstitious rabble.

---

8. *The Chicago Statement on Biblical Hermeneutics, reprinted in* A Guide to Contemporary Hermeneutics: Major Trends in Biblical Interpretation 21, 22–25 (D. McKim ed. 1986).

They are independent thinkers who insist on a right to their own means for seeking knowledge of the world, and they deny the right of the state to tell their children that their worldview is wrong.

On this vision, a public school curriculum perceived as secular and modernist is a grave and obvious threat to the efforts of parents to raise their children in their religious belief with its hermeneutical implications. Thus, the question that moves the debate—who shall control the education of children?—is starkly posed. Liberalism may insist that the public schools should be neutral on questions of religious belief, but the parents will no doubt protest that this insistence is simply window dressing for something more sinister. What the schools are offering, the parents will charge, is not a neutral curriculum, but one that can only call into question—or place into ridicule—their most cherished religious beliefs. For those whose Biblical hermeneutic insists on literalism and inerrancy, the tension between a disdainful science and an unchallengeable core belief is plain.

One early response to the tension was the effort to ban the teaching of Darwinian evolution. Many have forgotten that in the *Scopes* case [12] this ban was justified not as a means of protecting a particular religious view from contradiction, but rather as a way of easing the move toward modernization of the science curriculum in the public schools of Tennessee. In affirming the conviction of Mr. Scopes for teaching evolution theory, the state supreme court held that the legislature could make the judgment that popular prejudice would make a sophisticated science curriculum impossible unless, at least for the short term, the curriculum omitted all discussion of the origin of humanity. This justification might have been a smokescreen, but if sincere, it was neither foolish nor venal. It might even represent a compromise between the demands of some citizens for a modern science course for their children, and the insistence of others that the state not trivialize their core religious beliefs.

I do not mean this to be taken as a call to ban the teaching of evolution, but only as a suggestion that the ban might, in some set of historical circumstances, have represented wise policy. Of course, historical circumstances may change, and by the time the Supreme Court, in *Epperson v. Arkansas,*[14] brushed aside a ban on the teaching of evolution as a plain violation of the establishment clause, the statutes still on the books in many states apparently were not being enforced. The tension, however, had not died. With the political rebirth of the Christian fundamentalist movement beginning in the mid-seventies, the objection of parents to what their schools were teaching took on a new form, driven by a new insight: in a political world emphasizing rationality and pluralism, the effort of parents to protect their children from what they considered antireligious indoctrination by the state would have to present itself as both rational and pluralistic. By calling their

12. Scopes v. State, 154 Tenn. 105, 117–18, 289 S.W. 363, 366 (1927).

14. 393 U.S. 97, 107–09 (1968).

interpretive conclusions "science," the parents chose a fresh face that would, they hoped, survive constitutional scrutiny.

The courts, however, have viewed this fresh face as a subterfuge. The Supreme Court, in *Edwards v. Aguillard*,[15] has rejected entirely the effort to make creation theory a part of the science curriculum, but the judicial hostility predates *Edwards*. Certainly, there was little sympathy in the forceful opinion of Judge Overton in *McLean v. Arkansas Board of Education*,[16] the first federal court case dealing with the merits of a facially neutral statute requiring equal classroom time for evolution and creation. * * *

* * *

Judge Overton * * * relied on expert testimony to conclude that scientific creationism could not pass the establishment clause test because *it was not science.* * * * It is as though the command of the first amendment is not to cherish religion, but to cherish science.[21]

From the beginning, the constitutional case against creationism seemed bound up inextricably with the scientific case against it. This seems to me a profoundly mistaken course. A statute simply cannot be said to further religion on the ground that a majority of scientists do not believe that it furthers science. So what if the "scientific" case for creationism is appallingly shoddy and naive? What has this to do with constitutionality?

We live in a world in which epistemology may sometimes reflect religious belief—a world in which religious belief may move people to decide, quite sincerely, whether to accept or reject both moral and factual propositions. Consequently, there is little except the conflict with science to distinguish religiously motivated legislation requiring the teaching of creation theory from religiously motivated legislation to implement the Biblical injunction "Thou shalt do no murder"—or religiously motivated legislation in response to the Roman Catholic bishops' call for a more equitable sharing of the nation's wealth. A prohibition of murder, like a forced redistribution of wealth, might be religiously motivated; but only the teaching of creationism conflicts with natural science.

* * *

COPING WITH FAITH: RELIGION AS HOBBY

Suppose * * * that every member of the legislature accepts the hermeneutic of a literally inerrant Bible. Suppose that the same legislature now examines the curriculum. The legislators are furious to learn

---

15. [482 U.S. 578] (1987).

16. 529 F.Supp. 1255 (E.D.Ark.1982), *aff'd,* 723 F.2d 45 (8th Cir.1983).

21. Steven Goldberg has deduced from the Constitution's language and history what he calls the "implied science clause,"

which holds that "Congress may legislate the establishment of science, but shall not prohibit the free exercise of scientific speech." Goldberg, *The Constitutional Status of American Science,* 1979 U.Ill.L.F. 1, 1.

that only evolution theory is offered in the science classroom. The liberal critic might say that the legislators are furious because evolution runs counter to the teachings of their religion, but to make that the end of the matter is simplistic. Yes, the teachings of evolutionary theory are doubtless contrary to what the legislators hear in church and read in the Bible, but they are more than that, too. To the devout fundamentalist who accepts the principles of literalism and inerrancy, evolution theory is not simply contrary to religious teachings; it is *false*. Nor is it false in some intuitive or metaphysical sense. Based on the interpretive tools with which members of the legislature are accustomed to understanding the universe, it is *demonstrably* false.

The liberal, convinced that the legislative tools are bad ones and that the tools of science are superior, might shift into epistemology, contending that science deals with *knowledge* about the natural world, and is based on evidence, whereas religion is simply a system of *belief,* based on faith. One may criticize the implicit balancing of the relative merits of empirical evidence and spiritual faith, and many have done so. But I am not even sure why the legislators should concede the initial proposition, that one involves knowledge and the other does not. Here, I am put in mind of Wittgenstein, who observed:

> But I might also say: It has been revealed to me by God that it is so. God has taught me that this is my foot. And therefore if anything happened that seemed to conflict with this knowledge I should have to regard *that* as deception.[43]

This, of course, is precisely the logic that motivates many Christian fundamentalists to oppose the teaching of evolution or support the teaching of creation theory. They are informed by God's revelation; no artifice of mortal man can contradict that; and any "evidence" that the revelation is incorrect is either erroneous or deceptive.

This is the worldview of Christian fundamentalists. This is more than what they believe. In any sensible use of the word, this is what they *know*. Their fury that their children are taught in school something contrary to what they know to be true is like the fury of the black parents when my eighth-grade history teacher told us about the happiness of the slaves. There is no apparent reason to take the fury of the creationist parents less seriously, once one grants their right to their own epistemological choice.

If on the other hand the liberal refuses to accept the claim that the devout religionist knows rather than simply believes, then the argument that religion is nevertheless cherished stumbles near the edge of a frightening and perhaps unbridgeable precipice, yawning with the prospect of the humiliating dismissal of what liberal thought claims to cherish. If the arguments of the parents offended by the teaching of evolution are entitled to less weight than the arguments of the parents

43. L. Wittgenstein, On Certainty 47e   1969).
para. 361 (D. Paul & G. Anscombe trans.

offended by the teaching of racist history, the reason must surely be that the second set of arguments is clothed in an appeal to liberal rationality and the first is not. The black parents, perhaps, can "prove" the racist history wrong; whereas the "proofs" offered by the creationist parents are irrational, which is to say, crazy.

* * *

If * * * liberalism continues paying lip-service to a principle of "neutrality" while in effect permitting official indoctrination in a philosophy that runs contrary to deeply held religious beliefs—then what is left for the parents who want to rear their children in a belief in Biblical inerrancy? One possibility is exit: the parents might try, after the example of the Amish, to have their children excused from the objectionable instruction. This solution, however, has three obvious difficulties. First, by being forced to be the ones to opt out, to act differently from their classmates, the children whose parents oppose the teaching of evolution risk all the psychological trauma usually cited by liberals as the reason that an opting-out privilege cannot save the constitutionality of organized prayer in the public school classroom. Second, there is a dramatic slippery slope problem, as one imagines parents removing their children from one course after another because of conflict with religious knowledge, until, finally, the children are no longer receiving any education apart from home instruction. Third, as we know from *Mozert v. Hawkins County Public Schools*,[46] when parents do try to remove their children from objectionable courses of instruction, the state may try to keep the children in class. By refusing to excuse the children from instruction, the school would be telling the parents what Justice Douglas implied in his partial dissent in *Wisconsin v. Yoder*:[47] your children's education is not yours to choose.

D. AID TO PAROCHIAL SCHOOLS

The issue of government aid to parochial schools has received more of the Supreme Court's attention than any other question arising under the establishment clause. In part that can be explained by the political power of the contending forces requesting and opposing such assistance. But the other half of the explanation is the intrinsic difficulty of the legal questions that aid presents. It is in this context that the Court formulated the three-part rule that it used to apply across the board in establishment clause cases. Under *Lemon v. Kurtzman*[1] the Court asked about purpose, effect, and entanglement.

The Court regularly held that the government had acceptable secular purposes for giving aid to parochial schools. They do, after all,

46. 647 F.Supp. 1194 (E.D.Tenn.1986) (rejecting state's effort to force students to use textbooks offensive to parents' religious views), *rev'd sub nom.* Mozert v. Hawkins County Bd. of Educ., 827 F.2d 1058 (6th Cir.1987), *cert. denied,* 56 U.S.L.W. 3569 (1988).

47. *See* 406 U.S. 205, 244–45 (1972) (Douglas, J., dissenting in part)[.]

1. 403 U.S. 602 (1971).

provide a good education for their students, and that is something we want all young people to have. The hard questions always had to do with effects and entanglement. The articles by Freund and Garvey in this section focus on the problem of religious effects.

Paul Freund, writing before *Lemon* was decided, explores the effects that school aid has on taxpayers and the patrons of parochial schools. He argues that by withholding assistance we can best promote the establishment clause values of voluntarism, mutual abstention (of church and state), and neutrality. Implicit in his analysis is the assumption that any form of aid to the educational process promotes the religious objectives of religious schools.

John Garvey examines that assumption in some detail. He argues that it is sometimes true and sometimes false. Grants for tuition or for construction, for example, will inevitably promote the religious mission of parochial schools. But we should be careful about making the same assumption about tax deductions and assistance in kind, whether of materials (like books and maps) or of services (like remedial reading and math). Garvey's detailed analysis suggests, contrary to popular belief, that the Court's school aid rules are fairly sensible. There are a few notable exceptions, however. One is the Court's most recent effort in *Grand Rapids School District v. Ball.*[2]

PAUL A. FREUND, PUBLIC AID TO PAROCHIAL SCHOOLS

82 Harv.L.Rev. 1680, 1684–1687, 1691–1692 (1969).

Since June 10, 1968, a discussion of state aid to parochial schools can profitably start with the Supreme Court decision of that date in *Board of Education v. Allen.*[1] The case was brought by members of a local school board to enjoin the Commissioner from enforcing a law of New York, enacted in 1965 and amended in 1966, that requires them to lend textbooks, under stated conditions, to students enrolled in grades seven to twelve of parochial and private, as well as public schools. The statutory conditions are that the book be required for use as a text for a semester or more in the particular school and that it be approved by a board of education or similar body, whether or not designated for use in any public school. By judicial interpretation in New York, this duty embraces the loan of "secular," not "religious" textbooks. * * *

[The Supreme Court upheld the New York law, relying on its decision in *Everson v. Board of Education,*[9] which had allowed state reimbursement of bus fares for children in parochial as well as public schools. Freund argues that the decision in *Allen,* which involved materials used in the educational process, does not necessarily follow from the decision in *Everson,* which involved a kind of general welfare

---

2. 473 U.S. 373 (1985). See also Aguilar v. Felton, 473 U.S. 402 (1985).

1. 392 U.S. 236.

9. 330 U.S. 1 (1947).

benefit. But, he continues, it] is not enough * * * to maintain that precedent was reinterpreted in the New York case. After all, the newer majority may have read the Constitution more recently, or they may have read further in Robert Frost than "Good fences make good neighbors"—may in fact have reached the lines:

> *Why* do they make good neighbors? Isn't it
> Where there are cows? But here there are no cows.
> Before I built a wall I'd ask to know
> What I was walling in or walling out,
> And to whom I was like to give offense.
> Something there is that doesn't love a wall,
> That wants it down.

To translate Frost into legal prose, why does observance of the ancient religious guarantees of the first amendment continue to be important? Beyond ancestral voices, are there now any grounds of policy or polity that are threatened? Three such grounds need to be considered: voluntarism in matters of religion, mutual abstention of the political and the religious caretakers, and governmental neutrality toward religions and between religion and non-religion. * * *

The policy of voluntarism generates least tension between the free-exercise and non-establishment clauses. Religion must not be coerced or dominated by the state, and individuals must not be coerced into or away from the exercise or support of religion. The school-prayer decisions [11] reflected the principle of voluntarism on both counts: taxpaying families could not be required to support a concededly religious activity; nor could pupils, by the psychological coercion of the schoolroom, be compelled to participate in devotional exercises. When the state provides textbooks, taxpayers are forced to finance books selected by sectarian authorities for instruction in denominational schools maintained at considerable expense to preserve and strengthen the faith. Of course those schools serve a public purpose; that is why the loan of textbooks was held valid in the early *Cochran* case,[12] before the religious guarantees were thought to be embodied in the fourteenth amendment.

It will be argued that if the general taxpayer is coerced for an improper purpose where public funds buy parochial school books, the parochial school families are similarly coerced into paying taxes to support public schools, which, to be sure, their children are legally free to attend but which they regard either as an enemy of all religion, or, if "secularism" itself be deemed a form of religion, then as a friend of a repellent kind of religion. Note that this argument does not deny that the principle of voluntarism is violated by aid to parochial schools; the argument pleads rather by confession and avoidance, relying on an argument of reciprocity or fairness or neutrality. * * *

11. Abington School Dist. v. Schempp, 374 U.S. 203 (1963); Engel v. Vitale, 370 U.S. 421 (1962).

12. Cochran v. Louisiana State Bd. of Educ., 281 U.S. 370 (1930). * * *

If textbooks were selected by the public school authorities to be used in public and parochial schools alike, the problem of voluntariness for the taxpayer might be mitigated somewhat, but by no means removed. * * * [But t]he parochial schools might well consider their own autonomy—their voluntarism—compromised. In certain school districts the reverse might obtain: for the sake of uniformity the school authorities would be pressured into selecting books for the public schools that were particularly desired by the parochial schools. In that event there would be a double loss of voluntariness by the general taxpayer.

This risk of intrusion from one side or the other points up a second policy embodied in the religious guarantees—mutual abstention—keeping politics out of religion and religion out of politics. * * * For the identity and integrity of religion, separateness stands as an ultimate safeguard. And on the secular side, to link responsibility for parochial and public school texts is greatly to intensify sectarian influences in local politics at one of its most sensitive points.

The third policy—in addition to voluntarism and mutual abstention—is governmental neutrality, among religions and between religion and non-religion. It is this policy that is chiefly relied on by proponents of public aid. The concept of neutrality is an extremely elusive one, generally raising as many questions as it answers, because it depends on sub-concepts like comparability and on definitions (whose?) of religious and non-religious activities, on a determination whether it overrides the policies of voluntarism and mutual abstention, and on a decision whether in any event it requires or only permits public aid. Let me illustrate one difficulty of definition. One might suppose that "neutrality" requires the law to deal even-handedly with Jehovah's Witnesses and Unitarians. Yet in the school prayer cases Unitarians (speaking generally) succeeded in eliminating all ceremonial prayers from the public schools, while in the flag-salute case Jehovah's Witnesses succeeded only in getting themselves excused from a ceremony that to them was at least as unacceptable and religious in nature as the prayers were to the Unitarians.[13] In fact, the Witnesses regard the flag salute as the profanation of a religious gesture, a bowing before idols, a Black Mass in the schoolroom. And yet their claim was recognized only to the extent of excusal, exposing them to the repugnant ceremony. Why? Because the prevailing, dominant view of religion classifies the flag salute as secular, in contravention of the heterodox definition devoutly held by the Witnesses. Neutrality, that is, does not assure equal weight to differing denominational views as to what constitutes a religious practice.

Nor is there any general principle that requires the state to compensate those who out of religious conviction incur a handicap under law. Pupils in public schools may (perhaps must) be excused on their religious holidays; but it scarcely follows that those pupils are not responsible for the work they miss, even if they must resort to the expense of private

---

13. *Compare* West Virginia State Bd. of Educ. v. Barnette, 319 U.S. 624 (1943) *with* Abington School Dist. v. Schempp, 374 U.S. 203 (1963).

tutoring. Businesses that close on Saturday as a religious observance and must close on Sunday under the law are disadvantaged materially because of religious faith; but exemption from the Sunday laws is not required.[15] The state requires a certain formal ceremony to render a marriage valid in law, and provides magistrates at public expense who are available to satisfy this requirement. For those couples, however, whose religious faith compels them to hold an ecclesiastical ceremony, additional expense is involved, either to the couple or to their church or both. Must the state therefore compensate the minister or the bridegroom and bride? Would it help their case to insist that no true marriage can be celebrated without churchly blessing and that a ceremony before a judge is anti-religious, a profanation subsidized with public money? Would not the answer be: If your religion prevents you from availing yourself of the public facility and impels you to make a financial sacrifice for the sake of your faith, surely the spirit of religion is the better served by your act.

* * *

Are there, then, any forms of public aid to parochial schools that should be sustained? I would enumerate the following, which are general non-religious state activities that operate in effect to mitigate certain costs borne by parochial schools or their patrons:

1. General welfare services for children, wherever they may be located, including medical examinations and hot lunches.

2. Prizes and awards in general academic competition, usable by the recipients as they please, like veterans' benefits that constitute deferred compensation.

3. Shared time instruction in the public schools, treating participating parochial school children as part-time public school children.

Institutions of higher learning present quite a different question, mainly because church support is less likely to involve indoctrination and conformity at that level of instruction.

One final observation. In facing the issues that will soon be raised—provision of textbooks not on loan or not in form requested by pupils, or books of a character or for use in schools different from the circumstantial presumptions in the New York case; unconditional grants for specified areas of learning; lump sum grants—three courses are open constitutionally: to hold the aid mandatory, to hold it permissible, and to hold it impermissible. The mandatory result seems least pre-figured, notwithstanding the logical course of the argument from "neutrality." A choice between the permissible and the forbidden is in essence a choice whether to leave the issue to the political process in each state or locality, or to defuse the political issue. Ordinarily I am disposed, in grey-area cases of constitutional law, to let the political process function. * * * The religious guarantees, however, are of a different order. While

---

15. *See, e.g.,* Gallagher v. Crown Kosher Super Market, 366 U.S. 617 (1961).

political debate and division is normally a wholesome process for reaching viable accommodations, political division on religious lines is one of the principal evils that the first amendment sought to forestall. * * * Although great issues of constitutional law are never settled until they are settled right, still as between open-ended, ongoing political warfare and such binding quality as judicial decisions possess, I would choose the latter in the field of God and Caesar and the public treasury. This basic preference may help to account for what otherwise may seem a too rigid, and not sufficiently permissive, view of constitutional commands.

JOHN H. GARVEY, ANOTHER WAY OF LOOKING AT SCHOOL AID

1985 Sup.Ct.Rev. 61, 62, 73–85.

[In *Grand Rapids School District v. Ball* [a] the Supreme Court struck down several forms of aid to parochial schools. The problem, the Court said, was that the aid had the effect of advancing religion, in violation of the rule laid down in *Lemon v. Kurtzman*.[b] John Garvey argues that the Court reached this conclusion too hastily. It ought to take more seriously the question whether a particular form of aid actually causes forbidden effects.]

[The Grand Rapids] school district offered two programs in the parochial schools. One (Shared Time) provided remedial and "enrichment" math and reading, art, music, and physical education. These were taught during regular class periods by full-time public school employees, in rooms "leased" (at $6.00 per room per week) from the parochial schools, with materials supplied by the public school system. The other (Community Education) offered such courses as arts and crafts and chess in voluntary classes at the end of the school day. These were taught in large part by instructors already teaching at the schools where the courses were offered. No attempt was made to monitor either program for religious content.

The Court held both programs unconstitutional under the *Lemon* antiestablishment test because they had the effect of advancing religion. This effect, the Court said, might occur in three ways. First, the teachers might "become involved in intentionally or inadvertently inculcating particular religious tenets or beliefs." There was no evidence that this had happened, but the Court found evidence unnecessary since the classes weren't monitored and no one had any incentive to report violations. Second, the programs might subsidize the schools' religious function by providing "direct aid to [their] educational function." Third, "the programs may provide a crucial symbolic link between government and religion[.]"

* * *

a. 473 U.S. 373 (1985).   **b.** 403 U.S. 602, 612–613 (1971).

[*Grand Rapids* mentions three different theories about how government aid can cause forbidden effects. A close reading of the cases discloses four more—a total of seven.]

1. *Purpose.* The most obvious reason for holding government responsible for private * * * religious activity, is that it has intended its assistance to cause such effects. One would expect the law to be rather unforgiving in blaming government for effects when it has such a purpose, much as it is in blaming a defendant for remote damages caused by intentional torts or in finding complicity in someone else's criminal conduct. The issue is pretty much hypothetical, though. The courts rarely find evil intentions in government assistance programs.[83]

2. *Opportunity.* As a practical matter, when we say that the government has caused improper "effects" we do not mean that its conscious objective is to achieve such results. We do not even mean that the government has unwittingly made something happen. There are voluntary actions by people in the institution that intervene between the government's act and its "effects," and it would be strange to say that the government "made" those people engage in religious * * * activity. What we really mean, most often, is that the government has provided an opportunity for the institution to misbehave. It is as though the government has left the keys in a parked car, which a thief drives away. Or better, it is like the opportunity for harm that a Dram Shop Act seeks to prevent.

* * *

The Court has * * * flirted with the Opportunity Theory for aid to religious colleges. *Roemer v. Maryland Public Works Board* held that a state could give noncategorical grants to private (including religious) colleges, provided the schools segregated the funds in separate accounts, agreed not to spend the money for sectarian purposes, and accounted for the funds at the end of the year.[88] The important thing was the assurance that the government's money would not itself be misused: "if secular activities can be separated out, they ... may be funded."

The government can often avoid the consequences of this theory by providing assistance in kind rather than in cash. That technique has succeeded for books, tests, and diagnostic services delivered to parochial schools on their premises * * *. Such aid is thought to be self-policing: it does not create any opportunity for abuse and so cannot be said to cause any forbidden effects. It is as though the bartender in the dram shop gave his customer a glass of water rather than something more potent. * * *

3. *Infection.* One justification for reaching out beyond the grant program to other parts of the institution might be called the Infection

---

83. The purpose prong of the *Lemon* test has been invoked only in cases where the government itself has engaged in religious activity. See, *e.g.,* Wallace v. Jaffree, 105 S.Ct. 2479 (1985); Stone v. Graham, 449 U.S. 39 (1980).

88. 426 U.S. 736 (1976).

Theory. The idea is that misbehavior elsewhere in the school (upstream, as it were, from the grant program) can infect the use of government funds and should therefore be covered as well. The Infection Theory thus adds one link to the chain described in the previous section.

* * *

Grand Rapids relied on the Infection Theory for its first effects argument. The Court found that "the presence of the [parochial school] environment" might cause even public school teachers to "conform their instruction to the environment." There is a kind of fox-guarding-the-chickens plausibility to this with regard to the Community Education program, which was taught in large part by parochial school teachers hired *pro hac vice* by the school district. It is downright implausible as to the Shared Time program, which was taught almost entirely by full-time public employees who had no connection whatever with the schools to which they were assigned.

* * *

4. *Benefits.* This theory is something like the Infection Theory run in reverse. The Infection Theory holds that * * * religion[ ] upstream from the grant program can flow into and corrupt it. The Benefits Theory holds that an innocent grant program can sometimes provide a benefit to [religion] downstream. * * *

One example of the Benefits Theory is tuition grants, which can be passed on from one program to another. * * * *Committee for Public Education v. Nyquist* [forbids giving them] to parochial school students.[98]

A different kind of example concerns government aid that is used up in program *x* with side effects on program *y*. * * * *Grand Rapids* may * * * have had something like this in mind when it said that "state programs providing [instructional materials and services] advance[ ] the 'primary, religion-oriented educational function of the sectarian school.' " The Court may have meant that remedial reading classes make the school's own reading classes a more effective way of putting religion across.

* * *

These arguments stretch the idea of causation quite far. There is a sense in which Grand Rapids has contributed to the propagation of religious faith. But it has in the same sense contributed to the spread of pornography, the belief in creationism, and the growth of the Republican party since those are all things that increased literacy will lead one to read about.

5. *Freed-up funds.* * * * The Freed-up Funds Theory says that, even if the government aid is not itself abused, and even if it has no benefits that spill over into other programs, the institution may work

98. [413 U.S. at 783.]

new harm with the money that government aid displaces in its budget.
* * *

Like the Benefits Theory, this theory holds that the government causes all the ripple effects that flow from its assistance. [There are] two obvious weaknesses with this idea. First, the government aid may not really cause any diversion of funds. If someone gives me an automatic garage door opener, I won't have more money to spend on other things, if I should never have purchased a garage door opener for myself. Second, if money is freed up, it may be very hard to tell where it goes, and it may not go toward forbidden acts. * * *

* * *

A third kind of problem with the Freed-up Funds Theory is that it applies to a surprising variety of causes. One may say that remedial reading services free up money for teaching religion, but one could with equal justice point to city sewer services as a cause of the same effect. If the city did not provide sewer service, the parochial schools would have to install septic tanks, and you can buy a lot of catechisms for what you'd spend on a septic tank.

It is true that reading is part of the curriculum (a point emphasized in *Grand Rapids*) and sewers are not. But that actually counts against this theory. When school money earmarked for septic tanks is freed up and spent on religion, there is a net gain in funded religious activity. School money budgeted for the curriculum, however, is already going for religious activity, so moving it somewhere else may cause no new harm.
* * *

6. *Proof problems*. The paradigm cause-and-effect relation in all the theories I have discussed so far is one where the government provides an opportunity for harm that the institution exploits. [All of these theories focus on the program or activity funded by the government's grant,] though activities elsewhere in the institution may also be covered if they infect, or benefit from, or are funded by money freed up by, the government's program. But suppose that the government contributes half the cost of building a school library and that the school contributes the other half. It would be arbitrary, given the way libraries are built and paid for, to say that the government's money built one part of the library and the school's another or that the government's money paid for the first twenty years of its useful life and the school's for the remainder. Even if the effect we worry about is misuse of the government's money, the impossibility of tracing it requires us to say that the "program or activity" here is the recipient's program, not the grant program. This is what the * * * cases say about construction grants.

* * *

7. *Symbolism*. The other effect on which *Grand Rapids* relied, unlike all of those up to this point, has nothing to do with the recipient abusing opportunities. The Court said that the government would also improperly aid religion if it "convey[ed] a message of ... endorsement or

disapproval of religion." In *Grand Rapids* the message was sent via symbols: "the symbolic union of church and state" in one joint enterprise. It's as though the school paid for religious activity with its own money, but its partner the government said, "We are in this together."

* * *

The obvious problem with the implementation of this theory is defining the scope of the joint venture. * * * *Grand Rapids* * * * said that the scope of the joint venture * * * was determined by the public's (and especially the parochial school student's) perception:

> [The question] is whether the symbolic union ... is sufficiently likely to be perceived by adherents of the controlling denominations as an endorsement, and by the nonadherents as a disapproval, of their individual religious choices. ... The symbolism ... is most likely to influence children of tender years.

* * *

There is [an irony hidden in] the Court's conclusion about symbolic effects. Remember that we are speculating about people's impressions of how the government views its joint venturer's religious activity. It seems as though the government could neutralize any symbolic effects by making perfectly clear that it did not approve of what its partner was doing. [It could, for example, monitor the school to make sure that religion did not creep into the joint venture. That is what the state of New York did in *Aguilar v. Felton.*[c] The problem is that under *Lemon's* three-part test this method of preventing symbolic effects is forbidden by the rule against institutional entanglement.]

BIBLIOGRAPHY

Religion in Public Life

1. *Religion in a Liberal Democracy*

Robert Audi, *The Separation of Church and State and the Obligations of Citizenship,* 18 Phil. & Pub.Aff. 259 (1989).

Stephen L. Carter, THE CULTURE OF DISBELIEF: HOW AMERICAN LAW AND POLITICS TRIVIALIZE RELIGIOUS DEVOTION (1993).

Stephen L. Carter, *The Religiously Devout Judge,* 64 N.D.L.Rev. 932 (1989).

Comment, *The Establishment Clause and Religious Influences on Legislation,* 75 Nw.U.L.Rev. 944 (1980).

Daniel O. Conkle, *Different Religions, Different Politics: Evaluating the Role of Competing Religious Traditions in American Politics and Law,* 10 J.Law & Rel. 1 (1993–94).

c. 473 U.S. 402 (1985).

Edward B. Foley, *Book Review,* 92 Colum.L.Rev. 954 (1992) (of Perry, Love and Power).

John H. Garvey, *A Comment on Religious Convictions and Lawmaking,* 84 Mich.L.Rev. 1288 (1986).

Frederick M. Gedicks, *Public Life and Hostility to Religion,* 78 Va.L.Rev. 671 (1992).

Frederick M. Gedicks, *Some Political Implications of Religious Belief,* 4 N.D.J. of Law, Ethics & Pub.Pol. 419 (1990).

R. Kent Greenawalt, RELIGIOUS CONVICTIONS AND POLITICAL CHOICE (1988).

Sidney Hook, RELIGION IN A FREE SOCIETY (1967).

Scott C. Idleman, *The Role of Religious Values in Judicial Decision Making,* 68 Ind.L.J. 433 (1993).

Scott C. Idleman, *The Sacred, the Profane, and the Instrumental: Valuing Religion in the Culture of Disbelief,* 142 U.Pa.L.Rev. 1313 (1994).

Sanford Levinson, *The Confrontation of Religious Faith and Civil Religion: Catholics Becoming Justices,* 39 DePaul L.Rev. 1047 (1990).

Christopher Mooney, PUBLIC VIRTUE: LAW AND THE SOCIAL CHARACTER OF RELIGION (1986).

Thomas Nagel, *Moral Conflict and Political Legitimacy,* 16 Phil. & Pub.Aff. 215 (1987).

Richard Neuhaus, THE NAKED PUBLIC SQUARE: RELIGION AND DEMOCRACY IN AMERICA (1984).

Michael J. Perry, LOVE AND POWER (1991).

Michael J. Perry, MORALITY, POLITICS & LAW: A BICENTENNIAL ESSAY (1988).

A. James Reichley, RELIGION IN AMERICAN PUBLIC LIFE (1985).

Frederick Schauer, *May Officials Think Religiously?,* 27 Wm. & Mary L.Rev. 1076 (1986).

Lawrence B. Solum, *Faith and Justice,* 39 DePaul L.Rev. 1083 (1990).

Symposium, *Religion in Public Life: Access, Accommodation, and Accountability,* 60 Geo.Wash.L.Rev. 743 (1992).

Symposium, *The Role of Religion in Public Debate in a Liberal Society,* 30 San Diego L.Rev. 647 (1993).

Ruti Teitel, *A Critique of Religion as Politics in the Public Sphere,* 78 Cornell L.Rev. 747 (1993).

Garry Wills, UNDER GOD (1990).

2. *Civil Religion*

Robert Bellah, THE BROKEN COVENANT: AMERICAN CIVIL RELIGION IN A TIME OF TRIAL (1975).

Robert Bellah & Phillip Hammond, eds., VARIETIES OF CIVIL RELIGION (1980).

Timothy L. Hall, *Sacred Solemnity: Civic Prayer, Civil Communion, and the Establishment Clause,* 79 Iowa L.Rev. 35 (1993).

Norman Dorsen & Charles Sims, *The Nativity Scene Case: An Error of Judgment,* 1985 U.Ill.L.Rev. 837.

Robert C. Post, *Theories of Constitutional Interpretation,* 30 Representations 13 (1990).

Martin E. Marty, A NATION OF BEHAVERS Ch. 8 (1976).

Martin E. Marty, RELIGION AND REPUBLIC Ch. 4 (1987).

Sidney E. Mead, THE NATION WITH THE SOUL OF A CHURCH (1975).

Russell E. Richey & Donald G. Jones, eds., AMERICAN CIVIL RELIGION (1974).

Thomas L. Shaffer, *On Checking the Artifacts of Canaan: A Comment on Levinson's "Confrontation,"* 39 DePaul L.Rev. 1133 (1990).

Symposium, *Religion in Public Life: Access, Accommodation, and Accountability,* 60 Geo.Wash.L.Rev. 599 (1992).

Howard Vogel, *The Judicial Oath and the American Creed: Comments on Sanford Levinson's The Confrontation of Religious Faith and Civil Religion: Catholics Becoming Justices,* 39 DePaul L.Rev. 1107 (1990).

Religion in Public Schools

     1.   *Prayer, Moments of Silence, And Related Problems*

Ernest J. Brown, *"Quis Custodiet Ipsos Custodes?—The School Prayer Cases",* 1963 Sup.Ct.Rev. 1.

Jesse H. Choper, *Religion in the Public Schools: A Proposed Constitutional Standard,* 47 Minn.L.Rev. 329 (1963).

Kenneth Dolbeare and Phillip Hammond, THE SCHOOL PRAYER DECISIONS (1971).

Paul G. Kauper, *Schempp and Sherbert: Studies in Neutrality and Accommodation,* 1963 Relig. & Pub.Or. 3.

Robert Rodes, *The Passing of Nonsectarianism: Some Reflections on the School Prayer Case,* 38 N.D.Law. 115 (1963).

Thomas A. Schweitzer, *Lee v. Weisman and the Establishment Clause: Are Invocations and Benedictions at Public School Graduations Constitutionally Unspeakable?,* 69 U.Det.L.Rev. 113 (1992).

Rodney Smith, PUBLIC PRAYER AND THE CONSTITUTION (1987).

Geoffrey R. Stone, *In Opposition to the School Prayer Amendment,* 50 U.Chi.L.Rev. 823 (1983).

Arthur E. Sutherland, Jr., *Establishment According to Engel,* 76 Harv. L.Rev. 25 (1962).

Symposium, *Religion and the Public Schools after Lee v. Weisman,* 43 Case W.Res. 773 (1993).

2. *Equal Access*

Steven K. Green, *The Misnomer of Equality Under the Equal Access Act,* 14 Vt.L.Rev. 369 (1990).

Douglas Laycock, *Equal Access and Moments of Silence: The Equal Status of Religious Speech by Private Speakers,* 81 Nw.U.L.Rev. 1 (1986).

Rosemary C. Salomone, *From* Widmar *to* Mergens: *The Winding Road of First Amendment Analysis,* 18 Hastings Const.L.Q. 295 (1991).

Nadine Strossen, *A Framework for Evaluating Equal Access Claims by Student Religious Groups: Is There a Window for Free Speech in the Wall Separating Church and State?,* 71 Cornell L.Rev. 143 (1985).

Ellis West, *The Supreme Court and Religious Liberty in the Public Schools,* 25 J. Church & St. 87 (1983).

3. *Creation Science*

Charles Blinderman, *Unnatural Selection: Creationism and Evolutionism,* 24 J. Church & State 73 (1982).

David Caudill, *Law and Worldview: Problems in the Creation–Science Controversy,* 3 J.Law & Rel. 1 (1985).

Alan Freeman & Betty Mensch, *Religion as Science/Science as Religion: Constitutional Law and the Fundamentalist Challenge,* 2 Tikkun 64 (No. 5, 1987).

Gregory Gelfand, *Of Monkeys and Men—An Atheist's Heretical View of the Constitutionality of Teaching the Disproof of a Religion in the Public Schools,* 16 J.L. & Educ. 271 (1987).

Stephen J. Gould, *Justice Scalia's Misunderstanding,* 5 Const.Com. 1 (1988).

Edward Larson, TRIAL AND ERROR (1985).

Note, *Freedom of Religion and Science Instruction in Public Schools,* 87 Yale L.J. 515 (1978).

David A.J. Richards, TOLERATION AND THE CONSTITUTION Ch. 5 (1986).

4. *"Secular Humanism" And The Public Schools*

George W. Dent, Jr., *Religious Children, Secular Schools,* 61 S.Cal. L.Rev. 864 (1988).

Mary Mitchell, *Secularism in Public Education: The Constitutional Issues,* 67 B.U.L.Rev. 603 (1987).

Note, *"Public Education in Shreds": Religious Challenges to Curricular Decisions,* 64 Ind.L.J. 111 (1988).

Leo Pfeffer, *The "Religion" of Secular Humanism,* 29 J. Church & St. 495 (1987).

Paul Toscano, *A Dubious Neutrality: The Establishment of Secularism in the Public Schools,* 1979 B.Y.U.L.Rev. 177.

Paul Vitz, *Religion and Traditional Values in Public School Textbooks,* 84 Pub. Interest 79 (1986).

Aid to Parochial Schools

1. *Aid To Elementary And Secondary Schools*

Lee Boothby, *The Establishment and Free Exercise Clauses of the First Amendment and Their Impact on National Child Care Legislation,* 26 Harv.J.Legis. 549 (1989).

Jesse H. Choper, *The Establishment Clause and Aid to Parochial Schools,* 56 Calif.L.Rev. 260 (1968).

Jesse H. Choper, *The Establishment Clause and Aid to Parochial Schools—An Update,* 75 Calif.L.Rev. 5 (1987).

Comment, *Day Care and the Establishment Clause: The Constitutionality of the Certificate Program in S. 5, the "ABC" Bill,* 12 Geo. Mason U.L.Rev. 317 (1990).

Mark Gibney, *State Aid to Religious–Affiliated Schools: A Political Analysis,* 28 Wm. & Mary L.Rev. 119 (1986).

Murray Gordon, *The Unconstitutionality of Public Aid to Parochial Schools,* in THE WALL BETWEEN CHURCH AND STATE 73 (Oaks ed. 1963).

Michael W. McConnell, *The Selective Funding Problem: Abortions and Religious Schools,* 104 Harv.L.Rev. 989 (1991).

John E. Nowak, *The Supreme Court, The Religion Clauses and the Nationalization of Education,* 70 Nw.U.L.Rev. 883 (1976).

Elizabeth J. Samuels, *The Art of Line Drawing: The Establishment Clause and Public Aid to Religiously Affiliated Child Care,* 69 Ind.L.J. 39 (1993).

Louis J. Sirico, Jr., *The Secular Contribution of Religion to the Political Process: The First Amendment and School Aid,* 50 Mo.L.Rev. 321 (1985).

William Valente & William Stanmeyer, *Public Aid to Parochial Schools— A Reply to Professor Freund,* 59 Geo.L.J. 59 (1970).

Edwin West, *Constitutional Judgment on Non–Public School Aid: Fresh Guidelines or New Roadblocks,* 35 Emory L.J. 795 (1986).

2. *Aid To Higher Education*

Donald A. Giannella, *Lemon and Tilton: The Bitter and the Sweet of Church–State Entanglement,* 1971 Sup.Ct.Rev. 147.

Paul G. Kauper, *Public Aid for Parochial Schools and Church Colleges: The Lemon, DiCenso and Tilton Cases,* 13 Ariz.L.Rev. 567 (1971).

3. *Aid To Other Religious Institutions*

Boris Bittker, *Churches, Taxes and The Constitution,* 78 Yale L.J. 1285 (1969).

Wilber G. Katz, *Radiations from Church Tax Exemption,* 1970 Sup.Ct. Rev. 93.

Dean Kelley, WHY CHURCHES SHOULD NOT PAY TAXES (1977).

Note, *Government Aid to Religious Social Services Providers: The Supreme Court's "Pervasively Sectarian" Standard,* 75 Va.L.Rev. 1077 (1989).

Stephen Schwarz, *Limiting Religious Tax Exemptions: When Should the Church Render Unto Caesar?,* 29 U.Fla.L.Rev. 50 (1976).

John Witte, *Tax Exemption of Church Property: Historical Anomaly or Valid Constitutional Practice?,* 64 S.Cal.L.Rev. 363 (1991).

Chapter VII

THE FREE EXERCISE OF RELIGION

A. Introduction

First Amendment jurisprudence is divided between two clauses—the establishment clause and the free exercise clause—governed by two sets of rules. To the modern mind, accustomed to thinking in terms of rights, free exercise should be a more familiar notion. Like other freedoms (speech, press, "privacy") it identifies a realm of private conduct which the government is not allowed to prohibit. But that is only a formal description of religious freedom. The right becomes more puzzling and controversial when we try to give it substance.

What do we mean, for example, by freedom of *religion*? This is a question about the scope of the right. What sort of private conduct does it protect? Religion is not a natural activity like speech or sex. We build certain ideas and values into our definition of the term.

And what does it mean to say that the government can't *prohibit* free exercise? This is a question about the strength of the right. Government in a welfare state is omnipresent. Everything it does intrudes in one way or another on religious acts and institutions. Here again we need to make judgments about what kinds of interference we will tolerate.

We cannot talk intelligently about the scope and strength of religious freedom without first asking why we should protect the right. What values does it hold for us? How much do we cherish those values?

This chapter addresses these questions. Section B begins by discussing the value of religious freedom. Section C deals with how we define religion. Section D takes up the kinds of government action that the free exercise clause is concerned about.

Section E brings us full circle in our consideration of the religion clauses. If we assign a special value to free exercise, we seem to violate the establishment clause by giving preferential treatment to religion. Is there some way to give a consistent meaning to the two clauses?

B. THE VALUE OF RELIGIOUS FREEDOM

The readings in this section discuss why the Constitution protects religious freedom. The answer is not as obvious as you might think. The obvious answer is that we value religious freedom because it permits religious action—it lets us know and serve God. But there are two difficulties with this explanation. One is that there is no consensus about it. We are no longer "a Christian nation" or "a religious people," though we once might have been.[1] The other is the establishment clause. It would be paradoxical to say that the First Amendment views the knowledge and service of God as good things, when the establishment clause forbids the government to encourage them.

For these reasons, people who write about free exercise usually look for 'secular' justifications—they try to offer reasons that will appeal to everyone, believers and nonbelievers alike. That is the approach taken by John Garvey in the last article in this section. Michael McConnell bucks this trend. He argues that the main impetus behind the distinctively American principle of religious freedom was the desire of evangelical Protestant sects for a release from state control. They thought that state support for religion was bad because it stifled religious enthusiasm and initiative. State support was also inevitably linked to control. The most effective countermeasure was the one envisioned by Madison: to increase the number of religious sects and encourage the vigor of the small ones.

Robert Casad responds that this approach to free exercise suffers from the endemic weakness of religious justifications: it is inconsistent with the establishment clause. By promoting a particular institutional form of religion—a system of denominational churches—it favors one religious principle over others. Casad illustrates his point by noting that Madison's vision is at odds with the ecumenical movement that has been influential among Christian churches in the latter half of the twentieth century.

John Garvey offers a "secular" argument designed to avoid these difficulties. For the most part, he argues, the benefits of religious freedom accrue to religious believers. Freedom relieves them of the special harm they might suffer if they had to disobey God's law. It also releases them from the tension of conflicting duties. The hard problem is to explain why the rest of us should extend unique consideration to religious believers when there is little in it for us, and when there are many others also clamoring for special treatment. Garvey argues that we treat religion differently because it is just to do so. Religious people have special cognitive and volitional problems that the law can justly take account of.

1. Church of the Holy Trinity v. United States, 143 U.S. 457, 471 (1892); Zorach v. Clauson, 343 U.S. 306, 313 (1952).

MICHAEL W. McCONNELL, THE ORIGINS AND HISTORICAL UNDERSTANDING OF FREE EXERCISE OF RELIGION

103 Harv.L.Rev. 1409, 1513–1517 (1990).

The free exercise clause may well be the most philosophically interesting and distinctive feature of the American Constitution. Viewed in its true historical light, as the product of religious pluralism and intense religious sectarianism in the American states and colonies, with limited influence from the rationalistic Enlightenment, the free exercise clause represents a new and unprecedented conception of government and its relation to claims of higher truth and authority.

Until the Protestant Reformation, the separation of church and state was the product not of theory or design but of geopolitical reality. It was graphically illustrated by the throne of St. Peter in Rome and the throne of the king in each of the nation-states of Christendom. At times, the church was under the domination of the state; at times, though more rarely, the state was under the domination of the church. More often, the church and the state were independent powers, supported by different claims of authority, acting in varying degrees antagonistically or cooperatively one with the other. This separation, a product of a "catholic" church in a post-imperial world, was instrumental in staving off incipient despotism. Mankind's two great loyalties, to God and to country, were of necessity divided; claims of ultimate right were pitted against the power of the state. " 'To that conflict of four hundred years,' " according to Lord Acton, " 'we owe the rise of civil liberty.' "

The Reformation introduced religious factions to Western Europe, and with them, two novel dangers to public peace and freedom. First, the rivalry among religious sects broke out into bloody warfare, both between countries, as in the Thirty Years War, and within countries, as in the English Civil War and the Huguenot wars in France. Second, as the universal church was sundered, it became possible to form national churches, such as the Church of England, which could be more easily dominated by the government. Thus, a complete and enduring fusion of earthly and spiritual authority became a serious possibility for the first time since the fall of Rome.

The Enlightenment writers on the subject tended to concentrate on the danger of religious rivalry. Sectarian intolerance and struggle for hegemony was a major cause of unrest, violence, rebellion, and persecution. There were two promising ways to ameliorate and, if possible, eliminate such violence and persecution, and both had proponents among the thinkers of the Enlightenment. One solution was to suppress religious differences by establishing a national church and supporting it with public funds. This solution was proposed by Hobbes,[550] the youth-

550. *See* T. Hobbes, [Leviathan,] pt. III, ch. 42, at 293–95 * * *.

ful Locke,[551] and Hume,[552] among others. It would have two advantages: by unifying religion, it would reduce religious factionalism, and by guaranteeing financial support to the clergy, it would cause them to become indolent and subservient. The difficulty with this solution was that it would enrage dissenters from the established church (or at least the most intense among them) and might well exacerbate religious unrest. For this reason, the mature Locke proposed the second approach: to extend toleration to all (except Catholics and atheists), on condition that each religion adopt toleration as one of the tenets of its faith. Toleration, it was hoped, would calm the fevers of religious dissension. To the Enlightenment skeptic, convinced of the absurdity of the more intense varieties of religious expression and likewise convinced of the power of reason, this approach seemed to offer the additional advantage that reason, and with it rational religion, would prevail over the sectarians. Hence Jefferson's hope that with religious freedom in America, all would become Unitarians.

An aggressive interpretation of the free exercise clause would be incompatible with the Enlightenment theory of toleration. Free exercise exemptions are likely to encourage dissident sects to maintain practices at variance with the mores of society, and thus perpetuate the very religious factionalism that is the root of the problem. While deliberate oppression of minority religious groups is counterproductive, indirect measures that increase the cost and inconvenience of exotic religious practices likely will dampen the enthusiasm for religious differentiation and thereby reduce religious strife.

As with the establishment solution, however, the toleration solution seemed less than realistic from the American side of the Atlantic. Too many Americans had come to these shores precisely because they could not practice their faith in the controlled environs of Europe. Too many sectarians were spreading their views, and religious factionalism was already too deeply ingrained. Dissenters were a vexatious minority in Britain; in America they were (in the aggregate) a large majority, divided into many sects. And experience had shown that Americans were attracted—not repulsed—by the "irrational" surges of enthusiastic religion that peaked in the Great Awakening.

Madison, for one, grasped that the United States was not amenable to the Enlightenment solutions. In a letter to Jefferson, he stated that "[h]owever erroneous or ridiculous these grounds of dissention and faction may appear to the enlightened Statesman or the benevolent philosopher, the bulk of mankind, who are neither Statesman nor philosophers, will continue to view them in a different light." Religious sectarianism will not go away. Universal Unitarianism, even if desirable, is not going to come about. The Madisonian contribution, familiar to us from *The Federalist* Nos. 10 and 51, is to understand factions,

---

551. *See* J. Locke, Two Tracts on Government * * * 124–27 [(P. Abrams ed. 1967)].

552. * * * 1 D. Hume, History of England, ch. 29, at 552–553 (1851) * * *.

including religious factions, as a source of peace and stability. If there are enough factions, they will check and balance one another and frustrate attempts to monopolize or oppress, no matter how intolerant or fanatical any particular sect may be.

This point of view is consistent with an aggressive interpretation of the free exercise clause, which protects the interests of religious minorities in conflict with the wider society and thereby encourages the proliferation of religious factions. To increase the number of religious sects and the vigor of the small ones will not, as Locke appeared to believe, exacerbate the problem of religious turmoil. More likely, it will make religious oppression all the more impossible and therefore all the more unprofitable to attempt. Rather than try to foster an ecumenical spirit, the state allows each sect to promote its own cause with zeal. The Madisonian perspective points toward pluralism, rather than assimilation, ecumenism, or secularism, as the organizing principle of church-state relations. Under this view, the Supreme Court errs if it attempts to calm or suppress religious fervor by confining it to the margins of public life. It should welcome religious participation in all its diversity and dissension. The Court should not ask, "Will this advance religion?," but rather, "Will this advance religious pluralism?" The Court should not ask, "Will this be religiously divisive?," but rather, "Will this tend to suppress expression of religious differences?" Most of all, the Court should extend its protection to religious groups that, because of their inability to win accommodation in the political process, are in danger of forced assimilation into our secularized Protestant culture. The happy result of the Madisonian solution is to achieve *both* the unrestrained practice of religion in accordance with conscience (the desire of the religious "sects") *and* the control of religious warfare and oppression (the goal of the Enlightenment).

So understood, the free exercise clause also makes an important statement about the limited nature of governmental authority. While the government is powerless and incompetent to determine what particular conception of the divine is authoritative, the free exercise clause stands as a recognition that such divine authority may exist and, if it exists, has a rightful claim on the allegiance of believers who happen to be American citizens. The actual occasions for free exercise exemptions may be rare now, as in our early history; but the importance of the principle outstrips its practical consequences. If government admits that God (whoever that may be) is sovereign, then it also admits that its claims on the loyalty and obedience of the citizens is partial and instrumental. Even the mighty democratic will of the people is, in principle, subordinate to the commands of God, as heard and understood in the individual conscience. In such a nation, with such a commitment, totalitarian tyranny is a philosophical impossibility.

Dissenting in *West Virginia Board of Education v. Barnette*,[556] Justice Felix Frankfurter wrote:

---

556. 319 U.S. 624 (1943).

The constitutional protection of religious freedom terminated disabilities, it did not create new privileges. It gave religious equality, not civil immunity. Its essence is freedom from conformity to religious dogma, not freedom from conformity to law because of religious dogma. ... Otherwise each individual could set up his own censor against obedience to laws conscientiously deemed for the public good by those whose business it is to make laws.

So saying, Justice Frankfurter overlooked the unique American contribution to church-state relations and embraced instead the Enlightenment ideal of Locke and Jefferson. Locke and Jefferson may well have been animated, in Justice Frankfurter's words, by the "freedom from conformity to religious dogma." But that is not what the Baptists, Quakers, Lutherans, and Presbyterians who provided the political muscle for religious freedom in America had in mind. To them, the freedom to follow religious dogma was one of this nation's foremost blessings, and the willingness of the nation to respect the claims of a higher authority than "those whose business it is to make laws" was one of the surest signs of its liberality.

ROBERT C. CASAD, THE ESTABLISHMENT CLAUSE AND THE ECUMENICAL MOVEMENT

62 Mich.L.Rev. 419–426 (1964).

[In the last few decades, we have seen] some basic changes in the role of religion in American society and in the attitudes of the American people concerning religion in general.

One of these phenomena is the growth in power and influence of the Catholic and Jewish minorities—"shifts in status of the nation's religious forces" that are said by one noted writer to have "pointed up a significant new pattern of American religious pluralism which marks the end of the so-called Protestant era in American history."[2] Another is the development, largely within Protestantism itself, that is called the "ecumenical movement."[3] During the time when the "new pattern of American religious pluralism" has been developing through the growth of Catholic and Jewish influence to end the "Protestant era in American history," a new spirit of Protestant unity has been growing, marking the end of the separatist era in church history.

In recent years the Roman Catholic Church has begun to give tentative official support to the view that eventual reconciliation with

2. Kauper, *Church and State: Cooperative Separatism*, 60 Mich.L.Rev. 1, 2 (1961).

3. The word "ecumenical," as defined in Webster's New International Dictionary (3d unabridged ed. 1961), means: "of, relating to, or being a chiefly 20th century movement toward worldwide interconfessional Christian unity originating in Protestantism and now focused in a world council of churches that is supported by many Protestant, Eastern Orthodox, and other church bodies and that promotes through functional organizations cooperation on such common tasks as missions and work among students and through conferences mutual understanding on fundamental issues in belief, worship, and polity and a united witness on world problems." * * *

the Protestants is feasible and desirable. The acceptance of the ecumenical ideal by the Roman Catholic Church removes virtually all doubt that in the ecumenical movement organized Christianity is facing an upheaval of major importance, comparable perhaps to the Reformation. * * *

* * *

[These changes may require us to reconsider some assumptions about the First Amendment.] One [is] that the constitutional religious freedoms may have been designed, in part at least, as a declaration of a public policy favoring the separation of the Christian church into a large number of different sects. One of the framers of the first amendment, James Madison, expressed the opinion that the policy of the country ought to be to promote a "multiplicity of sects," and that the first amendment was designed to accomplish this end.[6] There have been no decisions of the Supreme Court actually holding this, although there ha[ve] been dicta suggesting that the first amendment has that meaning. It is logically difficult, however, to conclude that the policy of the United States positively favors multiplicity of sects, yet at the same time opposes the establishment of religion and favors the free exercise thereof.

The meaning of the establishment clause is not very well understood, even today. The recent decisions of the Supreme Court in *Engel v. Vitale*[9] and *School District v. Schempp*[10] make it fairly clear, however, that the clause proscribes not only tangible financial support and official preferences as between religious groups or doctrines, but also *any* official support of religion in general or of particular institutions or doctrines. The problem of what institutional form a religion is to assume is basically a religious question, answered by each religious group according to its own beliefs. Official public support of one institutional form over another would seem to constitute an establishment of the favored form. Few would argue that it would not be an establishment of religion as well as a restriction upon the free exercise thereof if a law, applying equally to all religious groups, Christian, Jewish or others, were to require that the organizational structure of all groups conform to congregational principles of polity. By providing official sanction for one form of ecclesiastical polity, such a law would establish the religious doctrines upon which that polity rests. Similarly, a law that does not require conformity to that polity, but encourages it over all other alternative forms, would likewise seem to be an establishment. * * *

Before *Engel v. Vitale* and *School District v. Schempp* the establishment clause was usually understood to require equal official treatment of

6. " 'In a free government,' Madison added, 'the security for civil rights must be the same as that for religious rights; it consists in the one case in the multiplicity of interests and in the other in the multiplicity of sects.' " Hunt, *James Madison and Religious Liberty,* 1 Am.Hist.Ass'n Ann.Rep. 165, 170 (1961). "He [Madison] believed it was best for the country to have a large number of religious sects, but it is doubtful if he ever dreamed that the process of splitting up would go as far as it has." 1 Stokes, Church and State in the United States 348 (1950). For fuller treatment of Madison's idea of multiplicity, see Cahn, The *"Establishment of Religion" Puzzle,* 36 N.Y.U.L.Rev. 1274, 1287 (1961).

9. 370 U.S. 421 (1962). * * *

10. 374 U.S. 203 (1963).

all denominations, none being preferred over another. It is now apparent that the establishment clause goes farther and requires not only that one denomination shall not be preferred over another, but also that religion itself shall not be preferred over irreligion. The Court's willingness to consider "religion" at a higher level of abstraction suggests, if it was not already implicit, that the impact of the establishment clause on the Christian religion does not necessarily have to be viewed at the denominational level. In this country we have tended to consider the Christian religion as being necessarily embodied in a varying number of denominational churches, but there is nothing absolute about this system of denominational churches. It is the product of historical forces that may now be largely spent. It is just as appropriate—perhaps more so—to regard the Christian religion as being embodied in one universal "church," with each denomination being viewed as a subdivision of that larger body. If the "church" is viewed at that level, instead of each denomination being considered a separate church or separate religion, it seems clear that a law requiring that larger "church" to adhere to the institutional structure of multiple sects would be an establishment of religion in the same sense that a law requiring denominations to adopt congregational polity would be. Likewise, it would seem that a law officially encouraging that larger church to assume the form of multiple sects in preference to a unitary, catholic institutional form would be an establishment, just as a law encouraging denominations to adopt congregational polity would be.

If the Madisonian principle of multiplicity of sects is deemed to be incorporated into the first amendment religious freedoms, then, a sort of paradox is produced. The first amendment itself would, in that event, accomplish what it specifically forbids—the establishment of religion—since it would officially support one institutional form, and perhaps prefer that form over an alternative form.

This is not a true paradox, of course. * * *

When the first amendment was adopted, the religious climate in America was such that the multiplication of sects was foreseeable as a probable consequence of the disestablishment of religion. If official support was removed from the established churches, they were in a less favorable position to compete with vigorous, relatively new groups such as the Baptists and Methodists, and less able to resist divisive schisms within their own institutional structures. But the fact that multiplicity of sects was a likely *result* of disestablishment at that point in history does not mean that the multiplicity of sects was the *objective* of disestablishment. Madison may have felt it a desirable objective, but it was desirable to him primarily for political reasons: to prevent the concentration of too much power in the hands of a few institutions and to facilitate the control of religious strife. Political expediency, however, is hardly more palatable as a reason for supporting the multiplicity of sects than as a reason for suppressing particular sects or for establishing a politically controlled state church.

There may be better reasons than political expediency, however. There were religious groups then, and there are some now, who regarded the multiplicity of sects as a valid religious principle; they supported on a religious basis the principle Madison accepted on political grounds.[17] The fact that some religious groups found religious support for the principle, of course, does not justify its adoption as official public policy. It does, however, tend to explain why the notion that the first amendment favors multiplicity of sects has received widespread support. The groups who approve the principle on religious grounds have supported the view that the Constitution embodies that principle, and those groups have comprised a large proportion of the population and, in some regions of the country, have constituted the most influential religious institutions.

If the first amendment must be read as encouraging the multiplicity of sects it could prove to be a serious impediment to the ecumenical movement, since the ultimate aim of that movement is to unify, not multiply, the sects. * * * There may be a danger in this situation, and especially so since it involves a field where basic ideas are in upheaval, as they seem to be today in the area of religious institutions. The ecumenical movement is having an ever-widening effect in changing basic, longstanding notions about the importance of denominational distinctiveness. It is inducing changes in theories as to the nature and role of denominations and probably in notions of religious freedom as profound as the changes wrought by the labor movement in theories relating to freedom of contract. Unless the courts are made aware of these changes they are likely to go on applying to present-day problems rules of law developed to meet the needs of an older order, without realizing that in so doing they are casting themselves in a partisan role in a struggle between the old and the new, in which the state should really be neutral.

The ecumenical movement cannot continue to grow in scope and influence unless the individual church members support the movement. It follows that if the ecumenical movement does continue to grow, it will indicate that more and more people are undergoing these basic changes in religious attitudes and aspirations. To be effective the Constitution

---

17. Certain religious groups, then as now, emphasize the extremely individualistic nature of religion. These groups reject creeds, dogmas and hierarchies—in short, all elements that tend to make the practice of religion uniform for all believers. These beliefs lead to congregational principles of polity and to the view that "any group of like-minded and professed believers have the right to organize themselves into a church." Sperry, Religion in America 9 (1945). Baptists and Quakers were leading advocates of this doctrine. Today the largest of the Baptist bodies, the Southern Baptist Convention, remains unaffiliated with the National and World Councils of Churches, and has thus far demonstrated little enthusiasm for the ecumenical movement. Theron D. Price, speaking unofficially of, not for, Southern Baptists, has said: "We tend—partly because we are busy with the work which we believe God has given us to do—to be oblivious to the need for wider unity [*i.e.,* wider than the spiritual unity all Christians share]. ... [I]t would be difficult to convince us that the visible reduction of the mystical body to one legal corporation would enhance the true unity of the Church." Price, *A Southern Baptist Views Church Unity,* in Nelson, Christian Unity in North America, 81, 87 (1958).

must not be seriously inconsistent with the religious views of a majority of the people.

JOHN H. GARVEY, FREE EXERCISE AND THE VALUES OF RELIGIOUS LIBERTY

18 Conn.L.Rev. 779, 786–796, 798–801 (1986).

THE INADEQUACY OF ACCUSTOMED SOLUTIONS

I have a few suggestions about directions to explore in the development of free exercise jurisprudence. Before taking them up, though, I want to mention some that I think may be dead ends. These include the kinds of values to which we have become most accustomed in our theories about other constitutional liberties.

A. The Constraining Influence of the Establishment Clause

The most striking feature of the free exercise clause is that it is coupled with the first amendment's injunction against the establishment of religion. Free speech and due process liberties have no such companions. Indeed, one of the most persistent justifications for protecting free speech is its role in promoting democratic self-government, an independent end that the Constitution itself establishes.

One consequence of the establishment of democracy is that we allow the government to promote speech, or democracy itself, by entering the market as a participant. The government can create public schools and require children attending them to learn the virtues of democracy and the evils of fascism. It can finance presidential election campaigns, and in doing so give more money to Republicans and Democrats than to Nazis.

The Constitution does not promote any particular social or scientific truth in the way it establishes a form of government, but we do see the attainment of truth as a worthy social objective, and we value speech because it serves that end. For that reason we allow the government to act in some ways to increase the quality and variety of speech. One example is rules allowing access to broadcast, and now cable, media; others include the Corporation for Public Broadcasting, and legislation like the Newspaper Preservation Act. We even spend public money to promote particular versions of truth: We teach evolution but not creationism in our schools; the National Endowments for the Arts and Humanities sponsor some kinds of art and literature but not others.

In all of these examples the government acts as a participant in, not a regulator of, the free speech market. We allow government participation because it is consistent with the values we think underlie freedom of speech. By forbidding the government to promote religion, on the other hand, the Constitution indicates that free exercise rests on a different set of values. We are very much hampered in arguing for religious freedom on the basis of its social consequences. We cannot say such things as that it promotes a religious society, or that it is an effective way of getting at the truth about religious issues.

The observation that free exercise cannot be supported by arguments about its social consequences is not meant to deny that religion affords a number of important social benefits. Religion has traditionally solemnized the social order by prescribing moral norms. It has served as a means for emotional expression and regulation. * * * But it is constitutionally a matter of indifference whether these purposes are served by religion, or by law, science, psychiatry, popular culture, or some other agency. The Supreme Court made that fairly clear in *Stone v. Graham,*[57] where it forbade Kentucky to advertise "[t]he secular application of the Ten Commandments . . . in . . . the fundamental legal code of Western Civilization and the Common Law of the United States."

B. *Autonomy As A Value*

[Not all arguments for freedom of speech are consequentialist. Some arguments hold] that speech is intrinsically valuable. The most persistent of these is the quintessentially liberal claim that speech is one important way in which we define ourselves as autonomous actors, worthy of human dignity. In listening to the speech of others, we learn the variety of ideas and principles from which we can choose our own life's course. In speaking, we create our identity and proclaim it to others.

Many have argued that the same value underlies the substantive due process liberty that the Court has protected in *Roe v. Wade* and subsequent cases. The Eleventh Circuit recently concluded, regarding homosexuality, that "[t]he Constitution prevents the States from unduly interfering in certain individual decisions critical to personal autonomy."[59] * * *

In each of these instances, the autonomy justification rests on certain assumptions about the good of human life and the essential unity of different civil liberties. "The vision [of the good], ultimately, is one of persons who, because of the effective exercise of their autonomy, are able to identify their lives as their own, having thus realized the inestimable moral and human good of having chosen one's life as a free and rational being."[61] According to this view, the sources of value are the ability to choose and the fact of choice—not the outcome of any particular choice. And all constitutional liberties, which provide protection for different kinds of choices, ultimately are sustained by that source of value.

[Some say that we should apply this same thesis to freedom of religion. And there] *is* some support for this view in what the Supreme

---

57. 449 U.S. 39 (1980) (per curiam).

59. Hardwick v. Bowers, 760 F.2d 1202, 1211 (11th Cir.1985), *rev'd,* [478 U.S. 186 (1986).]

61. [Richards, *Commercial Sex and the Rights of the Person: A Moral Argument for the Decriminalization of Prostitution,* 127 U.Pa.L.Rev. 1195, 1225–26 (1979)] (footnote omitted).

Court has done. In *Torcaso v. Watkins,* the Court held that Maryland had violated the "freedom[s] of belief and religion" by requiring state office-holders to declare their belief in God. So if the free exercise clause protects the freedom not to believe as well as the freedom to believe— that is, if the outcome of one's religious choice is irrelevant—then one might naturally conclude that what the Constitution values is the process of choice itself.

I nevertheless think it is wrong to say that the free exercise guarantee rests on the value of individual autonomy. * * *

* * *

* * * One [difficulty with this claim] stems from what at first appears to be a great virtue of the autonomy argument—its ability to offer a unified explanation for all constitutional freedoms. The difficulty is that, by attempting to cover too many activities, the argument offers too little protection. Consider the case of Simcha Goldman.[69] He claimed that the free exercise clause protects his right to wear a yarmulke while on duty at an Air Force hospital, notwithstanding contrary Air Force regulations. Whatever one thinks of the merits of Goldman's claim, no one would deny that it deserves more serious consideration than I would get if I wanted to wear a cowboy hat under the same circumstances.

The autonomy argument, however, has a hard time telling these two claims apart. I might truthfully say that wearing a cowboy hat is important not just for my image, but to my very conception of self. If my claim were sincere, Goldman and I ought to get the same degree of protection for our autonomous choices. But Goldman's claim is constitutionally stronger, for a reason that goes beyond autonomy to some *special* value of religion. Both claims are protected, in a weak way, as due process "liberties," but only Goldman's is explicitly mentioned in the first amendment.

A second problem with resting the free exercise guarantee on the value of autonomy is that many religious claimants would not agree with that explanation. The good envisioned by autonomy is *choosing* one's own "life as a free and rational being." But the religious claimant often sees things the other way around: It is God who chooses him, sometimes whether he likes it or not. Jews consider themselves the *chosen* people. Many Christians believe the same of *them*selves. One could try to finesse this difficulty by arguing that the religious claimant is still autonomous if he assents rationally to the course of action he sees God as having chosen for him. But if asked why the Constitution should protect his right to follow that course of action, his response would undoubtedly be that God willed him to, not that he had autonomously agreed.

69. Goldman v. Weinberger, [475 U.S. 503] (1986).

Some Suggestions for a Theory of Values

* * * I would like to conclude by offering a few suggestions about values that might deserve further exploration. I will discuss three in particular: avoiding special suffering; avoiding conflicting duties; and avoiding the social costs of nullification and civil disobedience.

A. Avoiding Special Suffering

One value that might underlie the free exercise clause is relief from the special mental torment suffered by claimants who are forced, through coercion or restraint, to violate religious norms. There is something very compelling about this in cases such as *Reynolds v. United States* [75] and *Wisconsin v. Yoder*, [76] where the defendant in a criminal action believes that he will face eternal damnation if he complies with the law. The predicament may be especially painful even in less extreme circumstances. The pain attendant upon compliance may be the loss of a surpassingly desirable good, rather than actual punishment.

This hedonistic principle takes account of the believer's present suffering, rather than of the loss that he suffers in contemplating. [78] By making the relevant good the avoidance of pain, this principle skirts at least one of the faults of the autonomy approach: It is consistent with the fact that religious claimants may not see themselves as "choosing" the commitments they fear to violate. The loss of bliss and the pangs of hell are no less awful to contemplate for one who is made to play the game than for one who opts in.

But hedonism pure and simple may share the other fault of the autonomy approach: It may not provide any way of distinguishing Simcha Goldman from the man in the cowboy hat. The question is whether one can say that the suffering from deprivation of religious liberty is somehow *special*. There are at least two sources of difficulty in proving that proposition. One is that compliance with the law may entail great emotional strain for reasons unrelated to religion. A soldier drafted overseas to risk his life in combat may suffer greatly at the thought of leaving his wife and children. The other source of difficulty is the great variation in the significance of religious acts * * *. Not everything protected by the first amendment is religiously required on pain of severe loss; one who believes that saluting the flag is simply disrespectful, not blasphemous, is also entitled to be excused.

Dean Choper has suggested that we can correct this fault in the special-suffering principle by taking account of the cause of suffering, not just the emotion itself. He argues that the religious claimant's pain is special because it derives from extratemporal consequences, not from the kind of temporal disabilities suffered by the man in the cowboy hat

---

75. 96 U.S. [145 (1878).]

76. 406 U.S. [205 (1972).]

78. The latter value, after all, is one that the Constitution could hardly enshrine next to the establishment clause. And such losses could not be measured in any objective way.

and the unbelieving soldier.[80] This is a nice way to complete the
hedonistic argument, because it provides an explanation for the uniqueness of religious liberty. The problem with Choper's suggestion, however, is that it threatens to remove coverage from a fairly broad range of
cases that most of us think should get first amendment protection. To
begin with, it might not apply to many matters of worship whose
abandonment, though seen as undesirable, would not be visited with
"damnation or some like consequence." And it is even troublesome as
applied to matters of moral behavior: "A strict Calvinist, for example,
might think that election to heaven is determined on some basis beyond
human comprehension. ... Many Christians are deeply unsure about
the precise relation of sins in this life to the nature of existence in a
possible afterlife."[82]

I don't mean to say that we should abandon either the hedonistic
value or the extratemporal consequences modification. It may be a
mistake for lawyers to assume, like physicists who seek to unify the four
forces, that there is only one ultimate principle supporting constitutional
freedoms. There may instead be a cluster of values, and this is one that
explains much of the importance we attach to free exercise.

B. Avoiding Conflicting Duties

This second value is not entirely distinct from the first. It looks at
the same kinds of moral dilemmas, but from a different perspective.
The hedonistic argument is utilitarian in the sense that it turns on the
individual consequences—pleasure and pain—that flow from recognizing
or failing to recognize religious freedom. The second value, on the other
hand, is nonconsequentialist: It says that there is something wrong with
forcing a conscientious religious claimant to violate a duty, even if he is
not primarily concerned about final rewards and punishments. The
focus is not the claimant's own feelings, because these are not the
claimant's concern. He is instead preoccupied with the one, or perhaps
the many, to whom he owes a duty, and whom he must cheat, fail, or
disappoint in order to comply with the law. The individual places great
value in keeping faith with such duties, and it is this value that religious
liberty would protect.

This approach, like the last, avoids the difficulty of assuming that
religious claimants "choose" the commitments they are so reluctant to
violate. A duty is no less binding because it is "natural"—arising from a
relationship or situation that the individual did not voluntarily enter—
than it would be if it were freely assumed.

Here too, though, there is a problem explaining what makes religious duties *special*. It is a common observation that "persons who
avow religious beliefs ... do not hold a monopoly on conscience." A
pacifist who believes that killing is absolutely wrong may act from a

---

80. Choper, [*Defining "Religion" in the First Amendment,* 1983 U.Ill.L.Rev. 579,] 597–601.

82. [Greenawalt, *Religion as a Concept in Constitutional Law,* 72 Calif.L.Rev. 753, 803, 804 (1984).]

conviction that he has a duty to his fellow man that is in no sense religious. But it is difficult to show how such an obligation is any less binding than the parallel claim of a Quaker whose duty has a religious source.

Still another problem with the value of avoiding conflicting duties is that it imperfectly describes the grounds for action posited by many nontheistic religions. Consider * * * the case of Steven Roy's daughter, Little Bird of the Snow.[85] Her claim to an exemption from the general requirement that applicants for food stamps and AFDC must use a social security number [did] not rest on a belief that doing so [would] breach a duty owed to her gods. Instead it [was] a kind of self-regarding concern dictated by a religious world view: that "the government's use of [her] social security number . . . will 'rob [her] spirit.'" That kind of claim is entitled to consideration (even if not recognition) under the free exercise clause. But the value of avoiding conflicting duties does not account for it.

C. Avoiding Nullification and Civil Disobedience

I said earlier that the existence of the establishment clause makes it difficult to argue for religious liberty on the basis of the social benefits that accrue from protection of freedom. But I think there *is* one kind of social interest the establishment clause permits us to recognize. This is the interest in preventing the kinds of harm caused by the eighteenth amendment: widespread disobedience; disproportionate investment of enforcement resources; and loss of respect for the law. It may be that repression of religious behavior, like suppression of drink, is unusually productive of these evils. If so, it is consistent with establishment clause values to minimize the harm by taking a laissez-faire attitude toward religious freedom. After all, the same arguments are made for legalizing marijuana and prostitution, but the law would hardly be said to canonize those activities by taking the arguments seriously.

The value of avoiding civil disobedience is not without problems. [One is that the argument] builds on policy (social utility) rather than principle. If conflicting social goals loomed larger than the one I have mentioned, the right would go up in smoke. A second problem is the familiar weakness shared by the first two values I discussed: What is so special about religion that makes its repression unusually likely to produce the harms referred to? Mightn't we just as well add marijuana and prostitution clauses to the first amendment, if suppression of those activities leads to the same kinds of problems?

* * *

D. Is Religious Exercise Special?

Each of the suggestions I have made for values that might underlie the free exercise clause—avoiding special suffering, avoiding conflicting

---

85. [Bowen v. Roy, 476 U.S. 693 (1986).]

duties, avoiding nullification and civil disobedience—depends on the assumption that there is something special about religion. Yet there are many other activities that can make roughly similar claims for entitlement to constitutional protection for those same reasons. In this section I want to make one suggestion about why religious claimants might be different from other people, and therefore deserving of special constitutional protection.

To put it bluntly, I think religion is a lot like insanity. There are two aspects to the parallel, just as there are two aspects to the most commonly used test for insanity.[94] The first is a cognitive aspect, which concerns defects in practical reasoning; the second is a volitional aspect, which concerns the ability to conform one's conduct to legal norms one knows to be binding.

First, as to the cognitive aspect. One can see several points of correspondence by considering the old *M'Naghten* test. One part of that test asked whether the actor, by reason of mental disease, did not know the nature or quality of his act.[96] The parallel problem of understanding natural events in a way wholly at odds with the rest of society occurs frequently in a religious context. Guy Ballard thought he communed with Saint Germain and shook hands with Jesus.[97] He was not exactly mainstream, but, as the Court pointed out, more orthodox believers are not all that different: "Religious experiences which are as real as life to some may be incomprehensible to others. . . . The miracles of the New Testament, the Divinity of Christ, life after death, the power of prayer are deep in the religious convictions of many." On occasion, the two problems—insane delusions and transcendent experiences—may even overlap.[99]

More typical are problems concerning *M'Naghten*'s second part, the actor's inability to know that his act was wrong. Religious people frequently make similar claims both in and outside the criminal context. They assert that God requires what society deems wrong, or more frequently, that God forbids what society permits or requires. Once again the problems of insanity and religion may overlap in cases where an actor, "because of a delusion, believes that what he is doing is morally right even though he knows it is criminal and condemned by society." In jurisdictions that ask about the defendant's understanding of wrongfulness (rather than criminality) such a belief will serve as an excuse.

---

94. The Model Penal Code states the test thus: "A person is not responsible for criminal conduct if at the time of such conduct as a result of mental disease or defect he lacks substantial capacity either to appreciate the criminality [wrongfulness] of his conduct or to conform his conduct to the requirements of law." Model Penal Code § 4.01(1) (1985).

96. The Model Penal Code gives as an example "[a] deranged person who believes

he is squeezing lemons when he chokes his wife." Model Penal Code § 4.01 comment 2 (1985).

97. United States v. Ballard, 322 U.S. 78 (1944).

99. One might point, for example, to instances of witch murder, where the actor does not believe that the victim is a human being. *See, e.g.,* Hotema v. United States, 186 U.S. 413 (1902).

The second, noncognitive aspect of the insanity test concerns problems of volition. These are cases where the accused, "as a result of mental disease or defect ... lacks substantial capacity ... to conform his conduct to the requirements of law." [105] I am reminded, in thinking of this aspect, of Martin Luther's response at the Diet of Worms: "Here I stand, I cannot do otherwise," or of St. Luke's gospel: "not my will, [Lord,] but thine." The thoroughly religious person may hope to give up his own volition altogether in favor of following transcendent directions.

* * *

* * * I think it is possible to draw from these parallels a hypothesis, if not a conclusion, about the special status of religion. Both aspects of the insanity inquiry, cognition and volition, are concerned with whether a person is capable of making a meaningful choice to comply with the law. The odd thing about religious claimants is that their actions are controlled by factors that "cannot be verified to the minds of those whose field of consciousness does not include religious insight." [110] The rest of us can assess only one of the options (the "real" one) presented by any choice, and cannot say how it stacks up against the alternative. It may be that the two options are so incommensurable that, for the claimant, there is no question of a choice. We protect their freedom, then, because they are not free.

C. What Is Religion?

We cannot apply the free exercise clause without understanding its terms. The most difficult problems have concerned the meaning of the term "religion." [1] This is an interpretive problem like the meaning of the word "speech" in the free speech clause. The First Amendment singles out some activities for special treatment, and leaves the rest to the weaker protection of the due process clause. It is thus very important to determine exactly what is covered.

The increasing religious diversity of the United States makes this job much harder than it once was. Many free exercise claimants will not belong to well known denominations within the Judeo–Christian tradition. Some will be adherents of Islam or of eastern religions. Others will belong to groups that are not only exotic but novel. Some will claim private beliefs unique to themselves. It is difficult to find a common thread running through all these claims. To take only the most obvious example, many (like Buddhists) do not believe in God.

In defining the term "religion" under these circumstances it is important to guard against cultural imperialism. The First Amendment

---

105. Model Penal Code § 4.01(1) (1985).

* * *

110. *Ballard,* 322 U.S. at 93 (Jackson, J., dissenting).

1. The precise language is: "Congress shall make no law respecting an establish-ment of religion, *or prohibiting the free exercise thereof* [.]" But there is no doubt that the word "thereof" refers to the term "religion" in the establishment clause.

should not favor western religions, or traditional religions, over others. But neither can it extend protection to everyone who wants it. That would invite false claims for special treatment. It would also dilute the strength of the free exercise clause. As we pointed out when dealing with speech, the more claims the clause covers, the less protection it can give them. Universal coverage by the free exercise clause would also create problems under the establishment clause. How can the public schools teach moral philosophy, behavioral psychology, and ecology if those beliefs are "religions?"

The Harvard Note with which this section begins tries to avoid the problem of cultural bias by defining religion in a way that takes no account of the content of belief. The test it employs instead is psychological: how strongly does the believer hold the affected belief?

Kent Greenawalt points to serious difficulties with this approach. It is, to begin with, both vague and ambiguous. And it will produce some surprising results. A drug addict's use of cocaine might be a matter of ultimate concern; an Orthodox Jewish prisoner's kosher diet might not be. Greenawalt emphasizes a variety of factors, but stresses that none of them is decisive. A practice is clearly religious if it includes a belief in God and an afterlife, a sacred text, an organization, rituals of prayer and worship, and a number of other features. But harder cases might look very different. The connection among them all is what Wittgenstein calls a "family resemblance"; Methodism and Ethical Culture may both be religions in the same way that football and chess are both games.

NOTE, TOWARD A CONSTITUTIONAL DEFINITION OF RELIGION

91 Harv.L.Rev. 1056, 1057, 1063–1067, 1072–1073, 1075–1082 (1978).

I. THE SUPREME COURT'S EFFORTS TO DEFINE RELIGION

* * *

[I]n *Torcaso v. Watkins* [45] * * * a unanimous Court struck down a provision of the Maryland Constitution which had been used to deny a Secular Humanist appointment as a notary public because he refused to declare belief in God. The Court reasoned that, under the establishment clause, government cannot force a person to profess either belief or disbelief in any religion, aid all religions against nonreligions, or aid theistic religions against nontheistic faiths. The Court thus gave wide reach to the term "religion." Among the beliefs the Court explicitly identified as religious were Buddhism, Taoism, Ethical Culture, and Secular Humanism.

The Court shortly made it clear that *Torcaso* was not an eccentric ruling. *United States v. Seeger* [49] and *Welsh v. United States* [50] were the

45. 367 U.S. 488 (1961).

49. 380 U.S. 163 (1965). [Seeger was convicted for refusing to submit to induction in the armed forces. He stated that he was conscientiously opposed to war in any form by reason of his "religious" belief.

50. See note 50 on page 596.

occasions for the most detailed consideration of the definition of religion yet given by the Supreme Court.

In *Seeger,* the Court resolved a conflict between circuits regarding the interpretation of section 6(j) of the Universal Military Training and Service Act of 1948. Construing the statute's requirement of belief "in a relation to a Supreme Being," the Court characterized the question as

> whether a given belief that is sincere and meaningful occupies a place in the life of its possessor parallel to that filled by the orthodox belief in God of one who clearly qualifies for the exemption. Where such beliefs have parallel positions in the lives of their respective holders we cannot say that one is "in a relation to a Supreme Being" and the other is not.

Although the *Seeger* Court couched the issue narrowly as one of statutory construction, its holding appears to have been constitutionally required. Certainly the Court violently strained the plain meaning of words and disregarded the evident intention of Congress to exclude nontheists from exemption. * * *

Of course, the "parallel position" standard is not free from ambiguity, since the criteria defining parallelism were left indeterminate. *Seeger,* however, does provide some partial resolution of the resulting ambiguities. It places within the ambit of religious belief all sincere beliefs "based upon a power or being, or upon a faith, to which all else is subordinate or upon which all else is ultimately dependent." While these notions of subordination and dependence have some of the same indeterminacy as the parallel position standard, they do make clear that the Supreme Court had [decided to protect] atheists and agnostics as well as members of traditional religions.

In *Welsh,* which also construed section 6(j), the Court extended *Seeger.* [By] holding that purely ethical and moral considerations were religious, it further blurred the distinction between religion and morality, at least when the conviction with which the latter is entertained approximates the intensity usually associated with more conventional religious belief. * * *

II. The Court's Definition and Contemporary Religious Experience

Arguably, there are as many definitions of religion as there are students of religion. Nonetheless, the Court simply cannot avoid the problem of definition. *Torcaso, Seeger,* and *Welsh* suggest a willingness, in contexts raising free exercise questions, to adopt an expansive definition of religion. That willingness comports both with the free exercise

Although the draft law required a "belief in a relation to a Supreme Being," Seeger left that question open. He stated that "his was a 'belief in and devotion to goodness and virtue for their own sakes, and a religious faith in a purely ethical creed.' " The Supreme Court held that he was entitled to an exemption. Ed. Note.]

50. 398 U.S. 333 (1970). [Welsh, like Seeger, was convicted of refusing to submit to induction. Unlike Seeger, he was unable to say that his beliefs were "religious." He said instead that his beliefs were "moral," and formed "by reading in the fields of history and sociology." Ed. Note.]

clause's concern for inviolability of conscience and with the diversity of contemporary religious experience. Indeed, the Court's approach closely parallels developments among students of religion. In *Seeger,* the majority explicitly relied on the views of several progressive theologians, notably Paul Tillich, and in so doing, tapped into one of the most respected, yet most expansive, traditions in the phenomenological approach to religion. Far-reaching and, to some, surprising consequences seem to flow from that reliance.

Tillich locates the essence of religion in the phrase "ultimate concern." [66] The word "concern" denotes the affective or motivational aspect of human experience; the word "ultimate" signifies that the concern must be of an unconditional, absolute, or unqualified character. The meaning of the term "ultimate" is to be found in a particular human's experience rather than in some objective reality.[67] Tillich's thesis, then, is that the concerns of any individual can be ranked, and that if we probe deeply enough, we will discover the underlying concern which gives meaning and orientation to a person's whole life. It is of this kind of experience, Tillich tells us, that religions are made;[68] consequently, every person has a religion.

III. Definition of Religion in the Free Exercise Context

A. *The Appropriateness of a Functional Definition*

* * *

The search for a definition is inherently problematic. Unless some distinguishing elements are chosen and some beliefs or behavior excluded, what purports to be a definition of religion would be merely a description—an open-ended compendium of historical experience. Limiting factors must therefore be chosen, either on the basis of inductive reasoning or in response to some a priori vision of the appropriate indicia of religiosity. * * *

Early attempts to define religion identified doctrines and tenets thought inherently common to all systems of belief worthy of characterization as religious. This approach was manifest in the requirement of a belief in a Supreme Being, a requirement definitively rejected·by the Supreme Court on both free exercise[99] and establishment clause[100] grounds. And no wonder: the Court was able with little effort to adduce examples of groups which profess no belief in a Supreme Being and yet are widely recognized as religious.

Of course, more tolerant variants of an approach that focuses on religious doctrine might be imagined. But the dangers of parochialism

---

66. P. Tillich, Dynamics of Faith 1–2 (1958).

67. P. Tillich, The Protestant Era 58, 87 (1948).

68. * * * P. Tillich, The Shaking of the Foundations 63–64 (1972).

99. *See* * * * United States v. Seeger, 380 U.S. 163 (1965) [.]

100. *See* * * * Torcaso v. Watkins, 367 U.S. 488 (1961) [.]

are not so easily avoided. Even the minimalist proposition that a religion must teach moral principles is flawed. A number of beliefs—including the Greco–Oriental mystery cults, for example—offer no moral or ethical principles to guide their adherents, but few would argue that their attempt to put their believers in contact with the Ultimate is not religious. Similarly, the superficially innocuous demand that a religious individual be committed to something beyond himself proves inadequate. Some mystical traditions and Eastern religions deny that any external reality exists or that a simple separation of internal (self) and external (not-self) is possible. So followers of the nondualist Vedanta tradition of Hinduism hold that the entire phenomenal world is an illusion and that the essence of godhead (Brahman–Atman) interpenetrates the individual.

Extreme tolerance is a conceivable response to the preceding line of argument. But a willingness to accept *any* belief as religious would serve no definitional function at all; it would suffer from the very open-endedness already described. Therefore, any useful catalog of acceptable beliefs must be finite. Yet any such catalog leads inevitably to the official proscription of some beliefs and prescription of others—to a species of state-authorized orthodoxy. Clearly the free exercise clause requires something more.

* * *

To remain true to the free exercise clause, then, a definition must proceed at a level of inquiry that does not discriminate among creeds on the basis of content, that does not circumscribe the very choices which the Constitution renders inviolate. What those choices are—and thus the meaning of religion for free exercise purposes—can therefore be limited only by a broader inquiry which looks at the role played by a system of belief in an individual's life and which seeks to identify those functions worthy of preferred status in the constitutional scheme. This is precisely the kind of inquiry at the root of the ultimate concern test espoused by Tillich and relied upon by the Court in *Seeger* and *Welsh*.

This approach is appropriate for at least four reasons. First, as noted above, it does not violate the idea of free exercise itself because it focuses on functional rather than content-oriented criteria. Second, it is not hopelessly open ended; on the contrary, it rejects any belief which for the individual is subordinate or capable of compromise. Third, while parochial to the extent that any definition formulated on the basis of human experience must be, the ultimate concern approach does as much as possible to avoid the dangers of religious chauvinism. Fourth, and most importantly, this test is peculiarly appropriate to the preferred status given to religious freedom by the first amendment. Indeed, what concerns could be more deserving of preferred status than those deemed by the individual to be ultimate?

B. *The Ramifications of a Functional Standard*

Two extensions, not thus far endorsed by the Court, are necessary to implement a standard based on ultimate concern. First, fidelity to the purposes of the free exercise clause demands that any concern deemed ultimate be protected, regardless of how "secular" that concern might seem to be. While full acceptance of the ultimate concern idea as developed by progressive theologians would lead to an expansive standard, this is exactly what the free exercise clause commands. Second, implicit in this approach is recognition that the only actor competent to decide what constitutes an ultimate concern is the individual believer. Autonomy of belief can be safeguarded only if the believer is entrusted with the task of ranking and articulating his own concerns.[110]

Admittedly, an expansive definition of religion entails potentially serious difficulties. Most importantly, there is at least some reason for concern that a functional definition would impede government programs and encourage fraudulent claims for religious protection. Neither objection is overpowering, however.

1. Impact on Government Programs.—In *Sherbert v. Verner,*[111] the Supreme Court crystallized the doctrine that there is a "zone of required accommodation" in which the state *must* use religious classifications to prevent direct or indirect burdens on religion unless there is an overriding state interest to the contrary. In *Sherbert,* the Court compelled South Carolina to modify its unemployment compensation system to accommodate the needs of those opposed on religious grounds to working on Saturdays but willing to work on Sundays instead.

Since many untraditional concerns could be viewed as religious under an expansive definition, it might be feared that the required exceptions and accommodations will imperil the effective implementation of government programs. * * *

These fears are overdrawn. Under *Sherbert,* exemption from observance of the law is not automatic. * * * While the unique importance of a religious claim to the individual places a heavy burden on the state, nothing in an expansive definition would prevent officials from proceeding with a program grounded in a strong state interest so long as

---

110. * * *

Clearly not every belief—not even all those quite strongly held—constitutes a matter of ultimate concern. How is the individual to decide whether a view is his ultimate concern or merely a matter of great importance to him? Much of the concern about the expansive approach reflects a fear that that approach is undefinable, hence illimitable. Tillich describes two characteristics which may be helpful. (1) An ultimate concern is an act of the total personality, not a movement of a special and discrete part of the total being. P. Tillich, *supra* note 66, at 4–8. Thus, the belief happens "in the center of the personal life and includes all its elements." *Id.* at 4. (2) An ultimate concern must be uncon-

ditional, made without qualification or reservation. *Id.* at 8–9. This attribute, in large measure an outgrowth of the first, prevents an individual from defining his ultimate concern conjunctively as "X and Y and Z." Each element conjoined implies a reservation or condition on the other elements. For example, should an individual try to define his ultimate concern as "helping my fellow men and achieving personal fulfillment," he runs afoul of problems of tradeoff. In some instances, a given action might advance one goal but only at the expense of the other. The goal the individual elects to compromise cannot be called ultimate. * * *

111. 374 U.S. 398 (1963).

they have explored, and in good faith rejected, seemingly less restrictive alternatives.

* * *

2. *Possibility of Fraudulent Claims.*—The more common objection to an expansive definition is that including "fringe" beliefs will encourage fraudulent claims for exemptions or privileges. If insincere assertions became frequent, and if no satisfactory means could be found to recognize them, the courts would be confronted with the hard choice between, on the one hand, granting all claims (and perhaps producing so many exemptions that government programs would be emasculated) and, on the other hand, denying all free exercise claims (and thus rejecting many that are sincerely religious).

While often used to justify the denial of free exercise claims, the fear that fraudulent assertions are more likely when dealing with small, unknown or unorthodox sects rests on somewhat shaky foundations. * * * An unscrupulous individual determined to avoid the draft, for example, could do so as readily by professing belief in a Supreme Being as by fabricating some less traditional belief. Thus, if the ambit of the term "religion" were contracted in response to the fraud argument, the unscrupulous would not be prevented from swearing false allegiance to a convenient creed. On the other hand, those genuinely moved by unorthodox beliefs would be faced with unacceptable alternatives: they could resist official commands and face penalties, follow those commands and thereby violate concerns deemed ultimate, or distort and falsely represent their beliefs in order more nearly to resemble the orthodox. * * *

* * *

Further, the courts are not completely powerless to resist false claims. Insincerity may sometimes be discovered through examination of extrinsic evidence, including patterns of inconsistent actions or statements. While some judicial language has warned against too close an examination of sincerity, there is no doubt that extrinsic evidence will in some cases provide a reliable tool for disposing of a false claim.

KENT GREENAWALT, RELIGION AS A CONCEPT IN CONSTITUTIONAL LAW

72 Calif.L.Rev. 753, 762–764, 767–769, 771–773, 802–810 (1984).

The Analogical Approach to the Constitutional Concept of Religion

* * *

Religion as a Complex Concept

Religion is a highly complex concept. As courts have occasionally noted, dictionary definitions of religion vary widely, and agreement upon a settled account of what makes something religious has been elusive.

The very assumption that some kind of "dictionary" approach will suffice may constitute a significant stumbling block. By a dictionary approach, I mean the identification of a single element or a conjunction of two or more central elements that are taken to be essential for the application of a concept. Thus, if religion is constituted by "belief in a Supreme Being," one would decide whether a doubtful instance involves religion by determining whether such belief is present. Under this approach, religion would be characterized by a condition that is both necessary and sufficient. A decision about the presence or absence of that condition would determine whether something was religious. Some other major suggestions about defining religion share with the Supreme Being standard a focus on one central feature, such as "ultimate concern" or "belief in extratemporal consequences." However, a single central element is not an inevitable feature of the dictionary approach in my sense. One might believe that two or three, or more, crucial features are all present in every genuine instance of religion.

Nevertheless, any dictionary approach oversimplifies the concept of religion, and the very phrase "definition of religion" is potentially misleading. No specification of essential conditions will capture all and only the beliefs, practices, and organizations that are regarded as religious in modern culture and should be treated as such under the Constitution.

A more fruitful approach to understanding and employing the concept of religion is to identify instances to which the concept indisputably applies, and to ask in more doubtful instances how close the analogy is between these and the indisputable instances. Such an approach can yield applications of the concept to instances that share no common feature, a result that the dictionary approach precludes.

Perhaps the best known presentation of this underlying idea is Ludwig Wittgenstein's suggestion that games have no common feature but rather family resemblances.[47] * * *

* * *

47. L. Wittgenstein, Philosophical Investigations ¶¶ 66–67 (3d ed. 1958).

66. Consider for example the proceedings that we call "games". I mean board-games, card-games, ball-games, Olympic games, and so on. What is common to them all?—Don't say: "There *must* be something common, or they would not be called 'games' "—but *look and see* whether there is anything common to all.—For if you look at them you will not see something that is common to *all*, but similarities, relationships, and a whole series of them at that. To repeat: don't think, but look!—Look for example at board-games, with their multifarious relationships. Now pass to card-games; here you find many correspondences with the first group, but many common features drop out, and others appear. When we pass next to ball-games, much that is common is retained, but much

is lost.—Are they all 'amusing'? Compare chess with noughts and crosses. Or is there always winning and losing, or competition between players? Think of patience. In ball games there is winning and losing; but when a child throws his ball at the wall and catches it again, this feature has disappeared. Look at the parts played by skill and luck; and at the difference between skill in chess and skill in tennis. Think now of games like ring-a-ring-a-roses; here is the element of amusement, but how many other characteristic features have disappeared! And we can go through the many, many other groups of games in the same way; can see how similarities crop up and disappear.

And the result of this examination is: we see a complicated network of similarities overlapping and criss-crossing: sometimes

The Analogical Approach to Religion in Ordinary
Usage and in Constitutional Law

To use the analogical approach to determine the boundaries of religion, one begins with instances of the indisputably religious, instances about which virtually everyone would say, "This certainly is religion." Such instances do not require a consensus about all the concept of religion signifies or about treatment of borderline cases. For example, no one doubts that Roman Catholicism, Greek Orthodoxy, Lutheranism, Methodism, and Orthodox Judaism are religions. Our society identifies what is indubitably religious largely by reference to their beliefs, practices, and organizations. These include: a belief in God; a comprehensive view of the world and human purposes; a belief in some form of afterlife; communication with God through ritual acts of worship and through corporate and individual prayer; a particular perspective on moral obligations derived from a moral code or from a conception of God's nature; practices involving repentence and forgiveness of sins; "religious" feelings of awe, guilt, and adoration; the use of sacred texts; and organization to facilitate the corporate aspects of religious practice and to promote and perpetuate beliefs and practices. This list could be expanded or organized differently. The main point is that among religions typical in this society a number of different elements are joined together.

Should any single feature be absent, religion, as far as general usage is concerned, could still exist. A set of beliefs and practices would still be religious, for example, if it were based on polytheism or nontheism rather than monotheism, if it failed to assert any claim between transcendental reality and proper moral practices, or if it did not involve any corporate organization. Religions need not share any single common feature, because no single feature is indispensable.[58]

Whether any features of the paradigm instances are, by themselves, *sufficient* to make something religious is more complicated. Some of

overall similarities, sometimes similarities of detail.

67. I can think of no better expression to characterize these similarities than "family resemblances"; for the various resemblances between members of a family: build, features, colour of eyes, gait, temperament, etc., etc. overlap and criss-cross in the same way.—And I shall say: 'games' form a family.

58. Whether some overlap of features would exist among any two instances of religion would depend on how many features of the indisputably religious are required to constitute religion. Very roughly, if something would not be considered a religion unless it exhibited six of the nine central features, any two instances would share at least three features. If only a few features were required to make a religion,

two instances of religion might have no feature in common. This possibility, raised by Wittgenstein's treatment of the word "game," see *supra* note 47, may seem strongly counterintuitive, until we reflect on how the words "religion" and "religious" are actually used. Individuals who reject all forms of corporate worship and organization, but who believe that they are capable of opening their hearts to God in moments of concentrated solitude are considered not only to have religious beliefs, but also to engage in solitary religious practices. Individuals who are strongly skeptical about any "higher reality," but who participate in secular versions of traditional corporate religious services, believing that such services promote inner peace and brotherhood, are thought to be engaged in religious practices.

these features have nonreligious manifestations. Professional and fraternal organizations have rituals and ethical codes that are not religious. Marxism presents a comprehensive view covering the deepest questions of human existence that is not usually considered religious. Ordinary practices of psychological therapy that help people assuage their feelings of guilt are not religious. Other features of paradigm instances, such as belief in God, may by themselves always be religious, but they do not always make the broader practices and organizations associated with them religious. A simple requirement that members believe in God would not alone make an organization religious, nor would commencement with a prayer make a legislative meeting religious. In seeking to categorize an organization or a broad set of practices, one must examine the combination of characteristics that constitute it. A final decision to consider something religious depends on how closely the combination of characteristics resembles those of the paradigm instances, judged in light of the particular reason for the inquiry.

In this brief discussion of the ordinary concept of religion, I have not explored the plausible claim that some deep characteristic such as "faith" or the "transcending of ordinary experience" does unite all instances of religion. My reason is that a common characteristic as vague and general as these would be little help for someone trying to classify beliefs and practices as religious or not. For legal purposes, one needs to concentrate on features of religion that are specific enough to be employed by judges and other actors in the legal system.

* * *

The Analogical Approach and the Courts

* * *

Among the earliest opinions grappling seriously with what makes something religious [is a case] deciding that the Washington Ethical Society [was entitled to a tax exemption] made available to churches. The opinion * * * was authored by Chief Justice Burger when he sat on the United States Court of Appeals for the District of Columbia.[70] Though the Ethical Society propounded no theist beliefs, the court determined that it was a religious corporation or society within the meaning of the relevant provision of the District of Columbia Code. The court accepted a broad notion of religion and found a strong similarity between traditional religious practices and aims and those of the Society. The Society emphasized spiritual values and guidance and the need for inward peace; held Sunday services with bible readings, sermons, singing and meditation, as well as Sunday school classes; and used "Leaders," trained graduates of established theological institutions who preached and ministered and conducted services for naming, marrying and burying. The opinion did not essay a statement of conditions that were necessary for a religion or church. Indeed, its indication that the

---

70. Washington Ethical Soc'y v. District of Columbia, 249 F.2d 127 (D.C.Cir.1957).

broad purposes of the tax exemption statute influenced its classification amounted to an implicit acknowledgement that what might be religious for one legal purpose would not necessarily be religious for another.   In terms of the analogical approach, the case confirms this Article's suggestion that the respects of analogy must be sensitive to the particular legal context.

* * *

In *Seeger* [76] and *Welsh,* [77] the Supreme Court stressed the similarity between the beliefs of the claimants and those of traditionally religious persons in relation to the reasons for an exemption from military service. Though these cases may be viewed as resting on a "dictionary approach" to religion that makes "ultimate concern" or "conscientious feeling" the indispensable feature, they may also be understood as employing an analogical approach to a statutory formulation of religion for which ultimate concern or conscientious feeling turns out to be the decisive aspect of analogy.

* * *

THE INAPPROPRIATENESS OF PROPOSED ALTERNATIVES
TO THE ANALOGICAL APPROACH

* * *

Ultimate Concern

The idea that the central feature of a religious claim is "ultimate concern" gained currency after *Seeger.*   In *Seeger,* the Supreme Court drew from the theological writings of Paul Tillich the suggestion that the ultimate concern of an individual is his God.   * * * "[U]ltimate concern" received systematic endorsement as *the* free exercise standard of religion in a 1978 Harvard student Note.[205]   Since the author displays deep sophistication about the nature and variety of religious belief, and mounts powerful arguments for a criterion of ultimate concern, criticisms of his account serve to establish the grave objections to the ultimate concern standard.

* * *

As a proposed standard for legal categorization, ultimate concern retains deep ambiguity and vagueness.   Plainly, it involves the relevance of something for one's life, not just the grandness of the questions answered by a system of belief.   Beyond this solid ground, we reach the ambiguities, which can best be introduced by a series of questions: Does everyone have an ultimate concern?   Does anyone have more than one? Is a person's ultimate concern determined by his cognitive beliefs or his

---

76. United States v. Seeger, 380 U.S. 163 (1965).   * * *

77. Welsh v. United States, 398 U.S. 333 (1970).   * * *

205. Note, [*Toward A Constitutional Definition of Religion,* 91 Harv.L.Rev. 1056 (1978).]

psychological attitudes? How does ultimate concern relate to absolute moral prohibitions? To one's deepest desires? For a claim to qualify as based on ultimate concern, what must be the connection between the act involved and that which constitutes the ultimate concern?

One virtue of the Harvard Note is that it does, at least implicitly, provide an answer to each of these questions. But the combination of answers is implausible in the extreme, if not intellectually incoherent. The answers to be found in the Note are: everyone has a single ultimate concern; this concern is what he psychologically cares about most and can be identified with his notions of absolute right and wrong; a legal claim is grounded in ultimate concern if it directly involves what the individual feels he absolutely must or must not do.

The Note's choice of a psychological approach to ultimate concern is understandable. We are all familiar, by introspection or acquaintance, with an honest intellectual belief that some things should matter more than they actually do in the way we feel and behave. A woman believes that salvation is the most important aspiration of any human and she believes that her remarriage will forfeit her hope of salvation, yet she remarries. At an intellectual level, one can say that she regards salvation as more important than the benefits of remarriage, but at a psychological level her priorities are reversed. The *Seeger* opinion left unclear whether the "parallel place" that a belief had to occupy was to be judged by intellectual or psychological criteria. However, the plurality opinion in *Welsh* adopted the psychological approach.[211] Such an approach concentrates on what individuals really care about; it permits successful claims by those who have strong feelings of conscience without a settled pattern of belief; and it relieves the courts from outside examinations of an individual's system of beliefs.

The Note's conclusion that each individual has one and only one ultimate concern is unsupported by argument. Many people care a great deal about a number of things—their own happiness, the welfare of their family, their country, perhaps their religion—without any clear ordering among these and without any single ordering principle for clashes between them. (Most people with traditional religious beliefs accept intellectually that religious concerns are ultimate, but their feelings and behavior are not always in accord with that premise.) Either such people do not have any ultimate concerns or their ultimate concerns have to be understood as amalgams of both the various things about which they care deeply and the ad hoc resolutions they make among them.

The latter possibility would gravely complicate the idea of ultimate concern. The Note plainly rejects the idea that such an amalgam of different values could constitute an ultimate concern, since a "goal the individual elects to compromise cannot be called ultimate."[213] How then do we classify those people whose scale of values is precisely of this sort?

211. Welsh v. United States, 398 U.S. 333, 339–40 (1970).

213. Note, *supra* note [205], at 1076 n. 110.

While the author speaks of a person who might "try to define his ultimate concern" in this multivalue manner,[214] the prevailing, undefended assumption is that no one could *accurately* describe his values in this way. That assumption blinks reality, leaving us with the uneasy conclusion that either all those people lacking a single ultimate concern have no free exercise rights, or the ultimate concern standard is infinitely more complex than it first appears.

The Note's assumption of a basic identity between what people care most about and what they take as absolute mandates of conscience is also unjustified. The author accepts Tillich's statement that an ultimate concern happens "in the center of the person's life."[215] The lives of people addicted to hard drugs may center around using and obtaining the drug, and they may be willing to do almost anything rather than be deprived of the drug. Yet they may not regard their obsession as one concerning conscience. On the other hand, some people believe they have absolute duties, derived from scripture or rational ethical thought, that limit the pursuit of their objectives but are not at the center of their lives. They may think it is absolutely wrong to receive a blood transfusion, for example, but they rarely even think about blood transfusions. Perhaps the response to this objection is that the person's ultimate concern is living according to God's will, which includes refusing blood transfusions; but the implications of this expansion of ultimate concern are startling.

When a person is devoted to doing God's will or living a good life, almost any of his judgments about right and wrong actions will be *connected* to his ultimate concern. These judgments include ones that are not absolute in the ordinary sense, such as "Unless someone will suffer greatly, we should use wine rather than grape juice because it better reminds us of God's love." If the question is whether the person can think of any reasons strong enough to overcome the preference for wine, the answer is "Yes." The judgment, though related to ultimate concern, is not absolute.

This somewhat abstract exploration of the possible significance of ultimate concern shows that further refinement is needed before "ultimate concern," or variants of it, can be put to general use by the courts. It also prepares the way for the major point of this section: claims may be religious even though they do not satisfy a standard of ultimate concern or absolute duty.

Though most modern religions both give answers to major questions of existence and offer an overarching focus for people's lives, some belief systems, commonly regarded as religious, have existed that do not make such claims. In these systems, how life should be lived has been determined on some other basis; and religious worship has been mainly a matter of placating the gods or enlisting their help for projects with preestablished value. If the ultimate concern test were accepted in any

---

214. *Id.*

215. *Id.* (quoting P. Tillich, Dynamics of Faith 4 (1958)).

of its versions, practitioners of these religions would have no free exercise rights.

If the test were understood as requiring a tight nexus between a particular claim and the ultimate concern of the claimant, the main impact of its restrictiveness would fall on members of traditional religions. Such a nexus between the claim and ultimate concern would exclude practices generated by religious reasons but not considered absolute duties. The use of wine during communion is one such example; another is a claim by an Orthodox Jewish prisoner to receive a kosher diet even though he believes that nonobservance is appropriate when one is "in extremis." Further examples may be found in many claims of religious organizations to be free from state interference in their decisions. A further difficulty with this restrictive version of the ultimate concern test is the inquiry into sincerity that it would generate. Courts would be in the position of assessing the truthfulness of assertions about intensity of commitment and unwillingness to compromise.

Expansion of ultimate concern to cover duties conceived as less than absolute cannot save it as *the* threshold standard for free exercise cases. If connection to ultimate concern were all that were required, the test would lose most of its bite as a useful tool for categorization. Moreover, it would embrace moral claims that would now be regarded as obviously nonreligious. Suppose a person is a thoroughgoing utilitarian and thinks that accepting jury duty will not maximize utility. His position is not absolute: he thinks submission would be better than wasting time in jail, but his view is derived from his ultimate commitment to the principle of utility. If the free exercise clause were construed to treat his claim and every other claim that ties remotely to the claimant's ultimate concern as religious, the clause would be separated both from any general understanding of what is religious and from the purposes that gave it birth.

D. EXEMPTIONS

The hardest recurring problem in free exercise law has been the proper treatment of neutral laws that inhibit religious practices. Such laws may forbid conduct (e.g. polygamous marriage, or smoking peyote) that is religiously required or sanctioned. Or they may require conduct (e.g. attendance at school, or payment of taxes) that is religiously forbidden.

The Court has gone through four phases in its thinking about this problem. It first proposed a distinction between belief and conduct: belief was entitled to absolute protection; but the government could regulate religiously inspired conduct on much the same terms as it could regulate comparable secular behavior. *Reynolds v. United States* held that the federal government could outlaw polygamy, even as to Mormons for whom the practice was a religious duty.[1] This standard, permissive

---

1. 98 U.S. 145 (1879). See also Cant-
well v. Connecticut, 310 U.S. 296 (1940).

as it was, was used in the 1940's and 1950's to strike down a number of state laws inhibiting religious speech.

The next step was a distinction between laws that imposed direct burdens (*i.e.* that made a religious practice unlawful) and laws that imposed indirect burdens. The statute in *Braunfeld v. Brown* [2]—a Sunday closing law that prevented Orthodox Jews from opening their shops on the Christian sabbath—was of the latter sort. Such a law, the court held, would be upheld if it was within the state's power, provided there was no less restrictive alternative available.

This was a step in the direction of the balancing test finally adopted in 1963. In *Sherbert v. Verner* [3] the Court dealt with a general regulation of conduct that had only an indirect effect on religion: South Carolina denied unemployment benefits to people who would not work on Saturday. Sherbert, a Seventh Day Adventist, could not work on that day for religious reasons. The Court nevertheless held the law invalid. In order to justify any substantial burden on religious conduct, it held, the government must show a compelling state interest and a means narrowly tailored to achieve that interest.

That was the rule in exemptions cases until 1990, when the Court at last held "that the right of free exercise does not relieve an individual of the obligation to comply with a 'valid and neutral law of general applicability on the ground that the law proscribes (or prescribes) conduct that his religion prescribes (or proscribes).' "[4] The case itself, *Employment Division v. Smith,* was unremarkable. It allowed the state to forbid the smoking of peyote, and to withhold unemployment benefits from employees fired for doing so. But the opinion forthrightly rejected the balancing test in favor of a clearer and less forgiving rule.

Smith does not mark the end of free exercise protection.[5] It goes without saying that states cannot discriminate against religion; a law that singled out religious conduct for harsh treatment would not be "neutral" in the required sense. But it is equally likely that *Smith* will not be the last word in the exemption controversy. Douglas Laycock discusses six types of cases where the Court might still grant special protection to religious belief and behavior. He notes, however, that this

2. 366 U.S. 599 (1961).

3. 374 U.S. 398 (1963).

4. Employment Division v. Smith, 494 U.S. 872, 879 (1990).

5. Perhaps the most important avenue of protection after *Smith* is not constitutional but statutory. In 1993 Congress enacted the Religious Freedom Restoration Act, 42 U.S.C. §§ 2000bb to 2000bb–4 (Supp. V 1993) (RFRA). Section Three of the Act provides:

(a) In general

Government shall not substantially burden a person's exercise of religion even if the burden results from a rule of general applicability, except as provided in subsection (b) of this section.

(b) Exception

Government may substantially burden a person's exercise of religion only if it demonstrates that application of the burden to the person—

(1) is in furtherance of a compelling governmental interest; and

(2) is the least restrictive means of furthering that compelling governmental interest.

RFRA thus restores the doctrine that was in place before *Smith* was decided.

is an optimistic view of the law's future course. If we make more pessimistic assumptions it is easy to see *Smith* as a recipe for religious persecution.

Freed and Polsby propose an attractive alternative to the current rule. They favor a kind of balancing that focuses on strategic behavior. They would allow exemptions in some cases where the Court's current rule does not. But acknowledging religious claims sometimes invites other claimants to feign religious scruples (to engage in strategic behavior) in order to get the same benefit. Tax exemptions are a good example. In such cases we should reject even sincere claims in order to avoid the costs of identifying strategic behavior.

DOUGLAS LAYCOCK, THE REMNANTS OF FREE EXERCISE

1990 Sup.Ct.Rev. 1, 39, 41–51, 54–61, 63–65.

[Douglas Laycock discusses the implications of *Employment Division v. Smith,*[a] which held that a state could forbid the use of peyote at a worship service of the Native American Church, so long as it did so under generally applicable laws. *Smith* discarded the rule of strict scrutiny that had been applied since *Sherbert v. Verner*[b] to laws burdening religion.]

THE PRACTICAL IMPACT: WHAT IS LEFT OF FREE EXERCISE?

* * *

* * * *Smith* announces a general rule of devastating sweep, but it also announces six overlapping exceptions and limitations * * *. The Free Exercise Clause never requires exemptions from formally neutral regulations of conduct, but:

1. This rule does not apply to regulation of religious belief and profession.

2. This rule does not apply to religious speech.

3. This rule does not apply to parental control of children's education.

4. This rule does not apply to unemployment compensation cases.

5. This rule does not apply to regulatory schemes that require an "individualized governmental assessment of the reasons for the relevant conduct."

6. This rule does not apply to laws that are not formally neutral and generally applicable.

* * *

a. 494 U.S. 872 (1990). **b.** 374 U.S. 398 (1963).

In the remainder of this section, I examine each of the exceptions and limitations in turn, reading them optimistically from the perspective of religious liberty.

1. *Belief and profession.*   * * *

This restriction could provide substantial protection against a potent source of formally neutral intrusions into churches: the whole body of modern labor law, including discrimination laws, collective bargaining laws, and wrongful discharge law. These laws provide few exceptions for churches, but courts have generally refused to apply them to ministers and other religious teaching personnel. There is no exception in the employment discrimination laws for sex discrimination by churches. Must religious schools employ unwed mothers as school teachers? Must faiths that teach a moral duty of mothers to care for small children in the home employ mothers of small children in paid work for the church outside the home? Must the Roman Catholic Church ordain women priests? Must churches employ or ordain practicing homosexuals under local gay rights ordinances? Can courts review the church's reasons for discharging a parochial school teacher, a pastor, or a bishop? All of these cases present an internal dispute between the employee and the church, and often there is a reform faction that supports the employee's position and an entrenched faction that resists it. If government cannot interfere in "controversies over religious authority," then courts should continue to dismiss most of these cases.

* * *

2. *Speech.*   * * *

Continued protection for religious speech is key to the many suits for fraud and intentional infliction of emotional distress now pending against high-demand religions. These suits are typically brought by disgruntled members and their families; they often produce multi-million dollar verdicts that threaten the very existence of the defendant religion. The trials of these cases are generally characterized by attempts to incite the jury to fear and hatred of a strange faith. But the liability rules of fraud and emotional distress are formally neutral.

* * *

If religious speech is protected and religious conduct is not, litigants will claim that much conduct that previously would have been protected under the Free Exercise Clause is now protected as speech.   * * *

3. *Parental control of education.* The Court's exception for the unenumerated right of parents to control their children's education would appear to make *Smith* inapplicable to a large body of litigation, mostly in the state courts, about conflicts between religion and state educational systems. The issues in these cases include intrusive regulation of religious schools, home schooling, and exemptions from public school curricula that undermine religious faith. Even without *Smith* the states have been winning most of these cases in the lower courts, but the

states have lost some, and they have lost the cases decided on the merits in the Supreme Court. Most of these issues remain open at the Supreme Court level, and apparently they remain subject to the compelling interest test.

4. *Unemployment compensation cases.* The Court's exception for the unemployment compensation cases is the most cryptic of all. At one point, it seems to be an arbitrary exception for unemployment compensation only, based on nothing but precedent, like the distinction between baseball and football in antitrust law. * * *

But the Court does offer a reason for the unemployment compensation exception, and the reason appears to have other applications. Indeed, the reason appears to have many applications, and to be a special case of the general requirement of neutrality. It requires separate treatment.

5. *"Individualized governmental assessment of the reasons for the relevant conduct."* The Court says that the unemployment compensation cases provide for "individualized governmental assessment of the reasons for the relevant conduct," and that "where the State has in place a system of individual exemptions, it may not refuse to extend that system to cases of 'religious hardship' without compelling reason." There are two points run together here. One is individualized assessment, and the other is non-religious exemptions. They will often appear together, but as a matter of logic and policy, they have independent force.

The Court does not explain why individualized assessment cases are to be treated differently, but the reason must be that individualized decisionmaking provides ample opportunity for discrimination against religion in general or unpopular faiths in particular. * * *

This is * * * true, of, for example, zoning, landmarking, and condemnation decisions. Zoning boards restrict the location of new churches, and what is far worse, restrict the ministries of existing churches. They sometimes discriminate against minority faiths. The administration of landmarking laws has burdened churches at rates many times higher than any other class of property. Older religious institutions with open space are sometimes special targets of eminent domain, because it is cheaper to buy open space than to destroy buildings and restore it. These land use cases are readily subject to analysis under the *Smith* exception for individualized assessments.

In such individualized decisionmaking processes, the Court's explanation of its unemployment compensation cases would seem to require that religion get something analogous to most-favored nation status. Religious speech should be treated as well as political speech, religious land uses should be treated as well as any other land use of comparable intensity, and so forth. * * *

The other point in the Court's explanation of its unemployment compensation cases is secular exemptions. If the state grants exemptions from its law for secular reasons, then it must grant comparable exemptions for religious reasons. * * *

* * *

The requirement that religious conduct get the benefit of secular exemptions is a requirement of broad potential application. American statutes are riddled with exceptions and exemptions for various special interests, small businesses, private citizens, and government agencies. The federal employment discrimination laws do not apply to Congress or to employers with fewer than fifteen employees. The law penalizing employers of illegal aliens does not apply to employers of household help. The Florida humane slaughter law exempts any person slaughtering and selling "not more than 20 head of cattle nor more than 35 head of hogs per week." And so on.

* * *

A set of exemptions so institutionalized and generalized that they do not even seem to be exemptions is the scheduling of government functions on the Christian calendar. The Court is so accustomed to this calendar that it appears to think of persons desiring to observe minority holy days as asking for special treatment. Consider a Jewish student who asks to make up an examination administered on Yom Kippur. Such a student is not seeking special treatment; he is seeking an accommodation equal to that already extended to Christians. The school's calendar is not formally neutral just because it never mentions religion. School never meets on Sunday; it never meets on Easter; there is a long break at Christmas, even in schools where the Christmas break falls at an awkward time near the end of the semester. School is the clearest example, but the point is general. Operating on a Christian calendar is a sensible accommodation to the Christian majority, but there is nothing neutral about it. Calendar exemptions for minority religious observance should be required, even after *Smith,* because the calendar is not neutral.

6. *Formal neutrality.* The Court in *Smith* never defines neutrality. But the Court does implicitly recognize the obvious dangers of evasion and abuse.

Consider first the case of formally neutral laws enacted for the purpose of suppressing a minority faith. [Imagine a law that banned] consumption of wine in public places where children are present. The Court says that a law is neutral if prohibiting the exercise of religion "is not the object of the [law] but merely the incidental effect." This language would seem to recognize that even a facially neutral law enacted with bad motive—for the "object" of suppressing a religion—is unconstitutional. * * *

* * *

The Legal Framework for Persecution

Smith announces a general rule that the Free Exercise Clause provides no substantive protection for religious conduct. It also notes enough exceptions and limitations to swallow most of its new rule. Everything seems to depend on judicial willingness to enforce the exceptions and police the neutrality requirement. The previous section assumed that *Smith's* exceptions and limitations are to be given full scope in the protection of religious liberty. This section assumes the opposite.

* * *

A. Formal Neutrality Without Exceptions

First, assume that the courts carefully scrutinize legislative enactments for bad motives * * * and the like, but that they narrowly interpret the *Smith* exceptions for internal church decisionmaking, speech, and parental control. That is, assume that the courts apply formal neutrality quite generally, but insist that it really be neutral. What results would follow?

One result might be more legislative exemptions for churches and believers. But if legislatures do not provide exemptions—if all the regulatory burdens of the modern state are laid on churches—churches would be severely damaged. The institutional damage to churches would be of two kinds. The first is simply the sheer burden of compliance. Rightly or wrongly, businesses complain about being strangled in red tape. But churches are not businesses; their product cannot be sold at a profit, and they cannot raise the price to cover the cost of regulation. They are largely dependent upon voluntary contributions, much of their cash flow is committed to charity, and a building in which to function is a large fixed expense. The demands of the modern regulatory state may severely constrain the religious mission.

Second, churches would frequently find that they simply cannot practice important parts of their faith, even within the enclave of the religious community. * * *

If this sounds alarmist, simply consider the range of regulatory issues mentioned [above.] If churches must share control of their institutions with unions and labor boards; if every church personnel dispute is resolved under secular standards with potential recourse to secular courts; if egalitarian sex roles may be enforced in church employment, or in the church itself as a place of public accommodation; if church schools must conform to secular models of curriculum, student discipline, and academic freedom; if church disciplinary processes are subject to secular standards of due process, or if any church discipline at all risks liability for intentional infliction of emotional distress; if all new ministries require notice to the neighbors and approval from the zoning board; if the Salvation Army cannot continue its ministry to the homeless unless it pays them the minimum wage; if nuns cannot carry the handicapped homeless up a flight of steps because the code requires an elevator; in short, if churches are neutrally subjected to the full range of modern regulation, it is hard to see how they can sustain any distinctive social structure or witness.

* * *

Legislative exemptions are hard to get because the political dynamic of the modern regulatory state recognizes no natural limits to the pursuit of secular values. New regulatory legislation typically results when some interest group successfully demands it, and when such legislation is successfully enforced, it is either by the interest group on behalf of private litigants or by an agency that is committed to the legislative goals. Both the interest group and the agency tend to be single-mindedly focused on the benefits of their legislation; it is not for them to balance competing interests. Thus, those who initiate and enforce much modern legislation tend to be wholly unsympathetic to claims that religious liberty requires an exemption.

If a church says that the sheer burden of compliance with particular legislation interferes with the religious mission, the interest group is unlikely to see that as an important enough reason to justify an exemption. If a church says that it is conscientiously opposed to compliance, the interest group is likely to see the church as an enemy, as a symbol of resistance to the goals of the legislation, legitimating other resistance by its moral or theological stance. If such a church can be forced to comply, that is an important victory in the larger fight to establish the goals of the interest group as unquestionably good things.

Many of the church landmarking disputes illustrate the first kind of clash. Proponents of landmarking seem genuinely unable to comprehend why churches object to maintaining their houses of worship as permanent architectural museums, at the expense of those who worship there, for the aesthetic pleasure of those who do not. It does not matter to the landmarkers that the building has become liturgically or physically obsolete, that it is designed for a congregation much larger than the one that now worships there, or that maintaining the building may absorb all the resources that might have gone into charity, evangelism, education, or other aspects of the religious mission. * * *

The conflict over student gay rights organizations at Georgetown University illustrates the second kind of clash. This dispute has so far produced ten published judicial orders and two Acts of Congress. The sums expended on litigation and legislative lobbying far exceeded any economic stake for either side. The stakes were political and symbolic: could gay students force a Catholic university to recognize their equal status, and subsequently, could Congress force the City Council to accept the legitimacy of religious refusals to recognize the gay students' equal status? It is hardly surprising that those who have devoted their time to leading the gay rights movement tend to see only one side to this issue.

* * *

B. FORMAL NEUTRALITY WITHOUT JUDICIAL SCRUTINY

1. *The risk of persecution.* So far I have assumed that even if *Smith's* exceptions to formal neutrality are allowed to wither, the Court will insist that formal neutrality at least be formally neutral. * * * If the Court will not do this much, it has created a legal framework for persecution.

I want to be very careful here, to avoid either overstating or understating the dangers. Religious liberty is one of America's great inventions. The extent of religious pluralism in this country, and of legal and political protections for religious minorities, is probably unsurpassed in human experience. I have no desire to deny that achievement. But a counter-tradition also runs through American history. There have been religious persecutions in the American past, and it would be foolish to assume that there will not be religious persecutions in the American future. There are localized religious persecutions in the American present, and if the Court gives those persecutions a way to escape judicial review, they will accelerate.

Persecution is a strong term, but it is the word I mean. Still, there are degrees of persecution. This country has never experienced the worst, and I am not predicting the worst. The strongest form of persecution is a systematic effort to kill all persons who believe in a minority faith, or who refuse to profess belief in the established faith. That has happened in other lands, but it has never happened here, and there is no apparent danger that it will happen here.

The next strongest form of persecution is a systematic effort to entirely eliminate the practice of a faith within a jurisdiction. This is what Cromwell did when he suppressed the Mass, and this is what the Court says Oregon may do to suppress peyote worship. * * *

* * *

2. *Past American persecutions.* At times Americans have had the political will for persecution, and in places they have it today. The history of religious tolerance in America reveals a gradually expanding circle of religious groups that are tolerated and even accepted, together with recurrent outbursts of public or private persecution of religions outside that perimeter.

The New England theocracy expelled dissenters, executed Quaker missionaries who returned, and most infamously, perpetrated the Salem witch trials. The political reaction to these trials broke the power of the theocracy in Massachusetts. Colonial Virginia imprisoned Baptist ministers for preaching without a license. But the largest and most important colonial religious persecution is relatively unknown. This was the total suppression of African religion among the slaves, what one historian has called "the African spiritual holocaust."

The best known victims of American religious persecution in the nineteenth century were Catholics and Mormons. * * *

· * * *

The Jehovah's Witness cases that reached the Supreme Court from the late 1930s to the early 1950s arose from the best known twentieth-century outbreak of religious persecution. The Witnesses were persistent and aggressive proselytizers, and their message was offensively intolerant of other faiths, and especially of Catholicism. Towns all over America tried to stop them from proselytizing, enacting a remarkable variety of ordinances, most of which were struck down. The Court's decision in *Minersville School District v. Gobitis*,[251] upholding the requirement that Jehovah's Witnesses salute the flag, triggered a nationwide outburst of private violence against the Witnesses.

* * *

3. *Contemporary persecutions.* These historical persecutions have * * * contemporary counterparts. * * * One is the treatment of the so-called cults, itself a derogatory term. I mean the unfamiliar, high-demand, proselytizing religions, recently arrived from Asia or recently invented on these shores: the Hare Krishnas, the Unification Church, the Scientologists, and others less well known. * * *

A loosely organized movement of private citizens is working to destroy these religions. The best known controversy has surrounded the movement's technique of physically abducting and "deprogramming" young adults who have joined high demand religions against the wishes of their families. But the anti-cult movement found a much more powerful weapon in tort suits for emotional distress and punitive damages. These suits have produced verdicts exceeding $30 million. Verdicts as large as $3 million have survived post-trial motions and remittiturs, and some of these verdicts exceed $5 million with accrued interest. Few minority religions can survive more than one such judgment; none can survive several. All Krishna temples and monasteries in the United States are now in receivership, execution proceedings, or subject to lis pendens filings, to secure just one of these judgments. The Supreme Court vacated the judgment for further consideration of the Krishnas' constitutional claims; if those claims are ultimately rejected, the temples and monasteries will be sold. Seizing places of worship is a time honored means of persecution: the Romans destroyed the Jewish Temple, and Henry VIII seized the Catholic monasteries, and both events are remembered centuries later.

These extraordinary judgments have resulted from the application of formally neutral tort rules in decidedly non-neutral ways. The typical plaintiff is a disgruntled former adherent of the faith, often joined by relatives. The torts commonly alleged include intentional infliction of emotional distress, invasion of privacy, fraud and misrepresentation, and false imprisonment based not on alleged physical restraint but only on claims of "brainwashing." The alleged wrongdoing typically consists of a series of communications, many of them communications about religious belief. Most of the sums claimed are punitive damages and

251. 310 U.S. 586 (1940).

compensatory damages for emotional distress, neither of which is measurable by any objective standard.

From beginning to end, these cases consist of subjective and intangible elements. Even with careful and unbiased effort, it is difficult to separate the actionable wrongdoing, where there is any, from protected religious exercise. These cases provide maximum opportunity for juries to act on their prejudices, and minimum opportunity for judges to control juries.

MAYER G. FREED & DANIEL D. POLSBY, RACE, RELIGION, AND PUBLIC POLICY: BOB JONES UNIVERSITY v. UNITED STATES

1983 Sup.Ct.Rev. 1, 22–26, 30.

[Here] is a * * * fruitful way to think about the free exercise problem, which has occasionally surfaced in the Court's free exercise decisions, though more frequently in dissenting opinions. Granting religious exemptions from generally applicable legal rules frequently invites strategic behavior—that is, lying about one's religious convictions in order to gain the advantage of the religious immunity. The danger that people may engage in insincere or strategic behavior, in turn, makes it necessary for government to develop a mechanism for inquiring into the *bona fides* of an assertion that one's religion requires one to deviate from a law that applies to others, for if this were not done, the integrity of the underlying governmental policy would swiftly be unraveled. The likelihood of such strategic behavior, and the accompanying need to adjudicate the sincerity of religious beliefs, were among the factors relied upon by the Court in *Braunfeld v. Brown*,[53] which upheld a state Sunday closing law as applied to Orthodox Jews whose religion requires them to refrain from doing business on Saturday. * * *

"Strategic behavior" is the right way to think about free exercise problems and "compelling governmental interest" is the wrong way, because strategic behavior analysis asks what a free exercise claim will cost if it is granted, while the "compelling governmental interest" approach simply labels a conclusion according to whether it should be granted without illuminating the factors that might bear on that conclusion. The question that is ultimately called to judgment in free exercise cases is simply how costly, in one way or another, recognizing a religious exemption will be. Two sorts of costs count in this connection: those attributable to the undermining of the state's policy by granting exemptions to concededly sincere claimants, and the costs entailed by efforts to insure that only sincere claimants actually do get the exemption. Some free exercise claims will involve mostly costs of the first sort, because the likelihood of strategic behavior is minimal. In other cases, where something of value can be obtained at the price of telling a hard-to-detect lie, both sorts of costs need to be evaluated.

---

53. 366 U.S. 599 (1961).

An example of the first sort of case is *Menora v. Illinois High School Ass'n,*[54] where Orthodox Jewish high school boys sought exemption from the rule against wearing headgear in interscholastic basketball competition because of religious custom of wearing a head covering at all times. The State pointed out that in the course of a basketball game, a *yarmulke* might fall to the gymnasium floor and become a slip-and-fall hazard for the players. If there are any likely costs associated with granting the sought-after exemption, they stem from the risk of injury which the State feared. It seems doubtful that there would be any incentive for basketball players to feign a religious injunction in order to be able to wear a head covering while playing competitive basketball. [*Wisconsin v.*] *Yoder*[a]—although it is often reckoned to be the high water mark of the free exercise tide—is a similar sort of case because it is difficult to envision many parents engaging in deceptive behavior in order to have the "privilege" of procuring less (free) education for their children than the State requires.

But *Braunfeld v. Brown* involves both sorts of costs, and the Court so analyzed the case. First, the Court described the reasons for a state's having one compulsory day of rest. If believers in the biblical sabbath were afforded an exemption from Sunday closing laws, this "might well undermine the State's goal of providing a day that, as best possible, eliminates the atmosphere of commercial noise and activity. Although not dispositive of the issue, enforcement problems would be more difficult since there would be two or more days to police rather than one and it would be more difficult to observe whether violations were occurring." The Court also recognized that a religiously based privilege to violate the Sunday closing law would be commercially valuable and that therefore a strong incentive would exist for people to manufacture religious convictions so as to obtain the economic benefit.

Similarly, *United States v. Lee*[57] involved both sorts of costs. Lee was an Amish carpenter who brought an action to establish his exemption from the requirement that he, as the employer of two Amish workmen, withhold social security taxes from their paychecks and pay the employer social security portion himself. His theory was that in the Amish community, care for the elderly is a matter of religious duty, and that it is sinful both to receive benefits from and to contribute to the national social security system. The Supreme Court unanimously rejected this claim, recognizing the danger that would be posed to the social security system if conscientious exemptions from it were allowed. The solvency of such systems depends upon their universality. Moreover, there is no conceptual difference between a social security tax and a general tax such as the income tax. Opening up the principle of conscientious objection to social security taxes would carry implications for income taxation as well. A tax system that allowed such conscien-

---

54. 683 F.2d 1030 (7th Cir.1982).

a. 406 U.S. 205 (1972). *Yoder* held that the state could not enforce its compulsory education law against Amish children, who objected for religious reasons to attending school after eighth grade.

57. 455 U.S. 252 (1982).

tious objection "could not function," said the Court, by which it meant that a largely self-assessed and self-policed tax system—whose functioning depends on its reputation for fairness—could not possibly survive such an exception. If a person could deduct from his tax liability some amount of money corresponding to an activity of government to which he had sincere religious objections, no doubt the country would swiftly become more religious, abuses would be widespread, and the apparent fairness of the system—not to mention its actual fairness—would suffer so greatly that honest taxpayers would appear to be fools and would therefore reduce their voluntary compliance with the system. Unless the government were content simply to surrender its tax base, then, it would have to establish some sort of administrative process to evaluate religious exemption claims on a case-by-case basis, as the Selective Service System used to do for those claiming conscientious objection to the draft. But of course, the tax objection board of inquiry would have a far harder job than Selective Service did. It would have not only to decide whether the objector's claim was a *bona fide* religious one. It would have to calculate how those religious scruples translated into a reduced tax liability. Not only would the religious scruples of the taxpayer be involved here—and these could of course change from year to year—but so also would the activities of the government, which change over time as well.

The concurring opinion of Justice Stevens more explicitly recognizes the economic incentive to acquire religious scruples that would flow from an open-ended availability of religious objections to particular governmental expenditures. His opinion also emphasizes the necessity of extensive inquiry into individual religious beliefs in order to contain the damage to the tax system. Justice Stevens makes this latter point more generally by explaining that the principal objection to an expansive interpretation of the Free Exercise Clause is "the overriding interest in keeping the government—whether it be the legislature or the courts—out of the business of evaluating the relative merits of differing religious claims."

* * *

Although Justice Stevens disagrees, *Sherbert* and *Thomas* [also] present formidable invitations to strategic behavior. Justice Stevens says that such behavior is quite unlikely, because the claimants would be asserting that religious scruples had led them to quit their jobs and that religious scruples that required so substantial a sacrifice would not likely be counterfeit. But there are any number of people, with any number of idiosyncratic or personal reasons, who want to quit their jobs. If they do quit, they will not be eligible for unemployment compensation benefits. On the other hand, if they feign religious objection to the work that they are doing and quit, pretending it is because of that objection, then they are entitled to unemployment benefits under the doctrine of *Sherbert* and *Thomas*—unless their dissembling were uncovered. Accordingly, such people certainly do have an incentive to manipulate the system once cases like *Sherbert* and *Thomas* make such manipulation possible, if not indeed easy.

Taken together, the run of free exercise cases indicate that, notwithstanding more recent pronouncements to the contrary, the strategic behavior problem remains of central concern to the Court. Viewed in this way, the results in *Sherbert* and *Thomas* must be considered anomalous and [cases like *United States v. Lee* make up] the mainstream of free exercise analysis.

E. CONFLICT AND RECONCILIATION

It has often been observed that there is a kind of schizophrenia in the way our constitutional law handles religion. Read one way the free exercise clause gives it special treatment. Read less sympathetically the establishment clause treats it with concern, if not suspicion. This is probably a modern problem. The founders did not entertain such love-hate feelings about religion, nor build them into the constitution. The problem is more difficult for us partly because the government does so much more work today. It regulates most aspects of our lives, pays for a vast range of goods and services, and plays a major role in shaping our culture. These activities bring it into close contact with religion in a thousand different ways. It is no wonder that the relationship has changed.

Still, we ought to be able to interpret the two clauses in a consistent way. That is the topic discussed in this section. Suzanna Sherry describes four possible solutions: (1) Read both clauses broadly, as the Court did in *Yoder* and *Lemon*.[1] This is irrational, because it means that religious exemptions are both required (*Yoder*) and forbidden (*Lemon*). (2) Read both clauses narrowly, as the Court did in *Smith* and *Weisman*.[2] This is also irrational, she argues, because it deprives both clauses of substantive content. (3) Subordinate the establishment clause to the free exercise clause, so that exemptions are required. (4) Subordinate the free exercise clause to the establishment clause, so that exemptions are forbidden. This was (almost) the state of the law for the two years after *Smith* and before *Weisman*. Sherry claims that (3) and (4) are the only possible solutions. We cannot reconcile the conflict in a way that gives meaning to both clauses.

Jesse Choper thinks we can. Our mistake lies in thinking that the establishment clause forbids laws that have a religious purpose. Any religious exemption will have a religious purpose almost as a matter of definition. *Lemon* is the villain. We should replace it with a rule that the government cannot (on purpose) coerce, compromise, or influence religious beliefs. Aid and exemptions that don't have these effects are all right. (Compare Choper's test with the "coercion" test used by

1. Wisconsin v. Yoder, 406 U.S. 205 (1972); Lemon v. Kurtzman, 403 U.S. 602 (1971).

2. Employment Division v. Smith, 494 U.S. 872 (1990); Lee v. Weisman, 112 S.Ct. 2649 (1992).

Justice Kennedy in *Lee v. Weisman,* and the one advocated by Michael Paulsen at page 503.)

Abner Greene also thinks we can reconcile the conflict, perhaps in the way described in Sherry's position (1)! He argues that religion is properly excluded from American political life because it makes reference to an extrahuman source of normative authority. (Compare Kathleen Sullivan's similar argument at page 518.) But precisely because religion must be excluded from politics in this way, religious believers should be exempted from laws that they were not allowed to share in making.

SUZANNA SHERRY, LEE v. WEISMAN: PARADOX REDUX

1993 Sup.Ct.Rev. 123, 125–127, 129–131, 134–136, 142–143, 145, 150–152.

In a series of decisions beginning in 1963, the Court held that where a neutral law of general applicability seriously compromised an individual's ability to follow his religious beliefs, the Free Exercise Clause required the government to grant an exemption unless there was a compelling reason not to do so. Although many claims for exemptions were rejected (especially in the waning years of the doctrine), either because the law was found not to impinge on religious beliefs or because the government's interest was found to be compelling, the Court required exemptions in at least four cases.[7] [One of these was *Wisconsin v. Yoder,* where the Court required the state to grant an exemption from its compulsory schooling laws to Amish parents who had religious objections to high school education. During most of this period, however, the Court simultaneously interpreted the Establishment Clause to prohibit such exemptions.]

The Court first fully enunciated the interpretation of the Establishment Clause that guided its decisions for more than two decades in *Lemon v. Kurtzman.*[12] The *Lemon* doctrine, which was announced in 1971[,] prohibited any government support of religion (financial or otherwise) unless the government action had a secular purpose, had a primary effect that neither advanced nor inhibited religion, and avoided "excessive entanglement" with religion. Although inconsistently applied, especially in the area of aid to parochial schools, the *Lemon* doctrine was uniformly acknowledged to be a broad interpretation of the Establishment Clause which invalidated a great deal of government support of religion.

* * *

FALSE RECONCILIATIONS

Neither *Lemon* nor *Yoder* is necessarily correct, although each reflects the core values of the clause it interprets. The Free Exercise

7. [*Sherbert v. Verner,* 374 U.S. 398 (1963); *Wisconsin v. Yoder,* 406 U.S. 205 (1972); *Thomas v. Review Board,* 450 U.S. 707 (1981); *Hobbie v. Unemployment Appeals Comm'n,* 480 U.S. 136 (1987).]

12. 403 U.S. 602 (1971).

Clause is designed to protect the exercise of religion from government interference. The Establishment Clause is designed to prevent the government from putting its imprimatur behind any one religion or religion in general. A broad reading of the free exercise principle of non-interference leads to *Yoder*; a broad reading of the establishment principle of no-imprimatur leads to *Lemon* (or some similar formula prohibiting the preferential treatment of religion). I will call these broad readings the "no interference" and "no discrimination" principles, respectively.

There are four possible pairs of "pure" interpretations of the religion clauses: (1) we might interpret both clauses broadly, as the Court did under *Yoder* and *Lemon*; (2) we might interpret both clauses narrowly; (3) we might subordinate core Establishment Clause values to the Free Exercise Clause by adopting only the no-interference principle; and (4) we might subordinate the core Free Exercise Clause values to the Establishment Clause by adopting only the no-discrimination principle. In order, the consequences of these pairings for the issue of exemptions would be: (1) exemptions are both required and prohibited; (2) exemptions are permitted but not required; (3) exemptions are required; and (4) exemptions are prohibited.

In adopting the first alternative, the Court created a paradox that justices and scholars have been trying to resolve ever since. It is noteworthy that every proposed reconciliation of the tension between the two clauses has adopted one of the two subordinating solutions. Despite repeated claims that it is possible to give full value to the core principles of both clauses without creating a direct conflict between them, every proposed reconciliation has either recreated the paradox or devalued one of the two clauses. The various attempts at reconciliation fall into two broad categories: (1) attempts to distinguish among the various types of burdens that exemptions or failures to exempt place on nonbelievers and believers, often discussed in terms of "coercion"; and (2) attempts to determine whether exemptions or failures to exempt constitute religious discrimination, often discussed in terms of "neutrality." I will deal with each in turn.

A. Coercion

A common approach taken by some proponents of a strong Free Exercise Clause is to interpret the Establishment Clause as prohibiting only government coercion of religion. This approach claims to effect a reconciliation of the two clauses. In fact, however, it "solves" the problem by devaluing the Establishment Clause and rendering it essentially redundant and therefore unimportant.

Jesse Choper has suggested that the Establishment Clause should be read to forbid only government action that has both a solely religious purpose and the likely effect of "coercing, compromising, or influencing religious beliefs."[29] It is therefore permissible to burden nonbelievers—

---

29. * * * Jesse H. Choper, *The Religion Clauses of the First Amendment: Reconcil-* *ing the Conflict,* 41 U.Pitt.L.Rev. 673, 675 (1980).

even to impose "substantial costs"—in order to relieve the burden on believers unless the non-believers' religious liberty is itself impaired, *or* tax funds are used to subsidize religious beliefs.   Although he concludes that *Sherbert* was wrongly decided because other taxpayers were required to subsidize Ms. Sherbert's religious refusal to work Saturdays, he approves of most other types of exemptions as mere accommodations of religion that do not burden the religious liberty of nonbelievers.   [Five members of the Supreme Court also endorsed a coercion test in 1992 in *Lee v. Weisman.*[38]

But the coercion test suffers from a number of serious flaws.   One is that it] makes the Establishment Clause redundant.   Any government action that coerces religious belief violates the Free Exercise Clause. Although virtually all commentators (and the Court) agree that direct coercion of religious beliefs violates the Free Exercise Clause, the redundancy problem is especially acute for those who take an accommodationist approach, since they include even indirect coercion among Free Exercise violations.   * * * If all governmental coercion concerning religious beliefs violates the Free Exercise Clause, a coercion-based Establishment Clause does not prohibit anything that is not independently prohibited by the Free Exercise Clause.

The [second] problem with the coercion requirement is that it conflicts with the plainest possible meaning of the Establishment Clause, for it would permit Congress to establish a church, as long as no one was required to join.

Even if the Establishment Clause prohibits more than government coercion, however, there is significant dispute about the extent to which it prohibits government favoritism toward religion.   This dispute takes the form of debate about discrimination and neutrality, to which I now turn.

B.   Neutrality

The central problem with the neutrality solution to the issue of religious exemptions is that, in this context, there is no such thing as neutrality.   If an exemption is granted, then the government (whether the legislature or the Court) facially discriminates in favor of religion, as when it exempts the Amish but not the followers of Thoreau from compulsory schooling laws.   If, on the other hand, no exemption is granted, then the government discriminates in effect against those with religious objections to the law, as when a compulsory schooling law fails to exempt the Amish.   * * *

Most proponents of accommodation recognize this difficulty, and counter with a call for substantive rather than formal neutrality. [Douglas Laycock is one of these.   He argues that] the government should "minimize the extent to which it either encourages or discourages religious belief or disbelief, practice or nonpractice, observance or nonob-

38.   112 S.Ct. 2649 (1992).

servance." [77] According to Laycock, although no government act in this context can be wholly neutral, we can distinguish between the minor encouragement of religion that occurs when an exemption is granted and the severe discouragement of religion that occurs when an exemption is denied. He offers as illustration the question whether to grant an exemption from Prohibition for the religious use of wine.

What Laycock * * * fails to appreciate is that whenever government attempts to remedy a de facto discrimination against religion by granting an exemption to religious objectors it creates an equally noxious de jure discrimination against nonbelievers. For the government to grant only religious exemptions sends a message that religious belief is valued more than nonbelief (or non-religious belief) and encourages religious belief. * * *

* * *

If some alleged reconciliations of the religion clauses achieve their goal by subordinating the Establishment Clause, others make the opposite mistake. Those who oppose exemptions for believers often fail to see that neutral laws, rigidly applied, constitute a form of discrimination against believers, contrary to the values of the Free Exercise Clause. These scholars' "reconciliations" simply interpret the Free Exercise Clause narrowly, thus subordinating its core values to those of the Establishment Clause.[c]

* * *

III. THE COURT'S RESOLUTION: PARADOX REDUX

In 1990, the Court finally resolved the paradox in one of the two possible ways. In *Employment Division v. Smith,*[104] it abandoned the *Yoder–Sherbert* line of cases (confining them to their facts) and announced that henceforth religious objectors had the same obligation to obey neutral laws as everyone else. Assuming that *Lemon* would still govern establishment cases, *Smith's* repudiation of the exemption doctrine yielded a consistent jurisprudence that coupled a narrow interpretation of the Free Exercise Clause with a broad interpretation of the Establishment Clause. Although immediately attacked by most commentators, *Smith* was the first glimmer of coherence in the Court's religion clause jurisprudence in twenty years.

As I have argued, there were only two ways for the Court to resolve the tension created by its broad interpretation of both the religion clauses—either to narrow its construction of the Establishment Clause or to narrow its view of the Free Exercise Clause. Although some might quarrel with the Court's decision to choose the latter course, one or the

---

77. [Douglas Laycock, *Formal, Substantive, and Disaggregated Neutrality Toward Religion,* 39 DePaul L.Rev. 993 (1990).]

c. Sherry cites as examples of this approach Philip B. Kurland, *Religion and the*

Law (1962), and William Marshall, *In Defense of* Smith *and Free Exercise Revisionism,* 58 U.Chi.L.Rev. 308 (1991).

104. 494 U.S. 872 (1990)[.]

other was necessary. Which course one prefers depends on which clause one thinks more important, but the burden of my argument has been to show that one of these two choices was essential. * * *

Although it resolved the paradox, however, *Smith* contained the seeds of an equally problematic conflict, which came to fruition only two years later in *Lee v. Weisman.* Although the Court in *Smith* held that exemptions for religious objectors are not constitutionally required, it also suggested that such exemptions are not prohibited if a legislature chooses to grant them. Thus, at the same time that the Court narrowed its interpretation of the Free Exercise Clause, it intimated that it was on the verge of narrowing its interpretation of the Establishment Clause as well. In *Lee v. Weisman* it did just that, unofficially abandoning *Lemon* for its much narrower coercion test.

Thus, the brief but coherent reign of a narrow free exercise jurisprudence and a broad establishment jurisprudence was almost immediately replaced by narrow interpretations of both clauses. In the context of exemptions, this means that exemptions are routinely permitted, but never constitutionally required. In its own way, this creates a paradox as puzzling as—and more troubling than—its predecessor.

The problem with the Court's current interpretation is that it leaves both clauses without substantive content, for no apparent reason. No theory of the underlying values of the religion clauses—whether neutrality, benevolence, or separationism—justifies a scheme in which the government is permitted but not required to grant exemptions. Permitting the legislature broad leeway to grant exemptions suggests that the purpose of the religion clauses is * * * to protect and nurture individual religious beliefs in the face of governmental pressure to conform, thus elevating free exercise values. But if that is the case, the clauses should also be read to require exemptions in circumstances where the pressure to conform is great and the need for conformity is minimal. Similarly, if—as the holding in *Smith* seems to suggest—the purpose of the religion clauses is to allow a secular government to operate independent of the varied religious beliefs of the citizenry, thus elevating Establishment Clause values, then accommodation of religion at the expense of nonreligion must be forbidden in order to preserve that independence. For the Court generally to permit but not to require exemptions achieves no goal that can be explained by reference to any possible purpose of the religion clauses.

JESSE H. CHOPER, THE RELIGION CLAUSES OF THE FIRST AMENDMENT: RECONCILING THE CONFLICT

41 U.Pitt.L.Rev. 673, 685–688, 690–692, 700–701 (1980).

[Choper writes in 1980 (before the Supreme Court's decision in *Employment Division v. Smith*[a]), when the tension between the Free

---

    a. 494 U.S. 872 (1990).

Exercise Clause and the Establishment Clause was more acute than it is today. At that time the free exercise test of *Sherbert v. Verner* seemed to require religious exemptions that the establishment clause test of *Lemon v. Kurtzman* forbade.[b]]

VIII.

[I]t is the "secular purpose" prong that is most troublesome in respect to reconciling the seeming antipathy between the Establishment and Free Exercise Clauses. Because this part of the Court's test flatly prohibits any government action that has a religious purpose, it would make virtually *all* accommodations for religion unconstitutional. Since * * * the primary goal of nearly all accommodations for religion is to avoid burdening religious activity, it is plain that their purpose is to assist religion. Thus, taken literally, the "secular purpose" requirement of the Court's Establishment Clause test would, for example, forbid the exemption of conscientious objectors from military service and Amish school children from compulsory education laws. * * * [T]he Court's interpretation of the Free Exercise Clause rejects these implications of its Establishment Clause test. Indeed, the Court has not only mandated religious exemptions under the Free Exercise Clause but has also strongly indicated its approval of a number of government accommodations for religion that were not constitutionally required.[77]

The Court's apparent inconsistency may be rationalized by concluding that its Establishment Clause principles simply give way in the face of a serious (or even arguably substantial) Free Exercise Clause claim. Indeed, this approach may be endorsed as wisely fulfilling the historic and contemporary aims of both clauses to further religious liberty. But while I do not believe that the Establishment Clause should be read to bar all exemptions for religion, I am also unwilling to totally ignore the Establishment Clause simply because government's purpose is to accommodate religion. Precisely because the Establishment Clause is designed to protect religious liberty, I believe that it should not be automatically read as subordinate to the Free Exercise Clause, but rather as limiting the extent to which government may act in behalf of religion.

My discussion will focus on the Establishment Clause. It makes no attempt to determine, once it is found that a religious accommodation is *permissible* under the Establishment Clause, when such accommodation may be *required* under the Free Exercise Clause. Rather, it concerns the Free Exercise Clause only by confining its scope.

IX.

My proposal * * * is that the Establishment Clause should forbid government action that is undertaken for a religious purpose *and* that is

---

b. Sherbert v. Verner, 374 U.S. 398 (1963); Lemon v. Kurtzman, 403 U.S. 602, 612–613 (1971).

77. *See, e.g.*, Gillette v. United States, 401 U.S. 437, 461 n. 23 (1971) (draft exemption); Arlan's Dep't Store, Inc. v. Kentucky, 371 U.S. 218 (1962) (dismissing for want of a substantial federal question an appeal testing the constitutionality of a Sabbatarian exemption from a Sunday closing law); Zorach v. Clauson, 343 U.S. 306 (1952) (released time program).

likely to result in coercing, compromising, or influencing religious beliefs. Thus, I disagree with the Court's articulated view that religious purpose alone renders government action invalid. Rather, it is only when religious purpose is coupled with threatened impairment of religious freedom that government action should be held to violate the Establishment Clause.

I wish to make clear that my position is not grounded in the idea that government promotion of religion serves secular ends by producing public benefits. If legislation designed to assist religion jeopardizes religious freedom, no public benefit should save it. Conversely, if state satisfaction of the religious needs of either the majority or a minority does not jeopardize any Establishment Clause values that have been identified, it should be held constitutionally permissible regardless of whether it serves some independent secular goal. Thus, the key to an Establishment Clause violation should be whether the government action endangers religious freedom.

To illustrate my view—and specifically to contrast it with prevailing judicial doctrine—I believe that *Epperson v. Arkansas*[78] was wrongly decided. In *Epperson,* the Court held that Arkansas' "anti-evolution" statute, which made it unlawful to teach the theory of Charles Darwin in the public schools, violated the Religion Clauses. The Court rested its conclusion on the ground that it was "clear that fundamentalist sectarian conviction was and is the law's reason for existence." I would not dispute the Court's finding that the statute had a solely religious purpose even if it could be shown that it produced derivative secular benefits such as the promotion of classroom harmony. But to rely on the nonestablishment precept to invalidate a religiously motivated law that creates none of the dangers the Establishment Clause was designed to prevent represents, in my view, an "untutored devotion to the concept of neutrality"[82] between church and state. Conceding that the law in *Epperson* "aided" fundamentalist religions, there was no evidence that religious beliefs were either coerced, compromised or influenced. That is, it was not shown, nor do I believe that it could be persuasively argued, that the anti-evolution law either (1) induced children of fundamentalist religions to accept the biblical theory of creation, or (2) conditioned other children for conversion to fundamentalism. [T]hose whose religious interests were not advanced by the law appeared to suffer no *religious* harm. Therefore, while the accommodation for religion in *Epperson* may not have been constitutionally required by the Free Exercise Clause, the law should have survived the Establishment Clause challenge. Even though it satisfied a private religious need, it did not, given the above factual premises, threaten religious liberty.

* * *

78. 393 U.S. 97 (1968).

82. School Dist. of Abington Twp. v. Schempp, 374 U.S. 203, 306 (1963) (Goldberg, J., concurring).

XI.

Several scholars have urged that the Establishment Clause is largely designed to implement the Free Exercise Clause, so that when the Religion Clauses clash, the Establishment Clause must be subordinated to the Free Exercise Clause.[88] The leading decision of *Sherbert v. Verner* may be read as supporting this view. In that case, Mrs. Sherbert, a mill worker and a Seventh Day Adventist, was discharged by her employer when she would not work on Saturday, the Sabbath day of her faith, after all the mills in her area adopted a six-day work week. South Carolina denied her unemployment compensation benefits for refusing to accept "suitable work," even though that would require her to work on Saturday. The Court held that this violated the Free Exercise Clause because "to condition the availability of benefits upon [her] willingness to violate a cardinal principle of her religious faith effectively penalizes the free exercise of her constitutional liberties." Under the Court's Establishment Clause test, however, any government action that has a religious purpose is forbidden, and, therefore, a Sabbatarian exemption would appear to be unconstitutional. It seems indisputable that when the state excuses Mrs. Sherbert from taking otherwise suitable work because of her religious scruples, the purpose of the exemption is solely to facilitate her religious exercise.

To avoid the stark impact of its Establishment Clause approach, the Court may have either totally subordinated the Establishment Clause's "no-aid" mandate to the Free Exercise Clause, or simply balanced Mrs. Sherbert's right to Sabbatarianism under the Free Exercise Clause against the "no-aid" principle of the Establishment Clause and found the former weightier. Justice Brennan, author of the *Sherbert* opinion, had previously advocated this approach for resolving the establishment-free exercise conflict: "[T]he logical interrelationship between the Establishment and Free Exercise Clauses may produce situations where an injunction against an apparent establishment must be withheld in order to avoid infringement of rights of free exercise." [91]

If, in a balancing process, the Establishment Clause's prohibition of aid to religion is viewed only as an abstract principle rather than as a means for securing religious liberty, then it is not surprising that the Court found it wanting in *Sherbert*. On the other side of the balance was Mrs. Sherbert's grave, immediate, and concrete injury—the very type of injury that the Free Exercise Clause was meant to prevent. Indeed, if the Establishment Clause is so abstractly viewed, then it is difficult to imagine any situation where it would not be subordinated or outweighed when measured against a colorable free exercise claim.

Under my proposal, the Establishment Clause would not be so viewed. Rather it would serve the underlying values of both Religion

---

88. *See, e.g.,* Moore, *The Supreme Court and the Relationship Between the "Establishment" and "Free Exercise" Clauses,* 42 Tex.L.Rev. 142, 196 (1963).

91. School Dist. of Abington Twp. v. Schempp, 374 U.S. 203, 247 (1963) (Brennan, J., concurring).

Clauses by forbidding laws whose purpose is to aid religion—including exemptions for religion from general government regulations—if such laws tended to coerce, compromise, or influence religious beliefs.

Mrs. Sherbert's exemption would fail this test. First, since those who refused to work on Saturdays for nonreligious reasons, such as watching football games or spending the day with their children, would be denied unemployment benefits under South Carolina's scheme (and could constitutionally be denied them under the Court's ruling), the sole purpose of Mrs. Sherbert's exemption was to aid religion. Second, the exemption results in impairment of religious liberty because compulsorily raised tax funds must be used to subsidize Mrs. Sherbert's exercise of religion.

The situation produced by the Court's decision in *Sherbert* is distinguishable from that in which the state allows all unemployment compensation claimants to refuse work on one day of their choosing in order to pursue whatever outside interests they might have. Even though some claimants might use the day for religious exercise, government has not conditioned the grant of public funds on a religious use, nor in any other way restricted freedom of choice as to how the money will be spent. While taxpayers may rightfully complain if Mrs. Sherbert's exemption is granted on condition that she use it for religious purposes, they may not object to Mrs. Sherbert's religious use of her leisure time.   * * *

* * *

Conclusion

My proposal for resolving the conflict between the two Religion Clauses seeks to implement their historically and contemporarily acknowledged common goal: to safeguard religious liberty.   * * * The proposal requires that a number of delicate, factual judgments be made—and some that I have advanced herein may well be subject to dispute. Nor have I attempted to set forth criteria for determining when an advantage to religion is so great as to impermissibly influence religious choice: that is left for case-by-case adjudication on developed factual records leavened by common sense. I have urged, however, that the Establishment Clause forbids such influence if accompanied by government action for a religious purpose.

Although the proposal will invalidate some accommodations for religion, I do not believe that it improperly diminishes the religious freedom guaranteed by the Constitution. For it is only when an accommodation would jeopardize religious liberty—when it would coerce, compromise, or influence religious choice—that it would fail. To subordinate the Establishment Clause in such circumstances would be to permit—or, indeed, sometimes require—government to implement one person's religious liberty at the expense of another's.

ABNER S. GREENE, THE POLITICAL BALANCE OF THE RELIGION CLAUSES

102 Yale L.J. 1611–1614, 1616–1617, 1619–1620, 1623, 1633–1635 (1993).

When the Supreme Court held in *Employment Division v. Smith*[1] that the Free Exercise Clause does not protect religious practices from otherwise valid laws that incidentally burden those practices, it followed a particular theory of democratic politics. That some laws might unintentionally burden certain religious practices is, said the Court, an "unavoidable consequence of democratic government [that] must be preferred to a system in which each conscience is a law unto itself." The Court was certainly right in one sense: To claim that conscientious objection to an otherwise valid law should exempt one from that law is to claim that one's values should prevail over the values chosen by the majority. Reading the Constitution to require such exemptions as a matter of right would indeed render each conscience a law unto itself. Although not stated explicitly, the Court's theory of democratic politics recognizes that there will be winners and losers in the political marketplace, where value competes against value for adoption as law. So long as one is able to participate in that competition, one cannot claim a constitutional right to avoid obedience merely because one's values were defeated by a competing set of values that one finds objectionable. Losers as well as winners are bound by the outcome of an open democratic political process.

By applying this theory of democratic politics in *Smith,* however, the Court revealed that it does not take religious values seriously as a special source of conscientious objection. In fact, neither the Justices nor commentators have articulated a theory of the religion clauses that accounts for the proper role of religion in politics. Without paying much attention to this issue, the Warren and Burger Courts read the Establishment Clause to invalidate legislation with a predominant religious purpose,[3] while reading the Free Exercise Clause to give individuals a prima facie right to exemption from laws that burden their religious practices.[5] But this doctrine often was accused of being internally inconsistent, on the theory that religious exemptions infringe Establishment Clause values. * * *

This Article seeks to explain the relationship between the religion clauses in a way that accounts for the proper role of religion in politics, and in so doing offers a new defense of the embattled religion-clause doctrine of the Warren and Burger Courts. In brief, I argue that the Establishment Clause should be read to forbid enacting legislation for the express purpose of advancing the values believed to be commanded

---

1. 494 U.S. 872 (1990)[.]

3. *See, e.g.,* Lemon v. Kurtzman, 403 U.S. 602 (1971); *see also* Edwards v. Aguillard, 482 U.S. 578, 590–91 (1987)[.]

5. *See* Hobbie v. Unemployment Appeals Comm'n, 480 U.S. 136 (1987); Thomas v. Review Bd., 450 U.S. 707 (1981); Wisconsin v. Yoder, 406 U.S. 205 (1972); Sherbert v. Verner, 374 U.S. 398 (1963)[.]

by religion. *Precisely because religion should be excluded from politics in this way,* my argument continues, the Free Exercise Clause requires the recognition of religious faith as a ground for exemption from legal obligation. Thus, I reject *Smith*'s implicit political predicate that all values may be offered for majority support to be enacted into law. If the Establishment Clause should be read to place a special burden on the role of religious values in politics, then those values should receive special treatment when they conflict with the values adopted by the legislature. Reading the Free Exercise Clause to require exemptions from law neither favors religion nor renders religious conscience "a law unto itself." Rather, these exemptions are merely the appropriate remedy for the damage that precluding religious values from grounding law causes religious people.

* * *

I. The Establishment Clause Proscription Against Enacting Religious Faith into Law

My central claim in this Part is that the Establishment Clause, properly understood, prohibits enacting religious faith into law, by which I mean enacting legislation for the express purpose of advancing the values believed to be commanded by religion. Although the Court and many commentators have accepted the notion that laws must have a dominant secular purpose, there is still considerable controversy over the role of religious values in animating the passage of law. I first discuss * * * what makes religious values different from secular ones and justifies at least their partial exclusion from the political process. I focus on what seems to be their chief distinguishing characteristic—their reference to an extrahuman source of value. Basing law expressly on values whose authority cannot be shared by citizens as citizens, but only by those who take a leap of faith, excludes those who do not share the faith from meaningful participation in political discourse and from meaningful access to the source of normative authority predicating law. Requiring that secular analogues be found for religious values, and demanding that the secular purpose be dominant rather than merely present and express rather than merely plausible, ensures that political debate remains a discussion of politics and not religion, and hence that nonreligious people have meaningful access to the terms of the political debate. * * *

* * *

[What chiefly distinguishes religious belief from secular belief is that] only religious belief involves reference to an extrahuman source of value, of normative authority. To be sure, I am defining "religious belief" in this way; I do not purport to divine a "natural" meaning of "religious belief." But there is reason to think that when most people speak of "religion," they are thinking of some such "reference out," some such reliance on a source of normative authority that is not based solely on human reason or experience. By far the most common criterion mentioned by scholars as definitive of "religion" is a reference beyond human experience to an extrahuman source of value.

* * *

Basing law on an express reference to an extrahuman source of value should matter for Establishment Clause analysis because such reference effectively excludes those who don't share the relevant religious faith from meaningful participation in the political process. Consider a law based on the maxim "you should love your neighbor as you love yourself"—a law enacting some form of Good Samaritan obligation, say. The legislature's reliance on that maxim might be based on express reference to facts about human behavior and conclusions reached about the causes and effects of such behavior. In that case, the law would not be based on a source of value beyond human experience. Although it might be hard or impossible to "prove" these conclusions and to "show" why they should lead to a particular law, at least the door is left open for dissenters to seek to alter the law based on arguments accessible to all involved. In this sense, reference to human experience can be seen as the common denominator for political debate. If, on the other hand, the Good Samaritan law were based expressly on the ground that God (or, more generally, any source of value beyond human experience) commands us to love our neighbors as ourselves,[28] then dissenters are left with the options of (a) converting to the relevant faith and thus gaining access to the source of values animating the law, (b) arguing with the religious believers about whether they have properly construed the commandments of their faith, or (c) persuading those believers that their faith is "false." Unless they come to share the faith, dissenters cannot meaningfully compete in the debate over how conclusions from religious faith should be enacted into law.

In other words, although secular as well as religious beliefs might not be provable, there is nonetheless a significant difference between expressly grounding law in premises accessible to citizens as citizens, on the one hand, and only to those with a particular religious faith, on the other hand. * * * When religious believers enact laws for the express purpose of advancing the values believed to be commanded by their religion, they exclude nonbelievers from meaningful participation in political discourse and from meaningful access to the source of normative authority predicating law. They force their "reference out" on others, disempowering nonbelievers. For this reason, it is proper to insist that law be grounded expressly in sources of value accessible to citizens as citizens, not merely to those citizens who happen to share a faith in a separate, extrahuman source of authority.

* * *

[But, you may ask, why in] a liberal democracy * * * aren't all arguments valid in political debate, subject to the possibility that listeners will reject them (which is likely to occur if the arguments aren't

28. *See Luke* 10:25–37.

widely accessible)? The position implicit in this question reflects a misunderstanding of the role of religion in political debate. Religious arguments cannot simply be "rejected" by those who don't share the faith of the people making the arguments. As a non-Christian, I can't meaningfully debate with a Christian whether certain values do or do not stem from her faith in Jesus Christ. The model of political debate implicit in [this] question fails to address debates that are dominated by an expressly religious position. In such instances, nonbelievers are not equal participants in the lawmaking process, for they lack access to the source of normative authority that is offered as the basis for the law they are told to obey.

II. Free Exercise Clause Exemptions as a Political Counterweight to Establishment Clause Disabilities

The *Smith* position against exemptions implicitly treats religious values as playing a full and uninhibited role in politics. If we insist upon a more limited role for religious values, then we eliminate the predicate for *Smith*'s aversion to Free Exercise Clause exemptions. [I]f the rules of the political game set by the Establishment Clause place a special disability on religious values—a disability that is not placed on secular values—then there is a powerful case for such exemptions.
* * *

In the lawmaking process, we are free to make political, moral, and philosophical arguments to support our positions. But the central point of the Establishment Clause argument made above is that the lawmaking process in a nontheistic government should not involve appeals to religious faith. In fact, one principal feature that distinguishes a country like ours from theocracies is the preclusion of law based expressly on religion. Religious belief goes a step beyond standard measures of justification for law: It involves a leap of faith to an extrahuman source of value. One can try to persuade others to take the same leap (by evangelizing and proselytizing, say), but the ultimate leap that religious argument calls for is different from what political, moral, or philosophical argument demands. Because of this difference, the latter should be part of public political justification; the former should not.

Enter the Free Exercise Clause. Lawmaking is a "contractual" process in the sense that if the political, moral, or philosophical arguments that we favor fail to attract enough support, we are bound by the resulting law even if it violates our political, moral, or philosophical sensibilities. Part of losing—of being the minority on an issue—is having to obey the law or to suffer the consequences. But precisely because we should exclude religious faith from being the express basis for law, an appeal to faith as the ground for a constitutional right of conscientious objection does not violate the "contractual" premise of obedience once one loses. The person basing a claim of conscience on faith hasn't lost the "faith argument" on the political playing field; if the process went as it should have, that argument was never allowed onto the playing field.

Sometimes the position that religious faith should be kept out of law is understood to forbid all legislative exemptions for religion. On this view, we separate religion from civil government by denying it recognition as the basis either for law or for exemptions from law. This position secures a sort of facial or formal "neutrality." But if we preclude faith from being the express purpose behind law, then exemptions are required to compensate religious people for the obstacle that this disability poses to their participation in the democratic process. Just as we grant special judicial protection to discrete and insular minorities who are effectively excluded from political power,[68] and just as we enhance judicial scrutiny when legislation blocks the channels of political change,[69] so should we recognize the need for religious exemptions from laws created by a process that is closed in an important way to religious people.

Thus, the Free Exercise Clause can be seen as providing a political counterweight to the Establishment Clause. If the latter should be read to prevent law from being based expressly on religious faith, then the former should be construed to make religious faith a ground for avoiding the obligations of law. In other words, a religious person can justifiably say, "You're keeping my religion out of your politics, now keep your politics out of my religion."

BIBLIOGRAPHY

The Value of Religious Freedom

Gerard V. Bradley, *Dogmatomachy—A "Privatization" Theory of the Religion Clause Cases,* 30 St. Louis U.L.J. 275 (1986).

Richard Delgado, *Religious Totalism: Gentle and Ungentle Persuasion Under the First Amendment,* 51 S.Cal.L.Rev. 1 (1977).

Mark Galanter, *Religious Freedom in the United States: A Turning Point?* 1966 Wis.L.Rev. 217.

Frederick Mark Gedicks & Roger Hendrix, *Democracy, Autonomy, and Values: Some Thoughts on Religion and Law in Modern America,* 60 S.Cal.L.Rev. 1579 (1987).

Timothy L. Hall, *Religion and Civic, Virtue: A Justification of Free Exercise,* 67 Tul.L.Rev. 87 (1992).

Marci A. Hamilton, *The Belief/Conduct Paradigm in the Supreme Court's Free Exercise Jurisprudence: A Theological Account of the Failure to Protect Religious Conduct,* 54 Ohio St.L.J. 713 (1993).

Leonard W. Levy, THE RELIGION CLAUSES (1986).

John H. Mansfield, *Conscientious Objection—1964 Term,* in 1965 Religion and the Public Order 3.

---

68. *See* United States v. Carolene Prods. Co., 304 U.S. 144, 152 n. 4 (1938).

69. For an extensive elaboration on this theme, see John Hart Ely, Democracy and Distrust (1980).

John Courtney Murray, WE HOLD THESE TRUTHS (1960).

Note, *Reinterpreting the Religion Clauses: Constitutional Construction and Conceptions of the Self,* 97 Harv.L.Rev. 1468 (1984).

Leo Pfeffer, CHURCH, STATE, AND FREEDOM (1967).

David A.J. Richards, TOLERATION AND THE CONSTITUTION Chs. 4–5 (1986).

Robert Rodes, *Sub Deo et Lege: A Study of Free Exercise,* 4 Relig. & Pub.Or. 3 (1968).

Michael J. Sandel, *Religious Liberty—Freedom of Conscience or Freedom of Choice?,* 1989 Utah L.Rev. 597 (1989).

Michael E. Smith, *The Special Place of Religion in the Constitution,* 1983 Sup.Ct.Rev. 83.

Clyde W. Summers, *The Sources and Limits of Religious Freedom,* 41 Ill.L.Rev. 53 (1946).

David C. Snyder, *John Locke and the Freedom of Belief,* 30 J. Church and State 227 (1988).

What is "Religion?"

A. Stephen Boyan, Jr., *Defining Religion in Operational and Institutional Terms,* 116 U.Pa.L.Rev. 479 (1968).

Joseph M. Dodge II, *The Free Exercise Of Religion: A Sociological Approach,* 67 Mich.L.Rev. 679 (1969).

George C. Freeman III, *The Misguided Search for the Constitutional Definition of "Religion",* 71 Geo.L.J. 1519 (1983).

Phillip E. Johnson, *Concepts and Compromises in First Amendment Religious Doctrine,* 72 Cal.L.Rev. 817 (1984).

Gail Merel, *The Protection of Individual Choice: A Consistent Understanding of Religion Under the First Amendment,* 45 U.Chi.L.Rev. 805 (1978).

Terry L. Slye, *Rendering Unto Caesar: Defining "Religion" for Purposes of Administering Religion–Based Tax Exemptions,* 6 Harv.J.Law & Pub.Pol'y 219 (1983).

Ninian Smart, THE PHILOSOPHY OF RELIGION 3–39 (1970).

Sharon L. Worthing, *"Religion" and "Religious Institutions" Under the First Amendment,* 7 Pepperdine L.Rev. 313 (1980).

Exemptions

J. Morris Clark, *Guidelines for the Free Exercise Clause,* 83 Harv.L.Rev. 327 (1969).

John H. Garvey, *Freedom and Equality in the Religion Clauses,* 1981 Sup.Ct.Rev. 193.

Steven G. Gey, *Why is Religion Special?: Reconsidering the Accommodation of Religion Under the Religion Clauses of the First Amendment,* 52 U.Pitt.L.Rev. 75 (1990).

Donald A. Giannella, *Religious Liberty, Nonestablishment, and Doctrinal Development—Part I, The Religious Liberty Guarantee,* 80 Harv. L.Rev. 1381 (1967).

James D. Gordon III, *Free Exercise on the Mountaintop,* 79 Calif.L.Rev. 91 (1991).

Philip A. Hamburger, *A Constitutional Right of Religious Exemption: An Historical Perspective,* 60 Geo.Wash.L.Rev. 915 (1992).

Robert D. Kamenshine, *Scrapping Strict Review in Free Exercise Cases,* 4 Con.Comm. 147 (1987).

Douglas W. Kmiec, *The Original Understanding of the Free Exercise Clause and Religious Diversity,* 59 UMKC L.Rev. 591 (1991).

Douglas Laycock, *Formal, Substantive, and Disaggregated Neutrality Toward Religion,* 39 DePaul L.Rev. 993 (1990).

Ira C. Lupu, *Where Rights Begin: The Problem of Burdens on the Free Exercise of Religion,* 102 Harv.L.Rev. 933 (1989).

Paul Marcus, *The Forum of Conscience: Applying Standards Under the Free Exercise Clause,* 1973 Duke L.J. 1217.

William P. Marshall, *In Defense of* Smith *and Free Exercise Revisionism,* 58 U.Chi.L.Rev. 308 (1990).

William P. Marshall, *The Case Against the Constitutionally Compelled Free Exercise Exemption,* 40 Case W.Res.L.Rev. 357 (1990).

Michael W. McConnell, *Free Exercise Revisionism and the* Smith *Decision,* 57 U.Chi.L.Rev. 1109 (1990).

Michael W. McConnell & Richard Posner, *An Economic Approach to Issues of Religious Freedom,* 56 U.Chi.L.Rev. 1 (1989).

John T. Noonan, Jr., *How Sincere Do You Have To Be To Be Religious?,* 1988 U.Ill.L.Rev. 713.

Note, *Developments in the Law: Religion and State,* 100 Harv.L.Rev. 1606, 1703–1740 (1987).

Note, *Indian Religious Freedom and Governmental Development of Public Lands,* 94 Yale L.J. 1447 (1985).

Note, *Native American Free Exercise Rights to the Use of Public Lands,* 63 B.U.L.Rev. 141 (1983).

Note, *The Collision of Religious Exercise and Governmental Nondiscrimination Policies,* 41 Stan.L.Rev. 1201 (1989).

Stephen Pepper, *Taking the Free Exercise Clause Seriously,* 1986 B.Y.U.L.Rev. 299 (1986).

Steven B. Smith, *Free Exercise Doctrine and the Discourse of Disrespect,* 65 U.Col.L.Rev. 519 (1994).

David E. Steinberg, *Religious Exemptions as Affirmative Action,* 40 Emory L.J. 77 (1991).

Geoffrey R. Stone, *Constitutionally Compelled Exemptions and the Free Exercise Clause,* 27 Wm. & Mary L.Rev. 985 (1986).

Symposium, *New Directions in Religious Liberty,* 1993 B.Y.U.L.Rev. 1.

Mark V. Tushnet, *"Of Church and State and the Supreme Court": Kurland Revisited,* 1989 Sup.Ct.Rev. 373.

Conflict and Reconciliation

Bette Novit Evans, *Contradictory Demands on the First Amendment Religion Clauses: Having It Both Ways,* 30 J. Church and State 463 (1988).

John H. Garvey, *Freedom and Equality in the Religion Clauses,* 1981 Sup.Ct.Rev. 193.

Mary Ann Glendon and Raul F. Yanes, *Structural Free Exercise,* 90 Mich.L.Rev. 477 (1991).

Scott C. Idleman, *Ideology as Interpretation: A Reply to Professor Greene's Theory of the Religion Clauses,* 1994 U.Ill.L.Rev. 337 (1994).

Philip Kurland, *The Irrelevance of the Constitution: The Religion Clauses of the First Amendment and the Supreme Court,* 24 Vill.L.Rev. 3 (1978).

Ira C. Lupu, *Keeping the Faith: Religion, Equality and Speech in the U.S. Constitution,* 18 Conn.L.Rev. 739 (1986).

Michael W. McConnell, *Religious Freedom at a Crossroads,* 59 U.Chi. L.Rev. 115 (1992).

Note, *The Free Exercise Boundaries of Permissible Accommodation Under the Establishment Clause,* 99 Yale L.J. 1127 (1990).

Note, *Toward a Uniform Valuation of the Religion Guarantees,* 80 Yale L.J. 77 (1970).

Leo Pfeffer, *Freedom and-or Separation: The Constitutional Dilemma of the First Amendment,* 64 Minn.L.Rev. 561 (1980).

Steven D. Smith, FOREORDAINED FAILURE: THE QUEST FOR A CONSTITUTIONAL PRINCIPLE OF RELIGIOUS FREEDOM (1995).

Steven D. Smith, *The Rise and Fall of Religious Freedom in Constitutional Discourse,* 140 U.Pa.L.Rev. 149 (1991).

Regulation of Churches

Gerard V. Bradley, *Church Autonomy in the Constitutional Oder: The End of Church and State?,* 49 La.L.Rev. 1057 (1989).

Joanne C. Brant, *"Our Shield Belongs to the Lord": Religious Employers and a Constitutional Right to Discriminate*, 21 Hastings Const. L.Q. 275 (1994).

Carl H. Esbeck, *Tort Claims Against Churches and Ecclesiastical Officers: The First Amendment Considerations*, 89 W.Va.L.Rev. 1 (1986).

Carl H. Esbeck, *Government Regulation of Religiously Based Social Services: The First Amendment Considerations*, 19 Hastings Con. L.Q. 343 (1992).

Frederick Mark Gedicks, *Toward A Constitutional Jurisprudence of Religious Group Rights*, 1989 Wis.L.Rev. 99 (1989).

Douglas Laycock, *Towards a General Theory of the Religion Clauses: The Case of Church Labor Relations and the Right to Church Autonomy*, 81 Colum.L.Rev. 1373 (1981).

Douglas Laycock, *Tax Exemptions for Racially Discriminatory Religious Schools*, 60 Tex.L.Rev. 259 (1982).

Ira C. Lupu, *Free Exercise Exemptions and Religious Institutions: The Case of Employment Discrimination*, 76 B.U.L.Rev. 391 (1987).

Note, *Imposing Corporate Forms on Unincorporated Denominations: Balancing Secular Accountability with Religious Free Exercise*, 55 S.Cal.L.Rev. 155 (1981).

Shelley K. Wessels, *The Collision of Religious Exercise and Governmental Nondiscrimination Policies*, 41 Stan.L.Rev. 1201 (1989).

David J. Young & Steven W. Tigges, *Into the Religious Thicket—Constitutional Limits on Civil Court Jurisdiction over Ecclesiastical Disputes*, 47 Ohio St.L.J. 475 (1986).

Church Property Disputes

Arlin M. Adams & William R. Hanlon, Jones v. Wolf: *Church Autonomy and the Religion Clauses of the First Amendment*, 128 U.Pa.L.Rev. 1291 (1980).

Ira Mark Ellman, *Driven from the Tribunal: Judicial Resolution of Internal Church Disputes*, 69 Calif.L.Rev. 1378 (1981).

John H. Garvey, *Churches and the Free Exercise of Religion*, 4 N.D.J.L., Ethics & Pub.Pol. 567 (1990).

Patty Gerstenblith, *Civil Court Resolution of Property Disputes Among Religious Organizations*, 39 Am.U.L.Rev. 513 (1990).

Mark DeWolfe Howe, *Foreword: Political Theory and the Nature of Liberty*, 67 Harv.L.Rev. 91 (1953).

Paul G. Kauper, *Church Autonomy and the First Amendment: The Presbyterian Church Case*, 1969 Sup.Ct.Rev. 347.

Paul G. Kauper & Steven C. Ellis, *Religious Corporations and the Law*, 71 Mich.L.Rev. 499 (1973).

John H. Mansfield, *The Religion Clauses of the First Amendment and the Philosophy of the Constitution,* 72 Cal.L.Rev. 847 (1984).

Note, *Church Property Dispute Resolution: An Expanded Role for Courts After Jones v. Wolf?,* 68 Geo.L.J. 1141 (1980).

Note, *Church Property Disputes in the Age of "Common–Core Protestant-ism": A Legislative Facts Rationale for Neutral Principles of Law,* 57 Ind.L.J. 163 (1982).

Note, *Government Noninvolvement with Religious Institutions,* 59 Texas L.Rev. 921 (1981).

Note, *Judicial Intervention in Disputes Over the Use of Church Property,* 75 Harv.L.Rev. 1142 (1962).

Note, *Judicial Resolution of Church Property Disputes,* 31 Ala.L.Rev. 307 (1980).

William G. Ross, *The Need for an Exclusive and Uniform Application of "Neutral Principles" in the Adjudication of Church Property Disputes,* 32 St.Louis U.L.J. 263 (1987).

Louis J. Sirico, Jr., *Church Property Disputes: Churches as Secular and Alien Institutions,* 55 Fordham L.Rev. 335 (1986).

Louis J. Sirico, Jr., *The Constitutional Dimensions of Church Property Disputes,* 59 Wash.U.L.Q. 1 (1981).

Religious Freedom Restoration Act

Stephen M. Bainbridge, *Student Religious Organizations and University Policies Against Discrimination on the Basis of Sexual Orientation: Implications of the Religious Freedom Restoration Act,* 21 J.C.U.L. 369 (1994).

Thomas C. Berg, *What Hath Congress Wrought? An Interpretive Guide to the Religious Freedom Restoration Act,* 39 Vill.L.Rev. 1 (1994).

Christopher L. Eisgruber and Lawrence G. Sager, *The Vulnerability of Conscience: The Constitutional Basis for Protecting Religious Conduct,* 61 U.Chi.L.Rev. 1245 (1994).

Scott C. Idleman, *The Religious Freedom Restoration Act: Pushing the Limits of Legislative Power,* 73 Tex.L.Rev. 247 (1994).

Kenneth L. Karst, *Religious Freedom and Equal Citizenship: Reflections on Lukumi,* 69 Tul.L.Rev. 335 (1994).

Symposium, *The Religious Freedom Restoration Act,* 56 Mont.L.Rev. 171 (1995).

†